A Call to Mission
The Jesuits in China
The French Romance
Volume One
1842–1955

David Strong SJ

A Call to Mission
The Jesuits in China
The French Romance
Volume One
1842–1955

David Strong SJ

Adelaide
2018

Published by:

An imprint of the ATF Press Publishing
Group owned by ATF (Australia) Ltd.
PO Box 504
Hindmarsh, SA 5007
ABN 90 116 359 963
www.atfpress.com
Making a lasting impact

Table of Contents

Abbreviations

ARSI   *Archivum Romanum Societatis Iesu,* Jesuit Archives, Rome

ATF   Australian Theological Forum, Adelaide

DAC   Diplomatic Archives Centre, Nantes

NLA   Australian National Library, Canberra

CHPA   China Province Archives, Taipei

PF   Propagation of the Faith Archives, Rome

ASV   Vatican Secret Archives, Vatican City

FPA   Province of France Archives, Paris

SPA   Spanish Province Archives, Madrid

TPA   Province of Turin Archives, Gallarate

CPA   Canadian Provinces Archives, Montreal

HPA   Hungarian Province Archives, Budapest

AASI   Austrian Province Archives, Vienna

CaPA   Californian Province Archives, Los Gatos

UCAN   Union of Catholic Asian News

Preface

My inspiration for writing this book has been to keep alive the memory of 1,121 foreign Jesuit missionaries to the region of Jiangnan, China, from 1842 to 1950. Their heroism lies in the way they left the security of their own country, entered a completely foreign culture relatively unprepared, and persevered in their mission to 'save' the Chinese people by sharing the Catholic faith that they held so strongly. They worked with 286 Chinese Jesuits and a small number of Chinese secular clergy.

The period 1842–1950 is a discrete period for the Jesuits. They returned to China after the restoration of the Order in 1814 and this book covers the time of their presence in China until the Communists expelled them in the 1950s.

The aim of this story is to give an overview of all the missions of the region, from the time that Jiangnan was one mission in 1842 to the nine it became by 1950, and the contrasting understandings of Chinese culture. The narrative shows significant mission growth, especially in religious and secular education and social services, as well as the number of conversions during these years that formed the basis for the continuing faith of Catholics during the darker Communist years without European support. Jesuit comments on how Chinese culture contrasted with their own are enlightening, as was their attempt to adapt to such an alien cultural and social system.

The book indicates differences in missionary approaches between the various foreign missionaries, although there were more similarities than differences given the similar background that these missionaries brought to China. Finally, after some evaluation of the missions, suggestions are made in an epilogue about the future of the Catholic

Church in China and significant initiatives Jesuits have undertaken since 1950. An interlude about the development of the theology of mission in the Catholic Church indicates the growth in understanding of being a missionary.

This is the first time a general history of these missions has been written in English. It is not intended to be an in-depth analysis of these missions, but rather a story largely narrated from primary source material that might stimulate further in-depth research into regions or issues raised by this work.

The first mission came from the Province of France, and subsequent divisions of the Jiangnan region brought missionaries from the Provinces of Champagne (France), Leon and Castile (Spain), French Canada, Austria, Hungary, Italy and California to form separate vicariates. Background historical information on the political and social developments in China relevant to all the missions is dealt with in relevant detail in the narrative of the Jiangnan mission, and only repeated in passing or in greater relevant detail in the narratives of the other vicariates.

Research into the history of these nine missions required visits to the archives of the Jesuit headquarters in Rome, as well as the archives of all other provinces. These primary sources included letters, diaries, reports, reflections, and many statistics from the missionaries to home base, reporting observations on Chinese culture and encounters with the people and government officials. A variety of opinions are included to show contrasting responses of the European and Chinese missionaries to social, political or ecclesiastical situations.

These sources also focus on the administrative challenges faced by the missionaries, both internally and externally, such as the tension that existed between Roman directives and differing local missionary opinion, as well as descriptions of negotiations between the missionaries and various Chinese governments and how the missionaries survived during times of turmoil and revolt. The sources chosen for this work were those that especially highlighted these challenges that underlay how the European missionaries, as outsiders, and the Chinese interacted.

Letters and reports from Chinese Jesuits were particularly sought, with some cited from those Chinese who were literate in the prescribed Latin or French, usually critical of the methods of the European missionaries. Letters in Chinese were very few. Roman decrees from the Jesuit headquarters and from the Vatican were readily available, indicating the control desired by Church officials.

In addition, the archives of the French Foreign Ministry were a valuable source, detailing the close collaboration between the French government and the Catholic missions. The influence of the French protectorate on the missions is an important theme throughout this narrative. The Vatican archives, and those of the Congregation of the Propagation of the Faith gave additional insight into the reaction of Roman Catholic officials to mission activity, and the kind of advice sent to Rome from China.

In considering these sources, I was well aware that all letters sent to Rome or to home base reporting life on the mission were highly self-censored by their writers. Letters to Rome highlighted both achievements and difficulties encountered, especially financial and the recurring problem of insufficient manpower. Observations on Chinese culture or political situations were the opinions of the authors, and taken to be such: missionaries' perceptions frequently disagreed. Letters to family were more personal reflections, while those to the home province for publication in province mission periodicals not only gave information about the good work accomplished, but also indicated challenges that still required further support, usually financial. The support of lay co-missionaries was recognised as an important lifeline to the missions.

When discussing challenges relating to personnel, most of the letters are very cautious in their comments about the inadequacies of individuals. Instead, to meet this problem, some letters simply indicated what positive qualities were needed in missionaries, and especially in superiors. That was considered a more positive approach to superiors who needed to make future decisions considering Jesuit leadership and Jesuit community composition.

Particular mention must be made about the primary sources used for the account of the Hungarian mission. The main sources used were Roman letters, usually written in Latin or French. Letters in Hungarian were not used, as the author was not familiar with the language. This is a weakness in this chapter, as the Hungarian Jesuits presumably wrote some letters to the Hungarian provincial in Hungarian. Other sources might give a more positive view of mission work.

Peter Vamos has written a comprehensive account of the Hungarian mission of Daming, and his comments about individual Jesuits in English have been included in the endnotes. These obituaries give a more comprehensive, positive account of the contribution of individual Jesuits to the mission, especially about those who were noted in the text as having personal difficulties relating to their mission. By including letters relating to those Jesuits, the aim was to show the great strength and generosity of the Hungarian Jesuits who not only worked hard among the Chinese, but also tried to assist those confreres whose efforts were considered a hindrance the work of the mission. The openness and honesty of the Jesuits in these letters in commenting on internal challenges was particularly edifying.

Despite the 'thinness' of the narrative in this chapter, I hoped that using what sources were available in Latin, French or English might still give an overall perspective on the work of the Hungarian missionaries in English, touching upon external achievements and internal challenges. To write a history of the Jiangnan mission and to exclude the significant contribution of Hungarian mission would be incomplete. What has been written might stimulate scholars to further research.

Secondary sources cited are used mainly for providing a context for the mission narrative, for verifying primary sources, and for filling in important details that the letters and reports of the missionaries presupposed. Of particular assistance in this regard were Xiaoxin Wu and Mark Stephen Mir of *The Ricci Institute for Chinese-Western Cultural History* at the University of San Francisco. The Jesuit theological library at Centre Sèvres, Paris, was another important material source.

I would like to thank all the archivists and their assistants, who so willingly provided the appropriate documentation and gave ongoing assistance, including photos of the missions. They include Robert Bonfils SJ, Barbara Baudry and Peter Li from Paris, Daniel Peterson SJ from Los Gatos, California, Diego Brunello SJ from Gallarate, Theresa Rowat and Jacques Monet SJ from Montreal, Mihalik Béla Vilmos from Budapest, Elías Cerezo SJ and Anselmo Garcia SJ from Taipei, and Martina Lehner from Vienna. Special thanks are given to these archivists for providing the many photos in the book.

One significant challenge for a work of this kind is that all the archives, except for those of the Californian province, are in languages other than English. The narrative, therefore, involved translations from Latin, French, Italian, Spanish, German and Hungarian.

The book could not have been written without people who helped me by translating documents into English. Cornelius O'Donovan spent many hours translating German and Spanish documents, as did Louella Perrott with translation of Italian documents. Peter Vamos set up a connection for me with the Hungarian province archives in Budapest. Robert Kenderes also helped with translating parts of Peter Vamos' book on the Hungarian mission of Daming in Hungarian.

Further complicating the research were the Chinese place names. All were written in the Wade-Giles form, and needed translation into Pinyin. Louis Liu from Saint Ignatius' College in Sydney most generously undertook this task. Some names were impossible to translate or to locate, possibly because they originally appeared in a local dialect, and so were left in the original. The work would have been incomplete without his assistance and he has my enduring gratitude.

Further attempts were made to locate place names on the maps provided and this resulted in the location of more places. Special thanks are given to Lucia Cheung and Porson Chan in Hong Kong for contributions to this challenging task. However, even with energetic attempts to locate the modern place names on maps that had older names, our efforts were not always successful. Furthermore, some names in the research documents had different spellings, which further complicated locating.

The maps in this work are a re-designing of the mission territories based on maps found in Edward Malatesta's *The Society of Jesus and China*, and maps provided by the various archives usually found in province mission magazines. Place names have been changed into Pinyin. Much gratitude is given to John and Terry O'Mara from Big Image Sydney, whose staff designed these new maps. In particular my thanks go to Noel Conlon for this work.

Columban Father Noel Connolly gave valuable assistance for the research needed for the interlude on the theology of mission.

Special thanks also to our proofreaders, especially Noel Bradford. Many scholars gave valuable comments on various sections of the work. They include Paul Rule, Jean-Paul Wiest, Youguo Jiang SJ, Paul Mariani SJ, Peter Vamos, Gerald O'Collins SJ, and readers from the Provinces of California, Canada, Italy, Spain, and Austria. The history has been enriched by their comments.

The publication would not have been possible without the financial assistance of Frank Brennan SJ and the Australian Institute of

Jesuit Studies, Canberra, Australia. Michael Kelly SJ, the Executive Director of UCAN, and Hilary Regan undertook editing and bringing the book to its final completion at ATF Press Publishing Group, Adelaide. Their tireless efforts on the details of publication are much appreciated.

David Strong, SJ, Pymble, NSW Australia

Introduction

The Society of Jesus

With the purpose 'to serve the Lord alone and His Church under the Roman Pontiff, the vicar of Christ on earth',[1] Pope Julius III, on 21 July 1550, confirmed and approved the Society of Jesus founded by Ignatius Loyola as a religious order in the Catholic Church.[2] Within two hundred years, members of the Society of Jesus, commonly called Jesuits, became advisors of monarchs, missionaries to foreign lands, defenders of the poor and the papacy, making enemies of those jealous of their power and influence. Such enemies, who finally forced

---

1. Ignatius Loyola, *The Constitutions of the Society of Jesus,* translated by George E. Ganss (St Louis: Institute of Jesuit Sources, 1970), 66; cf. François Courel, 'La fin unique de la Compagnie de Jésus', in *AHSI,* 35 (1966): 186–211.

2. **Inigo Lopez de Omaz y Loyola,** or Ignatius Loyola, was probably born in the year 1491 in the Castle of Loyola near the town of Azpeitia in the Basque Province of Gipuzkoa in Spain. He was the last of thirteen children, born when Ferdinand of Aragon and Isabella of Castile governed Spain. In 1492, the last Moorish stronghold in Spain, Granada, fell, and Christopher Columbus discovered America. Fighting for King Charles to defend Navarre in 1515, Loyola was wounded at the garrison of Pamplona. During his convalescence, after reading the lives of the saints, he underwent a spiritual conversion and decided to serve God alone. He abandoned his former life as a nobleman, adopted the dress and lifestyle of a pilgrim, finally decided to undertake studies at the University of Paris, and with a group of like-minded men, offered himself and his companions to the Bishop of Rome. In 1540, the pope approved the group or 'company' as a new religious order in the Church, the Society of Jesus. Loyola died in Rome on 31 July 1556. Selected biographies of Loyola included by non-Catholic Mary Purcell, *The First Jesuit* (Md: Westminister, 1957) and Cándido de Dalmases, *Ignatius of Loyola, Founder of the Jesuits,* translated by Jerome Aixalá (St Louis: Institute of Jesuit Sources, 1985).

Pope Clement XIV to suppress the Jesuits on 21 July 1773, would have agreed with the description of them as 'the disturbers of kingdoms, the oppressors of nations, the masters of the world'.[3]

Up to the suppression of the Jesuits in 1773, they worked among the Turks, and natives of Canada, as well as among Lutherans and other separated Christians. They lived in hostile lands like Japan and China, as well as among the traditional Catholic faithful in Europe. At this time, there were 3,500 Jesuits in mission lands, 15.5 per cent of their total number.

The Catholic Church as missionary

The classical era of the Church's mission occurred during the first eight centuries, with the spread of Christianity to Greece, Rome and later to the Celtic and Germanic tribes. This period of Church history was characterised by respect for both the Christian message and the local culture. For Christianity to be accepted in a new region, it was necessary for the Church to understand and come to terms with the local culture, accepting what was good, while attempting to adapt and even change customs unacceptable to Christianity. This approach to mission required patience and tolerance: awaiting and fostering the gradual transformation of the local culture into something new.

However, by the ninth century, a great plurality of rites and structures existed, so changes occurred. The Church became concerned about unorthodox groups retaining pagan and superstitious forms under the guise of Christianity. In addition, secular powers realised the importance of developing unified and common structures within kingdoms. This resulted in greater uniformity in Church practices, and a new era of mission developed. European culture and Christianity, considered superior to other cultures and religions, was imposed on other nations and peoples.

With the expansion of Europe into the new world came the opportunity for a revival of the classical mission approach, which was applied especially by the Jesuit Order in China, India and Paraguay.

---

3. L'Abbé Martial de La Roche Arnaud, *The Modern Jesuits* (Longmans 1827) quoted in *The Jesuits, their History and Crimes* (Protestant Truth Society, London, n.d.), 5. A substantial polemical bibliography against the Jesuits exists, among which are included, Pascal's *Les Provinciales*; René Fülöp-Miller, *The Power and Secret of the Jesuits* (NY: Braziller, 1956). Much of the attack is against the Society for its orthodox Catholicism and anti-liberalism and is largely European in origin.

In a remarkable document addressed to the missionaries in China by the recently established Congregation *Propaganda Fide* in 1659, the importance of missionaries adapting themselves to others was stressed. It encouraged missionaries to preserve what was good, to respect national heritage and customs, not to seek to impose practices with rigid conformity, to avoid rash and hasty judgments. Local customs, rites and mores were not to be changed unless they were evidently contrary to religion and good morals. What was suitable for Christian Europe would not be the same in China.[4]

This period, however, was relatively short-lived, and was not a universally held approach to mission. The imposition of European Christian thought on indigenous cultures were the predominant form of mission endeavour until comparatively recent times, and resulted in severe losses to the local culture.

Whichever method missionaries employed, dangers existed. In attempting to utilise the local religion as a base for new religious ideas, syncretism was possible. China had a long history of absorbing religious sects into the mainstream of Chinese belief. It was into this world that the Jesuits entered.

Early Jesuits in China

The first Jesuit to be allowed to reside in China was the Italian, Michele Ruggieri, who was sent to Macau in July 1579 by Alessandro Valignano to learn to read, write and speak the Chinese language.[5]

---

4. *L'art chrétien chinois*, special number of *Dossiers de la commission synodale*, v/5 (Peiping, May 1932): 411, cited in J.R. Levenson, *Confucian China and Its Modern Fate* (London: Rutledge and Kegan Paul, 1958), 118.
5. Born **Pompilio Ruggieri** in Spinazzola, Puglia, in 1543, he obtained in Naples a doctorate in both civil and canon law, and was employed in the administration of Philip II. He entered the Society of Jesus on 27 October 1572 in Rome, taking the name 'Michele'. After his initial Jesuit formation, he volunteered for the Asian missions and left for Lisbon where he was ordained in March 1578 while waiting to travel to Goa. He arrived in India in September that year and began learning the language of the Malabar Coast. His gift for language made him an ideal choice for the Chinese mission, and so was sent to Macau with this mission in mind.

   Ruggieri wanted to become Chinese in order to win China, following the Jesuit tradition of being all things to all men. Ruggieri left China for Italy in 1588 in order to influence the pope to send an embassy to the Chinese emperor. This mission failed and Ruggieri retired to Salerno, where he died on 11 May 1607, having never returned to China.

Macau was to become the Catholic missionary base for missionaries to China as it had been for Japan. Matteo Ricci, another Italian, joined Ruggieri in Macau in August 1582 to prepare for a Jesuit mission to China.[6] After studying Chinese language and customs, the two Jesuits settled in Zhaoqing from 1583 until 1589, when a new viceroy expelled them. It was here that Ricci composed the first European-style map of the world in Chinese, as well as compiling a Portuguese-Chinese dictionary. Ricci then went to Shaoguan in 1589, followed by Nanjing and Nanchang in 1595. In 1598, he moved to the terminal port of Beijing, Tongzhou, on the Grand Canal, and first reached Beijing on 7 September 1598. His attempts to reach the emperor failed at this time, but in 1601 he was invited to the imperial court of the Wanli Emperor. Established in Beijing, Ricci influenced the court scholars with his Western scientific learning. He died on 11 May 1610, aged 57, and was buried in Beijing in the Zhalan cemetery.

Ricci and his successors were challenged as to how to align Confucianism and Christianity without reducing the latter to the former. Ricci attempted to discover what was good in the Chinese cultural tradition and to use this as a base for teaching Christianity. Both Christianity and Confucianism had a common ethical base, so Ricci built upon that foundation. This is called accommodation. Truth was not sacrificed, but attempts were made to find what truths in Chinese culture were compatible with Christianity. Where differences occurred, Christianity was to argue its case with Chinese tradition. Moreover, in attempting to accommodate to Chinese belief, not all truths of Christianity were taught at once, but rather they were gradually introduced as the neophytes were able to understand and were prepared to accept new doctrines. This method was sometimes misunderstood, sometimes condemned.

Ricci's approach was to respect the presence of God within Chinese culture; and so is called 'Sinification'. This is contrasted to 'Europeanism', which believed that Christianity and its European expression were one and the same, and ought to be imposed on other

---

6. **Matteo Ricci** was born on 6 October 1552 in Macerata in the Italian region of Marche. He first studied the classics and then law in Rome for two years. He entered the Society of Jesus in April 1571 at the Roman College, where in addition to his ecclesiastical studies, he also studied mathematics, cosmology and astronomy under Christopher Clavius. In 1577, he applied for the Far East missions and arrived in Goa, September 1578, and remained there teaching until assigned to Macau in 1582.

cultures.[7] Local custom and religious expression that differed from the European experience ought to be challenged and changed where necessary. The danger in this approach was not only that good local beliefs and traditions were frequently overlooked and the people bewildered, but that in equating Christianity with European thought, European cultural values and ideals were also expressed; much to the distaste of the local people.

The Ricci missionary approach of encounter, accommodation and adaptation to Chinese culture was finally condemned by Rome in various decrees culminating in 1742, which condemned allowing Chinese Christians to practise various Chinese rites to Confucius and dead ancestors. Future missionaries were ordered to take an oath of submission to this decree, which affected the Catholic missionary approach until 1939 when it was revoked.

The effects of the Rites controversy were significant for the future of Christianity in China. It destroyed Ricci's attempt to win the Chinese literati and officialdom; Christianity in the future tended to concentrate on the lower strata in Chinese society, and so lost much respect. The emperor Kangxi kept missionaries at Court for scientific and artistic reasons, but they were given little opportunity to evangelise. Later Manchu emperors condemned Christianity as subversive and actively persecuted it.

The struggle between the missionaries and the final decision from Rome contributed to the ruin of the Catholic missions. Latourette argued that after Kangxi, missionaries were not welcome to work in China, as they were seen as agents of foreign powers. In addition, the suppression of the Jesuits, the decline in religious zeal in France and the decline of Spain and Portugal as colonial powers, all contributed to the decline of Christianity in China.[8]

Jesuit restoration

As liberalism and rationalism emerged from the revolutions in Europe, however, the papacy needed support to stem the tide of the

---

7. Henri Bernard-Maître, 'La correspondence Becker-Brucker sur la question des rites chinois (1885–1907)', in *Recherches de Science Religieuse*, 54 (1966): 422.
8   Kenneth Scott Latourette, *A History of Christian Missions in China* (London: Russell and Russell, 1929), 153.

anti-religious sentiments inherent in these ideas. Members of the Society of Jesus had been working under the patronage of Frederick II of Prussia and Catherine II of Russia. These non-Catholic monarchs had refused to promulgate Clement XIV's Bull of dissolution because of disagreements with the pope, and a desire to use the Jesuits for education. When opposition to the Jesuits diminished, Pope Pius VII formally restored the Society of Jesus to the universal Church on 7 August 1814.

Traditional elements in the Society of Jesus were resurrected – the spiritual nature of its life, obedience to the pope, and work as educators and missionaries. But the world of 1814 was different from that of 1773. Gone were the missions in China, India and Paraguay, gone were the colleges, gone was the influence at court, while influence among the great Catholic families of Europe no longer mattered. The Society of Jesus existed again, but it realised that existence depended on the Papacy. They were once again the pope's men, totally one with the spirit of Rome.

It was in the context of this spirit that the Jesuits returned to China in 1842.

Historiography

Jean-Paul Wiest presented a framework for missionary histories in China. There were the 'in-house' histories that 'aimed to keep a missionary community aware of its roots and developments'. 'Official' histories were endorsed and commissioned by someone. 'Inspirational' histories were 'meant to edify the faithful and to arouse missionary vocations'. 'Secular' histories 'considered Christian missions as a religious manifestation of the broader socio-economic and political impact of the West on Third World countries'. And then there were missionary chronicles.

He noted that 'the bulk of these histories focused on the role played by the missionaries, with few observations from the local community or the role of the local people in the development of an indigenous form of Christianity'.

Wiest described missionary chronicles as 'detailed accounts of events arranged in order of time, lacking analysis and interpretation. While usually rejected as mission histories, they play an important part in the overall narrative under discussion. Such chronicles are not devoid of interpretation, as they depict the writer's interpretation of what events were significant by use of specific choice of words'. He believed that 'chronicles are important tools for further in-depth analysis of events, but their weakness lies in their hidden interpretative element that might mislead researchers'.

> Wiest saw official and in-house histories as those approved by Church officials, with the distinction that the former was for public use, the latter for private use only. These in-house histories provide detailed accounts of events, places and people in terms understood mainly by Church or missionary groups. Official histories aim at inspiring an outside readership by selecting the more significant data for publication. These histories are frequently criticized for leaving out failures or mistakes. It is accepted that all religious writing within the Catholic Church has been subject to censorship, and authors are all aware of this; so they exercise their own censorship on their writing. Religious history also wants to demonstrate the divine nature of the Church and God's work in the development and spread of the Christian message.

Inspirational mission histories were seen to emphasise spiritual values, as well as the dedication and heroism of missionary life.

The local socio-economic life of neophytes was vastly improved by missionary activity. Failures and mistakes were not usually included in the narrative, except to show how they were successfully overcome. The emphasis of these works was to edify the readers, rather than to present a history.

Finally, secular histories were believed to analyse

> The cultural, social, economic and political factors of missionary activity rarely touch upon the theological dimension. These works were concerned with what was empirically verifiable, but by doing so they neglected the supernatural or spiritual motivation and activity of missionaries that inspired the missionaries to develop indigenous communities.

The most relevant mission history should be one that combines the best elements found in the secular and the official approaches. Wiest goes further to suggest that

Mission history should be more than a secular history. The mission historian should also be a theologian. To omit the concept of spreading the Kingdom of God and the Church's vocation to evangelise would diminish mission history. A purely secular history could not understand the motivation of missionaries to go to the ends of the earth. Therefore, any history of missionary activity should combine the historical and the theological aspects of missionary life. The China missionary could not be totally understood without examining their methods and theology that underpinned their understanding of mission.

Ideally, a mission history should combine both the study of Western missionaries and their activity in the mission, and how missionary efforts combined with local responses to give rise to an indigenous Church. The story of the response of the indigenous people to Christianity perceived by the local people themselves is equally important in the narrative.

The role of the missionary historian is to give a voice to the past. A well-balanced mission history is not just a history of how structures, and theological concepts were implemented, but it is a history of encounters between peoples of different cultures.[9]

Another mission historian, Jean Charbonnier, emphasised the need for mission history to be viewed from the point of view of the indigenous people. Any appreciation of the missions in China should be approached primarily from China rather than Europe. Western historians needed to be critical of the evolution of Christianity in their own cultural context, and also be aware of the cultural context of China, both among the educated and the illiterate people.[10]

Paul Rule agreed with the concept of a Chinese-centred history, and argued for an ethnographic history that places the individual Chinese Catholic in their environment at the centre of the narrative.

Rule critiqued the historiography of China missions by enumerating the different styles of writing. He mentioned first, participant

---

9. Jean-Paul Wiest, 'The Contemporary Relevance of Mission History', in *Historiography of the Chinese Catholic Church, Nineteenth and Twentieth Centuries*, edited by Jeroom Heyndricks, C.I.C.M. Louvain Chinese Studies I (Leuven: Ferdinand Verbiest Foundation, 1994): 30–6.

10. Jean Charbonnier, M.E.P., 'The Interpretation of Christian History in China', Chinese and Christian Criteria, ibid., 37–51.

history, memoirs and formal histories written by early missionaries, such as the *lettres édifiantes*. He sees these histories as 'polemical and propagandist' that give an important 'feel and excitement of the pioneering encounters'. Then came the first surveys, the accounts of events in the voyages to the mission, and the struggles to establish the local Churches. These accounts are indispensable to the later historian. Institutional histories followed, sometimes criticised for not including the non-institutional spirit, but they too 'form a kind of skeleton' from which historians work. They focus on the evangelists rather than the evangelised who usually appear as statistics, achievements or failures. They don't appear as 'involved participants in a complex cross-cultural transaction'. George Dunne's *Generation of Giants* attempted to breach this divide, but was still heavily institutional. Narrative history, however, is always important from which new insights could derive.

More recent research has moved from concerns about 'accommodation', which was the challenge for the missionary, to 'indigenization' and 'contextualisation', which focuses on the young Church itself.

General historians of China and general history of religion by such authors as Arnold Rowbotham, Paul Cohen, Jonathan Spence, Jacques Gernet and many others have written about their subject for 'its intrinsic interest'. These authors have 'come to appreciate that missionary sources offer privileged insights into eras and geographical areas slightly if at all documented by other outside observers'. What is needed is 'an insider's history using outsiders' methods and language'.

Paul Cohen in his *Discovering History in China: American Historical Writing on the Recent Chinese Past* (1984) called for 'a China-centered history of China', stressing Chinese culture rather than Western culture 'for determining what is historically significant in the Chinese past'. Rule would rather use the term 'Chinese-centered' over China-centred, because the focus should be on the human subject, the Chinese Christian and how they come to believe in Jesus Christ, and how that changes his world view. Chinese culture is 'to an extent Christianised, but through the individual'.

Finally, Rule proposes an ethnographic history of the China mission. This focuses on description rather than explanation, understanding of the particular rather than generalisation, drawing upon the American symbolic interactionist school of anthropology for its basic theory, insisting that cultures are symbol systems and religion the highest meaning-making level of the culture. It follows Clifford Geertz's theory of 'the unraveling of the intricate interweaving of action and significance, meaning and intention, in specific events'. Historians of religion have largely neglected action for ideas, but 'actions often indicate intentions and meanings never articulated or at odds with the explicitly stated meanings'. Moreover, the accounts of actions are all that the historian has to work on. Assemblies, prayer practices, liturgical rituals, religious symbols and style of architecture have been comparatively neglected in the history of Chinese Catholicism.

What would an ethnographic history of Chinese Catholicism look like? Rule believes that it would tell the story, conveying 'something of the living experience of the lives it represents'. It would need to analyse seriously the written records of that Church, but with concern for intertextuality. It would take action seriously, 'regarding performance as a kind of text as significant if necessarily more opaque than words'. It would place religious ideas, motivation and experience at the centre of the narrative.[11]

Purpose of study

The aim in writing this history of the Jesuit missions in central China, 1842–1950, was to inform a wider audience of the motivation and missionary activity of Jesuits steeped in the European culture of the time as they encountered the contemporary culture of China. This period was a time of tumultuous change in the social and political life of China, and the Jesuits were challenged, not only to understand the traditional and current Chinese way of life, but also to understand the changes that were taking place, both locally and nationally, and how the presence of European missionaries might interact with these changes, while still upholding perennial Christian truths. Within the existing framework of their European religious experience, the missionaries were confronted with these changes that forced them to question and even sometimes modify their own self-identification. The many letters written by these Jesuits helped them to clarify their own Jesuit ideals, and how to adapt those ideals to the existing and changing circumstances that they encountered. This study looks at

---

11. Paul Rule, 'Chinese-centered Mission History', ibid., 52–9.

how the Jesuits attempted to resolve the contradictions and tensions that they experienced between the attachment to their traditional European religious ideals, and the reality of their lives in the changing social and culture milieu of everyday Chinese life.

The author is an insider to the task of understanding the nuances of Jesuit life, but an outsider to understanding the complexities of the Chinese character and way of life. Attempting to make this work as Chinese-centred as possible, the result was that it is primarily an analysis of how these religious Europeans understood Chinese culture and either made adaptations or rejected it. Some Chinese criticisms of missionary methods are available to indicate that the European missionaries largely failed to appreciate the complexities of the Chinese world, lived the life of Europeans, and tried to change the social and religious beliefs of the Chinese converts, usually isolating them from other Chinese. An outstanding exception to this was the Lazarite, Vincent Lebbe. The Jesuits, for the most part, and most of the hierarchy within China, rejected his style of missionary accommodation. Fortunately for the future of an indigenous Church, Rome supported Lebbe rather than the Jesuits.

Problems continually existed for the Jesuits in resolving the tension between the rhetoric of ideals, written rules and directives from Rome, and the lived Chinese reality, as well as the conflicts created by faith and secular experience. The outsider could be forgiven for not appreciating the significance of the power and strength of spiritual motivation behind daily activities, or for not really perceiving the reality of Jesuit life, as they attempted to reconcile their religious experience and ideals expressed in directives, with the reality of their individual lives. Many letters from missionaries pointed to these tensions, and indicated how they attempted to resolve them. Everyday challenges eventually won the day, be they external or internal. The external forces were the European culture, religious and secular, that acted upon the missionaries and made their task of missioning more difficult. They were rarely free to act instinctively in any important venture. The internal forces were the Chinese people themselves, their culture and social experiences. The changing Chinese political scene for supremacy continually complicated any action. While the local scene ultimately dictated missionary advancement, the European authority continually indicated what were acceptable procedures in any local situation.

In writing this history, the insights of two anthropologists were helpful. The first was Victor Turner because he dealt with the notion of community and the processes by which communities established their identities in themselves by ritual.[12] Then, Clifford Geertz has provided a methodology in the way he has suggested societies might be described. 'Heaven is a grain of sand' has been his constant theme. The whole is to be seen, even in the most particular.[13]

This study describes itself as a social and cultural history of the Jesuit missions in central China, 1842–1950; social in the sense of describing the interactions between the Jesuits themselves and with the Chinese; cultural in the sense of understanding the symbolic systems at work.

This type of social and cultural history gathers strength from viewing the sources out of which the narrative appears in a different way from the usual social, cultural or political analysis.[14] It attempts to be ethnographic in identifying the qualities of Jesuit religious life in the cultural and social context of China. Jesuit government spans a vast amount of documentation in which every aspect of life and governance are observed and reported on. In letters and articles, Jesuits constantly revealed themselves, their values, ideas and reactions to situations, sometimes indicating difference of opinions and ways of proceeding. However, not even the most honest self-measurement is beyond self-censorship. Among Jesuits, 'edification' was an important part of Jesuit culture, and this was obvious in much reporting about the missions and missionary activity.

This study looks at the way Jesuits from France, Spain, Italy, Austria, Hungary, French Canada and the United States, interacted with the Chinese in the Jiangnan region, by promoting the Christian religion. This was a distinctive period in the history of the Jesuits in

---

12. Victor W. Turner, *The Ritual Process* (UK: Penguin, 1969).
13. Clifford Geertz, *The Interpretation of Culture* (New York: Basic, 1973); also, cf. Robert Darnton, *The Great Cat Massacre* (USA: Penguin, 1984). Darnton's analysis of documents relating to a massacre of cats in eighteenth-century France shows how 'ordinary people made sense of the world, and how historians can enter into a period of history from the most particular events to draw more general social and cultural conclusions', from page 11.
14. June Philipp, 'Traditional historical narrative and action-orientated (or ethnographic) history', in *Historical Studies*, 20/80 (April 1983). Philipp argues that traditional narrative history is event-orientated, while ethnographic history is action-orientated, from page 352.

China, from the time they returned to China in 1842 to the time they were expelled by the Communists in the 1950s. It was also a dramatic period in Chinese history, with a dynasty change, battles between rival factions, and the impact of European invasion and its culture in influencing China into becoming a modern state. Into this world, in the footsteps of the European powers, the missionaries came to China to win 'souls for Christ'.

These Jesuit missionaries saw themselves as a tribe apart from the Chinese, a group of men rich in European tradition, essentially characterised by a life of faith that both motivated and sustained their religious life and activity. Jesuit spirituality was seen to energise, empower, and even to drive many to work hard pursuing 'the greater glory of God'. This spiritual ideal theoretically gave meaning to all other aspects of Jesuit life.

While all belonging to the Roman Catholic Church, and subject to its rules and decrees, as members of a Religious Order, they made perpetual vows of poverty, chastity and obedience. Poverty was understood to mean living a simple life after the example of Jesus of Nazareth; chastity enabled these men to be freed from family, and so available to all people, while obedience disposed them to readily accept the will of lawful authority 'for the glory of God' and 'the good of souls'. These vows were a mystery to the majority of the Chinese, and marked the Jesuits as a tribe apart.

In practice, interpretation of how these ideals were to be preserved when living in a culture that was totally different and unsupportive of these ideas was always a teasing reality. Jesuit religious life proposed 'separation' from the world, but this was always relative. They had also to be totally immersed in it, working with strength and vigour, teaching and offering spiritual nourishment to the many Christian converts in the Chinese villages. The demands of Jesuit religious life constantly clashed with pastoral demands, and superiors worked hard to ensure that religious life predominated when clashes occurred. The demands of ministry to the Chinese had to be in harmony with the demands of religious life.

In interacting with the Chinese, the Jesuits narrated their experiences and reflections that not only opened up their lives to new cultural experiences, but also gave a valuable insight into the European perception of China and the Chinese. It describes the way the Jesuits continued to operate their ministry with zeal amid natural disasters, wars, social disruptions, opposition, persecution and even torture and death. They were constantly challenged to modify their approaches with the changing times. This they found difficult because the adaptation required did not correspond to their European categories of thought and practice. Ultimately, this intransigence was their downfall. By the 1950s, it was impossible for two authoritarian bodies, the Communist Party and Roman Catholic Church, to co-exist, given ideologies that were diametrically opposed.

Criticism can easily be made of the European missionary for not understanding the Chinese psyche, and failing to understand and accept the changes that were taking place in Chinese society at the time. The notion of nationalism and sovereignty of the people did not fit the categories of Jesuit European mentality. While striving for neutrality between rival Chinese political factions, and emphasising a spiritual ministry to the Chinese, they struggled to come to terms with many decrees that emanated from the various Chinese governments, especially those that hindered their spiritual and educational ministry.

Accepting the French protectorate both aided and hindered missionary progress. It aided the spread of missionary contacts by offering support and even force when Chinese bureaucrats opposed the missionaries. It gave Chinese converts the security to know that when persecuted or simply unjustly treated, they could call on the European powers to act on their behalf. This support helped with conversions: being Christian brought social benefits to many poor Chinese, especially with education and relief support in times of floods or drought. The presence and influence of the European powers to modernise China ultimately benefited China by unleashing the desire among many reform-minded Chinese to fight for a modern state, equal in strength to the European nations that inhabited China.

However, the protectorate indicated to the Chinese that the missionaries were part of the European invasion and exploitation of China, and that they worked in collaboration with them. As the foreigners became to be hated for disrupting traditional Chinese ways of life, so were the Christian missionaries. Missionaries suffered persecution and death, more often from being European than from their spiritual offerings. Most Chinese wanted to govern themselves without European control, be that secular or religious. Responding to Chinese criticism that they were agents of European imperialism, the missionaries responded that their mission was entirely spiritual.

The missionaries constantly reassured themselves, their superiors in Rome or those in their home mission, or their mission supporters, by publishing great detailed statistics of the growth of each mission. The opening up of new districts, the increases in the number of converts, the establishment of mission houses, especially churches and schools, orphanages or medical stations, as well as the religious fervour of the new Christians, were tabled for all to appreciate. News of tragedies and setbacks were narrated to indicate the determination of the missionaries to overcome all challenges, sometimes with only the help of God. Spiritual and financial assistance from 'home' was deemed essential for the survival of the missions. Calls for more missionaries and finance were continually made.

Other continuing challenges for the missionaries were how to resolve the problem of Chinese language study for the newly arriving missionaries. These included the length of years given to the study, and the problem of many dialects. Many missionaries were not intellectually equipped to master the Chinese language that inhibited missionary effectiveness.

Questions raised about the most suitable language used in educational institutions was also a continuing challenge, with French being the main language chosen, but the more enlightened wanted greater use of Chinese. With the opening up of China to European culture and commerce, the demands for teaching English grew. The French Jesuits in Tianjin quickly accepted this in their institution, but the French Jesuits in Shanghai held out for many decades. However, with declining French manpower, and the need for missionaries from other Jesuit provinces, especially those that could teach English, they negotiated the assistance of Jesuits from the Californian province.

Much discernment took place related to the quality of theological formation of seminarians and the religious formation of catechists and catechumens. Related to this was the belief that despite declaring that the formation offered was similar to that in Europe, most Jesuit missionaries did not believe that the Chinese Jesuits had leadership qualities or were sufficiently qualified to teach in seminaries.

Jesuit observations on the social and political changes in China were an important ongoing part of the narrative.

With all these difficulties to overcome to bring the Gospel to the Chinese people, by the time the Europeans left China, and with most Chinese missionaries imprisoned, a significant legacy of many Chinese Catholics remained. From the 1950s, those converts who remained loyal to their faith were forced to go underground, and these became the nucleus of the restored Catholic Church in China under Deng Xiaoping from 1978.[15] Without the earlier work of the European missionaries, the Catholic Church in China would not have survived. Even the official suppression of religion by Mao Zedong and the subsequent persecution of Christians did not destroy the legacy of the European missionaries. While the Europeans believed that the Catholic Church in China would not survive without them, the irony is that it was the Chinese priests and religious who were criticised by the Europeans as unsuitable for leadership that supported the Catholic families in keeping their faith. The seeds sown by the European missionaries came to fruition in ways never anticipated by the Europeans, but occurred with the survival of an indigenous Church.

China is a striking example of the importance of the laity in the survival of the Catholic faith. After persecutions in the seventeenth and eighteenth centuries and the absence of priests, the Catholic laity kept the faith alive. They did this again after 1950. The Chinese Church was forced to initiate the 'era of the laity' well before it became popular after the Second Vatican Council (1962–5) in the wider Catholic Church. Today, with the Christian Churches in China under strict control from government agencies, the role of the laity in keeping alive the faith remains crucial for the future spread of the Christian Good News.

According to recent statistics relating to the Catholic Church in China in 2015, it is estimated that there are 112 bishops in Mainland China. Among them, 99 are in ministry. Seventy bishops are in the open Church community, eleven more than in 2014. In the underground community, there are 29, a drop of 13 compared to 2014. There are also 2,500 priests and 3,170 religious sisters in the open Church, a decrease since 2014. The open Church has nine seminaries, but the number of seminarians had decreased from 560 in 2014 to 424 in 2015. The underground Church also has ten seminaries with the number of seminarians declining from 300 to 200 between 2014

---

15. Deng Maomao, *Deng Xiaoping, My Father*, (NY: Basic Books, 1995).

and 2015. Minor seminaries have increased from eleven to twenty within the past year.[16] The Patriotic Church estimates that the Catholic population of China is approximately ten million, but this does not include those Catholics belonging to the underground Church.

These statistics indicate that Church leadership in China is healthy, but in much need of support as it balances communicating its spiritual message to the Chinese people, while remaining within the guidelines of the Chinese authorities. One important challenge for the Chinese Church is unity between open and underground Church communities. This will take much discernment, openness, dialogue and willingness to take risks, focusing on the future rather than holding on to the past.

---

16. UCAN News, via China Infodoc Service, 29 April 2016, quoting Anthony Lamb in *Tripod*, Spring edition, 2016.

Maps Volume 1

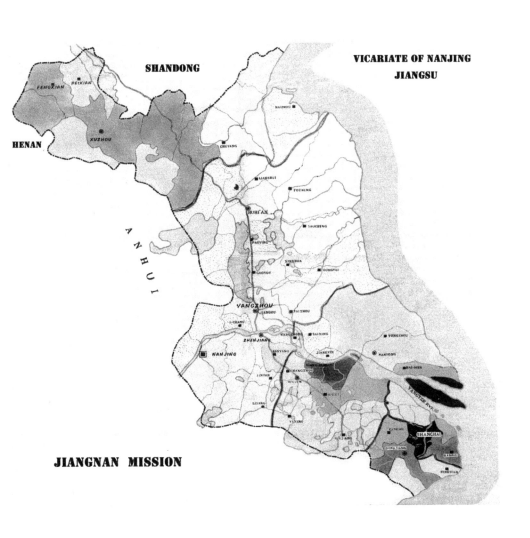

SHANDONG

VICARIATE OF NANJING

JIANGSU

HENAN

FENGXIAN
PEIXIAN

XUZHOU

CHUYANG

HAIZHOU

LIANSHUI

FOUNING

A N H U I

HUAI-AN

YANCHENG

BAOYING

XINGHUA

GAOYOU

DONGTAI

YANGZHOU

JIANGDU

I-CHANG

TAIZHOU

ZHENJIANG

YANGZHONG

TAIXING

YONGZHOU

NANJING

DANYANG

JIANGYIN

NANTONG

JINTON

CHANGZHOU

HAI-MEN

WUJIN

YANGTZE RIV.

LIYANG

WUXI

YIXING

JIADING

QINGPU

SHANGHAI

SONGJIANG

NANHUI

FENGXIAN

JIANGNAN MISSION

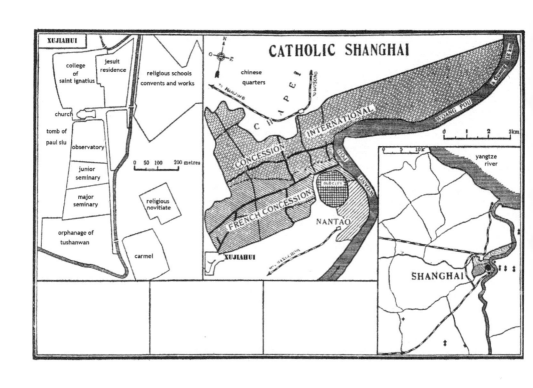

XUJIAHUI

college of saint ignatius

jesuit residence

religious schools convents and works

church

tomb of paul siu

observatory

junior seminary

major seminary

orphanage of tushanwan

religious novitiate

carmel

0 50 100   200 metres

CATHOLIC SHANGHAI

chinese quarters

N
O   E
S

C H A P E I

INTERNATIONAL CONCESSION

FRENCH CONCESSION

NANTAO

XUJIAHUI

TO NANJING

TO WUSONG

WOANG POU

OLD CITY

TO HANGCHOW

0   1   2   3km

0   5   10km

yangtze river

SHANGHAI

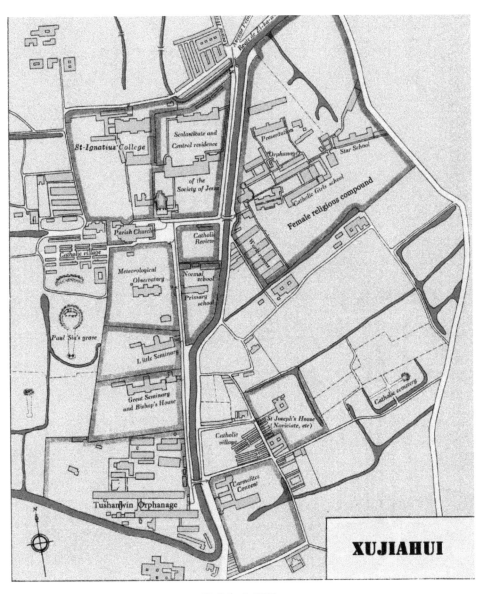

Xujiahui, 1930s.

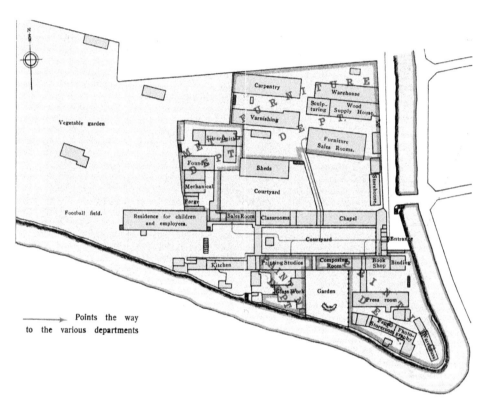

Tughanwan orphanage complex, late 1930s.

Chapter 1
Jiangnan Mission, 1842–1850
Province of France

Jesuits return to China, 1842–1850

There were no shipping companies accepting passengers to the Far East in 1840, so Fathers Claude Gotteland[1], François Estève[2] and Benjamin Brueyre[3] sought assistance from the French Jesuit Gustave François Xavier Delacroix de Ravignan (1795–1858)[4] and Bishop

---

1. **Claude Gotteland**, a Savoyard from the Province of Lyon, the designated superior of the mission, aged 40, a specialist in mathematics and physics, was born in Bossens (Savoy) on 12 June 1803 and died in Xujiahui, 17 July 1856.
2. **François Estève**, from the Province of France, aged 36, was born in Paris on 26 March 1807 and died in Xujiahui, 1 July 1848, aged 41.
3. **Benjamin Brueyre** was born in Tense on 20 May 1810, entered the Province of Toulouse on 19 September 1831, aged 21, founded the first seminary in Shanghai, February 1843, was superior of the Zhili mission from 1859–1866, and died in Xianxian, 24 February 1880.
4. **Gustave de Ravignan** was born at Bayonne on 1 December 1795 and died in Paris in 1858. He was an intelligent young man who eventually studied law and became deputy attorney general in 1821. He even served in the military. Then he entered the Sulpician seminary in 1822 for a short time before being received into the Jesuit noviciate at Montrouge. After his ordination in 1828, he taught dogmatic theology and preached missions and retreats in Europe and London, finally gaining fame with his conferences at Notre Dame. Here, he was proclaimed a worthy successor to the famous Dominican French preacher, Jean-Baptiste Henri Lacordaire. Subsequently, he was caught in negotiations between the Vatican and the French government, especially with Thiers and Béranger, 1843–5, which ended with the Jesuits temporarily withdrawing from France. His fame as a prominent preacher continued, preaching the Lenten sermons in 1855 at the Tuileries before Napolcon III and the Empress Eugénie. At his death, some called him 'the Apostle of Paris'.

1

Félix Antoine Philibert Dupanloup (1802–78).[5] They spoke to the Queen of France, Marie-Amelia, about the journey of these three Jesuits to China and, as a result, the Minister of the Navy gave the three priests free passage from Brest on the frigate *L'Erigone*, 27 April 1841, sailing for Manila, arriving on 23 September. After a few weeks rest, they reached Macao, 21 October 1841, on a German merchant-man *Paradise*. Not having a visa from Lisbon, the Jesuits were not welcome in Macao, and faced hostility from the Lazarists,[6] who were aware that they were being replaced in Jiangnan with these Jesuits. Permission was given to them to stay for only a short time during which they studied Chinese.

When transport became available, they left for Tinghai of the Zhoushan Islands together with a French Lazarist and two Italian Franciscans on the English transport *Maria*. After further difficulty finding transport to China, Gotteland and Estève were forced to embark on a British Navy ship, the *Anna*, arriving in Wusong, 11 July 1842.[7] From there, Chinese Christians took them by boat to the Catholic station at Pudong, facing Shanghai.

---

5. **Felix Dupanloup** was born at Saint-Félix, Savoie on 3 January 1802 and died in Lacombe, Isère on 11 October 1878. After choosing an ecclesiastical career, he was ordained priest in 1825, and while curate at the Madeleine was, among other duties, religious tutor to the Duc de Bordeaux and the Princes d'Orléans. Soon after, he gained fame as an orator, and as director of the seminary of Saint-Nicolas (1837–45). In 1844, together with Montalembert and de Ravignan, he fought for liberty of education that resulted in the Falloux Law. He was appointed Bishop of Orléans in 1849, where he became highly respected for his administration that extended to all aspects of diocesan life. He was elected a member of the French Academy in 1854. He always defended the Holy See and, at the Vatican Council in 1870, while not against the declaration of papal infallibility, he argued against the opportuneness of its definition. After the Franco-Prussian War, he was sent as a delegate from Orléans to the National Assembly, becoming a senator in 1875. He was undoubtedly one of the most able French bishops of his day.
6. The Lazarists, or Vincentians, were formally called the Congregation of the Mission (CM), a vowed religious institute of priests and brothers associated with the Vincentian family, a loose federation of organizations that claimed St Vincent de Paul as their founder. The congregation was constituted by the Holy See on 12 January 1633, its rule of life based on that of the Jesuits. In 1783, they took the place of the Jesuits in China after the Holy See suppressed the Jesuits worldwide.
7. Peter W Fay, 'The French Catholic Mission in China during the Opium War' in *Modern Asian Studies*, 4/2 (1970): 115–28.

Upon arrival, the bishop, Ludovico de Bési,[8] welcomed them, and suggested that they should first improve their Mandarin and learn the Shanghai dialect. They brought with them many cases of books and

8. **Ludovico de Bési** was an Italian missionary, born into a Catholic aristocratic family on 16 October 1805 in Verona. After ordination in 1829, he joined *Propaganda Fide* in January 1830. After a brief study of Chinese at the College of the Holy Family in Naples in 1832, *Propaganda Fide* assigned him to the China mission. After a short period working as a missionary and following ecclesial maneuverings, he was appointed administrator of the diocese of Nanjing and vicar apostolic of Shandong in 1839, arriving in 1841, but immediately appointed a pro-vicar and returned to Jiangnan, the contemporary Provinces of Jiangsu and Anhui, at the request of the Chinese priests and people. After various conflicts with local Christians, the Lazarists and the Jesuits, he left China for Europe and resigned his China post to Bishop Maresca on 3 June 1848. In 1850, he was appointed Apostolic Delegate in the Argentine Confederation. He attended Vatican I, during which he died at a retreat at Desenzano on Lago di Garda on 8 September 1871. Cf. R.G.Tiedemann, 'Ludovico de Bési' in *Ricci Roundtable on the History of Christianity in China*, biographies.

    Paul Mariani discovered further information about Bési, suggesting that a previously undisclosed letter indicated that Bési was removed from his appointment in China because of allegations of moral indiscretions, 'especially with the virgins' (304–5). cf. Paul Mariani, 'The Phoenix Rises from the Ashes: The Restoration of the Jesuit Shanghai Mission', Part IV, China and Beyond, in *Jesuit Survival and Restoration, A global history, 1773–1900,* Chapter 17, edited by Robert A Maryks and Jonathan Wright (USA: Brill, 2014), 299–314. This article of Mariani's is an excellent source on the early days of the return of the Jesuits to Shanghai. In the same volume edited by Maryks and Wright, Paul Rule has an article entitled 'Restoration or New creation? The Return of the Society of Jesus to China', 261–77, suggesting that the return of the Jesuits in 1842 was quite different from the earlier Jesuit mission to China, as they did not return to Beijing to continue the scientific and intellectual apostolate, and rather concentrated on pastoral work in Shanghai, focusing on the current needs of an emerging China. The returning Jesuits also had to take an oath against the Chinese Rites. This meant a break with the earlier period. Jeremy Clarke developed this point in his article in the same volume, 'The Chinese Rites Controversy's Long Shadow Over the Restored Society of Jesus', 315–30. Benoit Vermander SJ in *Jesuits and China*, Oxford Online Publication, April 2015 makes a further important contribution to the discussion of the return of the Jesuits to China. His work covers the whole Jesuit mission to China from the earliest days to the post-1949 period. In his description of the Second Mission, 1842–1949, he comments on the diversity of opinion among these Jesuits, such as between Gotteland, a traditionalist, and Vuilaume or Gonnet who expressed 'attitudes and methods' similar to the Ricci period. The context of the resumed Jesuit mission in 1842 was markedly different from that of the arrival of Ricci.

liturgical vestments. Local Chinese spread rumours that the 'foreign devils' had brought treasure with them. Soon bandits appeared to attack the Christians with their suspected treasures. As a result, Bési quickly dispatched some of the luggage with Estève to a village thirty kilometres south west of Shanghai.[9]

For pastoral reasons, Brueyre remained in Tinghai, but after the British forces evacuated the area, Bési recalled him to Wusong, arriving 23 October. He was sent as pastor at Yangshupu, on the West bank of the Huangpu River.

The region of Jiangnan had existed since 1667 and consisted of two Chinese provinces: Jiangsu and Anhui. The former was the richer of the two and had the larger population. Shanghai was the major city of the region and the commercial capital of China.

The arrival in Shanghai of the three Jesuits marked the resumption of mission works in China following the suppression of the Jesuits in the universal Church in 1773. When they arrived, there were only ten secular Chinese priests in the vicariate of Jiangnan, four of whom were pastorally ineffectual. In a letter to *Propaganda Fide*,[10] 1 December 1841, a missionary described the Christians of Jiangnan as 'ignorant, given to gambling, living in concubinage, and superstitious'.[11]

The Catholic Church in China

After the worldwide restoration of the Society of Jesus by Pius VII in 1814, Christian communities, together with Chinese priests, asked Rome for the Jesuits to return to China. The Christians of Beijing, remembering the importance of the scientific and cultural works of earlier Jesuits, wrote a letter in Chinese to the superior general of the Society on 25 April 1832 asking for some learned and zealous Jesu-

9. Fernando Mateos, SJ, Suppression and Restoration, 2014, quoting Joseph de la Servière, SJ, *Histoire de la Mission du Kiang-nan*, Tome I, 1840–1856, (Shanghai: Xujiahui, 1914): 53–4.

10. The Sacred Congregation for the Propagation of the Faith, commonly known by its Latin title, *Propaganda Fide*, was founded by Pope Gregory XV, 1622, to promote and coordinate mission work for the Church in non-Christian countries. In 1627, it established within itself a training college for missionaries the *Collegium Urbanum*.

11. M. Faivre to Propaganda, 1 December 1841, quoted in Boucher, H., *La Mission du Kiang-nan*, (Paris, 1900), 44.

its. The general replied that he would send Jesuits when requested by the Vatican. These Christians wrote again in 1834, this time to Pope Gregory XVI (1831–46), with a similar request.

The pope, a man who reflected the conservative attitudes of his time – opposing modernisation and democratic movements – was, however, a promoter of the missions, including the development of the indigenous clergy. In response to the petitions from the Chinese Christians, the pope sent Bési to China in 1833 to replace the elderly Bishop of Nanjing, Cajétan Perès-Pereira, who was based in Beijing. But it was not until 1839 that Bési was invited by the Catholics of Jiangnan to be their bishop. He arrived in 1841 and eventually replaced the Lazarists in the region with the Jesuits.[12] The Lazarists had wanted the mission of Nanjing, and were not happy with the arrival of the Jesuits. They had wanted the Jesuits to go to Shandong. Bési did not want two congregations working in the same region; he believed that it never worked. The Christians in Jiangnan were already divided in loyalties between the Lazarists and the Jesuits, but the majority supported the Jesuits. Moreover, Gotteland did not want to work alongside the Lazarists, nor did he want to go to Shandong, as he believed that was courting martyrdom because of the persecution of Christians in that area.[13] Rather, at the beginning of his ministry in China, Gotteland believed it was better for the Jesuits to work independently of any other religious order, and as for going to Shandong, he was not ready for a martyr's death.

It was the 1834 request to the pope and the superior general from 51 Christians representing the Jiangnan mission claiming pastoral neglect of the mission, and, reflecting the significant impact of earlier Jesuits, that had ultimate effect in the return of the Jesuits. In addition, Bési wrote to the superior general Jan Roothaan in 1839 supporting this claim, reinforced by a letter of 96 Christians from the Nanjing diocese in November 1838. On 30 January 1840, Cardinal Fransoni, Prefect of Propaganda, asked the general to send Jesuits to support Bési. This time the general agreed and asked the Jesuit Province of

---

12. David Mungello, 'The Return of the Jesuits to China in 1841 and the Chinese Christian Backlash', in *Sino-Western Cultural Relations Journal'*, 27 (2005): 12.
13. Gotteland to Guidée, Jiangnan, 19 August 1842. ARSI; Gotteland to Maillard, Jiangnan, 5 July 1842. ARSI (*Archivum Romanum Societatis Iesu*, Jesuit archives, Rome).

France to select three Jesuits capable of being missionaries in China.[14] In 1840, the Province of France had 278 members with 40 novices.

The 'old Christians' of the Nanjing diocese remembered and appreciated the presence of earlier Jesuits. Matteo Ricci (1552–1610), Julio Aleni (1582–1649) and Adam Schall (1592–1666) had been missioners in the region. The Catholic Church began in Shanghai in 1608, when Paul Xu Guangqi, the first Shanghai Catholic, invited the Italian Jesuit, Lazaro Cattaneo, to preach there. About 200 people received Baptism during the next few years, and the first Catholic church was built near Xujiahui. Other Jesuits followed, especially another Italian, Francesco Brancati, who worked in the area, 1623–65, baptising 2,300 people. He maintained good relations with the Xu family, and officiated at the burial of Xu Guangqi in 1633.[15]

Among the last ex-Jesuits working in the late eighteenth century, three European Jesuits did pastoral work in the Jiangnan region, 'the most literate and prosperous region of the country'. They were Inácio Pires (1724–76+), Martin Correa (1699–1786) and Bishop Gottfried Xavier von Laimbeckhoven (1707–87).

Laimbeckhoven, an Austrian, was Bishop of Nanjing from 1752–87, a man praised for his knowledge, zeal and virtue, who, during a time of great persecution of Christians in China, worked with patience and resolve, but not without fear, to support his Christian communities. Two Chinese Jesuits supported him, Mark Guan (1717–74) of Xuzhou, and John Yao (1722–96) of Huizhou, Province of Anhui. Laimbeckhoven arrived in Jiangnan, 6 May 1759, to work with a small flock of 1,500 Christians, which later grew to 24,000[16]. Former Jesuits outlived him working as secular priests, with the last ex-Jesuit, Louis de Poirot, dying in Beijing in 1813.[17]

---

14. Mungello, op. cit., p. 15.
15. **Xu Guangqi** (1562–1633) was a senior mandarin bureaucrat in Imperial China, and a disciple of Matteo Ricci; helping him with the translation of Euclid's elements of geometry. He was known in China 'as a great scientist, an incorruptible man and a patriot'. With his scientific knowledge, he helped transform existing methods of farming, irrigation and construction. He was a founder of the Christian community in Shanghai after receiving Baptism in 1603 (*Asia News*, 2 January 2015).
16. Joseph Krahl, SJ, 'China Missions in Crisis', Bishop Laimbeckhoven and his times, 1738–1787, *Analecta Gregoriana*, 137 (1963): 99.
17. Mungello, op. cit., 9.

The Papal Bull of Suppression of the Society was not promulgated in Beijing until November 1775. The years following were troubled with internal disputes among missionaries and persecution from the Chinese authorities that greatly affected both Christians and missionaries. Those Chinese Christians who survived the persecutions did so within the family, keeping alive the faith in the communities, supported by laymen and women, who led the rosary and litanies, as well as family rituals within the community. Priests visited the communities rarely: so lay leaders gave religious instruction, and were in charge of finances, paying catechists and promoting works of charity. Itinerant catechists baptised abandoned children. The work of the consecrated virgins[18] was of vital importance to sustaining Christians

---

18. Catechists played a significant role in the life of the Church. The assistance of lay Chinese catechists was essential to the evangelisation of China, as the foreign missionaries had poor knowledge of the Chinese language and culture. There were male and female catechists, who taught the essence of the Catholic faith to the local people, and had to undergo a long period of formation. They kept a record of missionary activities in the area, reporting and guiding the priest when he visited. They helped the priests with marriages and funerals. The female catechists were called 'virgins', who adopted the celibate life, and dedicated their lives to missionary work. They were the means for the missionaries to make contact with Chinese women. In the middle of the Qing dynasty, in Sichuan, they served as commentators and cantors at Sunday Mass, read passages from spiritual books, and explained Catholic doctrine. However, as they were not fully trained at this time, their influence was limited. They were, however, the backbone of the Church.

    Strict laws governed their selection. They must be 36 years old, and set a good example to others. There were virgin catechists and ordinary virgins. At the end of nineteenth century in the diocese of Zhili (Province of Hebei), there were 408 virgins, among whom 283 were teachers. Non-catechist virgins took part in the more general missionary life. In the second half of the nineteenth century, many vicariates ran special schools for the formation of virgin catechists. The pioneer was the Jesuit-run vicariate of Jiangnan, which in 1855, under Luigi Maria Sica, organised the virgins in Huang Tang, Shanghai, into a community. Joseph Gonnet continued this work in Zhili, with a training school in Xianxian in 1876. The influence of these virgins extended to non-Christians.

    By 1892, the training of catechist virgins became more structured and lasted up to five years, requiring a good knowledge of scriptures. In the early days, virgins lived with their families. Later, the virgin catechists were divided into two groups; one, the itinerary group, centred around the parish, but also moved out to the districts, while the second group was residential and assisted the priest at Mass on Sundays, helped in the administration of the parish and educated the local people. (This information was extracted from an article by

and contributing to the growth of the Church. The numbers of Christians increased, as did the number of Chinese clergy. Around 1800, there were about 75 priests in China, 50 Chinese and 25 foreigners.[19] In 1804, eleven priests ministered to 50,000 Christians in the three Provinces of Henan, Anhui and Jiangsu.[20] At this time, only five ex-Jesuits worked in China, all living and working in scientific and cultural works in Beijing as employees of the emperor, but they were also involved pastorally with local Christians.

With knowledge that the Society of Jesus still worked in Russia, Louis de Poirot wrote to Rome several letters from 1778 asking for Jesuits to return to China, but he received no response. He wrote again with the same request in 1804, after learning that the pope had re-established the Jesuits in the Kingdom of Naples. This time he received a positive response, and two Jesuits were nominated for China, but as no ship sailed from Lisbon to the Far East at that time, they returned to Russia.[21]

Europe at this time was recovering from the Napoleonic wars, and with the restoration of monarchy in France, Catholicism revived with a conservative spirit. This was in contrast to an age now changed by revolutions and liberal thought. Catholicism was experienced as opposing the new social and cultural form of democracy and liberalism. Following the hierarchic Church, the Jesuits were generally

Kang Zhijie, 'The Yeast of Evangelization: a Study on the Contribution of the Virgin Catechists', in *Tripod*, 33/170 (Autumn 2013). (Catholic Women in China.)

Further background information on the role of the virgins as examples of indigenous leadership, highlighting the role of Chinese women in faith education, is to be found in an article by Robert Entenmann, 'Christian Virgins in Eighteenth Century Sichuan', in *Christianity in China: From the Eighteenth Century to the Present*, edited by Daniel H Bays (California: Stanford University Press, 1996), 180–93. Entenmann suggests that the virgins in Sichuan were established probably as early as the 1640s, but began as an Order in 1744.

R.G. Tiedemann also has an article on the virgins entitled 'Catholic Religious Communities of Women (Foreign)' in *Handbook of Christianity in China, Volume 2: 1800 to the Present, Part Two: Republican China*, edited by R.G. Tiedemann (USA: Brill, 2010), 526–31.

19. Nicholas Standaert, SJ, 'The Chinese Mission without Jesuits', in *Yearbook of the Society of Jesus* (2014): 58. This article is a comprehensive summary of Christian life in China, 1775–1843.

20. R. Datin, SJ, *Un centenaire de la mission de Chang-hai, 1842–1942* (Paris 1943), 24–6.

21. Fernando Mateos, SJ, *China Province News* (April 2014), 22.

ultramontane, vigorous in supporting autocratic and monarchic structures. Their fortunes were linked to those of the papacy. Suppression had radically weakened their spirit of institutional independence. Despite every effort to be cautious and orthodox, the Jesuits were expelled from towns and countries by liberal and anti-clerical governments on 32 occasions between 1814 and 1848.[22] Many Portuguese colonies fell into British, French and Dutch hands, so they could no longer be generous with missionaries.

France in 1800s

Religious revivals in Europe in the 1820s led to a gradual expansion of missionary enterprise in China. This revival in France occurred among intellectuals influenced by the Romantic movements, and gave expression among the people in the form of sentimental devotions, especially those of the Sacred Heart of Jesus, the Immaculate Heart of Mary and the Holy Family. Other devotional demonstrations included the wearing of miraculous medals and scapulars, religious processions and pilgrimages and the cult of relics and saints.

The interest in foreign missions among the people of France led to the formation of the Association for the Propagation of the Faith, a lay organisation established in France in 1822, with the aim to support overseas missions. This organisation spread to other European countries and began a significant fundraising institution for the Catholic missions.

Another important organisation, the Holy Childhood Association, founded by Charles de Forbin-Janson in France in 1843 provided funds for the Baptism of non-Christian children in danger of death. Regular communications between the missionaries and the organisation kept alive this important lay collaboration.

The missionary zeal of Pope Pius VII led to the reorganisation of the Sacred Congregation for the Propagation of the Faith (*Propaganda Fide*), the restoration of the Society of Jesus in 1814, and the creation of new male and female missionary societies.[23]

---

22. John W. Padberg, SJ, *Colleges in Controversy, the Jesuit schools in France from Revival to Suppression, 1815–1880* (USA: Harvard University Press, 1969).
23. *Handbook of Christianity in China, Volume Two. 1800-present*, edited by R.G. Tiedemann (Brill, 2009), 278–81

Jesuits returned to France, 31 July 1814, by opening a noviciate with nine novices. By the end of that year the numbers increased to 70 novices. With a sympathetic King, Louis XVIII, but with ministerial opposition, the peaceful life of Jesuits was continually challenged. Technically the Mission of France was an unlawful institution, having been suppressed since 1764, so the Jesuits proceeded cautiously. They opened minor seminaries, primary and secondary schools, and provided home missions. By 1820, Jesuit numbers had so increased that the mission was raised to the status of a province. Opposition to them grew, not only because of their successes, but also because their presence symbolised the Catholic Church's opposition to the secular state. The Jesuits were the pope's men.

In 1828, the Jesuits' eight educational establishments were closed down. Then with the anti-clerical 1830 revolution, all Jesuits were expelled from France. Missionary activity resumed at this time, beginning with a mission to Syria. By 1836, with the tacit acceptance of Louis Philippe, the Jesuits returned to France. Their numbers so increased in succeeding years that the Province of Lyon was created in 1836 from the Province of France, which, in 1840, opened nine new colleges and residences. Opposition to the Jesuits continued during the 1840s, with Adolphe Thiers pressing for the suppression of the Jesuits once and for all. In 1845, Jesuit houses in Paris, Lyon and Avignon were closed. The 1848 revolution gave the Jesuits some breathing space, as the new government believed that they ought to modify their more extreme anticlericalism. From the 1850s, the Jesuits continued to expand in France.[24]

China and relations with the West

The China into which the new missionaries were sent in 1842 was largely rural, consisting of about 300 million farmers. These formed a separate class from the urban artisans, merchants, landlords, scholars and officials who numbered around 80 to 100 million people.[25] Any social change depended upon the educated elite and imperial officials

24. Cornelius Michael Buckley, SJ, *When Jesuits were Giants* (USA: Ignatius Press, 1999), 19–23.
25. John King Fairbank, *The Great Chinese Revolution, 1800–1985* (New York: Harper and Row, 1986), 23.

who were the ruling class, and it was they who advised the emperor. He decreed the official line, but this did not always filter down to the rural masses, many of whom rejected the Manchu rule. The spirit of the time communicated by the Manchus was 'backward and inward-looking, defensive and xenophobic'.[26]

China experienced many periods of seclusion from the outside world in its history, but it was never completely isolated. Over time, Arab, Portuguese and Dutch traders engaged in occasional direct or indirect trade, followed by the East India Company and the British. [27]

Diplomatic negotiations with China were attempted by the Dutch, Russian, Vatican and Portuguese, but met with failure. But the British were more successful after the embassy of Lord Macartney, 1792–3. This became the turning point in China's diplomatic and commercial relations, and a symbol of the changing relationship between China and the West. The encounter between Macartney and the emperor failed, with neither side prepared to make concessions regarding protocol or trading requests, and highlighted a clash of cultures, of different ways of viewing the world. The British wanted diplomatic and trading relations on an equal basis; the Chinese did not. Future failures by the British to secure trading rights inexorably drew China and Britain into conflict. Two wars followed, the First Opium War (1839–42) and the Second Opium War (1856–8), with the opium trade the immediate cause of the conflict. It was at this time that the Jesuits re-entered China.

Chinese officials worked vigorously to stop the opium trade, but it was too profitable for the British to withdraw. When negotiations broke down, British ships began attacking Chinese ships in the Pearl River delta from 3 November 1839. Further fighting followed, with the Chinese finally conceding defeat to the superior British forces. The Treaty of Nanjing was signed, the first of the 'unequal treaties' on 29 August 1842. The Chinese were humiliated and Western influence in China grew through trade. The United States and France signed further treaties in 1844, obtaining extraterritorial rights that allowed them to maintain separate legal, judicial, police and tax system in the treaty ports. French consulates were opened in Guangdong (1845),

---

26. Fairbank, op. cit., 36.
27 Michael Dillon, *China, a Modern History* (London/New York: Tauris 2010), 29–35.

Xiamen (1846) and Shanghai (1848). This became a most significant concession for the future growth of the Jesuit missions in China, with Shanghai their base. The French community in Shanghai at the time numbered about thirty, most of whom were Jesuits.

The treaty with France also gave them, and Chinese Christians, permission to practise Christianity in the five treaty ports without persecution. However, priests and Christians living in the countryside remained open to persecution. [28]

These treaties and the relationship between the Chinese and the Western powers were the seed beds for future clashes between the missionaries who relied on the foreign powers for support, and the Chinese who resisted the growing influence of Western culture and religion. It was continually difficult for the missionaries to divest themselves from European culture and to immerse themselves in Chinese culture.

Jesuits prepare for mission

When Gotteland and Estève received news that they were being sent to China, they were overjoyed. Gotteland expressed his gratitude to the superior general, Roothaan, telling him that he had prepared 50 sermons for the missions on ten subjects, but would treat 33 subjects in all on 'the great truths of our religion, symbols, sacraments, commandments, method and order of the Spiritual Exercises, devotion to the Sacred Heart of Jesus and Mary, as well as on Scripture and the works of the early Fathers, such as John Chrysostom'.[29] It could only be imagined how the Chinese would have reacted to sermons of this kind. Chinese neophytes would have had no understanding of these theological truths without more basic background information such as the scriptures. Mission methodology of preparing religious instruction without any idea of the readiness of the recipients to receive these ideas was typical of the time.

A month later, he was still overwhelmed with delight about being sent to China. He said the right thing about being not worthy 'because of my many faults', and had doubts and difficulties about the mission. At the time, he did not appear to have received any instructions about

---

28. Ibid., 36–41.
29. Gotteland to General, Vannes, 6 June 1840. ARSI.

the mission and what he should do, except for the advice 'to save souls and fulfil your ardent desires'. So he shared his concerns with the superior general, such as his desire to study Chinese in Naples. He wanted to know what powers he had as head of this new mission, with whom did he correspond, with whom did he meet when he arrived in Macau, and what he should say to him? Did he establish a Jesuit residence or should the group become missionaries? How should he react to the Chinese Christians? Should he teach a little science, mindful of the influence of the earlier Jesuits with regard to the sciences? Further questions occupied his mind: should he grow a beard, 'take a watch, two boxes of books, instruments?'[30] Only gradually did it occur to Gotteland that he was entering a completely different culture. He had no idea of how to conduct his mission or adapt his European theology to new circumstances. His knowledge of the successful work of earlier Jesuits in teaching science gave him some insight, and so he studied astronomy. It might be useful, as education was traditionally an important aspect of Jesuit mission work.

With no evident response from the superior general, he set to work in preparation for his mission. He met with the Society of the Foreign Missions of Paris[31] and put questions to them, which they answered cordially. He came to recognise the importance of reading and speaking Chinese, but had reservations about doing that at Macau. Furthermore, he believed he should make the voyage in lay dress to avoid upsetting the Portuguese. He already had a sense that he might not be welcomed in Macau. He indicated as well that he was aware that *Propaganda Fide* wanted quicker local ordinations from among the Chinese people.[32] This information was very basic for someone embarking on such a totally different mission from one in Europe. Jesuits assigned to China received little or no prior education about the land to which they were sent, nor how they might conduct their mission. They had to learn from experience.

Upon hearing that the Jesuits were being sent to China, the procurator of the missions from *Propaganda Fide*, a secular priest, Theo-

30. Gotteland to General, Vannes, 13 July 1840. ARSI.
31. The Society of Foreign Missions of Paris, *Missions Étrangères*, was established 1658–63, by Bishops Pallu and de la Motte. It was a congregation of secular priests who mainly worked in the foreign missions, especially in Indo-China and China.
32. Gotteland to General, Paris, 22 July 1840. ARSI.

dore Joset [33], wrote a warning note saying that while he welcomed the Jesuits, others did not want them, seeing them as an 'evil presence'. Local Portuguese missionaries in Macau were fearful, but when they arrived he welcomed them, and arranged for them to have a teacher of Chinese. He stressed the importance of European science for the Chinese, especially astronomy. Finally, he would arrange for the Jesuits to go to Sancian and Nanjing, which was currently in the hands of the English.[34] Missionaries to China at this time had little choice of being transported by any other means than the opium-carrying ships of the British.

Before leaving Europe, the Jesuits were required by *Propaganda Fide* to swear obedience to the condemnation of the Chinese rites issued by Pope Benedict XIV in 1742.[35] Missionaries to China accepted this papal decree without question.

The Catholic population of China in 1841 was approximately 250,000 out of a total population of 413 million.[36] The growth in the number of Catholics in China had not increased in proportion to the rise in the general population. However, Jiangnan appeared to have 20 per cent of all Catholics in China. The number of Catholics in the region in 1847 was 60,963.[37]

Approximately 50 European and 100 Chinese priests worked among the Chinese Catholics in 1841. The Europeans were Italian Franciscans, under *Propaganda Fide*, Portuguese and Chinese Lazarists, secular priests from the Paris Société des Missions Étrangères, and Spanish Dominicans from the Philippines. Each of the first three

33. **Theodore Joset**, 1804–1842, was the procurator of the Sacred Congregation for the Propaganda of the Faith in the Far East. He was a secular priest sent to Macao in 1833. He was later appointed the first prefect apostolic of Hong Kong, and settled there on 3 March 1842 after being banished from Macao by the Portuguese authorities. He was welcomed in Hong Kong by the British authorities who appreciated the spiritual assistance given by the Catholic Church to the Irish soldiers in their military.
34. Joset to Brethren of the Society of Jesus, Macao, 1841. ARSI. Joset to General, Macao, 8 November 1841. ARSI.
35. Mungello, op. cit., 16.
36. Ibid., 16, quoting Ping-ti Ho, *Studies on the Population of China, 1368–1953* (Cambridge, Massachusetts: HUP, 1959), 282.
37. Ibid., 17.

groups was represented in Macau by a procurator, the mission promoter.[38]

This was the unstable state of the Church in China at the time, but the political situation was even more complicated. The Jesuits arrived in Shanghai one month before the signing of the Treaty of Nanjing, but the climate in China was already one of hostility between the Chinese and the European powers. Arriving on the British ship did not help the welcome of the Jesuits in Shanghai, and Bési wrote to Pope Gregory XVI that the Chinese hatred of the Protestant English extended by association to European Catholics.[39]

With the approval of the Vatican and the superior general, Bési appointed Gotteland vicar general, in addition to being Jesuit superior. He also sent Estève to Pudong to work with a Lazarist priest.

One of the Jesuits' first communal acts was to renew their vows on 15 January 1843 at the missionary station of Tangkung, the same place where, 56 years before, Bishop von Laimbeckhoven had died, and where his memory was kept alive with relics of the bishop. This symbolic act linked the present Jesuits with that of their Jesuit predecessors.[40]

This same year, the superior general, Roothaan, formally entrusted the new Jesuit mission of Jiangnan to the Province of France, whose responsibility it was to provide the mission with personnel and financial resources.

Opening a seminary

One of the first tasks assigned to the Jesuits by Bési was to open a seminary. Initially it was to be in Zhoushan, where Brueyre had eight to ten students learning Latin and Chinese, but it was finally opened at Zhangpoqiao, 3 February 1843, with 23 students.[41] This shows the importance the French Jesuits placed on the development of an indigenous Church from the beginning of their ministry. They worked hard to train the future Chinese clergy and never compromised on their assessment of the suitability of these men for ordination.

---

38. Ibid., 17.
39. Ibid., 17.
40. Mateos, op. cit., 17.
41. Gotteland to Guidée, Jiangnan, 19 August 1842. ARSI.

Brueyre himself was studying Mandarin at the time, which he found difficult, but hoped that after a few months he would be able to teach the students the catechism. He was happy when the numbers at the seminary increased to 40. Bési provided funds and the seminary was organised along the lines of the Jesuit colleges in Europe.[42] Exams and compositions were held each week; during May, the litanies of the Blessed Virgin Mary were recited; Confessions were offered each month, while the rosary, prayers and two small examinations of conscience were said each day. The seminary was named the Sacred Heart of Jesus, and all students were enrolled in the sodality of that name, as well as in the Sodality of Sacred Heart of Mary, in order to 'pray for the conversion of sinners'.[43] The dropout rate among Chinese seminarians was high because of lack of Christian maturity and low level of general education before entering the seminary. But Chinese seminarians who survived this education generally accepted what was taught, while the more enlightened questioned the lack of relevance to Chinese culture.

Support for the seminary came from Rome in 1845, with an instruction addressed to all missionaries stressing the importance of the formation of an indigenous clergy. In a lengthy document, it traced the history of the priesthood back to apostolic times. Formation of suitable local clergy was essential for the propagation of the

---

42. *Ordo Studiorum* in the seminary, Nanjing, 1844. ARSI
    1. Introduction. Latin studies for two years, and Chinese studies for five or six years, from first year philosophy. Latin studies were considered important because of the recitation of the Divine Office. Students should not be ordained before their 25th year. Philosophy studies were undertaken for two years, and theology for four years. Generally, students were not accepted into philosophy before their 22nd year, while those under 12 years were not accepted to earlier studies.
    2. Order of Chinese studies and Latin.
      a. Chinese studies. They must have the capacity for the Baccalaureate.
      b. Latin studies. One hour a day, with the exception of feast days and Sundays. Exams monthly. There was a curriculum for a six-year period.
    3. Latinists.
      a. First and Second year – Latin grammar.
      b. Philosophy – logic and metaphysics.
      c. Theology – First year: religion and ecclesiology. Second year: *de Uno Deo, de oratione, de Incarnatione*. Third year: *de gratia*, Baptism and confirmation. Fourth year: the sacraments in particular and the 'last things'.
43. Brueyre to General, Jiangnan, 29 May 1844. ARSI.

faith. It further mentioned earlier Roman decrees on this subject, the first in 1626 recommending the formation of priests in Japan. Alexander VII followed this up with a decree to the bishops of Tongling, China and Cochinchina in 1659, pointing out that the appointment of mission bishops was to foster the growth of the local church through formation of local clergy who would be the best evangelisers. Other similar decrees followed in subsequent years.

This decree of 1845 made eight suggestions:

1) In order to promote the spread of the faith, the number of bishops should be increased by the division of existing regions.
2) The establishment of seminaries was to be undertaken with 'extreme zeal'.
3) The training of the seminarians should include teaching in 'science and piety', as well as teaching about how to exercise the 'dignity of priesthood according to the customs of the Holy See'.
4) Distinctions between European and local clergy should not exist.
5) All should be considered equal; the indigenous clergy were not mere assistants to the Europeans.
6) Assisting the clergy, lay catechists were important for the propagation of the faith. These should be men of 'irreproachable morals and an eminent faith'.
7) Furthermore, the clergy should not become involved in political matters, an instruction that went back to Alexander VII. They were not to take sides in political disputes and concentrate on their religious role in society.
8) Finally, the ecclesiastical leaders were encouraged to care, 'with prayer and penance', for all the institutions in their region, encouraging lay teachers and catechists, men and women, who supported the clergy in the religious education of the young. A synodal assembly was also suggested as a means of fostering the unity of faith and discipline, and for establishing 'perfect uniformity of conduct and of administration among the workers'.[44]

Soon after this time, efforts to promote the formation of indigenous clergy were advanced. One missionary, Joseph Gabet, a Vincentian

44. *Instruction de la sacrée Congrégation de la Propagande adressée aux archevêques, vicaires apostoliques et autres supérieurs des missions.* Rome, 1845, in Joseph Gabet, CM, *Les Missions Catholiques en Chine en 1846* (Paris: Valmonde, 1848), 68–75.

missionary to China and Tibet, became an ardent advocate of the importance of developing an indigenous clergy, even submitting his writing to Pius IX in October 1847. In his work, he spoke disparagingly of the corruption and 'moral degradation' of the Chinese people and their need to hear the Gospel, which would enable them 'to elevate their lives to a higher degree of humanity'. He made a strong case for local clergy based in the communities, as they understood the local people better than the European missionaries who were busy, constantly moving from community to community, unable to consolidate the faith of the local people. Unfortunately, the Christians saw the priests as foreigners, allied with the foreign invaders, and so were viewed with suspicion. The Chinese priests also showed 'antipathy' towards the European priests, because they observed the poor regard of the Europeans towards the Chinese people. Furthermore, the European priests were seen to treat the Chinese priests as 'serfs', and second-class people. As a result, unity among the clergy was strained. Finally, there was a strong requirement that the European missionaries become proficient in the Chinese languages. Without this, they could not communicate with the people adequately in either the communication of the faith, or in assisting the Christians in their disputes with the civil authorities.[45]

Early ministry

Gotteland and Estève were not idle after their arrival. In the first two years, 1842–3, they reported baptising 203 children of non-Christians and 68 adults. In addition, they heard 4,326 Confessions. Gotteland commented that it was difficult for the Christians to observe annual Confession, as a priest only visited their communities every two or three years. The six new Jesuits who arrived in 1844 reported pastoral progress. They looked after 40,500 Christians grouped around 215 chapels or churches, and baptised 280 adults and 703 children. In addition, there were 6,021 annual Communions. In each subsequent year, these numbers increased.[46] Recording statistics of their ministry was a significant means for the Jesuits to measure success or otherwise. Every

---

45. Ibid.
46. Joseph de la Servière, SJ, *Histoire de la Mission du Kiang-nan*, Tome I, 1840–1856 (Shanghai: Xujiahui, 1914), 148.

year, statistics from every mission were sent to the Jesuit headquarters in Rome and to *Propaganda Fide* according to a Roman pro-forma.

Estève did not take long to reflect upon the many differences in customs between the Europeans and the Chinese. In a letter of 1843 to Europe, he commented on these differences: in China they wrote from right to left; the place of honour was given to those on the left, rather than the right; in showing respect in the house, the Chinese kept their hat on, rather than take it off; the colour for mourning was white in China rather than black; sick people in Europe were put on a diet, but in China food was prescribed; in summer, Europeans had cold drinks, but in China they had very hot drinks; Europeans liked vegetables well cooked, but the Chinese liked them half-cooked and loved rice, tea and pork.

He reflected on the way the Chinese learned in schools: the students learned by heart what they have been taught, and only later were given an explanation of the material by the teacher. Learning the Chinese language was difficult for the Europeans, because many phrases were the opposite of the European construction. Other different customs were that the military profession was not considered honourable, nor was dancing popular; in arranging marriages, it was the husband that must provide the wife's family with a sum of money.

He viewed funeral rites as excessive, where the family showed great respect to the deceased with the son showing filial piety leading the ceremonies.

Another excessive custom observed was the sale of women and children, especially those related to the opium smokers. A child of eight or nine years could be sold for 15 to 20 francs. Missionaries suggested that Christian families buy these children, instruct them in the faith and baptise them. In this way, the Church would be considered a true mother to them.

The parents, without the consideration of the couple, arranged marriages; the law only required the children's consent, but they usually obeyed. Sometimes these marriages were arranged between under-aged children. For the Church to recognise these marriages, since the Council of Trent had not been promulgated in China, the Church did not require a priest to be present for the marriage to be valid.[47]

---

47. Letter of Estève, 1843, quoted in N Brouillon, *Mémoire sur l'état actuel de la Mission du Kiang-nan, 1842–1855* (Paris: Julien, 1855), 239–47.

Reflections like this showed that the missionaries were open to learning about Chinese culture and the environment in which they were immersed. With this knowledge, some were able to adapt European theological ideas more effectively to a race of people completely different from themselves. Furthermore, enlightened with this information about the Chinese, European friends and colleagues were better able to understand the Chinese and the challenges that European missionaries experienced in communicating the faith effectively.

In reporting to the superior general about the initial work of the Jesuits in the mission, Gotteland was concerned that he was unable to teach astronomy and mathematics, but he had come to an arrangement with Bési concerning the Jesuits' material wellbeing. The community kept the 'Rules for Priests', and they had a small house to reside in when they were ill. He expressed regret for opposing the presence of the Lazarists in the mission. Finally, the bishop had asked for more theology books, and he would like an Irish Jesuit to help care for the Irish soldiers in the resident British army.[48] Gotteland was more comfortable in administration than anything else, and was keen to indicate to the superior general that he was faithful to all Roman requirements. He was always the obedient and dutiful local superior.

The request for more Jesuits resulted in the arrival on 15 October 1844 of five more from France. They were Stanislas Clavelin, Joseph Gonnet,[49] Louis Taffin, Adrien Languillat[50] and Brother Pamphile Sinoquet. These new missionaries were sent to the prefectures of Songjiang and Suzhou. They became full of admiration for the gener-

---

48. Gotteland to General, Jiangnan, 4 June 1844. ARSI.
49. **Joseph Gonnet** was born on 31 December 1815 and joined the Society of Jesus at Avignon, 18 January 1840. He arrived in China, 15 October 1844, and worked first in the district of Pou-nè. He was appointed Superior of the Mission in Jiangnan, 23 November 1862; superior in Zhili on 20 May 1866 and again 18 April 1878, finally dying at Xianxian, 2 July 1895.
50. **Bishop Adrien-Hippolyte Languillat** was born in Chantemerle, France on 28 September 1808. He entered the Society of Jesus in 1841 as a priest and was consecrated bishop in 1856. He was named Apostolic Vicar of south-east Zhili, in the Province of Nanjing, and succeeded Bishop Borgniet in 1864 as Vicar Apostolic of Nanjing. He died at Xujiahui, Shanghai, on 30 November 1878. An appreciative obituary appeared in Colombel's history of the mission, 3rd part II, 4th vol. The episcopacy of Languillat, 440–55.

osity and faith of the leaders of the Christian communities who had kept the faith alive when priests were so scarce.[51]

Before the arrival of the first French consul in Shanghai, Louis Charles de Montigny in 1848, it was the English consul who protected French missionaries and their work. Stanislas Clavelin (1814–62), describing his arrival in 1844, spoke of his friendship with the British, but although they were the 'purveyors of the evil opium', they were powerful protectors of 'the true religion'.[52] This gave the Christians more hope because the mandarins were cautious in their reaction to Christianity.[53] However, while foreign protection resulted in more Baptisms, it created tension with the Chinese authorities, especially when the Chinese Christians refused to pay taxes. Bési rejoiced in this protection, unaware that this situation provoked hostility towards the Christians in Jiangnan.[54]

In their ministry, the Jesuits, feeling appreciated by the Christians, the bishop and Chinese priests, became aware that there were insufficient priests to meet the pastoral needs of the region. They believed that the lack of priests meant that the majority of Christians did not attend Mass on Sundays, but acknowledged they would call for the priest when someone needed the Last Rites. After an initial welcome by the Chinese, the arrival of Europeans resulted in the Christians becoming more timid. Teaching the catechism in the vicariate was undertaken, but concern was expressed that the Anglicans were spreading the word of the bible everywhere, through teaching and medical works, resulting in the displeasure of Bési, who denounced them as heretics.[55] This public expression of differences of approach to Christianity between the two Christian churches was a constant source of confusion among the Chinese.

Bési was disappointed that only five new missionaries arrived in 1844, expecting twelve. Other congregations also attacked the Jesuits for not supplying more men. The bishop became cool toward the Jesuits as a result. The departure of the Lazarists left a great void in

51. Joseph de la Servière, SJ, *La Nouvelle Mission du Kiang-nan*, 1840–1922, pamphlet, (Shanghai: Xujiahui, 1925). ARSI.
52. Louis Wei Tsing-Sing, *Le Saint Siège et la Chine de Pie XI à nos jours*, (Paris: Allais, 1968), 92.
53. Brueyre to General, Jiangnan, 29 May 1844. ARSI.
54. Mungello, op. cit., 19.
55. Brueyre to General, 29 May 1844. ARSI.

Jiangnan, but they remained on good terms with the Jesuits. Priests in the vicariate of Nanjing were reduced to twelve, which depressed Bési. He believed that for all his efforts, the mission was in a worse state.[56] He had 60,000 Christians to care for, and needed more priests. Many people died without the sacraments.

At this time, the Jesuit Province of France was sending missionaries to America. In 1831, four Jesuits were sent to Kentucky, rising to 22 in 1842. From 1832–6, five Jesuits were also sent to Syria, and in 1845 the Jesuits moved into Canada. In 1844, there were 39 French Jesuits in Kentucky/Canada and nine in China; in 1848, 93 Jesuits were in America, and 29 in China; while in 1856, there were 198 Jesuits in America and 38 in China. Obviously the mission priority of the Province of France was America.[57]

After studying Mandarin for three months, the newly arrived Jesuits were sent out to mission stations to replace the Lazarists, a task they found difficult. The 30-year-old, Stanislas Clavelin, sent by the bishop in 1845 to Chongming Island without the approval of the Jesuit superior, wrote about the shock he received when he arrived, having had no pastoral experience in Europe. As a true outsider, he was sent to replace two overworked and exhausted men in a strange country, ignorant of both the local language and customs. He felt alone without a guide or catechist, unable to understand anyone. When he informed his Jesuit superior and the bishop of these problems, he was told to resolve the problems himself. He managed to survive, and after two years achieved success, establishing nine new mission stations, baptising 312 adult Chinese and 1,400 children of non-Christian parents. He also had 300 catechumens.[58] Experiences like this one showed the resilience of the missionaries, and that with zeal and ingenuity, and no doubt improvisation, they were able to create something out of nothing, but it was a lonely task. This was a constant experience of the newly arrived missionary.

In another early letter, Clavelin outlined the many tasks that were expected of him.

> Visiting a district once a year, if possible, was usual. Each day, after baptising, instructing couples and marrying, and

---

56. Brueyre to General, Nanjing, 1844. ARSI.
57. Missiones Provinciae Galliae et Francia extra Europeam, statistics, Rome. ARSI.
58. Mateos, op. cit., 18.

administering to the sick, Confessions were heard. There
could be 20 or more a day that could take up to 10 hours in
the confessional. Instruction of the penitent was difficult, as
he could hardly understand what was said. At Mass, a short
instruction of 20 minutes was given. Many interruptions to
these activities occurred. Missionaries could be called to go
long distances to visit the sick by means of very slow transport,
and could take a day to accomplish. After administering to
the sick, baptising children and other necessary tasks, the
missionary return to home base, which was a good time
for making spiritual exercises. But upon the return, many
Christians could have been waiting for days for Confession.
Confessional work could go on until 11 o'clock at night,
after which the missionary retired until four or five o'clock
in the morning. But this was regularly interrupted by a sick
call. Some Christians had not confessed for 40 years, and a
number died before confessing and receiving the Last Rites.
On Sundays, two Masses were said in two different places
with short instructions given at each.[59]

Other missionaries shared similar stories of their daily routine. The
work was constant and draining, demanding much patience, but they
were strongly motivated to work for the good of China and 'the glory
of God'.

Other newly arrived missionaries suffered similar challenges to
Clavelin, and were unable to communicate with the educated Chinese, nor participate in local social ceremonies and traditional rites
prohibited by the Holy See. The only opportunity available was to
present the Gospel to the ordinary and poor people. These pastoral
placements of the Jesuits by the bishop, without consultation with the
superior, heightened tension between the Jesuits and the bishop.

It was not all bad news, as in the same year it was reported that
'two excellent Chinese boys' aged between 16 and 19 might be future
novices. The bishop did not object and 'despite his fragile state' was
still showing his support for the Jesuits. His interest in the seminary
was shown by his wanting a novena to be conducted to St Aloysius
Gonzaga among the seminarians. Brueyre, while working in the
seminary, was besieged with pastoral requests from everywhere, all

59. Clavelin to European confrères, January 1845, quoted in N Broullion, *Mémoire sur l'état actuel de la Mission du Kiang-nan, 1842–1855.* (Paris: Julien, 1855), 231–4.

of which could not be accepted. He saw much work available, but the newly arrived Jesuits were not available, as they needed to study the language first. The death of Brother Sinoquet, aged 46, the year after his arrival in China, was considered a blow to the mission, while Gotteland was not in good health, as 'he hardly ever sleeps and performs the work of four men'. The need for more men was crucial, and Bési declared that if the Jesuits did not provide more men, he would re-invite the Lazarists to the region.[60] This pressure on the superior general to send more Jesuits to China seemed to work, as in the next year, 1846, eleven men were sent.

Relationships between the Jesuits and Bési became strained from 1845. Gotteland felt the pressure of recognising the needs of the mission for more men, and the demands of Bési. He asked the superior general to be replaced. The tension between the bishop and the Jesuits was heightened over the question of the rights of the Jesuits and who had authority over what. The bishop wanted to control all money coming into the mission and wanted to rule all in his jurisdiction. Gotteland told him that the noviciate and the Jesuit houses of formation were under Jesuit authority, and that his primary obedience was to the Society of Jesus and only secondary to the bishop. Legal wrangles ensured, with *Propaganda Fide* telling Bési that he should consult the Jesuit superior before dealing with any member of the Society.[61] Gotteland's letters to Rome at this time, attempting to sort out juridical issues, were long and legalistic.

With the arrival of eleven Jesuits, largely from France and Italy, Bési asked the Society to send men to Shandong, which was also part of his administration. As there was only one Chinese priest in the region, Adrien Languillat was sent there on 26 October 1846. Brueyre, having just left the seminary, joined him on 24 February 1847. They took eight days to arrive at their destination. They found the climate of Shandong harsh and the Christians poor, and observed the ruins of churches caused by recent persecutions. Christians were fearful to approach the priests, while many had apostatised in their misery. After several months, Languillat had reconnected with several former Christian communities, finding 100 catechumens. This

60. Brueyre to General, Nanjing, 25 April 1845. ARSI.
61. Gotteland to General, Jiangnan, 15 February 1845. ARSI; Gotteland to Bési, Jiangnan, 1 November 1845. ARSI.

gave him some joy, but in September 1847, visiting the community of Majiadong, in east Shandong, the senior mandarin was violently opposed to the Europeans and their religion, despite the decree of tolerance given by the emperor. The priests were harassed and thought to flee, but decided against it, because it would set a bad example to the Christians. They were arrested with a catechist, interrogated and questioned about all things European and their religion. Languillat told the mandarin that he had come to China as a human being to make known the only true religion and to save souls. They remained eight days in prison with common criminals whom they instructed in the basics of the Faith.[62] They were later released.

Reflecting on China a year after he arrived, Theodore Werner (1817–54) wrote that his life had completely changed, trying to adapt to the 'habits, ideas and customs' of the Chinese. He admired the simplicity of the Chinese and their 'admirable faith'. He thought the priest to be a 'good reconciler' in local disputes between the non-Christians and the Christians. He bought two children, 25 sous for a boy and 15 sous for a girl, took them to the orphanage and placed them in the care of the virgins. He was horrified that some non-Christians strangled girl-children. Christians sometimes bought these children, while others either took them to the orphanages or gave them to the virgins.[63]

Similarly, the newly arrived Luigi Sica (1814–95) wrote about having responsibility for between 30–35 Christian communities, with each having between 50–400 Christians. Each district had one or two priests who administered the sacraments. The missionaries could not visit every Christian community in a year. He wondered if it was worth the effort for missionaries to spend six or seven years learning the Chinese language while 80 million people 'lost their souls'. Maybe it was better for the missionaries to learn Mandarin while still in Europe. He understood that many Chinese did not care much about pronunciation, preferring that the missionaries knew the significance of as many characters as possible.[64]

---

62. Joseph de la Servière, SJ, *Histoire de la Mission du Kiang-nan*, op. cit. 149–50.
63. Werner to MM Roze, Tours, 28 February 1847, *Lettres des Nouvelles de la Chine*, Tome II, 1846–1852, lettei 64.
64. Sica, Tcham-kim, to Jesuit scholastics in Naples, 13 July 1847, ibid, letter 74.

Political negotiations

Meanwhile, as a result of the Treaty of Whampoa with the French ambassador, Théodore de Lagrené, in 1844, the emperor, in an edict of 20 February 1846, ordered that the establishments formerly belonging to Christians must be restored to their owners, and that henceforth officers searching for and arresting harmless Christians should be tried. However, this was not sent to all governors, with some disastrous results for Christians.

The 30-year-old Mathurin Lemaître [65] (1816–63), having only just arrived in China, was appointed procurator of the mission: the person in charge of its overall material welfare. He was asked to negotiate with the Chinese authorities over the return of previously Jesuit-owned buildings. The result of these negotiations was that the Jesuits were given three plots of land in compensation for the non-restoration of some churches, but the old cemetery of the former Jesuits was not returned. One of these plots of land was for the cathedral of St Francis Xavier and the residence of Dongjiadu, built in 1847. On another piece of land, in the centre of the French concession, was the location for St. Joseph's Church at Yangjingbang, a Jesuit residence, and the Church of St Ignatius, built in 1848. The latter was situated in the zone of Xujiahui, near the tomb of Paul Xu Guangqi, a friend of Ricci. Gotteland bought this land in 1847 with funds from a Chinese Catholic family.

---

65. **Mathurin Lemaître** (1816–1863) arrived in China in 1846, and having negotiated with the sub-prefect of Shanghai over the return of former Jesuit property, was sent to Hai Men in 1848, where soon after, he experienced floods followed by famine. In 1851, he was appointed secretary to Bishop Maresca, and after Nanjing fell to the Taipings on 8 March 1853, Lemaître was able to speak with the Taipings, who respected the neutrality of the missions. Lemaître visited Catholic families on both sides of the war. From 1855, he was superior of the mission. After the Chinese war with Britain and France that began in 1857, Lemaître helped in the negotiations between the Chinese and Europeans. Worn out because of his work he died on 3 May 1863, after 17 years in China. The French consul, Edan, wrote of the esteem and affection of the Chinese authorities for Lemaître. They liked to consult him, believing that his impartial wisdom led to justice. He was seen 'as a mediator between heaven and earth'. Under his guidance, the Jesuits made 70,000 conversions in the south of the mission. Cf. *Cent ans sur le fleuve bleu, une mission des Jésuites,* (Shanghai: Xujiahui, 1942).

Xujiahui

Gotteland had a vision for the development of Catholic Shanghai. He wanted a Catholic centre, a seminary for the Chinese clergy, a school for boys and one for girls, an orphanage and a hospital. He also dreamed about building an astronomical observatory.[66] This dream gradually unfolded with an orphanage built at Tushanwan, and a college for boys, St Ignatius, both opened in 1850. His aim for the school was to educate the students from 'honourable Christian families' in 'piety', science, French language and Chinese literature. The missionaries envisioned that these students might become future helpers in the mission as teachers, administrators of Christian communities and catechists. In the first eleven years of the college, it educated 1,103 students, among whom were 10 Jesuits and six secular priests, seven Jesuit brothers, and 68 seminarians. [67]

The opening of a museum and observatory in 1871 was another step forward by announcing to the Chinese the importance of scientific investigation. It also showed continuity with the work of earlier Jesuits like Adam Schall and Ferdinand Verbiest. These works became known in the intellectual world through numerous academic publications. The Jesuit Pierre Heude (1836–1902), a naturalist (zoologist), had explored the interior Provinces of China, collecting specimens of flora and fauna and documenting his findings. He published the well-illustrated *Conchyliologie fluviatile* in Paris, as well as the *Memoires sonsernant l'histoire naturelles de 'Empire chinois.*[68]

The observatory, built next to the museum, became very significant for its meteorological observations, similar to the ones in Europe. It published monthly bulletins of observations, which were appreciated by ships that needed to know weather conditions in the Orient.

An astronomy section followed. Finally, Jean Chevalier undertook hydrographic studies of the Yellow River (Huang He/Hwang Ho) after 1897. Workshops for teaching carpentry, painting and sculpturing were also established. The products of these workshops were well used in the churches of the mission.

---

66. Mateos, op. cit., 20.
67. Boucher, op. cit., 62.
68. Pierre Marie Heude was born at Fougères, France, 1836, joined the Jesuits in 1856, and went to China, 1868, and died at Xujiahui in 1902.

The printing press at Xujiahui became a most important means of evangelisation in the mission by printing many works in Chinese for the Christians. Each month there was the *Messenger of the Sacred Heart* and a twice-weekly Chinese paper that was distributed to thousands. Under the director Angelo Zottoli (1826–1902), they published five volumes of *Cursus Litteraturae sinicas* that was the prelude to the greater work of an academic dictionary. Finally, European friends favourably received the *Variétés Sinologiques*, which were a collection of monographs on sinological topics such as Chinese history, Chinese science, as well as Chinese customs and language.

Religious sisters played a very significant part in the evangelisation of the mission. The *Auxiliatrices des* âmes *du Purgatoire* arrived in 1867 to work in the orphanage, as well as 25 sisters of Carmel in 1869 to pray for the work of the mission. In 1854, Sica established a religious group of Chinese Christian virgins called the Presentations of the Holy Virgin (*Seng-mou-yeu).* They grew rapidly in number; by 1898 they had 90 religious and made a significant contribution to running schools for girls in the mission. They also baptised, gave Christian instructions, and helped in organising the religious ceremonies in the local communities. [69]

The Xujiahui centre became a unique Catholic enclave in the Far East within Shanghai, the thriving European commercial centre of China.

This vision of Gotteland was hindered under the present bishop. From the beginning of 1845 Bési refused to give permission for a Jesuit noviciate, and tried to get the Italian Jesuits who had arrived in May 1846 to write to Rome with complaints against the French Jesuits, and especially against Gotteland. He even forbade Jesuits from performing priestly ministries in Shanghai.[70]

There were differences in approaches to mission work between the Italian and French missionaries. Bési noticed this and preferred the Italians; they were easier to work with, being more relational and adaptable than the more authoritative and rigid French.

Meanwhile, at the political level, having received reports from Shanghai, the French provincial, Ambroise Rubillon, wrote to the French Foreign Minister expressing gratitude and pleasure for

---

69. Boucher, ut supra, 58–73.
70. Mateos, op. cit., 20.

French 'patronage as we move to the interior of China'. He reminded the minister that missionaries represented France, and that by their works of charity, France benefited. But he was also aware that while some mandarins accepted the missionaries, in other areas missionaries were persecuted. He hoped that the mandarins involved in these cases would investigate these affairs.[71] French support in this matter was implied in the letter.

Disputes among Christians and missionaries

It was not only differences with Bési that the Jesuits had to contend. Chinese Catholics became critical of their methods in pastoral ministry. The Jiangnan Christians had memories of the earlier Jesuits who were learned, spoke their language and adapted Christianity to Chinese culture. The new Jesuits were experienced as not having sufficient fluency in the local languages to communicate adequately for pastoral work. In the haste to establish a firm base, they had not given themselves time to learn Chinese customs.

Before the Jesuits arrived, the local Catholic churches were alive, despite persecution. Chinese priests and catechists were well established in the Christian communities and had been running the churches with confidence without outside interference. 'Indigenous Chinese traditions had been incorporated into the Jiangnan churches to create a distinctly Chinese church'. The new Jesuits were different from the former ones; the earlier Jesuits needed to be cautious in their approach to the Chinese, fearing retribution. They were flexible and accommodating. The new Jesuits, backed by British forces, were more secure in their approach, and showed signs of arrogance, imposing European and Roman theology and rituals in a way that the Christian communities had not experienced and did not like.[72]

On Ash Wednesday 1846, Jiangnan Christians produced an open letter, or an 'essay in ten parts', expressing their reflections and concerns about the procedures of Bési and the Jesuits in their pastoral ministry in the communities, compared with their own long-estab-

---

71. Ambroise Rubillon SJ, to French Foreign Minister, Paris, 26 February 1846. DAC. Rubillon (1804–1888) was provincial of France, 1845–1851, and then appointed assistant for the Province of France to the superior general in Rome, 1851–1883.
72. Mungello, op. cit., 28.

lished customs. The tone reflected bitterness about the way the Christian communities were treated by the European priests, and indicated the pastoral differences that existed between the Chinese church leaders and the Europeans pastors.

Gotteland was upset by this letter and gave a long, detailed reply to the many objections that had been raised. In general, he expressed belief that the objections should never have been made in the first place; Christians were only required to obey their superiors. He explained that if conflict arose, then superiors would explain reasons for their action, and after an explanation, the complainant ought simply to obey and not speak scandal against the superiors. If they continued to hold subversive views, they committed 'evil and sin'. However, if they repented, they could obtain forgiveness. The priest had the authority to help people live good lives, as well as to help them to think correctly.

This response was arrogant and alienating to the Chinese. It showed Gotteland the outsider endeavouring to impose European rules on the Chinese without any understanding of their Chinese traditions or previous Christian rituals. His attitude was far from accommodating or helpful to inter-cultural relationships.

There were twenty-two objections to which Gotteland responded at length with passion and conviction of the righteous approach of the European priests. His replies indicated that the Jesuits had little or no sympathy with certain customs in the Christian communities that were not compatible with European Catholic theology and ritual.

The first complaint was that the European priests did not understand the Chinese, nor should they interfere with material customs of local Chinese. Gotteland replied that the European priests did not come to China to engage in material things, but to work for religion, which was a 'universal business of following Christ'. Christ did not deal with temporal matters, and neither should the priests. There seemed to be agreement on this matter, but the underlying suggestion by the Chinese was that European priests did interfere with the well-established Chinese way of life.

The Chinese Christians believed that the earlier Jesuits, like Ricci and his companions, were 'wise and respected', whereas the 'new' ones were ignorant of Chinese culture. Gotteland replied that the comparison should not have been made, as the times had changed. Earlier Jesuits, he claimed, did not visit the sick, nor explain the precepts of the Church, but rather gave themselves to intellectual tasks, and took seven years to study the Chinese classics. The 'new' European Jesuits studied Mandarin for two years, which he believed was insufficient to help them in visiting the sick or in explaining church teaching. However, they did the best they could, given the pastoral needs of the Christians.

Against the criticism that the Europeans did not preach to the non-Christians, nor expound Christian doctrine, nor confront superstitions, Gotteland replied that preaching was not the 'convenient medium of our days'. He said that when Jesus called someone to the faith, he used everyday images, not using great words, but told the truth 'in virtue and example'.

It was further claimed that the Christian religion, as presented by the Europeans, was not what Christ taught, but rather what the bishop taught. There was a perceived discrepancy between the two approaches. Gotteland responded that Christ taught his disciples to preach about 'the unity and Trinitarian God, and the Incarnation of the Word'. Furthermore Jesus wanted the 'bishops to depend on the pope, and the faithful on the bishops, observing the precepts of the Church, without which Paradise could not be attained'. He stressed that these doctrines, the doctrines of Christ, were in the heart of every Christian. The priests who came to China did so with the authority of the bishop to teach these truths. The people should obey. This response made no distinction between what Jesus taught and what the Church taught. For Gotteland, they were the same. This reflected well the European ecclesiology of the day, and Gotteland, proclaiming these truths, as he knew them, saw no reason to attempt to explain these truths in any other way. It was the only way he knew. He did not understand the existing beliefs and rituals within the Christian communities, as Ricci had done in the sixteenth century.

In response to the comment that the European priests were seen as spies of the British, and secretly communicated with them, Gotteland seemed to understand this comment, but admitted that the missionaries had no other means of arriving in China than in British ships. It was also 'the best means whereby letters to and from the pope were sent'!

Other complaints included criticism that the European priests did not speak many languages as the apostles did. They also objected to some liturgical practices, such as the directive for Chinese men and women to pray together. This latter demand contradicted the Chinese custom of the sexes praying separately and violated the Chinese sense of propriety. The European priests were not open to this custom, saying it was not the custom of the universal church.

Gotteland agreed with the criticism that the priests did not preach the scriptures by saying that the people would not understand them if they did. The Christians were not considered to have sufficient understanding of the faith to comprehend them; it was better for the priests to explain the catechism, especially the importance of the sacraments and the observance of the Commandments. The Chinese also objected to the prohibition of servants preaching. They were told that church law only permitted priests to preach. This was a power given to the priests from the bishop, and not given to just anyone. Besides, preaching required learning, which was considered rarely found among the Christians. Gotteland was as direct in his rebuttal to the Chinese, as they were in their attack on the Jesuits.

From the Chinese perspective, the instruction by the Jesuits was incomprehensible because of their lack of Chinese language skills. This was a significant difficulty when attempting to discuss the scriptures with the less educated Christians in the villages. The missionaries did not accept the Chinese offer of help at the time. Until the language skills of the missionaries improved, their influence among the Chinese was minimal. In the meantime, they involved themselves with setting up lasting structures for the mission.

The Chinese also raised questions about Church marriage laws and their application. Bési had forbidden traditional customs of contracting marriage ceremonies, while the universal Church laws regarding marriage were quite foreign to the Chinese.

The way money was distributed in the vicariate and the poverty of the missionaries were called into question. It was claimed that Bési and the Jesuits were extravagant in food and clothing. Earlier Jesuits were believed to have worn poor clothing and went barefoot, but the new Jesuits wore long and expensive robes.

Gotteland's response was that religious priests took and lived a vow of poverty, and that all money was spent on the needs of the mission. He wrote that the missionaries were only in China to save souls and, if they could not do this, then they would leave. Further criticisms included that the Jesuits could not understand the Confessions of the Chinese and were unable to communicate catechesis on this or about the other sacraments.[73]

The final major complaint concerned infanticide, with the question as to why after baptising a child, the mother was told not to suffocate the child. Christians believed that if the child was baptised it would go to heaven after death, but infanticide was an acceptable part of Chinese culture, especially if the child was a female. Not to smother the child would leave the child to a worse fate since there would be no one to protect the abandoned child. This justified their action. It was believed that few Chinese Christians followed the directive of the missionaries.

The Jesuits, earlier and present, condemned the practice. It was illegal in Chinese law, but the practice was common, especially in mid-nineteenth century Jiangnan. The main reason for infanticide was poverty and the inability of the parents to care for the child. Infants born to unmarried mothers were also killed, as were deformed males.[74]

Gotteland's response to the question was that to kill a child was against the will of the Church, which was an expected response, but this showed his lack of empathy with the Chinese custom in 1846.[75] It would appear that Gotteland, and the other Jesuits at this time, had little understanding of the social implications of the custom. It was sufficient for them that such a practice was unjust killing and should be prevented. To deal with this situation as best they could, they opened an orphanage at Tu San Wan in 1850.

Gotteland's responses to the Christians were defensive and uncompromising, and in doing so he clearly articulated his Roman theology. The hierarchical church was firmly established in the world, and everyone had his or her proper place in that hierarchy. Ultimately the Christians were expected only to obey: obedience to the rules was the expectation of the universal church.[76] Any local customs at variance with this vision were expected to change. Furthermore, there does not appear to be evidence that Gotteland was particularly inter-

73. Gotteland to General, Jiangnan, 26 May 1846. ARSI.
74. Mungello, op. cit., 40–5.
75. Gotteland to General, Jiangnan, 26 May 1846. ARSI.
76. Pius X, 'On the French Law of Separation', in *Vehementer nos*, (11 February 1906), Papal Encyclicals online. He told the Chinese Christians that they had only to obey the hierarchy. This attitude was strongly endorsed in the universal church.

ested in studying the Chinese classics. He was too busy dealing with administrative and pastoral situations.

Bishop Bési and the Jesuits

These objections clearly highlighted the tension between Bési and the educated 'old' Chinese Catholics. Bési also never had good relations with *Propaganda Fide*, so when he lost the support of his friend Pope Gregory XVI, who died in 1846, Bési decided to go to Rome to defend himself against growing criticisms. After laying the cornerstone for the cathedral in Shanghai, 21 November 1847, he departed for Rome with his secretary, Italian Jesuit Renato Massa, who had arrived in China with three of his other brothers who were also Jesuits, on 24 May 1846. Eleven Jesuits had arrived together on that date so that altogether 17 Jesuits were in the Jiangnan mission when Bési departed China.[77] Also present in the mission at the time were two secular priests from *Propaganda,* and five elderly Chinese priests, all serving 60,000 Christians.

The tension between Bési and the Jesuits reached the stage where he advised *Propaganda Fide* not to send any more French Jesuits to Jiangnan. *Propaganda* agreed, not because of Bési's request, but because they wanted it to be an Italian sphere of influence. In 1845, Pope Gregory had accepted the French government's demand that the Jesuits leave France. That was probably why so many were sent to China in 1846. Seven new Jesuits were sent to China in 1847, four of them French.

Meanwhile, following instructions, Massa had begun recruiting missionaries in Italy, with 30 showing interest, but with limited funds, only six Italian Jesuits arrived on 27 September 1848, joining the other six Italian Jesuits already in the mission.

Rome did not permit Bési to return to China because his presence was considered too disruptive. Acknowledging this, the Jesuits considered him 'too rigid and authoritarian, lacking in humility, and alienating his collaborators', but praised his 'zeal in government'.[78]

77. Fernando Mateos, SJ. List of Jesuits in the China Mission, 1842–1949, manuscript, Taipei, Taiwan. CPA.

78. Joseph De La Servière, SJ, *La Nouvelle Mission du Kiang-nan,* 1840–1922, pamphlet, (Shanghai: Xujiahui, 1925). Chapter One.

The episcopal years of Bishop Francisco Xaverio Maresca OFM (1848–1855)

The Italian, Maresca, a missionary from Hong Kong, was consecrated bishop on 23 May 1847, and appointed coadjutor Bishop of Nanjing on 1 December 1847, but when Bési resigned on 9 July 1848, Maresca became Bishop of Nanjing. He was much liked, gentle, affable, and worked well with people, as well as with the Jesuits. To resolve previous tensions between the Jesuits and the bishop, *Propaganda* confirmed the Jesuits right to order religious discipline of the Jesuits, but the right of the bishop to control all business and directions of the mission. Whenever conflict could not be resolved, the decision of the bishop was to be upheld. However, this decision did not eradicate all conflict between the bishop and the Jesuits, which continued until 1856, when *Propaganda* reconstituted the mission of Jiangnan as a separate vicariate from the diocese of Nanjing. The Jesuits administered the new mission at the request of Maresca in his final days.

To support the genial Maresca, the Italian Luigi Spelta OFM was appointed his coadjutor, a man who had Bési's forceful character, and so was a good foil to Maresca. He remained in the diocese until 1856.[79]

At the same time, there was a change of Jesuit superior. Augustin Poissemeux (1804–54) replaced Gotteland on 5 April 1848, and early letters to the superior general, indicated that he wanted the newly arrived Jesuits to spend time learning the Chinese language, with some undertaking special studies in order to influence the 'educated classes'.[80] More missionaries arrived that year, four from France, and six Italians.[81] One Italian, and three Frenchmen joined these the following year.[82] During the Maresca years, seven missionaries returned to Europe and seven died.[83]

---

79. Mungello, op. cit., 22.
80. Poissemeux to General, ZKW, 20 December 1848. ARSI.
81. Fathers Nicolas Broullion, Louis Froget and Jean-Baptiste Wuilbert, 20 March 1848, and Italian Fathers Francisco Adinolfi, Ignazio Catte, Agnello Della Corte, Luigi Massa, Angelo Zottoli, and French Father Jean-Francois Ducis, 27 September 1848.
82. Father Francesco Giaquinto, 24 January 1849; Fathers Louis Hélot, François Plet, Victor Vuillaume, 1 October 1849.
83. Fathers François Estève died 1 July 1848; Cajétan Massa, 28 April 1850, aged 29; Paul Pacelli, 2 June 1850; René Massa, 28 April 1853, aged 35; Louis Yvetot, 30

The question of whether any more French Jesuits should be sent to China was discussed in Rome, with the result that the pope revoked the decision of *Propaganda* not to send French Jesuits to China on 21 April 1849. Both Maresca and Poissemeux claimed that they only wanted peace in the mission.

Many of the letters from the mission superior to the superior general dealt with the right ordering of religious life among the Jesuits. They were keen to inform the superior general that the Jesuit rule of life was being observed. In one of his last letters as superior, Gotteland assured the superior general of the orthodoxy of the Jesuits concerning ecclesial procedures. He mentioned the need to teach the catechumens 'everything about the Faith according to law before baptism'. But to do this properly, the priest 'must know the vernacular language because he must interrogate the catechumen about his knowledge of the faith'. Church laws were obeyed concerning 'the time of baptism and the use of the sacred oils'. No detail of Church law was omitted. To help with teaching the catechumens, he requested more books, especially 'the catechism of the Council of Trent'.

Some acknowledgement of adapting to the local people was made when mentioning that the bishop had recommended the exercise of prudence in dealing with the Chinese, emphasising the need to show deference to the mandarins when negotiating business.[84] This call for greater sensitivity in personal relationships was praiseworthy, and one-step forward in establishing closer relations with the Chinese.

Following Maresca's installation as bishop in 1849, extensive flooding occurred throughout Jiangnan, followed by crop failure, pestilence, famine, and death in 1850. Many Christians asked for Confession before they died. Much devastation resulted, and Lemaître mentioned that 20,000 people drowned in Haimen alone.[85] Poissemeux recounted that in Huguang the non-Christians were eating one another, while the Christians stripped the bark from the trees to cook for the juice from the bark.[86]

May 1854; Augustin Poissemeux, 9 June 1854, aged 50; and Theodore Werner, 23 August 1854.
84. Gotteland to General, 7 April 1848. ARSI.
85. Quoted in Nicholas Broullion, *Mémoire sur l'état actuel de la Mission du Kiangnan, 1842–1855* (Paris, Julien, 1855), 88.
86. Ibid.

As a result of this disaster, many parents abandoned their children because they could not feed them. Seeing this, the Jesuits opened separate orphanages for boys and girls, initially at Xiaotongyuan, and later at Xujiahui.

Shanghai at this time was invaded with starving refugees, who were looked after by the missionaries and by the sub-prefect of Shanghai who opened a hospital, with financial support coming from the French consul in Shanghai, de Montigny. Catechists and Christian virgins attended the hospital baptising many dead children. The Jesuits also helped in the crisis, with Louis Hélot (1816–67) installing a ventilation system in the hospital, Cajétan Massa (1821–50) assisting as a doctor, and Nicolas Brouillon as the bursar of the bishop distributing necessary funds. They acknowledged in their letters assistance from the British and the Americans, but the French consul gave the greatest assistance, not only to the starving refugees, but also to the Jesuits themselves. They expressed happiness at the close connection between the French consulate and its protection of the Christian missions, which they believed was politically good for negotiating with the mandarins, and for increasing the importance of the French presence in China. Favourable commercial gain for France was believed to follow. The missionaries were seen as ambassadors for France. The bishops, too, were grateful for French protection of the missions and the Chinese Christians, as the protection was seen by the Europeans to help in their work of evangelisation. Some Chinese Christians, however, were acknowledged to use this protection to further their own ambitions.[87]

Support for the abandoned orphans came from the charitable organisation, Work of the Holy Infant, founded in France in 1843, for the Baptism of dead children, buying back and adopting abandoned children, and for the creation of orphanages. The Jiangnan mission generously benefited from this organisation. Sixty children had been rescued in the six months after the floods and famine, and many children were baptised.[88]

One result of the floods and famine was the increase in the number of bandit groups plundering the countryside near Shanghai. The local mandarins were incapable of keeping order. The Jesuit residence

---

87. Servière, *Histoire de la mission . . .*, op. cit., 164–9.
88. Servière, ibid., 173.

at Xujiahui was threatened, so the superior Poissemeux called de Montigny for support from the French troops to guard the residence. This was forthcoming, the bandits withdrew and the crisis ended.[89]

Having overcome these challenges, the Jesuits set about assisting the people devastated by famine, and the attacks from bandits. While many people were killed, many also sought Baptism from the missionaries. In Haimen, about 600 adults in danger of death, and about 2,000 children were baptised. The missionaries in other regions experienced similar scenes of poverty, despair and destruction as well. The missionaries themselves were exhausted from their attention to the sick and dying, with Estève, Cajétan Massa, and Paul Pacelli dying of typhoid.[90]

During this time of reconstruction within the mission, the Christians especially appreciated the opening of free primary schools. The missionaries considered schools as breeding grounds for the future of the mission. The secondary schools were also important, with four to five years instruction, teaching Chinese literature and religion, where they learnt about the faith. It was hoped that these students would spread their knowledge when they left school. Some even studied Latin for the priesthood, and acted as catechists under the direction of the missionaries.[91]

Chinese education

Gotteland reported extensively on the process of examinations and academic grades in China at the time. Education was open and free, but no institution or college as in Europe existed. There were 'small schools' of 20 to 30 students under a teacher, who engaged in preparatory studies for degrees. The studies depended on the local mandarins, who examined the students for 15 days before giving their recommendation as to who were the more successful. This was a similar system to the missionary schools in Shanghai, where there was a preparatory examination before presenting the students for the baccalaureate examination.

---

89. Servière, ibid., 169–70.
90. Servière, ibid., 175–6.
91. Letter of Poissemeux, 23 April 1850, quoted in Servière, op. cit., 172.

There were six types of exams. After the first exam, the second was for the baccalaureate itself, called the 'small exams'. The third exam was for the 'licence', and the fourth was the doctorate. More distinguished than the doctors was the fifth exam for 'learned academicians', presided over by the emperor. This exam was only taken in Beijing. The sixth type of exam was for bachelors, taken every three years for the rest of their lives. From the 'licence' upwards, the exams were called 'grand exams'.

The time for the baccalaureate exam was twice every three years, and those of the 'grand exams' once during the same period. The number of graduates was controlled locally. In Nanjing, at this time, there were 15,000 candidates for the 'licence'; only 114 would graduate.

The place for the preparatory exams was held in towns ranked in the third order, while those of the bachelors in towns of second order. The licence exams took place in the province capital, while the doctors and academicians were examined in Beijing.

The local mandarins were the examiners for the 'small exams', while the examiners for the doctors' degree came from Beijing to examine. In Beijing, the ministers of state examined the future doctors, while the exam for the academicians was reserved to the emperor himself.

The exams were written. Bachelors had to write two compositions, one in prose and one in verse. They were given a half-day or a whole day to complete, under the supervision of the inspectors. The 'licence' exams consisted in writing three compositions in prose and three in verse. Students were given nine days to complete the exercises, working, eating, and sleeping in small groups.

The subject matter of the exams was the teachings of thirteen books. The first four were compositions of the disciples of Confucius, dealing with moral and natural philosophy. They were called 'the four books'. Then there were the five sacred books, the *King*, of Confucius himself. The candidates for the 'licence' had to deal with three subjects taken from the 'four books of the *King*', and five other subjects given freely by the examiner. They were to write answers in prose only. The content for doctorate exams was the same as the 'licence'.

Results given by the examiners depended on the depth of the subject matter and the style. The books studied were taken from ancient sources that were full of wise maxims that students were not permitted to change. A Chinese teacher said that citing these ancient texts was comparable to Europeans citing the Bible.[92]

Gotteland was finding more time to study the Chinese educational system, which would have been important background knowledge for the Jesuits when organising the curriculum in mission schools. In communicating the high educational standards expected of the Chinese *literati*, Europeans learnt about other pedagogical methods than their own to achieve academic excellence.

Ecclesiastical plans

Personnel in the mission in 1849 numbered 38 Jesuits: 28 priests, five scholastics, and five brothers (which included two Chinese brother novices). They worked in 356 Christian communities, which had 195 churches and 101 chapels. The missionaries had baptised 308 adults and 331 children that year, while 485 marriages were blessed.[93] These statistics indicated an impressive growth in the mission in a short number of years.

Meanwhile, in Rome, *Propaganda Fide* called for a general synod of all Far Eastern vicars apostolic for the winter of 1849 in Hong Kong. They wanted a discussion on the orderly establishment of an ecclesiastical hierarchy for China. The vicars and mission superiors were to draw up exact boundaries of their ecclesiastical territories, while vicars apostolic would become diocesan bishops. The vicars apostolic objected to this plan, and the French government objected to the synod being held on British territory, so the idea was indefinitely postposed.[94]

However, plans for a combined meeting of vicars apostolic were not abandoned and, after much discussion over an acceptable meeting place, another council was called for on 7 November 1851 at Shanghai. Five bishops attended: one from Beijing, Henan, and Japan, and the two Jesuit bishops of Jiangnan.

The first question related to the establishment of the Chinese hierarchy. The majority agreed to this idea. *Propaganda* suggested

---

92. Gotteland, Shanghai, 22 January 1849, cited in Broullion, op. cit., 248–54.
93. Statistics on the China Mission, 1849. ARSI.
94. Patrick Taveirne, 'Missionary enterprise and the endeavours to establish an ecclesiastical hierarchy and diplomatic relations with China, 1307–1946', in *Tripod*, 54 (December 1989).

the appointment of six archbishops in the major Chinese cities, with jurisdiction approximating to the civil provinces. Only the bishops and priests of the archdiocese should elect them.

The formation of the clergy was given attention. The delegates rejected the idea of an abridged course of study for the Chinese. If the Chinese were not sufficiently literate, they should be employed as catechists rather than be considered seminarians. In the seminaries, the Chinese language must be the means of communication. Furthermore, young Chinese should not be sent to Europe for studies, except for the Chinese college in Naples, which had been established for them. A central seminary in Shanghai for all was considered good in theory, but was rejected for practical reasons. A suggestion that the seminarians might serve as catechists before ordination was considered a good idea, but it should not be imposed upon them. The delegates were also not in agreement whether it should be a general practice that the newly ordained Chinese priests work under the direction of the European priests for a time.

The formation of catechists was considered as almost important as that of the priests. The success of the mission depended in great part upon them. Married catechists should be preferred to celibate ones.

The question of ownership of ecclesiastical property was a delicate issue. Clashes between Bési and the Jesuits on this question had previously caused disagreement. *Propaganda* had wanted all funds to be centralised in the hands of the bishop, who would then distribute them according to need. The bishops rejected this, deciding to maintain the *status quo*, which was that temporal matters should be regulated in the missions of China according to the particular rules of each religious institute or mission.

The delegates were careful to reject the idea of a common catechism for China, but wanted the formula of prayers to be kept, even with Latin words that had been inserted by the earlier missionaries, as this was what the Christians were accustomed. To insert Chinese words would change the sense of the prayers, and might even affect the validity of Baptism. The translation of the prayers should be in Mandarin in the poetic style and in the local dialect of each region. Vestments at Mass should follow the customs of the country. There was no need for a common calendar; each bishop should publicise his own, according to the faculties given by Rome. The bishops encouraged the alternate chanting of the prayers between men and women, despite earlier disagreements about this practice. Public penances ought to be continued, while the virgins ought to be carefully supervised in their work.[95]

Attempts were made at this Shanghai council to account for some local adaptation of European seminary training. Mandarin as the language of communication was innovative. Pastoral experience as catechists for Chinese seminarians was also creative, while respecting Chinese sensitivities in the recitation of liturgical prayers was wise. Growth in the number of Chinese Christians would follow missionary respect for the sensitivity of the Chinese and their long-standing rituals.

Mission reports

Meanwhile on the Jiangnan mission, the new superior Poissemeux gave strong leadership to the Jesuits. Internal discipline in Jesuit religious life was paramount, as regulated community life gave life and support to the missionaries for apostolic mission. Presumably believing that the Jesuits were in need of reminding of the essentials of Jesuit religious life, he exhorted them to goodness and to keep the rules of the Society, and then gave detailed instructions on how to keep the religious vows. As for the spirit of poverty, they were not to give away anything without the approval of the superior, but he was happy with the spirit of poverty at Xujiahui. He then went on to give directives about what to wear and when, and prohibitions about borrowing books from the library without writing their name in the book provided. Religious discipline required superiors to legislate great detail for the harmonious daily living of the Jesuits.

Concerning chastity, Jesuits were to take great prudence in dealing with women, especially to make sure the 'crates', the barrier between confessor and penitent in the confessional, was to be in place, and to avoid frequent visits to the 'virgins'. The latter were only to visit the priest accompanied by other ladies. He counselled severity rather than familiarity with women, and never to be alone with them. In the evening, the priest should retire for prayer. Presumably these regulations would help the missionary with any temptations in regard to the women in the Christian communities.

---

95. Servière, op. cit., 190–5.

He was also very exacting with regard to the vow of obedience. Every priest was to write to the superior monthly concerning their spiritual ministry, and every four months concerning their health. This was important for uniformity under the superior. They should also write to Europe regularly, especially keeping the mission procurator advised about the mission so that he could inform the benefactors of the mission. In the residence at Xujiahui, Jesuits were not to visit the rooms of others, nor go into areas ministered by the brothers. Silence was to be kept in the rooms and garden. They must not interfere in the work of the superior, and avoid rumour and complaints. Accept the rulings of superiors.[96] Poissemeux must have been worried that some Jesuits were not sufficiently subservient. Yet, in all these directives, he was strictly applying the universal rules for the Jesuits, in whatever country they lived.

In 1851, Poissemeux was happy to report to the superior general about the religious zeal of all the Jesuits. Quoting the *Ratio Studiorum* about the importance of work for youth in schools, he was proud that the mission now had elementary schools for catechists, a Chinese school at Xujiahui, and a diocesan seminary. He believed that the students were advancing 'in piety and learning'.

His policy in the elementary schools was to select those who might more normally proceed to secondary education, but as he was concerned that some communities might not be able to support schools, they could be concentrated in the major centres.

Furthermore, he did not want colleges for catechists established in each district, but also grouped together in major centres. They should teach not only the Chinese language and Christian doctrine, but also prepare students who were at least 14 years old and 'of good character and keen to learn' for the baccalaureate. Fostering a religious or priestly vocation in some was advisable. For those students unable to provide for themselves financially, they could be subsidised by the Jesuits. It was important that religious studies be given daily.

He was pleased to note the recent opening of the Chinese college in Xujiahui. It was only for Chinese where Chinese studies and Christian doctrine was taught. The age of intake was 10 to 12 years, and only for those students with good prospects would normally be

96. Poissemeux to the Fathers, Xujiahui, 1850. ARSI.

admitted.[97] The letter gave many more detailed instructions. Very little was left to the initiative of the teacher. Poissemeux seemed to be a very controlling superior.

One year later, Maresca, writing to the superior general, said he was happy with the Jesuits and praised their good works. Conversions in the mission were due to these 'good French soldiers of Christ'. The emperor showed his dislike for Christianity by imprisonment and torture of a Chinese priest and two Chinese Christians, but 'God' later released them. Maresca had a strong spiritual belief in Divine Providence and His care. He believed that the schools were doing well, with the college at Xujiahui teaching 'science and piety'. A new chapel had been built by Louis Hélot at Xujiahui, and great confidence was expressed in the Jesuits who showed much zeal in setting up primary and secondary schools, orphanages for both sexes, and places of refuge, while baptising infants and 'infidels' and preparing catechumens. He was full of praise for Gotteland, and Hélot, who worked on the Cathedral for the bishop. He had appointed Brouillon his vicar-general.[98] The tone of Maresca's letters was positive and full of hope, grateful for the work of his collaborators.

In 1852, the Jesuit superior, Nicolas Brouillon (1816–55)[99], wrote that he was pleased with the increase in the number of Chinese receiving instruction, as well as for the provision of good education for those interested in the priesthood. He believed that a native clergy could more easily 'triumph over idolatry' than the foreigners. But to achieve this, missionaries had to have knowledge of Chinese customs and culture, and work with the level of Christianity that existed. He even advocated the promotion of a native episcopacy.[100]

From 60,000 Christians in 1842, there were 71,151 Catholics in 1852. In the years 1851–2, 448 adults had been baptised and there were 388 catechumens. There was a further increase by mid 1853, with a further 609 adult Baptisms and 530 catechumens. Working

---

97. Poissemeux to all and to the General, Xujiahui, 12 March 1851. ARSI
98. Maresca to General, Shanghai, 1 July 1851. ARSI.
99. **Nicolas Broullion** was born at Viéville, Haute Marne, France on 18 May 1816. He entered the Jesuits, 1 December 1844, and arrived on the Jiangnan mission, 20 March 1848. He was superior of the mission, 1851–1854, and died at Xujiahui, 8 July 1855, aged 39.
100. Augustin Brou & Gustave Gibert, SJ, *Jésuites Missionaires, un siècle, 1823–1923* (Paris, 1924), 45–6.

among the 369 parishes within the diocese of Nanjing were 1,450 virgins, very pious ladies, full of zeal who engaged in works of spiritual and corporal mercy.

Orphanages were considered a major work, and by the end of 1853 there were 197 children in the orphanages and 681 children living with Christian families. About 1,124 children had died after being rescued.

Education in the schools flourished. The total number of schools in the diocese in 1853 was 74, of which the virgins ran 30 for young girls. It was costly running these schools, with funds coming from the diocese, the Holy Infant Sodality, and alms received from *Propaganda*. After the civil war, when many of the schools were destroyed and required rebuilding, funds became scarce.[101]

The growth in the number of Chinese converts in the Jesuit mission was impressive considering that in the 1850s, it was estimated that the total number of Chinese Catholics in the country reached 330,000.[102]

Progress in the growth of Christian communities and the overall increase in numbers of Catholics since 1842 was impressive. The faith and zeal of the missionaries in the care of Chinese Christians influenced other local Chinese, with conversions following. European knowledge, sacred and secular, financial assistance and military protection was generally appreciated by the uneducated Christians whose living standards improved considerably, but separated them from other Chinese that caused future problems.

---

101. Broullion, op. cit., 193–225.
102. Kenneth Scott Latourette, *A History of Christian Missions in China* (New York: The Macmillan Company, 1929), 129.

Chapter 2
Jiangnan Mission
Uprisings, 1850–1898

While focusing on evangelisation, the missionaries were continually harassed by the presence of bandits and rebel groups that disrupted social harmony in the villages of the mission. The missionaries also had to accommodate themselves to the restraints placed upon them by the Chinese government, and to the many natural disasters that they encountered.

The Qing government, following forced agreements with the European powers after the Opium War, faced the consequences of the floods and famine of the early 1850s in the form of riots and disorder in the countryside. Peasant uprisings sometimes resulted in the rise of rebel organisations, which were common in Chinese history. The Imperial court feared these revolts as being a sign that they were losing the mandate of the Lord of Heaven to rule. The Qing dynasty itself had come to power as a result of social upheaval in 1644.

The government struggled against these uprisings that included the activities of a secret society known as the White Lotus. They were a disaffected group of minor gentry that supported the impoverished peasants against current economic and social conditions. Following the death of the Daoguang emperor in 1850, the new emperor, Xianfeng, young, weak and ineffective, left officials to run the Empire.

There were three significant uprisings in the nineteenth century: the Taiping Heavenly Kingdom in the south, the Nian in the north, and a series of Muslim uprisings in the west of the country.[1]

---

1   Michael Dillon, *China u Modern History* (London: Tauris, 2010), 65–7; and Jonathan Fenby, *History of Modern China* (England: Penguin, 2008), 18–19.

The Taiping rebellion

From 1850, of all the insurrections of the time, the Heavenly King-dom of the Taiping, capitalising on local poverty and corrupt admin-istration, was the most significant, and directly affected the life of the mission. It caused significant social and political upheaval, from the Provinces of Guangdong-Guangxi in the south to Nanjing in the north, and moving eventually further east to Xuzhou and areas south of Shanghai in 1862, which were areas of Jesuit missionary activity. It was a revolt that 'took up to 20 million lives, devastated wide areas of China, created a flood of refugees, and brought a shift of power that further weakened the throne'.

The movement was led by Hong Xiuquan, a disgruntled village teacher and failed imperial examinations student. He proclaimed himself 'the son of the Christian God', after a vision that told him to read the Christian Old and New testaments, as well as the writings of Confucius. He decided that the Manchus were devils and that he was given the commission to eradicate them and Confucianism. His cru-sade also reflected and flamed the racial tension between the indig-enous Han and the Manchus, which was rooted among the peasants.[2]

Hearing that this new movement was based on Christian teach-ing, the initial reaction of Westerners living in China was encour-aging, but when Hong claimed to be the younger brother of Jesus, such enthusiasm evaporated, and the Taipings were denounced. In order to preserve their commercial and diplomatic interests, they cre-ated a Volunteer Corps that assisted Li Hongzhang's Huai army in its struggle against the Taipings that were finally defeated at Nanjing on 19 July 1864.[3]

During the civil war, the British staged an attack on Guangzhou after the *Arrow* incident, on 9 October 1856, not ending until the city fell to British and French forces on 29 December. The initial incident occurred when Chinese authorities, suspecting the crew of piracy, boarded this British ship that was owned by the Chinese, but registered in Hong Kong and flying the British flag. The British consul demanded an apology that was not forthcoming; so the Brit-ish shelled Guangzhou with much devastation. Although the conflict

---

2. Fenby, ibid., 19.
3. Dillon, op. cit., 82–3.

had nothing to do with opium, the skirmish had been called the Second Opium War or, alternatively, the *Arrow* war.

The Treaty of Tianjin followed in 1858, which was a series of treaties with representatives of Britain, France, the United States and Russia. They demanded the opening of more treaty ports, the right to establish diplomats in Beijing, and to send missionaries into the interior of China. These demands were rejected in May; so the French and British forces occupied the Dagu forts that guarded the approach to Tianjin. The Qing government capitulated and accepted the May demands under protest, but later reneged on the agreement.

A joint British and French expeditionary force under Lord Elgin, occupied Beijing on 13 October 1860 and virtually destroyed the old Imperial Summer Place, the Yuanmingyuan, on 20 October. The Convention of Beijing followed, whereby the court agreed to respect the provisions of the Treaty of Tianjin, which was signed individually with Lord Elgin and the French envoy, Bros Gros, on 24 October.[4]

These treaties resulted in further Chinese resentment against the Western powers and, by implication, with the European missionaries.

Missionary reactions to the Taiping rebellion

In August 1853, Gotteland wrote to the French provincial of his concerns about the Taiping rebels arriving in the mission areas from the south that could not be stopped by the mandarins. The missionaries believed that the rebels were part of the Chinese secret societies called Triads: groups wanting a change of dynasty. They were known as 'Reds' because of the colour of their turbans. To counteract this threat, the Dao-tai of Shanghai asked for assistance from the European navies, but the consuls, wanting to maintain neutrality, refused.

On the morning of 7 September, Lemaître encountered a group of these Reds with armed sabres on his way to say Mass. He was not impeded, but he later heard that they had entered the village and killed the under-prefect. When the European concessions were considered under threat, the French consul asked for the support of the British who responded by sending sailors from their ship, the *Hermès*,

---

4. Ibid., 102–3. Dillon and Fenby have been used extensively in this narrative for modern, clear and precise background information on the political, social and economic history of China.

to guard the area. Shortly after, the French were able to send forces to guard the missionaries at Xujiahui.[5] The missionaries expressed gratitude to the French consul for his offer of assistance.

Greater danger to the mission occurred with the arrival of 20,000 Imperial troops outside Shanghai in mid September. While the rebels were uncontested, order reigned. But these troops declared themselves allies of the Taipings and prepared to march on Suzhou and Wuxi. They treated the Europeans tactfully, and that included the missionaries. Their soldiers guarded the cathedral at Tong-jia-tou. On 17 September, peasants in the village of Fa-hoa were massacred, and soon after their village was burned. Xujiahui was preserved with assurances from the rebels. After 17 months of stand-offs between the rebels, the Imperial army and the French sailors, peace was restored.

The hero of these days was Lemaître, who obtained the security of the residents at Xujiahui, as well as the crowd taking refuge in the Cathedral. He maintained order among the refugees, and stopped the rebels who were trying to force the doors of the Cathedral. Lemaître had also begun a hospital in October 1853 for the wounded of both sides, without any external help. Brother Jules Saguez (1824–55) and two French doctors from the *Cassini* helped him. By 1854, Lemaître had baptised 870 adults in danger of death as well, and they included mandarins and leaders of the bandits. French assistance was also given to Chinese Christians living in the suburbs of Shanghai.

The French consul asked the Jesuits to provide two missionaries to accompany the *Cassini* to Nanjing in the French attempt to negotiate with the leaders of the Taipings. Clavelin and a catechist were chosen. They were well treated in Nanjing during the negotiations.

After dealing with the rebels, greater dangers occurred when the Imperial troops came to the city.

During this civil strife and social upheaval, the missionaries expressed much gratitude for the protection given by the French legation. Maresca expressed this many times, saying that the protection stressed to the Chinese the importance of 'liberty of conscience and of religion'. Moreover, missionaries upheld the honour of France and with protection missionaries announced a new era of Christianity to the Chinese authorities. Religion, he said, could be a great force in unifying people. Moreover, the protection given was believed to be

---

5.   Servière, op. cit., 267. Letter Gotteland, 20 August 1853. *Nouvelle de Mission*, 3, 42.

important to get justice from the local Chinese authorities. Maresca continually informed the French Minister of the great work done by the missionaries.[6]

In writing to Europe, Maresca wrote about the civil war that disrupted the lives of everyone in the mission. The Imperial army pillaged local villages and set fire to houses, with the bullets of both armies flying over the houses of the missionaries. In the midst of this fighting, missionary work peacefully continued, as well as courses in the seminary and in the school. Maresca believed this was the result of the 'hand of God' that protected them. He hoped that this attitude of the missionaries would bring about many conversions.

The letter continued with great details of the battle from 7 September 1853, when the Reds attacked Shanghai, and how they occupied all essential buildings in the town. Some mandarins fired shots, but most fled. Soon an announcement was made telling the people not to fear, and to continue their usual occupation. Eventually, order was re-established in the town.

At the end of September, an Imperial army arrived to take Shanghai and five other fortified villages that were occupied by the rebels. On 29 September, fifty war junks arrived on the river and fired their weapons. They aimed at the town, but many missiles hit the suburbs, where they hit the poor people. This continued for a few days. Some troops came ashore and camped near Xujiahui. By 10 October, six to 7,000 troops were ready to retake the city from the rebels. The battle continued for a few days. The Imperial troops, despairing of taking the city, passed the time drinking, smoking and pillaging the countryside. The rebels, on their side, did not seem to have a leader capable of organising their forces. The missionary hospital in 15 days received 40 wounded, while 13 non-Christians in danger of death were baptised, with nine of them subsequently dying. An explosion on one of the British ships wounded six Chinese and several Filipinos. The Chinese asked for Baptism and the Filipinos went to Confession.

---

6. Maresca, Memo on the state of Catholic Missions in China, Shanghai, 29 June, 1852; Maresca to French Minister, Shanghai, early 1853; Maresca to French Minister, Shanghai, 1853; Maresca to French minister, 28 May 1853; Maresca to French Minister, 1 June 1853; Maresca to French Minister, Shanghai, 9 June 1853; Maresca, three letters to French Plenipotentiary in China, 26 February, 24 March, 2 August 1853, DAC.

During all these events, the seminary, school, orphanage, and Jesuit residences remained undisturbed. Throughout the mission, work flourished with adult Baptisms of children, and an increase in the number of catechumens and children in schools. The Christians, despite the terror of war, showed great faith, and distinguished themselves from the non-Christians by abandoning themselves to Divine Providence.

At Nanjing, however, the Christian communities were much distressed, following rough treatment from the Taipings. Beijing also reported persecution from the Imperial forces. Other areas of the mission had not given reports.[7]

Due to the chaos caused by the Taiping Rebellion around Shanghai on 13 May 1854, the Chinese Imperial government ceased to function. The French, British and American consuls established a set of local bylaws under which foreign residents, represented by an assembly of landowners, chose a Shanghai Municipal Council to set tax rates to be imposed on all residents including the Chinese, in order to finance public works and the police force.

After a clash between the French and the rebels on 6 January 1855, during which a French sailor was mortally wounded, war broke out between them, the result being that the Taipings finally left Shanghai in February 1855.

Writing in 1856, Clavelin spoke about the great patience and resignation of the Chinese Catholics during the Taiping occupation. They were tired, suffered from hunger, often slept under the stars or in pagodas, reciting prayers, looked after orphans, and baptised many abandoned babies.

The Taiping war actually helped many in Shanghai economically. Some Chinese Christians did well through their connection with the missionaries and the French. The missionaries indicated that the progress of the mission depended much on the protection of the French, 'It is an honour to have your presence'.[8] They spoke about their work of 'Christian civilisation' and the good name they brought to France, stressing the importance of the French concept of 'liberty'.[9]

---

7. Maresca, to the central councils of Lyon and Paris, Shanghai, 19 October 1853, in Broullion, op cit., 323–52.
8. Broullion to French Minister, Shanghai, 3 January 1856. DAC (Diplomatic Archives Centre, Nantes).
9. Lemaître to Chargé d'Affairs, Shanghai, 6 April 1856. DAC.

They saw themselves as setting the Chinese free from their backward civilisation.

While dealing with the Taiping rebels, internal Jesuit administration continued. After the synod of vicars apostolic in 1851, a plan arose to give the Jesuits the district of south-east Zhili (diocese of Beijing), with Gotteland as vicar apostolic. Rome decided to wait, not wanting to upset the potential clash between the Jesuits and Spelta about the ordination of Chinese seminarians. The Jesuits said that they were not ready, but the bishop thought otherwise. The Holy See sent a visitor to Jiangnan, Pierre Fournier, rector of the Jesuit scholasticate at Laval, France. He suggested that a Jesuit replace Maresca who was old and sick, and that Spelta be sent to another region. Maresca died on 2 November 1855 and *Propaganda* suppressed the diocese of Nanjing, sent Spelta to the vicariate of Hupeh in April 1856, and the Jesuit André Borgniet[10] was appointed the first vicar apostolic of Jiangnan in 1856. The Jesuits also received the region of south-east Zhili, with Languillat appointed vicar apostolic of this region.

During the reign of Maresca, the increase of Chinese Christians had been only modest: from 60,963 in 1847 to 74,296 in 1857. Schools flourished: student numbers increased form 2,988 to 4,812. There had been 21 European and five Chinese priests in 1847, which increased to 35 European and six Chinese priests in 1857.[11]

In the aftermath of the Taipings, Bishop André-Pierre Borgniet (1856–1862)[12]

Writing to the superior general soon after his appointment as vicar apostolic, Borgniet mentioned that he wanted to appoint the new

10. In an article by Henri Cordier on Bishop Borgniet, he wrote: Borgniet's main work in China was helping catechumens. He introduced devotions to the Sacred Heart, Mary, and St Joseph, as well as monthly devotions. In 1857, he introduced retreats. In his time, schools increased from 260 in 1855 to 400 in 1860.

11. Joseph de la Servière, *La nouvelle mission du Kiangnan, 1840–1922* (Shanghai: Xujiahui, 1925).

12. **André-Pierre Borgniet** was born 14 February 1811 in Mainz, Germany. He entered the diocesan seminary of Arras and was ordained priest in 1835. He joined the Jesuits on 6 December 1845, and on 24 October 1847 arrived in Shanghai. He died in Changchiachuang, Hebei, on 31 July 1862, aged 51.

superior Lemaître as his vicar general, and lamented the deaths of Léon Fornier and Augustin Massa (1813–56).[13]

When France and Britain were at war with China from 1859–60, Christians fled south to Xujiahui. Although the Taipings were stopped in their approach to Shanghai by the Anglo-French forces, they attacked Tushanwan and the orphanage, assassinating René Massa and a number of children.[14]

When Borgniet gave a report of the mission in 1859, he was only 48 years old, very active and involved in governing the mission. He described the size of the mission as requiring 20 days travel to reach all parts. Christians lived amid much misery because of famine and the civil war. The number of non-Christians was between 50 to 70 million. He respected the virtues of the non-Christians and indicated that they showed an aptitude towards Christianity. The young especially were believed to be keen to accept mission education.

The mission was the same as the former Province of Nanjing, but divided into Jiangsu and Anhui. The episcopal residence in Shanghai was modest, available for visiting priests for consultation or for those wanting to make the spiritual exercises. The seminary was in the same building near the church in which there were five new Chinese priests and seven clerical students who had finished theology. Later, they became teachers or catechists. The building housed also five theologians with four European scholastics, and nine juniors studying Latin in preparation for philosophy. Students at St. Ignatius' at Xujiahui studied literature and were sufficiently educated to be considered for the seminary.

The new prefectures of Jiangsu and Anhui were the former Province of Jiangnan. There were very few Christians in Anhui, the majority being in the prefectures of Songjiang and Suzhou, situated in the far east of Jiangsu.

The overall number of Christians in the mission was 75,352, with 5,766 in the Shanghai district. The Christians were 'poor, timid and despised'. Most were 'well instructed in the doctrine of the faith' and 'its exact obligations'. They cared for the non-Christian children by feeding them and teaching them about the faith.

---

13. Borgniet to General, Shanghai, 31 August 1856. ARSI.
14. Servière, *La nouvelle . . .* op cit., ch 3.

Europeans in Shanghai were courteous towards the missionaries and generous when required. Protestant missionaries were prominent in the city, preaching and distributing Christian books among the Chinese.

In the mission schools, there were 3,833 male students and 1,163 females, taught by 291 male teachers and 90 females in separate schools. Two priests taught theology in the seminary and another two in the college at Xujiahui who, together with nine Chinese teachers, taught 93 students. In the orphanage at Tushanwan, with two priests, there were 140 students studying the arts.

As for the clergy, there were 11 Chinese and 29 Europeans priests, as well as four Jesuit scholastics and five brothers. The missionaries were considered 'pious and morally upright', working in mission stations or teaching the young in seminaries, colleges or schools. The Chinese priests were likewise 'pious, obedient and cared much for the salvation of souls'. The bishop was pleased with them.

In order to avoid any scandal, women were excluded from all houses of the missionaries. The latter dressed in a long toga 'of varying cloth according to place and climate, acceptable to all'.

All missionaries studied the local dialect for at least one year, and when they travelled they took catechists who acted as companions and negotiated with the local people. All studied Mandarin, but only a minimum was considered sufficient, because many local people in the Nanjing mission didn't understand it. Many local dialects existed within one province, and as missionaries moved around, they had to study a new language. In addition, in any one place, the European language of English, French, Spanish or Portuguese might be found. Facility in speaking different languages was considerably advantageous for the missionaries and, in most cases, indispensable.

As was the custom of the universal Church, the regular clergy were all dependent on the vicar apostolic, while the religious were accountable to their own superior for religious discipline. They lived from communal expenses. The Jesuit religious superior was also the vicar general of the diocese.

Christians and non-Christians held all missionaries in high esteem. The Europeans worked in mission districts or in education, whereas the Chinese clergy worked only in the mission stations.

There were no congregations of women, but the 'virgins', considered 'upright and virtuous', were indispensable co-missionaries, preparing the children for Baptism and teaching the basics of the faith.

No grave abuses appeared among those Christians who lived the Christian life, but all Chinese shared human misery. The non-Christians found Christian beliefs and rituals incomprehensible. The Christian faith was preserved and propagated by the preaching of the Word of God, the administration of the sacraments and the founding of schools.

The mission survived the challenges of the civil war because of the zeal and unity of the missionaries united with their flock. Moreover, the educational institutions were considered a means of preaching the Gospel.[15]

In a further report to *Propaganda* in 1861, Borgniet described Jiangnan as in a 'state of disruption and disorder because of the civil war'. He rejoiced that Xujiahui, the city of Shanghai and its suburbs, were under French protection and, therefore, safe. He gave thanks that the missionaries and Christians were under the protection of troops and ships, especially in those areas outside the city where the rebels held sway. He feared for the many Christians in the outlying stations. Wuxi was totally in the hands of the rebels, as was Somhiang and Pauni. In God he placed his total trust. Many refugees from the outlying districts had come to Xujiahui for protection. Many had been violated and there were reports of abduction.

More joyful information was shared that one Jesuit scholastic, Emil Chevreuil, who had arrived in China in May 1859, had been ordained and was working in the Xujiahui area. However, sad news was that two priests, one Jesuit and one Chinese priest had recently died. The minor seminary had 34 alumni, but many who were not considered suitable were dismissed. In the city schools and suburbs, there were 520 alumni, among them about 90 non-Christian boys. He was pleased that the mission cared for both Christian and non-Christians, all of whom had both physical and spiritual needs. More than 500 non-Christians – men, women and boys – had been baptised in the current year, while First Holy Communion was given to both boys and girls after a period of probation, and then celebrated

---

15. Borgniet to Sacred Congregation *Propaganda Fide*, Shanghai, 1860. ARSI.

with solemnity. The non-Christians were always impressed with solemn Catholic ceremonies.[16]

Gratitude for French protection was constant and genuinely expressed in letters from 1858. In 1861, Borgniet was grateful to the French Minister for the provisions in the Treaty of Tianjin, as it would help promote 'the moral regeneration of the non Christian population who we evangelise.'[17]

The French protection was effective. Following petitions from the missionaries, the French legation constantly placed pressure on the Chinese authorities not only to prevent rebel attacks on Christian communities but, if damage occurred, compensation was demanded.[18] The role of the French consul at Shanghai was considered crucial to the development and even the survival of the mission. While this pleased the European missionaries, it did not please the local Chinese authorities, resulting in friction and distrust toward the Europeans.

One example of this was a letter sent by some Chinese Catholics to the pope, which, in turn, was sent to the superior general, who asked Borgniet to comment, which he did. Lemaître added his comments. He noted that of the authors, one had apostatised during the persecution, and notified the emperor of this. Another became mixed up in political affairs, and having left his post given to him by a Chinese priest, stole some furniture. The issues involved the allocation of money for the building of churches and the accusation that the Jesuits forced seminarians to enter the Jesuit noviciate. In fact, no one had yet entered, and many requests had been refused. Three deacons had asked to join.

Lemaître believed that the 'new Christians' were only Christians in name, and some lose their initial fervour, especially during the many troubles they endured during the war and persecution. Most, despite these difficulties, remained faithful, while others died during the troubles. These were the true Christians. Some criticisms were calumnies and others were 'doubtful truths'. Despite these hurtful

---

16. Borgniet to Cardinal Barnabo, Shanghai, 29 September 1861. ARSI.
17. Borgniet to French Minister, Shanghai, 31 May 1861. DAC.
18. Report of the Minister of Foreign Affairs and an official communication to the governor of Jiangsu concerning the influx of Christian refugees to Shanghai, 1861. DAC.

accusations, the missionaries persevered doing 'good works for the glory of God'.[19] This was the end of this matter under discussion.

During the reign of Borgniet, the seminary produced its first three priests in 1858, while the Jesuit novitiate opened at Xujiahui on 29 May 1862, with 11 novices under the novice master Angelo Zottoli.

In 1859, Pius IX asked Spelta to do a visitation of the Chinese missions with the intention of establishing a Chinese hierarchy, which had already been requested by six bishops in 1849. Spelta died in September 1862, but had sent his report to *Propaganda* on 8 June 1862. Borgniet did not want to ordain young Chinese clerics without prior pastoral experience. Some proved to be excellent potential priests. Fears had been expressed that Chinese priests were being ordained too early, without sufficient education. However, during the civil war, French Jesuits were happy with the work of the Chinese priests. Commenting on the character of Chinese seminarians, it was believed that they were 'less expansive' than the French, but were nonetheless 'solid'. They were not enthusiastic, but worked from 'reason and faith'; they were studious, serious about philosophy and theology, and 'persevering and tranquil amid the difficulties of the civil war'.[20]

One of the advantages of the war had been that the Catholic families living at Xujiahui received additional spiritual help from the missionaries. Marin Desjacques, who had arrived in China only on 9 February 1856 with five other Jesuits, administered to the sailors of all nations in Shanghai in 1861, as he spoke English and was liked by all.

Diplomatically, M de Bourboulon, the French minister at Beijing, obtained from Prince Kong an imperial edict revoking all the old laws against the Christian religion on 15 April 1862. The missionaries believed this to be the best news since the times of the Emperor Kangxi.[21]

Despite the suffering of the Christians during the civil war, they were not only helped by the presence of the French and British military forces, but they received generous donations from a number of French charities, which helped develop educational and health services in the mission, as well as rebuild destroyed church buildings.

---

19. Lemaître to missionaries, Shanghai, 1861. ARSI.
20. Letters of Lemaître, 26 May 1862, and 20 September 1857, quoted in Servière, *Histoire . . . op.cit.* Tome II.
21. Ibid.

Letters by Jesuit superiors to Rome were usually heavily self-censored. The Jesuit custom in writing letters was expected to give edifying comment on Jesuit life, while criticism or disagreements were generally hidden, obscure, or not mentioned. The appointment of Jesuit consultors to the superior, who also wrote letters to Rome, was a counterbalance to the former. Information that they gave sometimes offered a differing perspective on local affairs.

One such consultor, Louis Taffin (1810–64), vice-superior of the residence at Xujiahui in 1863, believed that the Chinese should have been more involved in evangelising the non-Christians instead of working at Xujiahui. Rather, they might have been more involved in accompanying the missionaries on their travels, serving Mass, writing letters, and instructing some ignorant Christians who presented themselves to receive the sacraments. He believed that they would work more effectively if they were more adequately educated for the work.

He appreciated that the students in the school received a good education 'in piety and solid instruction' and hoped that they would further their education to become good catechists. But he observed that most of them only wanted a 'noble and lucrative position in society'. Most worked eventually for the local European businessmen 'to the detriment of their souls'. His wish was to find leaders among the students who might want to learn the job of catechists. In this way, the 'fruits of the mission' would increase, especially among the poor people of the countryside, who lived simple lives away from the commerce of the 'old Christians' in the city.

To meet this goal, the Jesuits needed not only to find such men, but also to provide the necessary finances and manpower to educate them. This was a difficult objective: to work zealously with the 70,000 Christians would require 20 or more catechists. What finances existed would be better spent on this project that on building or rebuilding destroyed churches.

The students at the boarding school at Dongjiadu were among the more intellectually capable, sent by the Jesuits from the surrounding districts. It was the hope that after some training, they would return to their districts to exercise their 'zeal and trade'.

The same idea of the multiplier effect might occur by uniting the 'virgins' and the 'widows', who already showed 'zeal and constancy'. They could then work with the young girls. The two girls' schools that

Taffin already directed did not give him much consolation, because he considered that the students were 'dissipated'. The training of more female teachers would better serve the preparation of these students for Baptism.

Country students in the elementary schools were 'subtle and docile', and had a good spirit. External students living nearby were 'dissipated, argumentative and without piety or devotion'.[22]

The relationship between the Jesuits and the French consul was very close. They wrote letters to each other when a Jesuit died, and thanks were expressed when a minister was changed or departed from China. The minister gave his sympathy to the Jesuits with the death of Lemaître in 1863, praising him for serving both the Chinese and Europeans well for 17 years. Reciprocal gratitude was given to the French government for the gift of 75,000 francs to help rebuild destroyed chapels and Church buildings after the war.[23]

The annual report on the mission was an important means of communication among the Jesuits. That of 1864 spoke about working in the two Provinces of Jiangnan, which before the invasion of the rebels comprised between 50–60 million people, with 51 Jesuits and 13 Chinese priests. Eight European Jesuits had died between 1862 and 1864.[24] In addition, in a year and a half, about one third of the apostolic workers died from sickness or fatigue, as well as many Christians in certain districts. In the border district of Zhenjiang, more than a third died. Happily in the districts of Hai Men, Chongming and Shanghai, less affected by the devastation by the rebels, there was an increase in the number of Christians. In the whole of Jiangnan there were 70,136. Added to this were between 2–3,000 European Catholics in Shanghai. The number of catechists decreased from 4,000 before the invasion to 1,825 in July 1864.

The material losses were incalculable. In 1860, there were 382 churches and chapels; in 1862, there were 230. Fortunately, with the generous help of the French government and from Chinese indemnities, some of these churches were rebuilt.

---

22. Taffin to General, Shanghai, 6 March 1863. ARSI.
23. Desjacques to French Minister, Shanghai, 2 July 1863. DAC.
24. They were Stanislas Clavelin, André Borgniet, Louis Pajot, and Victor Vuillaume in 1862; Mathurin Lemaître and Hubert Pingredon in 1863; Louis Taffin and Francesco Giaquinto in 1864.

In the 315 schools, the numbers of students and teachers increased. In the outlying districts, five primary boarding schools were established, teaching children a 'full religious and literary education'. Those who showed special aptitude were sent to the college at Xujiahui or to the minor seminary. The Xujiahui College was for children of 'good families', and for those showing greater intelligence. At the end of their studies, the Chinese students received the baccalaureate. During the rebellion, exams had been suspended. The subjects taught included Chinese literature, French, Latin, geography, mathematics, and the 'beaux-arts', which included design, painting and music. In 1864, there were 110 students.

Attached to the college were the major and minor seminaries, where there were 18 students in theology and philosophy and 38 Latin students. It was felt important to point out that these institutions were not 'lacking in piety and science of the European institutions', and that the students made good progress in studying the French language.

The education of young girls was not neglected in the mission. Besides the elementary schools, there were 70 boarding schools for those between 13 and 25 under the supervision of the 'good, Christian virgins'. The girls were taught Chinese literature and were considered 'no less capable of education than their European counterpart'.[25]

The superior general sent Michel Fessard as visitor to the mission from December 1865 to May 1866. He wanted the French model for seminary training and for the Jesuit scholastics with adaptation to the local situation. The importance of the work of the catechists was recognised. He told the superior general that the Jesuits were very faithful to their vocation and that 'God was blessing the mission'. He was impressed with the mission statistics from 1845–65: 32,723 adult Baptisms and 44,844 Christian infants baptised. In 20 years, the Jesuits had sent 88 priests to China, of whom 30 had already died. The rest worked in 414 Christian communities among 73,684 Christians.[26] It was never clear what significant adaptions 'to the local situation' in seminary training ever occurred.

---

25. *Annales Domus* Xujiahui, 1863–78. A report of the Mission of Kiang-nan, 1 July 1863 – 1 July 1864. ARSI.

26. A. Colombel, below in footnote 43, 3rd part II, 4. 1865–1878, 30–49.

Bishop Adrien Languillat (1864–1878), mission protection and prosperity

With the death of Borgniet in 1862, the search for a new bishop resulted in the appointment of Adrien Languillat who had first been appointed vicar apostolic to south-east Zhili in 1856, but was then translated to Jiangnan in 1864. Soon after his appointment, the bishop paid his respects to the French Minister and requested the renewal of French protection of the mission. Recent incidents were mentioned, where two Christians were the victims of a brutal attack, and were thrown in the river and drowned. The minister was asked to obtain justice for this outrage from the Chinese.[27] Action was taken, and the bishop later expressed his gratitude for the 'effacious protection' for 'the honour of France'. He believed that the missionaries would not be able to function 'without new help given at the blessed hand of our Mother country'.[28] To prove the effectiveness of this protection he sent the minister the latest statistics for the mission in 1865, indicating the growth of the mission: the number of Christians was 71,152 living in 17 districts with 404 Christian communities. There were 4,372 catechumens, as well as many schools. He stressed the importance of education in the work of the mission.[29]

During his episcopate, 78 European Jesuits arrived in China. From 1865, missionaries obtained permission from the Zongli Yamen to buy property in the interior of China. Li Hongzhang met with Languillat and they bought some land outside Kia-koan for a priest's residence near a former church. Other residences were built near the Yangtze at Anqing, capital of Anhui, and at Yangzhou, as well as at Xuzhou at the end of 1866.

In the years following the civil war, the mission underwent material prosperity, with buildings rebuilt with finance from compensation from the Chinese authorities or from France. New women religious were introduced into the mission and 12 Chinese candidates were received into the Society. Yet, there were local issues of conflict between the Jesuits and mandarins over implementing the imperial edict allowing the missionaries to work inland. Also, the viceroy of Nanjing did not want Christian missionaries. As a result, the French

---

27. Languillat to Minister, Sienhsien, 3 February 1865. DAC.
28. Languillat to Minister, Shanghai, 2 July 1865, 12 September 1854. DAC.
29. Languillat to Minister, Shanghai, 21 September 1865. DAC.

consul threatened Li Hongzhang with military action.[30] Finally, with the help of the French army, the Jesuits entered Nanjing, but this caused local reprisals. Long negotiations followed, with the Jesuits going to Nanjing and the old church restored to the Christians, as well as a residence. Another residence was given at Anqing.[31]

This was followed up with the French telling Prince Kong that Catholic churches, schools, cemeteries and other former church land that was included in the Treaty of Peking should be restored to the Christians in Jiangnan. Specifics were given. The prince replied that he had directed the officials to accede to this request.

The consul general also requested new passports.[32] There was a constant request for passports for new missionaries, as well as requests for the renewal of these passports. This applied also to non-French missionaries, but 'only if they speak well of France'.[33] As well as dealing with disputes between missionaries and the Chinese government, the French also intervened in disputes between Christians and non-Christians. This action did not please local Chinese authorities.

In a further report to Paris in 1867, the French minister in China noted that the Catholic religion met with hostility, mainly because it was seen as a 'doctrine of foreigners'. The decrees of the recent treaties did not help the situation. The missionaries were believed to use the French protection only in dealing with the Chinese government in extreme cases. But in reality, the missionaries went to the French minister on most issues, especially to seek justice for wronged Chinese Christians, or for compensation from the destruction of property.

The minister believed that there were two factions within the Chinese government, one group that understood that China could not remain isolated and therefore should engage with the European powers, and those who didn't want change. In disputes, the Chinese government showed itself to be very weak.

The Chinese found it very hard to accept the 1860 treaty. Three French missionaries had been killed since that time, as well as many Chinese Christians. Many neophytes had been exiled and all their goods confiscated; 'all for embracing the Catholic religion'. In

30. French Consul General to French Minister, Shanghai, 20 February 1864. DAC.
31. De Carrière to French Minister, a memo, Jiangnan, January 1865. DAC.
32. Consul General to Chinese government, Shanghai, 10 April 1865. DAC.
33. French Consul to Paris, Shanghai, 1867.

conclusion, he stated that the Chinese government was hostile to both the Catholic religion and the foreign powers.[34]

In the annual report to Rome from the vicar apostolic for the years 1866–7, he concentrated on internal affairs, indicating especially the development of the mission, shown in the annual statistics, and in the courses given in the educational establishments.[35]

In the minor seminary there were 68 students, 51 of these completed the junior course. A complete course as prescribed by the Council of Trent was not offered, but rather 'a remote preparation for the sacred studies'. This time was a test of their vocation. Many Chinese priests could not read or write their own language, and so they started with literature studies and then proceeded to Latin for three years, Gregorian chant and liturgical ceremonies, as well as two hours a week on the Chinese language. In the second year, they learnt the 'Catechism of the Council of Trent', the epistles of St. Jerome, and the works of Cornelius Nepos (Roman biographer) and Ovid. In the third year, they studied 'more complex grammar', with excerpts from the Fathers, Sallust and Virgil. Lectures were in Latin.

In the major seminary, there was a two-year course in philosophy in which they studied logic, metaphysics and mathematics, as well as moral philosophy, theodicy and physics. Repetitions were given twice a week for an hour. Theology studies for three years included moral theology, church history, canon law and sacred scripture.[36] These theological courses were similar to any theological course of studies in Europe.

Following the desire of his predecessors, Languillat was keen to foster the growth of the indigenous clergy and was open to the idea of a Chinese bishop in charge, which was something new for the French missionaries. He declared that establishing a Chinese Church under a Chinese bishop was the reason why European missionaries were in China. The minor seminaries and work in the 146 villages of Jiangnan were a good start in this process of promoting a local Chinese church.[37]

---

34. Memo addressed to M le Comte de Lallemand, French Minister plenipotentiary in Beijing on Religious Affairs in China, Paris, 6 January 1867. DAC.
35. In 1866–7: 414 Christian communities; 73,684 Christians, 1,562 Virgins, 345 schools, 5,548 alumni.
36. A report on the mission from the vicar apostolic, Nanjing, 1866–7. ARSI.
37. Languillat to General, Paris, 11 October 1867. ARSI.

Languillat saw the mission need to increase the number of women religious to work with Chinese women, especially in the field of education. So, during a visit to Europe in 1867, Languillat obtained the services of the 'Religious Helpers of the Souls in Purgatory', founded in 1856, and the Carmelites from France to assist the Daughters of St Vincent de Paul and the Sisters of Charity who were already in China.[38]

Other letters from missionaries at this time showed concern about the procedure for the Baptism of babies. It was particularly sad to see that bandits left their children behind to die when they left a village, while one Chinese family refused to allow a child to be baptised, preferring to let it 'suffer eternally in Hell with its ancestors rather than be baptised and go to Heaven'. Another missionary saw this attitude as the 'work of the devil'.[39] European missionaries did not understand the reasons for this attitude or why unwanted children were abandoned to die. Changing such practices was a challenge.

Challenges to mission work, 1869–1870

In May 1869, Pierre Heude (1836–1902), having only arrived in China in 1868, reported that he was well received by the prefect of Lu'an and the two sub-prefects of Ing-chang and Heshan, receiving full liberty to promote the Catholic religion. The catechumens he described as being 'solid in the faith', but fearful before the priest arrived, and very ignorant. These fears dissipated quickly during the visit and the population seemed to be well disposed to receiving the faith.

No permanent priest resided in many places; the Christians simply relied upon a visit from time to time. But, in the centre of the province, in the capital Anqing, Heude lived in a small house previously provided by Adrien de Carrière. A number of groups of old Christians resided in the area and it was the centre for a growing number of catechumens, especially after the Taiping war. The Christians of Ningguo asked for priests for their district, and so Joseph Seckinger and Heude were sent there. In Choei-tong, they found about fifty former Christians from Hubei, and especially helped the sick and poor.

---

38. Colombel, below in footnote 45, cf. footnote 130, 127–8.
39. Various letters to Rome, Shanghai, 1867 and 1 July 1869. ARSI.

Trouble began in November 1869 in Anqing when young students arriving for exams attacked the priest's residence and looted it. Despite the presence of the priest, they threatened him with death and the destruction of the residence. Heude fled when the situation became critical, and the residence was ransacked. The mandarins only appeared when the deed had been done: they simply took the keys of the residence and kept it safe. Seckinger, from Anhui, visited the town and called on the mandarins, but they refused to see him.

Several days later near Anqing in the sub-prefecture of Jiande, where there were centres for the catechumens, the mandarins were disturbed by the growth in the number of conversions. Having heard of the attack on the residence in Anqing, they launched an invasion of the catechumens. Opposition to the Christians grew because of their protection from the Europeans. Soon after, war broke out in the sub-prefecture and, on 8 December, Christian houses were invaded and eleven burnt down. Twenty-two people were killed. Similar occurrences happened elsewhere. Persecutions had broken out in Se-tch'oan, with two foreign missionaries and a number of Christians killed. The reaction of the French minister in Beijing, Count Julien de Rochechouart, was immediate, sending French vessels up the Yangtze to Nanjing on 24 December 1869, demanding reparations from the governors of the provinces involved in the destructions. Demands were made according to the treaties and were accepted by the Chinese representative, Ma-sin-i. The presence of the French fleet was believed to inspire a healthy respect for the Europeans.

In accordance with the settlement, the missionaries were given a large area for development and troublemakers of disturbances were punished. In addition, the viceroy 'solemnly recognised the honesty of Christianity' and affirmed permission for it to be spread in the Empire. The rights of the French missionaries were recognised to rent and buy land, and to build churches and residences in all the provinces. Transgressors of this law would be severely punished.

However, lower officials did not share these official declarations. When Seckinger went to Anqing in January 1870 to claim the new land, difficulties were presented. A different piece of land was granted. Still peace did not reign, but following further disagreements, and continual intimidation from the French fleet, finally settlements were reached, with the Chinese humiliated once again.

Another challenge occurred when the enemies of the missionaries in 1870 accused the European priests of stealing orphans, killing them, and tearing out parts of their anatomy for 'magical operations'. The simple people began to believe these stories, with subsequent attacks at Anqing against Seckinger and Heude. The enemies were stirred up by Tcheng-kouo-choei, who exhibited much hatred against the Europeans. He went to Nanjing in 1870, vowing revenge against them. The missionaries were asked to leave Nanjing, but they refused. A new prefect in Nanjing decided to protect the missionaries, but attempting to placate their enemies, he decided to inspect the residence, and found no bodies of children. Ma-sin-i sent 100 men to guard the residence, and attested to the innocence of the missionaries. At the same time five criminals held in detention were decapitated in an attempt to placate the crowd. It was announced that they had stolen children. Tcheng-kouo-choei, seeing that his coup failed went to Shandong and Tianjin where he and his men attacked European houses killing two priests, six sisters, the French consul, and several French and Russian residents. This sent fear among the priests in Nanjing and among those in the interior of China.

Even in Shanghai, the *dao-dai* issued a proclamation to the people against those who wanted parts of dead children for sale. As fears grew in Shanghai among the European settlements, they formed a voluntary militia for protection. Access to the concessions was forbidden to the Chinese locals. The French had seventy armed men. Guards were placed all the way to Xujiahui. With this common threat, political and religious rivalry disappeared. The US consul and Protestant ministers expressed solidarity with the Catholic missionaries. They even talked about the glories of martyrdom. At a service in the church of St Joseph in Yang-jing-pang for the victims of the massacre, the British, Russian, German, Italian, Spanish, Portuguese and Chinese – and above all, the French, Catholics and Protestants – were all united in sentiments of sadness. The consuls of all nations and officers of all navies, and about a dozen Protestant ministers were present.

Special prayers were made to the Blessed Virgin in the chapel on the hill of Sheshan near Songjiang. The missionaries believed that their prayers were answered when the 'grand judge' of Jiangsu gave the fathers the protection of Chinese soldiers to guard the cathedral at Xujiahui. By the end of July, all danger had been averted, thanks to the presence of the European navies.[40] Thanks were given also to the mandarin, Ma-sin-I, who saved the works of the mission in the southern capital and who, in communication with the emperor, criticised the mandarins of Tianjin who tolerated the bandits. Unfortunately, on 2 August he was assassinated in Nanjing, but the identity of the assassin was never proven. One Chinese was accused and executed, but it was doubtful that he was the true assassin.

Ecclesiastical negotiations

Meanwhile, Languillat was absent from the mission attending the Vatican Council in Rome in 1870, accompanied by the Jesuit Louis Sica as his theologian. His role in the council was identified as 'modest but active'. He did not intervene in the general sessions but worked hard in the commissions. He did not miss any general sessions, congregations, sacred ceremonies or meetings of bishops, and spent the rest of his time in his room in prayer and reading. He voted with the majority in the definition of papal infallibility, but within the group of 62 who voted '*placet juxta modum*', agreed but with modifications.[41]

While in Rome, the cardinal prefect of *Propaganda* called a meeting of all the vicars apostolic from China. They agreed on a division of China into five regions that would hold a synod every five years. A lively discussion occurred about the establishment of the Chinese hierarchy, but with no clear agreement. However, all were agreed against establishing an apostolic delegation in Beijing. They were pessimistic when discussing the formation of the native clergy; they thought the Chinese were incapable of supporting the needs of the faithful in the long term. Curiously, they asked *Propaganda* not to flatter the Chinese priests in their correspondence, observing that the Chinese students in Europe were of lesser quality than those who were in their own mission. Other topics discussed were clerical studies, guidelines for the admission to religious life, the way of living among European and Chinese religious, the wisdom of establishing a liturgical calendar unique for China, common customs for days of fasting and abstinence, and rules for the administration of the sacraments.

---

40. Servière, op cit., 164–78.
41. Ibid., 180–2.

They also wrote to the Emperor Napoleon III thanking him for the blessing of the French protectorate, which enabled the missionaries to freely move around the Chinese Empire, to preach, build churches and charitable institutions. For this, the emperor replied by thanking the bishops for their work 'in the interests of religion and of the European civilisation'.

The year 1870 was not the most settled one in Europe. The Franco-Prussian war broke out on 16 July 1870, and Piedmontese troops entered Rome on 20 September 1870. Languillat, having attended the fourth session of the Council on 18 July, obtained permission from Pius IX to leave Rome. He went to France with Sica, visiting Versailles, Laval and Blois. While waiting for the pope to suspend the Council, he decided to send Sica back to China with Bishop Dubar, the vicar apostolic of south-east Zhili, but they were arrested in Marseilles and kept in prison for eight days before being permitted to leave on 4 October 1870. When the Council was indefinitely adjourned on 20 October, Languillat left France from Marseille on 27 November, arriving in Shanghai on 13 January 1871 with three new Jesuit missionaries, Hippolyte Joret, Joachim Chevalier and Victor Laperrelle.

During his stay in Rome and France, Languillat held meetings with local Jesuit superiors concerning mission affairs, about which he communicated with the missionaries upon his return. Teaching questions were given priority. Before the Chinese seminarians began Latin studies, they ought to be prepared for the baccalaureate. A new European college in Shanghai was to be established. The recruitment and formation of the catechists was considered one of the more important works of the mission. In principle, it was also agreed to establish a Chinese periodical. The mission was divided into five sections, each with a local superior: Nanjing, with three ministers – Xuzhou, Songjiang, Pudong, and Hai Men with Chongming.

It was believed that the main means of propagating the faith among the non-Christians was through the Christian families, while the medical work in the pharmacies, and the distribution and explanation of holy images helped. The calumnies recently arising from the work in the orphanages required great prudence in dealing with these issues by those in charge. The Baptism of children ought to be performed in a hidden place by well-instructed catechists and virgins, while the adoption of orphans by Christian families was considered the best option.

Following up on these issues, Languillat sent out a directive to the missionaries on 16 June 1871, about how they ought to conduct their activities and religious procedures. Mention was made of the professions of faith required by the Councils of Trent and the Vatican, and of the vow relative to the Chinese ceremonies. He reminded them of the prudence needed in dealing with the mandarins in order to avoid tension, of the importance of education for catechists, of the main Chinese superstitions, of the administration of the sacraments, and how to work with the virgins and other mission collaborators. The consecration of the vicariate to the Sacred Heart of Jesus was made in the cathedral and in all churches and chapels of the mission.[42]

Political concerns

Some time before, in 1857, the English Consul, Sir Rutherford Alcock, a former friend of the fathers at Xujiahui, reflected on the work of the missionaries in a memorandum entitled 'Tolerance toward the Christian religion'. In it he blamed the excessive zeal of the missionaries for the persecutions (both Catholic and Protestant). The protection of missionaries by invading forces did not help the Christian religion itself and was a cause of irritation among the mandarins. 'The worst enemies to Christianity in China are the missionaries and the Western powers who have declared too easily to protect them'. This document was shown to all the representatives of foreign powers on 8 June 1871. It was an enlightened opinion, not commonly shared at the time.

In discussions with the European powers over the massacres in Tianjin, the members of the Zongli Yamen submitted a memorandum. In it they asked for the suppression of the Christian orphanages, suggesting that they be open to inspection by the mandarins. This was rejected. It also raised the former objection to mixing males and females in Christian churches and, finally, they asked that the missionaries return to Europe. They accused the missionaries of abusing power, and asked them to renounce the way they supported Chinese Christians in clashes with the mandarins. They objected to the treaty rights, and the passport rights to preach the Christian religion throughout the Empire. The mandarins wanted to have the right to inspect the Christian communities. They particularly objected to

---

42. Ibid., 183–8.

the treaty clause giving the missionaries the right to purchase property without the permission of the local mandarin, and concluded with the comment that if the Christians and non-Christians could not live in harmony with one another, the missionaries should not be permitted to preach their religion in China. Chinese authorities were becoming more vocal in objecting to European methods of working in China that failed to respect Chinese traditions and way of life.

The response by the diplomats was unanimous rejection of these proposals. But the principles proposed in the memorandum inspired the mandarins in the provinces, and clashes with missionaries continued up to 1895.

Mission developments

Meanwhile, discussions took place in the mission about developing the intellectual apostolate. Jesuit superiors, mindful of the intellectual heritage of the Jesuits of the earlier period in China, wanted to have a presence in Beijing, making use of the specific intellectual talents of some of the Jesuits. Gotteland, Jean-François Ducis (after 1848) and Hélot were among those who had fostered this idea. The constancy of the pastoral demands in Jiangnan had stalled this idea. With the arrival of Henri Le Lec in 1865, who had knowledge of meteorology from the Jesuit observatory at Stonyhurst, England, in addition to teaching science in the seminary at Tong-jia-tou, the making of meteorological observations with instruments that Le Lec had brought with him from Europe commenced. Auguste Colombel arrived in 1869, and together with Le Lec worked on developing the idea of establishing an observatory. Pierre Heude, a naturalist, was sent to study Chinese fauna and flora and to establish a museum in 1868, which was finally built in 1883.

At a Jesuit consultation in August 1872, it was decided to formalise these scientific ministries. The area of meteorology and scientific observations was assigned to Augustin Colombel[43], with an

---

43. Augustin-M Colombel (1833–1905) wrote the standard work on the Jiangnan mission, *L'histoire de la Mission de Kiang-nan*, (Shanghai: Imprimerie de la Mission Catholique à l'Orphelinet de T'ou-Se-wee, 1899). There are three parts in five volumes, 1549–1898. In the last section of the fifth volume (1127–418) is a necrology of the names of 65 Jesuits (European and Chinese) who died, 1879–1899, followed by very detailed obituaries. This volume ends with an appendix on Protestant missions, 1149ff.

observatory to be built at Xujiahui, which would give a daily bulletin of observations published in Shanghai and sent to Europe. Heude worked in natural history, and a museum was to be built. Researching the history and geography of China was given to Louis Pfister, while 'Diverse Publications' in Chinese were given to two Chinese scholastics, Joseph and Matthias Ma.

Work on the construction of the observatory began in February 1873. From this time, the first monthly observations appeared, and in 1874, an English Journal *The Shanghai Courier* began publishing daily observations on the evening of the previous day. Colombel handed over the observatory work to Dechevrens who specialised in magnetic observations, while meteorology was given to Le Lec. From 1877, Chinese assistants were employed. The observatory was popular with the officers and sailors of Shanghai, as well as with many visiting foreign navigators.

Other developments within the mission included the introduction of the female religious order 'Helpers of the Souls in Purgatory' who worked in the education of female children of Europeans in Shanghai. They also cared for the orphans. St Joseph's College for young boys was established and the opening of the college of St Francis Xavier was announced for 21 September 1874. Teaching in these schools was elementary: reading, writing, study of grammar, English and French language, history, geography, arithmetic, and the explanation of Christian doctrine for Catholic students.

A new church, St Francis Xavier, was under construction in the American concession, with the first stone turned on 29 November 1874.

The care of the elderly of both sexes was undertaken, with a double hospice provided in 1867, as well as a hospital near the church at Lao-dang, between 1870–1871.[44]

The two missions within Jiangnan were quite different. The area north of the Yangtze, comprising Anhui, consisted mainly of new Christians, whereas the region south of the Yangtze, included sections of Chongming and Hai Men, comprised almost entirely of old Christians. After the war of the rebels in the region south of the river, the humble work of the missionaries continued, but they were con-

---

44. Servière, op. cit., 189–200.

stantly supported by French troops, ready to assist with any clashes with the mandarins.

In the north, Joseph Seckinger was praised for his pioneering work. At Zhenjiang he built a residence, a pharmacy, an orphanage and three schools. Christian communities existing before the war almost entirely disappeared, while the new ones established largely comprised immigrants and converts. It was a town of educated and business people; so converts were rare. By 1878, there were only between 350–400 Catholics. At Yangzhou, Seckinger bought a house in 1866 that had been rented by de Carrière, around which he established a Christian community of 425 by 1875. Other houses were bought within the region, but each resulted in a struggle with the mandarins. Many Chinese did not want 'Seckinger's religion' in Anhui, and Seckinger's security was constantly threatened.

French legation

Much correspondence between missionaries and the French consul occurred over property disputes from 1876–7. Auguste Foucault wrote two letters indicating concern about the destruction of property, the persecution of Christians and the murder of secular priest Ouang, killed owing to anti-Christian feeling. He was accused of killing and burying two men. The missionary asked for French support with the Chinese authorities. The new Jesuit superior, Louis Chauvin, added his weight to this request, saying that a resolution of these problems was 'good for China', and mentioned, in particular, the persecution of Christians in the districts of Ningbo, Kowang-te-zhou and in the suburbs of the Province of Anhui. He did not spare the consul any details. At Ningbo, the Chinese spoke about 'the European religion' with anger, and criticised the Christians for refusing to worship idols and the ancestors. This divided the community. Chauvin believed that the success of the mission depended much on the French protection. Except for the areas mentioned, Chauvin reported that peace reigned in other parts of the mission. The protests to Nanjing must have worked, as Chauvin reported at the end of 1876 that there was peace in the region of Ningbo, and the enemies stopped attacking the Christians. He thanked the minister for his intervention in obtaining justice for the mission. But he was still not satisfied, and submitted an evaluation of material loses during the persecutions of 1876, demanding indemnities from the Chinese.[45]

The consul expressed frustration with Chauvin, and criticised the Jesuits for not showing 'their usual prudence and habitual calm in the Ouang affair'. The killers of Ouang had been found and executed.[46] He obviously did not share this feeling with Chauvin, who, the following year continued his request for compensation. While thanking the minister for his help, he mentioned another case of persecution of Christian fisherman on 25 August 1876 that he witnessed on the way to Xuzhou. He said that the men were accused of 'piercing men on paper', and were tortured. He wanted justice and an indemnity, pursued with 'strong representation from you', 'for the liberty of religion and for the good order given to Chinese Christians'. Chauvin did not let up with the consul, and wrote again the following month with complaints about clashes over land ownership in the villages.[47]

The representation worked, and Prince Kong agreed to pay an indemnity resulting from the destruction of Church property, and also agreed to rebuild other destroyed buildings.[48]

Languillat's legacy

Considerable progress in the development of the Christian communities of Jiangnan occurred during the reign of Languillat. From 1866–79, the number of European priests increased by 13, and the number of Chinese priests increased by 12, while the number of Christians increased by 20,463. The number of catechumens reached 8,000, while annual Confessions and Communions increased considerably. This growth was admirable, especially considering that outside the Shanghai area a priest only visited districts once a month. The local catechists held together the Christian communities that in turn were admired by other Chinese villagers.

---

45. Foucault to French Minister, Shanghai, 17 October 1876; Chauvin to Consul, Shanghai, 16 November, 1876; Chauvin to Minister (re Ning-Kofou), Shanghai, 25 November 1876; Chauvin to Minister, Shanghai, 23 December 1876, DAC.
46. Consul to Minister of Foreign Affairs, Shanghai, 5 February 1877; Consul to Minister, Shanghai, 24 February 1877. DAC.
47. Chauvin to Minister, Shanghai, 22 February 1877; 4 August 1877; 3 September 1877. DAC
48. Prince Kong to Minister of France, Beijing, 13 August 1877. DAC.

The work in the schools was also considered a great success. From 259 boys' schools in 1867, there were 363 in 1879, with the number of Christian students increasing from 2,620 to 4,015. Non-Christian students increased from 1,251 to 2,913. It was a similar story for the girls' schools. In 1867, there were 106 schools, teaching 1,401 Christians and 107 non-Christians, while in 1879 there were 297 schools with 3,438 Christians girls and 244 non-Christians. Overall, the number of teachers increased from 255 to 413 over the same period.

The importance of the work of the Holy Infancy grew after the war. For the year 1861–2, 15,557 non-Christian children were baptised, with 4,094 joining the orphanage or were adopted by Christian families. By 1879, they had registered 17,611 non-Christian Baptisms.

The number of Christian communities increased from 416 to 584, moving into new prefectures. The only prefectures without Christians were Xuzhou and Haizhou.

Languillat was praised for his strong leadership and his collaboration with colleagues, especially with the Jesuit superiors. Luigi Sica (1814–95) praised his 'right intention, piety, and brotherly love for the Society'.[49]

Bishop Valentin Garnier (1879–1898)

Languillat's successor as vicar apostolic in Jiangnan was Valentin Garnier, nominated bishop on 21 January 1879. He had arrived in China on 3 February 1869 as a priest, and was immediately assigned to Chinese language studies. In 1872, he worked in the mission station of Songjiang with Francisco Adinolfi, and in 1875 was religious superior of the Nanjing section, responsible for the mission districts of Nanjing, Ningbo, and Yangzhou. Immediately prior to his appointment as vicar apostolic, he was vice-rector of the major seminary and college in Xujiahui, as well as director of studies.

Soon after his consecration as bishop on 27 April 1880, he submitted a report on the Jiangnan mission for the years, 1878–9, which was the custom of the vicar apostolic every year.

In the eastern part of the mission, there were 660 adult Baptisms during the year, but only 1,218 serious catechumens. The most productive region was Tchangzhou, where mainly the virgins undertook

49. Servière, op. cit., 320–1.

the work. At the hospital in Tong-jia-dou more than 300 'vagabonds' were baptised each year, with more than 100 of these dying after being baptised.

Garnier gave thanks to God for the 'old Christians', but the heads of the districts expressed concern that work among them took up much time and energy, which they preferred to expend in converting the non-Christians. Preparation for Confessions also took too much of the missionaries' time. They preached 6,854 sermons and gave retreats to schoolteachers, administrators, virgins and Christians of both sexes.

The work in the schools was not neglected, with enrolments increased by 1,450 over the previous year. The European school for boys in Shanghai was popular, even among Protestants. Students appreciated the work of the fathers who carefully prepared them for First Communion. Theatrical performances were popular. The school for girls in Shanghai ran by the 'Mères Auxiliatrices' was a success with 138 students. There was another school at Caotiancuntang in the interior. Overall for the mission, the number of non-Christian students increased: at the school for girls, 35 out of 46 students were non-Christians. Garnier put great hope in two boarding schools, one at Tou-si for girls and at Jiangyin for boys. There was need to 'reconstruct' the college at Xujiahui to make it more 'solid and healthy'. More than 100 students studied the sciences and natural history, while meteorology and magnetics were encouraged.

In 1878, a Chinese newspaper was inaugurated: at first it was twice monthly, and then weekly. It had Chinese priests as director and publisher. Other Jesuits and academics assisted in the production, which was published at the orphanage at Tushanwan. Circulation, even outside the mission, was more than 900.

A Chinese priest set up a hospital for opium smokers in the sub-prefecture of Tsang-go for those wanting to rid themselves of the habit. They currently had 25 patients, and it was hoped that kindness offered to them might result in conversions.

The picture was not so bright in the Western part of the mission. It had only 5,337 Christians in 13 districts, taking in the whole Province of Anhui and part of Jiangsu. Few conversions occurred that year, with only 160 adults baptised, and only 500 catechumens. Garnier noted that the priests were strict about admitting anyone to Baptism, as these people would form the base of new Christian communities. The recent persecution had taken its toll in the area.

In the section of Ningbo repairs were made to the large church at Choei-tong, while apostates were returning slowly to the church.

In the section of Nanjing-Yangzhou, the missionaries worked well in strengthening the faith, but acted with prudence to ensure a solid faith was established. Catechists and virgins were brought into the area from the east, but not in the number that was desirable.[50]

Mission visitation

After a visitation of the mission, 1879–80, François Grandidier, former provincial of the Province of Champagne, submitted a report to the superior general indicating that he thought a malaise existed in the mission for a combination of many reasons. The first related to the attitude of the vicar apostolic, Garnier, who was experienced by some missionaries as 'too jealous of his authority, and rigid in the interpretation of regulations', even more than earlier vicars apostolic. Grandidier dismissed this attitude as untrue, and stated that Garnier only wanted to be visible to missionaries and Christians in the region. It was accepted that he governed strongly, but 'only according to the Institute of the Society of Jesus and the Jesuit superiors'. He showed 'the highest esteem and complete confidence' in the Jesuits. However, his weakness was that he did not have an 'expansive spirit', and held strongly to certain ideas. He was inclined to speak directly and acted against or without the advice of his council.

Some missionaries found the Jesuit superior Chauvin a challenge. They accepted that he had a 'strong intellectual and moral fibre' and was a just man, 'righteous and prudent, and an excellent religious' and 'an excellent superior'. But he was 'more austere than amiable, and not very communicative'. His tastes were exclusively serious, and he was 'very professional and exact in affairs'. He was not a joyful person in company, did not encourage others, and had a mournful appearance, with a tendency not to mix with people.

The mission appeared sterile. The progress of the gospel was not as fast as people wished, nor was the growth rate comparable to other

50. Garnier, A report on the Mission of Kiang-nan, 1878–79, Shanghai, 2 September 1879. ARSI.

missions in China. The missionaries tended to concentrate on working with the 'old Christians', but scarcely gained new ones. The discouragement did not appear to stem from this, but rather that the
missionaries took themselves too seriously. In fact, increases did
occur from time to time. In the east, the difficult area, new Christians
were found, and many non-Christian infants were 'baptised and sent
to Heaven' each year. In the vast regions of the west, where 20 years
ago there were not many active Christians, the apostolate flourished.
Each year new initiatives were undertaken, schools opened and
churches built. New Christian communities were established, despite
the persecutions of 1876, which did temporally halt progress. Aposta-
sies resulted, while others had responded negatively to the missionaries, but recently conversions had once again occurred.

One reason for the slow rate of Chinese conversions was believed
to be the character of the Chinese people, who were naturally scepti-
cal. Depression among the missionaries at the lack of conversions was
believed to be a 'lack of a supernatural spirit, relying too much on
natural rather than supernatural means'. This was a common Jesuit
response to challenges of this kind. Jesuit superiors believed that the
missionaries were not putting enough belief in the providence of God
to support them in difficult times.

Grandidier reflected that when the Jesuits arrived in China they
knew practically nothing about China, while he believed that the present situation did not reflect 'our Institute'. He was concerned about
the health of the missionaries in 'such a bad climate'. He observed
poor quality teaching and 'mediocre religious formation'. Moreover,
the Province of France sent men to the mission of 'inferior quality',
with exceptions, but generally they were mediocre Jesuits. To overcome this, he suggested that the province send scholastics to China
only after they had finished philosophy in Europe. They would then
be 'better formed', and better able to acclimatise to Chinese conditions. Chinese novices might be sent to Europe for formation: in this
way the 'traditions of the province and the spirit of the Society of
Jesus' could be maintained. There was no follow up on how to educate
new European missionaries about China and its culture before they
left Europe.

The visitor noted rivalry between the eastern and western regions
of the mission, which heightened discord. The regions differed not
only by language, mandarin in the west, and a patois in the east, but

also by culture in the way people responded to the missionaries. The east had most of the old Christians living in Christian communities, with missionaries visiting each community at least each year to regularise marriages and administer the sacraments. The west had few neophytes or Christian communities. The ministry there was to visit the few Christians and attempt to evangelise the non-Christians. The missionary in the east was well supported financially, not only locally, but also from the proximity of Shanghai, but it was different in the west, where there was little local financial support. Those missionaries in the east complained of being overworked, while still seeking new developments. Those in the west complained that their Jesuit colleagues did not give them sympathy in their mission, and that superiors did not give them sufficient help. Some spoke of abandonment, as some districts were without missionaries. Moreover, they felt isolated from other Jesuits.

The missionaries reflected about mission methods: distinguishing between the conservation and propagation of the faith, between good pastors and poor ones, between established parishes and mission stations. These discussions were considered dangerous. But such discussions were a most important opportunity to assess mission priorities and challenges.

There was talk about dividing Jiangnan into two vicariates. It was suggested that this be discussed at the next mission synod at Hankou.

Pleasure was expressed about the success of the European school situated in the area of the French concession, near the Church of St Joseph. It was for the children of foreign origin: Europeans, Americans, Japanese, Filipinos and Eurasians, without exception of religion. The education offered was culturally Christian. Some missionaries criticised this kind of school, but Grandidier believed that it helped those who lived in the colony and was good for the mission. Some people, he added, wanted a school for the Chinese children as well.

One missionary commented that contributing to the general malaise was overwork. For example, one man directed both the observatory and a Chinese periodical. It was recommended that no expansion of works in the mission occur.

On the positive side, Grandidier gave praise for the classical education given at the college at Xujiahui, which prepared students for public examinations, and recommended students for the seminary. He praised the work of caring for the abandoned infants, and for the orphanage for boys at Tushanwan, where the boys were given a technical education. The two hospices for Christians in Shanghai had 80 places for both sexes. The virgins were recognised as being great help in the schools, crèches and orphanages, especially caring for the sick and dying children. The work of the European sisters was invaluable to the mission, especially in the education of Chinese children. But they also ran a school for foreign children in Shanghai. The Sisters of St Vincent de Paul ran a general hospital for Europeans.

Overall, Grandidier believed that the mission was in good shape.[51] With a population of 50 million in Jiangnan in 1880, there were 97,000 Christians, with 86 priests, 14 of whom were diocesan, that being one mission priest for 581,000 non-Christians and 1,228 Christians.[52]

Chinese political developments

While the Jesuits were trying to resolve internal issues, and reflecting upon how to influence new Chinese converts, external factors also weighted upon them that constantly inhibited mission progress.

The Xianfeng emperor Yinzhu died on 22 August 1861 and his five-year-old son, who reigned under the title of Tongzhi, succeeded him. The young emperor died unexpectedly on 12 January 1875, and the Empresses Dowager Cixi appointed a four-year-old, Zaitian, his successor, who was enthroned on 25 February 1875. Cixi became the effective ruler of China until her death in 1908.

Surprisingly, the Tongzhi reign ushered in a new era for the Qing dynasty. The recent rebellions had been crushed, central control re-established, and the social values of Confucianism promoted.

In relation to the Western powers, war broke out again between China and the west, when, citing the murder of the French missionary Auguste Chapdelaine, France joined Great Britain in launching the Second Opium War in 1857. In the Treaty of Tianjin on 27 June 1858 that followed, the French gained the right to build churches, hospitals, orphanages, schools and cemeteries. While this treaty facilitated the expansion of mission work, it continued to cause resent-

---

51. Grandidier to General, Shanghai, 25 March 1880, ARSI.
52. Statistics on the number of priest-missionaries in Asia, Africa and Oceania, compared to the number of infidels and to the number of Christians, a report, 1880. ARSI.

ment among many Chinese, who viewed Christianity as imposed upon them by the unwelcome Westerners.

Further Western attacks on the Manchus occurred in September 1860, when 8,000 French troops won a battle at Palikao near Beijing. Then they sacked the Summer Palace, an act considered by most as one of sheer barbarism. The Beijing Convention that followed authorised the western powers to establish legations in Beijing and required China to create a Ministry of Foreign Affairs. Then the foreign troops assisted the Imperial Chinese troops crush a Taiping rebellion near Shanghai. Further inroads into Chinese sovereignty followed in 1861 with the French being granted territorial concessions in both Tianjin and Nanjing, and the Shanghai concession increased by 23 acres. The Catholic missions made the most of these new concessions by expanding mission activities within the concessions, and urging the French consuls to negotiate more effectively on their behalf with the Chinese government through the new Ministry of Foreign Affairs.

Following these defeats, Chinese defence against the Western powers became a high priority. This was to be accomplished by what became to be known as the 'Self-strengthening Movement', which acknowledged the need to use Western technology.

Zeng Guofan and Li Hongzhang undertook modernisation of the defence forces. From 1865, Chinese ships and guns were modernised with the help of Western technology. The China Merchants Steam Navigation Company was formed in 1872, and the Tianjin Naval Academy in 1880. These and other reforms were sometimes criticised by those who believed it would be better for China to study non-military Western technologies, such as railway construction and electricity.

Following the occupation of fifteen Treaty Ports after the Treaty of Tianjin, the Western powers developed strong bases for commercial activity. Chinese middlemen were active in trading negotiations with the Westerners. Warehouses, offices and foreign settlements grew where the Europeans lived. Missionaries followed in the wake of the economic barons, promoting medical and educational services to the local Chinese. The local Chinese communities were affected by these developments, and many Chinese became involved in these enterprises as labourers, domestic servants, interpreters or employees. While not engaged in this commercial activity, the missionaries certainly benefited from this growth of Western influence. Graduates from mission schools could gain employment with Western enterprises.

In order to cope with the creation of foreign enclaves, two important concepts emerged, that of concessions and extraterritoriality. The former were areas ceded to Europeans for their exclusive use following the treaties. They included Tianjin, Hankou, Guangzhou and especially Shanghai. Some concessions were rented from the Chinese; others were purchased, as in Shanghai. Foreigners maintained responsibility for local administration, including policing, and maintenance of roads and sanitation.

The system of extraterritoriality meant that the foreigners were governed by the laws of their own country rather than by Chinese law. In the French concession in Shanghai, the *Code Napoleon* was enacted. Overseeing the whole system, Western diplomats were accredited to the Qing court in Beijing, each having consular officials in each Treaty port. The missionaries continually and effectually furthered their cause with the Chinese government through these consuls and the French legation in Beijing.

The European concessions in Shanghai were completely separated from the Chinese settlements. Racial prejudice and antagonism, with many clashes of culture, resulted. The Chinese were generally resentful of this invasion of their land, but were helpless to resist, while many made the most of the situation.

The spread of European influence at this time furthered the cause of the Christian missions, both Catholic and Protestant. Education and social services were developed along European lines that rendered valued service to many Chinese, while some saw the importance of studying the Chinese language and culture, following the model of earlier Jesuit missionaries of the seventeenth and eighteenth centuries.[53]

Sino-French War

Military conflict between China and the Western powers escalated from the 1880s. This directly contributed to the weakening of the Qing dynasty. The first significant one was the Sino-French War, which was the result of a long-standing dispute between China and

---

53. Dillon, op. cit., 104–10.

France over Annam, the northern part of modern-day Vietnam, involving France's right to trade with Annam.

Political interest in eastern Asia was given new impetus under Louis Napoleon, who saw an opportunity for France in the Far East as a means of reviving national and dynastic prestige, especially after his disastrous Mexican adventure. Persecution of missionaries in 1858 in Annam gave Louis the occasion to send troops to take Saigon, and in 1862, he imposed a treaty on Annam, giving France Cochin China, as well as a protectorate over Cambodia.

While trade in Annam was an important aspect in discussions with China, France hoped that the Mekong River had the potential for trade in Yunnan in southern China, and so, if tapped, it promised to strengthen the French national image, and at the same time serve as a challenge to England. When this plan failed, the French turned towards Tongkin and the Red River as a better link to Yunnan. England was concerned with this move, as it wanted the West China trade to proceed west to Calcutta or Rangoon rather than to Hanoi,[54] and so any development of French activity in Tongkin and Yunnan must be considered part of Anglo-French rivalry in the east.[55]

Meanwhile, the French forces took Hanoi and the delta region in 1873 after failure to secure mining rights in Yunnan. This action embarrassed France because at this time she was not interested in colonisation, but only trade and riches; not obligations, but national prestige. Further conquest was stopped, and the French-Annam Treaty was signed in Saigon on 15 March 1874, which allowed France to trade, promote Christianity and exercise overall sovereignty over Cochin China, the part of southern Vietnam.

However, further aggression by France in Annam resulted in its annexation by France in 1884, declaring it a French protectorate. This angered the Chinese, considering this territory a tributary state of the Chinese empire. However, a treaty was signed on 11 May 1884 between France and China, in which China agreed to open Yunnan and Guangxi to trade with France, while withdrawing its troops from Tongkin. Neither side complied fully with the agreement; fighting broke out and spread along the coast into China. French forces

---

54. S.H. Roberts, *History of French Colonial Policy*, 2 vols. (London: King and Son, 1929) II, 424.

55. Henry McAleavy, *Black Flags over Vietnam* (London: George Allen and Unwin, 1968), 283.

attacked and destroyed the naval dockyard at Fuzhou and blockaded the Yangzi ports. China capitulated and a treaty was signed in Tianjin on 9 June 1885.[56]

The result of this war was that China returned to its 'ancient ways', but new political, military and social ideas grew out of this conflict with France. In the short term, China gained more from the war than France. The latter received a blow to her national pride and international image. Dreams of a great empire in the east were not realised and, in fact, trade with China itself suffered. France, no longer enthusiastic as an expansionist power, gained the protectorate over Annam and Tongkin, but China, although suzerainty rights were lost, still continued a presence and was an influence in the region. Overall, weaknesses in both China and France were highlighted.

Internationally, the war resulted in a signal to other powers to stake claims against China in Burma, Manchuria and Korea. In all these negotiations, the French failed to rival British interests in the East.

In China itself, future French influence became mainly political, relying on a military presence that continually supported the spread of Catholic missions and defended them against local oppression and destruction. The French legation found the missionaries useful in communicating French culture to the Chinese. This, they believed, enhanced their prestige. Many Chinese thought differently.

Roman intervention

During the Sino-French War, Pope Leo XIII asked the Guangxu Emperor for protection for missionaries and for the Chinese converts. When the emperor gave a favourable response, Li Hongzhang suggested that a nunciature might be established in Beijing. The pope agreed and appointed Antonio Agliardi (1831–1915). France strongly objected to this proposal as it cut across their designs to continue exercising French influence in China through the protectorate. The pope postponed the appointment. But discussion continued about whether it was time to establish a Chinese hierarchy, with two archdioceses: Beijing and Nanjing. Li Hongzhang agreed to this, as he saw the move as religious, non-political and good for maintaining

---

56. Dillon, op. cit., pp. 110–1.

unity. He agreed that the pope could establish a Chinese hierarchy at any time, and then appoint an apostolic delegate. Bishop Favier, the vicar apostolic of Beijing, did not favour the protectorate, the French legation accusing him of being anti-French, and they continued to be protective of their own position. Negotiations continued between the Church and the French government, and between Li and the Zongli Yamen. Finally, the French government vetoed the plans on 6 September 1892 and the pope backed off, indicating how important he considered the protectorate for the missions.[57] This was obviously a political settlement, but the Roman ecclesiastical authorities were not happy with the French protectorate. They wanted the missionaries responsible only to the Holy See, thus indicating that their mission was essentially spiritual.

French protection

The protection of missionaries had considerable advantages for France, with the French using the missionaries to promote their language and culture. Yet the treaty negotiations regarding the movements of the missionaries caused considerable unease with the Chinese, because they were conceding Chinese rights to the foreigners. Of particular disgust was the clause giving the right of missionaries to buy property in all towns of the Empire and to construct buildings. This clause did not appear in the French text, only in the Chinese one, and was the cause of continual friction in the years ahead. Negotiations between Berthemy, the French minister in Beijing and the Zongli Yamen on details of how property might be acquired in the interior of China resulted. In 1865, it was agreed that provincial authorities were not to place any obstacle to missionaries acquiring property provided they agreed that the property was for the Christian community, and in whose name the property was registered.

The Chinese also ceded to the French legation the right to issue special French passports to the missionaries. This right was later given also to Spanish and Portuguese missionaries, but the German legation, while happy for the French to assist their missionaries, did not cede the right for the French to issue passports for German mis-

---

57. Patrick Taveirne, *Missionary enterprise and the endeavours to establish an ecclesiastical hierarchy in and diplomatic relations with China, 1307–1946*, op. cit. 62.

sionaries. Eventually, all missionaries came to accept French protection, because no other European power offered such help to the Chinese Christians as did the French.

Apart from the right for the missionaries to reside in all localities, to rent or buy property, and to construct churches and houses, Alphonse de Bourboulon, the French minister to China, also obtained the rights for Chinese Christians to be exempt from taxes relating to the national cults and to abolish measures previously enacted against Christians.

The Holy See accepted this role undertaken by the French government to protect the missionaries; it was very convenient, as the Vatican at the time had no other European power to exercise similar rights. The pope had no means to negotiate with the Chinese and the time was not right for the appointment of a Vatican nuncio. Furthermore, if the Holy See had wanted to end the French protectorate, it would have had opposition from the French missionaries who were 'very attached to their Fatherland'. These missionaries formed three-quarters of all Catholic priests in China, and considered themselves as agents of France.

It should be questioned if the protectorate was useful for France. There were continual disagreements between the missionaries and the Chinese officials that the French legation was asked to arbitrate. The French did not object to this role as the missionaries kept the French legation informed about local issues. The legation became the centre of information for all Chinese provinces, giving the French a special role in China. This role gave them prominence in the country. British prestige was gained through commerce, while territory disputes gave attention to the Russians. The French undertook the protectorate without any mandate from the Holy See, while recognising that such a role might eventually cause problems for them with both the Holy See and the Chinese government.[58] They were not wrong.

In a pamphlet written by a Protestant minister in Shanghai, mention was made of the rising wave of anti-Christian and anti-foreign sentiment from the autumn of 1884, with special mention of the anti-French sentiment because of the legation's aggression on behalf of French missionaries. Factors seen as contributing to this situation were race-hatred in Guangzhou against the Europeans over the

---

58. G. Gogordan, *Direction politique*, no 29, Eureg no. 676, Peking, 12 April 1886. DAC.

opium trade, and the pretensions of the Catholics, who had done much to prejudice the Chinese against Christianity. To support this latter proposition, mention was made of the priests assuming privileges of official rank to gain influence over the people. This angered the mandarins and gentry who were jealous of this privilege. Priests also claimed privilege of sanctuary for the Chinese in their churches, and claimed protection over Chinese converts, preventing the civil power to act against them. Sometimes even the guilty were protected. Finally, Catholic priests would make strong demands to visit the mandarins when difficulties arose, which displeased officials. Hostilities with France did not help dampen local hostilities, and most outbreaks of fanaticism were condoned by Chinese high officials, who did nothing to stop the violence, and even encouraged it. The final suggestion was that the status of Chinese Christians should be clearly defined, and that they be well treated.[59]

True to form, missionaries in Jiangnan were not supine in seeking help in negotiations with the Chinese authorities over the damage done to property after pillage at Xuzhou on 10 October 1884. No mention of indemnities was made, but in the negotiations, the Chinese agreed to pay the costs for rebuilding. Thanks were duly given to the minister for his intervention.[60]

Later, German (1891) and Italian (1888) governments placed their missionaries under their own care. Despite protests from the Holy See and the French government, Italy assumed full responsibility to represent all Italian missionaries in China in 1902. More and more, missionaries in China were increasingly looked upon as agents of imperialistic powers. An imperial decree issued 15 March 1899 stated that since Catholic clergy were given official rank and allowed to participate in Chinese civil affairs, there was no need for foreign diplomatic intervention on their behalf. Henceforth missionaries could have recourse themselves at the local level without recourse in Beijing.[61] In attempting to do this, the missionaries frequently failed, and ultimately had to rely on the political and military force of the French government.

59. Rev. R.H. Graves, DD, Memorandum on the persecution of Christians in China, pamphlet, Shanghai, 1885. DAC.
60. Garnier to Minister, Shanghai, 28 August 1886. DAC; Garnier to Minister, Shanghai, 30 June 1887. DAC.
61. Taveirne, op. cit., 63.

Anti-foreign and anti-missionary movements

Large-scale anti-foreign movements grew during the later part of the nineteenth century. Cultural superiority of the Chinese dominated any Western incursions into the Kingdom. The main challenge to the Chinese was restricted to Guangzhou and Shanghai, and later to other treaty ports: the rest of China was unaffected. Before 1860, the number of missionaries was too small to have created major conflicts with the Chinese people. At that time, missionary activity was restricted to the treaty ports. But after the Anglo-French expedition of the 1860s, when China was opened up to missionary activity, guaranteeing Chinese the right to practise Christianity, as well as the right for the missionaries to move around freely and purchase land, this led to a growth in missionary activity and converts among the Chinese. From 1860–70, it was estimated that the number of Chinese Catholics increased to 400,000. But this incursion into Chinese culture fuelled sentiments of resentment against the European powers.[62]

While Chinese culture and tradition was deeply rooted in Confucianism, and Buddhism was also widely accepted by the Chinese, Christianity was seen as inseparable from the colonial invasion of China. Missionaries were protected by the Europeans, and grew under the system of the unequal treaties. The Chinese resented the idea of the Europeans that Western culture was superior to their own. While there were differences between the religion of Christianity and Confucianism as a school of thought and way of life, hostility between the two groups derived mainly from cultural, social and political conflicts, rather than religious questions.

Confucianism considered foreign customs and cultures as heresy, and Christianity was seen as a threat to their influence among the Chinese people through Christian preaching, and educational and medical establishments. Confucian intellectuals became unfriendly.

---

62. Kuang-sheng Liao, *Antiforeignism and modernization in China, 1860–1980* (Hong Kong: The Chinese University Press, 1984), 39. In Henrietta Harrison's, *The Missionary's Curse and Other Tales from a Chinese Catholic Village*. Series: Asia, Local Studies/Global Themes (USA: University of California Press, 2013), she describes the reaction of a Chinese village whose combination of folk beliefs and Catholic rituals, came in conflict with the orthodoxy of Italian Franciscan missionaries. This story indicated that the conflict between the Chinese and foreign missionaries was not restricted to the Jesuit missions.

The Christian prohibition of ancestor worship upset Confucians, while the Christian belief in the equality of all before God, clashed with the Confucian belief in social hierarchy, each person with their own place in society, from the emperor down. This order was the basis of social relationships, and must be preserved as essential to Chinese society.[63]

The gentry were also antagonistic toward Christianity. They were the social group that had political and administrative roles in Chinese society. They closely identified with Confucian traditions and values, having been educated in Confucianism. They represented the cultural leadership at the local level and engaged in public works and cultural activities. They were persons of influence.

Part of the role of the gentry was education and cultural affairs. With the arrival of the missionaries, their preaching, teaching and counselling threatened the position of the gentry. Preaching Christianity was an insult to them, as it was to Confucianism.

Their hostility toward the Europeans grew as well, following the many humiliating military defeats. The activity of the missionaries was equated to the European invasion of China. The gentry were disturbed by the success of the missionaries among the Chinese people, many of whom were grateful for the Western help they received.

Anti-Christian literature circulated in many provinces in the 1860s, which resulted inevitably in anti-missionary incidents, including pillage, destruction and deaths. This provoked the missionaries to seek protection from the Chinese government, backed up by the French protectorate. Local magistrates were pressured into dealing with these cases and punishing rioters. This further antagonised the gentry.

In summary, the main aspect of anti-foreignism, 1860–1884, was that most incidents were independent of each other, caused by local responses to missionary activity. In the early 1880s, anti-missionary incidents generally became less frequent and less serious, but anti-missionary activity grew again in 1884 after the Sino-French War.[64]

During the 1890s, anti-foreign hostility gradually developed into a widespread movement, which could easily be ignited by a single incident. The attitude of the imperial government was sympathy with

63. Kuang-sheng Liao, ut supra, 40 1.
64. Ibid., 42–4.

the movement. The unequal treaties were seen as an insult to the imperial government, while the activities of missionaries frequently challenged the local authorities that then lost face in the eyes of the people when they were overridden.

The anti-foreign movement, closely connected with the anti-Christian movement continued, with the imperial government trying to appease anti-foreign sentiments. But eventually the Dowager Empress decided to support the Boxer movement in 1900 to expel the foreigners.

The effect of the anti-Christian movement on Chinese politics was that anti-Christian sentiment provided a common ground for the gentry and others to combine in opposing the missionaries. Furthermore, the development of anti-foreignism led to the gentry's acceptance of violence in their struggle, their opposition to Christianity being based on the need to preserve Chinese tradition and culture from foreign influence. In this opposition, the conscientiousness of the nation gradually emerged; the genesis of Chinese nationalism was conceived in this movement.[65]

A further study by R.G. Tiedemann, viewing the north China plain on the eve of the Boxer rebellion, sought to find the underlying causes for a growth of conversions in this area during a time of much violence. He looked at the distinction between anti-missionary conflict, anti-foreignism, and anti-Christian violence. The first type of conflict was opposition to the presence of missionaries that arose in the context of local politics, and frequently centred around the acquisition of property in order to build churches and residences. The second type represented opposition to foreigners, their ideas and economic and military penetration. Chinese xenophobia was an important factor in the Boxer Rebellion. The third type was expressed in conflict between Christians and non-Christians, especially with the Chinese gentry, who objected to Christianity on ideological grounds. And so, 'anti-Christian strife derived predominantly from endogenous circumstances'.

The north China plain included the Jesuit vicariate that embraced the northern Jiangnan mission in the Provinces of northwestern Jiangsu and northern Anhui, and the border area of Shandong-Zhili. In the 1890s, the Jesuits wrote about the presence in the mission

---

65. Ibid., 45–7.

of the Righteous Harmony Boxers and the Big Sword Society, both forerunners of the anti-foreign and anti-Christian Boxer movement of 1899–1900. In the Shandong-Zhili border, Christianity had been established since the beginning of the eighteenth century, which was a solid base for the spread of Christianity. But in the Shandong-Jiangsu-Henan border there was little missionary work before the 1880s. Yet, in the 1890s, the area produced considerable growth in the number of Christians, especially in South Shandong worked by the German Society of the Divine Word, and in Xuzhou worked by the Jesuits.

Tiedemann suggested that the growth in Christianity was due neither to spiritual nor material benefits to the Chinese, but to 'the political incentives which Christianity offered' in a violent social environment caused by the scarcity of resources. The success of the missionaries in cases of litigation with the civil authorities was usually successful, showing the Chinese their privileged status, and the effectiveness of their power and influence.

But this power rested upon coercive foreign power, exercised especially through the French protectorate. This process of foreign intrusion accelerated after the Sino-Japanese War, 1894–5. The missionary enterprise in China was long associated with imperial expansion. However, while the Jesuits constantly wrote about their pride in being French, and the importance of spreading French culture in China, it was not true that the Jesuit mission had a 'purposeful collusion' with the French imperialists, but it certainly benefited from its protection. The Jesuit missionary aim was strictly spiritual: the conversion of the Chinese through the acceptance of Christianity.

However, this distinction of aims between the imperial government and the missionaries was not always obvious or clear to the Chinese gentry, especially when observing the aggressive actions of missionaries to receive justice for their Chinese converts or compensation from the authorities for damage to Church property caused by the bandits. In the eyes of the Chinese, the cause of the foreigners was also not helped either by this aggression.

But among the poor, weaker groups in rural communities, hassled by violence and natural disasters, the missionaries provided protection and survival. The converts were not all misfits and criminals; in fact, most converts came from those trying to seek justice from criminal elements in society or in the government. The latter, usually imbued with the Confucian ethos, which was already declining in influence in China, objected to the people associating with the foreign religion, which often challenged some traditional Chinese social customs such as bribery. The missionary provided a safe haven for all in an ever-increasing chaotic China.[66]

Life on the Jiangnan mission, 1885–1889

The Jesuit missionaries found life rewarding in 1885, and continued to reflect upon their ministry. They acknowledged that the study of Chinese antiquities would help them find God's action in Imperial China. But the only way they knew how to achieve this was to replicate Church organisation like that in Europe. In China, there were 800 priests in 37 missions with 500,000 Christians. In each vicariate, the bishop had a seminary, and each Christian community had a school with both male and female teachers, and numerous chapels as well as hospitals and orphanages. There were also 'devote congregations'. In the previous 14 years in Jiangnan, there had been an increase of 30,000 Christians, with 300 new churches or chapels. The optimism expressed was that the future of China did not rest on fighting, but 'in the Church alone, with its teaching of the Decalogue, the catechism, the Gospel and the holy Roman Catholic Church'. The Chinese people were 'simple in obedience, docile in their conduct, generous to hear the message, and towards the missionaries, polite and adaptable'.[67] In commenting on the assistance given to the missionaries by the virgins, they were consoled by the majority of them who were 'zealous, dedicated and with devotion'. Some were given to 'great mortification, some fast three times a week, some walk for an hour fasting to attend Mass', but while not all were equally good, the number of scandals were very few. Those in Pudong gave great service.[68]

---

66. R.G.Tiedemann, 'Christianity in a violent environment. The North China Plain on the Eve of the Boxer Uprising', edited by Jerome Heyndricks, *Historiography of the Chinese Catholic Church, 19th and 20th Century* (Leuven, 1984), 138–44.

67. Letter to Provincial, Nanking, 23 March 1887, in *Lettres de Jersey*, VI/III (December 1887): 372–3. The *Lettres de Jersey* was a periodical published by the Jesuits from the Channel Island of Jersey from 1882–1930, with articles of interest about Jesuit works. It was a popular means of communication between the Jesuits in China and those in Europe.

68. Dominic Gandar, an article *Le Christianisme au Pou-tong'*, ibid., 390ff.

Social issues always concerned the Jesuit missionaries, and one more obvious problem was extent of the opium trade. The missionaries encountered many Chinese whose lives were destroyed by addiction. In 1887, there was a report on opium, which was so much part of the Chinese way of life. Opium came to China from two sources, India and the local opium. In India there was 'a culture of the poppy'; it sold for 3,250 francs a case. The annual exportation was 45,000 cases, worth 165,750,000 francs. Within China, it was grown mostly in the north. The Chinese government tried in vain to restrain this culture of the poppy. In 1885, thirteen million pounds of crude opium arrived in China, which gave 7,060,000 pounds of opium to smoke. A smoker consumed three pounds a year. The Indian opium only supplied 2,687,000 smokers, scarcely one per 100 of the Chinese population. However, the use of opium was universal in the empire, and Chinese customs officials were in connivance with smugglers in the trade.[69] Reforming the individual addict was rare. Moreover, the Church refused to baptise any known addict, indicating its objection to the use of the drug.

Support from local Chinese officials for social reform was a continual battle. Encounters with Chinese locals in rural villages were not always friendly. Auguste Ledru, who had arrived in China only two years previously, gave a lengthy account of one such encounter in December 1889, in the village of Hong-tchang-tan, during which his catechist, Cheng-ko, was murdered. Consultation with the local military mandarin was friendly. He investigated the case and sought reparations from the locals, but denied culpability. As a result, the missionaries continued to be menaced by the people, who accused the mandarin of being a friend of the Europeans.[70]

Despite these interruptions, ordinary missionary life continued. With particular reference to the Anhui region in 1889, it was reported that the priests from Shanghai continually visited the Christian communities in the outlying areas to preach, say Mass and administer the sacraments, covering an area that had 20 churches, and two to three thousand Christians. Clovis Bienvenu and Henri Doré were well established in the north, with the catechists holding the line, while John Bedon travelled the highways and byways of T'ai-p'ing

---

69. Note on Opium, *Lettres de Jersey*, VI/1 (April 1887): 164–6.
70. Ledru to Goulven, Tong-men, 1889, in *Lettres de Jersey*, 9 (1890): 37–42.

and Huzhou living in a new residence. He brought together about 60 people for instruction in preparation for Baptism. At Shuidong, together with Joseph de Barrau, he had a model parish with 1,200 Christians, administering the sacraments and dealing with the many needs of his parishioners. Severe Bizeul visited his five to six hundred Christians each Sunday. There were the usual problems of little money to spend and clashes between the Chinese Christians and the non-Christians. Bizeul travelled with two mules, a catechist and a porter. Travels could take up to five hours at a time, during which he could certainly say the rosary, and even the breviary if the conditions were right.[71] The missionaries continually communicated mission successes, local challenges, and some failures. All with the aim of receiving more support from Europe.

When writing from the village of Niang-jia-jiao, within the mission district of Wuhu, in the region of Anhui, Paul Delorme reflected on the non-Christians in the region and the obstacles to their conversion. He noted that non-Christians were friendly towards the priest, and that Chinese authorities were exteriorly friendly. A non-Christian doctor, an educated bachelor, was impressed with the concern of the priest for the sick, and grateful for the gifts given to him for his troubles. He knew 20 other 'notables' in the area who were friendly.

So why were there not more conversions? The soil was not fertile. He had baptised only 120 to 130 Christians, and as for other Christians, they were only Christians in name. Non-Christians respected the priest and thought of him as rich and powerful. They talked about converting, but were not very serious about it. The main obstacles to conversion were seen to be opium, a habit that was practically universal, and 'bad morals', which were deplorable. No details were given. If a third priest was made available, and spent time in the village, there might be more catechumens, as there once had been.

The people were seen as very ignorant, even the Christians. An example was given of one notable non-Christian trader, when visiting Hankou, mistook the foreign consuls for priests, believing them to be very powerful with the traders. The faith of many families was weak, the children in the missionary schools were good while at school, but when they returned to their village and their homes, the faith meant very little. These were generally the 'new Christians'.

---

71. Bizeul to Delaunay, ibid., 44–8.

The majority of those receiving Baptism were the elderly or those children in danger of death. There were few others. This story might appear to be depressing, but at the same time Delorme expressed joy at being in China, and would not want to leave. Whatever the challenges, he found joy in listening to the Christians singing their prayers in full voice in a district where not long before 'the Devil ruled'. And whatever the faults of the Christians, they slowly grew daily in faith. Delorme believed that faith was all God's work, and that he was happy to serve.[72] This attitude was the common attitude of the missionaries, especially when the difficulties seemed insurmountable.

Protestant missions

Jesuits regularly commented on the progress of the Protestant missions or recorded their activities in order to compare and contrast their work with that of the Catholic missions. They were usually not very complimentary comments, as the Protestants were seen at best as competitors, or at worst as heretics.

It was reported that the Protestant missionaries held a meeting in Shanghai, the first in 17 years, when only 10 missionaries were present. At this conference, there were more than 400, representing 45 Societies that worked in China.

The Englishman, James Hudson Taylor (1832–1905), founder of the 'China Inland Mission', was the guest speaker, and he suggested a plan that would 'convert China in five years'. Despite an exterior sign of unity, there was disunion and antagonism about practical means to achieve this aim. There was discussion and disagreements about which translation of the Bible should be used. Should there be an authorised version? Should the Bible be in Chinese? Should a commentary be given? A compromise suggestion was that each Society could do as they wished, provided everyone abstained from all doctrine. They agreed that the existing translations of the Bibles used were largely unintelligible to the Chinese, and so, Christ could not be understood. The Bible should speak for itself. This was basic to

---

72. Extract from Delorme to Rochemontaix, Niang-hia-Kiao, 19 March 1890, in *Lettres de Jersey*, ibid, 52–5. Camille de Rochemontaix, in 1890 was superior of the Jesuit house in Rouen, and wrote several books of history.

Protestant belief. About 600,000 Bibles were distributed annually and they asked the government for tax exemption for the importation.

The Catholic comment on this meeting was that Protestants only preached under the shadow of Catholicism, but that they did good work with their medical teams. They asked the government to abstain from importing opium, and they valued an increase of female missionaries to work in the schools for girls, especially to combat the barbaric custom of the deformation of feet.

One Protestant Chinese missionary from Shanghai said that he had not found one true Christian. He was advised to wear Chinese dress and not to marry.[73] Other issues raised were whether it was better to wear Chinese or European dress, and how to act towards Roman Catholic missionaries, European or Chinese, in the interior of China. The response to this latter question was that as Romans Catholics were in error, Protestants should work to replace them in the eyes of the Chinese. To the question as to what should be preached to the non-Christians, the reply was that the unity of God is all that they are able to understand; the doctrine of 'expiation' was 'too evangelical' for them. The age for Baptism was discussed, and it was agreed that it should be administered around the age of reason, for children between four to six years old. They wondered whether the Chinese classics mentioned 'the true God'. It was said that Dr. Eskin believed that the Supreme Being mentioned in the Classics was the true God. He also believed that all Asia had been monotheistic before becoming polytheistic.[74]

There is no evidence that the Catholic missionaries valued any aspect of the theological missionary approach of the Protestants to conversions. Both considered the other in error. The Protestants concentrated on preaching the gospel, while the Catholics basically taught the doctrine of the Catholic Church, which was considered the way to salvation. On medical facilities and education, the two Christian churches were not very different, except that the Protestants had more money to spend on these means of evangelisation, which was the envy of the Catholics.

---

73. Extract from a letter of Bizuel, 30 August 1890, Shanghai, in *Lettres . . .* op. cit., 186–8.
74. Ibid., *Lettres . . .* 1891, 10, 40–1.

Missionary reflections on the 1890s

When reflecting about the Chinese motives for converting to Christianity, it was generally believed that the motive was not supernatural, but rather a means to improve themselves, or at least to seek their own advantage. The Chinese Christians were 'not so poor, and not so rich', but they were very honest and respected. The Catholic religion had a reputation for strict justice, which many Chinese wanted as well as protection. Missionaries were seen to have power and influence to right wrongs. Honesty was rewarded. Bienvenu referred to his parishioners as 'strong, proud and gallant boys'.[75] Some missionaries communicated very positive attitudes towards the Chinese converts, but others were not slow to mention also their faults.

Baudoux believed that the Western powers wanted to end the imperial dynasty, and gave rifles to the rioters. The Chinese converts were seen as 'the crème in a mass of iniquity' of 'good character, sober, temperate, affable, polite, flexible, without exaggerated vices, and patient, but also attached to the earth, without faith, only reflecting upon their material interests'. He found it hard to understand their conscience. While very few references were made about the Chinese rites, it appeared that they were part of the mind-set of some missionaries, for Baudoux made reference to one educated Chinese gentleman who told him that the Chinese only made memory of Confucius in their rituals, and nothing more.[76] Of course, the missionaries had taken an oath to accept the banning of Chinese rites by the Catholic Church.

Instructing catechumens took the missionaries much time. They were serious about discerning whether the catechumen was genuinely committed to becoming a Christian. Probation might take a year or two before Baptism, as the Chinese found it hard to renounce their superstitions. Chinese rituals relating to births, marriages, anniversaries, and death of parents, were seen to be 'all impregnated with paganism'. Baptism could mean exclusion from the family, which would bring shame on the individual who was socially exposed if he

---

75. Extract from a letter of Beinvenu to Pierre, Mao-kia-wo-tse, 9 March 1889, in *Lettres de Jersey*, (1890–91): 9–10.
76. Letter from Baudoux, Tchong kia-tchoang, 3 October 1891, in *Lettres de Jersey*, 11 (1892): 61–3.

did not make the required ancestor worship. Converts were considered very brave.[77]

On the survival front, the mission reported difficulties with pillage, burning and massacres, followed by much harassment. In Mongolia, authorities passively watched the massacre of Christians and supported the attacks. While seeming to act, the government sent troops, but the Christians had already been killed. They punished some 'poor miserable wretches', who were believed to be far from culpable, while the real villains who were more significant went free. More locally, there were reports of burning, and again, while a few were caught, most went free. To support the idea of lack of support from the Chinese authorities, it was noted that they had refused to register new land purchases by the missionaries, which indicated to the people that they were against the missionaries.[78]

In his five-year report of Rome, for the years 1888–93, Bishop Garnier highlighted the persecution against the Church and the Chinese Christians, because of 'the calumnies spread by the educated Chinese and other perverse men', assisted by the ill-will of the mandarins who barely tolerated the missionaries, and who obstructed the assistance the mission required according to the treaty obligations. This persecution had been going on for two years, with the aim to extinguish the Catholic religion, and have the European missionaries expelled from China. They burnt and destroyed most missionary residences, Christian churches, colleges, schools and orphanages. It all began in May 1891, with the burning of the main house and church outside the city of Wuhu, which had been built some years before by the Jesuits as the central residence for 33 missionaries who worked in the Anhui district. The rampage spread then to other places in the vicariate, with fires and the destruction of property. Depopulation resulted. More than 22 churches with schools attached, residences, orphanages and other church buildings were destroyed.

However, the destruction could have been worse, except for the intervention of the French delegation and warships. The mandarins were compelled to calm the people, while compensation for damages was demanded of the Chinese.

---

77. Letter of Goulven, *Lettres de Jersey,* ibid., 234–6.
78. Letter of Biesse, Long-sai-kong, 19 March 1992, *Lettres . . .* ibid., 236–8.

On the positive side, it was reported that, at the end of 1888, there were 132 priests in the vicariate. But, in the following five years, 16 European priests and three Chinese priests had died. The Jesuit scholastics, European and Chinese, numbered 32, and there were 30 seminarians, 670 Christian stations and 697 churches. In July 1893, the number of Christians was 105,357, and each year there were 1,700 adult Baptisms. Finally, the establishment of a school for foreigners in the American concession was considered a blessing, as was the advent into the vicariate of other religious orders, especially women.[79]

Further destruction of mission property took place with the arrival of 21 bandits and robbers at Tai-tao-leou, where they entered the Christian compound, seized the best catechist, beat him and left him for dead. Much pillage also took place. The robbers expressed opposition to the missionaries and their work, especially for building a residence. They referred to the missionaries as 'devils from Europe'.[80]

Soon after, and despite recent attacks and destruction, Leopold Gain reported to the bishop that he was happy with attendance at Mass, 'almost as many women as men'. In the morning, the whole village, non-Christians as well, wished the priests well and made the prostration before the Lord of Heaven, and then another to each of the priests. The catechumens came and offered vows and a small present to one of the priests. During the day all the non-Christians of the village came and wished him a happy new year, and made the prostration.[81]

There was more action in Tai-tao-leou in 1896, when bandits attacked the Catholic compound and wanted money. When this was refused, they pillaged the residence. Joseph Thomas, a seasoned missionary, was arrested by a group of 50 to 60 brigands on the bank of a small canal, but was saved by a group of soldiers from the imperial army. The brigands then took all the other families of the village, with their cattle, horses, and asses – all that was transportable. Six brigands were killed and thirty wounded. The irony of situations like this was that those bandits killed were among those the missionaries came to save.[82]

79. Garnier, Quinquennial report to Rome on the Vicariate of Kiang-nan, from end of 1888 to end of 1893, Shanghai, 2 March 1894. ARSI.
80. Gain to Superior, Heou-kia-tchoang, 29 August 1893, in *Lettres de Jersey*, XIII/1 (May 1894), 3.
81. Gain to Garnier, Heou-kia-tchoang, 8 February 1894, op. cit., 5.
82. Thomas to RP Le Cain, on ship In the Imperial Canal, 6 February 1896, in *Lettres de Jersey*, XV/1, (January 1896).

After this incident, there were disasters at Xuzhou. The Jesuit residence was pillaged, and as the brigands found nothing, they burnt everything. They then burnt the houses of other Christians in the community. These rebels from Shandong had occupied the districts of Heu-zhuang, Tai-fao-leou and Majing. Twenty Christian communities were destroyed and 1,000 Christians were left as refugees. Indemnities once again were sought from the mandarins for this destruction.[83]

In 1897, Pierre Pérrigaud at Fong-t'ai hien expressed happiness at the way the Chinese converts came together in groups forming 30 families, with each having a 'prayer school', while Eugène Goulvin at Tai Hu reported that he was happy teaching between 50 and 60 catechumens each day. With an increase of conversions at Jianping, Eugene Gasnier found that his church was too small for services. Other missionary letters expressed joy in their work and they were pleased with the progress of spreading the faith. They saw a 'rich harvest' in China, and were encouraged by the increase in conversions and the number of catechumens. One missionary was pleased to note that the non-Christians respected the catechists in his village. Maybe this was because the catechists were seen to be living a better life from working for the missionaries and for being under foreign protection.

But there was disappointment as well, as when Christian families 'made sacrifices to their ancestors'. One Jesuit went so far as to attempt to denounce one family to the sub-prefect for doing such a 'diabolical act'. It was reported that the family repented! Some missionaries even believed that the devil was seen at work when difficulties were encountered. Human respect, fear and timidity were believed to prevent conversions.

Jesuits were seen as hard working, but there were an insufficient number of them for the many needs and opportunities available. Some reflected that the Chinese were 'lazy, with a hostile spirit'. The Christians were believed to be really 'weak Christians, ignorant of Christianity'. They didn't work with 'desire or zeal', and so their influence in the villages did not result in the number of conversions desired. Some Jesuits were very harsh and intolerant of the Chinese

---

83. Letter of Ferrand, Shanghai, 8 July 1896, in *Lettres . . .* op. cit., 378–9; letter of Gain, Xuzhou, 29 June 1896, 379–81.

and their customs, and lacked patience in gradually influencing them to an alternative life.

The missionaries continued to comment on the progress of the Protestant missions. It was again mentioned that their missions flourished because they had plenty of money, but that did not necessarily result in conversions. It was not appreciated when they entered into the Jesuit domain in Shanghai. Such competition was not to be tolerated.

While the Chinese authorities in Shanghai valued the presence of the Jesuits for the day-to-day advantage that they brought with European support, there was distrust and certain fear when they saw the number of Chinese converts brought about by the Jesuits.

Within the mission, tension between the Jesuits and the Chinese secular clergy was ongoing. Culturally they were experienced as very different, 'lacking in missionary zeal, but associated more closely with the Chinese people' than the Europeans. This suspicion of the Chinese clergy and their culture was carried over when evaluating Chinese Jesuits. It was claimed that if the Chinese Jesuit brothers were carefully chosen and trained, they would be good religious, but if they increased in numbers, and considered themselves superior to the European Jesuit brothers, they would be seen as more Chinese than Jesuit. There was always the belief that being a European Jesuit was always the best, and that the Chinese Jesuits were expected to rise to the high standards of the Europeans. Many European missionaries failed to appreciate what positive contribution the local clergy/religious could bring to the missionary work. The Jesuit approach was to Europeanise the Chinese, with only minor cultural concessions.

Wanting to be seen as successful in their work, the Jesuits shared statistics that indicated mission growth. They were pleased that in 1894 there were 14 novices, seven Chinese and six others, while the number of Jesuit Chinese priests continued to increase. There were 26 at this time.[84] After all, the main aim of the European missionaries was to establish a local Chinese Church, and these increases in Chinese vocations were a pleasing indication that their aim was being realised.

Contexting the work and influence of French missionaries around the world in 1897 indicated that the number of their conversions compared with the total populations was slow, and far from satisfy-

---

84. Letters from Jesuits, 1897, in *Lettres de Jersey*, XVII/1 (May 1898).

ing their ambitions. Their work in 'infidel countries' was considered one of the Jesuits' most important works. The Society of Jesus had 3,687 men in foreign missions, while of the 776 French missionaries, 348 were in China. The description of the mission fields was that 'the work is immense'. It would have been most unexpected to read that the Jesuits were ever satisfied with the progress of their work, considering that their spirituality always sought the greater good and better ways of evangelisation.

Christian press in Shanghai

One of the more important means of Christian evangelisation was the use of the press. Shanghai alone had many Catholic and Protestant periodicals. The Jesuits published a twice-weekly Chinese journal, *I-wen-lou*, which aimed at the 'educated public of the East'. There was also the monthly *Messenger of the Sacred Heart* in Chinese, mainly for Catholics. The *Variétés* covered many topics 'in order to protest, and to refute, to warn and to make clear, to avenge and to establish the truth'.

The Catholic press was slow to enter the field of communications, and various attempts for French journals failed. Much of the press was in the hand of the English Protestants; the *Reviews* were all in English, such as the *China Review*. The Protestant journals were: *The Chinese Recorder, The Child's Paper, Illustrated News, Missionary Review, China's Mission* and *the Medical Missionary Journal*. Protestants claimed that they reached twice the number of people than the 'Papist missionaries'. But the Catholic missionaries retorted that there were only about 35,000 Protestant in China, compared to 500,000 Chinese Catholics!

The Protestants claimed that the English language had dethroned the French, and that Protestant preachers had replaced the Jesuits of the Ricci period in the domain of Sinology. However, the Protestant journal, *The North China Herald* that appeared from 1879, claimed that the Catholic missionaries were distinguished by their scholarship and were critical of the mediocrity of the Protestants.

The *Chinese Recorder* supported the idea that the modern Catholic missionaries didn't distinguish themselves like the Jesuits of an earlier era. In another edition, they wrote about the tremendous influence of the Jesuits. 'The Order aspires to dominate Catholicism'. 'The Church is a vassal of the Jesuits who are independent and autonomous'. 'The Lazarites are secretly administered by the Jesuits, the clerical police of the entire world'. They stated that 'not all the protestant missionaries are belligerent'. Despite these efforts to praise Catholics, some Protestants spoke with scorn about the miracles that occurred through 'blessed water', about the private Confession of women, and the extravagance of worship witnessed by 'the power and wealth of the Catholic missionaries'. Furthermore, the Chinese government had tried for 20 years to have an official inspection of Catholic works, both educational and charitable institutions, but to no effect. They further believed that the Franciscans and the Dominicans had a higher level of morality and theology than the Jesuits, and accused the Jesuit Ricci and his successors of tolerating idolatry and, in particular, modern Jesuits who tolerated ancestor worship in the Christian homes. They believed that the Catholic Church had recourse to magic to save souls by the monopoly of 'blessed water and consecrated bread'. Moreover, after conversion by the Jesuits, the Chinese converts passed from the jurisdiction of the State to that of the Church. Finally, 'the celibate sensual priest is the corruptor at home and its name is legion'.

In *Journeys in North China*, the Jesuits were identified as not showing any intelligent zeal to elevate or enlighten the Chinese people. Catholic schools were believed to give basic instruction, but did not help transform the lives of the Chinese by searching for truth. Many other items appeared in this journal, highlighting the animosity of the Protestants towards the Jesuits, as well as expounding different theologies.

After reporting on these Protestant prejudices against the Jesuits, Louis Gaillard, a missionary since 1885, believed that the Protestants were the main enemy of the Jesuits in China: their influence hindered Jesuit ministry. While Jesus was almost unknown or scorned by the majority of the Chinese, and despite the opposition from other European Christian traditions, Gaillard believed that the Jesuits had been faithful to their educational tradition and to Chinese scholarship.[85] Many would disagree with him that the Protestants were the Jesuits' main enemy in China, but his sentiment expressed the strong feeling against the Protestants held by some Jesuits.

---

85. Gaillard to Fr. M . . . The Catholic Press in China, Shanghai, in *Lettres de Jersey*, XIII/1 (May, 1894), 41–56.

Protestant missions, 1890s

Concern about the activities of the Protestants continued, usually comparing them unfavourably with their own efforts.

At the Nanjing University (American, Methodist-Episcopalian) living languages were emphasised, especially English, and there was a commerce and sciences school, and a bible school for theologians and preachers. It had a hospital, gave free consultations, and dispensed to all classes of the public.

The foreign Christian Missionary Society has a second hospital, and the Quakers opened a third, run by an American lady doctor. Elementary schools were also opened, with American ladies running some schools for girls. They also cared for women's illnesses.

Nanjing also had two government schools run by European Protestants. There were German officers at the military school and English teachers at the naval school. While these were not specifically religious schools, the Protestant teachers attached ensured the likelihood of 'promoting heresy'.

These Protestant establishments at Nanjing were important for providing numerous resources that the Catholic mission did not have. They had the added advantage that they lectured in English, and so influenced commerce, industry and administration.

In Shanghai, the Protestants had missions, schools, hospitals and a medical school. These missionaries were very hard working and zealous. They sought conversions through their liberal schools, while in the hospitals they taught modern science. They had a boarding house for boys and one for girls run by two deaconesses, and a hospital administered by two doctors helped by their wives. They lived as Americans or English, and were not too solicitous to observe Chinese customs.

The number of conversions to Protestantism was considered far less than those of the Catholic missions, despite the huge financial outlay, and despite the fact that Catholics really tested the Chinese before admitting them to Baptism, and so refused many.

What then was the French influence? If this declined, what would happen to the Catholic missions, especially if the French protectorate disappeared?

In December 1895, a new code of Chinese laws was promulgated. It reinforced earlier articles against the Christian religion: any European who preached this religion and made conversions was to be imprisoned or garrotted. Chinese who assisted in making Christians would suffer the same fate. A more recent imperial decree stated that the Christian religion was on the same level as that of secret societies.[86]

In an article by Dr John Stevens published in the *Methodist Review*, he wrote that he believed that the governing classes had a change in attitude towards the missionaries and their works. There was still an attitude of hostility, but the number of incidents had diminished. The mandarins recognised that the West had knowledge and 'prudence' that the Chinese lacked. So they turned to the West for help.

However, it was different with the Chinese masses. They appreciated the multiple activities of the Church, and so there was an increase in the number of conversions and seekers. At Fujian in 1895, there were 20,000 followers, and of these, 5,000 converts. There was also a growing demand for Bibles and Christian tracts. Medical works and education units were in much favour. Even the mandarins asked the missionaries for help with Western sciences. The Sino-Japanese War showed the Chinese their weaknesses, while the 'humble edification' of the missionaries in their work influenced the Chinese. In the eyes of Christians, the Chinese Empire was ruled 'not by a legitimate ruler but by the prince of darkness'.

On the ninetieth anniversary of the entry of Protestant ministers into China, there were 3,000 missionaries, with 80,000 Chinese Protestants. Some of the Protestant propaganda had been against Catholicism and other non-Christian Chinese religions.[87]

The Jesuits recognised the good works of the Protestant missionaries in regard to education and medical services. But the differences in theological approach to mission must have confused the Chinese, and expended missionary energy that might have been better used in evangelisation.

Sino-Japanese War

Meanwhile, relations between China and Japan deteriorated. Despite being close neighbours, they responded in different ways to the incur-

---

86. S. Adigard, 'Protestant establishments at Nanjing and Chang-King (Sichuan)', Varia, in *Lettres de Jersey*, XVI/1 (May 1897), 514–16.
87. J. Stevens, Extension of Protestantism in China, in *Lettres de Jersey*, XVII/1 (May 1898), 36–8.

sions of Western imperialism. Japan began modernisation with the Meiji Restoration of 1868, when modern-minded samurai, recognising the power of the West, overthrew the weak Tokugawa Shogunate.

Japan looked for overseas expansion, and Korea became the first country of conflict. Korea had been a tributary state of China for centuries, but Japan had been trying to open Korea to trade since 1876. China reacted to this threat by sending a diplomat to Seoul to ensure the Korean connection with China. When Korea underwent a military revolt in 1882, China was given an excuse to send troops to Seoul to restore order, and from 1882–94, China maintained a strong presence in Korea.

Another revolt occurred in Korea in 1894 by the *Tonghak*, a radical nationalist sect, having grown in strength from 1866, following the incursions of the American and Western powers into Korea. To counterbalance Western influence, Japan attempted to establish diplomatic relations with the court in Seoul, while at the same time coming to an agreement with China that neither would intervene in Korean politics without informing the other. With the outbreak of the *Tonghak* revolt, China broke this agreement by sending 1,500 troops to suppress the rebellion. Japan countered by sending its own forces, and the two countries found themselves at war on Korean soil.

China was determined to maintain its influence in Korea, as was Japan. With the build up of opposing forces, on 23 July, Japan occupied the imperial palace in Seoul. Hostilities with China broke out on 25 July 1894 after Japan sank a British ship transporting Chinese soldiers to Korea. Both sides declared war on 1 August. The Japanese bombed the port of Weihaiwei and the battle at P'yŏngyang resulted in a Chinese defeat. The Japanese army occupied the whole of Korea, and even seized Chinese territory across the border. China finally settled for peace on 12 February 1895.

The Treaty of Shimonoseki was signed between the two countries on 17 April 1895, in which China agreed to the complete independence of Korea, and tributary to China from Korea would cease. The Liaodong Peninsula, the Pescadores Islands, and the island of Taiwan with its connected islands, were ceded to Japan. China was to pay an indemnity to Japan of 200 million *taels*. In addition, Japan was accorded Most Favoured Nation Status with the right to trade in another four ports. An additional right was given to navigate vessels along the Yangzi as far as Chongqing, and along the Grand Canal from Shanghai to Xuzhou and Hangzhou. Japan was also given permission to manufacture goods on Chinese territory. This gave Japan great leverage with China in the years ahead.

The outcome of this war changed the nature of the relationship between China and Japan. Japan's victory showed China the effect of modernisation. The balance of power had changed, with Japan in the ascendency. Japan's desire for colonial regions continued, with its sights firmly set on China.[88]

The victory of Japan in Korea and humiliating to China and indicated its weakness in relation to Western modernisation. This resulted in many in the Imperial court determined to modernise China, and the Hundred Days Reform.

The Hundred Days Reform

The emperor agreed to a program of social reform and modernisation, which was not popular with conservatives in the Qing court. A new group called the

Self-Strengthening Society urged the court to implement radical social reform that included a move toward a constitutional monarchy. The court reacted by proscribing the Self-Strengthening Society, but popular support for reform continued. The emperor, still sympathetic to the reform movement, signed a decree on 11 June 1898, supporting the movement. Thus began the 100 days. The list of reforms requested included the creation of a cabinet style of government, a national assembly, a constitution, and a Bureau of People's Affairs to include the scholar-gentry in the reform program.

The reformers proposed a 'modern education and examination system, the abolition of the system of extraterritoriality, the promotion of agriculture, medicine, mining and trade, as well as the modernisation of the military, the police and the postal service'.

This reform program was unacceptable to the ruling conservatives in the court, and using the Empress Dowager, attempted to stop the reform movement. Before the emperor could outsmart the empress by imprisoning her, she acted first by coming out of retirement and had him placed under house arrest in the Lake Palace, where he

88. Dillon, op. cit., 111–14.

played no further part in the affairs of state. The reform movement ended on 21 September 1898.

From 1898 until her death on 15 November 1908, Cixi became the ruler of China. Although the Hundred Days had ended, it was not the end of the reform movement, the impetus for change was too strong, and continued up to the revolution of 1911, a time too late for the Qing.[89]

Scramble for concessions

China's weakness following the war with Japan also indicated to the Western powers that the time was ripe for making further territorial concessions from China. The more powerful nations wanted to establish their own spheres of influence, not keen that Japan alone should share the spoils.

Germany had a long-standing interest in the Province of Shandong. Its main rivals here were Japan and Russia. On 1 November 1897, two German Catholic missionaries were killed in Caozhou, and their churches badly damaged by bandits: groups of xenophobia Chinese that evolved into the Boxer movement. In response to this, the German ambassador to the Qing court, Baron von Heykink demanded the right to sink mines and build railways in Shandong, and claimed the right to lease the Bay of Jiaozhou. The Zongli Yamen rejected these demands, and on 4 December, German forces entered the town of Jiaozhou that lay at the head of the bay, thereby gaining a foothold in China.

In response to German action, the Russians sailed into Lüshun (Port Arthur) on 18 December 1897, and on 27 March 1898, China and Russia signed a treaty granting the Russians the lease of the ports of Lüshun and Dalian for 25 years, and also giving them the right to build the first phase of the South Manchurian Railway.

The French were not to be outdone by these actions. They sailed into the harbour of Guangzhou, April 1898, and sought a lease of the Guangzhou Bay for France, while would facilitate French influence in Yunnan and Vietnam. An agreement for this was finally negotiated, 16 November 1899.

---

89. Dillon, op. cit., 115–17.

Britain also signed a lease to use the Kowloon peninsula for 99 years, and also took control of the port of Weihaiwei in Shandong, 1 July 1898.[90]

These seizures of territory strengthened Western influence in China, and while some Chinese wanted to use Western technology to strengthen China and gained by collaborating with them, large scale resentment grew against the West for invading China, which highlighted China's weakness. This resentment by many Chinese carried over to the European missionaries who were seen as emissaries of Western imperialism. The result was increased Chinese opposition both to the Western powers and to the missionaries, who were to suffer much from these activities of the West.

---

90. Idem., 117–18.

Chapter 3
Boxer Uprising and Aftermath (1898–1912)
Effects of the Imperialist Wars on Jesuit Missions

The resentment felt by many Chinese following the annexation of Chinese territory by Europeans during 1898 resulted in growing unrest in the empire. The Chinese felt humiliated and defeated after the invasion of Russia, Germany, England and France, and by the concessions demanded after their defeat. As a result, a new wave of anti-foreign fervour grew among the Chinese; all sectors feared further foreign aggression. Unrest became more prevalent in the Shandong area, the region of earlier foreign incursions. The imperial government showed its weakness in being unable to control foreign aggression and in its control of many parts of China. While anti-Christian attacks continued to increase, hostility had shifted to opposing foreign aggression, rather than Christianity. The immediate concern of the government was the future of the nation, and its survival at the hands of the Europeans.

A further challenge for the Imperial government arose from the rise in the number of members to 'secret societies': groups seen as brigands causing trouble everywhere. The raiding of villages came from the White Lotus and the Boxers who attacked the homes of the rich, assaulted and killed people, and set fires to houses. The mandarins, while promising to protect the people, usually did not, as they were as frightened of the bandits as the ordinary people. Europeans were threatened and killed. Other stories of similar attacks were reported.[1]

Among the more significant nation-wide anti-foreign groups at the end of the nineteenth century were the Boxers. They grew out

---

1. Letter of Gouverneur, Hien-hien, in *Lettres de Jersey*, XVII/1 (May 1898).

of the Big Sword Society and the Plum Flower Boxers, two of many secret societies that flourished at this time. Its members believed that spirits would protect them from bullets. Many Chinese who were already hostile to Christianity joined this Society in great numbers. Their slogan was 'Support the Qing and Destroy the Aliens'. After initially burning Christian buildings and killing missionaries in Shandong, with resulting protests from the Europeans, the governor of Shandong, Yuan Shi-kai, stopped these anti-Christian activities.[2]

According to the missionaries, the reasons for the hostility toward the Christians were multiple. They experienced Chinese opposition to the Christian faith, as it clashed with traditional Chinese religions, and could not be integrated into it. The missionaries, refusing to compromise with other cults and superstitions, aroused suspicion and hostility among the Chinese by putting themselves above the civil power and by prohibiting all Chinese rites. Christianity seemed a dangerous sect.[3]

The missionaries did not appear to be aware, or at least did not care, that their theology clashed with the Chinese religion, or that Chinese converts became foreigners in their own country, having to abandon ancient traditional rites such as ancestor worship. These practices were deemed superstitious and should be suppressed. European Christianity at this time saw themselves as beacons of light fighting the forces of darkness.

Another cause for hostility toward Christianity was the missionaries' nationality. Despite being in a foreign country, the missionaries still saw themselves as essentially European. While trying to gain the mind and hearts of the Chinese people, their countries were invading China. The missionaries were sometimes perceived as agents of the foreign powers, and even spies for the invading armies: this hindered evangelisation. Some missionaries believed that attacks upon them

---

2. Kuang-sheng Liao, *Antiforeignism and modernization in China, 1860–1980* (Hong Kong: Chinese University Press, 1984), 50–1; Handbook of Christianity in China, Volume Two, op. cit., 338ff.

3. Elisa Giunipero, 'The Boxer movement through the eyes of European missionaries', in *The International Conference on the Boxer Movement and Christianity in China*, (Hong Kong, June 2004), 173, quoting Luciano Morra, SJ, *I Boxer e la Chiesa cattolica in Cina nei secoli XIX e XX* (Rome: Gregorian Pontifical University, 1996); and Jacques Gernet, *Cina e Cristianesimo*, (Casale Monferrato, Italy: Marietti, 1984), 72–114.

were caused as retaliation against the invasion of foreign forces, who were humiliating China militarily, economically and socially. The mission stations were particularly vulnerable because the missionaries were the only Europeans who were unarmed. Furthermore, the introduction of the railway and steam navigation upset those who worked traditional means of transport. This also heightened action against the missionaries. They were also seen as belonging to a powerful Church, backed by the European powers, with the resulting fear that Christians would become a separate group within society, and so disrupt Chinese social harmony.

The Jesuit missionaries of Jiangnan did not appear to be aware that being foreigners hindered their mission, as they were willing and happy to take advantage of privileges granted to them as outlined in the Unequal Treaties. They intervened in lawsuits in defence of the Christians, whom they believed to be victims of prejudice, knowing that if the case did not go their way, they could enlist the support of the French government. Non-Christians and mandarins resented this interference in Chinese law, and hostility resulted. In addition, Chinese converts were exempt from paying the quotas offered to the temples and pagodas. Moreover, the missionaries rejoiced in triumphalism, which was seen in the building of large cathedrals and churches, and in the performance of elaborate liturgical ceremonies: all to impress the local people and to symbolise the superiority of European culture to that of the Chinese.

The French protectorate was recognised implicitly as one of the main causes of the persecution. French Jesuit missionaries of Jiangnan generally rejoiced in this protection, and even saw it as an important means by which the missionaries could spread the Gospel. The imperial government wanted to deal directly with the missionaries, but as this did not generally result in favour of the Christians, the missionaries rejected this suggestion and supported the stronger and more reliable French intervention. This alignment with the foreign power did not support the missionaries' cause.

A local cause assisting the rise of bandits and the Boxers was the natural calamities that pervaded the period. There was a prolonged drought at the time that resulted in famine and starvation. This triggered acts of brigandage against the Christian missions and their properties, because they were seen to be rich and able to be exploited. Rather than religion being the main reason for the attacks, it was the demands of physical hunger. Some peasants seemed to believe that the current calamities were the direct result of the presence of the foreign missionaries and their converts, as they offended the 'heavens' with their new religious practices contrary to traditional Chinese beliefs.[4]

The French minister in Beijing monitored the attacks on Christian communities throughout the troubles, as the missionaries constantly reported any troubles. The consul was told about the pillage and burning of the priests' residence at Ne-zie, 17 kilometres south-west of Xujiahui in August 1898. The exorbitant cost of rice led to famine; so bandits attacked rich houses, either non-Christians or Christians, to find rice. Then they attacked church property hoping to find provisions, found none and left, but the next day they returned to burn the church. Government soldiers tried to guard the residence, but failed. There was a rising fear among Westerners/missionaries about the severity and scale of the attacks on church property. The consul reported further attacks on church property in north Jiangsu. The Jesuits Prosper Paris and Henri Doré kept the consul informed of developments. Meanwhile, the Germans were taking matters into their own hands to protect their interests.[5]

In the midst of these attacks, Bishop Valentin Garnier, vicar apostolic of Jiangnan, died aged 74 on 14 August 1898, which caused sadness in French diplomatic circles, as he had always shown courtesy to the consulate, and had recognised the 'vigilant protection' given by the French government to the Catholic missions.[6]

Meanwhile, the French minister was claiming indemnities from the Chinese government for the recent destruction of mission buildings. He successfully obtained $18,000 for the Jesuit mission of Shanghai for the destruction of Ne-zie and Tao-ci. The Jesuits were grateful for this speedy resolution.[7]

With the increase in the number of rebel groups, especially in Shandong and northern Zhili, the Empress Dowager issued a decree in favour of the missions on 5 October 1898, probably the result of some pressure from the European powers. She ordered local authorities to protect the missionaries and 'their good works'. All missionar-

---

4.   Giunipero, ibid., 173–8.
5.   French consul to French Minister, Shanghai, 10 August, 11 August 1898. DAC.
6.   French consul to French Minister, Shanghai, 15 August 1898. DAC.
7.   French consul to French Minister, Shanghai, 24 September 1898. DAC.

ies were to be treated 'cordially'. She was upset especially about the troubles in Suzhou, because of the false rumours against the missionaries, with resulting fights that the local authorities were unable to prevent. All missionaries working in the interior of China were to be treated with 'respect and politeness', and all disputes between the local people and the missionaries were to be resolved 'immediately and without exception'. The people were commanded to live in harmony with their Christian neighbours, while mandarins not following this decree were to be punished.[8] The French minister, in Beijing on 27 October, reassured the superior of the Jesuit mission that the threats against them would cease in the light of this decree.

By 1899, Jesuit missionaries recognised that the nature of the brigandage marked the beginning of 'a new rebellion'. Peace reigned in February that year, but the community was on guard during nights. They had been building fortifications at Chai and Feihe, which were well defended. At this time, famine was seen as a greater fear among the people than the brigands, with many beggars quickly becoming wasted and emaciated. The people were so desperate that they sold young girls and exposed small children to the elements. Brigandage followed these conditions. By June, while noting that the notables of Feihe were friendly toward the missionaries, the district continued to be in poor shape as a result of floods the previous year and the current drought: no wheat or sorghum was available. The countryside was a desert and people died or moved to another village. The famine was an open invitation for further difficulties.[9]

Albert Wetterwald at Weit-s'ounn described 1899 as a 'frightening and unsettling' one. The village was on a war footing, with a local militia made up of 19 squads of 10 men each. Even the old people were energetic in assisting the defences. In September that year, he described the arrival of the Big Swords Society disrupting the region of Zhao-jia-zhoang. Seven Christian villages were pillaged and several Christians were taken captive. There were no deaths or burnings. The civil authorities and military were active during this time, and the main body of the rebels went back to Shandong, where Bishop Johann Baptist von Anzer, the vicar apostolic in Yanzhou, had been

---

8. Decree of the Dowager Empress in favour of the mission, Beijing, 5 October 1898, in *Lettres de Jersey*, XVIII/1 (June 1899).
9. Chevalier to Superior, Fei-ho, 25 February, & 22 June 1899, in *Lettres de Jersey*, XIX/1 (January, 1900).

active in seeking assistance from Beijing. The military attacked the Boxers, but the governor of Shandong was known as an enemy of the Europeans.[10]

The superior of the mission of south-east Zhili, Henri Maquet, in reporting to the French provincial, described the secret societies as wanting to end Christianity and expel the Europeans. A chapel was burnt down in Fouzheng, while there was much disorder in Gaizhou, Kou-zheng and Jing-zhou. The mandarins were incapable of preventing the disorders. In Kou-zheng, bandits attacked with a 'so-called imperial letter' telling them 'to protect the throne and destroy the foreigner'. Armed with guns, swords, pistols and lances, they set fire to the chapel, threatened the veteran missionary Paul Denn, and demanded of the mandarin '500 ounces' of money.[11]

By Christmas, the Boxers had already despoiled many Christian communities. The French consul was informed, who, in turn, complained to the local Chinese viceroy, but he proved to be ineffective. The Chinese government was torn in every direction by the secret societies. They grew in numbers as they proceeded from village to village, recruiting followers with the incentive that as they invoked magic spells and the devil, they would be given special powers to defend themselves against attackers. Before going into battle, the Boxers burnt short sticks of incense and 'invoked the devil'. At Tong-tai-guo, even though the more strongly armed Chinese soldiers were in place to confront them, still much damage to houses occurred.[12]

From January 1900, the *North China Herald* reported increasing violence and destruction wrought by the Boxers. From Zhili, there were reports of Catholic chapels destroyed with many refugees fleeing the area. There were threats to the Catholic cathedral at Xianxian and at Hejianfu. All the missions south of Zhili and NW Shandong were uneasy, and military protection alone saved them for further

---

10. Wetterwald to Laurent, Weit-s'ounn, 26 February 1899; extract from Wetterwald, Tchao-kia-tchoang, 20 September 1899 in *Lettres de Jersey*, XIX/2 (October 1900).

11. Maquet to Provincial, 29 November 1899, in *Lettres de Jersey, ut supra.*

12. Mangin to Desmarquest, Tientsin, 20 December 1899; Gheslin to Jesuit in Enghien, Tchang-kia-tchoang, 17 December 1899; Wantz to Jesuit Brothers, Tchang-kia-tchoang (Xianxian), 1 January 1900, in *Lettres de Jersey, ut supra.*

violence. The Boxers attacked the Chinese converts first. It appeared that the Boxers were allies of the empress.[13]

Reports in February noted the increased in violence by the Boxers in Zhili and Shandong. The Christians in the north were persecuted, with the cry to drive out the foreigners. A not unbiased press noted that the Christian converts became members of the Church in order to obtain help in lawsuits. The example given for this view was that two German priests in Shandong were killed and another was targeted by the Boxers for helping in a lawsuit against a rich Chinese man. Germany intervened. To end European protection would be handing missionaries over to their enemies. It was claimed that the Catholic missionaries wanted political power and so endangered the whole missionary work in Shandong. In support of this claim that missionaries wanted power, it was noted that the priests demanded the same official rank as the Chinese officials. The Jesuits desire for social status was no help to the Chinese Christians.[14]

By June, it became clear that the Imperial court supported the Boxers because they supported the Dynasty, and that the attacks by the Boxers were aimed at both foreigners and missionaries alike. As the governor of Shandong condoned the attacks and was no help to the Europeans, foreign troops moved into Shandong. There was a meeting between the English and the French ambassadors who agreed to take up arms against the Boxers and any opposing group. They asserted that the desire to rid China of Europeans would fail, while expressing support for the emperor, but not the empress. New French, English, German and American forces were being sent to China. Li Hong-zhang was reported to declare that the empress had ordered him to Beijing from Guangzhou in order to suppress the Boxers and make peace with the European powers. He stated that the Boxers were only a fanatical anti-Christian rabble, and thought that Chinese converts and missionaries were to blame for the troubles, especially among the Catholics. He did not think that the Boxers had any political motives, and the empress was entirely misled and misinformed about the state of affairs. It was the duty of the viceroys to protect life and property, both foreign and Chinese. He would behead

---

13. *North China Herald,* 10 January, 17 January, 24 January 1900. NLA (Australian National Library, Canberra).
14. Ibid., February 1900. NLA.

the leaders of the Boxers, send the others home and make peace with the European powers. Li was later told to stay in Guangzhou, while Prince Duan controlled Beijing.[15]

There were reports of 100 casualties in two days of fighting in Tianjin in June. The French settlement was destroyed by fire, and Tianjin itself was under threat. Beijing made no response. The revolt against the foreigners came as a surprise to some foreigners, who believed that they were weak in response to the obvious threats. Western guns did not easily threaten the Boxers. It was the Japanese who lead the forces in retaliation. Two Yangtze viceroys, Lui Kun-yi and Tan Chitong, were mentioned as giving support to the embattled Europeans against the Boxers. In Jiangsu and Anhui provinces where the Jesuit missions were established, the revolutionary societies and disbanded soldiery were reported to be 'very troublesome'.[16]

The European military force sent to relieve the Europeans in Beijing in June made little advance until 1 September. News from the Shandong area reported burnt churches, as well as the death of foreigners and hundreds of Christian converts. Tianjin was looted and in ruin, and relief came only after a bombardment lasting six days (17–23 June). The relieving force consisted of 300 British and 1,700 Russians. Because of its exposed position, the French settlement suffered the most. The river was filled with corpses. Until rain arrived on 1 July, there had been no rain, and no crops, which led to pestilence and famine. Catholic missionaries were murdered along with Chinese Christians in Manchuria. The Boxers even killed some Chinese officials. It was believed that the Boxers had infiltrated the Court and were influencing some Manchu princes.[17]

By August, it was reported that Prince Duan was in league with the Boxers (from 16 July) and that they wanted to kill all foreigners in Beijing. All foreign legations but two had been destroyed. Foreigners went to the British legation, which was constantly being shelled.

There was an exaggerated report claiming that the Boxers were 'losing their spirit' in Beijing, and that some foreigners were returning to their own houses. It was expected that the relieving army from Tianjin would not expect much resistance. Meanwhile murders con-

---

15. Ibid., 6 June, 20 June, 23 June, 24 June, 25 June, 27 June 1900. NLA.
16. Ibid., 21 June, 23 June, 24 June, 25 June 1900. NLA.
17. Ibid., 11 July 1900. NLA.

tinued in the provinces: five foreigners in Shansi, and also some in Baoding and Zhejiang.

Li Hong-zhang claimed that the empress had no part in the attack on the legations, but rather it came from a group around Prince Duan. Moreover, it was claimed that the empress had regained control of the bandits, despite one Chinese general wanting to rid China of all foreigners, not only the missionaries. Li wanted the Europeans to believe that the empress was a friend of the foreigners, and that the enemy was Duan and the Boxers. He memorialised the throne, urging repression of the Boxers.

Meanwhile, the Jesuit settlement of Xujiahui in Shanghai became a refuge for missionaries from the interior, both Protestant and Catholic.

Lord Salisbury, the British Prime Minister, suggested that the Boxers had not always been against the missionaries: so, why the change? He suggested it was because of European imperialism into China.[18] This was an enlightened response.

By August, massacres were being reported. The French consul at Jantai announced the murder of Jesuit missionaries at Daming: Augustin Finck, Raphael Gaudissart, Omer Neveux, Celestin Cézard, Valentin Gissinger and Xavier Keiffer. The death of the Japanese chancellor, Sugiyama, by decapitation occurred when he entered Beijing against the orders of Duan that stipulated that no one was to enter or leave Beijing. It was on 13 June that the Boxers first attacked the legations, with the slogan from 14 June, 'slay the foreigners'. The empress first issued a decree to suppress the Boxers, and then changed her mind to 'rid China of all foreigners'. Kang Yi had convinced the empress that the Boxers were invulnerable to bullets, despite the fact that there were bodies everywhere. But the empress probably would not have seen them. This change of mind by the empress empowered the Boxers. In the Imperial court, there were two factions: the Chinese group that opted for restraint, and a Manchu clique that wanted war.

All during June the Boxers attacked foreign commercial buildings, and the German minister was murdered. The Boxers even murdered any Chinese who opposed them or any that were associated with foreigners.[19]

18. Ibid., 1 August 1900. NLA
19. ibid., 8 August 1900. NLA.

The Jesuits in Xuzhou, prefecture of Jiangsu, were well established, and had won a victory over the Big Sword bandits in 1896, gaining an apology with indemnities, and the promise that the local authorities would protect the church. The Christian community grew in strength as it continued to seek justice for its people.

When the Boxers moved towards the village of Wu-fou-tang in 1900, they found it well defended. They first attacked the non-Christian section of the village, and the imperial soldiers did nothing, as they were the friends of the Boxers. The Christians then abandoned the village, taking some of their wounded with them as the Boxers headed north. It was believed that Bishop Pierre-Marie Alphonse Favier [20] in Beijing was in negotiations with the Imperial Court, but there were no results. Between Pooting and Beijing, at Gaojialou, 60 Christians had been killed, burnt in their chapel.

June was a chaotic month in this prefecture, with reports that the Boxers attacked Wu-fou-tang and Caijian, with many massacres. Large numbers of refugees resulted, with the mandarins showing no authority. Even some catechists fled south to save their families and to care for the sick. Albert Wetterwald was critical of the 'cowardess' of the 'old Catholics', whom he expected would have been more steadfast in the support of others. The missionaries stayed with the people, marshalling the local militia. Rémi Isoré organised a Christian self-defence force, while Wetterwald did the same at Weicun. He claimed that his defences had caused the Boxers to hesitate as early as November 1898, and by 1900, the village triangle of Weicun-Pengcun-Zhaojiazhuang had become the centre of Christian defence in the Wei district, while in outlying areas, Christian communities and buildings were destroyed. Wetterwald reported that the Boxers were seen for the first time on 3 July, appearing on the dike towards the southwest, 800 metres away from Kata. On 17 July, they appeared on the plains of Daming. The Christian militia led by Wetterwald con-

20. **Bishop Pierre-Marie Alphonse Favier** (1837–1905) was born at Marsanny-la-Côte, France, and entered the Lazarists (Vincentians), 1858. He arrived in Beijing, July 1862, and in 1897 became coadjutor to the vicar apostolic, succeeding him two years later. He obtained an imperial decree placing Catholic bishops socially equal to Chinese governors, which was not well accepted. He lived through the siege of the Beitang (North Church) during Boxer Rebellion, 1900, and afterwards condemned the excessive force of the European forces against the Chinese rebels. He died in Beijing.

fronted the Boxers as they approached and attacked them, forcing the Boxers to retreat. Some 68 Boxers were killed.[21]

In his report of the persecution at Chen-zhou, Henri Wibaux mentioned the death of Jesuits Rémi Isoré and Modest Andlauer on 21 June. About 100 Boxers went on to Lao-pai-zun on 23 June, but the villages were well armed, killing seven Boxers. Other villages were also saved, but there were many deaths. On 26 June, the mandarin of Chen-zhou went to Wang-lao-seu, appealing to the Christians to renounce their faith, and to lay down their arms. They replied that they would rather die than renounce their faith. The Christian population of Wang-lao-seu was 70 on 5 December 1899. Of these, the Boxers killed 48, fourteen left the village, and one apostatised.[22]

After the retaking of Tianjin on 15 July, documents were found to incriminate the Chinese officials of the Zongli Yamen with the Boxers, with requests for swords, money and food. The Yamen had listed the names of all the Boxers in the surrounding villages, which made it good for mopping up operations later. On 14 July, supervised by the Jesuits, Xianxian was saved by 12,000 men from among 30,000 refugees. The Boxers suffered many losses from attacks beginning 4 July.

Beijing under siege

On the fall of Beijing, 15 August 1900, Kang Yi and Tong Fuxiang were left in control of the city, with Li Hong-zhang expecting to negotiate with the allies. The Boxers made up 65 per cent of the empress's imperial guard, and she left only 45,000 Chinese troops in Beijing to face the allied advance. Just before she fled Beijing, with the emperor forced to join her, she killed Chinese officials friendly towards the

---

21. Journal of Albert Wetterwald, May–July 1900, Fan-kia-kata, 23 October 1900, to his mother, in *Lettres de Jersey*, XIX/2, (October 1900). Other works on the Boxers are Robert A. Bickers, and R. Gary Tiedemann, *The Boxers, China and the World*, Langham, (Md: Rowan and Littlefield, 2007) (on line); Paul H. Clements, *The Boxer Rebellion*, (Columbia: Longmans, 1915); Joseph W. Esherick, *The Origins of the Boxer Uprising* (California: University of California Press, 1987); Diana Preston, *The Boxer Rebellion* (New York: Berkley Books, 2000); International Conference on the Boxer Movement and Christianity, Taipei and Hong Kong, 10–14 June 2004.

22. *Lettres de Jersey*, 1901.

foreign legations, those who had too high an opinion of foreign troops and those who had too low an estimate of the Boxers. She left for Shansi on 11 August.[23]

The British were peeved that the Russians reached Beijing first, but were consoled that they reached the legations first. At the final victory, the number of foreign troops in Beijing were 8,000 Japanese, 5,000 Russians, 3,000 British, 3,000 Americans, 2,000 Germans and 2,000 French, Italian and Austrians. The British were quick to note that the French did very little. Russia occupied the Summer Palace. Yi Lu, the viceroy of Zhili, committed suicide, together with his family. Foreigners expressed the wish to stay in China, but wanted continued protection under the Treaty Rights. The allies sought the whereabouts of Prince Duan, but he was not to be seen, while the empress sought protection from the Russians rather than from the other allies. It was noted that at Suzhou, 86 men were executed, while relief with rice was provided for the starving.

From the diaries of the siege in the British legation, it was learned that the Chinese began shelling the legations from 12 July, whose food was reduced to eggs given to them by the Chinese, as well as horse meat. Thirty French marines and ten Italians defended the Catholic cathedral, called the Xishiku church or Beitang, together with some 2,000 Chinese converts. Their provisions ran very low by 26 July. By 9 August, starvation was setting in, with children dying. There was fear of disease. On 14 August, there was a very heavy attack from the Chinese; at 3pm the Sikhs arrived, followed by other troops, bombing the gates on the east and north. The Beitang was relieved: 400 converts had been killed; 76 children had been blown up in a mine explosion; 10 French and five Italians were buried within the walls. The details given by Bishop Favier indicated that their ordeal was far worse than at the British legation. From 20 June to 15 August, the legation had been completely cut off, with no news of any kind.[24]

After the fall of Beijing, it was the Russians who assumed some leadership among the allies, influencing the return to Beijing of the empress and the court, with a return to imperial rule. Britain feared

---

23. *North China Herald*, 22 August 1900, LXV/1724. NLA.
24. Ibid., 19 September 1900, LX/1728. NLA.

Russian influence against her interests, as well as any further 'carve up' of China when new settlements were negotiated.[25]

The European allies had to solve the question of the future of the empress. Some wanted her banished and the emperor restored together with his reform programme implemented. A more radical opinion was to overthrow the present dynasty. To exile the empress would not be permitted by most viceroys and governors who supported the Europeans, while most Chinese were believed to welcome the reinstatement of the emperor.[26]

Causes of the rebellion

In discussing reasons for the Boxer rebellion, there was immediate criticism of Catholic missionary priests for their political interference in negotiating with Chinese magistrates on behalf of their converts. Protestants did not do this. The Imperial Court, rather, suggested the cause was foreign aggression. In reply, it was thought that this had its roots in Chinese opposition to the Catholics. The outbreak of the rebellion immediately followed the granting of official status to the Catholic missionaries.[27] Protestant missionaries were perceived as not disliked as missionaries, but rather as foreigners. But the missionary was the face of the foreigner. Well-informed Chinese blamed the land grabbing of the European Powers as a cause of the trouble.

Many factors contributed to the rebellion. Included were the attitude of those Chinese officials who were recognised as agents of foreign forces, the Chinese people, the spirit of Western peoples, foreign trade, the Catholic Church, Protestant missionaries, and the general history of China's relations with the West. What if the Catholic missions had been independent of the French protectorate or free of European political manipulation? Christianity was not destructive by nature, and did not attack the Chinese political system. Protestant Christianity was a power for change: it fought injustice, was eager for liberty, and passionate for progress. The missionary was always on the side of the people.

---

25. Ibid., 5 September 1900, LXV/1726. NLA.
26. Ibid., 26 September 1900, LXV/1729. NLA.
27. Ibid., 17 October 1900. NLA.

Peace negotiations

The harm experienced by the missionaries from this rebellion was immense. Three Catholic bishops lost their lives, as did 31 missionary priests and about 30,000 Chinese Catholics. The Protestants lost nearly 2,000. Much property was destroyed, including the famous Nantang church in Beijing. The slaughter was particularly felt in Zhili, Shanxi, Mongolia and Manchuria.[28]

In the negotiations with the Europeans, Prince Jing and Li Hongzhang were the Throne negotiators with the Allied Powers. Meanwhile, Chinese Christians were still being persecuted. They were told to recant their religion or suffer confiscation of property. Lying hidden in Beijing were 20,000 Boxers ready to re-take the city with Prince Duan when he returned. There were also many Boxers on the route between Beijing and Tianjin.[29]

In the clean up, Russia was the dominant allied power in negotiations with the Chinese, especially about Manchuria, their region of interest, which worried the British. The allies condemned to death Chinese officials who supported the Boxers, and those who killed missionaries at Baoding. Prince Duan, when he returned, together with the Boxers presented their own peace terms to the allies. They wanted the return of all land to China, and for all foreigners to leave China. All remnants of European technology, especially the railways, were to be removed.[30] Of course, this was totally unacceptable to the Allies.

For the rest of the 1900s, negotiations over the peace were frustrating for the allies as the Chinese procrastinated, even hinting about another outbreak of war. The Europeans did not trust the words of the Chinese officials. Even Prince Jing, the chief negotiator, was once known to be against the foreigners.[31]

The Catholic Church hierarchy complained to the French minister that the press had blamed religious propaganda as a cause of diplomatic embarrassments. They denied that religion produced fanatics and persecutors, rather holding the view that the unpopularity of the missions was because of their solidarity with the foreigners. Notwith-

28. Cary-Elwes, op. cit., 224.
29. *North China Herald,* 24 October 1900. NLA.
30. Ibid., 7 November, LXV/1735; 14 November LXV/1736. NLA.
31. Ibid., November to December. NLA.

standing these impressions that acknowledged the close relationship between the French and the missionaries, the bishops wanted to keep the protectorate, which they believed was important to the French, because the European penetration of China would ultimately bring about transformations in the country. Moreover, the Catholic missions relied on the protectorate for safety and security. Yet they queried whether the treaty arrangements of 1860, as well as that of Berthemy in 1865, and the imperial decree of 15 March 1899, where bishops were equated to Chinese magistrate, gave the impression that the church was being too much involved in politics.

They wanted Chinese Christians to be able to sit for Chinese political and military exams at all levels, as well as for them to be exempt from official rites at pagodas. As well, they wanted Chinese Christians to abstain from superstitious ceremonies in the temple of ancestors.

Further requests were made of the French for help concerning the murder of Europeans and the destruction of Church property. Compensation was not considered sufficient; the 'criminals must be punished'. Moreover, the Church wanted the Secret Societies suppressed, or at least to have their influence diminished. Finally, the use of opium should be reduced, and Europeans should continue to have full access to the Empire.[32] The Catholic Church had no intention of relinquishing its close connection with the French legation. Indeed, its very survival might depend upon its support.

The Jesuit mission of Jiangnan in 1900

With the death of Bishop Garnier in August 1898, and the death of coadjutor Jean-Baptist Simon, bishop for 45 days, dying from a fever in 1899,[33] Bishop Prosper Paris (1846–1931) became the new vicar apostolic of Jiangnan in 1900. He had arrived in China in 1883, and later as a Jesuit superior, and kept close contact with the French

---

32. Catholic Church Hierarchy to French Minister, Shanghai, 15 November 1900. DAC. The letter had 14 signatures, including the Jesuits of Jiangnan, Bishop Paris, and Fathers Henri Boucher (Rector of Xujiahui) and Jean-Baptist Rouxel (Procurator).
33. **Jean-Baptist Simon (1846–1899)** was born in the diocese of Nantes, entered the Jesuits on 25 August 1868, and arrived in China on 18 October 1886. He was sent initially to Nanjing for 11 years, 1886–1897, and later to Shanghai as rector of Xujiahui. Garnier wanted a coadjutor as he was in his 72nd year.

consul, frequently expressing gratitude for the 'close collaboration between the French government and the church' for developments in Shanghai and elsewhere in the mission. There was an issue discussed between them from 1898 about setting up an 'interpreters' school', which would assist the French. The French consul thought the Jesuits would be interested in the idea because of their great interest in promoting French influence in China, and since they already had a College of Translators at Xujiahui involved in the translation of books. Paris was cautious about this plan, and no firm arrangement was made, suggesting further discussion on the matter.[34] Such collaboration might appear to be too close, given the tension in holding the balance between religious and political questions.

With annual reports to Rome, the Jesuits kept their superiors well informed of progress in the mission, and commentaries upon the present political and social conditions in China. In 1900, despite these upheavals in parts of the mission, with the destruction of property and the dispersal of converts, it was reported that considerable mission growth took place.

Rome was told that the total number of Catholic missionaries in China in 1900 was around 900, of whom 471 were Chinese priests. Proportionally, the number of Chinese priests relative to the foreigners grew during the following decades. The number of Chinese Christians between 1890–1900, increased from about 550,000 to 720,000. This expansion was particularly evident in the rural areas of China. Increases in the urban areas occurred among those keen to acquire Western knowledge taught in the missionary schools.

At this time, the Catholic Church in China was divided into 41 dioceses and vicariates, while the Jesuit mission of Jiangnan still embraced the two Provinces of Jiangsu to the east and Anhui to the west with a total population of 50 million people. The former had 12 prefectures and 67 sub-prefectures, while the latter had 13 prefectures and 55 sub-prefectures.

Apart from Shanghai, the mission was divided into 19 sections comprising 100 districts. Jiangsu had 10 sections with 59 districts; and Anhui, nine sections with 41 districts. A district was the combination of a number of Christian communities under the jurisdiction

---

34. French Consul to French Minister, Shanghai, 23 October 1898; Paris to Consul, Shanghai, 21 October 1898. DAC.

of a missionary, whereas a section comprised several districts, and had a minister at its head, who directed the missionaries and Christians in his sections.

Besides the Jesuit vicar apostolic, there were 137 Jesuit priests, of whom 23 were Chinese; 15 Jesuit scholastics (Jesuits in training), five of whom were Chinese; and 30 brothers, 13 being Chinese. In addition there were 22 Chinese secular priests, as well as 18 major and 24 minor seminarians. Younger aspirants, the 'Latinists', numbered 28. There were two religious houses of men: 20 'Petits-Frères de Marie', at the school in Hongkou, and 31 catechists belonging to the Chinese congregation of the Mother of God.

Women increased in influence in the mission, especially by the 770 'virgins' whose work in schools was considered indispensable. They also baptised dying children, cared for orphans and church property, as well as administered to the Christians in the communities in a host of human circumstances, especially during times of drought, famine and disease. Congregations of religious women assisted them: 27 Carmelites (16 Chinese); 86 'Auxiliatrices du Purgatoire' (30 Chinese); 29 Sisters of St Vincent de Paul; and 127 Chinese Presentations.[35]

In another letter, Paris outlined the progress at the College of St Ignatius at Xujiahui. Its aims had always been to increase 'piety' and to educate the students from 'honourable Christian families' in the sciences and in 'Chinese letters', in order to prepare them for future academic preferment. The emphasis on producing leaders was important. In the 11 years since its foundation, the college had produced 10 Jesuit priests and six secular clergy, as well as seven Jesuit brothers, and 60 seminarians (24 remained in 1900).[36] Vocations to the priesthood or religious life were always a sign to the Jesuits of a successful apostolate.

Effect of the rebellion in the Jiangnan mission

The effect of the Boxer rebellion was not felt as much in the Jiangnan mission as in the Zhili mission to the north. However, in 1901 at Qingjianpu, after petitioning the mandarins for six months, Auguste

---

35. State of the Mission of Jiangnan, Bishop Paris, 1 July 1900. ARSI.
36. Bishop Paris, 'The mission of Jiangnan, its history, its works', 1900, a report. ARSI.

Debesse reported the arrest of the chief of the brigands, Wang-hai-tao, who, in the previous October, gave trouble in the vicinity. His group burnt down one Christian community, harassed, tortured and killed people, but the police were not keen to follow up on this case, because they said that the brigands belonged to the neighbouring Province of Jiangxi, where the arsonists continued to terrorise the countryside.[37]

As a distraction amid death and destruction at Bozhou, Joseph Dannic reflected upon the Chinese funeral rites, which were very important, even for the simple people. They showed great respect and reverence for dead relatives, with mourning taking several days. Dannic described the Chinese as having a 'human heart', as all other mortals, but they were 'a slave to traditions', even more than in Europe. This was in contrast to the way they treated unwanted or dead children when they exposed the bodies to the elements. He was horrified with this practice.[38]

An imperial decree was promulgated in 1902. It declared that the court loved and protected the people. Christians and non-Christians were treated with the same kindness and no distinction was made between them. The court wanted all to be united and enjoy peace. Viceroys and governors were instructed to live in peace with non-Christians and Christians alike. In Henan, where churches were destroyed and Christians killed, the governors were instructed to arrest those culpable and bring them to justice according to law.

Missionaries had been in China for 200 years with the intention of helping the people. However, there had been some bad people, who, in the name of Christians, caused trouble. They duped the missionaries with untruths and went to the mandarins demanding redress. The missionaries did not have good relations with the local mandarins because they were considered unjust.

When Catholic accusations arose, the mandarins ordered their men to seize those accused, and more than often imposed upon the people a heavy indemnity. This antagonised the people further against the missionaries, who were only trying to achieve justice for

---

37. Debesse to Troussard, T'sing-chan-kiao, 9 April 1901, in *Lettres de Jersey*, XXI/1 (January 1902). Paul Troussard was rector and master of novices in Laval, Province of France.
38. Dannic to Lecointre, Po-tchéou, 29 April 1901, in *Lettres de Jersey*, XXI/1 (January 1902).

the people. Both sides needed to dialogue without jealousy or aversion. Bishop Favier in Beijing was very just and understanding. Discussions were held how to prevent such evils in the future. No longer would bad people be permitted to become Christians, and if Christians broke the law, the mandarin ought to punish them as with the non-Christians.[39]

A comment on the imperial decree by Jesuit Pierre Guimbretière mentioned that despite all the treaties between China and the European Powers, despite all the edicts coming out of Beijing in the previous three decades, and despite even the recent repression of the Boxers in 1900, the Imperial Court had been impotent to prevent deaths and destruction; the victims of recent years were sufficient proof. The decree was favourably received in both the Chinese and foreign press. The Protestant press of Shanghai was either exercising flattery or was ignorant of the information narrated. The *Echo de Chine* congratulated the Court for its 'excellent' decree about what it intended to do, but there were other decrees less favourable to the Europeans. Was this latest decree sufficient to protect them? The future was hard to predict, but missionaries should be neither defiant or ungrateful, and certainly not imprudent. Whatever happened, they must put their trust 'in God's decrees' that they believed protected them and the Chinese Christians.[40]

A further commentary by Xiang-xue-wong was critical of the mandarins in the recent troubles involving negotiations between them and the missionaries. He focused on the need for the mandarins to protect the life and wellbeing of all missionaries in China. All non-Christians and Christians were in future to be under the laws of the Empire. Therefore, all dealings must be treated according to justice and the laws. He praised the 'grand words' of the emperor attempting to decree peace, but it was difficult to have peace between non-Christians and Christians when some mandarins were 'half fearful and routine-minded', while others were 'ignorant and partial'. The mandarins were ignorant of the terms of the treaties relating to the Christians, and such ignorance made it impossible for them to judge justly. When faulty judgments were given, discontent between the

---

39. Imperial Decree, 8 April 1902, in *Lettres de Jersey*, XXI/2 (August-September 1902).
40. Imperial decree in favour of the Christians, extract of letter from Guimbretière to French scholastics, in *Lettres de Jersey*, XXVII/1 (April 1908): 4.

disagreeing parties continued. The missionaries, knowing the law, should teach Christians what they can or cannot do. Everyone, then, would obey the laws of the Empire.[41]

Negotiations on a peace settlement between the allied powers and between them and the imperial court were long and tortuous, with many disagreements. Finally, more than a year after the relief forces arrived in Beijing, a treaty was signed on 7 September 1901. There were 12 articles in the Boxer Protocol, as it was known. It required an apology for the murders of the German ambassador Baron Clemens von Ketteler, and the Japanese diplomat, Mr Sugiyama, as well as the demand for death sentences or banishment for senior officials of the court, and suspension of official examinations for five years in towns in which foreigners had been murdered or ill-treated. In addition, by an imperial edict on 29 May 1901, China agreed to pay foreign powers an indemnity of 450 million Customs *taels*, with annual payments to be made until the end of 1940. The Legation Quarter was to be recognised as a foreign quarter in which no Chinese had the right of residence, and its own troops and police would defend the legations. The foreign powers were given the right to occupy 12 towns to give them access to the sea. Edicts were to be given forbidding membership of anti-foreign organisations, to be published in all country towns throughout the Chinese empire. Finally, the Zongli Yamen was to be reorganised as a Ministry of Foreign Affairs, while the foreign governments agreed to withdraw all troops, apart from the legation guards, from Beijing by 7 September 1901, and from the region of Zhili by 22 September.[42]

This very one-sided Protocol was humiliating to the Manchu government, from which it never recovered. It did not endear the Chinese to the presence of the Europeans and, by implication, to the missionaries.

Russia/Japanese relations

The Japanese, having proved their superiority over China at the Treaty of Shimonoseki in 1895, played a significant role in the suppression of the Boxers. Japan's main rival in Asia was Russia, which over the

41. Ibid., 5–6.
42. Dillon, op. cit., 130–1.

years had been pushing its influence eastwards, finally establishing
a naval base at Vladivostok, a port within striking distance of Japan.
Fearful of a possible alliance between France and Russia, some Japanese politicians favoured a Japanese/Russian alliance, but this was
aborted with the news of the creation of the Anglo-Japanese Alliance
on 30 January 1902. Meanwhile the Russians established themselves
in Manchuria, causing concern among the British, Japanese and Chinese. Russia signed an agreement with China on 8 April 1902, for the
withdrawal of Russian troops from Manchuria and the re-establish-
ment of the imperial authority. However, Russia did not withdraw
its troops by 1903, and in October took control of the government
offices in Shenyang. By December, Russia indicated to Japan that
it would no longer negotiate over its position in Manchuria. Japan
lost patience and broke off diplomatic relations on 8 February 1904,
and launched a naval attack upon Port Arthur on the same day. Both
countries declared war on each other.

The Japanese troops vastly outnumbered the Russians, while its
navy was also superior, having more naval bases. Russia at this time
was internally weak with internal disturbances, while Japan was rising in industrial strength. The Japanese navy and land forces finally
crushed the Russians, who were forced to sign of Treaty of Ports-
mouth on 5 September 1905. Russia had to accept Japanese dominance in Korea and Manchuria. Both agreed to withdraw troops from
Manchuria, except for the Liaodong Peninsula, and Japan obtained a
lease of Port Arthur from the Chinese government. It also obtained
exclusive rights to the railway between Changchun and Port Arthur,
the South Manchurian Railway, which was to become an important
vehicle for Japanese expansion into Manchuria and China in later
years.

Japan also consolidated its position in Korea by appointing a Resident General in Seoul to control foreign affairs. Korea came under
Japanese control until it was formally annexed in 1910, and remained
so until 1945. China not only lost Korea as a tributary state, but was
also faced with the growing power and influence of Japan on its
north-eastern frontier.[43] This aggression by Japan was only the beginning of its expansion into China. As Japan's expansionist dream in

---

43. Ibid., 132–5.

Asia continued to grow in strength and determination, everyone in China had reason to be concerned about Japanese intentions.

Social and political change in China after 1901

After the rebellion, political and social changes in Chinese government became necessary. The 1898 Hundred Days Reform movement formed the basis of these changes, proposed by the less conservative court officials in the absence of the Empress Dowager Cixi. While acknowledging that these reforms were probably too late to save the dynasty, they indicated the way forward that helped create the conditions necessary for the revolution of 1911. In April 1901, a new government department, the Bureau for the Promotion of Political Affairs, was created to implement education, military and administrative reforms.

The education edict in January 1901 created the basis for a modern educational system, partly modelled on Japan. A new network of schools was to be established, following the system set up by Yuan Shikai in Shandong. Scientific and technical education was included in the curriculum in order to encourage industrialisation. Traditional methods of teaching and examination were abandoned, and students were sent abroad for the first time, mainly to Japan. Yanjing University, the precursor of Peking University, was founded in 1902, while a Ministry of Education was created in 1906.

The weakness of the Chinese army and navy became obvious when compared with the strength of the European powers and Japan; so modern weapons and military training methods were introduced under new provincial academies on 1 September 1901.

To replace the Zongli Yamen, a Foreign Ministry was created in 1901. A Ministry of Trade followed in 1902, as well as Ministries of Police, Education and War in 1906. On 1 September 1906, an edict endorsed the principle of constitutional government for China.[44]

With the death of the Empress Dowager on 15 November 1908, a day after the death of the emperor, who was suspected of being poisoned, political change continued. In 1909, the idea of constitutional government became a reality with the convening of Provincial Assemblies, whose members were elected by a limited suffrage of

44. Ibid., 135–6.

scholars and landowners. These became a focus of opposition to the central government. In February 1910, delegates from these assemblies demanded that a national assembly be convened. An undertaking was given that a parliament would be in place by 1913. In the meantime, in April 1911, a 'cabinet of princes' was created as a first step towards 'a cabinet parliamentary system'.[45]

The rail network in China was sparse, foreign owned and operated. They were not significantly economical, but grew in importance for the opposition they attracted from the Chinese, arising largely from popular superstition and xenophobia generated during the Boxer Rising. The central and local governments tried to assert greater control over the railways. New financial agreements between the European powers and China included a deal over financing them. Following an Imperial Court edict in May 1911, the nationalisation of all the main railway lines was promulgated. Opposition to this decree came not only from commercial interests, but also from nationalistic and anti-Manchus.

Xenophobia was rife in China. In 1905, the Chinese Chamber of Commerce called for a boycott of American goods and other business organisations in Shanghai. The *Tatsu maru* incident of 1908 resulted in demands to boycott Japanese goods. The incident concerned a Japanese ship, the *Tatsu maru*, believed to be smuggling weapons into China on behalf of the revolutionary organisation, the *Tongmenghui*.[46]

The Boxers did not disappear after the main action in Beijing. It was reported that the Boxers were still causing trouble around Shanghai in 1906, and when the French consul complained to the Chinese government, Prince Jing promised to take action against the bandits. The leaders were later subdued and calm resulted, but a strong movement to rid China of foreigners remained.[47]

At the same time, there was a report from the French navy reporting Christians killed and residences destroyed at Ou-Yan. The Jesuit Peter Lémour, minister at Anqing, said that the troubles came from local Boxers who still proclaimed that the foreigners were the cause of all troubles in China, and that they humiliated the people. The

---

45. Ibid., 137–8.
46. Ibid., 138–9.
47. Prince Jing to Chargé d'Affaires, Beijing, 14 May 1906, DAC.

mandarins lost face with the demands of the foreign consuls, and the English still gave the Chinese opium. They believed that the Chinese hated the foreigners, and especially the soldiers. It was suggested that the Europeans ought to keep the laws of the empire.[48]

The modernisation of government structures facilitated negotiations with the foreign powers, but growing foreign influence, especially by the Japanese, resulted in growing opposition to all things foreign and the rise of revolutionary movements.

Revolutionary organisations

The earliest influence on the revolutionary movement at the time came from Zou Rong, who had written a popular book, *The Revolutionary Army*, in 1903 on his return to China from Japan, where he had associated with exiled revolutionaries that included members of the Revive China Society. He was arrested in Shanghai and died in 1905. His work was patriotic and anti-Manchu, arguing passionately for a political revolution in China. He attacked the Manchus for their repression of the Chinese population during the seventeenth century, together with current major political figures in government such as Zeng Guofan and Li Hongzhang for accepting appointments under the alien Qing dynasty.

Radical student movements and revolutionary books continued to proliferate. The most significant group was the Revive China Society, established by Sun Yat-sen in Manila in 1894.[49] Sun moved to Honolulu to attract supporters, but with little success. Residence in Hong Kong followed, where he set up headquarters in 1895, with a branch of his party in Guangzhou. An uprising planned for 26 October 1895 failed. More than 70 rebels were arrested, with its leaders executed. Sun fled to Japan.

In Tokyo on 30 January 1905, the Revive China Society and other radical groups merged to form the United League (*Tongmenghui*) under the leadership of Sun Yat-sen. At the time, membership numbered about 400, but increased to 10,000 by 1911. It did not have

---

48. Memo from the French Navy, 1906. DAC.
49. For an account of the life of Sun Yat-sen and his worldview, cf. Peter Barry, MM., 'Sun Yat-sen and Christianity', in *Tripod,* 31/162 (Autumn 201).

a coherent program and was organisationally weak, but in 1912 it became an important part of the Nationalist party, the Guomindang.

After the death of the Dowager Empress, there were a number of unsuccessful insurrections against the Manchu government by revolutionary organisations. The first was on 19 November 1908 when Xiong Chengji led a revolt in Anqing, the provincial capital of Anhui province, and a Jesuit mission centre. A second revolt took place in February 1910 by the New Army in Guangzhou, where an assassination attempt was made against the Manchu regent. A major rising, the Guangzhou Rising, attempted a coup d'état on 27 April 1911, in Huanghuagang. The elite of the Tongmenghui were killed, while others fled to Wuhan, waiting for better days. There were also other riots and upheavals that contributed to a general malaise, and a feeling that revolutionary upheaval was imminent.[50]

Mission reconstruction

After the main suppression of the Boxers, the Jesuit missionaries began rebuilding mission stations, especially in the north.

But it was not just bandits of various kinds that had harassed the missions. Natural disasters also took their toll. At Chongming in October 1906, Jules Le Chevalier blessed a new chapel dedicated to Our Lady of Loreto. It was the occasion of a feast, with four missionaries invited, but the festivities were dampened by the arrival of a typhoon, with flooding in the lower areas of the island and in parts of Hai Men. The blessing went ahead, but on a smaller liturgical scale. The chapel was twice the size of the previous one. Five other chapels were also restored. This was costly, and the usual funds from France were not forthcoming (for reasons the recipient of the letter knew).

In addition, numerous floods raised the price of rice to an exorbitant high. Only Divine providence was expected to help the situation. Rebuilding extended to five new schools to accommodate the increasing number of converts. The most urgent need was teaching the faith to the children. However, Le Chevalier believed that his present troubles were not to be compared with the current persecution of the Catholic Church in France at the time.

---

50. Dillon, op. cit.,140–1.

A final plea for mutual prayers was requested, expressing a strong faith that 'the Father of divine mercies' would come to their aid.[51] This faith of the missionaries was ever evident during times of challenge, be they from natural disasters and the consequences, or having to rebuild after the destruction inflicted upon them by bandits. The strength of this belief was the greatest single factor that sustained the missionaries in their work, and was an important source of their success in conversions.

The reference to the troubles in France at the time was the enactment of the 9 December 1905 law on the separation of Church and State, establishing the secular character of the French state and society, and the programme of *laïcité*. The funding of religious groups by the State ceased. The power and influence of the Church gave way to the charter of the rights of man; church law gave way to the national constitution. Church ceremonies of Baptism, marriage and burials were replaced by the civil registration of births, marriages and deaths. Patriotism and nationalism were emphasised by replacing religious-sounding street names with patriotic names. The Enlightenment ethics of civic virtue and social harmony triumphed over Christian ethics. The result in France was a division between laicists and clericalists, culminating in the development of opposite cultures: on the one side, the predominating secularist culture of the ruling liberal bourgeoisie; and on the other side, the rear-guard, clerical and royalist, later papalistic, counter-culture of a conservative Catholic minority. The Catholic Church began to move into a cultural ghetto,[52] when the government expelled religious orders. This enabled more priests to be sent to the missions. Sixteen new Jesuit missionaries from the Province of France arrived in China between 1905–6.

Having been in China for 15 years, and in spite of terrible struggles, such as the new movements in society, financial problems, and living among people without a 'solid base of conscience and honesty', Eugène Rouxel believed that it was his faith that sustained him.

Reflecting on what was happening in China at the time, he believed that the Japanese had out-smarted the Chinese by endorsing a civilisation that had its origins in Christianity. The Chinese did not know

---

51. Extract of letter from Le Chevalier, Tsong-ming, October 1906, in *Lettres de Jersey*, XXV, unique (1906): 58–9.
52. Hans Küng, *Can we save the Catholic Church?* (UK: Collins, 2013), 169–70.

too much about where they were going, but they were recovering and were becoming more like their neighbours. They were readily imitating them in externals, seeing the distance between the two nations in purely materialistic terms. They embarked on schools, but without discernment, as the students only imagined themselves becoming aware of all the European and Japanese tricks within 15 days. In fact, the students imposed the curriculum on the teachers. The government made the mistake of sending thousands of young Chinese to Japan, where, most of them became anti-dynastic and revolutionary, and the Court, in fear of a revolution, had forbidden their re-entry into China. But despite all, the missionaries took these events calmly. China was in a period of chaos, with the radical movement speeding up their influence.

The task of the missionaries during this more peaceful time was to advance the work in education. Rouxel also happily reported that he had recently baptised nearly 100 adults in a year, but there were other missionaries who had been more successful.[53]

The peaceful time did not last, if it ever existed. There were reports of troubles in Anhui in 1910, with the destruction of the church at Jin-jia-pou, and at Ou-wei-zhou the mission residence was burnt down and the Christians maltreated. The burning of the church came about when the Chinese authorities refused to pay an indemnity for the destruction of another church at Yangliuwan. Was it the action of the Boxers? The French consul took up the issues with the governor of the Province of Anhui.[54]

Disturbances continued in the province. There was a report of the burning of a chapel in the Catholic mission in Jiangsu, with further destruction following. The Jesuit superior, Joseph Verdier, went to Nanjing to claim reparations. The consul opined that the movement was not anti-foreign, as the Christians had not been molested; the attack was simply the action of inhabitants in this area who were 'very turbulent'.[55] This seemed a naïve comment in the light of ongoing disturbances against Christians in the area.

Normal mission life continued despite the interruptions caused by the arrival of bandits of one kind or another. In his annual report

53. Progressive movements, an extract from the letter of Rouxel, Ou-hou, 13 February 1907, in *Lettres de Jersey*, XXV, unique (1906): 59–60.
54. Minister de Margerie to Minister Paris, Shanghai, 11 March 1910. DAC.
55. Consul, Shanghai, to Minister, Beijing, 17 August 1911. DAC.

to Bishop Paris, 1909–10, Henri Chevalier-Chantepie, a missionary since 1904, was pleased to recount that the number of Baptisms in his area had increased, as well as the number of Communions. He put this increase down to the recent visit of the bishop and the graces of the Holy Spirit. In his district of Sui-ning-xian, there were 364 Christian families living in 16 centres. He wrote about the 'great evil' of making Christians from those who wanted material gain from the missionaries. He was generally happy with the schools, and particularly those for the very young children. One problem in these schools was that the children only spent six months of the year in the mission school, and then they returned to the non-Christians schools in their villages, and if the Christians were not numerous in the village, the temptation was not to send the children back to the mission school. In the two schools at Suining, the students were taught English, so that they might gain employment with the railways that were developing in the area. This was a popular move with the people.

The previous two years had been ones of scarcity and poverty, but hope was sustained by an increase of 70 Baptisms over the previous year, and with the catechumenate of 30–40 women and 20–30 men. But there was sadness with the apostasy of one family.[56]

Another report of 1910 from Léon Ferrand in Xiaoxian, also in China since 1904, wrote about the misery of the lives of his Christians during this period of scarcity, and the sadness in seeing some get rid of their children, especially girls, as they were no longer able to feed them. They were sold to wealthy people, or given over 'to vice', presumably prostitution. He was able to save some baptised children, but when the parents came to ask for food that he did not have, he felt so helpless, as he was as poor as they were. It would be wrong to give money because both Christians and non-Christians alike would overwhelm him. He compromised by allowing some baptised widows to remain a few weeks at the catechumenate for women with their small girls too young to be admitted to the school. Another effect of this time of misery was the growth in the number of beggars. They moved south in the hope of finding food or charity. This was a potential source of vice, as they sold their girls for food. The year had been a very hard one, but despite all these difficulties, the faith and fervour

---

56. Chevallier-Chantepie to Bishop Paris, annual report, 1909–1910, Xuzhou East, in *Lettres de Jersey,* XXX/1 (June 1911): 27–9.

of the Christians had not faulted, with the numbers at Sunday Mass pleasing.[57]

Around the same time, Gain from Xuzhou reported that despite the floods, he was delighted with the growth of the mission. Since the first Baptism in the district in 1888 up to 1 July 1910, there had been 38,999 Baptisms, of which 23,118 were adults. During the famine following the floods, the number of Baptisms increased, and there were currently 34,918 catechumens.[58]

Further descriptions of the local scene included that in Guoyang eight out of ten families lived only by makeshift means, mainly begging, with one meal a day of wild herbs, picked up on the wayside. The floods that ruined the fields of wheat, sorghum, peas, millet and potatoes resulted in famine, as well as the inability to pay debts and taxes. Depression set in among the rich and the poor alike, increased by the arrival of very strong typhoons. The people questioned whether they should migrate as they traditionally did in hard times. They lived day by day, and even ate dog or dead bodies. Thieves and brigands were more frequent than ever, terrorising families. Eight captured brigands were crucified and some were beheaded. In the south, the rice fields were passable and rice could be bought if people had any money. The Christians were no worse or better off than anyone else. The mission was not able to feed the thousands of starving people, as there was no food to go around.[59]

Establishment of the republic (1911–1916)

These natural disasters described by the missionaries contributed to the rise of banditry and other revolutionary groups that, while originating locally, taken collectively became a national threat to the Qing government, and ultimately resulted in the formation of a republic.

Various factions within China challenged the Qing government. The desire for a republic became more important than support for a constitutional monarchy, while the long-standing division between the north and the south grew in importance. There were supporters

---

57. Annual report, Ferrand to Bishop Paris, Siao-hien, 1910, in *Lettres de Jersey,* XX/1 (June 1911): 29–30.
58. Gain to Provincial, Xuzhou, 10 October 1910, up supra, 31.
59. Floods and famine in Ing-tcheou-fou, extract from various letters of Joseph Dannic, Kouo-yang, October 1910, *Lettres de Jersey,* up supra, 64–7.

of the Qing dynasty who wanted to retain as much of the old system as possible, and revolutionaries who wanted to change everything. These differences were symbolised in the opposing political views of Yuan Shikai and Sun Yat-sen. The economic underdevelopment of China and the control of China's key resources by foreign interests underlaid these issues.

Eventually Sun was elected provisional president on 29 December 1911, whose duty it was to set up a provisional government to deal with the foreign powers, reunite seceded provinces, and bring back Mongolia and Tibet into the sphere of influence.

Yuan Shikai, already prime minister from 7 November 1911, and head of the Beiyang Army from 27 January 1912, demanded the abdication of the emperor. A provisional parliament was convened on 28 January 1912. On 12 February, the emperor Pu Yi abdicated, Sun stepped down, and Yuan Shikai took power and was declared president on 15 February 1912. After his inauguration as provisional president on 9 April, the National Assembly was transferred to Beijing, which once again became the Chinese capital. This move strengthened Yuan's power in the north, which was controlled by his army, and weakened the power base of southern parties.

Under a new system of parliament, the number of political groupings increased. The Tongmenghui was transformed from an underground secret society into an open political party. In alliance with other groups, a coalition was formed called the National People's Party, under the inspiration of Song Jiaoren. The Guomindang that emerged from this grouping became the largest political alliance in the first parliament. It stood for the unification of China, the development of local government, the abolition of racial discrimination, improvement in the standard of living, and the maintenance of national peace. With many political groups, the government was far from stable to establish solid government. Yuan Shikai alone with his military strength dominated.

Song Jiaoren worked hard to strengthen the power of the Guomindang, and in the first parliament it commanded a majority among the parties with 360 seats. His actions were not acceptable to the military elite, and he was assassinated at the railway station in Shanghai. Those involved in his death eventually came to a violent death, while Yuan Shikai, being fearful of the rise of the Guomindang, could not be completely cleared of his implication in the assassination.

Yuan continued to work against provincial governors who supported the Guomindang. Military forces associated with the Guomindang retaliated, deposing the military governor of Jiangsu, Li Leijun, and declared war on Yuan in July 1912. The Provinces of Anhui, Jiangxi, Guangdong and Hunan declared their independence from Yuan's government. The troops of Yuan reacted by retaking Nanjing, and suppressed the uprising that was called the Second Revolution. Sun fled to Japan in August 1913 in fear of his life, together with many Guomindang supporters. These regrouped forming the Chinese Revolutionary Party in July 1914, with political allegiance to Sun.

Opposition to Yuan continued within China. On 13 October 1913, Yuan instructed the arrest of members of the provisional assembly in Jiangxi who had supported the military against him, and on 4 November he dissolved the Guomindang, and so the Assembly was unable to meet because of an insufficient quorum. Yuan went further to dismiss all representatives in the provincial assembly who were also members of the Guomindang. Then he replaced the National assembly with a Political Conference, a group completely under his control, meeting for the first time on 15 December 1913. A new constitution was inaugurated; with the term of office of the president lengthened to ten years, after which he could be re-elected. Yuan had established himself as a military dictator for life.

During World War I, Yuan Shikai declared Chinese neutrality on 6 August 1914. On 15 August, Japan issued an ultimatum to Germany to withdraw her naval fleet from Japanese and Chinese waters, and to hand over to Japan its lease on the territory of Jiaozhou. Britain accepted this move. Japan declared war on Germany on 23 August 1914, and moved its troops into Shandong, occupying Qingdao on 7 November.

On 18 January 1915, Japan presented China with Twenty-One Demands, which would, if accepted, cede to Japan control over key areas of the Chinese economy and government. China would become a 'partial colony' of Japan. Yuan accepted the majority of these humiliating demands, because it was suggested that Japan supported his move to become emperor, which in fact did not occur because of mounting opposition. He died on 6 June 1916. The era of the warlords shortly followed.[60]

---

60. Dillon, ut supra, pp. 145–58.

Yuan's rise to power increased the tension between his government in the north and the Guomindang in the south. It also facilitated further encroachments of Japan into China, and the anxiety about this by European powers. The missionaries watched these developments as the various waring parties invaded mission domains, with particular anxiety about the 'Communists' from the south. Increased Western interference in Chinese affairs followed, not the least to protect the missionaries.

Chapter 4
The Jesuit Mission 1912–1921
Aftermath of the Republic

Immediately after the proclamation of the republic, letters from the Jesuit missionaries indicated that social life within the mission was generally more settled than in previous years, but they were also aware that this situation would not last given the philosophical differences between the two main waring parties struggling for power in China, together with the random attacks from bandits.

Paul de Geloës reported in 1912 that after a previously difficult year, the current one was more joyful because the harvest was the best in 40 years. The farmers had sold their crop, and they even thought of buying back their wives and girls!

Moreover, the republic was established peacefully, but not without challenges. There were mixed results: the government did not have enough money, and too many soldiers had not been paid, which resulted in brigandage. But Catholicism was approved and respected, and superstitious cults were abolished. Pagodas were to become justice tribunals. All their 'pit-bellied men, their small imps in copper and bronze' disappeared with amazing speed, with magistrates no longer obliged to attend sacrifices.

A former Chinese student in Berlin wrote to Auguste Haouisée on 22 August 1912, giving his assessment of what was needed for a future China. He believed that a monarchy was best for China, but wondered who should rule. Hope needed to be sustained in the midst of the existing critical situation. Under the Manchu dynasty, China had been sick, eventually becoming fatal. But after the revolution, China underwent a violent illness, which could cause death, but had the chance to heal itself. The sadder question was not the development of the political regime, but the lack of will and the dedication of the Chinese people. Certainly a religious spirit would be a great remedy, but how was this to be communicated to the Chinese? It would be a great task, taking several centuries. Now that the philosophical positivists were in vogue, the Christian doctrine was a much better 'hypothesis'. He hoped that the work of the missionaries would prosper rapidly, and exhorted the missionaries to work more with the lower classes, as most Chinese Christians had no faith in religion: they were Christians for some material benefit. He wanted the missionaries to give the Chinese more 'metaphysics' than 'miracles'. The Christian religion had no need for miracles, which were taken as mythology. Philosophical considerations would be sufficient to indicate the truth. This would give respect for the faith.[1] Such suggestions might have appealed to some educated Chinese, but would not be widely understood by the lower classes.

Eugène Beaucé made further comments on the existing situation in December, writing that young China had nothing for Europe to envy. Much confusion of ideas existed. He was not keen on the ex-president Sun Yat-sen, who offered China 'socialism, communism and evolution'. In quoting Darwin, Sun spoke of China less in terms of militarism, and more of humanity and justice. He appealed to his young listeners with the great principles of democracy, socialism and fraternity. He understood the defence of justice and humanitarianism, but not the barbaric effects of militarism. With these ideas communicated to the future leaders of China, what would eventuate?

The writing of the Rev. G.H. Fitch in *The Chinese Recorder*, December 1912, page 721, further distressed Beaucé where Fitch recounted the visit of a Chinese gentleman who innocently gave him some articles. They were nothing less than an approval of socialism by the abolition of the family, calling for a union of socialists in China with those in Europe, and proposing a new religion which was to be a mixture of Buddhism, Confucianism, Daoism, Christianity and Islam.

However, Mr Parker in the *Asiatic Quarterly Review* expressed less pessimistic about the future of China, hoping that the government would respect religious liberty. He respected Yuan Shikai, who he believed knew how to act and act rapidly. He called the new republic a 'government by telegraph', with decrees, decisions, and orders of the

---

1. 'The young China', letter of Fr. de Geloës, Se-Tcheou-fou, 5 September 1912, in *Lettres de Jersey,* XXII/1 (June 1913): 31–2.

president to the different provinces in the government gazette, which Parker called 'parliamentary'! Parker believed that this time provided an 'excellent opportunity' for the missionaries in the whole country, and for every sect.

Furthermore, Parker approved that the Chinese were given works of charity, care of the sick, education of the young, the teaching of science and the struggle against opium. However, it would be an error to rely upon 'empty dogmas', to renew old rivalries between Catholics and Protestants, to take in worthless Christians, to interfere in legislation and administration, to re-learn the 'political-spiritual' faults of the Jesuits and Dominicans of two centuries ago, or to run the pope or the Anglican Church as a political party. The Chinese were quite as capable as foreigners to freely develop their own form of Christianity.[2] In reporting these views, Beaucé indicated his concern that even the different Christian Communions struggled for agreement on essentials for the path forward.

Meanwhile, some areas of the mission reported attacks from brigands, such as in Xuzhou in October 1912: hundreds of brigands arrived both from the east as well as the west. As the defences were very good, the peasants were able to respond by organising and fortifying themselves in the larger villages.

At Peixian and Wutan mission houses and chapels were burnt and turned upside down. Republican soldiers were responsible for shooting many people, burning their villages, taking away their wives and girls, as well as their cattle, and removing anything else that could be taken away as booty. Two resident priests, Henry Frenken and Zen, left for Shanghai.[3] Not even government soldiers could be trusted.

The missions experienced attacks from a variety of brigands, and Joseph Dannic, from Guoyang, gave a more detailed account of the types of brigands that the missionaries experienced. As the occasion arose, he believed that everyone at Guoyang was more or less a thief. During the troubles of the last year, such was the mentality of these people that to be called a thief or brigand did not tarnish the reputation of the people. There was no disgrace to be called a thief and punished.

---

2. Letter of Paul Beaucé, 16 December 1912, ibid., 32–4.
3. Across Jiangsu. Brigands in Xuzhou. Extracts from *Nouvelles de Chine* (8 October 1912), in *Lettres de Jersey*, ibid., 36–9.

He distinguished three kinds of brigands: brigands properly so called, the regular soldiers, and the 'satellites' of the mandarins.

The first group of brigands were those who, in bad years, were mainly those who were starving from extreme necessity. Also, there were many soldiers who had European guns. There were 100 bandits in this region, a dozen runaway soldiers, and 90 other rogues with primitive weapons, lances, knives, sabres and, above all, torches and matches to set fires. Sometimes they seized venerable old men and held them for ransom. Most of the time, families paid the bandits something as an insurance against fire. One night, the bandits set fire to stacks of straw and nearly all the peasants fled, leaving their belongings to the brigands. They took money, grain, clothing and animals, and sometimes burnt the houses. Some peasants took up arms against the bandits and were killed, while others fortified their villages with walls, retiring each evening behind the walls with their families. Sometimes these villages were attacked for some weeks by the brigands. If they could not defend themselves, they sent some money to the bandits as a peace offering. Frequently, the brigands employed tactics to deceive the villages.

The second group lived in the village, and were paid and recognised by the republic. There were four to five hundred in Guoyang armed with rifles of every kind. Since the fall of the emperor there was no longer any real authority, with no idea of patriotism. It was believed that the Europeans were intent on taking over China. Meanwhile, these bandits drank, eat, played for money and amused themselves with the girls – 'that was their ideal'. They understood only one thing: the government ought to pay them better, without which they would compensate themselves from the villagers. When the soldiers arrived, the brigands were gone with their riches. The soldiers then fleeced the poor. They accused the owners of being in league with the brigands, and they, in turn, pillaged in the same way as the genuine brigands. They were feared more than the first group.

The third group were essentially a Chinese institution, not Manchu. They were also trouble-makers. They were not soldiers, but 'torturers, rural policemen, or wardens'. There was not an honest man among the satellites. They were considered a vile, low caste. They were the ears, eyes and hands of the mandarins, outside the law. When the mandarin was short of money, he went to war with the satellites precisely in the direction where there were no real brigands. The satellites told him where to find the rich villages: he trumped up a charge, and the satellites took whatever they wanted: clothing, money, animals, and sometimes a wife. There was not a month that the local prefect did not sell five women under these conditions. While the brigands and the soldiers contented themselves with pillage, the satellites were more subtle and persecuted their innocent victim, who sometimes lingered in prison for many months undergoing horrible tortures. The previous month, Dannic protested to the mandarin that the satellites had taken a dozen Christian families. The mandarin responded that was the Chinese custom. The brigands were socialists in the sense of the *psai-pang*, 'It is better to be a dog than an honest man'.[4]

The life and influence of Ma Xiangbo

Ma Xiangbo was one of the most significant and influential Chinese Christians of this period for the way he attempted to combine Western learning and Chinese culture. He constantly challenged the foreign missionaries to appreciate better traditional Chinese learning.

His association with the Jesuits began when St Ignatius' College, Xujiahui (Xuhui gongxue), opened with a restricted curriculum in 1850 during a time of famine with about 12 students from peasant families needing care. Later, there were more flexible programs catering for all levels of learning, even providing for entrance into the Civil Service Examination. Non-Catholics were included among the students.

Ma Xiangbo was one of the earliest and the most notable Chinese students, who began at the college from the age of 11. He was born in Dantu, Jiangsu province in 1840, into a traditional family of scholars, and eventually learned seven languages: Latin, Greek, French, English, Italian, German and Japanese. Even while being educated by the Jesuits in a Western environment, Ma was always essentially Chinese, showing an attitude similar to the scholar gentry of the late Qing, but his patriotism did not extend to the emperor. One of the early aims of St Ignatius' College was to teach sufficient French to the Chinese students so that they might become interpreters for the French consulate in Shanghai, helping them in diplomacy and commerce. Ma

4. Three kinds of brigands. Letter of Dannic, Kou-yang, 8 November 1912, in *Lettres de Jersey*, ibid, 49–53.

refused to use his French for this purpose, and was very critical of the attitude of the French Jesuits who showed discrimination against Chinese students. While at Xujiahui, Ma became friends with two Italian Jesuits, Angelo Zottoli and Francesco Adinolfi, but with no other Jesuit. Zottoli was principal of St Ignatius' in 1852, and their friendship was based on a mutual respect for each other's culture. The French Jesuits thought the Italian priests set up the Chinese students for disagreements with the French. Tension between the two Jesuit nationals grew.

Presumably because of the influence of Zottoli, Ma entered the novitiate of the Society of Jesus on 29 March 1862, and was ordained in 1869. His seminary training was in both Chinese and Western learning, but he was influenced especially by the Jesuit Matteo Ricci's explanation of the 'True Meaning of the Lord of Heaven'. During his life in the seminary, he experienced constant tensions between his perception of Chinese society and culture as opposed to that of the West, as well as the differences between the Chinese and foreign missionaries.

He was so capable that he was appointed principal of St Ignatius' College where he emphasised Chinese studies, in contrast to the French Jesuits, who, while including Chinese in the curriculum, gave emphasis to traditional Western Jesuit education. This did not please his French superiors, so Ma was removed from this post as principal and moved into astronomical studies in 1875, which did not please him. This was a time when nationalism was on the rise in China, especially among the gentry, which included Ma's family. Ma had no desire to be 'a French Jesuit', and seeing that they did not treat the Chinese Jesuits equally, he finally left the Jesuits, 15 August 1876, believing that his talents could be better exercised for the benefit of China outside the Society of Jesus. The French missionaries were not distressed with Ma's decision, believing that he was anti-foreign, and also 'anti' any social inequalities in his own country. It was true that he always sympathised with the lowest strata of society seeing the hardships they endured.

Ma resented the foreign missionaries biases against Chinese Catholics, especially their ignorance of Chinese culture. This lead him, in conjunction with Ying Lianzhi and Chen Yuan, in revising and reprinting the seventeenth and eighteenth centuries works of Matteo Ricci and Adam Schall. In doing this, he was casting critical light on the contemporary foreign missionaries. Ma blamed the rising anti-Christian sentiment among the Chinese people on the foreign missionaries who relied so much on the foreign secular power. Furthermore, he was critical of the foreign bishops who used absolute power, the educators who did not promote scientific studies, and the missionaries who seemed incapable to respond to the anti-religion movement. He saw the Chinese priest as a lackey of foreign missionaries, who had no 'voice' in the running of the mission. He disliked the way foreign missionaries were excessively critical of the Chinese people and their officials in their letters to Europe. He believed that only one or two out of ten missionaries were able to speak Chinese, and only a few Chinese priests could write ordinary Chinese. Hence, there was little communication possible among them. Foreign missionaries needed to learn the Chinese language and communicate in it to avoid misunderstanding and mistrust. These views were supported both by the Jesuit curia and the popes in Rome. Furthermore, he was critical that the local bishop was rarely seen, so that the Church made little impact upon society, while anti-religious activists had become extremely popular. Anti-religionists adapted themselves better to contemporary society, working with the government, attracting new members, founding schools and promoting modern science.

After leaving the Jesuits, he joined a Chinese embassy to Japan in 1881, and another mission to Korea in 1882.

Between 1914–18, Ma expressed his views of wanting a Chinese church. He asked that foreign missionaries who wanted to work in China renounce their government of origin, get Chinese citizenship, and have a working knowledge of the Chinese language and schools of learning. This proposal led to the subsequent slogan of the 'Three Self Movement': self-administration, self-financing, and self-propaganda among Chinese Catholics. He saw the foreign missionaries as 'basing their work on national power', rather than on the Ricci method, which he strongly endorsed, as the basis of the Catholic tradition in China.

After his wife died, Ma returned to Xujiahui in 1898, and took up work as an interpreter. He continued to advocate that the Church should adapt itself more to Chinese culture, and communicate the message in the Chinese way. In the early twentieth century, Ma was still unhappy with the way the French Jesuits held onto power, he found that they did not even trust the Chinese translators in understanding French.

Despite these tensions in his relationship with the Jesuits, Ma founded Aurora Academy (Zhendan xueyuan) at the site of the old Jesuit observatory of Xujiahui on 28 February 1903. The initial enrolment was 24 students. The academy specialised in the translation of Western books necessary for the modernisation of China, and in the development of textbooks in the sciences and liberal arts. A two-year curriculum was offered with students required to study Latin and specialise in one European language – French, English, German or Italian. They were also given the option to study the liberal arts (philosophy, geography, politics, sociology, economics and international law) or sciences (physics, chemistry, mathematics, astronomy and the natural sciences). Within this framework, the traditional Confucian way of learning (master-disciple) was preserved, and on Sundays public debates were held, a long-established practice of Jesuit education.

In September 1904, François Perrin, a Jesuit from Anhui, took over the direction of the studies, as the French Jesuits became uneasy with Ma's leadership. In August 1905, Ma resigned as president of the academy and joined 128 students who voted against the changes introduced by the Jesuits. They opened a new school, which they called Fudan gongxue, later Fudan University.

Meanwhile, the Jesuits reorganised the Zhendan academy, and developed it into a full-fledged school of higher education, with initially a two or three-year course of studies, and finally a four-year curriculum in liberal arts and sciences. By 1906, 172 students had enrolled. A five-year medical course was introduced in 1912.

In 1917, the name Zhendan Academy was changed to Zhendan daxueyuan and in 1930 to Zhendan daxue (Aurora University). In 1932, the university's four faculties of law, literature and arts, science and engineering, and medicine, were registered with the government. In the same year, a Chinese president was appointed, Hu Wenjao (1932–52), following various Jesuits since 1905. In 1934, 113 students from 22 different countries were enrolled.[5]

Despite the dominant French atmosphere in the academy after the removal of Ma as principal, the Chinese came to respect the academy for its academic performance, and showed the Chinese that the Jesuits valued tertiary education.

---

5. Patrick Taveirne, CICM, 'Catholic Higher Education in China', in *Tripod*, 26/142 (Autumn 2006).

However, despite religion being an obvious part of the culture of the institution, the Jesuits were disappointed that only a few converts resulted each year.

In 1919, when asked for his views on the missionary church, Ma expressed hope that Catholic missionaries would adapt more to Chinese culture, learn from the Protestants who got on well with modern society, establish links with official Chinese circles, set up schools and teach science. He wanted Chinese and foreign priests to have equal rights, the Chinese language promoted, and the standard of education in both Chinese and Western studies raised.

Meanwhile, he became secretary to Li Hongzhang during the 'Hundred Days' and the 1911 revolution.

Ma was critical with the administrative structure of the Catholic missions that were divided up among the religious orders, with Church affairs governed by each Order, and decision-making frequently made outside China. Every nation put the needs of its own citizens first, and gave them administrative positions in each vicariate. The Chinese Catholic Church was not in the hands of the Chinese people. Furthermore, there was at this time no overall missionary planning, with each religious order administrating its own affairs: so the efficiency of evangelisation was compromised.

The Vatican, agreeing with much of Ma's assessment of the missions, expressed dissatisfaction with the way the foreign missionaries operated in China in a papal letter, *Maximum Illud,* in 1919. The pope expressed his desire that the Chinese people run their own church. The response of the bishops to this papal request was cool; the letter was uncirculated. However, the Bishop of Jiangchang in Sichuan, Jean-Baptiste de Guebriant (1860–1935)[6] gave such an enthusiastic response that the pope appointed him papal visitor of the Catholic missions in 1922. His recommendations endorsed the promotion of a Chinese Church, and so the pope set in motion his desire to send a permanent Vatican representative to China. After discussions with

---

6. **Jean-Baptiste Budes de Guébriant MEP** was born in Paris, and joined the Paris Foreign Mission Society in 1883. He was ordained priest in 1885, and sent to China. In 1910 he was appointed vicar apostolic of Xichang, Szechwan Province, and then moved to Guangzhou in 1916. After his election as superior general of his Order in 1921, he implemented a policy of handing over the missions he administered to the local church once they were established. He rejoiced greatly at the appointment of the first six Chinese bishops in 1926. He died in Paris in 1935.

the Chinese government, the pope appointed Archbishop Costantini apostolic delegate, with the aim of trying to disestablish the missionaries from the protection of the French legation. Ma was happy with this letter, and translated *Maximum Illud* into Chinese for its dissemination.[7]

Commenting on events after the establishment of the republic, Ma saw the anti-Christian movement of the 1920s in China, not as one arising from an ignorant mob like the Boxers, but rather as one from the cultural elite of China, while the anti-religion movement was seen as a continuation of the May Fourth Movement.[8] Warlords were backed by foreign powers. Ma continued to promote the idea that China's successful resistance against foreign aggression depended upon national solidarity, self-improvement, the guarantee of human rights and democracy, as well as the abolition of totalitarianism.

Following the 18 September 1931 clash between China and Japan, Ma urged the Chinese to cease the civil war and unite against the Japanese invasion. In 1935 he wrote the 'Declaration of the Shanghai Culture Rescue Movement' with Sheng Junyu and Zuo Taobei. He was executive officer of the United China Rescue Association in 1936 with Song Quingling and He Xiangying, and in January 1937 he was appointed a councillor to the National Government in Nanjing. He died in 1939.[9]

Ma was the most significant Chinese Christian to challenge the foreign missionaries and their missionary approach to the Chinese. He was an insider who experienced the Jesuit system firsthand. While unfortunate that the European missionaries rejected him and many of his ideas, Costantini and the Vatican supported his ideas in their quest for an independent Chinese Church. It would be this vision that ultimately succeeded.

---

7. William Hanbury-Tenison (trans), *The Memoirs of Jin Luxian*, Vol. 1: Learning and Relearning, 1916–1982 (Hong Kong: Hong Kong University Press, 2012), 23.
8. The May Fourth Movement, 4 May 1919, occurred when 5,000 students from Peking University demonstrated over the discrimination against China at the Treaty of Versailles. The students stood for modern Western education, challenging China's backward tradition, and Confucianism. The emancipation of women was an aspect of the programme. The movement could be seen as the forerunner of the Chinese Communist Party.
9. Ruth Hayhoe and Yongling Lu (eds), *Ma Xiangbo and the mind of Modern China, 1840–1939* (New York: Sharpe, 1996).

College of St Ignatius' (Xuhui gongxue), Xujiahui, and education

Saint Ignatius' College was probably the most well-known and influential Jesuit institution in the Jiangnan mission. On 28 September 1910, there were 132 students: 68 older Christian students, and 64 younger ones. Of these, there were 35 non-Christians, while 40 studied Latin, 20 French and 61 English. Despite the French orientation of the college, it is significant that by this time Chinese students understood that the English language would better serve their future prospects in Shanghai rather than French, hence the greater number of students studying English.

Also included in the school curriculum was the catechetical program offered to non-Christians. For the year 1910–11, it consisted in the first semester the following topics: the commandments linked to the idea of a legislator, proofs for the existence of God, 'natural prayers', order in the world, 'the egg and the spoon', conscience, revelation, truths to believe, how the bible was composed, the reasonableness of belief, faith and Baptism (of desire). Then they learned about the reasons to believe in God, and his attributes of being all-powerful, good, all-present, unity and the Trinity. And finally, God the creator, conserver; Angels and men, the nature of man: soul, spirit, and immortal. In the second semester, they learned the Creed in the form of the history of religion, and the Old and New Testament.[10] This was a comprehensive program for any Catholic school in Europe at the time. It would be most interesting to know how the Chinese non-Christian students understood these theological concepts. But it must have influenced some, as at this the college expressed pride that they had produced 72 secular priests and 37 Jesuits.

However, all was not perfect at the college, for it was reported that in November 1910, the students were not happy with the standard of teaching in general or, in particular, with the quality of Chinese teaching at St Ignatius College.

Student restlessness, in the exercise of 'liberty' was reported from Foochow College on 21 October 1910. This was perceived to arise from the Japanese books available. Even unions were formed. In response, it was proposed to them that they practise the following virtues: kindness, punctuality, cleanliness, economy, diligence, perseverance, faithfulness, patriotism, honesty and purity. Discipline

---

10. College at Xujiahui, *Ephemerides*, No. 1, 18–25 (September 1910). ARSI.

was necessary. It could only be imagined how the students would have reacted to this spiritual exhortation to conformity to traditional Christian virtues at a time when the Chinese nation was about to explode into civil war.

Student unrest and clash with teachers continued into 1911. Students believed that the education of Chinese students in the missionary schools was inferior. Good teachers, paid well, were needed. The students were exercising a sense of nationalism and free speech. This upset the teachers saying that this attitude led to a 'dissipation and lack of interest in studies, and less hard work'. The teachers were uninterested in nationalism, and many believed it was more than a distraction, but an evil that was to be opposed.

The 1911 revolution had its effect upon the college at Xujiahui. Rebels were at Wuchang on 11 October. Students were interested to hear about the advance of the rebels, while some were with them in spirit: 'Today China rises, as with the Portuguese of old, against the tyranny of the dynasty. Fathers have fear!'[11]

The revolution did approach Xujiahui, as on 3 November, Shanghai gave in to the rebels, but the Jesuits did not tell the students for fear of frightening them. When the students were told the next day, they were over-joyed at the news, but classes continued as usual. The students saw Shanghai as 'liberated from the symbol of servitude' of the queue. In time, each student cut his hair. The non-Christian students became more critical of the discipline of the Jesuit system, but they settled down eventually. In fact, the revolution brought new students.

Obviously the students were full of enthusiasm for the ideas of a new China. In July 1911, at a conference of students in Beijing, they discussed the importance of modern subjects in the curriculum such as evolution of science, sociology, psychology, morality, comparative religion, and the relationship between religions, science and contemporary thought. Education, public hygiene, the problem of communication, and whether to romanise the different Chinese dialects were also discussed. Should classical Chinese be spoken? It was thought the latter was impossible.[12] Education in China was in the melting pot: there was little order, poor teachers, and little uniformity. Much reformation was needed.

---

11. Ut supra, 1911.
12. Ut supra, No. 3, 1 December 1911.

The St Ignatius' students were excited by the changes indicated by the revolution, such as the formation of a new National Assembly, and the election of a president. The prefect of studies at Ignatius' received an invitation from Gilbert Reid on behalf of the International Institute of China to a conference of all those who worked in China and on missions with the purpose of finding common ground to work together for the future of the new China. This indicated the spirit of co-operation that was developing in the field of education.[13]

Overall in China, the number of foreign missionaries in 1912 were 1,836 men, 1,337 women not married, 1,379 married – a total of 4,552. The number of schools were 2,557 primary with 56,732 students, and 1,172 middle schools with 45,801. At St Ignatius' College, there were 289 students with 155 'externals'. In the boarding section, the boys were divided into Christian and non-Christian dormitories, and then into junior and senior. At Xujiahui, there were 285 beds for students.[14]

The curriculum at St Ignatius' took nine years: two years in the preparatory courses, where all learned French, but they didn't study Chinese. They then progressed to the primary section for three years, and secondary for four years. In the first year of secondary all studied French, and in the following years there was a choice between Latin and French. In discussions about which foreign language was the best for the study of European science, English was considered the most important. Chinese was also considered very important.[15] The French missionaries were very slow to acknowledge this.

The Jesuits were continually conscious of the work done by the Protestant missionary, as seen by the number of detailed reports that were made about their work, and the comparison between the two Christian approaches. Quoting a Protestant article comparing Protestant and Catholic schools, it was observed, perhaps with a degree of jealousy, that the Protestant schools were 'built sumptuously, perfectly managed with capable and numerous personnel'. They offered an elite education with the aim to direct their graduates into running the affairs of China. The YMCA was important. In each village, they had four pastors: one for parish services, one to direct the

---

13. Ut supra, No. 4, 1 January 1912.
14. Ut supra, No. 7, 1 May 1912.
15. Ut supra, 1 March 1913.

schools, one for 'scientific propaganda', and one to receive visitors to their well-appointed apartments. On the other hand, the 1,500,000 Catholics were considered 'serious Christians of God and church'. The Protestants believed that some priests claimed that Catholicism was 'the religion of cultivators and people of sadness', and that wanting to evangelise the 'bourgeoisie', they did not succeed. Catholic missions were not as rich as the Protestants who had 7,000 primary schools with 138,000 students, as well as 128 modern schools with 5,000 students. The Protestant ministers were not sympathetic to the idea of a Chinese clergy having official government status as the Catholic clergy did. From 1899 to 1909 the number of Catholics increased two fold. From 1889 to 1906, the number of Protestants increased fourfold, but the number of Catholics were three times larger than the number of Protestants. The Protestants believed that Catholics were incapable of forming a Chinese clergy, whereas the Protestant had a body of Chinese 'leaders' working in the missions. Finally, the Protestants believed that they were optimistic about mission work, whereas the Catholics were pessimistic.[16] Each Christian denomination gave little praise to the other for achievements in evangelisation. Sectarian issues were always present.

Vincent Lebbe (1877–1940)

One of the most influential Catholic missionaries in China during these years was the Lazarist missionary Vincent Lebbe, a man whose opinions about mission methods were controversial and usually challenged by the French Jesuit missionaries and the European vicars apostolic. He was of mixed Flemish and English descent, and joined the Lazarists at 18 years of age. He left Marseilles for Beijing on 10 February 1901, and immediately showed his interest in all things Chinese. He was critical that the missionaries mainly spoke French, a language that the Chinese did not understand, and that in their relationship with the Chinese priests, they only wanted them to be pious and obedient. It was his belief that the Boxers killed missionaries mainly because they were European. When he taught scripture in the seminary in Beijing, he was criticised by the rector of the seminary

16. Ut supra, No. 1, 1 October 1913.

for turning away the seminarians from the spirit of humility by treating them as equals.

It soon became clear to the authorities that Lebbe was not a conformist, and was outspoken on what he perceived as the wrong approach to missionary practice. He told the local bishop of northern Zhili, Stanislas-François Jarlin, that he was concerned that the missionaries were presenting themselves as a race apart from the Chinese people. The bishop did not appreciate this comment, replying that the current Church methods of evangelisation were the experience of centuries, and that Lebbe was not to change it. Lebbe's apprenticeship was to be challenging, as he strongly believed that he should help the Chinese to be themselves.

Lebbe was transferred to Tianjin, but before he left Beijing he approached Jarlin again to comment that he worried that the Chinese did not have the same rights as the Europeans. How could missionaries make Christians of them, and not let them love their own country? Jarlin told him not to worry about such things, and simply work as a priest, hearing Confession, help in the catechumenate, and 'leave the rest alone'.

Despite this advice, Lebbe continued to pursue his own vision in which he strongly believed. He imitated the politeness of the Chinese in their rituals of greetings, opened the door of the priests' house all day, which was usually closed, stopped the 'k'ou t'ou' to priests, spoke the Chinese language, and was accessible to all. He was always on the move, working among the Chinese each day, wearing a blue cotton Chinese garment, modest, and indistinguishable from the Chinese except for his use of a bicycle. This lifestyle did not please the bishop or other missionaries.

Lebbe was heavily involved with Catholic Action in Tianjin, together with his friend Antoine Cotta (1872–1957). They had a 'burning heart and apostolic zeal' in forming the Union of Chinese Catholic Action (UACC). It had its own press and was good at propaganda. Its members became good apostles in promoting Christianity. Lebbe organised a conference for non-Christians: he rented a room, and appointed a catechist to welcome visitors. He gave talks each evening for two hours. All kinds of people attended, and the outcome was considered a great success. Two conversions each day were reported.[17]

Lebbe and Cotta had been influenced by the writing of the French secular priest Léon Joly in 1907, in which he criticised missionary priests for neglect in the formation of an indigenous clergy. Joly outlined the obstacles to this as the need for real collaboration between mission and politics, the inadequate advancement of the Chinese clergy, the failure to create viable independent Christian congregations, and the failure to consecrate Chinese bishops to administer their own vicariates. This writing opened up the debate between Europe and China concerning the future of the Church in China. Jesuits criticised Joly for exaggerations and generalisations.[18]

Tianjin became a separate vicariate on 27 April 1912. Lebbe was appointed president of the Propagation of the Faith and went to Europe essentially to get financial support for the schools, and recruit vocations. While in Louvain, he met Cardinal Mercier who appreciated Lebbe's missionary views, especially regarding the creation of an indigenous clergy with their own bishop.

The Chinese clergy, Lebbe believed, were excellent, but it took up to ten years for them to become a priest. In contrast, the American Protestants had considerable resources, unlike the Catholics, and promoted the idea that they were progressive, whereas the Catholics were seen as reactionary, 'old', 'imperialist'. He thought that the English were hostile to the Republican movement, while the French were more popular because they were 'republican and rationalist'. He praised the Chinese intellectuals for being very reasonable, and who valued education. When they converted to Protestantism, they became more liberal than their pastors. In Northern China, there were ten times more Protestants than Catholics, and they had ten times more resources. Lebbe liked the Chinese, seeing the Chinese

---

17. Ut supra, No. 6, 1 February 1914.

    Antoine Cotta was born in Cairo on 7 January 1872, and went to France in 1891 to join the Congregation of the Mission. He served in Madagascar between 1898 and 1905, and in China from 1906–1919. Being forced out of China by his Lazarist superiors, he went to the United States and joined the Maryknoll Fathers. He died in 1957.

18. Léon Joly, *Le christianisme et l'Extrême-Orient* (Paris: Leithielleux, 1907). Roy G. Tiedemann, 'The Chinese clergy', in *Handbook of Christianity in China*, 2, op.cit., 575–7.

Christians as 'fervent, zealous, faithful and admirably generous'.[19] In
sharing these views, Lebbe challenged the Church establishment.

Back in China after his visit to Europe, Lebbe's superiors praised
his zeal in promoting Catholic Action. He had founded the daily
newspaper *I che pao* in 1915 to further its ideas. He was implaca-
bly opposed to the French Protectorate and became a strong voice
for a truly Chinese church. Superiors feared the consequences of his
actions, and so he was banished to Shaoling in South China, as far
away from Tianjin as possible.

Lebbe now had time to reflect upon missionary methods in general. He identified four, which he summarised as the legal method, the
Spanish method, the method of good works, and the alms method.
All these he considered defective, and proposed a fifth method, that
of love.[20] This was considered a naïve and a highly radical approach
to mission, given the political and social turmoil of China at the time,
which the Church authorities approached best by association with
the French protectorate demanding justice for its missions.

Undeterred by Church opposition, after a retreat in September
1917, Lebbe outlined his philosophy: patriotism for the Chinese,
establishment of a national clergy, and the Chinese Church to be free
of foreign protection. This did not go down well among the European missionaries, nor with the French legation, but the pope, Benedict XV, confirmed these views in 1919, with the promulgation of his
encyclical, *Maximum Illud*.

In 1920, Lebbe went to Paris to work with Chinese students, but he
also went to Rome to see the Prefect of Propaganda, Cardinal van Rossum, and Pope Benedict XV, who was the great promoter of indigenous
churches, with the proposal to appoint Chinese bishops. They agreed,
even allowing Lebbe to suggest suitable candidates. Despite this good
reception, Lebbe was not to return to China in the short term.[21]

---

19. Ut supra, No. 2, 1 November 1913.
20. Cary-Elwes, op. cit., 237.
21. Chanoine J Leclercq, *La Vie du Père Lebbe* (Paris: Tournai, 1964). Subsequent to
    this story, Lebbe returned to China after the appointment of the Chinese bishops in
    1926. Bishop Sun asked him to go to his Hopei diocese, a rural region, centred on
    Kao-kia-chuang. Archbishop Costantini, the newly appointed Apostolic Delegate to
    China, protected Lebbe from the displeasure of traditional European missionaries.
    In 1928, he founded the Brothers of John the Baptist, an Order based on humility,
    poverty and renunciation, and he lived with them, leaving the Lazarists in 1933.

However, in 1927, Lebbe did return to China and worked under a Chinese bishop. He founded two Chinese religious congregations, and was fully involved in the patriotic war of resistance against the Japanese. He was captured in 1940 and died in Chongqing. His legacy was to show the Church the way to become fully Catholic in China, by creating an authentic Chinese Church, and recognising Chinese human and cultural values.[22]

Mission struggles, 1916–1917

The formation of the republic did not bring peace to the country. The northern government military and the southern armies fought each other for dominance, not counting local skirmishes of disgruntled soldiers and impoverished bandits. These continuing disturbances directly affected the missions.

Louis Hermand gave an account of the troubles at Jiangyin in Jiangnan on 22 July 1916. Soldiers gave themselves over to pillage in the town, villages and countryside, wounding and killing a number of people. It lasted for a few days, but not before the locals, who defended well, killed several soldiers. The military leaders made several executions before calm was restored. Gratefully, the churches were not affected.

A few days later, he wrote that 1,500 northern soldiers left Wuxi to fight revolutionary troops from Jiangyin. The soldiers met in a skirmish at Jia Ding, south of Qing Yang, but after a few shots, the 'nordists', the northern army, returned to Wuxi, where they killed an inoffensive Christian citizen near the church. Then, on 25 April, there was another skirmish at Jia Ding where two soldiers were killed. Hermand and his fellow missionaries claimed that they had nothing to fear as they had the French flag flying together with the colours of the mission.[23] Confidence in foreign support was not always a guarantee that the mission would not be attacked, but bandits did generally

---

22. Claude Soetans, 'Apôtre et Chinois: Vincent Lebbe' in Heyndricks, op. cit., 206ff. Other works on the life of Lebbe include: Leopold Levaus, *Le Père Lebbe, Apôtre de la Chine Moderne* (Paris/Brussels, 1948); Albert Sohier, 'Père Vincent Lebbe: Prophet and Missionary', in *Prophets in the Church,* edited by Roger Aubert (New York, 1968), 113–29.
23. The troubles from Kiang-Yng, Letter of Hermand,in *Lettres de Jersey*, nouvelle serie, XXXIV/1 (January 1920):100–3.

leave the mission buildings unharmed, not from respect for the missionaries, but mainly in fear of foreign retribution.

There were stories of mission life 'among the brigands' during July 1917 that, while the brigands did not harm the mission at Dai Tao Lou, they swarmed over the countryside, pillaging and demanding ransoms from the villages. Some villages were so well defended, like that at Fengxian, that the bandits were stopped, but occasionally someone was wounded, and attended to by the priest. But life in the villages continued as usual. The coming and going of bandits/rebel soldiers was an integral part of daily life. Later that year, the villages of Tai-ping and Houxian were pillaged. Sometimes government soldiers engaged them, usually with success, sometimes capturing and decapitating them, sometimes successfully arranging a withdrawal from the village. At Yao-wan, in October, Hermand refused to act as an intermediary between the villagers and the brigands, or between the brigands and the soldiers, so as not to be compromised, but he did ask the rebels not to kill or burn the village. The soldiers of General Zhang-Jin-yao at Gan-zhoang-ba, among whom were a number of Christians, while everyone else wanted them to exterminate the bandits, decided to give them a pardon if they consented to become soldiers. This they accepted: 1,800 of them. At Dai Tao Lou, in November, the rebels came and went, but they never disturbed the Christians or the priest, they only wanted food from the Christians. This care was attributed to that of Divine Providence, and Pierre Ancel would exhort the Christians with the words, 'If you believe in God, he will protect you'. He also used these words to unite the villages in their defences. He had seven or eight villages, a little apart, armed with rifles, well organised in defending the walls of the villages. The missionary gave money to help them. In appreciation, some villagers agreed to send their children to the missionary school. Twenty-four years previously, many of these families were enemies, and now these same families gave their help and money to protect the missionaries. It was to their advantage to do so.

The district of Dai Tao Lou was founded in 1893, with 64 Baptisms; in 1900 there were 87 Baptisms and 2,214 catechumens; in 1903, the district was divided into two, the northern part formed north Fengxian. In 1910, it had 2,340 Baptisms and 1,673 catechumens. In 1915, there was a new division, forming the district of central Fengxian. At the last count there were 1,895 Baptisms. So, in 25 years, after two divisions, the district had nearly two thousand Christians, indicating the growth of the Church in the region. And this occurred despite the continual presence of rebels who opposed the Europeans, despite the anarchy caused by the revolution, and despite bandits who occasionally harassed the countryside. Ancel attributed this growth to the 'hand of God' that attracted the good people, impressed that charity and love triumphed over evil.[24] Spiritual reflections on either the resolution of troubles or the progress of the mission were always given to indicate the motivation of the missionaries, and the faith they had in the active present of God in their evangelisation.

Describing the situation in the region of east Xuzhou and Haizhou in 1917, Hermand wrote about many calamities, some permanent, some occasional. The first concerned the floods that occurred along the vast plain around the Imperial Canal. They wreaked havoc, destroyed the crops, and created famine among the people. Then followed the drought, the ground becoming 'clayey' or sandy. The sun burnt all the crops of wheat, sorghum and millet – everything dried up. Then came the plague of grasshoppers that devoured what grass or crops were left. The farmers worked hard to fend them off, but they were too numerous. Brigands then arrived. The modern ones were formidable, well organised, and better armed than the soldiers, with abundant munitions. They had modern arms, recently manufactured in Japan, Germany, England or America, as well as bugles and trumpets with the French trademark. The regular Chinese soldiers sold the rifles to them. Many of the brigands were soldiers who had deserted, bringing with them arms and munitions. The brigands were well informed as to who had arms when they arrived in a village, and how many rifles were in the houses of the villagers. When they took possession of the village, they expected the people to hand over these weapons and, if they refused, they were harassed, tortured, or taken as hostages. But the brigands in this area were not cruel or violent;

---

24. Letters from, Ancel, Tai-tao-leou, 27 July 1917; Couturier, Fong-hien, 20 July 1917; Michelin, T'ai-p'ing, 8 September 1917; Hermand, Kao-lieou, 11 October 1917; de Geloës, Yenteou-les-palais, 15 October 1917; Hermand, Yao-wan, 16 October 1917; le Biboul, 13 October 1917; Ancel, Tai-tao-leou, 26 November 1917; Hermand, Kao-lieou, 25 November 1917, *Relations de Chine*, VI, 1918–1921, 22–32. Cf also, Louis Hermand, *Les étapes de la Mission du Kiang-nan, 1842–1922*, for a more detailed description of the geography of the region, and the travels of the missionaries, and the results of evangelization.

there were thieves and assassins among them, but also honest men who were down on their fortune, poor and destitute, or were in trouble with their families, and joined the bandits as the best path for the future. The main activity of the bandits was thieving: what food they could find, an animal, a wife or daughter. Some expounded socialist slogans, with 'War on the rich; generosity to the poor'.

The last group that harassed the area were the police. They were a civil or municipal guard, who in the villages, and in the countryside were a type of armed militia to defend the people from the brigands. But in order to do this, they expected the people to pay for the purchase of rifles and munitions to defend the village, in addition to paying a bribe to the leaders to do their job. When the brigands came, the police were useless, telling the people to hide, and then they hosted the brigands with food and tea.[25]

Mission progress

In a report on the work of the missionaries of Jiangsu during the following two years, 1918–19, it was noted that on 4 May 1919, the superior general had separated Anhui and Jiangsu into two regions, with Henri Gilot, vice superior of the former, and Joseph Verdier, the new superior of the latter. Each region was autonomous, but under the authority of the same vicar apostolic.

The number of Christians in Jiangsu increased by 4,172, and of these there was 2,227 ordinary adult Baptisms. There were a further 2,578 Baptisms of adults in danger of death, mainly occurring in the hospitals. While pleased with this result, the increase in numbers was not as good as in the years preceding the revolution of 1911. The main reasons given for this decrease was the lack of security in the region with the continual incursions of the brigands into the villages that were trashed, with hostages taken, and brigands doing whatever they wanted. The so-called ill-fated soldiers of the regular army occupied the villages. They were former government officers and soldiers. During their occupation, the catechumens were frightened to come to the residence of the priest for instruction, and it was impossible for the missionary to visit them. As for the rest of the population, they

---

25. Letter of Hermand, 'In the country of 10,000 calamities', 1917, in *Relatio de Chine*, VI (1918–1921), 168–75.

took refuge in the large-walled villages, sometimes at a distance, following the coming and going of the bandits. They had to abandon their houses, but took with them their children, food, cooking pots, herds, and other personal goods, in order to avoid the requisitions of the bandits, and also the harassment of the soldiers who followed the bandits, taking everything that was left by the bandits. In these circumstances, missionary activity became impossible.

A further cause given for the reduction in the number of catechumens was that during the times of flood, famine and drought, the number of Baptisms was good, the schools were well attended, and the people depended on the charity of the missionaries, but when better times arrived, with good crops and sufficient food, they became more self sufficient, and religious questions were not relevant.

The section of Hai Men, a region where life was hard, with a poor population, reported a respectable number of adult Baptisms, as did the section of Zhengzhou. But it was different among the 'old Christians' near Shanghai, where the conversion of non-Christians was rare. Joy and hope was expressed with 158 adult Baptisms and 2,249 catechumens that year among the 'new Christians' in the section of Songjiang. In a new area of Fengxian, there was hope thanks to the generosity and work of M. Loh-pa-hong and some of his colleagues who each Sunday catechised the non-Christians of good will and prepared them for Baptism, speaking publically on religious questions before a respectful and attentive crowd. Their generosity extended to the building of new schools for the catechumenate in Fengxian.

Pudong also reported a small increase in converts with 52 adult Baptisms during the year, and also along the banks of the Huangpu River. Meanwhile, older Christians were still faithful, with plenty of Communions of devotion. However, in the neighbouring areas around Shanghai, among the Christians who were employed as workers, domestics and small merchants in the town, there were 3,000 adults who did not approach the sacraments. The missionaries believed that this was because of their love of money, the pleasures that were present in communications with Shanghai, and mixing in the non-Christian environment in which they lived. Moreover, the Christians were extremely subject to human respect. In their relations with the non-Christians, far from influencing them towards the Christian religion, they were more influenced by the non-Christians. These people needed special help, but the missionary resources were too stretched already with the foundation of new churches and chapels.

The schools of Jiangsu were very important for the missionaries. They had 224 schools for boys with 9,500 Christian students, and 3,806 non-Christian students. There were also 541 schools for girls, with 9,011 Christian students, and 1,498 non-Christians. The salary of the teachers, 437 males and 711 females, was a heavy strain on missionary finances. In the areas of new Christians, it was difficult for the families to pay school fees. Many of these children boarded and were cared for by the missionary during the school year. Some families paid in kind with food. Overall, there was a great need for more money to finance both the existing and new ventures in the mission. Support from benefactors was much appreciated.[26]

The missionaries were required by Rome, both from Jesuit headquarters and the Holy See, to publish detailed annual statistics of the work of the mission. This covered the personnel on the mission, the missionary districts, the number of Christian communities, the number of Christians and catechumens, and the numbers of those who received the sacraments of Baptism, confirmation, extreme unction, and marriage. As schools were an important work, the number of schools were recorded, as well as the number of Christian and non-Christian students in different categories.

For the year July 1917 to July 1918, statistics were given for the two major provinces: Jiangsu and Anhui. In the former province, details were given for Shanghai and ten sections. From these figures, success or failure was judged.

Jiangsu had 754 Christian communities, 184,974 Christians and 31,432 catechumens. That year, the sacraments were well received, with 2,423 adult Baptisms, as well as many thousands of infants at the point of death. There were 789 schools, teaching 18,405 Christian students and 5,346 non-Christians.

In Anhui, there were greater numbers in every category. The number of Christian communities was 1,188, with 251,242 Christians and 90,495 catechumens. There were 4,821 adult Baptisms. They had 1,461 schools, teaching 23,730 Christian students and 7,865 non-Christians.

Overall comparative statistics for the total mission were given from 1847–1918, which showed extraordinary growth. In 1917–18,

---

26. Le Jiangsu durant l'année apostolique 1918–1919, according to the reports of the missionaries, *Relatio de Chine,* ut supra, 206–10.

there were 200 priests, 1,188 Christian communities, 251,242 Christians, 90,495 catechumens, 7,433 adult Baptisms, and 44,999 Baptisms of non-Christian children. The only decrease from 1912 was in the number of Christian communities.[27]

With constant written communication between the missions and Jesuit headquarters in Rome, the superior general was always kept well informed of issues relating to the missions, and letters from Rome to the missionaries in China usually reflected some concern that Rome had with the administration of the mission. After the ordinary exchange of letters, special decrees were issued when a particular need was perceived to require support from higher superiors to enact change. One of these decrees in 1918, issued by the superior general, Wlodimir Ledóchowski, was on the necessity of studying the Chinese language, a theme continually mentioned in letters from Rome over the decades.

Indigenisation

In this letter of Ledóchowski, he insisted on the serious study of the Chinese language among the Jesuits, as the custom of the Society was to learn the language of the place where they worked. This was important, not only in the exercise of the Jesuit mission, but also so that the missionaries could enter better into the mind of the Chinese, their families, their thought patterns, speaking and writing. Jesuits were required to learn about the Chinese intellectual and moral heritage, and become familiar with the language, institutions, customs, habits, ceremonial and all etiquette of the Chinese. This was the approach of Matteo Ricci, Adam Schall, and many Jesuits in the sixteenth and seventeenth century in China. Furthermore, Jesuits needed to adapt themselves to the needs of the situation: times had changed. Even in what had not changed, methods required changing. The great transition that the Jesuits had in China was the promotion of current scientific knowledge and evangelisation. In accommodating to the Chinese culture and becoming more one with the people, it was possible that the Chinese would become more accessible to the Jesuit philosophy of the natural and Christian law, as well as the doctrines

---

27. Table of works for the apostolic year, July 1917 – July 1918, in *Relatio de Chine*, ut supra, 84.

that were preached. In the schools and university, Jesuits should teach the mathematical sciences, physical and natural, and apply these to 'production'. There should also be a course in medicine. All courses should be taught in the Chinese language, as this would help Jesuits relate better to the Chinese intellectual elite, by showing 'our cordial and intimate engagement, always tempered by reserve and religious discretion, and imbued always by supernatural charity'. This approach would contribute to the Christianising of Chinese society. It would even further the expansion of Christian civilisation in other parts of the world. Finally, the superior general wanted Jesuits to become true Sinologists, especially through publications in special disciplines.[28]

This letter is significant for the reference of the superior general to the missionary methods of earlier Jesuits, such as Ricci, in relating to accommodation to Chinese culture and customs. He wanted the Jesuits to adapt more to the local culture, presumably within the restrictions imposed by the Holy See that forbade acceptance of Chinese rites. He also wanted the Jesuits to share Western scientific knowledge as being in complete agreement with traditional Jesuit missionary practice.

A further letter was received in Jiangnan from the superior general in response to information he had received from some Chinese priests in Zhili when *Maximum Illud* was received in the mission in 1920. These priests complained that the French Jesuits were critical that the encyclical had been ill considered and showed insufficient knowledge of the conditions in China. They were shocked further when superiors had tolerated the reading of an article in *Echo de Chine* that asserted that the pope was rash in promulgating the encyclical. Furthermore, they were aggrieved that they had not been given the opportunity to meet de Guébriant during his visitation of the mission in January 1920.

In response, the superior general encouraged the mission superior to develop a Chinese clergy, secular as well as religious, on an equal footing with the Europeans, and to prepare them for responsible ecclesiastical office. In this statement, he echoed the views of

28. Vlodimir Ledóchowski, The Study of the Chinese language, Zizers, 28 October 1918, in *Lettres de Jersey*, ut supra, 63–9.

Rome and was not supportive of the cool response of the mission to the papal encyclical.[29]

When the vicars apostolic of China met in Shanghai, 15–19 February 1920, issues raised in the encyclical were discussed, as well as other questions of common concern about how to present Christianity to the Chinese while avoiding the suspicion that Christianity was a foreign religion, controlled by the European nations. What associations were organised among the Chinese Christians that they might help convert their compatriots? What was the best method of evangelisation for the catechumens? What fruits could be expected? The bishops compared the Catholic missionary endeavour with that of the Protestants, praising their propaganda and organisation, and looking at the causes of its success, but also wondering how to 'neutralise its evil influence'. They recognised the need to reconsider the administrative divisions within each vicariate, and to plan a general synod for the whole of China. Looking at the Christian communities, they wondered what changes were needed to attract non-Christians. How were the zeal and competence of the missionaries, as well as results of apostolic effort measured? The dedication of the Chinese clergy must be maintained, while at the same time increasing the number of European missionaries. In 1920, 963 Chinese and 1,417 foreign priests served 1,994,483 Catholics in 52 missions. Over the following decade, the numbers of missionaries and Catholics increased.

Further issues raised included how to maintain the spirit of poverty, obedience and hard work among the missionaries who frequently worked in isolation and mixed with the secular world. Missionaries needed to adapt to the customs of the people, to work for the conversion of the non-Christians, to preach themselves, and not rely solely on the catechists and laity. The best missionaries needed identification, European and Chinese, in each vicariate. In the seminaries, zeal was required to recruit talent, and to develop suitable programs and methods, to be approved by the Holy Father, as a means of elevating the culture of the local clergy. It was acknowledged that the Chinese clergy needed to be treated with respect, like the Europeans. According to their capacity, they should be appointed to all positions of authority in the administration of the mission. The schools showed a

---

29. Roy G Tiedemann, 'The Chinese Clergy' in *Handbook of Christianity in China*, 2, op. cit., 580–1.

shortage of special higher studies required for professional training. The question of how to proceed with admitting non-Catholics to the schools and colleges was raised, and financial matters were discussed at length.[30]

This plenary meeting of the vicars apostolic raised many significant issues for the growth of the mission and the indigenisation of the Chinese Church. While reiterating belief in the superiority of European culture, they realised that growth in awareness of important aspects of that culture among the Chinese would only result if they were more conscience of how best to adapt aspects of their culture to the Chinese culture.

Education

In a report on the mission for 1920–1, it was noted that Catholic schools could not provide a comparable salary for teachers compared to the government or Protestant schools: so the quality of missionary teachers was inferior to them. The good teachers left for rival schools or for administration in the railways, where they were given three to four times the salary they were getting in mission schools. Therefore, the reputation of these decreased, with families not sending children to them. However, while the Protestant and non-Christian schools were sending their graduates into the 'revolutionary movement', the more serious families, even non-Christians, not wanting their children to fall into the hands of the young 'bolshevists', were turning toward the missionaries. The number of students at the Jesuit school at Xujiahui and Aurora University was increasing. At Yangzhou, on the Imperial Canal, a village of educated families facilitated the establishment of a French school with 'European sciences' in 1919, which became a preparatory school to Aurora University. It had immediate success with about 40 enrolments from these families who were grateful to the missionaries for a Catholic education. Unfortunately, most secondary and 'superior' teaching in the mission regions, except for Shanghai, was in the hands of non-Christians or Protestants.

Despite so many difficulties, the number of students in the missionary schools increased slightly. The number of Baptisms increased by about 4,000, but the number of catechumens had diminished by

30. Report on a meeting of Vicars Apostolic, 15–19 February 1920. ARSI.

1,000, while the numbers of those receiving the sacraments increased. Xuzhou had the highest increase, followed by Shanghai. This was expected, as these major towns were well supplied with priests who regularly provided the sacraments, whereas in the rural areas, where the priest rarely visited, the strength of faith among the Christians was not as evident. The missionaries expressed pleasure with these statistics, which indicated to them that their missionary work was producing results. A further comment was made that the Chinese in the more settled areas, the 'old Catholics', responded better to the missionaries than did the people in France to their priests at that time.

In outlying parts of Xuzhou, the missionaries expressed concern about the formation of groups of young people into civil guards to assist the regular government soldiers defend the village against the attacks from bandits. It appeared to them that these young men were 'being corrupted with Chinese superstitions' existing among the soldiers, and were abandoning their religious faith. The missionaries had complained about this to the local mandarins, but without much success.

Overall, pleasure was expressed that, despite the current 'state of anarchy' in China, neophytes came to the missionaries in greater numbers in those areas where there were more priests available for evangelisation. There was a final plea for resources to further fund the mission works from the readers of *Relatio de Chine*.[31]

China after Treaty of Versailles, 1919

While the Jesuits' missions continued to grow, despite disruptions around them, there were significant developments on the political front in China that would bring about further challenges to the missionaries in the future. China had entered World War I against Germany and Austria on 14 August 1917, so was admitted as an ally to the peace negotiations at Versailles that ended on 28 June 1919. According to the treaty, all German-owned properties were to be returned to China, except for sections of Shandong that were given to Japan. The Chinese government refused to ratify this latter clause, which was to be cause for future dissention between China and Japan.

---

31. The Apostolic Year in Jiangsu, 1920–1, *Relatio de Chine*, 3, 1922, 13–16.

Japan's Twenty-One Demands in 1915 had earlier aroused Chinese nationalist fervour. But the humiliation that followed the Treaty of Versailles resulted in demonstrations led by students that culminated on 4 May 1919 in Beijing and Shanghai. They objected to the Chinese acceptance of the Japanese demands. Strikes and boycotts followed these demonstrations, which became known as the May Fourth Movement. Sun Yat-sen supported the movement, endorsing its spirit of patriotism. This movement paved the way for the foundation of the Chinese Communist Party in Shanghai in July 1921, and the revival of the Nationalist Guomindang. The growth of the Communist Party became an important social and political reality in Shanghai and elsewhere in China.[32]

Shanghai between 1919–27 was a decade of prosperity. The influence of foreigners grew. In the International Settlements foreigners built their own parks, churches, schools and hospitals. Foreign missions flourished, as did sporting and cultural clubs, charitable organisations, and Western style buildings. Commerce and trade developed. Factories and warehouses were built, and Westerners had their own postal services and newspapers, of which there were a dozen daily and weekly papers in different languages. There were 20 foreign banks. Many Chinese shared in the growth and influence of Western culture in Shanghai, but it also stimulated the growth of Chinese nationalism from 1919 that opposed this Western invasion.

Missionary ministry, 1920–1921

Reporting from Xuzhou in 1920, Joseph Dannic wrote with some degree of pessimism about his work. Six European and five Chinese Jesuit priests worked and socialised well together, but the Chinese secular clergy felt themselves inferior to the Jesuits. This did not contribute to necessary collaboration among the missionaries. This section of the mission had previously flourished for 20 years, but was presently 'in decay'. Very few students or catechumens came to the schools, as they were drawn away for railway employment, or attracted to the government and Protestant schools that gave a practical education. The greatest difficulty Dannic experienced was the evangelisation of women because of the lack of female teachers. Being so far from

---

32. Dillon, op. cit., 175–7.

Shanghai, and different in local customs, language and culture, the district failed to attract female teachers. He was also depressed that his superiors in Shanghai did not appear to give Xuzhou the attention it deserved, with everything centralised in Shanghai, which had flourishing mission works. Smaller neighbouring vicariates with less Christians had a boys' school, or a hospital run by European nuns. Protestant missions were growing in popularity. His section only had five catechists, and only the occasional Extreme Unction (Last Rites) was called for. Moreover, the region was the main area for the bandits, although 1920 was a less troubled year. Relations with the mandarins were courteous, and correct. They administered just treatment, but generally ignored the missionary. Even when great work had been done in the past, as in the time of René Lecointre (1912), who gave everything he had and was very knowledgeable about the Chinese, the results were very mediocre. Nearly all the Christians were labourers: no one was wealthy. Dannic saw this as a bonus, as all the rich Chinese had several wives at once, as was the Chinese custom, which was a stumbling block to becoming a Catholic.[33]

In the eastern part of Xuzhou it was reported that the previous year (1919) brought 'glory to God', because the region had suffered much at the hands of soldiers turned bandits who destroyed villages 'without mercy'. They even captured a local missionary, Henri Chevallier-Chantepie, and imprisoned him for six days, but released him unhurt without the demand for a ransom being paid. He later wrote to the French legation from Souxian about his ordeal, saying that when he was released they kept his administrator who had been captured with him. Although the bandits treated him well, they threatened to kill him if government soldiers attacked. Fortunately, they had held off.[34]

Because of the bandits, Christians were scared to go outdoors in most districts. The catechumenate was rarely visited and the number of adult Baptisms diminished. It became more and more difficult to enrol boys or girls into mission schools so that they might learn the catechism, prayers, and prepare for Confession and Holy Communion. Parents did not trust the missionaries, but some children came to the priests voluntarily. Sadness was registered that many Christians did not have their children baptised, even hiding the children from

---

33. Dannic to General, Xuzhou, 30 November 1920, ARSI.
34. Hermand to Vice Consul, Yaowan, 30 July 1920. DAC.

the missionaries. Girls were educated without Baptism and then married to non-Christians.

Each missionary cared for between 2,000 and 3,000 Christians, a strenuous task considering the vast distances they were called upon to make. Similar sadness was expressed that the region didn't have schools, hospitals, dispensaries or orphanages like Shanghai at the other end of the vicariate. Like Dannic, it was believed that the superiors in Shanghai showed no interest in these local concerns.[35]

The European priests frequently made comments to the superior general about the qualities of the Chinese priests with whom they worked. Opinions differed considerably ranging from high praise to much criticism. In the Xuzhou section of the Xuzhou region, Pierre Bonay commented that the Chinese secular priests did much of the work: they were good workers and had good will, but they lacked sound 'spiritual formation', which generally meant that they did not respond to the local scene the same way as the European missionaries. Bonay was critical of them for not attacking the 'modern spirit' in China. They spoke about 'democracy, emancipation, liberty, equality and human rights with approval, and read the daily Chinese newspaper, which was full of this spirit'. Although there was no direct attack upon religion, discussion of these issues was considered 'a bad influence'. Among the Chinese priests, some seemed to have a 'supernatural spirit', but not many. Some indicated that they were not keen on religious orders, believing that obedience stifled initiative. They came from peasant stock and were 'coarse'. They showed signs of 'haughtiness and arrogance' with the ordinary Christians, and 'a certain obsequiousness' towards the Europeans. They appeared 'arrogant with the civil authorities and the educated Chinese'. Some priests in the region for ten years had never even seen a civil authority, but worked with zeal among the 5,000 Christians committed to their care. Bonay accepted that the Chinese clergy were necessary for the future of the mission, but requested that a better selection of them be made initially.[36] It was extremely difficult for the Western missionaries to come to terms with Chinese nationalism, and they fought against this modern development.

---

35. Hermand to General, East Xuzhou, 6 January 1921. ARSI.
36. Bonay to General, Soutseu (Jiangnan), 24 January 1921. ARSI.

In a report to the superior general from Hai Men, at the other end of Jiangnan, Joseph Ducoux reported that his best news was the arrival of two young Chinese priests in the region, which enabled the missionaries to open up two new districts. There were currently 11 priests in the section: three European and eight Chinese – four Jesuits and seven secular priests. The southern districts were more consoling to work than in the north. Baptised Christians in the area numbered 16,526, with an increase that year of 411. Christmas Day celebrations were successful: the priests travelled to eleven locations registering 3,200 Holy Communions. Christians in this area were poor, simple workers who showed deep faith. With few brigands present, it was a peaceful place for the apostolate to flourish. In the primary school at Hai Men there were 85 students (72 Christians), of whom there were 36 'Latinists', those interested in studying for the priesthood. The section had already given 15 priests, eight of whom were still living, while currently there were two major seminarians. Better students were sent to the school at Xujiahui that had 21 currently enrolled.

The Jesuits were proud of their 16,000 Christians, the result of 100 years working in the area. But did this constitute success? The 411 increases that year came mainly from an increase in births from Christian families. Only 156 adult Baptisms were registered. The people of influence were not converted, and it was a challenge for the missionary to know how to reach them. The Church wanted greater influence in China, but hard working Christians did not have time for anything else: so missionary influence was minimal. The catechists were not valued because they were paid so little, and many catechists were only so in name. A 'catechist' in China should more accurately be called a 'domestic': a Mass server, companion to the priest, a writer. The role required no special zeal; in reality, they were mere employees.

In contrast to this growth in the south, the Jesuits saw the vast northern section of the mission making little progress with conversions, because it was a very non-Christian area. The villagers were particularly superstitious, had plenty of material resources and maintained the traditional Chinese intellectual culture.

Ducoux was critical of the apostolate to the 'higher classes' in the north. There was no connection with the rich, middle classes. At Nantong, a large city, well populated, open to progress, and well organised, the Jesuits left this city to the Protestants who influenced the educated Chinese through their educational establishments. The

Jesuits, outside Shanghai, worked hard in the rural areas 'saving souls', finding plenty of work there to satisfy their zeal, but they did not look elsewhere. The smaller apostolate to the poor was easier to manage. Personal problems such as missionary 'clumsiness', their foreignness, and their imperfect knowledge of the Chinese language and culture also existed. All these factors impeded other alternatives.

He also criticised Jesuit central administration from Shanghai for lacking initiative, treading traditional apostolic paths, preferring a peaceful, uniform apostolate, and rejecting any new initiative as a novelty. There was no confidence shown to those missionaries working in the field. In particular, the customary consultation process among the Jesuits had broken down. The vicar apostolic sought advice from the Jesuit superior alone, and engaged in no wider consultation. He even showed no interest in those missionaries who visited Shanghai. When meetings were held, they usually centred on matters of 'religious perfection', or consultations concerning the appointment of new superiors or about those who were due for final vows in the Jesuits. Most business discussions related to the works in Shanghai, ignoring advice from the 'real mission' in the rural areas. Moreover, the recent papal encyclical, *Maximum Illud*,[37] which was excellent, had no response in the Catholic press. Did superiors have difficulties with it?

---

37. *Maximum Illud*, On the Propagation of the Faith throughout the World, Apostolic Letter of Benedict XV, November 30, 1919. In this letter the pope was critical of superiors of missions who established Catholic enclaves, and who did not reach out to many non-Christians at their doorsteps, nor accept help from others. The true missionary went out to seek helpers from wherever he could. It was only important that 'in every way . . . Christ be proclaimed' (Phil.1–18). This missionary activity was not to be restricted to men, but to women also, who could run schools, orphanages and hospitals. Mission superiors needed 'to secure and train local candidates for the sacred ministry'. The pope believed that the local clergy understood the local people better than the missionary, and had better access to places where a foreign priest would not be tolerated. To achieve this end, the local clergy needed to be well trained and well prepared, equal to that of a European, and not just accept being assistants to foreigners. All clergy must work together as equals, so that the local clergy would one day give spiritual leadership to their people. The pope attacked the notion among some missionaries that they were working as agents of their own country, rather than being ambassadors of Christ. The overall emphasis of the letter was the need to recognize the need to develop the local church. (*Maximum Illud* online)

On a more positive note, joy was expressed with the success of the minor seminary at Hai Men. This section of the mission was seen as fertile for vocations, despite the poverty of the people with its associated difficulties. Fifteen priests had already graduated from the area, while others had been sent to Xujiahui, where the education was exceptionally good. However, at the human level, there were problems for local seminarians in Shanghai with the climate, health, age, and the study of languages, money, and a lack of a 'get-together' environment. Many candidates to the priesthood were lost. If changes were not made at Xujiahui to accommodate these rural candidates, there would be need for a regional seminary, but that would require men and money, which probably inhibited the bishop and Jesuit superior from acting upon the advice.[38]

Meanwhile, the Jesuit superior, Joseph Verdier, was currently preoccupied with problems resulting from the lack of manpower and finance. He was pleased to report that the American Jesuits had agreed to send men to China, and to have them working among the English-speaking Catholics of Shanghai, and at St Francis Xavier College. Furthermore, their presence would bring some American money into the vicariate. But, Verdier still wanted more helpers, suggesting the Salesian Order, the Marists or Canadian Jesuits. He was against the idea of setting up a section with only Chinese priests, as 'their spirit is not good'.[39] This was a continuing attitude of the French Jesuits.

In the Nanjing/Yangzhou section of the vicariate, Jules Crochet had much to communicate. He described his 1,000 Christians as 'not good quality', and of his five missionaries, one Chinese was too ill to even leave his room. Another priest had a 'nervous illness' and could not do much work, another Chinese priest was over 60 years old, so that left two young priests, one Chinese who had just arrived and was finding his feet, and Beaucé, who worked very hard, especially in the French school at Yangzhou. Crochet looked forward to the advent of the Spanish and Italian Jesuits whom he had heard were to take over Anhui. The French had long abandoned the region, which was currently administered by four elderly French priests. The region needed a 'strong and vigorous working'. He was pessimistic that the proposed division of the vicariate would benefit the region, as the

38. Ducoux to General, Hai Men, January 1921. ARSI.
39. Verdier to General, Shanghai, 23 January 1921. ARSI.

secular clergy were too few in numbers. However, he was in favour of Chinese priests working their own region, an idea that was contrary to that of his superior Verdier.

Crochet had been in China for 42 years, and was one of the oldest French missionaries in the vicariate. He believed that the French were too chauvinistic as French, and much too exclusive as Jesuits. They opposed the presence of other missionaries, while leaving 'souls in distress', an attitude recently condemned by the pope in his encyclical. The bishop did not seem to want American missionaries in Shanghai, but they were needed because many English-speaking children went to the Protestant schools or to those run by an English-speaking religious order.

He did not approve that Shanghai should appear to be 'everything in the mission'. In Yangzhou, the third most important section in the province after Nanjing and Xuzhou, there still remained some 'old Catholics'. Also present were about a dozen Protestant missionaries from three different dominations: American Anglicans, Inland Mission and Baptists, with a boarding school for 100 boys, several schools for girls and a hospital. The Chinese did not like the Protestants who had establishments for mixed sexes. This shocked local sensitivities. The Chinese wanted the Jesuits to open separate schools for boys and girls, and to provide a modern education that respected national customs, but there were no missionaries for this work. The introduction of an English-speaking congregation would produce instant success. The Chinese had great admiration for the American Protestants: they opened schools, and founded hospitals and other charitable works. They set up committees for disaster relief in isolated regions, and were perceived as being 'disinterested philanthropic'. Of the 2,000 Catholics in Shanghai, two-thirds spoke English (from the Philippines and Portugal) and they resided in the parish of the Sacred Heart.

The French missionaries saw the American Protestants as different to themselves, with more workers than the Catholics. Considering their numbers, the Catholics could do little more.

Crochet was proud of the new French school at Yangzhou, with Eugène Beaucé in charge, supported by some wealthy Chinese families who valued education, and who wished to send their sons to Aurora University in Shanghai. Teaching was considered the best path for the future of the region, with funds given from France.[40]

---

40. Crochet to General, Kaoyeou, section Yangzhou, 11 February 1921. ARSI.

Crochet, with so many years of experience in China, showed that he had learnt much wisdom in his criticism of the French missionaries, and praise for the educational and social work of the Protestants. He was more aware of the sensitivities of Chinese culture than many of his European confreres, and was more open to the possibility of an independent Chinese vicariate than many others.

Chinese priests

However, while most French missionaries continually criticised the Chinese priests, both Jesuit and secular, who worked with them, Etienne Chevestrier, who worked in Pudong, appreciated the zeal and hard work of the Chinese priests: they fulfilled all obligations, which were often difficult, without fear of fatigue, and despite obstacles created by the language barrier, or from ill will from less fervent Christians. However, he observed that the Christians said that the European priests were more zealous than the Chinese. He accepted that the foreign missionaries faced the difficulty of language, and of understanding the spirit of the Chinese people. It was only after many years that the Europeans adapted appropriately to the Asiatic mentality. They found it hard to deal with the weaknesses of the Chinese character and with non-Christian influences. The Chinese had a very ordinary understanding of morals and character, according to European standards. Moreover, the Europeans had a double superiority over the Chinese: personal authority, and 'a great precision of spirit'. As regards preaching, the Chinese priest was easier to understand, but the European gave better instruction. The Chinese priest had little authority over his compatriots, as there was 'no order among the Chinese'. They did not 'affirm a principle' because it was a law, rather it was their custom to engage in discussion, and then for each to make concessions in order to reach a consensus. Compromise was the result, which did not always please the European priests, because they considered European theology 'the best and true, allowing no compromise'.

There were continual discussions among the European missionaries about the ability of the Chinese priests for administration. The French Jesuits did not believe that they had the ability, and did not want to work under them. Furthermore, there was fear that the Christians would not obey them because they had 'low self image'.

Based on experience, fear was expressed that when an older missionary lived with a younger missionary, after a short time they separated, each taking a different portion of the Christian community in
their district, largely because the older priest did not dare to impose
himself upon his assistant, who made it clear that he did not wish to
follow the directions of the older man. Chevestrier's analysis of the
relative influence of the European and Chinese priests in the mission,
as well as the difficulty each had in relating to the other, highlighted
the continuing challenge the European missionaries had in furthering the aim of establishing a truly independent Chinese Church.

Chevestrier made further comments about a clash of ideas among
the missionaries about how to run schools. His particular concern
was the main school in Pudong. Chevestrier bemoaned that the discipline and moral formation of the students declined after his term as
director. His successor, 1916–17, was a secular priest who was overworked. In 1918, a Jesuit, who also worked hard in the school, succeeded him, but was upset that he could not give the desirable amount
of time needed to run the school appropriately. With much effort, he
stimulated interest in studies, and increased the number of courses,
especially music, art and physical education. Chevestrier, who criticised the amount of money spent on 'these brilliant and noisy useless
subjects', did not appreciate this initiative, as he believed it was simply
an exercise of showing how modern and innovative they were. The
priest in this district said that he could not direct both the school and
the Christian communities, and there were many debts to pay. The
resolution of this crisis was that Chevestrier was sent back to direct
the school that was also experiencing financial difficulties. He agreed
with his predecessor that one missionary should not be asked to run
both the school and the Christian community. His superiors told him
that there were insufficient men available to meet this request, but
that a Chinese priest might be available in the future for work in the
communities.[41] Chevestrier continued to press his case.

Jesuit conference

Records of shared Jesuit reflection on their work are minimal. The
superior at Xujiahui, called one such conference in 1921, where com-

---

41. Chevestrier to General, Pudong, 25 February 1921. ARSI.

monly held ideas were discussed. Missionaries were reminded of the warning of *Propaganda Fide* on 6 January 1920, and of the superior general on 21 December 1920, not to be involved with Chinese secular affairs: be neutral in politics. This was a continuing challenge for the missionaries, who generally did not approve of Chinese nationalist aspirations. Yet, at the same time, they expressed their own pride in being French, and for French dominance in missionary work in the Orient. They rejoiced in the French protection, despite other European countries abandoning it, because they believed that the protection helped the Chinese Christians when they were persecuted. They agreed that the European missionaries should work toward an independent Chinese Catholic Church, and that they would survive eventually without European missionaries. There was acceptance of the idea that European missionaries must work within the spirit of the Chinese constitution, respect good government rules, and be on good terms with the mandarins, avoiding litigation where possible. There should be no threat to the Chinese of foreign intervention, and religion must be set free from French national interests. It was observed that papal instructions might be interpreted as being critical of the methods of the European missionaries, while passing over the methods of the Chinese priests. They reaffirmed that the sole aim of the missionaries was to seek converts and to save souls. Politics must not interfere with this.[42] The French were saying that being French, with French protection, fostered mission development, but that interference in local political debates did not help evangelisation, except when local ideas clashed with Christian principles. That they were working toward an independent Chinese Church was not always apparent, especially to the Chinese, but it was encouraging that they re-admitted the aim.

Chinese Jesuits reflect

Existing correspondence from Chinese sources about mission methods was rare, but one letter in 1921 highlighted the tension that existed between the European missionaries and the local Chinese. Mathias K'ang, a Jesuit scholastic, believed that the prime aim of the

---

42. Conference of Jesuit Superiors during the holidays at Xujiahui, July-August 1921. ARSI.

missionaries was to propagate French culture. He saw that an independent Chinese Church was 'the necessary principle of religion', but to achieve this the mission needed money and men of talent. He was critical of the European 'principles of government', that did not explain how missionaries should relate to the people, nor how to develop the talents and influence of the local Christians. European missionaries were not seen to adequately educate the Chinese priests to become pastors, appointing them only as assistants. Westerners saw the Chinese as inferiors, and there was no apparent indication of any preparation for an independent Chinese Church. However, the Western missionaries were better at handling local difficulties with the mandarins and with Chinese Christians. To improve the situation, the self-image of the Chinese priest needed enhancement. They must promote the love of God and of their country. Lou Ba-pong was a hero to the Chinese for his work for the Church in Shanghai, but Europeans saw him as a 'nuisance of a man'.

There was need to establish a 'Bureau of Studies', which might combine Chinese and European research to look for better ways to reach Chinese upper classes. This could be achieved through books and articles, an idea supported by Paschal d'Elia, but reading journals did not necessarily result in conversions. Personal interaction with the upper classes was essential, but the Europeans were not good at isolating influential people in the Christian communities who might then minister to the influential classes.

The seminarians were the 'solid rock' of the Catholic religion; they needed to be well educated, men of talent who set a good example, practised charity and who were good at preaching. It was better to sacrifice the talents of a dozen men who wrote books, and have them educate the seminarians, as they were the future Chinese missionaries. Administrators also needed to be trained to help enhance the Republic. Unfortunately, the aim of Aurora and the College at Xujiahui was seen to propagate and extend French influence. This was the opposite of what the Chinese wanted. The French were not seen to have a nationalist (Chinese) spirit, and so did not have their best interest at heart.[43] Moreover, there was insufficient trust between the European missionaries and the Chinese priests.[44]

---

43. So-Jen to Fr. P'e, 17 November 1921. ARSI.
44. K'ang to General, 26 May 1921. ARSI.

K'ang had very few supporters among the French Jesuits because of his critical attitude. Some wanted him dismissed from the Society. But he was among the more articulate Chinese priests who were acutely aware of the shortcomings of the European missionaries, as well as accurately observing the tensions between the European and Chinese priests. His suggestions about how to resolve those tensions were not popularly held among the European Jesuits.

Chapter 5
The Division of the Vicariate of Jiangnan, 1922–1924

A new chapter in the history of the Jesuit mission in Jiangnan occurred with the official decree of the superior general in October 1921 separating the two civil Provinces of Jiangsu and Anhui, and establishing a new vicariate apostolic of Anhui, as well as creating a new vicariate of Nanjing, which was previously the vicariate of Jiangsu. Both vicariates would be under the care of the Society of Jesus. This division took place because the large number of Christians in the Jiangnan mission could not be managed adequately.

The general recalled that the Province of France had worked hard since 1842 in developing the vicariate of Jiangnan, praising the great progress that had been achieved thanks to the zeal of the missionaries.

The civil Province of Anhui was divided into three regions under a single vicariate apostolic of Anhui: the region of Wuhu was given to the Jesuit Province of Castile, Anqing to the Province of Léon, and Bengbu to the Province of Turin. Each of these regions would have its own religious superior dependent upon their own provincial, but all would be under the same vicar apostolic, according to Canon Law 295, pertinent to the government of missions. As for the missionaries, the priests of the Province of France who worked in Anhui would remain in the region, together with the Spanish or Italian missionaries who would take over their posts when they arrived. Then the French would return to the mission of Jiangsu, unless another agreement was made between the superiors. The priests of the three provinces assigned to Anhui would work in the section assigned to them by their province, while other priests could remain temporarily with mutual consent.

The properties owned by the Province of France would be given to the new missions, while a visitor from France would supervise this distribution. The decree was enacted, 1 January 1922.[1] In the whole mission of Jiangnan in June 1922, there were 237 Jesuits; 256 had died on the mission; 51 returned to Europe; and 25 left the Society of Jesus.[2]

The Propagation of the Faith in Rome issued some notes regarding the new vicariate of Anhui in 1922. The region in 1853 had about 400 Christians. During the Taiping rebellion (1852–64), the region experienced difficulties, with many poor families from Henan and Hubei migrating to Anhui. Many non-Christians were converted.

In the northern section of the province, Bengbu, the vast plain that was the civil district of Huai-se-dao, there were 360 Christians in the Xuzhou area in 1868, but by 1906 there were five districts, 24 chapels, 1,513 Christians, and 2,256 catechumens.

In the central section, around Anqing, an area of mountains and plains, the number of Christians had grown from 20 Christian communities in 1868 to five districts, 18 Christian communities, 1,089 Christians, and 1,873 catechumens in 1906. There were other areas, including Lou-an, where there were five districts, 17 chapels, 738 Christians, and 1,643 catechumens.

In the southern part, the most distant and mountainous area where Wuhu became the centre of the mission, by 1906 there were five sections, 22 districts, 112 Christian communities, 7,601 Christians, and 5,230 catechumens. At this time, the whole Province of Anhui had been evangelised. From 1906–21 the number of Christians rose from 9,900 to 70,000.

The population of Anhui in 1920 was seventeen-and-a-half million people, while the language of the new vicariate was Mandarin, but in the south, a dialect was also spoken, especially in Huizhou. In the north, around Anqing, conversions were easier, whereas east of Anqing and Wuhu, there was hope for conversions from the indigenous people and from immigrants. The latter were considered good to convert, but the former difficult, because they were 'lazy, untrustworthy and had poor morals'.

---

1. Decree of General, relative to the division of the mission of Jiangnan, 17 October 1921, in *Lettres de Jersey*, XXXVI, new series, T111, (1922): 450–1.
2. Louis Hermand, SJ, *La Mission de Nanking, 1922–1932* (Shanghai, Xujiahui: Imprimerie de la mission, 1923).

There were Protestant churches and houses in all sections of Anhui, where they had large schools and hospitals. They had about 170 missionaries, mostly American.

Primary and secondary Catholic mission schools for boys and girls existed in every area, but there were no 'confraternities' or hospitals. The catechumenate was strong in each district, but no special funds were provided for this work. Each section had an orphanage, which received help from the work of the 'Holy Infants'.

Statistics published for Anhui, 1919–20, were:

	Districts	Communities	Christians	Catechumens
Bengbu	14	132	24,464	22,645
Anqing	18	97	7,412	15,566
Wuhu	26	223	28,972	16,570
Total	58	452	70,848	54,761

The Wuhu Christians were considered good and intelligent. Converts often came in the hope of temporal help, and didn't completely give up their idols. Many were poor and not always able to provide financial help to fray mission expenses. Wuhu became the headquarters of the vicars apostolic because the major Chinese officials were in that town.

Each Christian community had a small chapel with rooms for the priest and catechist; they were poor but suitable. In each district, there was a major residence and church, as well as schools for both boys and girls, and a place for the catechumens. As for the national composition of the missionaries, Italian Jesuits were in the majority in the north (8), while the Spanish were the majority in the other two areas (26), with the French in smaller numbers in each region (14). There was only one Chinese Jesuit, and he was stationed in Bengbu.

The numbers of Chinese secular priests in the region were two in Bengbu, eight in Anqing, and two in Wuhu. There were also four major seminarians for the vicariate studying at Xujiahui, but it was hoped that a local seminary might be established, because the living difficulties at Xujiahui were considered detrimental to health. Girls wanting to be religious were also sent to Xujiahui.[3]

---

3. Relatio de novo Vicariate Anhui, Propaganda Fide, 1922. ARSI.

Missionary social challenges

Meanwhile, in the Nanjing mission, life was challenged, yet again, by famine. Joseph Ducoux, in China since 1901, announced that while 18,000 children of non-Christians had been baptised over the previous four years, many would appear to have been abandoned children. He rejoiced that some of these children who were baptised before dying were 'singing God's praises in Heaven for eternity', but he was saddened that many of these children who were brought to the church came from poor or cruel parents who could not support them. No law existed that prevented parents from killing their children, especially the girls. They suffocated them or threw them on rubbish tips or drowned them. Some were rescued and sent to mission orphanages.

This happened especially in times of famine, when not only children were abandoned, but also the poor sold their animals, utensils, wives and furniture in order to buy several bushels of the indispensable *Lang-ché*. It was considered better to sell human beings rather than to see them die of hunger. The famine was so bad at this time that only two in ten people had enough grain, and in one village of 30–40 people, only one person had sufficient food. The presence of brigands added to the misery of the people.[4]

The missionaries continually expressed concern about infanticide, especially common among the poor. They found it challenging to save these children. In 1921, 6,836 children were received into the orphanages, while others were received into non-Christian establishments. The proportion of those who died was about 75 per cent; the remainder were sick or maladjusted. Missionaries attempted to prevent children from being sold or enslaved or sent into prostitution. Unfaithful or maltreated women were a strong temptation to murder. It was a Chinese custom that after the death of parents, girls were not permitted to offer sacrifice to their ancestors. Around Hankou, it was the custom to raise two boys and one girl, and them to kill the surplus, particularly if they were girls. The method of killing was to drown them in cold water immediately after birth. In recent times, infanticide was extended to boys. The areas most connected with the

---

4. Letters of Ducoux, Grimaldi, Goulet and Hermand, in *Lettres de Jersey,* XXXVI, new series, T111, (1922).

infanticide of girls were along the south coast of China and in the neighbourhood of the great lakes.[5]

A general report of the mission of Jiangsu, 1920–1, was a little more encouraging, despite financial concerns due to inflation. Increasing costs and the poverty of parents with school-aged children hindered growth. The Christians were generally too poor to help the mission; survival was the main concern. Inability to pay the salaries of the teachers in the school resulted in acquiring teachers of inferior ability. Government schools paid three to four times the salary of mission schools.

As a general social ferment of nationalist ideas grew, so did student activism. It was noted that non-Christian schools let their students become involved in 'revolutionary movements', whereas the Christian families generally did not like this and turned to the mission schools for support. Both St Ignatius' College in Xujiahui and Aurora University benefited from this trend.

Except for Shanghai, secondary and tertiary education was in the hands of the non-Christians or the Protestants, but despite this, together with social difficulties, the number of students in mission schools had not diminished, and even increased that year. The number of Baptisms had also increased by 4,000, but the number of catechumens had decreased by 1,000. Students at mission schools responded well to their teachers, while the religious fervour among Christians was good, if indicated by the number of Confessions and Holy Communions. The 'old Christians' were a continual source of consolation to the missionaries who still supported the mission, while groups of Christians in some areas organised armed groups to counteract the activities of the bandits. Unfortunately, superstition still existed among the young people who sometimes fell away from their religious practices.[6]

Other issues raised at this time were continuing complaints about the lack of priests to minister the regions. Reasons given for missionaries not being sent to the villages were that too few were able to speak Mandarin, and that older priests could not cope in the mission stations. Special mention was made about the perception that the Chinese priests were not suitable to hold positions of authority

5. Infanticide in China, *Relatio de Chine*, no. 4 October 1922.
6. The apostolic year, 1920–1921, in Jiangsu, *Relatio de Chine*, 1, January 1922.

in areas where there was troubles with brigands, especially in Gao-liu and Haikou, as they were not as good in dealing with the Chinese authorities as were the Europeans. Pastoral problems included mixed marriages, getting families baptised, encouraging Christian children to attend school or catechism classes, as well as dealing with old non-Christian superstitions. When considering candidates for Baptism, it was important to be 'prudent and hesitate to baptise' until the person was committed. Longer probation and instruction should outweigh the desire to register numbers. Some Chinese needed time and confidence before they made the commitment to become Christians.[7]

Tensions with the Chinese

Rising tensions occurred in the mission especially relating to administration, and concerning relations with the Chinese priests. Analysing the situation in 1922, Gustave Gilbert commented that Jesuit government was 'too centralised, autocratic and inflexible'. Decisions were made without consultation and missionaries were labelled as approved or otherwise. Superiors were too few and distant, and they found it hard to nominate subordinate 'Ministers of Sections'.

However, it was his concern for the Chinese clergy that occupied most of his letter. He saw a rising tide of resentment among the Chinese clergy relative to the Europeans. This emerged in a recent affair at Tianjin between the two groups. He thought that 'the Catholic cause was in peril and the missions compromised', while the spirit of the time was 'disturbing'.

He viewed the Chinese as 'politically volatile, intellectual, and commercial', among whom friends had been made. Missionaries had divergent views about the timing of an autonomous Chinese Church. On the European side, there were supporters of the Chinese clergy, but 'others were not always sincere despite what they said'. Some European missionaries underestimated the Chinese clergy, and this irritated the Chinese. With this attitude, tension would only continue. The Chinese clergy needed 'a solid formation to make up for the race characteristics', and absorb 'the Christian ambiance given by God to European priests'. A Chinese Church required 'men of prudence and supranational disinterestness', but the Chinese soul was 'so

---

7. Hermand to General, Xuzhou, Oriental Yaoway, 1 January 1922. ARSI.

difficult and complex to penetrate'. Despite these deficiencies, Gilbert believed that they had 'many gifts which make them apt to exercise their ministry'.

Finally, he was concerned about the 'angry' Chinese students who came back to China after studying in Europe. They expressed ideas that were contrary to traditional Chinese values, and denigrated the value of religion in society.[8]

Cultural tensions between the European and Chinese missionaries increased during 1922. Verdier alerted the superior general to this when he defended the European missionaries against criticism received from *Propaganda Fide* in December 1920, that the European missionaries were not culturally sensitive to the political and social movements currently alive in China. He acknowledged that some Europeans were not sufficiently discrete in their comments about conflicting Chinese clashes, while some even advocated 'an expansion of the French'. Verdier made no apology for French being taught at St Ignatius', Xujiahui, or for lectures being given in French at Aurora, because 'the university needed the support of the French government for survival'. He believed that without France, 'Catholicism would be reduced in China to several isolated Christian communities'.

Furthermore, he was critical of the attitude of the Chinese priests, who, while seemingly 'unmoved by pressure of patriotism' around them, were critical of the French missionaries for 'political involvement'. This probably meant involving themselves in Chinese affairs. Verdier believed that the tensions between the Chinese and European priests were dangerous. He cited that Chinese priests were quick to notice all that was disadvantageous to foreigners in documents from Rome, while expecting immediate realisation of directions given in favour of the Chinese. They accused the Europeans of disobedience to the 'Holy Father and Fr. General'. The result of this disaffection among the Chinese priests was that they became suspicious, ready to take a different path to the Europeans and disagreeing with them, despite the best intentions and sacrifices of the Europeans. Their attitude was reinforced by the current anti-foreign climate in the wider Chinese society, leaving them open to confuse the distinction between the political and the spiritual in their lives. Furthermore, they endorsed the movement toward greater independence for the Chinese, and

---

8. Gilbert, Notes on the Mission of Jiangnan south, May 1922. ARSI.

supported the move for a new mission region controlled totally by Chinese clergy.

Verdier further criticised the Chinese Jesuits because he did not believe that they would ever 'be completely detached or disinterested'. He saw the Chinese temperament as 'very supple, one that was never fixed'. They were flexible to everything, and remained impenetrable to everything and to everyone. They seemed 'elusive to all spiritual formation'; they accepted it externally, but internally they reverted to their primitive notions of spirituality, showing that the interior had not been penetrated. Life in the novitiate or seminary was a time of waiting, and a time they must go through to arrive at their chosen way of life. Verdier claimed that he admired 'the deep piety of the Chinese, but riches and authority destabilised them'. To their disadvantage, they could not resist the 'disorders of groupings', and listened to 'stupid rumours'. Perpetual adaptation and change became the joy of their existence. They waited patiently for the day of exercising greater liberty, and were not good communicators. Hence, Verdier wanted very strict entry requirements for the Chinese into the Society of Jesus. Novices needed deeper internal formation. In 1920 Verdier accepted into the Jesuit noviciate three scholastics and four brothers; and in 1921, three scholastics. Overall, Verdier was not keen on the Chinese priests, and did not believe that any Chinese Jesuit was fit to be a superior in the Order.[9]

The Mathias K'ang affair

The Chinese Jesuit scholastic, Mathias K'ang, continued to draw criticism from the French Jesuits for his outspoken opinion of them. It began with his letter to a Chinese secular priest in April 1922. He wrote about his 'plans for the progress of religion after independence of the Chinese church'. He wanted Chinese priests as 'Ministers' and European priests as 'Assistants' in the mission sections, claiming support from the superior general. A response from the vicar apostolic of south-east Zhili, Henri Lécroart, and some Europeans, was that 'the Chinese were not up to it'. The vicar told the Chinese that 'it was up to you to prove your ability in the administration of a section'. He was not far from the European opinion about the Chinese priests when

---

9.   Verdier to General, Chinkiang, 23 February 1922. ARSI.

he claimed that to achieve the independence of the Chinese Church, indigenous clergy had to be well prepared and educated; they needed 'virtue and learning'. But he and the Chinese differed as to the means, the latter wanted 'independent teachers who would not restrict us. We need initiative'.[10]

There was a response to this from the French Jesuit, Pierre Bonay, a few months later in a letter to the superior general. He described K'ang as 'difficult', one not having confidence in the superiors in China, and that he betrayed the higher interests of the Chinese Church in his criticism of the French missionaries. His patriotism was 'exasperating'; he had the mind of students in the 'New China', which was considered dangerous to the future of China. These people spent their days in meetings to foment revolt, write pamphlets and stir up trouble in schools, interrupting students, as well as disturbing the general public.

K'ang 'upset the good order and peace of the Society and in the mission. He was a dangerous man'. It was a mistake to think of sending him to France for studies, as his time in Europe would give him time to absorb nationalist ideas that were current at the time, and when he returned he would be a 'sower of discord'. Given the 'sheep like mind of the Chinese, they would follow him'. Even in the seminary, his companions considered him 'an evil spirit, opposed to superiors, very obstinate in his ideas, difficult to guide, giving bad example'. His spiritual and religious formation was considered defective. During an experiment after the study of philosophy at Anqing, 'he did nothing'. Jean Noury treated him with 'excessive goodness in giving him total liberty and no control'. During theology at Xujiahui, he showed 'anti-authority independence'. He continued to smoke, and others were amazed that he did not leave the seminary, but even more surprised that he went to France to join the Society of Jesus. Bonay continued in his criticism that K'ang was 'a malcontent, harsh critic, almost a revolutionary, which hides pride'. But K'ang was not alone with these faults; Bonay believed that 'this duplicity was an innate thing in all the Chinese, it was in their customs, in their blood'. Those Jesuits in the seminary saw this 'all the time'. They said it was a 'delicate matter to form the Chinese in China', it was better to send them to Europe under the guidance of an 'eminent director'.

---

10. K'ang to Pierre Siao, secular priest, 21 April 1922. ARSI.

He objected that K'ang said that French missionaries were only promoting French influence. K'ang did not see the 'supernatural promotion of the gospel in China, and the very humane propagation of French influence'. Bonay was peeved that while in France, K'ang pleased his superiors, as he did with Noury, despite being critical about the French Jesuits' attitude toward the Chinese. Bonay pointed out that K'ang did not value the number of Jesuits who had died from fatigue and sickness while serving the Chinese, without caring for the promotion of French culture. The French, he claimed, worked with great zeal to form a Chinese clergy in order to make the Chinese Church independent, but it would take a long time to realise this ideal. Bonay believed that the Ricci method of evangelisation by inculturation was good for its time, but it was currently out-dated. K'ang was wrong to believe that only the Chinese clergy were right, and that the French missionaries only wanted to expand French influence. The final shot at K'ang was that he believed that the foreigner treated the Chinese contemptuously, 'as if they were negroes'.[11] The Jesuit superior, Verdier, supported the views of Bonay about K'ang.[12]

Bonay and Verdier were very defensive about French missionary methods, and traditional Jesuit formation that they imposed on the Chinese scholastics and seminarians. They showed little understanding of the sensitivities of the Chinese, especially their sense of nationalism, which, ironically, the French claimed vigorously for themselves. K'ang had no intention of being supine in the face of French authoritarian control. Basically he wanted the French Jesuits to understand better Chinese aspirations for their country, and for the Chinese Jesuits to be given respect and understanding, even when their views clashed with the French. He considered it his right to challenge those French traditional attitudes that he believed hindered the growth and development of the Chinese people. French Jesuits did not tolerate dissent. In the light of this criticism, it was amazing that K'ang, the seminarian, was accepted into the Society of Jesus in France.

Maybe these serious disagreements between European and Chinese missionaries prompted the superior general to show concern

---

11. Bonay, Section Minister, to General, 13 June 1922. ARSI.
12. Verdier to General, re K'ang, Shanghai, 7 July 1922. ARSI.

about 'a general malaise in the mission'. Eugène Beaucé[13], rector at Xujiahui, did not seem to be aware of any malaise, but suggested that the idea may have come from Chinese scholastics studying in Ore or Jersey (France), who had been absent for a few years. The only trouble that he could imagine related to the mission superior, Verdier, but he gave no particular details.[14]

Despite this opinion, the superior general thought there might be problems in the mission, and so sent his special advisor, a visitor, to inspect and report on the mission. In his report, the visitor ignored the tensions that were evident in the mission at the time between the Chinese and European, and concentrated on the internal discipline of Jesuit life, which was always paramount in the minds of Jesuit superiors. Exactitude in observance of religious discipline according to the Institute of the Society was always deemed the most important. It was this that gave identity and cohesion to the Order, wherever they were in the world.

The visitor, J. Hoeberechts, Jesuit mission superior in Indonesia from 1923, gave the usual spiritual exhortation to engage 'in conversions and live in charity among themselves'. He did not find disunity among the different nationalities of Jesuits, and praised those at Xujiahui for 'zeal, great piety, and exact discipline'. Superiors should exercise a spiritual leadership, while the spiritual father should give 'points' for meditation to the Jesuit brothers at least once a month. The *crates*, the grill in the confessional between the priest and the penitent were to be used, especially to hear female Confessions. No touching the young or closed door when speaking to them was per-

---

13. **Eugène Beaucé (1878–1962)** was one of eleven children, of which two became Jesuits. He entered the Society on 7 September 1895 at Canterbury. He was assigned to the Jiangnan mission in China in 1903, and with six others arrived on 5 October, and began the study of Chinese. He was ordained in 1908, and from 1910 taught in the college at Xujiahui. After tertianship in Europe in 1912, he returned to China, and engaged in pastoral work in Hai Men. This was followed by an appointment as rector of Xujiahui that included all the works of this compound. In 1929, he succeeded Verdier as superior of the mission. After this term of office, he was made superior of Yangjinbin, residing at the church of St Joseph. He returned to Xujiahui as rector of St Ignatius College, as well as master of novices for twelve years. After leaving China, he because bursar of the mission from Hong Kong. *China Province News*, (November 1987), 30–1. CHPA (China Province Archives, Taipei).

14. Beaucé to General, Xujiahui, 16 July 1922. ARSI.

mitted. Jesuits should always have a Jesuit companion when going outdoors. Visits to 'externs', that is, anyone not a Jesuit, without permission of the superior was forbidden.[15] Superiors were always most solicitous to safe-guard the reputation of the Jesuit and avoid scandal.

Then in a separate letter to the superiors, he suggested that 'spiritual books' should be available in each section of the mission for meditation purposes. The availability of drinks was to be limited to special days, and only poor clothing was to be worn. He took up the long-standing debate about the length of time European missionaries study Chinese, but directed that they have at least one full year to study, 'under a European priest with a Chinese professor'. After initial study, the missionary might be sent to another Jesuit in the districts where theoretical knowledge could be put to practical use. He had obviously heard criticism of the lack of consultation in the mission, and so told superiors to consult with their advisors (consultors) 'on all matters of greater moment or difficulty'.[16]

Notwithstanding this spiritual exhortation and reaffirmation of universal Jesuit discipline and ways of proceeding, the 'K'ang affair' did not disappear. In May 1923, K'ang, then a priest in Europe, wrote a lengthy letter to the superior general strongly outlining his position, and those of most Chinese Jesuits, concerning the problems relating to the European missionaries, and the differing visions for the future of the Chinese Catholic Church.

While the French Jesuits frequently demanded a strong theological formation for the Chinese, the latter complained that the formation they received was 'insufficient'. The French had long claimed that the Chinese lacked a 'spirit of abnegation and sacrifice'; the Chinese suggested that the Europeans should take their own advice in relation to the wishes of the pope about furthering the establishment of a truly Chinese Church. The differences between the Jesuit superiors and the Chinese seminarians frequently resulted in ill will; the Chinese felt that they were treated as 'strangers'. K'ang insisted that he only wanted greater unity among all, according to the wishes of the pope.

He was aware of the great number of foreign missionaries in China: 1,352 in 1921 spread between 13 different congregations of eight larger nationalities. There was no unity or co-ordination between

---

15. Hoeberechts to Mission, Xujiahui, 1 October 1922. ARSI.
16. Hoeberechts to superiors and consultors, Xujiahui, 1 October 1922. ARSI.

these groups. Of the 1,352 missionaries, 690 were French, who were not good at cooperation or providing unity. Many differences arose from the 'concrete and psychological differences' between the groups. The Europeans considered their work 'perfect', with scarcely any possibility of improvement. They did not listen to the Chinese, or if they did listen to suggestions, the result was that they were considered 'malcontents and critical'. A proposition from a Chinese was hardly ever accepted, whereas one from the French was readily considered. As a result, even speaking to one another was rare. The Chinese did not like the arrogance and self-righteousness of the French.

K'ang accepted the European missionary goal that they were not in China to extend the temporal interests of their country, but they should make it clear to the Chinese that they did not equate 'Catholicity with nationality'. He found it ironic, and rightly so, that the Europeans condemned the nationalist aspirations of the Chinese, but extolled those of the French. This was a continuing blind spot among the French missionaries. Because the French had been the main protectors of Catholicism in China, they automatically promoted French culture, and desired to implant something of France into the heart of China. K'ang accepted the view of a Chinese student who, while praising the missionaries, was critical that they controlled everything without thinking they were in an 'autonomous country, even if it was weak'. He did not see that the missionaries came to China for the love of the Chinese.

K'ang rightly questioned what ideas were given to the missionaries about China in Europe before they arrived in China. What did they know about the Chinese and their politics, of their sense of 'inferiority and political humiliations'? The Chinese also judged the Europeans by what they said about the Chinese. He quoted a European priest as saying that the Chinese 'taste was weird, with an atrophied heart, and narrow intelligence', or another priest who claimed that they 'were incapable of anything and so cannot be independent'. Rightly, this did not endear the Europeans to the Chinese. Extraterritoriality was seen as another great obstacle to the missionaries in China, but many European missionaries considered its abolition after the Great War as a great blow.

In south Jiangnan, K'ang was critical that there had been 57 Chinese secular priests, and except for seven or eight, the majority were 'indifferent, cold and cause difficulties to our missionaries'. They were polite, but lacked confidence. From seminary days, they had not had good relations with the European missionaries, and especially with superiors. They had 'insufficient supernatural virtue to see the heroic sacrifices of the missionaries for the salvation of the Chinese'. Some Europeans praised the holiness of particular Chinese priests, but were critical of the faults of others, without seeing their own. He was critical of the opposition to Vincent Lebbe, who was eventually removed from his posts in Shandong for promoting the opinions of the Chinese Catholics, as well as European spiritual and theological formation received by the Chinese seminarians. The academic courses given in Chinese language and culture had little application to the reality of modern-day Chinese culture.

K'ang was prepared to admit that the Chinese needed more 'supernatural abnegation and sacrifice'. Many Chinese Catholics were on good terms with the missionaries, but the more influential and educated were not. Younger Catholics were experiencing more freedom and were less dependent on the missionaries. They wanted to know why Chinese priests were not given more administrative authority within the mission; they were full of ideas, but their expressions of Chinese nationalism were not appreciated by the French, despite the fact that the French were nationalistic themselves for France. Chinese Jesuits studying in France wanted to expel the European Jesuits from the Jesuit schools in China, because they were seen as more interested in France than China. They opposed student interest in Chinese politics, and tried to change new nationalist ideas in China espoused by many Chinese students. As for the non-Christians, they were seen as supporting the students, with many of them in the interior of China 'imbued with rationalism, materialism and agnosticism'. Christianity was considered 'an ally of capitalism and militarism'. Even Protestant missionaries were criticised for not appreciating 'Chinese customs, morals and their character'. Chinese students in America and Europe were particularly critical of missionaries.

Ultimately, K'ang was not confident that there was a solution to improving the relationship between the Chinese priests and the missionaries, as both groups were incomprehensible to each other, 'mysterious and impenetrable'. The Chinese kept their thoughts to themselves. They needed to be encouraged to be more spiritual, while the Europeans should choose the most gifted among the Chinese, and co-operate with them in building up a local Chinese church, and not 'lord it over them' with European ideas.[17]

This was a most significant letter, expressing, with some passion, the position of most of the Chinese priests, and certainly among the more reflective and articulate. They were expressing the thoughts of the exiled Lebbe, the apostolic delegate and even the pope, in trying to get the European missionaries to be more appreciative of the Chinese priests with their ideas and visions for a Chinese Church. Many Europeans did not understand the Chinese, or how to educate them for the new China, or to discover what they could contribute to mission methods. They had fixed European ideas for the formation of the clergy, and ministry among the people, that was universal in the Catholic Church at the time. Adaptation, such as Ricci had done in the sixteenth century, did not concern them but, rather, they imposed a rigid and dogmatic education on the Chinese, requiring of them docility, humility and obedience as the most important virtues for any priests. Creative initiative was never encouraged, even among themselves; that was reserved to superiors, who then told the others what to do. Consultation in the mission was not experienced as a priority in Jesuit ways of proceeding.

There was a postscript about the K'ang Affair in 1924 when K'ang was in Ore Place, France. The rector wrote to Rome that he was concerned about his apostolate among the Chinese. He wore 'lay clothes' when visiting Chinese students, and was told to seek permission for this from the Cardinal of Lyon, which he refused to do. He received Chinese students in the parlour, and it was impossible to control to whom he wrote, or what letters he received. It was also impossible to assign a companion when he went out on visits. He had no other complaints other than these.[18] These comments would have been typical of a rector of the time, always concerned about in-house religious discipline, for which he was responsible and accountable. Such activities of K'ang would not have been acceptable behaviour in any Jesuit house in Europe at the time. K'ang later returned to China and worked in the Italian mission, Bengbu, under Bishop Huarte.

17. Mathias K'ang to General, Hastings, 14 May 1923. ARSI.
18. Letter from Rector of Ore Place re P Mathias K'ang, 1924. ARSI.

Chinese students in Europe

The reported attitudes of Chinese students studying in France that K'ang mixed with were criticised by the European missionaries. M Painle-ve and M Cai Yuan pei, rector of the National University of Peking, had founded the Franco-Chinese Institute in Lyon in 1921. They assisted, at the time, 120 young Chinese students, paid by the French government. There were three categories of students: those from well-off families – considered atheists, who followed courses in Beijing; students of 'sufficient' wealth, who followed courses at professional schools in Beijing, Shanghai and Guangzhou; and those who were less fortunate, having only finished their secondary education. When they returned to China, some did industrial work, but a good number become involved with the law or government ministries.

These students were believed to be 'all democrats', admirers of Rousseau, proud of their nation, and they looked to the West for ideas and status. They were strong patriots, not only for the good of China, but of the whole world: 'internationalism mixed with social-ism, consumerism, anarchism and even bolshevism'. With Russian influence some were 'declared anarchists'. Science was all-important to them, and they denied 'the existence of God, the human soul and the supernatural order'. They were against religion, and anti-Catho-lic, expressing their views in journals. In France and Belgium seven weekly newspapers and two monthly reviews in Chinese were pub-lished, all anti-Catholic. One, in particular, was against the Catholic missionaries in China, with the slogan, 'fight religion and defend the country'. They claimed to be insulted by the actions of Westerners in China, and believed that the Boxer Rebellion was a natural reac-tion against missionaries. They admired France for its education in science, philosophy and French literature, and for the 'energy and patriotism of French political figures that want to suppress the power of the Catholic Church'.

Some of these students wanted 'complete freedom'; others simply wanted to improve themselves and develop an international spirit. The means believed to do this was to absorb the 'French way of life', social and familial, but they did not want to mix with French stu-dents. The local Jesuits desired to make friends with these students, and suggested a Chinese priest as chaplain, one who was 'intelligent, cultured and with a large heart', but foreigners were forbidden entry into the Institute, which meant that they reinforced their own ideas among themselves.[19]

The French missionaries in China could never accept the anti-religious attitude of these Chinese students studying in Europe, nor the extreme political views they expressed praising socialism and bolshevism. In defence of these students, they were young and impressionable in the face of a wide range of philosophical ideas prevalent in contemporary France. They were angry that the Catholic Church in China did not support the movement toward a new China, and so they looked for alternative organisations that might support the movement toward a strong and modern China. Religion as seen by the Chinese was not liberating, and frequently critical of the Chinese and its culture. Change suggested by the missionaries for the betterment of china did not always resonate with the reflective and educated Chinese. In fact, they believed that Catholic Church hindered the modernisation of China, keeping it subservient to European influence.

Indigenous clergy

The indigenous clergy were a significant part of the Jesuit mission in China, and symbolised one of the main aims of the Catholic missionary, namely to establish a local, autonomous Church. Stressing the importance of this aim, the first institutional establishment of the Jesuits after their return to China in 1842 was founding a seminary in 1843, forty-six years after the death of the last Chinese Jesuit, Jean Yao. There had been 44 Chinese Jesuits in the Chinese Empire during the seventeenth and eighteenth centuries. But Chinese secular priests continued to minister to the Christian communities during those centuries.

In the modern era, three new Chinese priests were ordained in 1858 in Jiangnan, and were described as 'having admirable zeal' and for being humble. They were considered well trained, their formation having been based on the training of Jesuit scholastics in France, such as instruction in the catechism, preaching in the refectory, learning French, and methods of instruction that included 'proclamations,

19. Document, 'The Chinese Students of Lyon', Lyon, Easter Sunday, 1924. ARSI.

circles, weekly repetitions, and examinations, as in France'. This news would have pleased religious readers in France, but it can only be imagined how the Chinese seminarians understood such a European education.

The vicars apostolic in succeeding years reported pleasure with the Chinese priests, who worked well with the same vigour as the European missionaries, but they generally observed that the Chinese needed more 'solid virtue and humility', as well as 'greater piety'. The European missionaries rendered great service to the mission, but more indigenous clergy were needed. Vocations needed promotion by teaching Chinese students 'the practice of solid virtue, and above all, humility'. A pious and well-instructed clergy was just as important in China as in Europe. In 1859, Latin was taught at the college of St Ignatius and in the seminary in Xujiahui. There were few vocations, 1856–60, probably the result of the Taiping rebellion, which caused much pain and suffering to the mission. In 1860, the college and minor seminary at Xujiahui were separated, and a new school was founded at Tong-jia-tou. Students in the schools were encouraged to enter the clerical school; nine accepted, rising to 14 in the first month.

At the end of 1866, there were 44 students in the minor seminary, divided into two categories: 32 seminarians, who were less certain of progress to the priesthood, studying Chinese and Latin; and 12 students studying Latin grammar, destined for the major seminary, which was founded at Xujiahui in 1877. From 1864–78, the number of Chinese clergy did not increase. At this time, there were 13 Chinese Jesuit priests working with the Europeans.

Valentin Garnier, bishop from 1879, considered the work of the Chinese priest the most important. He set up boarding schools for students in the outlying districts, helping those interested in the seminary, as at Mao-jia-zhen. From 1883–1902, this school gave nine priests, some brothers, many schoolteachers, catechists and administrators of Christian communities. At the end of Garnier's time, there were 21 Chinese secular priests and 17 Chinese Jesuits.

Bishop Paris transferred the minor seminary from Tong-jia-tou to Xujiahui on 11 November 1900, and in July 1901, the minor and major seminaries were united at Xujiahui. There was a reduction in the number of seminarians in 1913, as a result of the turmoil in the country during the preceding years. In 1910–11, there were approximately 60 'Latinists', with numbers growing in 1920 to between 75 and 110. Missionaries sought children who were 'pious, virtuous, loyal and intelligent', qualities deemed necessary for a good priest. At the end of 1921, there were 80 Chinese priests in Jiangnan; 60 were clergy of the diocese of Nanking and 20 were Jesuits.[20]

European missionaries were criticised as having cultural superiority and even arrogance by those who favoured a quicker development of the Chinese Church for not encouraging Chinese vocations, and for not encouraging the development of a local Chinese Church. The Jesuits of Jiangnan fostered Chinese vocations from the beginning, even if the training of seminarians was European centred, with Rome insisting that Chinese seminarians have a sound grasp of Latin. But this was the only system of formation that they knew, and the European model of Church was not only mandated by Rome, but was considered the best for the Chinese. Hindering the process of handover to the Chinese was the belief of most European missionaries that the Chinese priests were not adequately formed in theology, nor were they sufficiently gifted in administration to lead the Chinese Christians. In other words, they were not considered ready for a handover. But if these Chinese priests were deemed deficient in theology, spirituality and administration, surely the blame must be placed on the Jesuits who were assigned to teach and mentor them. The theological training would seem to have had only minimal effect on many of the Chinese.

The advancement of the Chinese clergy to run their own Church was slow. For the whole of China, while the number of prefects apostolic increased from 54 in 1920 to 144 in 1948, only 22 were entrusted to the Chinese clergy by 1935. In addition, while the number of foreign priests increased from 1,364 to 3,091, the number of Chinese priests increased from 963 to 2,661 over the same period.[21] The balance of power still rested with the foreigners.

---

20. Report on the indigenous clergy of Jiangnan, an abridged history of the seminaries, 1843–1921, *Relatio de Chine*, 1, January 1922.
21. Roy G. Tiedemann, 'The Chinese Clergy', *Handbook of Christianity in China*, Volume Two, op. cit., 571.

The French protectorate[22]

Reinforcing European influence on the Chinese Christians was the close connection between the European missionaries, who were mainly French, and the French government. This union became controversial over the decades, with most European missionaries grateful for support given. But there were a growing number of missionaries, mainly non-French, and the Holy See that had reservations about the Church's alignment with the European power.

As late as 1922, the vicars apostolic in China expressed appreciation to the ministry in France, voicing their support for French protection, while bemoaning the recent French government decree suppressing missionary orders in France. They claimed that this action would affect the Chinese missions and would 'diminish the French influence abroad'.[23]

There were political supporters for continuing the French protection, who believed that by supporting the French missionaries they were also promoting French culture and trade.

In 1922, a document was produced outlining the history of European protection for overseas European missionaries. It traced the development from the original Portuguese protection, the *Padroado*, from 8 January 1454, given to King Alphonse V by Pope Nicholas V. This applied only for protection to Asian missions. Unhappy with this exclusive right, *Propaganda Fide* came into existence in 1622, and exerted papal influence on the missions. Louis XIV sent five Jesuits to China in 1683, thus breaking the Portuguese stronghold in China. Especially after 1858–60, France took over protection of Catholic missions, as detailed in the Treaties of Whampoa, 1844, Tientsin, 1858, the Conventions of Peking, 1860, and Berthemy, 1865. All European missionaries, even non-French, were issued with special passports by

---

22. Ernest P. Young, *Ecclesiastical Colony: China's Catholic Church and the French Religious Protectorate* (Oxford: Oxford University Press, 2013) is a comprehensive secondary source on the French Protectorate covering similar material referenced in this work discovered in the archives of the French Foreign Ministry, the Vatican Secret Archives and the archives of *Propaganda Fide*. Notes and bibliography in Young's book offer important material for further research and reflection.
23. Memorandum from Vicars Apostolic to the Minister in France, protector of Catholic Missions in China, 24 April 1922. DAC.

the French legation, which set the European missionaries even more apart from the Chinese.

The right to the French protectorate was legalised in the Convention of Peking in 1860. It was the right to protect in China all persons and institutions called 'Christian', even Chinese. In 1862, the emperor excused Chinese Christians from all taxes related to the Chinese cults. In 1855, there were 700 European Catholic missionaries in China, more than 500 were French, as well as 200 Italian, Spanish, Portuguese, German, Austrian, Dutch, Belgium and British. On 22 May 1888, the pope and Cardinal Simeoni gave France protector rights over all Catholic missionaries. Leo XIII, who praised France for its patrimony, sanctioned this again in 1898. Spanish missionaries remained under the protectorate, but the Italians sought protection from the Vatican from 1922, after Archbishop Costantini became apostolic delegate to China. He objected to the French protectorate, and influenced Pius XI on 28 February 1926 to raise objections to the protectorate, and encouraged the advancement of the native clergy. From this time, the Vatican began to distance itself from the French protectorate, and attempted to abolish extra-territoriality.[24] This document supported French fears that its protection might be undermined by pressure from the Vatican.

The French were well aware of the implications of the protectorate, for as early at 1900 they weighed up the arguments for and against it. Against the protectorate they observed that it was an intolerable anomaly for one State to protect subjects of another State who do not profess the dominant religion. The presence of missionaries in the interior of China protected by France was a source of continual discord and quarrels and an obstacle to the exercise of legitimate authority. It was not to France's advantage to have continual discussions and quarrels with the Chinese government. Finally, there was irony in that France, which promoted a lay and anti-clerical state, should oversee religious proselytism in China.

The arguments given for the protection were that the missionaries were a source of information; they helped spread French culture among the Chinese. This also happened in the French schools run by missionaries. Finally, missionary expansion was believed to facilitate

---

24 Paper on the protection of Catholic missions in China and Diplomacy, October 1922. DAC.

the spread of French industry and commerce.[25] It was these arguments that continued to influence the French government to fight for continuing the protectorate, but it is doubtful that the French missionaries actively promoted French colonial interests.

The French legation in China was also concerned about the rise of an anti-Christian movement in China in 1922, especially among the students. Memos received gave many quotes from radical students: 'All our national humiliations have also been caused by Christianity', 'Christianity is invading China along with militarism and capitalism', 'religion has two ingredients, superstition and fraud', 'religion obstructs the progress of science, preserves the influence of the aristocratic class, maintains inequalities between the rich and poor, and retards the development of individual qualities', 'Christianity destroys true reason, obstructs progress, and disgraces human history', 'the Christian religion stupefies our intelligence, fetters our nature, disgraces our personality, pollutes our brains, and suppresses our conscience'.

These were strong criticisms of Christianity and useful slogans for stirring up trouble against the Christian missions. One observation from the legation was that the anti-Christian movement originated in Shanghai, and relief was expressed that the movement did not appear to be anti-foreign. However, they were watching developments, noting that the rebellious students had associations in Beijing, Shanghai and Guangzhou that were hostile to Christianity. The German legation shared its belief that in Tianjin, while there were gangs of robbers in the region, there was no increase of revolutionary movement, and no anti-foreign feeling. It was a similar story from Shanghai. However, the French minister writing to the British ambassador believed that while the causes of student unrest in Sichuan were complex, there was 'general social malaise, complaisance of Chinese bureaucracy', student powerlessness, and the desire to play a greater role in the political debate. Bolshevist propaganda was also bearing fruit among the students.[26] Meanwhile, in the north, in Xianxian, the Jesu-

---

25. Document concerning the Protectorate. Mission of M de Lagrené to China, 1843–44, Paris, 10 May 1900. DAC.
26. Memo, Anti-Christian Movement. Storm of agitation against Christians, Christianity and religion still spreading. Most government schools joined the movement and issued anti-religious declaration, Guangzhou, 25 April 1922; 'The non-religious or anti Christian movement spreading to Beijing, Tianjin

its complained to the minister that there was no response from the police to their request for help against 'bandits, brigands and secret societies'. The mandarins did not help, and the government soldiers were cold and even hostile.[27] Help from the legation was requested.

The French legation was active during the latter months of 1922 on behalf of the missions. One memo dealt with the capture of the Italian Jesuit Mario Grimaldi, some seminarians and eight Chinese students abducted by bandits at Yingzhou and taken to Henan. The missionary residence as well as the whole village had been burnt. The governor of Anhui, Ma Lien Jia, after being contacted by the legation, responded by saying that he would do all in his power to have those captured released, and punish those responsible. Shortly after all were released, except Grimaldi, who was later found at Baofeng, with the brigands demanding $20,000 ransom. A month later, Grimaldi was released. The French minister wanted to ask for compensation from the Chinese government over the Grimaldi affair and to rebuild the village. The Jesuits agreed and asked for $60,000, which was the French right under the treaties. The Chinese replied with silence over monetary compensation, but agreed to apprehend the bandits. Discussions continued.

There had also been concerns about bands of brigands in Honan, which threatened missionaries and property. The government had been asked for military help, but it was ineffective, which weakened its ability to 'fulfil its international obligations' of protecting the missions.[28]

An article was circulated concerning the French protectorate in 1923. It recalled that the French missionaries represented France and, without them, France would not be known in China. All Catholics were under French protection, with German Steyls the exception, as

and Shanghai', *Asiatic News Agency,* Beijing, 5 April 1922; *North China Standard,* 25 March 1922; The Young China Society, 'Religion against women's rights'; 'Anti-Christian movement', April 1922, *North China Standard*; Memo, 'The anti-Christian Movement, Tianjin, 3 April 1922; Memo, 'Anti-religious agitation in Guangdong'; Circular 180, Beijing, 23 June 1922; French Minister to British Ambassador, June 1922, DAC.

27. Debeauvais to French Minister, Xianxian, 4 April 1922, DAC.
28. Concerning the protection of people and property, 1922–32; memo 54, Beijing, 8 November 1922; memo 16 November 1922; memo, 27 November 1922; telegram to legation, from Catholic mission Shanghai, 13 December 1922; French Minister, Beijing, to French Consul, Shanghai, 31 January 1923. DAC

they were under the German protectorate. There was concern that the French government was about to lose its protection. In 1886, there had been talk of a papal nunciature. The Chinese empress was hostile to the French protectorate, and the English added their voice for a nuncio. However, after the intervention of M de Freycinet, Pope Leo XIII backed off. So the protectorate was saved until 1918, when Beijing again asked for a nuncio. France again objected and the project was dropped. However, an apostolic delegation in Beijing was finally established in 1922. With this announcement, the French became anxious once again, as France was well represented by French missionaries. Initially, most French missionaries were pleased with the delegate Costantini as he declared his role to be purely religious. However, there were changes in missionary activity in China with the influx of missionaries from Austria, Germany and Spain. Despite this, French missionaries were still in the majority teaching in schools, which were considered the most powerful means of spreading French influence. There were 6,315 schools teaching 155,569 students, learning Latin and French. Aurora University, with 300 students, also teaching in French, was much admired.

In a country where there were constant epidemics, wars and famines, the missionaries gave considerable help in developing the country, through schools, hospitals, French hospices, pharmacies, orphanages, and trade schools. During wars or attacks by bandits, French missionaries received French government protection from their concessions in Beijing, Shanghai or Tianjin; an action appreciated by the Chinese Christians. All missions, except German, hoisted the French flag.

The French legation appreciated the French missionaries for being a great source of information. Humanitarian aid given to the Chinese in times of famine or attacks by bandits was reported to the legation so that they might share this 'wonderful information' with the rest of the world.[29] All this was aimed to promote the glory of France.

Costantini read this article and thought that *Propaganda Fide* in Rome should be informed of its contents. The diplomatic battle between the Vatican and France heightened.

---

29. Bauduin Belleval, 'The French Protectorate', in *La Politique de Pekin* (29 July 1923). PF.

Meanwhile, a Jesuit wrote about the anti-French missionary feel-ing among other religious congregations, which he believed led to anti-clericalism. What was needed was to reinforce the 'honour of true France, of Catholic France'. The exclusive rights of the French missionaries were considerable and appreciated, and as a result, the number of Christians had increased three-fold in 20 years. However, he was aware of difficulties, especially that the Chinese believed that Catholicism was a French religion, or at least, a European one, while the Protestants were seen as an American religion. Where were the American Catholics? The Chinese wanted to learn English, because it was the language of commerce, and the European missionaries did not speak English well or teach the language much.[30] This letter showed the ambivalence of the French missionaries, endeavouring to hold in tension the desire to be French, and promote French culture, while at the same time aware of the limitations of the French protec-torate, and the minor influence that the French language and culture had among the Chinese.

Archbishop Celso Costantini, Apostolic Delegate[31]

The appointment of Costantini by the Vatican as apostolic delegate to China in 1922 was a direct confrontation to the French protector-ate. The Vatican had wanted to wean Catholic missionaries from the political influence of the French government. This move made the French ministers in China nervous. With the advent of his arrival in Guangzhou, the French consul general, writing to the local vicar apostolic, either naïvely believed or diplomatically stated that he thought that the object of the appointment of the delegate was to have 'amicable conversation between the Holy See and our ambassa-dor in the Vatican'. He expressed the wish to accompany him around Guangzhou and to introduce him to the Chinese authorities, with

---

30. De la Brousse, 'Statistics and geography of the mission', in *Relatio de Chine*, (May-August 1923).

31. **Celso Costantini** was born in Italy, 1876, and appointed Apostolic Delegate to China, 1922–33. From 1935–53 he served as Secretary of the Sacred Congregation of the Propaganda of the Faith in Rome. In 1935, he was created cardinal, and died on 17 October 1958. For a detailed appreciation of Costantini, see Francis Chong, CDD, 'Cardinal Celso Costantini and the Chinese Catholic Church', in *Tripod*, 28/148 (Spring 2008).

whom 'I have traditionally dealt with on religious matters'. He wanted to be informed of the intentions of Costantini in visiting Guangzhou so that he could inform the Generalissimo and the civil governor.[32]

When informed of this welcome by the consul general, Costantini replied that his visit was to the missionaries; his job involved the 'internal affairs of the vicariate', so that the visit, therefore, was both private and religious, which excluded all external manifestations that might give a political motive. He thanked the consul for his offer, but, if he chose to visit the Chinese authorities, the vicar apostolic would accompany him.[33]

Costantini's role in China was to set up the Apostolic Delegation, and to work on matters relating to the French protectorate. He believed that everyone in China was happy with the first plan. He wanted to set up a commission of Chinese priests who represented the seven Catholic vicariates, while on the question of the French protectorate he stated that 'civil matters are best handled with local authorities rather than with the French consul'. He wanted the Apostolic Delegation to be seen as a centre of unity for the various missions.[34]

Shortly after Costantini's arrival, the French consul general in Shanghai expressed some anxiety about his presence in China. He reported that he was a young (47 years old), intelligent Italian patriot who talked much. He understood that the Jesuits were disturbed by his arrival as delegate, seeing him as 'a serious menace to our protection'. They feared that he favoured the Chinese nationalist tendencies always advocated by the Chinese clergy. Among them was an element that had direct connection with the Vatican and wished to diminish the influence of French priests and their administration. Moreover, the delegate seemed to favour the methods of the Protestant American missions, whose schools and hospitals were most successful.[35]

Costantini strongly believed that the purpose of the missionary was to establish a local church, governed by its own people, fully incarnated in its own culture. But sometimes, he believed, foreign missionaries blurred the distinction between spreading the Kingdom of God, and furthering the interests of the Western power to which

---

32. M. N Beauvais, French Consul General, Guangzhou, to Fouquet, Vicar Apostolic, Guangzhou, 30 November 1922. PF (Propagation of the Faith Archives, Rome).
33. Costantini to Fouquet, Guangzhou, 2 December 1922. PF.
34. Costantini to Grimaldi, Vicar Apostolic, Anhui, Hong Kong, 5 December 1922. PF.
35. Consul General, Shanghai, to French Minister, Peking, 26 December 1922. DAC.

they belonged. They projected a dual loyalty; to the local church and to their country of origin, and when there was a clash, the latter usually won. Exceptions to this process were the methods of the Jesuits of an earlier period, Roberto de Nobili and Matteo Ricci, as well as the contemporary Lazarite, Vincent Lebbe, who inculturated the Christian religion into Chinese culture, trying to avoid, as much as possible, the appearance of European imperialism. Communicating the Catholic religion in European categories by missionaries educated in European culture to such a culturally diverse culture as the Chinese was a great challenge. Costantini wanted to redirect the role of the foreign missionaries toward developing an indigenous church, liberating it from the political influence of the French protectorate. He was aware of the existing tension between the Chinese and foreign priests, and encouraged the vicars apostolic to promote the local Chinese clergy in the administration of the vicariate. He even suggested the appointment of Chinese bishops, and promoted the renewal of the apostolate among Chinese intellectuals. He stressed the pastoral character of his mission, refusing 'protection' from the French and other foreign legations, because he believed that this protection was one of the main obstacles to the growth of the Church in China. He believed that the missionaries did not have much understanding of the 'new China', currently engaged in a struggle for radical renewal, nor did they appreciate that the Chinese authorities and non-Christians hated intervention by foreign powers in domestic disputes. He preferred personal diplomacy.

On a visit to Hankou in July 1923, a Franciscan, Kovac, told Costantini why he believed that Christianity was not progressing more quickly in China. They included the negative effects concerning the Church's prohibition of traditional Chinese familial rituals, the continuing humiliation of the Chinese resulting from the interventionist policies and military presence of the foreign powers, the tension among missionaries relating to the methods of presenting Christianity, and in the ways they should adapt Roman Catholicism to Chinese culture.

Costantini wrote about wanting an 'apostolic methodology' for China. Missionaries were expected to move beyond founding a mission, and establish a Church. To achieve this, a Chinese hierarchy was deemed to be necessary, according to the papal encyclical, *Maximum Illud,* and the missions should be handed over to the local clergy as soon as possible. Costantini called the present situation 'territorial feudalism'. He found some vicars apostolic unwilling to surrender even a part of their territorial jurisdiction to create new ecclesiastical territories. Many missions maintained the Chinese clergy in subordinate roles to the European priests, who would not even allow other foreign religious groups into their territory. Costantini was not impressed.

In 1923, he proposed to Rome the establishment of one or two ecclesiastical territories that would be governed by bishops selected from among the Chinese clergy. He called for a National Synod in 1924, and in 1926 created the Chinese vicariate of Xuanhua, formerly part of the Beijing vicariate. Then, Pius XI on 28 October 1926 consecrated six Chinese bishops in Rome. In this, Rome exercised strong leadership in promoting a Chinese autonomous Church.

Costantini's next move was to build stronger ties between the Chinese government and the Holy See. The Chinese liked this idea. Then he encouraged lay Catholics to take a more active part in the national revival, a plan supported by the pope. In 1927, a Catholic University (Fu Jen) was founded, approved by the government in Beijing. Some missionaries feared that this might mean the end of the French protectorate, and that all foreign missionaries might be expelled. Costantini was willing to take the risk in order to oversee that the Church in China became Chinese in every aspect. The suggestion that a second university be established administered by the French Dominicans was opposed, as Costantini thought the proposal might be seen as a further expression of the French protectorate and 'cultural aggression'. He worked hard to regain China's independence and national dignity, always justifying his comments from the methodology of the early Church.[36]

In his report to headquarters in Rome in 1923, Costantini commented on the political and social conditions in China. He mentioned 'financial and administrative disorder, brigandage and the indifference of people' (400 million of them) that were mainly preoccupied with material matters, since most lived in poverty. The rise of Bolshevism, and the new influence of America and Japan were significant. The military of the government could not cope with the challenges

---

36. Arnulf Camps OFM, 'Celso Costantini, Apostolic Delegate to China, 1922–1933, the changing role of the foreign missionary', in *Tripod*, 44 (1988): 9–12; 40–6.

facing them. But, despite devastation and turmoil, there was always hope for the Church.

His main concern was the continuing question of the French protectorate, which he called 'a scandal'. He wanted the apostolic delegate to take over the protection of the Catholic missions. He hoped that the upcoming Synod in 1924 would give the church its independence and liberty, having 'unity under the Pope'. Missionaries would then negotiate directly with the local Chinese officials.

Protection had led to many locals believing that Catholicism was a French national religion. One mandarin was surprised to learn that Costantini came from Italy, suggesting that he should be French, because 'the Christian religion is from France'. The question of remuneration from the Chinese, sometimes extracted by the government officials from the poor people for crimes against the missions, did not advance the cause of Christianity. Chinese Christians liked French protection, because it made them special and safe, but it isolated them from other Chinese. Having recourse to the supreme authority, Costantini mentioned that 'Jesus made no mention of secular protection for his missionaries'. The delegate believed that association with the political power impeded the liberty of the Catholic Church. Protection should come from God alone. Human protection was not needed. This comment conveniently ignored the history of the Catholic Church from the times of Constantine when the Church had close connection with political powers, and frequently needed and accepted political support.

He believed that foreign protection of Catholics in China for the propagation of the faith had not helped 'in any respect'. He noted that missionaries objected to this by saying that they needed this help when persecuted. In reply, Costantini again referred to Jesus' words about not worrying about what to do, but simply trust in Him. No one protected the early Christians, and many became martyrs.[37]

Costantini was very focused on the question of the French protectorate, truly believing that it was unwise at least, and convinced the Vatican to pursue the political idea of transferring protection of the missionaries from France to the Holy See, a non-politically aligned organisation. That, he believed, would help evangelisation. The missionaries were not keen on this idea, as they rightly observed that

---

37. Costantini to Propaganda Fide, 1923. PF.

the pope had no political clout to stop attacks on the missions, only the threat of foreign intervention was effective in China. Furthermore, with the protection of the foreign powers, many Chinese were converted, rejoicing that they received special protection from their enemies. Being Christian gave them security, and new possibilities, despite being isolated from their non-Christian neighbours. From conversion figures given by the missionaries each year, no one could deny that the missionaries were making converts. Also in the background was the tension between the pope and the French government that was pursuing a line of secularisation and oppression of the church. Costantini would have been aware of this.

In his own account of his mission in China, Costantini's initial reflections in 1922 were to assess the best means of bringing the Chinese people to Christ. All ecclesiastical hierarchy was foreign, and missionaries belonged to religious orders. The Catholic religion appeared to the Chinese as a foreign importation, tied to foreign political interests. Most missionaries were opposed to the Lazarites, Lebbe and Cotta because they had written to Rome for the creation of a Chinese hierarchy. He believed that the position of foreigners in China was based on a structure of privileges and sanction. Religion was tolerated only by virtue of foreign treaties.

By 1923, Costantini was aware of a 'new China' emerging, restless and wanting change. The missionaries' call on foreign diplomats to intervene in disputes was hated by the Chinese authorities and non-Christians. He saw that the Chinese had problems with Christianity because of their own 'inertia and atavistic traditionalism', because the missionaries were against filial piety and ancestor rights, and because Chinese national pride resisted the influence of Western culture. Moreover, many Chinese could not accept the imposition of the strict moral law of Catholicism. Since 1900, missionaries were blamed that China had been conquered and humiliated. The Chinese were not a mystical people; they were 'practical and materialistic'. The divisions among Christians, Catholic and Protestant especially were seen as a source of scandal.

As a start to his reform, Costantini ordered the abolition of the custom that Chinese Catholics kneel before the missionaries, to be replaced with a bow. He was uncomfortable that the treaties placed the missionaries above the Chinese, protected by foreign governments and exempt from Chinese laws. He objected to missionaries being placed on equal footing with the Chinese sub-prefects.

In 1924, he reflected on the opinion of the vicars apostolic that numerous non-Christians, especially from the poor classes, came to Catholicism to find 'refuge, aid and protection'. He agreed that the missions had recruited a remarkable number of catechumens. Protection by missionaries gave assurance to catechumens and Christians who had been brought before local Chinese tribunals, which sometimes resulted in the conversion of entire villages. However, some common law criminals had also placed themselves under the protection of the mission, which was not 'honourable for religion'. For many Chinese, accepting Christianity signified in some way 'renouncing the past glory of China'.[38]

While not in a position to offer material assistance to the missionaries facing local problems, Costantini's influence changed the way Catholic missions in China operated, at least externally. He appointed new Chinese vicars apostolic; arranged money to be sent to China from *Propaganda Fide*; dispensed missionaries from Canon Law, and gave ecclesiastical permissions, without the missionaries having recourse to Rome. New Catholic foundations were approved, or disapproved, while he dealt with internal Church problems. He presided over the first Chinese Synod in Shanghai, chose Chinese bishops, and sent annual statistics and other regular information about China to *Propaganda Fide*. Rome had never been better informed of local conditions in China.[39]

Life on the mission, 1923

Verdier wrote to the superior general expressing his concern about the malaise among the vicars apostolic in China because of the attitude taken by Rome towards them; it was one of coldness. Bishop Jean de Vienne, Tianjin (1923–46), returned from Rome saying that *Propaganda Fide* showed no interest in his mission. Bishop Paul-Marie Reynard, Eastern Chekiang (1910–24), on a similar visit, reported that Rome did not know about the existence of Chinese clergy in

---

38. Costantini, Cardinal Celso, 'Christian Evangelizers, builders of foreign missions or of a Chinese Church?' in Jessie G Lutz Ed., *Christian Missions in China, evangelists or what?* (Boston: Problems in Asian Civilizations, 1965), 21–5.

39. For more detailed analysis of Costantini's vision for the Catholic Church in China, cf., Sergio Ticozzi, PIME, 'Celso Costantini's Contribution to the Localization and Inculturation of the Church in China', in *Tripod*, 28/148 (Spring 2008).

most vicariates. But, Pope Benedict XV wanted 'China for the Chinese', therefore the need to ordain Chinese clergy. The bishops' reaction was one of defiance from perceived criticism coming from the Chinese priests and the apostolic delegate. Verdier questioned the judgment of Costantini, 'having been in China only one year', as well as for the advice he received. He was also critical of Costantini after a meeting at Hankou to prepare for the Catholic Synod in Shanghai in 1924. He thought that those present did not represent the diverse regions of China, the meeting was too hastily convened with little time to prepare, and resolutions were imposed without a vote. Verdier was at pains to support the vicars apostolic against the apostolic delegate by insisting that they had been generally supportive of the 'recruitment of Chinese helpers'. The work of Lebbe, his influence on the delegate and at Rome, was much discussed among missionaries. While Verdier acknowledge Lebbe's 'apostolic zeal, knowledge of Chinese language, his austerity and influence among the Chinese', he criticised 'his lack of judgment and discernment that diminished his cause'. He feared that on their visit to Rome, Lebbe and Cotta would not present an unbiased opinion of the good influence of the European missionaries, and hasten the ordination of the Chinese bishops. The idea of a totally Chinese vicariate did not please, because he, and most Jesuits, did not believe the Chinese clergy were ready for this responsibility.[40]

The Jesuits, true to their historical tradition, were keen observers of the local scene, reflecting upon what they were experiencing. Keeping one eye on the work of the Protestant missionaries, Pierre Ancel continued observations about them in 1923. He showed appreciation for their work in education, prayer meetings, promotion of prayer and evangelism, as well as a daily bible reading movement. They opposed 'lotteries and opium', preached in prisons, established stewardship for its patrons, and assisted with gaining good jobs on the railways and the post office for its followers. They had street processions, conferences on health and hygiene and baby shows. They showed films at their YMCA centres. At the Protestant University at Nanjing, all students assisted at daily prayer, even external ones, and they lost points if they did not attend. Despite all this, it was perceived that Protestant results at evangelisation were 'thin'. Catholics

---

40. Verdier to General, Shanghai, 19 November 1923. ARSI.

offered 'much greater treasures', as they 'change souls, attack the passions of the world and lead to God'.[41] While being somewhat gracious in showing appreciation for the work of the Protestants, there was always the belief that the Catholic missions achieved better results than the Protestants.

Joseph Hugon believed that the three great enemies of China were 'the politicians, the military and the brigands'. He saw the first part of 1923 as 'a sad history'. The Chinese parliament was in trouble with the Constitution, with few people taking any notice of government decisions. There was talk in France about the Republic of the North and the Republic of the South, but this was far too simple. Theoretically, there was only one Republic of China, but it was divided and needed reunification. The central power was weak, while the provinces were practically autonomous, and more often than not, at war with one another. It was the military leaders, the Marshals, who were responsible for this disorganisation. Li Yuen Hong was deposed as president, which resulted in no cabinet. Three ministers formed a 'Council of Regency of the Republic', which ran the country. Watching numerous Chinese alliances, the foreign powers seemed to think that the Beijing government consisted of Li Yuen Hong, together with the cabinet of the all-powerful leader of Manchuria, Marshal Zhang Zuo lin, and Marshal Cao Kun, with Wu Pei fu from Henan behind the scenes. But, in effect, the power rested in the three main semi-independent Provinces of Guangzhou, with Sun Yat-sen, Manchuria, ruled by Marshal Zhang Zuo lin, and Yunnan under the control of Marshal Tang Ji yao.

In the north, war always menaced between the various factions. There was constant threat from bandits; more than often they were former soldiers who sought out the rich to plunder. The missionaries, who had little money, were frequently spared these attacks. There were exceptions, the more recent one being the capture of Grimaldi in Anhui, but he was later released. Another form of brigandage occurred when bandits boarded the river ferries as first-class passengers, then, when they were *en route,* would seize the captain and officers and proceed to pillage the passengers. Sometimes brigands were bribed by the government to join the regular army.

---

41. Ancel, 'Catholics and Protestants in China', in *Relatio de Chine* (September-December 1923): 171–3.

On the diplomatic front, Japan evacuated Shandong, but kept considerable interests in the region: commerce, mines and industry were all in the hands of Japanese firms. The railways were sold to China. While China still had sovereignty over Shandong, the situation was fraught with danger.[42]

For Hugon, the end of 1923 brought hope, not resulting from the political chaos, but from the progress of the Catholic missions and from the forthcoming Catholic Synod in Shanghai. China should be considered a most important part of the world for evangelisation, with more than one-third of the world's non-Christians.

Meanwhile, Marshal Cao Kun was elected president at the end of 1923, but Sun Yat-sen and Zhang Zuo lin opposed the appointment. Peace did not reign among the 'Barons of the Empire'. Discord reigned between Nanjing and Shanghai, while the bandits were also unhappy.

Against this backdrop, the Christian missions continued to flourish. Hugon estimated that in China proper, mainly in the 18 eastern and southern provinces, there were 1.8 million Christians. In the Jesuit missions of Zhili, there were 601,533 Christians, and in Jiangsu, 195,863. The figures for Zhili were considered remarkable since the province was relatively uninhabited, and Christians were only 1.9 per cent of the total population. It was this region that suffered much during the Boxer uprising, with 20,000 martyrs. Of nearly two million Christians, two-thirds were neophytes. In 1900, there were only 600,000 Christians, but one million in 1910 and two million in 1922. Also, there were 2,610 priests, each priest in charge of about 800 Christians, which was about the same ratio as in France. But the number of practising Catholics in China was far superior to that of France.

The challenge for the missionaries was how to reach the many non-Christians in the country. The missionaries noticed that when there was a sudden rise in the number of conversions in one region, the number of catechumens ceased to grow. Wisdom dictated that the missionaries should then move on to new areas to evangelise new non-Christians; too many priests were engaged with these more stabilised communities. To reach new areas, more priests were needed. Europe could not continue to meet the demands of the missions, especially after the depletion of the male population after the Great War,

---

42. Hugon, 'Short story of China', *Relatio de Chine*, ibid., 173–80

so America was filling the gaps in China. The American Maryknoll congregation and the American Franciscans were in Guangdong and Hubei provinces, respectively. But the growth in the number of priests must come from China's own seminaries. That was already happening. Currently, there were 1,082 Chinese priests for 1,480 European priests. In 14 vicariates, the number of Chinese priests was higher to that of the Europeans. Each vicariate had seminarians, the total of which was about 2,492. It was estimated that in 15 years, the number of Chinese clergy would double. These figures were very encouraging for the missionaries. With the division of vicariates underway, totally Chinese ones were already beginning to emerge, as in Baoji, a division of the vicariate of Hubei S.O.

Other challenges were constantly present in the Christian communities. The brigands were active in 1923, even killing or capturing several missionaries. The damage to the communities from pillage and the destruction of buildings was considerable. But this problem was not as basic as the rapid growth of a materialistic civilisation in China, with the official teaching being anti-Christian, fed by the propaganda of the Bolshevists. To meet this challenge, the missions needed to develop intellectual centres. The Protestants had already built ten universities, while the Jesuits had *Aurora* in Shanghai, and the *École de Hautes Etudes* in Tianjin. Educational influence was seen through the work of the meteorological observatory in Shanghai, and the secondary college in Xujiahui. No one should forget the scientific and mathematical influence of the earlier Jesuits, Ricci, Schall, Verbiest and Gerbillon, whose work won the approval of the emperor that enabled their colleagues to work among the people in the provinces. Both aspects of mission activity were important. Hugon, like all Jesuits, was quick to compare their work with those of the Protestants. He mentioned that they only had between three to 400,000 adherents in China, while their posts 'in the bush' were far inferior to that of the Catholics. The Catholics worked with the poor.[43]

All letters from the mission reflected self-imposed censorship, in that according to the rules of the Society of Jesus, communication within the Society should be 'edifying'. A good image of the pastoral ministry of the Company should be presented. Jesuits were counselled to be careful in what they wrote; so anything approaching scan-

---

43. Hugon, ibid., 298–303.

dal was either omitted or very carefully worded. Any such mention to superiors in Rome was usually sent under special seal, what today would be called 'confidential'.

Very few 'scandals' were discovered in the various archives, but there were two in 1923. One involved Zingale, an Italian priest, who had 'difficulties with superiors'. He had been two years in China, and he did not please because he would not go where he was sent, and would not obey either the provincial or the superior general. Superiors in China had asked European superiors to recall him, but they did not. He even received a letter from the Sacred Congregation for Religious in Rome ordering him to France or to face dismissal from the Society of Jesus. Finally, he was suspended from his priestly duties because of his disobedience, and was later dismissed from the Society.[44]

Then there was the case of a Chinese priest Joseph Sen, who was accused of having an affair with a 20-year-old woman, and admitting her into his bedroom. It transpired that the accusation had come from a disgruntled catechist Pie who had been dismissed by Sen for being untrustworthy. There was no question of a 'crime' being committed, just indiscretion. Sen had an unblemished reputation for many years before, but once denounced, Sen's reputation was tarnished, and he had to leave his district. Pie was 'jubilant', but he was locally known as 'an evil man', living in luxury in the mission house; that was why Sen dismissed him. Missionaries claimed that many Christians at Anhui were 'notorious liars', and had been against the missionaries for 40 years. Before Sen, another Jesuit of the district, Dourandieu, also had a false accusation made against him, but he was later cleared.[45]

Most annual reports to the superior general in Rome were expected to follow a pro-forma, largely answering pre-determined questions relating to the spiritual life or observance of the Jesuit rule. Some Jesuits kept strictly to answering the questions, others deviated from the norm to inform the superior general about other matters he should know. Someone in Rome read the letters, noted what was

44. Noury to Apostolic Delegate, Shanghai, 29 August 1923, ASV (Vatican Secret Archives, Vatican City).
45. De Bodman, Yangzhou, to Verdier, Vicar Delegate, 29 October 1923; Mgr Paris to Apostolic Delegate, Shanghai, 28 November 1923; Sen to Apostolic Delegate, Toukadou, 20 January 1924; Cheng to Apostolic Delegate, Nanjing, 26 January 1924. ASV; Crochet, to Mgr Paris and Verdier, Yangzhou, May 1923, ASV.

considered important and ignored the rest. If reports were good, no immediate response was made.

Reporting about the mission life for 1923, Noury indicated that he was not happy about the division of the Jiangnan mission in 1921, or about discussions of future divisions. He was most probably not alone in this opinion. There had been discussions about a new bishop and vicar: no one was found acceptable. He thought Verdier was a good superior, but Schellier, writing at the same time to the superior general, commented that while Verdier was a good administrator, he was 'not paternal or suave'. For Noury, he thought essential qualities to be 'ministers' (leaders) of sections were 'poverty and obedience'. There was no mention of any other qualities, such as the ability to relate to the Chinese. As there was continuing reluctance to promote Chinese priests to leadership positions in the mission, he proudly announced that, in 1923, two Chinese 'ministers of regions' in the mission had been appointed.[46]

Schellier also believed that 'poverty and obedience' were essential missionary qualities, and that the Chinese priests were very deficient in that regard. He thought that they should only be admitted to the Society as 'neophytes'. Furthermore, he did not think that the spiritual level of the mission was high, as there was no obvious ardent desire 'for prayer and zeal for perfection'. Jesuit leadership in the mission was not sufficiently supernatural, but 'too human instead'. While he considered that there was a 'good religious spirit' at Xujiahui, 'reserve and discretion was totally lacking'. As for the mission, he suggested that superiors should give to other missionaries those sections of the mission that they were unable to serve. The division of the mission was necessary, but the idea of a Chinese vicariate would only be accepted 'under holy obedience'. The Chinese were not ready to assume this responsibility, nor were they capable of governing in the Society. Only two names could be considered, Joseph Tsang and Simon Zhu. He preferred Tsang, because Zhu was 'not intelligent and stubborn, self-centred, vain, partial and vindictive'. He did not value poverty, and was too close to his family and friends. As with Noury, he made comments about his fellow Jesuits who had authority. Apart from Verdier, he thought Beaucé, the rector of Xujiahui, was a good superior because he was 'very supernatural and united

46. Noury to General, St Joseph's Church, Shanghai, 29 January 1924. ARSI.

to God, very charitable, dependable and mortified, very straight and given to detail'. He thought Noury was a man 'of good judgment and charitable', while Biboul and Piet did not seem to have the required gifts for Jesuit government.[47] These comments make clear the virtues Jesuits believed necessary for good governance in the mission.

The First Chinese Synod, Xujiahui, 14 May to 12 June 1924[48]

A milestone in the history of Catholic missions in China was the Synod of 1924. It was very carefully prepared, bringing together all the Catholic mission leaders of China, and was a significant dream of the apostolic delegate, Costantini. A lengthy agenda had been circulated in 1923 to all the missions for reflection, which became the basic document for the final decrees. It was a very Roman synod, with no Chinese bishop present, that strengthened the discipline of Rome in all mission activities, with no apparent appreciation of how the Christian message might be best communicated to the Chinese. Present were 59 vicars or prefects apostolic, among whom were three Jesuits, Paris (Nanjing), Lécroart (Zhili SE), and Huarte (Anhui), as well as Jesuit religious superiors: Verdier (Nanjing), Debeauvais (Zhili SE), Barmaverain (Anhui), Ruiz (Anhui), Arguelles (Anhui) and two Chinese priests, Lucas Yang and Firminus Sen. The results were recorded in extremely detailed 1,004 pages containing 891 regulations, strongly endorsing Roman canon law and ecclesiastical control.

Reinforcing the missions' primary duty, the first decree reaffirmed allegiance to the Holy See and to all that it taught, especially canon law, applying it to China. However, the end of the mission was to proclaim the Gospel and prepare for a Chinese Church. The Catholic religion must be free from political suspicion, and not be seen by the Chinese as belonging to one or other nation. The universality of the Church under Christ was stressed. The name on Catholic buildings was to be *Tien Chu T'ang* (Catholic Mission), with no national flag flying. Obedience was to be given to the civil authority, legally constituted. All questions of protection were to be referred to the Holy See. Missions should not engage in commerce of any kind, nor engage in

47. Schellier to General, Aurora, Shanghai, 2 February 1924. ARSI
48. Anthony Lam, 'Archbishop Costantini and The First Council of Shanghai (1924)', in *Tripod*, 28/148 (Spring 2008).

any political or commercial association or social disturbances, or act for Chinese Christians in civil or criminal cases. In the erection of buildings, Chinese architecture was encouraged.

The papal decrees, *Ex Illa die* (1715), *Ex quo singulari* (1742), and *Ex quo* (1752), as well as that from *Propaganda Fide* (1895), were to be obeyed in full, with no concessions to Chinese rites or superstitions, such as the rites before the tablets of ancestors, or funeral rites, or the Chinese customs of concubinage, slavery or infanticide. The 'emancipation of women' was rejected, because it would dissolve the marriage bond, but the dignity of women should be restored.

Missionaries were to write in Latin, according to the custom of the universal church (not in a European language, as was frequent). Scripture was to be translated into Chinese, while the catechism for the catechumens was to include the sign of the cross, prayer on Sunday, the 'angelic salutation' (the Angelus), the Apostles Creed, the precepts of God and of the Church, the seven sacraments, the acts of faith, hope and charity and contrition. Catechists could baptise when no priest was present, as well as instruct catechumens. Rules were given for how to give the Sacraments, the rituals for burial and the care of cemeteries. Nothing was left to chance or individual initiative. Obedience to the rules was expected.

Missionaries were to learn the Chinese language, preferably for three years under the guidance of expert tutors, and should be involved in 'social action' according to the social papal encyclical of 1891, *Rerum Novarum* (On Capital and Labour). The lives of each missionary were completely regulated. To be recognised, priests must wear the Roman soutane, either white or black. Outside the house, they may wear the Chinese 'toga' with the Roman collar, according to local custom. The abolition of the *K'o t'ou* before the priest was reaffirmed; only an inclination of the head or body towards them was permitted, but the genuflection before bishops was suitable, as in the universal church.

The role of the Sacred Congregation of the Propagation of the Faith was, in the future, to handle all ecclesiastical questions, while the role of the apostolic delegate was to assist the growth of Christianity. He should be informed of mission questions, and when changes in mission superiors occurred. He was also to arrange divisions of vicariates.

Within the Jesuit vicariates, it was noted that the Jiangsu-Nanjing mission had 195,864 Christians, while that of Anhui were 73,912. Divisions of these vicariates were in preparation.

A section dealing with the relationship between the European and Chinese priests decreed that no distinction must exist between the two. In conversation between them, Latin or Chinese was to be used. There must be no expression of European nationalism, which was considered a 'false love of one's own country'. Indigenous vocations were encouraged, but care should be taken that they were suitable, that is, that they were at the standard of education required by Roman law.

The importance of education was stressed. Some schools in China were good, but others taught 'revolution, socialism, materialism and freethinking'. These schools were considered to 'poison society in the future'. Catholic schools were to counter-balance these 'evil ideas'. Aurora University was considered a leading light, but secondary schools needed development, always supported by the parish primary schools. All these schools should follow the government programmes, as well as provide religious education according 'to the rules of Holy Church'. As for seminary studies, Roman syllabuses were to be used.

It was the hope of the Synod to 'shed light, give direction for the struggle against these perverse errors and to form good vigilant soldiers who will bring honour to the Holy Roman Catholic Apostolic Church, and work towards the salvation of our country'.[49]

The French Foreign Ministry was concerned about this Synod with its political implications for France. They particularly noted the clause 'our fatherland is China', and the request that missionaries abstain from helping commercial interests of their own country. The Catholic religion was not to be seen to be part of one nation, but was a universal religion, and finally, they were wary about the mission houses being called 'Catholic Mission', without any mention of European nationality.[50]

---

49. The General Synod of Shanghai, proposed agenda, 1923; Acts of the Council, 1924, PF; *Primum Concilium Sinense*, 14 May to 12 June 1924, (Shanghai: Xujiahui, 1930), ARSI; General Synod of China, Shanghai, *Relatio de Chine*, 1 (January 1925).

50. *Primum Concilium Sinense*, ut supra. DAC.

French visitation, 1924

The apostolic delegate asked the vicar apostolic of Nanjing, Bishop Prosper Paris, if he would send a priest to Beijing. The Jesuit superior replied that there was no priest that could be found, and that the one requested by the delegate could not speak Mandarin, and so would have difficulty being understood by the people.[51]

Jesuit community life would surely have tensions among people of different personalities, nationalities and 'ways of proceeding'. While admitting that 'dissension in community had nearly disappeared', a complaint was made against Robert Jacquinot de Bessance, who was noticed 'alone with women in the library'. This was considered scandalous. Moreover, Jacquinot committed further 'sins' by 'working independently of the superior', and by 'lacking in love of the common life'. But it was admitted that he had great influence in Shanghai among Europeans. Even Protestants consulted him, and some non-Christians were converted.[52] This letter was indicative of recurrent attitudes within Jesuit communities. The most important factor in the life of the Jesuit was 'community life', and if someone spent more time working in his apostolic ministry than living within the community he was criticised, no matter what good work was being achieved. This happened with Jacquinot and also with Pierre Teilhard de Chardin, the famous Jesuit palaeontologist.

The French Jesuit provincial, Félix Mollat, reinforced this approach in the report of his visit in 1924, which almost entirely concentrated on Jesuit community life and religious discipline, despite the fact that the region, and nation, was in the midst of a civil war. The report reflected universal Jesuit discipline, with only minor references to the fact that they lived in China. Much of what was written could have been applied to similar situations anywhere in the world.

Concerning the formation of Jesuits in China, Mollat continued the discussion about the length of time spent learning Chinese: he wanted it to begin in the second year of the novitiate. Clothes worn by missionaries might adapt to Chinese culture. Reflecting on the 'intellectual life', he wanted established a 'group of writers', and suggested that both books and the Gospels be translated into the local

---

51. Vicar Apostolic Nanjing to Apostolic Delegate Beijing, Shanghai, 3 January 1924. ARSI.
52. Le Baboul to General, Sacred Heart Church, Shanghai, 30 January 1924.

Shanghai dialect. The role of the 'spiritual father' was important for the spiritual development of Chinese seminarians, while those who showed promise might be sent to Rome for 'further studies', such as a doctorate in theology. Retreats should be given to the secular clergy, while studies in the seminary could be 'modified courses in science and humanities'. He encouraged a chair for Chinese languages and literature, and a course in sociology. Even the establishment of a Chinese observatory was suggested. He responded to the question of teaching English in the Shanghai schools, by suggesting that the Californian Jesuits might be able to promote the English language in Shanghai. In each district of the mission, there should be a prayer school, an elementary education in small Christian communities, primary schools in the larger Christian communities for the poor, and superior primary schools for 'externs and non-Christians'. If the Shanghai Jesuits wanted a boarding section of the school that taught English and French, it would be better to invite the Marist Brothers to perform the task; the Jesuits should remain with day students only, teaching French and Chinese. This would be the best preparation for Aurora University, where instruction was given in French.

Mollat also commented on the 'government of the mission', code for how the mission was run. He liked Beaucé for being prudent, good, and with a 'supernatural spirit that led to confidence in others'. But he was less intelligent than his predecessors and got 'lost in detail'. His letters were 'too long and a little confusing'. He needed assistance in his work, but from someone who would not upset his 'sensitivity'. He took great care in visiting the sections of the mission. In general, Mollat was happy with the superiors of the mission, whom he found 'wise and very devoted'. Henri Gilot and Joseph Verdier were 'a little partial in their government, dismissing those who didn't agree with them, especially those who had initiative, such as Joseph Ducoux. Relations between superiors and district missionaries were rare and insufficient'; the latter felt isolated. Ministers of sections did not always write to the superior general once a year, and there was insufficient consultation among the Jesuits. Some missionaries complained that they were not well known in Rome. There was a malaise among the missionaries concerning the proposed establishment of an independent Chinese vicariate. They did not want one because they continued to believe that the Chinese clergy were not ready for such responsibility.

To promote Jesuit life, the idea that vocations to the Jesuit brothers might come from the orphans at Tushanwan did not bear fruit. Too much was expected of these orphans considering their background. The novice master considered himself more like a 'child invigilator', and wasted an assistant (a socius). He found that by temperament, the Chinese novices were not open and even secretive. This made it difficult for the European superiors to give the 'desirable intellectual and spiritual formation'. Even the best of them did not have 'the idea of true dependence or true poverty required by religious life'.

Mollat found the spirit of religious life in community to be good, the differences between the European and Chinese were mainly in temperament, and ideas about Chinese nationalism. Charity reigned, but not 'union of minds and hearts'.

He found that some Chinese Jesuits did not seem as 'holy, abnegated or with zeal' as their previous generation. Young Chinese missionaries 'tended to be critical, and lacking in generosity': even lacking in 'love of the missionary vocation or of China'. They had become too European 'instead of becoming truly Chinese with the Chinese'. The Europeans, especially the French, were also too nationalistic for France. They found the Chinese to be 'ambitious, impatient to excess of all things foreign, and incapable of sincerity and discretion'. They did not keep the rule of 'socius' when they went out. They were critical of the Chinese brothers for having 'too much liberty, abusing poverty and reading newspapers'. There were many other minor details of religious life that needed improvement, so he suggested a mission 'Custom Book' to remind all of their obligations. He discovered that this was not a welcome idea, especially from those who favoured 'mediocrity' in religious life. Finally, he thought the Jesuits were too free in the use of medication, such as antipyrine (used for relieving fever from 1884) and cocaine. Superiors also wanted to restrain the use of tobacco and alcohol.

The apostolic life among the missionaries was good, but the political events of recent years made evangelisation difficult. The Europeans were not confident in the success of the formation of the Chinese clergy, which added to concerns about the apostolate. Despite good numbers of seminarians in training at Xujiahui, the major seminarians were restless and even defiant. Entry into the minor seminary needed to be more rigorous.[53]

53. Notes of the visit to Jiangsu by RP Mollat, French provincial, Paris, 1924. ARSI.

Around this time, Joseph Hugon believed that the necessary qualities for a good missionary included good health, good humour, great detachment, energy, adaptability, gentleness and a spirit of prayer.[54]

Division of the mission

As the rest of the country braced itself for civil war, the Jesuits were discussing among themselves and with the apostolic delegate how best to divide the mission of Jiangnan that had too many Christians to manage. It seemed that a region with about 32,000 Christians was considered sufficient for any one vicariate to manage. Above that number, a division was required.

The decision by the apostolic delegate to divide the Jiangnan vicariate was not well received by many in the mission, but more level heads realised that the Province of France could no longer supply men for the mission, and resources in the mission were already strained, with insufficient finances, and missionaries growing older and sick.

When the decision to divide was made, consultation took place about how many new vicariates should be formed, and if one of them should be run by the Chinese clergy, according to the wish of the apostolic delegate.

Noury and Verdier suggested that Canadian Jesuits take the Xuzhou area (12 prefectures and 45,000 Christians), the Chinese clergy be given Hai Men and Chongming (19 prefectures, 32,000 Christians, and 22 priests), and south of the river to be retained by the French.[55] Verdier wrote that the French missionaries were 'happy with a Chinese vicariate', but warned that the Xuzhou region would be harder for them to run, as vocations there were rare. West of Shanghai and in Nanjing, Christians and vocations were not numerous. The two sections of Pudong and Pounce-east (south of the river) had more Christians, but few vocations. Here, the Christians were richer, and so more difficult to administer. Shanghai was considered a bad influence on the Christians. The Chinese had asked for Shanghai, but

---

54. Joseph Hugon, *La Mission de Nankin* (Paris: Vanves, 1925).
55. Noury to Assistant, Shanghai, 17 March 1924; Verdier to General, Nanjing, 3 February 1924; Verdier to General, Shanghai, 27 April 1924. ARSI.

Verdier did not think that a Chinese bishop in such an international city was wise.[56]

The creation of a Chinese prefecture apostolic was discussed because *Propaganda Fide,* via the apostolic delegate, wanted it. The Jesuits reluctantly accepted it, as did Bishop Paris and Verdier, but they were against it, saying that the Chinese were not yet ready for this responsibility. The Hai Men region suggested was the oldest Chinese Christian community, with Christians relatively numerous with some vocations, and a well-formed social-minded clergy.

Opinions differed between the European and Chinese priests as to which part of Jiangsu to give to the Chinese. The Europeans stressed the importance of a clear division giving each an apostolic field with less 'conflict of interests'. It should not be too large during 'this time of trial'. The Chinese wanted a well-organised prefecture, easy to administer with a good number of Christians and Christian communities, which would be a fertile region for vocations. They wished to have 'face', that is, a prefecture that honoured them, and one that would have confidence in them. The Europeans would not allow their preferred region of Shanghai. Figures for the number of Christians ruled out Nanjing, Anhui, and Xuzhou. Moreover, Nanjing was a strong Protestant base. That left Xuzhou, Shanghai or Hai Men. Bishop Paris and Verdier wanted Chongming and Hai Men, north of the river for the Chinese. The French province wanted Shanghai and surrounding districts, sections of Xuzhou, Dangzhou and Nanjing. The advantage of Paris' suggestion was that it pleased the Europeans, while the Chinese would have a well-developed region. The disadvantages were that the Chinese might be unhappy because Chongming was 'poor and miserable'. The rest of Hai Men was underdeveloped, and so difficult. Above all, they would lose 'face' administering a region with few resources. There was no major Catholic town, too few priests and seminarians. Another suggestion was to give the Chinese the Xuzhou region, which was a more prosperous area, so the Chinese would save 'face', but the Europeans were less agreeable to this idea. A further possibility was to give the Chinese sections of Pudong and Punan or sections of Chongming and Hai Men or sections including Songjiang.

A second question was when and how to divide Jiangsu. It was agreed that it should be done, as the mission was too large for the

56. Verdier, ut supra, 27 April 1924.

French province affected by persecution and war, with resulting lack of vocations. Each region needed more missionaries. Verdier wrote that if the Society could not help with the divisions, it would be necessary to find other religious orders. The division should take place as soon as possible, 'but with prudence'. Whatever the division, it should be 'for the good of souls'.

Opinions from the Jesuit consultors of the vicariate were that there was no Chinese Jesuit capable of governing according to the Jesuit Institute (Schellier); give north of the river to German or Austrian Jesuits (Beaucé); French Jesuits were already overstretched looking after Jesuit common works in Shanghai to move out to the 'bush' to convert non-Christians (Noury); and Lorando suggested that the division would happen, so give the regions of the north, Xuzhou and surrounding areas (with 46,000 Christians and 16,000 catechumens) to other Jesuits, as there was unity around the Mandarin language, and an autonomous secular Chinese vicariate in the south. [57]

In discussing the division of the Jiangnan vicariate, the French acknowledged that they needed assistance to run the mission, even with help from other religious orders if no Jesuit province would help. A change in attitude was also shown by acceptance of the wish of the apostolic delegate to establish an independent Chinese vicariate, even if reluctantly. In reality, the establishment of a Chinese vicariate would enable the Europeans to see that the Chinese could administer a region, but in a Chinese way.

---

57. Memo concerning the division of the Mission of Jiangsu, 1924; Extracts from consultors letters on the division of Jiangsu mission, 1924. ARSI.

Chapter 6
Civil War and Anti-Christian Activity
1925–1928

Amid internal discussions in the Catholic Church about the divisions of vicariates, the country was moving toward civil war. During 1925, there was an increase in anti-Christian propaganda. Reports were coming into the French legation with slogans like 'Christianity is a poison to the Chinese'; 'Christianity was the place where was born the diplomats who sold our country'; 'Christianity is the soul of international capitalism'. Christianity was believed to serve imperialism in order to conquer China, with priests as spies of imperialism. The history of Christianity in China was seen as a way to conquer China by means of opium and treaties to protect missionaries. This was given credence when Germany occupied Tsingtao after two missionaries were killed. 'The cross was a symbolic form of phallus worship' was another slogan. Furthermore, Jesus Christ was called 'a false idol, egotistical and vengeful'.[1]

These strong anti-Christian sentiments stemmed from the close connection of Christianity with the conquering European powers, which were seen by some as destroying China. The agitators were largely young, educated, nationally-minded Chinese who did not want propagated any ideas, religious or Western, that might hold back the material development of China and its people. The spiritual mission of the European missionaries was frequently obscured by their own nationalist spirit in promoting European ideas, without discerning whether they were good for China. They believed that European culture and Roman Catholicism were far better than what currently

---

1. Letter re anti-Christian propaganda, January 1925. DAC.

existed in China. The missionaries vigorously promoted both, often to their detriment.

Movements against Christianity in Zhili had been increasing over the years. France needed to realise that the anti-religious movement was also a political problem. These movements, essentially 'non-religious associations', that promoted science against faith, and the spirit of intellectual freedom against obscurantism, could lead to anti-foreignism, especially as Bolshevism was on the rise.[2]

The French legation closely monitored these movements, observing the existence of an 'anti-Protestant League' at Shanghai University with Li Ping Ziang as leader. They were concerned about the 'secret societies' that had the same end: 'abolish all authority, make all brothers, all people equal in privilege and wealth, attack foreigners, destroy religion, all riches of the country belong to the people and should be returned to them'. The example of Russia was encouraged, which indicated the influence of Bolshevism in these ideas.[3]

The civil war raging in Jiangsu and Zhejiang from 1924–5 meant that the work of the missionaries was in 'constant threat of obliteration'. On 30 May 1925, in Nanjing Road, Shanghai, students distributed leaflets against the foreigners in general and the Japanese in particular. Banners displayed were: 'Death to the Japanese, death to the English, death to the foreigners'. The police opened fire and killed four Chinese, with 30 wounded, of which five died later in hospital in Chantong Rd. This incident was considered a tragedy, as it indicated that foreigners were hated, especially the English and Japanese. The English were symbolised by a tortoise, the French by a pig, and the Japanese by a dog. Japanese and English goods were boycotted, which paralysed trade. They were called 'the exploiters of China'. Most of the students were believed to be Bolshevists.[4]

By the end of December 1925, the anti-Christian movement was considered 'a national movement with its centre in Guangzhou'. The movement appeared to develop during 1921 at the World Christian Students Federation that held its international convention in Beijing. In 1923, the 'Young China Society' met in Suzhou, and declared that 'Christian education was anti-nationalist because Christianity came

---

2.   French Consul, Tianjin, to French Minister, Beijing, 23 February 1925. DAC.
3.   Memorandum to French Minister Beijing, 26 February 1925. DAC.
4.   Report from Fr. Henri Dugout, *Etudes,* 20 April 1925.

from foreign countries'. This was called 'cultural invasion'. The movement was strongest in Guangzhou and Shantou, forceful in Ningbo and Shanghai, alive in Beijing, but not in Tianjin. The Guomindang believed in freedom of religious belief, but the Communists were anti-Christian. The Anti-Christian Alliance met from 22–24 December 1925, declaring that 'by magic training of missionaries, Chinese Christians had become the forced slaves of imperialists'. In order to gain perfect freedom for China, Christian propaganda needed to be checked. Shanghai was singled out as the 'stronghold of Christianity' and its influence very strong, especially through its 'liturgy aggression'.[5]

During 1926, French missionaries and, surprisingly, the apostolic delegate as well, sent petitions to the French minister in Beijing seeking help against the anti-Christian movement.[6] Specific complaints received included those concerning the Chinese army stealing from villagers, and about a band of anti-Christian students giving out pamphlets to people, exciting them to action against foreigners.[7]

The French minister in Beijing was so concerned with the anti-Christian and anti-foreign riots by students in Beijing that he registered a complaint with the Chinese foreign minister. The students opposed the introduction of foreign culture, the spread of Christianity, and the Christian religion. Chinese converts were called 'servant dogs', and Chinese students were urged to leave all mission schools. Teachings given by 'foreign slaves' were to be ignored, and mission schools should be suppressed. The French minister called this 'a serious happening' that denounced the Franco-Chinese treaties, as well as the 'liberty of civilised peoples', and demanded that the government stop the demonstrations. Somewhat ambiguously, the Minister of Public Instruction arrested agitators, but informed the mission schools to conform to all rules and ordinances of his department. In reply, the French minister asked for assurance that this rule would not restrict the liberty of conscience that the missions enjoyed, and was in accordance with the agreement between France and China.

Recent outbreaks of attacks on missions included those at Suiyuan, where property was confiscated, as well as at Sichuan, with the

5. *North China Herald*, 26 December 1925. DAC.
6. Letters to French Minister, Beijing, 1926. DAC.
7. Missionary priest to French Minister, Shijiazhuang, 6 January 1926. DAC.

arbitrary imposition of taxes, and in Jiangxi, where the right to buy and sell property according to the Berthemy Treaty was threatened. The formation of an Anti-Christian Federation aimed to abolish religious teaching and to forbid the Christian religion. The Chinese government must not allow this according to the treaties and to the principles that were the basis of the Republic of China's constitution.

There was concern about the publication of two pamphlets in January 1926, one in French from Zhengzhou (Henan) attached to the walls of the Catholic Mission of Nan-gong (Zhili), and the second in English sent to Shanghai from the students at the Jesuit 'Institute des Hautes Industrelles' in Tianjin. In the first pamphlet signed by Tcheng Tcheou from the Anti-Christian Federation, he declared that the Christian religion deceived and oppressed the people. It was the 'grand canon of imperialism' that capitalist countries brought to China to ensnare the people. It brought death to China. The English pamphlet was more strident in its condemnation of Christianity. The heading was 'Down with Christianity', a religion that was 'a tool of world imperialism', was not scientific, helped keep the people weak and in slavery, fooled the feeble minded, and especially young students. Christians were claimed to consort with 'despicable vagrants and outlaws'; they took advantage of the unequal treaties and influenced local lawsuits. They occupied Chinese premises by force and intervened 'with the freedom of matrimony'. The pamphlet was a clean sweep of all Christian influences in China.

Ironically, the apostolic delegate asked the French legation what it had done during the anti-Christian disturbances, and was sent copies of the letter to the Chinese minister and of the pamphlets. Copies of these were then sent to Rome.[8] Did Costantini simply want to be kept informed of actions taken by the French legation, or was it more subtly his way of collecting data that would later be used against the French protectorate in favour of Rome? In dealing with the Chinese government, the French had greater influence than the apostolic delegate, who did not have the threat of force of arms.

Meanwhile, from the Jesuit mission, Verdier reported to the superior general that the war between two military leaders in Shanghai and in the Province of Zhejiang (south-west of the mission) had resulted in much suffering by the Christians. Xujiahui had been threatened

---

8.   French Minister, Beijing, to Chinese Foreign Minister, Beijing, 6 February 1926. PF.

but was saved by French sailors. About 6,000 refugees gathered in
Xujiahui, and several churches in Wuhu had been destroyed. With
reference to the division of the vicariate that continued during this
time, Verdier was negotiating for French Canadian Jesuits to be sent
to China, but currently he was not impressed with the newly arrived
Spanish priests, who showed 'complete indifference to the needs of
their subjects'.[9] A few days later, Verdier mentioned in another letter
to the superior general that he had received a letter from the apostolic delegate informing him of the approval of the establishment of a
new Chinese diocese, as foreigners were no longer acceptable at this
time of Chinese nationalism.[10] This desire of the delegate to further
Chinese causes was further reinforced when he disapproved of the
proposal to open an English-speaking church in Shanghai, which was
to exclude Chinese. He said that the proposal was against the 'custom
of the church', and would not be diplomatic in the troubled times with
the Chinese. He recommended an English-speaking church that had
Masses in Chinese as well as in English.[11]

Chinese language concerns, 1926

The question of teaching the local language to the foreign missionaries was a continuing concern for Church officials, not only because
of its necessity for communicating with the Chinese, and also as a
sign to the Chinese that the foreigners were serious about sharing in
Chinese life and customs.

The Chinese Jesuits generally did not approve that the French
language was the main medium of instruction in mission schools.
The Chinese Jesuit, Joseph Zi, prefect of studies at the seminary in
Xujiahui, writing to the superior general in 1926, raised the question
of the unsuitability of using French as the language of instruction at
Aurora University, as many Chinese could not understand the language or did not want to use it. He noted that the Protestant universities lectured in English, which the Chinese preferred. In addition, he
was not happy with the standard of education received by the young
Chinese Jesuits.

9. Verdier to General, Shanghai, 26 March 1925. ARSI.
10 Verdier to General, Shanghai, 31 March 1925. ARSI.
11. Costantini to Beaucé, Beijing, 25 October 1925. ARSI.

He reflected that it was dangerous to speak about China in general, as there were so many diverse regions reflecting different mentality and language use. Therefore, the formation of seminarians should be considered on a regional basis, and even within regions. In the seminary at Xianxian, there was a Latin course for students who came from different regions and did not understand each other. Latin was the unifying language. It was difficult for the Europeans to understand the complex Chinese mentality. Many foreign missionaries never went beyond the treaty ports, the concessions or the legations, and never visited the interior of China, which was never comprehended by many missionaries. Very few were proficient in a Chinese language.

The superior general, in an instruction to the Jesuit superiors of Shanghai on 15 August 1919, had commented that the education given to the Chinese should be in proportion to the ability of the Chinese to understand (*ad modum recipientis*). Chinese scholastics should be given similar 'literary and scientific' studies as European scholastics, according to their capacity, and be formed to reach the same standard as their European counterparts. This was seen to be impossible at Xianxian, where the students were incapable of following closely classes in the style of those given in Florence or Laval (France). Was it not Jesuit policy to form Jesuits 'to the measure of their divine gifts rather than to realise some general formation'?

Zi further suggested that Chinese language study ought to begin before the end of philosophy. Others said it should begin during juniorate studies (earlier studies of the humanities). Instead of doing regency in Europe, they could go to language school in Tianjin and then study theology and tertianship in Europe. This more concentrated study of the language would be more appropriate for missionary work.

An outline of studies was suggested. In the novitiate, studies of the history and geography of the missions and of the province might be undertaken. Juniorate studies could include linguistics, philology, and a classical course of grammar and phonetics. In philosophy, the principles of ethnology and natural history might be included, with missiology and the history of religions during theology. Rules for missionaries would be suitable during tertianship. He claimed that Chinese scholastics were not capable of profiting from the study of French classics, yet he also wanted them to spend time in Europe, which would usually be in France, so understanding the French language would help.[12] This Chinese perspective of studies wanted the best offered by the Europeans, but with greater adaptation to the Chinese language and culture.

The following month, the bishop, Prosper Paris, took up the discussion of the study of the Chinese language. He made the distinction between what was required by the ordinary missionaries, and for those who were academics. He believed that one- year study was sufficient for the missionary, with more years allocated for the scholar. He was not in favour of sending young Chinese to Europe. Jesuit superiors should 'clearly know China, the Chinese, the lives of the Christians and everything about our apostolate'. He did not believe that Jesuits in Europe understood the requirements for missionaries in China.

Paris was aware of the different Chinese dialects, and the difference between the written and spoken language, with Mandarin spoken in the north of the mission, with different modalities, and the language of Shanghai spoken by almost all in the mission. He wanted all missionaries to be able to write and speak both languages in order to communicate with others, and to read an ordinary newspaper, letters and current books on 'doctrine and prayers'. There could be no missionary activity without this. He would like the European scholastics to study the written language during philosophy studies in Europe. When they came to China with these basics, a full year of study of the written language under a personal tutor in classical Chinese would be essential. This should be followed by a study of the spoken language: Mandarin first, and then the Shanghai dialect, both with competent lay tutors. Further studies and practice were encouraged.[13]

The superior general followed up on these ideas with his own ordinance. He reminded the missionaries that St Ignatius wanted all Jesuits to learn the language and culture of the place to which they were sent. Those destined for China during juniorate and philosophy studies should become acquainted with the history and geography of the region, and its current way of life. They should also have a working knowledge of English. When they arrived, two years or more studying the Chinese language under the guidance of the best

---

12. Zi to General, Xujiahui, 26 January 1926. ARSI.
13. Bishop Paris to Jesuit superior, Shanghai, 15 February 1926.

teachers was recommended. After this, the scholastic should go for a year into the mission areas to apply his knowledge. Tertianship should be in Europe until one can be arranged in China.[14] In this letter, the superior general showed his attempt to understand what preparations missionaries needed when assigned to China, and what was required when they arrived.

Roman intervention in China

While the Jesuits were discussing their own issues, the apostolic delegate and Rome were working on further interventions in China. The ideas of Lebbe and the apostolic delegate, Costantini, on behalf of a Chinese Church, were well supported in Rome. As a result of these interventions, in June 1926, Pius XI wrote to the bishops of China 'against some erroneous opinions on the subject of the works of the Church among the people' of China. He spoke of his 'solicitude' for the work of the missions. He reminded them of his previous letter, *Rerum Ecclesiae* (28 February 1926), where he championed the rights of the local clergy, and strongly urged the foreign missionaries to work for the establishment of a Chinese Church. Since then, he had been concerned about the way the young Chinese ridiculed the work of the Church, thinking that the main aim of the Church and the missionaries was not purely 'religious and spiritual', but served the political ends of foreign nations. This was an obstacle to the independence of the missionaries, and to the just national claims of the Chinese. In the history of the Church, she had not only propagated the greatness of Christianity, but had supported the people against tyrannical governments. Missionaries had traditionally been on guard against the prejudiced interests of foreign nationals. To this end, European missionaries should not only educate the Chinese clergy to help them in their mission, but work with them to replace the Europeans, as soon as numbers permitted. He rejoiced in the increased number of Chinese clergy, which he saw as the result of the seeds sown by the European missionaries, and who currently helped govern the Chinese Church. He was pleased that during his pontificate, he had

---

14. Decree of ARPN General, on the subject of Chinese studies for missionaries, Rome, 3 September 1926, in *Lettres de Jersey,* Vol. XL, Nouvelle Série, T.VII (1926–7): 56–7.

raised some independent Chinese vicariates, in the prefectures of Puqi, Hubei (12 December 1923), and Anguo, Hebei, (15 April 1924). The two Chinese prelates of these vicariates were the first Chinese to be present among European vicars apostolic at the Church Synod in Shanghai later in 1924.

The pope continued instructing the missionaries that the Church was not to be seen as interfering in civil affairs, or for promoting the interests of foreign powers. All should obey the laws and customs of the country, respecting the dignity and authority of legitimate civil authority. If sometimes foreign governments offered their protection, it must never be used to the detriment of the local people, but only to extricate those who were being unjustly treated. The Chinese government should protect its citizens, and the missionaries as well, amid dangers, while the Holy See would protect the Catholic missions from arbitrary and unjust treatment: they should not rely on help from foreign nationals.[15] The pope was having an each-way bet.

This letter paved the way for Roman follow up a few weeks later when Cardinal van Rossum, on 30 March 1926, announced the decision of the pope to consecrate the first six Chinese bishops.[16] In an accompanying letter, the pope urged all missionaries, once again, not to be agents for foreign powers in China. The pope consecrated the new bishops in Rome on 28 October 1926; the first ethnic Chinese to be made bishops since Lo Wen-sao in 1674.[17] In his homily during the consecration, the pope expressed hope that this occasion would be a new beginning for the Church in China, exhorting the Chinese bishops to take up the 'pastoral baton' by preaching and baptising. He spoke highly of the 'scientific, artistic and literary' culture of the Chinese. In taking this step, the pope showed great trust in the Chinese clergy, believing against the advice of many foreign vicars apostolic,

---

15. Letter of Pius XI to the Chinese bishops, Rome, 15 June 1926, in *Lettres de Jersey*, XL, Nouvelle Série, T.VII (1926–7): 52–5.

16. Van Rossum to Costantini, Rome, 20 March 1926, PF.

17. **Lo-Wen-sao** (1616–1690), was born in China of Chinese parents, and was a Dominican priest from the Philippines Province, ordained in 1656. He courageously supported the Jesuits in the debates over the Chinese rites, faithfully defending the Chinese. His religious confreres did not approved of this stance, and the Dominican master general did not approve his appointment as bishop. After attempts in the Philippines to prevent his consecration, including his arrest, he was consecrated in Guangzhou in 1685, by Bishop Bernardin della Chiesa, 15 years after his nomination as bishop.

that it was time for the Chinese to take greater leadership in their own churches. Politically, it was a wise move, showing that amidst the anti-Christian movement then current in China, the Catholic Church did value the gifts of the Chinese to run their own affairs.

This event was the realisation of the dream of Costantini to provide the basis for an autonomous Chinese Church, but it raised difficulties with the existing European vicars apostolic, many of whom indicated open opposition, citing yet again that the Chinese were not ready for this responsibility. European standards were high, and the mode of operating in the vicariates was European, with little appreciation for Chinese sensitivities, which in many aspects was different to the Europeans. Only those Chinese clergy who acted with the same zeal, poverty, humility and obedience as the Europeans were considered acceptable missionaries. One might wonder if these European missionaries would ever consider the Chinese clergy ready for government of their own church. They had been educated by the foreign missionaries; so why were they not yet ready for governing their own region? Was their education deficient or were they considered unsuitable because of temperament or culture? In assessments given about the suitability of the Chinese clergy for administration, the foreign Jesuits usually focused on personal character deficiencies.

The six Chinese bishops consecrated included the two previously nominated for Puqi and Anguo: Odoric Cheng He-de OFM and Melchior Sun De-zhen CM. The others were Philip Zhao Huai-yi (Xuanhua, Hebei), diocesan priest from Beijing, secretary to the apostolic delegation; Joseph Hu Ruo-shan CM (Taizhou, Zhejiang), consultor at the Shanghai synod; Aloysius Chen Guo-di OFM (Fenyang, Shanxi), also a member of the synod; and Simon Zhu Kai-min SJ (Hai Men, Jiangxi). Those who were religious were nominated by their respective religious superiors as being 'men of confidence'.[18]

Upon the announcement of the nomination of the Jesuit Simon Zhu Kai-min to Hai Men, Costantini wrote a congratulatory note to Bishop Paris, praising him for promoting the indigenous clergy, and gave praise for those European missionaries who had 'planted the seed' for the faith among the Chinese.[19] A few days later, he

---

18. Louis Wei Tsing-sing, *Le Saint-siege et la Chine de Pie XI à nos jours* (Paris: Allais, 1968), 128–32, 137–8.
19. Costantini to Bishop Paris, Beijing, 4 August 1926. DAC.

announced the nomination of the bishops to the Chinese vicariates, saying that the pope praised the missions and that he had care for them. He stressed that missionary activity was intended for the Chinese, and only second to serve the interests of the foreign state. In consecrating the Chinese bishops, the pope was showing the universality of the Church, which pleased the pope very much.[20]

The Jesuit reaction to the consecrations was cautious. With the announcement the Jesuits accepted the news, there was obvious unity, and a celebration was held. Chinese Christians were very happy with the news, but the Jesuits, especially those in Hai Men, the new Chinese vicariate, expressed mixed feelings.[21]

When Costantini arrived back in China with the six new Chinese bishops on an American boat, the French legation in Beijing expressed fears that this was another symbolic act that Costantini was trying to avoid any connection with the French protectorate. It was noted that the consecration of the bishops coincided at a time of 'great anarchy in China', with hostile influences among the Chinese Bolshevists and 'Young Turks' being expressed against religion in Guangzhou. The legation was proud of French missionaries who had good relations with the local Chinese population, in contrast with the attitude of 'certain other national religious'. The question of the sharing of property among the old and new vicariates was raised, with the comment that the administration of capital given to the new vicariates would continue to be administered by the foreign bishops.[22] The French minister was wary of the administrative skills of the Chinese bishops.

Costantini remained concerned about the French protectorate. He mentioned to Rome that the French government still wanted to protect Chinese Catholics. He was against the idea that the new Chinese bishops should go to the French consul 'in times of necessity' against their own government. All missionary matters should be handled by the apostolic delegate. Moreover, the Berthemy Convention was a treaty between China and France, and did not involve the Holy See. He was suggesting that the Holy See and China should have a treaty. Meanwhile, the Jesuits preferred to go to the French legation

---

20. Costantini to Chinese vicariates, Beijing, 7 August 1926, *La Politique de Pekin*, 22 August 1926. DAC.
21. Beaucé to Assistant, Xujiahui, 10 August 1926. ARSI.
22. French minister, Beijing, to French minister, Paris, 11 September 1926. DAC.

for protection rather than the apostolic delegate. It was also reported that the Chinese Communists were told by Russia to provoke Western powers to intervene in issues arising between missionaries of local authorities, even if they had to 'pillage and massacre' in order to get them into conflict. They wanted the fall of Marshal Zhang Zuo lin, and encouraged the Communists to maintain discord among the foreign powers and to be particularly watchful of Japan.[23]

Civil War, 1925–1929

While the Catholic missions were working out their own issues, the political situation in China deteriorated. It accelerated with the massacre of Chinese students in Shanghai on 30 May 1925 by agents of the British police, following a disturbance in the international concession, sparked off a series of incidents all over China, protesting against the foreign aggressors. The civil war that followed not only indicated objection to the control exercised by foreigners, but also worked against the works of both Catholic and Protestant missions that were protected by these foreign powers. It was a strong warning, taken seriously by the Chinese clergy, but not by the foreign missionaries.[24]

The causes of troubles in China from 1911, but increasing from the spring of 1920, were incessant inter-factional warfare, as well as foreign imperialism. Internally there was fighting among the marshals in the north, and between northern and southern armies, aggravated by Russia. Foreign imperialism included the foreign concessions, leased territories, the unequal treaties, and restriction upon tariffs. Aggressive mission activity compounded the problems.

The 1858 Arrow War, the Taiping and Boxer Rebellions, and the revolution of 1911 that led to increasing chaos in China, were all given as examples of imperialism.

The rise of Chinese nationalism was a direct result of foreign imperialism. It was born from a Chinese inferiority complex verses the West: Westerners lived better in China than the Chinese. Even worse, the Westerner witnessed China's failures and shame. The aims of the nationalists were to expel the foreigner and have China for the Chinese. In observing this increasing hatred, Westerners sensed the

---

23. Costantini to Cardinal van Rossum, Beijing, 13 November 1926. PF.
24. Louis Wei Tsing-sing, up supra, 137.

unfavourable influence of Russia that exploited China's anti-foreign-ism and encouraged chaos in society. Russia was not seen as seeking the welfare of China.

The British saw the anti-Christian agitation as only secondary to anti-foreignism, rather than the opposite, as the French legation sug-gested. During the conflict between the Northerners (Nationalists) and the Southerners (Communists/Kuomintang), the majority of missionaries were evacuated from the south to Nanjing and Hankou. There was mass destruction of Christian buildings, murder, rape and looting. In Zhejiang, the cemetery was destroyed, with the bones of missionaries killed in the Boxer Rebellion scattered. Both National-ists and Communists attacked Christianity. The 'Christian General', Feng Yuxiang, made attacks on missions, with missionaries from Shensi and Kansu evacuated. Civilians were treated inhumanely. Anti-foreignism was on the increase at all levels.[25]

From Haizhou, it was reported that 1927 had been a bad year for the missions in China because of the war between the two main com-batants, together with troops of brigands that terrorised the coun-tryside when the soldiers moved south. This affected the work of the mission: conversions had been good up to the arrival of the troops.[26]

On the evening of 23 March 1927, two days after taking Shang-hai, the National Revolutionary Army entered Nanjing under fire from British and American warships that were attempting to pro-tect foreign possessions from looting by the pro-Communist militia. Foreigners and their property were attacked, which surprised the for-eigners because this had not happened before during the Northern Expedition. This illustrated that xenophobia was a significant aspect of Chinese nationalism.

Less than one week after the coup in Shanghai, Chiang Kai-shek established his National Government in Nanjing, claiming to be the legitimate government for the whole of China. Southerners accepted the Guomindang as well as much of the north excluding Manchuria, and those loyal to the former warlords.[27]

Joseph Verdier, the superior of the Jesuits, was present in Nanjing at the time of its capture and reported that the attack came suddenly

---

25. 'The foreigner in China', *North China Daily*, Shanghai, 1927. DAC.
26. Hermand to General, Haitchcou, 1 February 1927. ARSI.
27. Dillon, op. cit., 208–9.

and quickly, with violence that had not been expected. The northern army present at the time had respected foreigners and their property, but that changed with the arrival of the southern army. When they arrived, Protestant missionaries left, fearful for their lives. Jesuit missionaries had previously fled Li-zhui, which was in the path of the advancing southern army. Verdier informed the British Consul about this incident. Placards were displayed announcing peace and order to the China people, but also incited pillage to the houses of foreigners. At Wuhu they occupied the Jesuit house, but there was no violence. Chinese religious and priests were sent to Shanghai. These troops came from Hunan, 'with a red band around their arm', demanding money that they thought the missionaries held for the northern army.[28]

After the taking of Nanjing, it was noted that the death of two priests, Claudio Vanara, an Italian, and Henry Dugout, killed by southern soldiers affected the Jesuits. The killings were seen as part of a 'wave of xenophobia and hate against religion' that had been witnessed in the south of China, and moved north with the advancing Cantonese army. On the morning of 24 March, people from Hunan attacked the English and Japanese consulates and other foreign establishments, especially Standard Oil, where some foreign refugees fled, but they did not touch a single Chinese house. At 6am, they forced the doors of the Jesuit residence and searched the place looking for money. The soldiers, followed by the people, pillaged everything inside and outside the house. Verdier was able to leave after two hours by bribing a soldier, and retreated to a more secure house, where Augustus Bureau later joined him in the Nanjing area. The following day, the French ship *L'Alerte* arrived at Nanjing, and was able to secure the release of the two priests. The Jesuits 'thanked God for his Providence', but it was hoped that they also thanked the French navy. The Jesuits had lost everything, including the death of two priests from the college.

On the evening of 25 March, the *L'Alerte*, with the two priests, a Jesuit brother, Andrew Tcheng, and a French lady, returned to Shanghai, but not before an assurance from the invading soldiers that they would bury the dead priests. They did nothing: some Christians performed the burial after the soldiers had dismembered the bodies.

---

28. Verdier, Nanjing, March 1927. PF.

From this time, the lives of European priests in the interior of China appeared to be at risk, and even more so when the foreign powers demanded reparations.

The same report mentioned the taking of Shanghai on 22 March in the afternoon, by the same troops. As the southern troops approached, Aurora University was closed on 21 March. At Xujiahui, toward 5pm on the same day, 2,000 southern soldiers attempted to force themselves into the compound and occupy the Jesuit houses, but were stopped by French sailors who defended Xujiahui. The advancing soldiers halted and camped outside the compound, while some joined other soldiers in the attack on Shanghai.

This was a testing time for the missionaries, who decided to move its people from Xujiahui into the foreign concessions in Shanghai until peace was restored. Fears were expressed that if the southern army became masters of Shanghai, Jesuit ministry would become impossible. In particular, teaching in the schools, colleges and in the university would be affected, if stories from Guangzhou were to be believed.

Not only were mission buildings, churches, residences and schools pillaged and destroyed in many places, but also mission property was threatened with confiscation. Signs indicating the 'Catholic Church' were being replaced with 'Common Property'. Nanjing, Zhejiang and the Chinese territory of Shanghai were the most threatened.[29]

Before the taking of Shanghai, the Jesuits had reported that the southern soldiers were all around Shanghai, with many having gone to Hai Men and to the north. Some troops were already moving from Shanghai towards Nanjing via Lake Taihu. They had occupied two Christian communities of Joseph Sen, destroyed the residence and 'profaned the Church'. Refugees were going to Shanghai from the west, Son-Kong and surrounding villages. Anhui was in their hands, and they occupied the residence of Bishop Vincent Huarte and pillaged all the religious houses. It was similar at Yun-zao with Jean Noury.[30]

The French legation was being kept informed of events. Even before the taking of Shanghai, it learned about violence in Wuhu, when Brother Blas Buruaga was wounded by gunshot 'from a propa-

---

29. Beaucé to General, Shanghai, 2 April 1927. ARSI.
30. Report from Xujiahui, 17 March 1927. ARSI. Jean Noury had been in China since November 1901.

gandist of Yantsao'. Other reports were that the Jesuit residences were being occupied by troops and property destroyed in Jiangsu.[31]

Finally, the situation was so serious that the French Minister of Foreign Affairs in Paris sent a message to the Jesuit procurator in Paris that all French citizens were to be evacuated from the region of Xianxian that was threatened, and even suggested that all Church authorities leave the missions. If any choose to stay, they should inform the French legation in Beijing.[32] This was communicated to the superior general in Rome, who immediately wrote to the Jesuit superior in Shanghai informing him of this advice for all French citizens to leave danger areas, and that they stayed at their own risk. He advised the Jesuits to remain at their posts as long as possible, despite the danger: that was the Jesuit tradition, even to accept death.[33] In receiving this message in Xianxian, the superior, Jean Debeauvais, said that the Jesuits were told to go to an 'open port', either to Tianjin or Shanghai. He questioned the right of the consuls to give this order, as many Chinese would be very happy to see the end of foreign missionaries. He felt that if the Jesuits left at that time, they might never be permitted to return. To leave the mission station should not be a decision of foreign consuls or Chinese Christians. Should war break out between China and a foreign power, the Jesuits would have to work as Catholics and not as foreign nationals. The apostolic delegate could replace the foreign powers in granting immunity for Catholic missions and giving legal status to the Church in China. Debeauvais seemed to be supporting the idea of the apostolic delegate to transfer Catholic protection from the foreign power to the Vatican, which he said, other missionaries agreed with him. But as this differed from the official view among the Jesuit missions, he wanted this letter to be private and confidential.[34]

A report from Emil Bonay on earlier events from Wuhu indicated that the northern troops had left and the southern revolutionary troops had arrived. This prefecture had a long history of Bolshevist agents. In nearly all the villages they had secret clubs, largely Communist. These clubs recruited from the Protestant schools, the peas-

---

31. French Minister, Shanghai, to French consul, Hankeou, 18 March 1927. DAC.
32. French Minister of Foreign Affairs, Paris, to Jesuit Procurator, Paris, 15 April 1927. ARSI.
33. General, Rome, to Beaucé, Shanghai, 26 April 1927. ARSI.
34. Debeauvais, Xianxian, to Apostolic Delegate, Tianjin, 25 April 1927. PF.

ants, the employees of the commerce houses, the unemployed, and outcasts of the areas, as well as those who were older or more simply utopian. Beyond these more or less secret clubs, nearly all the population were supporters of the southerners and the national revolutionary army. They alone said the propaganda could save China from the so-called oppression of the foreigner, and bring to the people riches, peace and honour. At Wuhu, these revolutionaries came from outside the city, organised the clubs, provided arms, and prepared the village for attacks from the northern army. There were rumours in the Chinese press that they would attack the missions, take the missionaries hostage, and if they did not talk, kill them. Protestant ministers were ordered by their consul to go to Shanghai. Only the doctor at the hospital and an American church minister remained. All the children from the Jesuit schools were evacuated by 14 March. Bonay and some religious sisters left for Shanghai on 17 March, while the director and an older companion guarded the girls' school.

The Communists occupied the whole district of Gong-sou, and after the soldiers left, the clubs took over, closed the school and forced the catechist to leave. At the Jesuit residence at Wuhu, the Jesuits left gradually, Joseph Sen was sick and James Ling was tired; so Bonay sent them to Shanghai on barges, together with the sacred vessels and some money. He remained with Simon Zhu. Communication with Shanghai became impossible.

The southern rebels arrived on the evening of that same day. There was no battle as the northern army had already left. The clubs took over the government of the village in the name of Tsiang Kai-che. The government prefect had disappeared together with the 'notables': 'We were governed by children'.

On 23 March, the first soldiers arrived at the Jesuit residence. They took over the boys' school for the soldiers' residence. Later, they took over the Jesuit residence. They insulted Bonay and wanted to take him prisoner, but at a meeting of the people, not one word was spoken against him. Zhu was so scared that he went to Gao-zang-ou, not far from Wuhu, where there was a chapel, but no priests' residence. He soon after moved much further away to Gong-ce.

The army of Sun-chuan fong occupied the village, which had been incorporated into the army of Tsiang Kiai che. Bonay was held prisoner in his room in the residence, unable to see any Christian. On 30 March, after receiving letters from his superiors in Shanghai, he decided to leave Wuhu by barge along the Imperial Canal to Shanghai. Twenty-six Christian villages in the region were occupied and pillaged by soldiers or clubs. They incited the people against the missionaries and said that they were 'enemies of religion'. They claimed that the Chinese had only one religion, *Suen wen*: 'one doctrine whose three principles were a mixture of Communist thoughts, socialism and a hatred of all that was not Chinese', including the foreigner.[35]

The apostolic delegate had been kept informed of these developments, but he was unable to do anything. Bishop Paris wrote to him that he feared that war between China and the foreign powers could erupt. All Jesuit foreign missionaries had been sent to Xujiahui in Shanghai, leaving the Chinese priests in the districts. Many chapels had been destroyed.[36]

By mid-May, it was reported that fears in Shanghai had diminished. There had been a struggle between the moderate and extreme Communists but, in general, peace currently reigned. Some Jesuits had returned to their outlying posts, but others could not because soldiers occupied their residences, as at Wuhu, Zhanjiang and Nanjing. It was better in Shanghai, with some classes resuming at Aurora University. At Xujiahui, all work continued as before. It was reported that when soldiers from either the north or the south entered a village, they asked for the European priest, so calm was only on the surface.

Much movement among the opposing armies was experienced. The northern soldiers returned and occupied all areas north of the river from Hai Men to Anhui, but they showed respect for the missionaries. When the southerners replaced them, missionaries worried. Under the northern armies, Jesuit missionaries were able to continue their work, but many other missionaries – including three bishops, Sisters of Charity, Franciscans, Recollects and Passionists – all took refuge in Shanghai.[37]

The reaction of the foreign powers to the massacres of missionaries was swift. The French consul approached Noury to find out the feeling of the bishop and the mission regarding compensation for the death of the two Jesuits in Nanjing. The American and English legations sought recompense for their dead. Noury replied that the Jesuits

35. Bonay to Jesuit superior, Xujiahui, 14 May 1927. ARSI.
36. Bishop Paris to Apostolic Delegate, Shanghai, 17 May 1927. ASV.
37. Beaucé to General, 18 May 1927. ARSI.

wanted nothing. In response to this, the consul said that the Jesuits were placing the French in an inferior position diplomatically if compensation was not sought. Moreover, the consul of Italy wanted recompense for the death of Vanara, saying, 'we have to protect the life of our nationals', while the French consul wanted indemnity for the death of Dugout, for the same reason. The Jesuit's negative response was supported by the apostolic delegate.[38]

A report of damage done to the properties of the Nanjing mission was made to the French consul on 26 May 1927. Mention was made of the destruction of the church and school at Hansimen and at Xiakuan, but the main problem was the soldiers occupying the Church, mission buildings and residences. Virtually all houses and properties of the Catholic missions were occupied by troops. Protestant chapels were less affected; they had notices forbidding entry to soldiers, but they were used as recruitment centres, conference rooms or schools. Chang Kai-shek issued orders that soldiers were to evacuate these buildings or be punished.[39]

Meanwhile, in Nanjing, on 18 April, Chiang Kai-shek established his National Government, in opposition to the left-wing Wuhu administration of Wang Jingwei. There were then two rival national governments, both claiming legitimacy of the nationalist movement. When threatened by the Nanjing army, Wang Jingwei eventually joined Chang Kai-shek, and expelled the Communists from his administration. A united government was formed by August 1927.

The National Revolutionary Army continued their march north, finally taking control of Beijing on 6 June 1928, and Tianjin on 12 June. Beijing, the northern capital, was renamed Beiping – 'northern peace' – so as not to confuse that Nanjing, the southern capital, was to be the only capital city of the new government.[40]

Visitation of the Mission, October 1926 – February 1927

With tensions everywhere in the mission and civil war raging around them, the provincial of France, Félix Mollat, visited the mission,

---

38. Extract from letter of Beaucé, Nanjing, 21 December 1928, concerning the massacre at Nanjing, March 1927; Notes on a meeting at Nanjing, 24 March 1927. ARSI.
39. Inspector of Security to French Consul, 26 May 1927. DAC.
40. Dillon, op. cit., 208–10.

and his report was typically Jesuit: similar to earlier visitations from France, he concentrated on issues relating to the internal functioning of the Jesuit communities, some of which may have been supportive.

His ideal missionary was one who exercised 'poverty, abnegation, and zeal', and he was pleased to note that the intake of 'drink and smokes' was acceptable. Mortification of personal ideas was considered essential, as ideas divided people. Jesuits needed to hide their ideas or keep quiet: this was essential for 'union of hearts' among Jesuits. He was not happy about the inadequate response to the papal decree about the need for all to learn the Chinese language. He noted that some priests knew no Chinese. He expected Shanghai Jesuits to know both Mandarin and the Shanghai dialect. There was nothing new in these suggestions.

He observed that French Jesuits were hard on the Chinese Jesuits. He found that the Chinese were good religious, attached to their vocation and very zealous, but accepted that the Chinese 'thought' differently from the French. They were 'child-like, too open to the ideas of others, and without verifying their ideas', and were quick to complain about the European Jesuits. Some Jesuits, like Joseph de Servière, had 'an inconceivable chauvinism' that did not help in bringing the two groups together. The Chinese brothers were criticised for being 'less understanding of religious life, with closed minds, and more ambitious for positions of authority'. He did not seem to approve of the ideas of the Chinese Jesuits or ask why they thought the way they did.

Mollat wanted Jesuit education to focus on the Chinese elite, who would, in turn, instruct the 'ignorant and poor Christians'. In the seminaries, 'spiritual fathers', both Chinese and French, should be more active in the formation of Chinese students. He was happy to learn that at Xujiahui, twelve Chinese entered the seminary each year. Chinese priests were concerned about the amount of French taught in the colleges, but he understood this, as French was a prerequisite for Aurora University. Chinese students were not keen on studying Chinese, as they saw their lay Chinese teachers lacking authority in the institution or having insufficient knowledge of how to teach. He favoured the idea in the ongoing discussion about Jesuit scholastics going to Europe for theology and tertianship, indicating that studying in China would show a lack of 'a certain scope that the great scholastics of Europe are able to give'. This idea showed that the French Jesuits did not believe that they had the sufficient resources to educate the Chinese students theologically, nor did they articulate the need to offer anything other than a European theology. That was all they knew. There was no awareness that the Chinese might be better prepared as priests by applying what they had learnt within China's milieu.

The conclusion to the visit from the provincial was the observation that the 'conversion of China is a completely supernatural work . . . missionaries must be men of God . . . if possible, saints'. This was a statement that could be made to any missionary in the world. For the missionary, their work was 'the work of God'; they were simply God's workers in establishing His reign, but the statement lacked helpful advice about how this might be accomplished in the Chinese context, especially at a time when the missionaries were fighting for the survival of the mission. In fairness to the provincial, it would have been almost impossible for an outsider from France to understand the external challenges facing the missionaries, or to offer helpful advice, as he had no personal experience of China, and could only comment in the light of his European experience after listening to what he heard during his short stay in China.[41]

Petition for a new Chinese vicariate in Pudong

Inspired by the creation of the Chinese vicariate in Hai Men, Chinese Catholics of Pudong petitioned that Pudong also become an independent vicariate. In support of their claim, they mentioned the desire of the pope that Chinese clergy should govern their own church, rather than Europeans. They thought it their natural right, especially following national independence.

They justified the call for a division by claiming that the current eleven Chinese priests who worked in the area held the region together when the foreign priests were sent to Shanghai during the recent occupation by troops. This gave the Chinese priests confidence in their own ability to govern. There were one million people in Pudong, with 40,000 'old' Christians, as well as 130 churches or chapels. It was noted that at the seventieth anniversary celebrations of the college at Xujiahui, 13 Jesuits and 16 secular priests had come from Pudong. There were currently 20 Pudong priests employed in

---

41. Report on the visitation to Jiangnan by French provincial, Mollat, 24 February 1927. ARSI.

the vicariates of Nanjing and Hai Men. Eminent among them were: Laurent Li, Andre Tsang, Sen Gni, Pierre Tsang and Ignacio Kiong. It was believed that there were a sufficient number of Pudong clergy with acceptable ability who could lead a new vicariate, and a sound infrastructure for government was already in place.[42]

Much discussion among the Jesuits of the vicariate of Nanjing followed, and they were strongly against this suggestion, believing that, while one day Pudong might become a separate vicariate, the current time was not right. Bishop Paris was critical of the petition, belittling the authors as young and inexperienced, inspired by a spirit of Chinese nationalism, an attitude the missionaries could not accept. Some said that a 'teacher in a non-Christian school' inspired the letter, while another said it came from a Chinese priest. Whatever the source, the bishop disclaimed that the region had a sufficient number of local priests to make a new vicariate viable. Many priests in Pudong came from the neighbourhood of Shanghai, and the number of seminarians was exaggerated. In fact, Pudong Catholics were not considered 'good at giving sons to the Church'. He advised Costantini not to take the petition seriously, as 'the authors were not worthy'. Furthermore, serious Christians did not want the division. If it went ahead, the area would become agitated and divided. Further problems would arise when peace returned.[43]

The Jesuit chancellor of Aurora University, Peter Lefebvre, was less complimentary in his choice of words to express his disapproval of the idea of a new vicariate in Pudong in response to a letter from the apostolic delegate. He saw the evil genius behind the idea of independent Chinese vicariates as Vincent Lebbe, who he saw as 'dangerous like all troublemakers'. He saw him as the one who caused a 'schism' between Chinese and foreign missionaries, especially at a time when the latter were suffering from brigands and Communist occupation. Collaboration was needed between the two groups, not division. He believed Lebbe's writing promoting Chinese independence were the expression of an 'exaggerated nationalism; a modern heresy, which sees the nation as an end in itself, with the danger of lessening the apostolic spirit which China has so much need'. He saw Lebbe's pro-

---

42. One hundred and twenty Catholics of Pudong, Zie Tsong-kie, to Jesuit Superior, Shanghai, 7 September 1927. ARSI. A similar letter was sent to the Apostolic Delegate, 12 September 1927, with a copy to Propaganda Fide. ASV.
43. Bishop Paris, Shanghai, to Apostolic Delegate, Shanghai, 13 October 1927. ARSI.

motion of xenophobia and denunciation of the current European vicariates as unfair. Lefebvre accepted that the church should not be under the tutelage of France as it once was, but this protection was the 'instrument of Providence used by the popes to establish the Catholic faith in China'. These rebels accused the European missionaries as being 'colonial agents' of their own country, and so were enemies of China. This was considered insulting to the Europeans who 'had left their country and sought only the Kingdom of God and the good of souls'. The promotion of 'exaggerated nationalism' by 'scatterbrains' like students, seminarians and even young priests in their clubs and hostels, made ordinary foreigners and missionaries alike as 'undesirable'. They accused foreign missionaries of not obeying the Holy See, and for not educating seminarians adequately for the new Chinese nation. This was only one side of the argument, 'flattering the Chinese, and depressing the foreigners'.[44]

The apostolic delegate communicated with the writers of the petition from Pudong, indicating that the Holy See would make a decision relating to the request when peace and order was established in the region. He mentioned that there were current discussions about further eight divisions of vicariates. Hai Men with more than 35,000 Christians was already a separate vicariate. Bishop Tsu had informed him that the Chinese priests in Pudong wanted a division from Shanghai.

Aurora University, Chinese students and the delegate

The French legation became more aware that power was slipping from them in maintaining the French protectorate. They had a copy of a letter that Costantini had written to Bishop Paris concerning the killings of the priests Dugout and Vanara. Costantini suggested that the Church should not ask for an indemnity because it was contrary to the present attitude of the Church.[45]

The legation continued to be concerned with the determination of the apostolic delegate to end the French protectorate. It was mentioned that despite his courtesy, Costantini had given the impression that the time of privileges resulting from the treaties had passed, and

---

44 Lefebvre, Aurora University, Shanghai, to Apostolic Delegate, October 1927. PF.
45. Costantini, Beijing, to Bishop Paris, Nanjing, 25 July 1927. DAC.

that sooner or later foreign nations ought to renounce them. The best interests of the Catholic Church would be to become detached more and more from the temporal powers that had given aid and protection to help them propagate their faith and to give them security.[46]

Agitation among the Chinese students at Aurora University came to the attention of the delegate. Some former students asserted that few conversions took place at the university because of an anti-Chinese atmosphere in the place. Lectures were in French, and should be in Chinese. The university had 'bad press', as many students were considered reactionaries. It was reported that a former rector of Aurora in a lecture in France, had said of the Chinese: 'southern Chinese were weaklings; those of the north, brigands. All Chinese were semi-savages'. This would not have endeared the French missionaries to the Chinese if it were true.

It was claimed that the authors of the French periodical, *Le Croix*, were anti-Chinese, while 'all former students of Aurora were anti-clerical'. The chaplain to the Chinese students in France, Abbé Boland, made the comment that instead of being a centre for the apostolate, former Aurora students appeared to be 'an instrument of European imperialism'. His thesis was that if China did not become Catholic, the fault lay at the feet of 'the nationalism of foreigners', because the Chinese were 'the most tolerant of men'. He attacked the French protectorate, and believed that many Chinese converts were 'rice Christians'. Furthermore, he was a supporter of Vincent Lebbe and disliked the approach of Europeans missionaries trying to impose a European style on Chinese villages. Christians were non-nationalists and the Chinese liked Lebbe because they believed that he understood the Chinese and China. Finally, he praised the apostolic delegate who seemed to understand China well. However, despite this affirmation, Costantini wrote to Boland asking him to be more prudent in word, always trying to preserve the unity of the church. Boland replied, thanking the delegate for his advice.[47]

The debate over Aurora continued. The Jesuit, Alexandre Brou, responded by commenting on the article in the *Bulletin de la Jeunesse Catholic Chinoise*, which claimed that Aurora was neither Catholic

---

46. French Consul, Shanghai, to French Minister, Beijing, 17 November 1927. DAC.
47. 'L'université de Aurora', in *Bulletin de la Jeunesse Catholique Chinoise*, l'Associatio Catholica Juventutis Sinensis, ACJS, Louvain, 37 (January 1928), 16–20. PF.

nor Chinese, that title being reserved for the Benedictine University in Beijing. Aurora was considered to be too French. As for the reference to the derogatory statements about the Chinese made by the Jesuit rector, Brou could not name the source, but it appeared to be former Catholic students of Aurora who wrote the comment. Most former students of Aurora were considered anti-clerical. Brou believed that Aurora's mission was to make conversions and to educate Chinese students to become 'elite and patriotic Chinese'. They needed the 'virtues of justice and charity', as well as 'love of country'. To claim that Aurora was 'an instrument of European imperialism' was extreme.

The Abbe Boland responded that he believed that 'scatterbrains' made the derogatory comments. Bishop Jean-Baptiste-Marie Budes de Guébriant, in Paris, did not want to see the priests in China feel condemned. Others also came to the rescue of the Jesuits. It was also commented that there were differences of approaches in China between the French Jesuits and the supporters of Vincent Lebbe. Boland asked if Aurora was 'a reactionary centre', and anti-Chinese, and was subject to the criticism that it was 'an instrument of European imperialism'. Brou responded that while many students of Aurora were anti-clerical, there were annual Baptisms, and even some non-Christian graduates supported the missionaries.[48] Brou's response to the criticisms was moderate and calm, making some apologia for the Jesuits at Aurora.

At the same time, Costantini wrote to the rector of Aurora, praising the university and the Jesuits for their work, but suggested that the language of instruction might be better in Chinese rather than in French. He quoted an article in *Nouvelles de Chine*, 2, February 1928, 'Le Catholicism en Chine', claiming that the Jesuit missionaries spread the French spirit in China. Aurora University was named. Costantini did not think this was good publicity 'in these difficult times'. He observed further that present Chinese nationalism gave the Church new 'delicate challenges'. The Church must avoid all political comment in its schools, neither Chinese nor anti-Chinese, and leave no doubt about respecting legitimate Chinese patriotism. This was not just a question of justice, but also about the future of Church schools in China.[49]

---

48. Augustin Brou, 'Concerning an article on Aurora', in *Lettres de Jersey*, 41 (1927–8).
49. Costantini to Rector Aurora, 1928. PF.

Lefebvre responded defensively to this criticism by saying that the teaching of science in French was necessary, because the Chinese language did not have words to explain scientific concepts. The preparatory course in the catechism was given in Chinese, but the more complex course was given in French, for the same reason as the above. He believed that the students preferred the course in French. In addition, it was difficult to find a priest who could teach these courses well in Chinese. When preaching in the church, there were sermons in both Chinese and French. He attempted to reassure the delegate that Aurora students were capable of understanding Christian doctrine in a foreign language and 'could follow instructions'.[50]

Attacks on the mission

Even during the obstacles presented to the mission establishments during the war, between 1 July 1926 and 1 July 1927, the mission grew with five new Christian communities, and the number of Christians and catechumens each increased by nearly 3,000. There were also nearly 2,000 adult Baptisms. This indicated that the mission offered some hope and security to the Chinese people who were suffering disaster and ruin from the marauding armies and bandits. Total villages had been abandoned.

Jesuits reported to the superior general about disruptions in their mission districts. Henri Gilot at Xuzhou mentioned that his residence was occupied by troops for 50 days, and mercenaries continued to harass the village, while Stephen Chevestrier, recently appointed to Song-gang east, also mentioned that troops occupied both the church and school for a week. He consulted the French consul who arranged through the Chinese commander who was his friend, for the Nationalist troops to withdraw, which they did. Communist bands were crossing the territory as well, also occupying church buildings. As a result of this incident the French consul went to Shanghai to have discussions with the Jesuit superior.[51]

Little by little, order was restored to the establishments at Xujiahui. They resumed operations, with the College of St Ignatius, at the end

---

50. Lefebvre, Aurora, Shanghai, to Costantini, June 1928. PF.
51. Gilot to General, Xuzhou, 20 January 1928; Chevestrier to General, Song-Kaong east, 2 February 1928. ARSI.

of May 1928, enrolling 400 students. Aurora University opened again with 130 students, despite criticisms by nationalist-minded students. After an excellent report from the nationalist government in September, 100 new students presented themselves. Also, a new faculty of Letters was introduced, separate from the Law faculty, teaching French, English and Latin. Chinese Jesuits were still uneasy with French being the main language of teaching in these institutions. They wanted all subjects to be taught in Chinese, as Chinese students did not understand French well. Even history and geography of China was taught in French. Use of the Chinese language was a minimal request.[52]

It was a different situation in the countryside with several mission residences invaded in September 1927 by troops moving through the villages of Puqi, Lo-ka-bang, Wu-ding, Kun-se and Song-gang. The girls' school at Wuhu did not open again until the end of November.

The inspection of mission buildings in Nanjing by Augustus Bureau in October 1927 revealed much destruction. He took up residence in a small room in a corner of the destroyed girls' school. Help from the French legation was soon forthcoming. The Count de Martel, the French Minister, visited the region of Yangtze, and was received by government officials. After discussions, he was able to give assurances to the missionaries that they would be able to regain all their former buildings.

It was in the north that skirmishes between the warring armies continued. It was noted that the armies of the north had a better reputation than those of the south in respect to the missionaries and their property. But this was damp praise, as both were guilty of pillage.

On 21 February 1928, Joseph Hugon, who had only arrived in October 1926, was captured by brigands and taken to their headquarters where he remained for three weeks. He experienced excessive cold, and was stripped of his habit, which was replaced by rags full of vermin. He slept on boards, without covering, amid dirty and gross gaolers. One day, he was taken to the countryside, thrown into a hole and buried alive. Thinking quickly, he made a hole through which to breathe, and little by little disengaged himself, but hearing several rifle shorts around him, he acted as if dead. In the evening, the brigands came to look for him and took him to prison. Finally, he was released through the efforts of the Jesuit minister of the section and a neighbour. Full

52. Zi to General, Xujiahui, Shanghai, 19 January 1928. ARSI.

of courage, he returned to his post and ministry, but weakened by his ordeal he contracted typhoid, was brought to Haizhou and died on 4 April 1929. Brigands could be more dangerous in the countryside where there was little protection.[53]

Chinese magistrates could not protect the missionaries from soldiers or brigands. If forced to leave their posts, they returned as soon as it was safe. They showed 'tenacity, patience and energy'. The Chinese priests suffered the same as the Europeans, which showed that it was obviously religion that was being attacked. Statues, images and crosses were destroyed.

Fear was expressed at this time that if the Bolshevist revolution took over China, it would be the end of religion. The future looked bleak in 1928. Missionaries believed that only the Catholic religion was able to change China, 'totally saturated with paganism and innumerable faults'. Society needed to be based on the 'principles of humility, charity and the true Gospel'.[54]

Status Quo of proposed new vicariates, 1928

Amidst so much disruption in the mission districts, discussions continued more peacefully in Shanghai on the viability of creating new vicariates. They included the following.

Xuzhou

The first Christians in this area dated from 1890–1900. When missionaries first arrived, there was no trace of earlier missions. Since

---

53. Antoine Saimpeyre, 'La Mission dans la Tourmente', in *Lettres de Jersey*, XLI, Nouvelle serie, T. VIII (1927–8): 91–105.

    Joseph Hugon was gifted as a writer, poet, literary critic and orator, with a passion for philosophical speculation. He had entered the Society of Jesus in 1910 and offered himself for the China mission in 1914, but was not sent until 1921. In preparatory studies for work as a missionary, he concluded that 'assimilation is fundamental for a missionary, it is not a luxury, it is a duty . . . to study the Chinese, their history, customs, geography and not merely their language . . . to become truly a Chinese'. He had only worked for four months in the district when bandits apprehended him. Cf. *China Letter*, The Jesuits of California, 33 (Fall 1939): 9. CaPA.

54. Responses to several questions asked by Fr. Echeverra de Grenade upon the situation in Jiangsu, 1928. ARSI.

then, progress was rapid. The overall population was low because the people were often afflicted by local brigands and by food shortages. Growth occurred because of the migration of poor peasants from surrounding areas in times of famine. The increase was more than 1,000 per year.

The territory contained eight sub-prefectures. It was in the extreme northwest of the Province of Jiangsu and touched three Chinese provinces: Anhui, Henan and Shandong. The centre of the mission, and of the region, was Xuzhou, where Protestants ran a hospital and some schools in the city. Some Muslims were also present. Xuzhou was also the centre of communication for the whole country, as it was situated at the crossing point of two main railway lines.

Since the 1912 revolution, the Chinese government encouraged the Jesuits to work in the towns. But, from 1927, while the authorities left the mission in freedom and peace, progress in apostolic work was inhibited by the frequent passage of groups of bandits or soldiers. The future was becoming more uncertain. Missionaries had to negotiate with the military authorities that occupied the mission residences and schools. During 1928, while there were 50,975 Christians, in general, the neophytes were not very fervent, but this varied according to the periodic troubles in the area. Some converts came from very good families. These neophytes gave practically nothing to the missionaries, except a meal after Mass or when they visited families to give the Last Rites. They themselves were very poor and in need of help. Any new buildings came with assistance from the vicariate of Nanjing.

In the region, there were 18 churches, as well as residences, and 130 chapels. Financial support for the region came from Rome; there was nothing from the government. Each year, the migrating bandits and soldiers ransacked the schools. Twenty priests worked in the area, largely French-Canadian Jesuits, and Chinese seculars who came from the southern Province of Jiangsu, where they preferred to work. While French Jesuits had worked in the area since the beginning, the Canadians had been present for only about three years. There were a good number of catechists and schoolteachers, but their education was so limited that they were not much help to the missionaries. Thirty Presentation sisters, all from the south and educated at Xujiahui, ran schools for girls. There was no question of starting a seminary during the troubled times; some seminarians went to Xujiahui, and two seminarians were currently studying theology. There were boarding schools for boys in the main towns, and one for girls. Xuzhou had two schools for educating catechists, one for boys and one for girls. Each missionary had a catechumenate attached to the central church, but there was no orphanage or hospital.

Jiangsu-east (Yangzhou – Gianyungang)

These two sections had 3,560 Christians, but it was a 'difficult and ungrateful apostolate' because mandarins would not give permission for a permanent residence: a moving water barge was used for a residence. Stories circulated of missionaries sealing children, and killing them, with eyes removed. Riots were always feared. This was also a non-Christian area, with 72 pagodas: 'a kingdom of the devil'. In the north-east, bandits were endemic.

The geographical limits to this section were: Shandong to the north; Xuzhou to the east (Anhui); and the Yellow River (Huang He) and Hai Men to the south. It contained ten major towns with one million people. The Protestants had several hospitals and schools, but the Catholic missionaries did not believe they had much influence. The government was not keen to give property rights to the missionaries, while 'superstition and indifference' were seen as the major obstacles to evangelisation. As the people were poor, and could not afford school fees, schooling was free. The missionaries lived on gifts from benefactors. The main residence for the missionaries was at Yangchow. Twelve missionaries, all French except for two Chinese seculars, worked the region. Mandarin was the only language of the region, which made missionary work difficult for both European and Chinese priests who came from Shanghai. Moreover, the Chinese priests were not seen by the Europeans as having the same missionary zeal as they had. Catechists were rare: only three or four teachers, as well as a few aides, worked in the schools. A school for catechists was required. Religious communities of nuns worked in the hospitals and schools at Yangchow, and there was no seminary. Any seminarians were sent to Xujiahui.

Jiangsu central (Nanjing)

Nanjing itself was little developed, with only 3,546 fervent Christians, while Xuzhou had good communities of fishermen. As in other areas,

the mandarins opposed missionaries building chapels in the countryside. Protestants worked hospitals and schools in the main centres
of Nanjing, Xuzhou and Wuxi. The greatest obstacle to evangelisation
was in the towns: there was too much 'wealth and pleasure, and corrupt morals'. In the countryside there was 'indifference'.

Twenty-six priests worked in the region: 20 Chinese and six
Europeans. Most secular priests were 'really zealous', but did not
want to work among 'the lost sheep'. They did not like working long
hours in the confessional or in the education of children. Moreover,
rumours of scandal were heard that some of them were too familiar
with women.[55]

A reflection on the mission from a newly arrived missionary

Sometimes first impressions of the mission are worthy of attention,
because they are fresh, and undiluted from fixed ideas transmitted
from missionaries of long-standing in the mission. One Jesuit at
this time was Fernand Lacretelle,[56] who, having arrived in China on
1 October 1927, wrote about his early impressions of the mission.
He saw the main missionary challenge to be the conversion of non-
Christians (19 million in the Jesuit mission). The work of the mission
was to strengthen the existing Christians and to prepare for an independent Chinese church.

He observed that the difference between the Chinese priests and
Europeans was that the Chinese were 'more refined and complex'
than the Europeans. Their reactions were generally the opposite of the
Europeans. They were very sensitive, but rarely showed it externally.
Freedom to express opinions in a straightforward manner could be
taken as rudeness by them. What Europeans considered deception
was for the Chinese 'elementary politeness'.

The foreign missionaries arrived in China with good will and
the desire to 'give themselves entirely to the Chinese'. But there
were communication problems between the two groups, as words
expressed were understood differently. The foreigners found this very
frustrating, which led to lack of patience, 'a natural dissatisfaction',

55. Status quo of areas designated for new vicariates, 1928. ARSI.
56. Fernand Lacretelle became a significant Jesuit in the mission, especially in the
late 1940s, cf. Ch. 10, footnote 1.

and even mistrust of the Chinese. This made the life of the missionary 'practically intolerable' and diminished the effectiveness of the apostolate.

For the Chinese, words were 'always only analogical to the sentiments of the heart'. Many times they did not pay attention to the words spoken or even 'declarations of affection'. They judged all by their acts. It was only after much observation that they gave their confidence to the foreigners.

The 95 secular priests in the mission were considered better educated than Chinese priests in other missions, because of the high standards at Xujiahui. They were good priests, but they lacked the 'spirit of adventure, abnegation, and zeal for the kingdom of God'. They needed to be 'supported, encouraged and loved'. Among themselves they showed little unity, lacked mutual confidence or a sense of collaboration.

One important challenge for the foreign priests was that of language: most were unable to speak the Chinese language fluently without interpreters. Speaking the language was essential to maintain the unity of the mission between the Chinese clergy and the foreigner. Many secular clergy were content to rid the mission of the Jesuits, but the Jesuits needed the secular clergy. Maybe one solution to the problem was to divide the mission into more vicariates for the Chinese, and retain one for the Jesuits.

Pastoral work, where the missionary and people met, was vital to the mission of the vicariate. Intellectual works were seen as 'food for pastoral work'. The Protestants relied much on education in schools and hospitals in their mission, without the personal follow up with the people. Mainly the foreign Jesuits did this work as the Chinese Jesuits were too few in number, and the secular priests lacked zeal.

Lacretelle was pleased with the Jesuit institutions in Shanghai. The College of St Ignatius' expanded over the years, with numbers increasing to include non-Christian students. However, its principal work was to educate Christians. The orphanage at Tushanwan was in difficulties because of lack of manpower. It should be given to other congregations of religious. Aurora University ought to move toward a more obvious Chinese education, but this could be a problem, as it still received subsidies from the French government. He was not keen on the suggestion that the mission should have a 'house of writers' because of insufficient manpower.

Lacretelle appreciated many Chinese Jesuits: Joseph Waong was 'an excellent man, intelligent and competent and has sound doctrine'; Beda Tsang had literary talent, and was a 'man of action' who had much influence in Shanghai; and Louis Waong was a 'real apostle', having great scientific and spiritual influence at Aurora. Others that he noted being pastorally effective were Joseph Zen, Ts'a and Louis Ou, but the others 'were ordinary'. He could not suggest a suitable Chinese master of novices.[57] Overall, Lacretelle gave an accurate description of many of the ongoing issues in the mission at the time, with wise suggestions about how to involve the Chinese more in educational works.

Jesuit studies

During the relative peace in Shanghai, Jesuit superiors also found time to discuss questions relating to the education of Jesuit scholastics. It was decided to concentrate them in Xujiahui, despite poor health conditions in Shanghai, but Nanjing or elsewhere appeared to offer worse conditions, and Xujiahui was probably safer than elsewhere. Moreover, Xujiahui already had good residences, a good library, and good teachers. Paul Beaucé said that the teaching there was as good as any seminary in France. However, there was a problem with language. In Shanghai, a dialect was spoken, but in the schools, Mandarin was taught. He admitted that after two years he could not understand Chinese, not 'even one sentence'. In Shanghai, there was no motivation to learn Mandarin. He advocated that the scholastics be sent to Gianyungang, where they spoke Mandarin, but he was not keen on a language school in Beijing because of the poor climatic conditions. Despite social and political disruption taking place in the country, and many mission works suspended, the Jesuits were also planning for the future of the mission by assigning Jesuits to post graduate studies in France and Rome.[58] This showed the hope they had in the future, which was an expression of their faith in the work undertaken for promoting the glory of God. Following the comment about the high quality of seminary teaching, it might be asked that

57. Fernand Lacretelle, 'The actual situation, the problem to resolve', no date, but probably 1928, ARSI.
58. Consult on scholastics in China, Xujiahui, 20 January 1928. ARSI.

if the seminary teaching in Shanghai was as good as that in France, why were the French Jesuits in China always complaining about the deficient training of the Chinese priests?

The Protectorate: the Holy See and the Delegate

Meanwhile, Costantini was still working on the question of the French protectorate. The French legation was rightly concerned that the delegate was campaigning against it. They would not be surprised if the delegate told the missionaries not to have recourse to their respective consuls concerning mission affairs.[59]

In a report to Rome, Costantini believed that eventually there would be a revision of the unequal treaties, including the protectorate. At present, the Chinese government could not guarantee the Berthemy Convention, as they had little control over the country. The missions must not be abandoned, but there was a need for new diplomatic agreements from which all may benefit. Italy, Portugal, Belgium and Spain wanted a new treaty. As long as France insisted on the protectorate, it did not serve its own needs or warrant sympathy with the Chinese people, in fact, the opposite was true.[60]

Bishop Zhu in Hai Men believed that there was a campaign against the French Jesuits, but while most people in the mission supported them, he admitted that some wanted independence from the foreigners. He praised the French Jesuits and wanted more of them in his diocese.[61] He had much to be grateful to them, especially for his promotion to the episcopacy.

There had been some discussion about the possibility of the French Canadians coming to China to maintain a new vicariate centred on Xuzhou. The French Jesuit, Edward Lafortune, the current superior of Xuzhou, was not happy with the proposal because the five Canadians presently in the area lacked knowledge of the Chinese language and culture, nor 'were (they) versed in the ways of evangelisation'. To make a new mission viable, they would need more priests. At the

---

59. French Consul, Hankeou, to Charge d'Affaire, Beijing, 18 September 1928. DAC.
60. Costantini, Memo on the French protectorate of the Catholic Missions, 29 October 1928. PF.
61. Simon Tsu to General, Hai Men, 26 November 1928. ARSI.

moment, only George Marin was capable of governing. He suggested that the provincial of French Canada visit the region in 1929.[62]

Meanwhile, the superior general in Rome had been receiving reports, even from the pope, that the Jesuits of the mission did not have good relations with the apostolic delegate, and that they disregarded his instructions. The pope was not pleased. It was important for the Jesuits to show 'fidelity to the Holy Father and the Delegate'. And so, he made three points. The first concerned the question of the native clergy. He wanted the foreign missionaries to show more appreciation of them, exercising 'a more positive cooperation'. He wanted the local clergy completely integrated, 'not in tutelage': equal in all respects to the Europeans. He understood that some Europeans had prejudices about 'the aptitude and maturity of the Chinese', but this must cease. In both word and 'in heart', missionaries must show full submission to the pope's wishes.

The second point raised related to adaptation to Chinese customs and culture, and to the Chinese character. In his criticism, the delegate had appealed to the 'glorious traditions of the Society', which reflected the ability to adapt to local customs and culture. To reflect this more obviously, it was suggested that Jesuits abstained from smoking and alcohol in order 'to give edification and expression of poverty'. The mission must avoid anything that might be considered rich.

The third piece of advice was that it was important for the Jesuits to show more reliance on Divine Providence than on the French government. The mission should not rely on the French for 'back up' and protection in times of crisis. In such moments, the directions of the apostolic delegate should be followed when clashes occurred. Furthermore, the Holy Father was saddened that the only two vicars apostolic who did not thank him for his letter sent to the bishops of China were the two Jesuit vicars apostolic.[63]

The climate in China was changing concerning the activities of the Catholic missions. The Sino-French Treaty of 1860, giving missionaries permission to live in the interior of China was changed in 1928, so that new buildings were subject to the permission of the local authority, and these acquisitions were to be limited to necessary buildings,

---

62. Lafortune to General, Xuzhou, 5 December 1928. ARSI.
63. General to Mission Superior, Rome, 20 December 1928. ARSI.

and excluded all commercial use. No longer did the missionaries have full rights to property, but all was given to them on loan.[64]

The French legation was concerned with these developments. It noted that Noury, the Jesuit procurator, the one who handled Jesuit temporal affairs in the mission, and also collaborator of Bishop Paris, had information that Costantini wanted to change the relationship between the Catholic Church and the Chinese government. Moreover, Bishop Paris was to go to Nanjing to see MCT Wang, seeking direct relations between the Catholic Church and the government in crisis situations. The French Jesuits knew that it was France who had given them permission to establish and maintain their works in China; they relied on France alone. Now, the Jesuits were very unsettled by this new development. Under obedience, they were unable to openly oppose this move. The legation asked the question how the apostolic delegate could disavow the treaties between France and China. He could not. Also the Vatican was not a party to the treaties of 1858. The French minister was also to see MCT Wang. After this meeting, Wang indicated that he wanted to avoid mixing the spiritual affairs of the Church with the political interests of the foreign powers. Meanwhile, the French legation watched Costantini's every move. Many memos were shared about the situation, indicating particular concern that some foreign missionaries had renounced the protectorate.[65]

The French had no intention of renouncing their rights over the Catholic missions without a fight. A somewhat strident article by Jean Dreffer concerning the future of the French missions in China appeared in *Le Journal de Pekin*, in which he stated that the threat to the French missions in China was not from the lay government in Paris, but from the Nationalist government in China, and especially the Vatican. The history of the connection between the French missionaries and France dated back to the signing of the unequal treaties of 1858 and 1865 establishing the French protectorate over all Catholic missions. He believed that France and Catholicism were the same. Of the 43 apostolic vicariates, 21 were French missions, with a total population of 263 million people. French was taught in their schools. The Nationalist government of China wanted to suppress the unequal

---

64. Statute concerning foreigners in China, *Journal of International Law,* July–October 1928. ARSI.

65. French consul, Shanghai, to Charge d'Affairs, Beijing, 2 November 1928 (plus shorter additional memos subsequently). DAC.

treaties and the concessions granted. The Holy See was compliant, not being enthusiastic about the French protectorate. Changes were already made concerning the ownership of property. In the future, all Church property was on loan and locally owned. Also, in a letter dated 1 August 1928, Pius XI called for 'the liberty and security of common law'. This recourse to 'common law', he believed, meant the 'ruin of the French protectorate' and replacing the French missionaries with Chinese clergy.

Dreffer believed that the ruin of the missions had been rapid since the end of the civil war. From the appointment of the apostolic delegate in 1922, he dealt with the Chinese government concerning Catholic affairs in place of the French minister. He subscribed to the belief that the Chinese clergy had been educated for a long time, 'strictly controlled and always subordinate'. Then there was the consecration of the six Chinese bishops in 1926, and Beijing, previously under the administration of the French Lazarists for 150 years, was given to the Chinese clergy as a separate vicariate. These moves displeased Dreffer, who represented many French missionaries.

Finally, Dreffer claimed that the French protectorate had given the Catholic missions 'prestige', while concessions made to the Chinese government would not help the missions in the future. The 'recall' of French influence had begun.[66] This was a pessimistic appraisal of the future of the Catholic missions, but showed the passionate belief held by most French priests in the importance of the protectorate.

---

66. Jean Dreffer, 'The future of the French Missions in China', in *Le Journal de Pekin* (30 December 1928). PF.

Chapter 7
A New Beginning, 1929—1933
Consolidation after the War

On 22 January 1922, Costantini made an official visit to the president of the Chinese Republic, and held discussions with the Minister of Foreign Affairs, M Wang. Considering the expansion of foreign influence in China and the internal movement toward an independent nation, Wang wanted in future to deal with the representative of the pope, and not with foreign legations concerning matters relating to the Catholic missions. In suggesting a new agreement with the Catholic Church, it was proposed that the government would guarantee the liberty of religion, recognise the right of the missions to own property, and the right to open schools to be run according to government programs. The government guaranteed not to interfere in seminary programmes, except for reasons of public order or health. In reaction to this meeting, '*Le journal de Shanghai*', the publication of the French concession, made the comment that Costantini's diplomatic activity with the Chinese government aimed to end the French protectorate over the Catholic missions in China.[1]

Later, at the General Council of China in 1929, in relation to the protectorate, it was decreed that the Church must obey all laws of the Republic of China, but did not exclude the laws that recognised the rights of other nations to protect Catholics. Meanwhile all questions regarding protection of the missions were reserved to the Holy See, but in litigation matters, assistance could be sought from foreign consuls. Good relations with foreign authorities ought always to be upheld. It was further suggested that the missionaries should not readily approach the consul for protection over clashes with the

---

1. Louis Wei Tsing-sing, op. cit., 137–8.

Chinese authorities, unless all other avenues to maintain the rights of the Church failed.[2] Not only was French protection not officially abolished, but also it was even approved when all other avenues of negotiation failed.

In reporting to the superior general on the state of the vicariate by the new coadjutor bishop, Auguste Haouisée, a missionary since October 1903, and consecrated bishop on 3 October 1928 to assist the ageing Bishop Paris, he began by asserting that 'everyone was suffering from depression'. Missionaries felt a 'little abandoned, unbalanced, discouraged', largely because of some accusations that were being made over differing opinions from the apostolic delegate. It was true that Bishop Paris had 'little sympathy for the delegate', as the delegate had accused Paris of being less than generous concerning divisions of the vicariate. Moreover, Paris thought that the delegate should concern himself more with details. Costantini was seen to want to please the Chinese and 'disgruntled Christians', with the aim to accede to their requests as much as possible without listening to objections. This upset Bishop Paris who was accused of not giving Dongjiadu to the secular clergy with a secular priest as superior. This would have happened if such a person could have been found. Several secular priests supported Paris' opinion. This criticism followed a previous one stating that the mission did not support the pope's directions; that was the result of communication problems with the promulgation of the pope's letter, and was 'absolutely false'. The local clergy in the vicariate received even better education than seminarians in France. Further criticisms were that the vicariate gave to the Chinese priests mainly the areas inhabited by the well-established Christians, while the Europeans were sent to the new areas. This also was not true; in fact, the opposite was frequently the case. Furthermore, it was claimed that the European missionaries did not sufficiently adapt to the Chinese culture. This was 'calumny'; Jesuits lived the Chinese life, spoke their language and respected their customs. Chinese politicians said that the Europeans had a 'colonial spirit'. These were very defensive statements, but at this time the tide had turned against the attitudes of the foreign missionaries in favour of the local clergy, and it was necessary for the foreign missionaries to put their case, address rumours, restate facts, and attempt to clarify misunderstandings.

---

2. Synodal Decree of the General Council of China, 1929. DAC.

Haouisée accepted the creation of the new vicariate of Xuzhou under the authority of the French Canadian Jesuits. There were three sections in the vicariate with 50,000 Christians. He also suggested that the Californian Jesuits might take up the region centred on Yangzhou, or at least establish an English-speaking college. He joined most other Jesuits in believing that the establishment of a new indigenous vicariate in Pudong was premature. It did not have the resources to survive on its own, being currently dependent on Shanghai for much assistance.

Some future directions for the vicariate were to make greater use of the laity through Catholic Action, the Apostleship of Prayer and Sodalities, as well as the press through *Revue Catholique* and the *Messenger of the Sacred Heart*.

He ended his letter again seeking support from Rome against the unjust, demoralising attack upon the European missionaries. He called for greater unity between bishops and missionaries, and totally rejected the rumour that the missionaries worked directly for France. He insisted that 'we want a free united China in Christ'.[3]

Haouisée was determined to keep communications with Rome open, supporting the European missionaries in the vicariate. In the same month, he wrote a lengthy letter to *Propaganda Fide* on the state of the Church in China, and especially in the vicariate of Nanjing.

He believed that the stability of the Nationalist government in Nanjing was exposed to three dangers: the size of China, with no one leader able to impose order; the Communists, with advisers from Russia; and the War Lords, re-arming during peaceful times. This affected the apostolate. In the countryside, the Communists were a continual threat, forcing Christians to become Communists and preventing them from attending church. The threat of war was continual, with the occupation by 'independent troops' who burnt, stole and destroyed everything. Moreover, the new government laws that prevented the possibility of buying new land, added to the misery of the missionaries. While future ministry was not looking good, the missionaries carried out their tasks of rebuilding schools and buildings destroyed.

Issues relating to the relationship with the apostolic delegate were prominent in the communication. He praised Costantini for gain-

---

3. Haouisée to General, Shanghai, 9 March 1929. ARSI.

ing the confidence of the government, but was critical for the way he made 'simple promises on very serious questions', and was simply 'wrong in some situations'. On his visit to Shanghai, Costantini publicly praised the Jesuits, while continuing to have serious reservation about them. Trust was not great. There were discussions about possible new Chinese vicariates. One was that the Chinese be given the vicariate of Nanjing or that of Shanghai. The latter would create difficulties for the French Jesuits, but more importantly, it would be very difficult to find a Chinese priest capable of administrating this vicariate; it was a 'delicate and difficult place', with possible clashes with the Jesuits over 'seminary rules', and the need to be competent in financial matters. Moreover, the vicariate of Shanghai was considered one of the best in China: a Chinese bishop would need to have 'stature' in the European community. Bishop Zhu was being considered for Shanghai or Nanjing. Shanghai was not recommended, because of financial questions relating to his brother. If Nanjing was chosen, it needed to be remembered that Zhu did not speak Mandarin, and the clergy of Hai Men did not want him to leave Hai Men. A better choice for Nanjing was Luc Tchang and, if Shanghai, Mao was considered the best.

Still on the defensive mode, Haouisée made a case for the European missionaries over criticism of their educational methods. Contrary to the criticisms of Aurora, the main aim of the institution was to provide a 'superior education', which was considered indirect evangelisation. Conversions were made. Students came from all over China because of the good reputation for serious work, dedicated teachers, and an opening to 'foreign science' and to a foreign language. It was believed that if Aurora only taught in Chinese, most students would leave. The problem with teaching in Chinese would be which one to choose among the many dialects. Chinese students from different parts of China did not understand each other. Moreover, even if teaching were in Mandarin or in the Shanghai dialect, as the delegate required of all seminaries, European teachers would still be needed to explain 'technical terms', especially in science. Teaching in French seemed to be the unifying language, and it was used 'not because of nationalism, but in the interests of the students'.

Jesuit superiors were criticised, probably from Rome, for not sending seminarians to Rome for theology studies, but in reply, it was said that if any had sufficient 'health, intellect or morals', they would be sent because of the 'advantage of a Roman culture'. But, the seminary at Xujiahui was at least as good as any European seminary in 'dogma, moral theology, pastoral, liturgy and preaching'. The 27 major and minor seminarians had a good spirit, and their examination results were 'good to very good'.

This refuted continuing criticism made against the foreign missionaries for their inferior education of the Chinese clergy. Haouisée further claimed that the 172 Chinese priests from the seminary in the vicariate were well educated by 'excellent professors from Europe'. Jesuit missionaries were totally aware that they came to China to found a local Church with Chinese priests who would eventually replace them. They worked hard to produce this result. In the schools of the vicariate, the better students were selected and sent to the seminary. Chinese students had entered the minor seminary each year since 1913, but the social and political conditions at the present time in China inhibited more entries.

Some believed that the attacks upon the foreign missionaries created an 'atmosphere of mistrust, suspicion and even apathy' in the vicariate. Some Europeans talked of going back to Europe, which was undesirable. The Chinese priests were treated as equals; some Europeans worked under Chinese superiors. Reviews and conferences regularly presented European missionaries as 'agents of the foreigner and cast discredit on their work'. Slogans were many and derogatory: 'They have done nothing serious here', 'They have not adapted', and 'Missionaries are colonial agents'. These 'calumnies' depressed the missionaries: all wanted unity not divisions. All missionaries, including the Chinese, worked for a 'united China, free for Christ'. Finally, Haouisée believed that the vicariate was 'faithful to the directions of the Holy See: *sentire cum Ecclesia*' (to think with the Church).[4]

When in Rome, Haouisée visited the Vatican Cardinal Secretary of State, 1914–30, Pietro Gasparri, who asked the question whether the French missionaries were 'too nationalistic'. Concerning the protectorate, he mentioned the desire of the pope to detach the Church from France, but he had no objection if the missionaries asked France for 'protection'. The cardinal was happy for French sailors to help guard Xujiahui when it was under threat, despite the disapproval of

---

4. Haouisée to Propaganda Fide, Shanghai, March 1929. ARSI.

the apostolic delegate.[5] The missionaries were to make much of this distinction given by the cardinal in the future, that while the vicariate should move away from French influence, the military support of France in special situations was acceptable to the Holy See. This was tested later in the year, when a petition, citing the need 'to maintain the sovereignty of China and to avoid malcontents', was made to the French consul in Shanghai to remove French sailors that were protecting Xujiahui, to be replaced by Chinese government forces.[6] This did not take place. No one trusted the competence of government soldiers.

Educational initiatives

In 1921, a directive was given to the Chinese priest P'é to open a 'Normal School' at Xujiahui. Since 1917, potential teachers in the schools of the vicariate were given a course in elementary pedagogy. At the end of the course, students were given a 'certificate of success', which was recognised only by the missionaries. Over the years, about 37 graduated from these courses and became good teachers in the mission primary schools. While pleased with this initiative, it was felt that the course given should be more substantial. Ten students were in the first intake in 1921, while in 1928 there were 101 students. The conditions for admission were a letter of recommendation from the priest in charge of the section, together with a certificate from the 'superior primary school', as well as an entrance examination. The limiting age was 15 years. The 101 students came from all eight vicariates of the mission. Three languages were spoken, and unity among the students was good.

The students had more than 30 hours of classes a week, and a course in religion was optional, outside the official class times, for five hours a week. A course in pedagogy was given in the third year. There were also music classes and other electives, such as physics and chemistry. The courses given were considered 'very liberal and modern'. Graduates had to work in the mission for five years, but for those who had paid their own way during studies, they were only required to work for three years, and were paid a salary.

5. Haouisée, Rome, to General, Rome, 25 March 1929. ARSI.
6. Hsu-Mo, Shanghai, to French consul, Shanghai, 3 August 1929. DAC.

Initially, the school had three teachers, but by 1928 there were twelve working in the school, including three Chinese: one for mathematics, one for social sciences and one for 'associated sciences'.

The parish school at Xujiahui served as a feeder school for the Normal School. In 1924, both schools had the same director, and Normal School students taught in the primary school under supervision. Graduates of the school were so enthusiastic about their experience at the school that they edited a periodical, *Trait d'union*.

Life in the Normal School included religious services in the chapel of St Ignatius' College, especially on feast days. Most students took Communion and said the rosary daily. At the beginning of each year, there was a silent retreat for three days, as well as devotions to the Sacred Heart and St Joseph throughout the year, and occasional benediction of the Blessed Sacrament. The Apostleship of Prayer was introduced, while St Joseph, the patron of carpenters, was also made patron of the school. Examinations were held monthly and at the end of the semester, while the sports played were football and tennis. Discipline in the school was strict: permission was required to go to see visitors, to enter the dormitory, leave school or to speak with different groups. Absolute silence was required in the dormitory, while in the refectory, grace was said before meals. There was a lecture at midday in the Shanghai dialect, and in the evening in Mandarin. The spirit of the school was one of 'family and love'.[7]

The influential layman, Lo Pa Hong, who had been very generous to the Jesuits, had also made a request for a Chinese/English College in Shanghai. He observed that five new American Jesuits had arrived in Shanghai in September 1928, and he thought highly of them, especially Pius Moore. He thought that they would be good to work in a new college after they had finished studying Chinese. Many 'noble Chinese families' came to Shanghai from China's inland to avoid the troubles, and they had children to educate. There was Aurora University for the French, St Ignatius' at Xujiahui for the Chinese, and one other school, Xavier College, Horghew, that taught English, but this was only for European children. Protestants had many colleges and a few universities that taught both non-Christian and Christian children English. He believed that it would be a good initiative for the

7. Yeu, J., 'History of the Normal School at Xujiahui', in *Lettres de Jersey*, 42 (1928–9).

Jesuits to start an English-speaking school, and he offered land in a good position in Shanghai for the purpose.[8]

Diplomatic manoeuvring

The apostolic delegate and the French legation were constantly manoeuvring over who should exercise protection over the French missionaries. Costantini informed Rome about an article that was inspired by the French minister in China in the *Journal de Shanghai*, on 6 February 1925, that criticised the Vatican mission in China and Costantini in particular. It quoted M Briand in Paris who claimed to have no interest in 'Christian propaganda' in China, but was in full support for 'French propaganda'.[9] Criticism was also registered from the Jesuit Licent, commenting on Henri Garnier's book, *Le Christ en Chine*[10]. Costantini had complained to his superior in Xianxian, who replied that he would deal with Licent, and hoped that there would be no further problems.[11] Such criticism of Church officials and its policy was never acceptable in the open press.

There was a further article in *Le Journal de Shanghai*, critical of Costantini's political intensions. It mentioned Costantini's reassurance to the Young Chinese Catholic Association that Catholicism would not interfere with their civil rights or their legitimate patriotism. He praised those missionaries who supported these ideas, and offered prayers for peace and progress in China. With the threat of Japanese activity in China's north, Costantini sent a message to all the heads of Catholic schools telling them to 'remain outside all political movements in China, be it interior or exterior. Political questions don't concern us; we must only preach the gospel'. Students should be taught to respect legitimate authority, while missionaries were to obey the civil authorities. Furthermore, Costantini stressed that the Catholic Church favoured the development of China, and the devel-

---

8. Lo Pa Hong to General, Shanghai, 27 February 1929. ARSI.
9. Costantini, Shanghai, to Cardinal van Rossum, Rome, 17 February 1929. PF.
10. **Henri Garnier** (1882–1965) entered the minor seminary in Dijon at the age of 12, and after a visit by Bishop Favier in 1902, Garnier joined him in Beijing. In 1905, he was ordained priest, and worked as a secular missionary. A meeting with Vincent Lebbe resulted in the book *Le Christ en Chine* in which he attacked Lebbe and the Roman plans for a native church.
11. Costantini, Beijing, to Cardinal van Rossum, Rome, 22 February 1929. PF.

opment of the Chinese Church with Chinese clergy at every level. The recent consecration of six Chinese bishops indicated that the pope believed that the Chinese Church was now sufficiently developed to live by itself. Many missionaries, including the Jesuits, did not believe that the Chinese Church was ready for this transition. European missionaries held high standards for Chinese clergy education, aiming to be equal to the best in Europe.

From this information, the French believed that Costantini was wooing young Chinese to his cause, and while not wanting the Nationalist government to see the Catholic Church as an adversary, wanted the government to respect 'full liberty of conscience; not hostile to religion'. Unfortunately, with troops already occupying Jiangsu, Nanjing had no authority in that place.[12]

Meanwhile in France, the 150–200 Chinese students attached to the 'Institute Franco-Chinese' in Lyon were recognised for their antireligious and even revolutionary ideas: not a sound base for evangelisation among them. This was the organisation with which K'ang had worked, but with his return to China in 1926, Gaultier had been appointed chaplain. However, the Abbé Boland from Louvain, travelling through French in December 1928, declared that he was chaplain to the Young Chinese Catholics in Europe, nominated by *Propaganda Fide*[13]. Despite being ignored by Boland, Gaultier organised a conference for him entitled, 'The Evangelisation of China and the Political foreigner', which turned violent. The result of the conference was the thesis that 'if China was not Catholic it was singly the fault of the nationalism of the foreigners, because the Chinese were very tolerant and friends of strangers'.

---

12. Editorial, 'The Apostolic Delegate and the Chinese Revolution: 'Triple Demons' (Sien Wen), *Le Journal de Shanghai*, 8 March 1929. PF.

13. Boland to Propaganda Fide, Louvain, 6 February 1929. PF. There were 104 Chinese students in Belgium at the time, and André Boland's student organization received 22,000 francs per month for them. Boland himself received an annual salary of 50,000 liras from Propaganda. So it seemed that he was an official chaplain, at least in Belgium. In 1922, he had been asked by Vincent Lebbe to welcome Chinese students to Belgium, and he later wrote of this experience in *Mes petits enragés*. He joined Lebbe in founding a lay missionary institute, the *Lay Auxiliaries of the Missions* in August 1937, with the opening of a house of formation for students in Brussels in October 1937. Boland and Lebbe had already formed a new group of priests, *Auxiliary Priests of the Missions* in 1926. Boland later worked in the Belgium resistance against the Germans from 1941.

Boland was against the French protectorate, seeing it responsible for the opposition of the Chinese against Christianity. He believed that the protectorate assisted the 'good-for-nothing', or the poor, who became Christians in order to obtain protection and food provisions from the missionaries. The ordination of the six Chinese bishops was an important sign of the Chinese church being liberated from 'foreign tutelage'. Boland wanted to 'repair the evil done to China by the Europeans'. Gaultier reasserted that the foreign missionaries also wanted the independence of China: China for the Chinese. Missionaries were happy to accept common law in China. But the students had lost confidence in the foreign missionaries, and were critical of their 'excesses'. Boland's visit to Lyon had only stirred up the divisions, which heightened their estrangement from the foreign missionaries, and then against the faith itself.[14]

At the end of 1929, Costantini reported to Rome that despite social disruptions in the missions, there was an increase in the overall number of Christians in China. From 1927–9, the increase was 29,080. The number of missions had increased 17.30 per cent, from 28 to 42. Disappointment was expressed that the number of conversions had not been greater. The reasons given for this were the dispersion and emigration of people because of brigands and epidemics. The greatest loss was in Hopei (Zhili) by 9,859, while Jiangxi also suffered a lost of 8,360. However, he was pleased to report good numbers of seminarians: 4,765 (838 studying philosophy and theology), while there were 2,465 in secondary schools and 1,462 in primary. He considered these students well educated.

Among the Jesuit vicariates he mentioned the following statistics:

Xianxian, (Bishop Lécroart): 57 foreign priests, 47 Chinese, 138,910 Catholics, and 2,619 conversions, which were an increase of 0.14 per cent over the previous year.

Nanjing (Bishop Paris/Haouisée): 103 foreign priests, 83 Chinese, 194,120 Catholics, and 2,001 conversions, an increase of 0.78 per cent.

Wuhu (Bishop Huarte): 26 foreign priests, two Chinese, 34,152 Catholics, and 591 conversions.

---

14. Gaultier, Fouvière, Lyon, to van Rossum, Rome, 8 April 1929. PF.

Anqing: 19 foreign priests, 21,457 Catholics, and 208 conversions, an increase of 1.12 per cent.

Bengbu: 15 foreign priests, 35,553 Catholics, and 587 conversions.[15]

The French foreign ministry published statistics of the number of missionaries in Catholic missions in the world in 1930. They were proud that France had the greater number, 4,182, followed by Italy with 1,078, and Belgium with 1,062. The French government also noted with concern that the Italians no longer wanted French protection. They believed that the Holy See and Fascist Italy were interested in trying to end French dominance/protection in the Catholic missions.[16]

Despite protestations from the apostolic delegate and Rome, the French legation continued to be called upon by missionaries in moments of crisis. Louis Hermand had been attacked, while the Spanish priests, Zacarías Hidalgo and Ismael Avito in Anhui, were held prisoners by Communist forces. The Chinese government went after them, but the bandits retreated with the priests to the mountains, demanding a ransom from the Chinese authorities. The Spanish legation was happy for the French legation to intercede. The pair ended up in Honan, but while not badly treated, prison conditions were unhealthy. The French legation did not succeed in negotiating with the rebels. It was suggested that better progress to release the priests might have been made by seeking the assistance of the Russian ambassador who had good relations with the Communists.[17]

A further incident involved the missionary Sen at Fengxian, who wanted to build a school. He received permission, which was later revoked. This led to confrontation and Sen was taken prisoner by bandits, probably Communists who were in the area. They demanded a ransom of $55,000. Sen was later found and released. Communists later captured Tomás Esteban on 25 July 1932. The Chinese ministry of Foreign Affairs was unhappy with the intervention of the French in these local matters, and approached the French legation to ask the missions to deal directly with local Chinese officials. If they didn't

---

15. Costantini, Beijing, to van Rossum, Rome, 31 December 1929. PF.
16. Statistics of the Catholic Missions in the world, 1930. DAC.
17. French Consul General to President Provincial Governor of Jiangsu, 23 April 1930; Noury memo to French consul, 6 August 1930; Bishop Frederico Melendro to French Minister, Anqing, 23 January 1931; French consul, Chengtou, to French ambassador, Beijing, 20 March 1934. DAC.

get satisfaction they should take up the matter with neighbouring Chinese officials.[18] Meanwhile at Xujiahui, Chinese authorities had requested the French admiral to withdraw sailors from protecting the Jesuit compound. The Nationalist government accused the Jesuits of not trusting them. Concern was expressed that the Jesuits needed to establish confidence with the Chinese government for the future good of the Church in China. The admiral was approached, accepted the reasoning of the Jesuits, but replied that it was up to the French consul to order the withdrawal, and he refused.[19] The French legation in China was not ready to give up their rights over missionaries. The French foreign minister in Paris was informed that while there had been only 41 vicariates in 1910 there were currently 98, and while the protectorate was seen as imperialist and a humiliation to the Chinese, it was important for them to continue their mission, as even twelve non-French missions used the protectorate.[20] In negotiations with rebel groups that harassed the missionaries, the Nationalist government was generally ineffective; the French legation generally had more influence, except with the Communist groups.

The question of who was to guard the Jesuit compound at Xujiahui continued. In a letter from Cardinal van Rossum to the superior general, it was noted that the French troops were withdrawn from guarding the main building of the compound, with the French legation looking for other means to protect the buildings of the mission. The missionaries believed that then they only had God to guard them. They argued that the reason they had guards in the past was that they needed strong help from the armed bandits that moved through the area. For example, in January 1925, the attack on Shanghai had been sudden and unexpected. Over 7,000 refugees arrived. In 1927, with the arrival of the southern army, the spirit of the population changed: nationalist ideas grew, as did anti-foreign sentiment. The number of Communists increased and the French military was no longer held in respect. Volunteers guarded Xujiahui at this time. Once again, the

---

18. Memo concerning the capture of Fathers Hidalgo and Avito by Red Army, Nganhoei, 1 May 1930; French consul, Chengtou, to French ambassador, Beijing, 20 March 1934; Henry to French Consul, Xujiahui, 25 November 1930; Haouisée, Shanghai, to French consul, 27 April 1931. DAC.
19. Noury to Beaucé, Shanghai, 10 May 1930. ARSI.
20. Legarde, Charge d'Affaires, Beijing, to Briand, French Foreign Minister, Paris, 30 June 1930. DAC.

French consul and the French admiral gave protection to the Jesuits, considering the situation an emergency. Sailors occupied the observatory. There was also a threat to the international concessions. Without their presence, Xujiahui was subject to destruction as had happened at Nanjing on 24 March, with the death of Vanara and Dugout. The danger was ever present, with the rector pressurised by the invading army that wanted to occupy the property and the church. The response to the army was that they should obey their commander who had forbidden them to occupy Catholic establishments. However, the Jesuits had no trust in that order: French sailors only could allay their fears. Nor could they trust the promises of the local Chinese authorities to guard the premises in the place of the French sailors. The mayor of Shanghai was approached for help to guard the property, but the letter was unanswered. The presence of the French sailors was some guarantee of safety for the foreigners in Shanghai.

Concern was expressed at the attitude of the apostolic delegate to these developments. While telling the Jesuits that he understood why they had sailor guards, he then wrote to Rome complaining about the Jesuits having them. Haouisée told the pope about the situation in Shanghai, and the pope agreed that it was natural law to take the necessary means to save both lives and property. Cardinal Gasparri also agreed, and these comments were communicated to the superior general. However, this was not discussed with Cardinal van Rossum, who had been receiving criticism of the Jesuits from both the apostolic delegate and some discontented Christians.[21]

The jostling between the apostolic delegate and the French legation broadened in 1934 into diplomatic exchanges between Paris and the Holy See. The French were obviously becoming more anxious over the protectorate. The French foreign ministry wrote to its ambassador in Rome about concerns with the new apostolic delegate, Archbishop Mario Zanin, who followed Costantini's plan to exercise authority over the Catholic missions. Costantini certainly weakened the French protectorate. The French government did not engage in the debate of July 1928 with Costantini who wanted a revision of the Treaty of Tianjin, 1858. Instead, the French ambassador to the Vatican dealt with Cardinal Gasparri, who suggested there should be no change. There was obviously some disagreement in Rome about details of the

---

21. Beaucé, a report, Shanghai, 1931. ARSI.

protectorate between the Vatican Secretariat of State and *Propaganda Fide*. Nationalist aspirations among Chinese nationals did not assist French aspirations.[22]

The ambassador replied that as a result of a meeting between Zanin and Chiang Kei-chek, on 19 June 1934, the Chinese government stated that it wanted direct relations with the Holy See rather than continue with the French Protectorate. This was seen as the result of the influence of Chinese Catholics and of some Chinese priests who were campaigning to suppress the protectorate. Nationalist aspirations in China were again seen as the main problem. The ambassador rightly questioned whether China could give the same protection to the missions currently given by the protectorate. He believed that the Holy See would prefer security from the French protectorate rather than unknown protection from the Chinese. His perception was that France was being left out of the negotiations between Rome and China.[23]

Mission progress in 1930

Continued harassment of the missions followed the massacre in Nanjing of 1927. Mission stations were occupied and raids occurred from Communists and other brigands, who no longer held the missionaries with former respect. Local Chinese authorities were difficult, there were disagreements among Christians, and the general hatred of foreigners grew. Despite these challenges, the missionaries hung on at their posts and evangelisation continued to grow.

Bishop Paris was the centre of unity in the mission, and much respected, as was his coadjutor, Haouisée. The arrival of Jesuits from the Province of California was the source of much joy and hope, as had been the local response to the arrival of the French Canadian Jesuits. There was a new faculty of letters at Aurora University, and construction of a Museum of Natural History had begun. At Nanjing, the church and parish schools had been repaired and the Jesuit residence reconstructed. The Californian College quickly filled with students, but sadly, the principal, Pius Moore, would not enrol Chi-

22. French foreign ministry to Charles Roux, French Ambassador, Holy See, 2 June 1934. DAC.
23. French Ambassador to Holy See, Rome, to French minister, Paris, 9 July 1934. DAC.

nese students, despite earlier promises that he would. In the outlying mission stations, the central schools were full of students, while a new parish, Our Lady of Peace, was opened in the workers' quarters of the International Concession. A second church in an 'English parish' was planned for both foreigners and Chinese.

Some hostility toward the missionaries was seen to diminish when non-Christians sent their children to the mission schools, saying that the non-Christian and Protestant schools did not have discipline, nor expect hard work, or show 'respect or morality', while they had confidence in the Catholic schools that exercised those virtues. Even some Chinese officials sent their children to these schools. With stable and peaceful government, the future looked more promising.

However, despite these hopes and signs of progress, there were many difficulties. With the Jesuit missions so close to the government capital, the missionaries experienced the general hostility to foreigners, despite personal sympathy to individuals. Exaggerated nationalism was seen to be 'hysteric'. Xenophobia existed everywhere, even among the Chinese priests. Priests were called 'running dogs of foreigners and imperialists'. Battles between opposing forces continued, with the Communist bands and opposition from local authorities particularly unsettling. This inhibited new initiatives and former zeal among the missionaries because of the uncertainty of the future.

The problem of insufficient numbers of missionaries continued. To meet the needs of the mission, more young, active priests were needed. Current priests were ageing and tired in most sections. Sixty missionaries out of 275 were 60 years or older. Division of districts was needed. There was also a lack of good superiors and leaders in the sections. The Chinese priests were considered good 'in general piety and zeal', but in the districts where they worked, Christian life had diminished, as had the number of catechumens. Sadly, the Christians preferred a European priest to minister to them, as the Chinese priest was generally not very communicative, and somewhat casual in ministry, rarely making demands of the Christians, and hardly ever obeyed by them. While numbers increased in some mission schools, their future was threatened by government requirements. The schools of prayer and primary schools were not currently affected, but secondary schools had to be approved. This became difficult because of the teaching of religion. The vicars apostolic were tending to close secondary schools because of these new decrees.

Fears were also expressed about the future of mission properties, especially after the Nanjing government suppressed the right to buy property and no longer recognised existing rights. There was belief that respect for the Catholic Church was diminishing. According to law, all Catholic property rights were threatened, despite assurances of the Chinese Minister of Foreign Affairs that nothing had changed. Trust in the government had eroded.

Concern over the attitude of the apostolic delegate continued. Externally, he was courteous and respectful toward the Jesuits, but hearing his accusations against Bishops Paris and Haouisée tended to lessen Jesuit confidence in him. The main issues of contention were French nationalism, Jesuit objection to a new Chinese vicariate in Pudong, and his establishment of a new Carmel convent at Jiaxing, in competition with the Jesuit Carmel at Tushanwan. Haouisée went out of his way to show confidence and deference to the delegate, but his letters went unanswered. The delegate believed that the Jesuits were opposed to his direction that mission schools and properties be recognised by the Chinese government. The Jesuits believed that they did not need recognition. Moreover, the delegate was believed to have too easily abandoned the official right of the Church in China to both possess land and to have recourse to the previously agreed treaty rights.[24]

Reflections

While these disagreements continued at leadership level, a discussion was initiated concerning the catechumenate and the education of catechists took place among the missionaries. This was an important debate as catechists were one of the most vital means of evangelisation open to the missionaries.

Many questions were raised concerning the necessity and the duration of the catechumenate. One line of action suggested was to confer Baptism on all who sincerely wanted it, and who showed that they lived good, moral lives, abandoned idolatry, had regularised their marriages, and restored ill-gained goods, without the need to pass through the catechumenate. Would it be sufficient for the Christianisation of China to rely solely on the grace of the sacrament and

---

24. State of the Mission of Nanjing to Propaganda Fide, July 1930. PF.

reduce the actual time of preparation for Baptism and initiation into the Christian life? Did the Church need to make a decision to limit the catechumenate and conditions for Baptism? Or rather, should each vicariate make its own rules?

By choosing catechists from among the Christian elite, did that stop or slow down the recruitment of Chinese clergy? What would be a reasonable approach: to separate catechists from the clerics, to group them into a fraternity, or to group them into a religious institute?

One suggested theological response followed the opinion of the Jesuit Pierre Charles [25] in the *Bulletin des Missions*, in which he suggested that there was no strict obligation to prolong the catechumenate before Baptism if there had been sufficient instruction, and there was evidence of the practice of the Christian life. In this case, Baptism would be seen more as a consecration rather than the end product of instruction into a virtuous life. Obligatory catechumenate only required summary teaching of the essentials of the faith. Only a minimum knowledge should be expected of adults seeking Baptism.

Conclusions to the debate were that Roman decrees over time didn't impose a prolonged catechumenate; they were looking for perseverance in the future; they wanted solid instruction, proved by practice; and that such decisions about the length of time for instruction should be left to the individual vicars apostolic. The Council of Shanghai in 1924 said that the catechumenate should be of short

---

25. **Pierre Charles** was born 3 July 1883, Schaerbeek, Bruxelles, and died Louvain, Belgium, on 11 February 1954. He was a philosopher, theologian and missiologist, who sponsored the annual *Semaine missiologique de Louvain* from 1925, taking over these seminars from the Jesuit Alphonse Lallemand who began them in 1923. In these seminars, he fostered the idea of the inculturation of the Christian faith among the indigenous people within their own culture relating to the concept of marriage, the family, the role of women and the liturgy. During his formation as a Jesuit he became conscious of the international dimension of Christianity. He was a companion of Pierre Teilhard de Chardin and shared his theological world view. In 1914, he became a professor of theology at the Jesuit theologate at Louvain. His preferred subject was the Incarnation of Christ, which led him to develop original ideas about sharing the Christian faith among peoples of different cultures. This led to his 'Theology of Mission' or missiology. In this subject, he defended the idea that in mission countries the local Church should be autonomous, advocating the decolonisation of peoples and Churches, and encouraging the education of local clergy and the nomination of indigenous bishops. His seminars were very successful and were published in *Dossiers de l'Action missionnaire*. 1926-9.

duration for the 'ignorant and old', but all needed instruction before Baptism concerning the essentials of the faith.

Haouisée's response to this debate was, first, that catechists were not employed to make them priests; in fact, most catechists were not sufficiently able to become priests. Second, they could be brought together as a 'confraternity' or 'a pious association'. Third, quoting Pierre Charles, he agreed that catechists accompanied the missionary, and should not be used as domestics. Christians admired the catechist, and it was with pride that he 'serves the foreigner'.[26]

Other reflections centred on governance in the mission. Discussions between the mission and Jesuit headquarters in Rome concerning the erection of Xuzhou as an independent mission under the control of the Canadian Jesuits had been ongoing for some time. Haouisée pointed out to the superior general that the problem still existed of small numbers of men available for this mission, and also that no particular Jesuit seemed suitable to lead the mission. He offered three solutions: train a suitable leader and change nothing at the present; make a French priest already in the mission vicar apostolic, which was proposed by the French Canadian provincial; or divide immediately and erect the Xuzhou mission with the Canadians, independent of Nanjing, that would provide priests, and also name a superior of the mission, as in Anhui. Most preferred the third proposal. Maybe Edouard Lafortune would be 'capable of governing'.

The question was also raised about establishing an English college for Chinese and foreigners run by the Californian Jesuits. It was felt that it should not be established in Nanjing because of political instability and the indiscipline of students. Also, there would be no protection for the priests from anti-foreign campaigns or Communist propaganda. The Californians should be employed immediately, but many of them didn't want to go as missionaries to the interior. Land might be bought for them between Aurora and Xujiahui, with the intention of starting the school in 1931. It should offer a classical education rather than a commercial one, as the Marists already had one such school. They should prepare for the Cambridge examinations or some American university with some courses in French in order to prepare students for Aurora University or even for the seminary. There was a problem with Moore, the superior, who wanted the col-

---

26. Payen to Vicar Apostolic, Nanjing, 1930; Haousée's response, 1930. ARSI.

lege to be named 'Foreigners school, opened primarily for foreigners'. This must not happen; it should be 'primarily for Chinese'. The mission preferred the school to be called an 'English school' conducted by American Jesuits in order to prevent possible difficulties from the Chinese government. The school should be for both native and foreign pupils with separate classes for each group. The new college would be a day school, not boarding, and, initially, be exclusively for Catholic students carefully selected. Maybe later it might open its doors to non-Christians. Various names for the college were proposed, with Gonzaga the one chosen.

In sharing his challenges with Roman superiors, Haouisée described his life as 'continually strained', with pastoral visits, ceremonies, feasts, visits for Rome, correspondence, and necessary visits in the absence of the Jesuit superior. The wider horizon in China was always changing: the growth of Communism, brigands in the country, kidnapping in the city, anti-Christian laws in the schools, and civil war. His formula for peace was ultimately 'to rest in the hands of God'. To further the mission, zealous priests and Christians were needed to promote such religious devotions as the Apostolate of Prayer and Sodalities, as well as Catholic Action. Greater use of the press would be beneficial with a weekly or monthly 'Catholic Review'.[27]

There was a special need for the appointment of a Jesuit superior of the mission. The various candidates to succeed Beaucé were Joseph Verdier, Ives Henry or Pierre Lefebvre. Verdier was thought to be too pessimistic, but a good administrator in difficult circumstances. Henry was 'paternal, optimistic, supernatural and open to new initiatives, but a little impulsive'. Whereas Lefebvre would seem to be the most acceptable to the secular clergy, but was little informed about the life of the missionary. He could be abrupt in manner, and not sufficiently firm in his decisions. Haouisée thought Verdier to be the best.[28] Discerning this information, the superior general appointed Lefebvre Jesuit superior on 6 January 1932. He also held the titles of delegate of the vicar apostolic and inspector of schools.

A further debate among the Jesuit missionaries focused on the relative emphasis to be placed on old or new ministries. The traditional works of the Jesuits in China were the observatories, which were

27. Hauousée, Shanghai, to General, Xujiahui, 11 August 1930. ARSI.
28. Hauousée, Shanghai, to Assistant (Boynes), Rome, 5 December 1930. ARSI.

considered superior to those of the Chinese government or even to those in England and Hong Kong. Aurora University was considered among the best in Chinese society – highly regarded everywhere in China. Even sons of non-Christian government ministers were students, while former students were already in government ministries in Nanjing. The periodical *Revue Catholique* had a pleasing circulation.

But to develop these works, the mission had insufficient qualified priests. Of the present 129 Jesuits, twenty-five were over 60 years old, and seven were still in studies. There were also 50 Chinese priests who were highly respected, and were leaders in the mission districts. The intellectual apostolate for the future did not look good, as the proportion of intellectual Jesuits currently sent to the mission was inferior to the intellectuals already in the mission. The works already established were not considered 'brilliantly lead', not because of ill will, but because of lack of personnel capable of leadership. All missionaries worked to their capacity. The main work of the mission was directly pastoral in the outlying districts, but only 60 missionaries were directly involved in these areas. The emphasis of this mission was evidently educational rather than directly pastoral.

The current need was to consolidate old works rather than to start new ones. Existing works could be reinforced by collaboration with other missionary congregations in all Jesuit missions in China, especially in the ministry of the press and in higher education. The establishment of a 'Chinese Bureau' could be a great support to missionaries by publishing useful works, such as the *Revue Sinologique,* and by encouraging one another in these times of disruption to mission work by armed groups. The library at Xujiahui was probably the best in China. It was particularly rich with Chinese books.[29]

New external threats

The political landscape of China was continually changing. The Chinese Communists had established a strong base in the south of China, centred initially around Jinggangshan, a remote mountain stronghold on the borders of Hunan and Jiangxi in October 1927, and then in the southern part of Jiangxi province in November 1931. The influ-

---

29. Notes from Goulet on a *memoire* of D'Elia, Shanghai, 26 February 1931. ARSI. Eduard Goulet was the Roman secretary for the missions.

ence of Russia in the formation of Chinese Communist troops and government was evident, with the arrival in China of Adolph Joffe, the Russian Comintern representative. They continually engaged in battles with the Guomindang forces, until the Nanjing troops were withdrawn from the south to engage the armies of rebellious marshals in the north that were advancing on Tianjin and Beijing. Civil war continued on two fronts for the central government of Chiang Kai-shek. The movements of rebel groups continued to harass mission districts that became desperately in need of funds. In addition to these threats, floods occurred in 1931 that threatened 20 million people in Hunan, Hubei, Jiangsu and Anhui (Bengbu).[30]

Throughout the history of China, the roaming of bandits throughout the country spelt the end of a dynasty. This was seen during the Han, Tang, Ming and Manchu dynasties.

The Communist Party was emerging as the main political force in China. A provisional body of the Chinese Communist Party (CCP) was set up in Shanghai in August 1920, and formally constituted at the First Congress of the CCP in Shanghai on 20 July 1921. The most prominent delegates at this conference that survived later interparty ideological conflicts were Mao Zedong and Zhang Guotao. At its second congress in Shanghai, July 1922, under the influence of the Comintern, it was agreed that they should form an alliance with the Guomindang (KMT), operating in Guangdong province, under the leadership of the revered Sun Yat-sen, known as the First United Front that lasted 1923–27. This period of co-operation involved a series of military operations that culminated in the Northern Expedition, with the aim to create a united republican China amid the fragmented chaos created by the warlords in the north. The Northern Expedition was formally launched on 5 September 1924, at a conference in Shaoguan, in the north of Guangdong, close to the border with Jiangxi.

The relationship between the warlords was complex, with territory occupied passing hands regularly. There was Feng Yuxiang, of the Zhili faction, who controlled most of the north and north-western regions, and seized Beijing on 23 October 1924. He sought a peace conference to end military rule, and appeared to be moving toward

---

30. Secretary Apostolic Delegation, Nanjing, to van Rossum, Rome, 8 August 1931. PF.

an alliance with the Guomindang. His main rival in the north was the Manchurian warlord, Zhang Zoulin. The Fengxian armies controlled Manchuria, Shandong, and much of Zhejiang, Anhui, Jiangsu and Nanjing. Zhang retook Beijing in early 1925. The Zhili forces under Wu Peifu controlled most of Hubei. In October 1925, another Zhili warlord, Sun Chuanfang, claimed control over Zhejiang, Fujian, Anhui, Jiangxi and Jiangsu. Guangdong and Guangxi were under the control of the forces of the Guomindang.

Sun Yat–sen died in Beijing on 12 March 1925, aged 58, and Liao Zhongkai, the administrator of the Huangpu Academy and one of the chief architects of Soviet-Guomindang co-operation, was assassinated. This gave Chiang Kai-shek and other non-Communists the opportunity to enhance their influence. They arrested many Communist leaders and took control of the Huangpu Academy.

The National Revolutionary Army (NRA) grew rapidly from 1924–6, and then moved northward, first to support the Hunanese warlord, Tang Shenzhi, who had been attacked by his rival warlord from Shandong, Wu Peifu. Chiang Kai-shek became the commander in chief on 9 June 1926, with the aim of following Sun Yat-sen's philosophy of the need to protect the welfare of the people, overthrow the warlords, implement the Three People's Principles, and 'complete the National Revolution'.

The army moved into Hunan, taking the capital, Changsha, on 1 July, and then moved into Hubei, taking the towns of Hanyang and Hankou, on 6 and 7 September, and Wuchang on 10 October. Other units took the treaty port of Jiujiang, Jiangxi province, on 5 November and Nanchang on 8 November. By the end of 1926, the NRA had taken all the major cities of the Provinces of Hunan, Hubei, Jiangxi and Fujian, and was in control of almost the whole of central China south of the Yangzi River. During 1927, they moved northeast, taking the cities of Hangzhou in Zhejiang, Hefei in Anhui and finally Shanghai and Nanjing were occupied in February and March. The reason for the rapid success was due to local support from the peasants and workers in the cities, as well as the division and feuding among the northern warlords.

The relationship between the Communist and non-Communist members of the Guomindang was never stable, but the leaders of the NRA on their northern journey found the Communists useful with their many contacts in towns and cities, who activated local party

cells and trade unions. This disrupted the local scene, with strikes
and protests resulting. Chiang Kai-shek was much less sympathetic to
the Communists than Sun Yat-sen, and by the time the NRA reached
Shanghai on 22 March, he was uneasy with their influence and
authority and decided to purge them and abandon the United Front.
Supported by Chiang's underworld friends in Shanghai, especially
those belonging to the Green and Red gangs, on 12 April 1927, he
attacked any group associated with the Communist Party. Between
400 and 700 were believed to have been killed, and many others were
wounded or disappeared. This action of Chiang's was sometimes
called 'the Shanghai Coup'. In response, the Communists set up the
Wuhan government under Wang Jingwei on 17 April 1927, with control over the three Provinces of Hubei, Hunan and Jiangxi, but they
were no challenge to Chiang and his forces that entered Nanjing on
24 March, and set up their own government on 18 April. After various disagreements between the two groups, the Communist Party
formally dissolved their alliance with the GMT on 15 July 1927.

The CCP retired to the countryside, and on 1 August 1927, unrest
in Nanchang, Jiangxi province, escalated into an insurrection led
by Ye Ting and He Long, celebrated as the Nanchang Rising. From
this group, the Workers' and Peasants' Red Army was created, but
surrounded by KMT forces, it was forced to retreat eastwards into
the hills. This was the birth of the Red Army. The Communists took
Guangzhou in December 1927 and Changsha in July 1930. This was
followed by many insurrections in villages and countryside in Hopei,
Hunan and Jiangxi. In Jiangxi in 1930, of 81 *hsiens*, 33 were Communist; 23 were somewhat Communist; and 20 were infiltrated, that
amounted to 76 were under Communist influence.[31]

In 1931, it was reported that in Jiangxi, the Reds massacred 186,000
people, and two million people became refugees. Over 100,000 houses
were burnt, and both rice and wheat crops destroyed. After taking the
villages, the Reds set up their own offices or committees, rejecting all
'reactionaries', which meant educated people, property owners, merchants, government officials; anyone opposed to the Reds. If money
was not given to them, people were killed.

31. Yang Chien, 'The Communist Menace in China', in *Lu Politique de Pekin*, 30 (1931). PF; Dillon, op. cit., 179–84, 189–93,196–8, 208–13.

Another tactic was to form groups of young people, 13–23-year-olds, called 'the young *avant garde*' of the Red Army. People 23–40 years old became the 'Red Guards'. Communists destroyed all the social and economic organisations of China. They confiscated property and commercial goods, and employed the workers and journalists by offering them an increase in salary. One catch cry was: 'take the land, refuse to pay taxes'.

The Nationalist government responded to these invasions by sending 200,000 troops into Jiangxi alone against the army of Chu The and Mao Zedong that had 50,000 rifles and more canon. Villages frequently changed hands from one army to the other. The establishment of a 'Red Bureau' was very active in Jiangnan.[32] These activities affected the mission directly when the Communist 10th Red Army on 17 December 1931, captured the Jesuit Estaban, and a ransom of $10,000 was demanded. The French legation immediately asked for his release, but the Chinese government offered no help. Esteban wrote asking for the ransom to be paid, but it was not.[33] It was thought that he died at the end of April 1934, but this was never confirmed.

Mission Issues 1931–1933

The much-awaited American school in Shanghai, Gonzaga College, was opened on 7 September 1931. Entrance requirements were that students should have completed eight years of primary education before entry into secondary school. It was a select school, a Catholic institution of higher learning, training 'young men for moral and intellectual leadership', just like other Jesuit secondary schools around the world. No boarders were enrolled, and all teachers were Jesuits holding university degrees. They offered a four-year classical high school curriculum, which was preparatory to a four-year college course leading to a BA or BSc degree at Aurora University, the Catholic University of Peiping or any other university in America or Europe.[34]

32. 'The Communist Menace in China', *North China Daily News*, Shanghai, 26 May 1931. PF.
33. Capture of Fr. Esteban, 17 December 1931 by Communists (10th Red Army), Mission Wou-yuan (Anhui), taken to To-king (Jiangxi). DAC.
34. Conspectus Gonzaga College, Shanghai, conducted by American Jesuits, First Year opens 7 September. Entrance Examinations for all applicants. ASV.

There was always concern among the Jesuits when questions were raised about creating new vicariates. Missionaries continued to wonder why *Propaganda Fide* was intent on multiplying divisions of the mission when there were so few missionaries, little money or 'scarcely a new Christian'. Were all these divisions for the greater glory of God, it was asked? The proposal for a vicariate of Nanjing was puzzling when there were so few mission works there, and difficult to build a college since the 'massacre' of 1927. No secondary school for girls, nor hospital or medical centre, no houses of brothers or communities of sisters existed. Nanjing needed help, not separation.[35]

Verdier also made personal comments concerning the proposal for the new independent vicariate of Nanjing with the Jesuit, Bishop Zhu from Hai Men as the new vicar apostolic. Bishop Paris only had 'mediocre confidence' in Zhu, as his administration in Hai Men 'left much to be desired'. The discontent of his subjects was public knowledge, as he favoured his family in certain matters. The man was not intelligent, either in his way of living or in common sense or in flexibility in governing. To promote him would not be wise. Moreover, Nanjing as the seat of government demanded a man already well proven in leadership ability. As the apostolic delegation was also in Nanjing, many religious matters would need to be discussed with the vicar apostolic. He could not recommend a Chinese Jesuit suitable for such an important post.[36]

Haouisée, also, while accepting the idea of an independent Chinese vicariate in Nanjing, found it hard to suggest the name of a Chinese priest that might lead the vicariate. The very unstable civil conditions in Nanjing at the time might suggest that this was not the right time for a new vicariate.[37]

Meanwhile, Costantini having retired as apostolic delegate on 1 February 1933, for health reasons, it was left to the new delegate, Archbishop Mario Zanin,[38] named by the pope on 29 November

35. Couturier, Nanjing, to Assistant, Rome, 12 August 1931. ARSI.
36. Verdier, Xujiahui, to Superior, Shanghai, 26 September 1931. ARSI.
37. Haouisée, Shanghai, to Apostolic Delegate, Nanjing, 11 July 1932. ASV.
38. Archbishop Mario Zanin was born in Italy, 3 April 1890, ordained priest, 3 July 1913, consecrated bishop, 7 January 1934, and appointed apostolic delegate to China, 7 January 1934–1946. Subsequent appointments followed as Apostolic Nuncio to Chile, 1947–53, and to Argentina, 1953–1958. He died, aged 68, on 4 August 1958.

1933, to pursue the division of the vicariate into two new ones: one for the secular clergy in Nanjing, and the other, Shanghai, for the French Jesuits.[39] However, the apostolic delegation could not decide upon the appointment of a new vicar apostolic for Nanjing.

As the deliberations continued, Zanin summoned Haouisée, accompanied by Lefebvre, to a meeting in Nanjing. The delegate did not find pleasing any of the secular clergy nominated for the position as vicar apostolic, and said that he wanted a Jesuit, either Joseph Zi or Luc Yang. The Jesuits replied that they did not think that either priests were suitable, because currently they 'did not give satisfaction'. But the delegate was insistent, and they replied that of the two priests, Yang would be the more suitable. They discounted Zi because they thought that his judgment could not be trusted, as he 'allowed Chinese books of dubious doctrine into the scholastics library'. Presumably he was 'infected' with nationalist views, and so was suspect. Zanin appeared impatient for a nomination, and both Chinese clergy and Christians could not understand the reasons for the delay in the appointment. It was thought that if Yang were appointed, he would need much support. He was a 'good religious' and would accept the position, but would be very afraid when he heard the news. Zanin agreed with the concern about the way the new vicariate of Nanjing might be administered, because of its position of prominence within the Catholic Church in China. Because of political implications of the appointment, he wanted a European Jesuit to become vicar to the new Chinese bishop. He need not have a specific title, but live in Ricci College, Zhenjiang, which was only one hour away by train from Nanjing, where the Jesuits had a residence. Zanin was enthusiastic about this idea, but the appointment would be a very delicate one, as the man would really be a 'personal advisor'. The idea did not please the two Jesuits, but they suggested that Haouisée could continue to give advice to the new appointee.[40]

The search for the new bishop continued, and in the interim, Haouisée who had been appointed vicar apostolic of Shanghai in 1933, remained administrator of Nanjing until the appointment of Paul Yü Pin in 1936.

---

39. Apostolic Delegate, Beijing, to Haouisée, Shanghai, 17 December 1933. ASV.
40. Lefebvre, Shanghai, to General, Rome, 25 November 1934. ARSI.

In letters to the superior general, Jesuits could be very critical about confreres who did not conform to the regular discipline of the religious house. In doing this, they knew that they would receive support from Roman officials. Even acknowledgment of good work performed in an external ministry would always be tainted if the person were not a 'good religious'. Robert de Jacquinot was one such Jesuit. It was noted that while he celebrated Mass devoutly, and heard Confessions in the church when called 'with exactitude', at other times he was scarcely seen. Externally, his relations with other members of the community were peaceful and charitable, but there was no 'genuine benevolence, fraternal and mutual, nor union of souls, nor cooperation'. He exhibited 'pride, arrogance, distance, and contempt of others'. However, he was praised for being 'an excellent worker' visiting many hospitals and people in need, including non-Catholics. He was president of the Famine Committee in Shanghai, helping many missionaries with money, which was distributed to poor families.[41] These external good works could never mitigate faults considered important for fraternal union in Jesuit community life.

Jacquinot was one of the most influential Jesuits in Shanghai at this time, so much so that Chiang Kei-chek invited him to a reception at Nanjing together with other religious leaders to elicit their support, and to find out ways that he could support the missions. At the end of the discussions, a group was formed to inform Chiang of the needs of the missions, and especially to seek his encouragement to support the teaching of religion in the schools of the mission. He was informed that Catholics did not have a political mandate, and didn't comment on the Japanese question or on Manchuria. Only the pope or the apostolic delegate could speak on these questions. A Protestant prayer service was held to pray for the safety of China.

Chiang told the group that his mother-in-law had influenced him to become a Christian, as it might help him to avoid disorders in his life. He admitted that China was in grave danger from the Japanese and the Communists, and he asked for help from the Christian churches.

Chiang did not appear to have 'a supernatural motive to convert or have a sincere desire to be a Christian'. He wanted to be popular with the group, and not only because of the recent Manchurian

41. Lorando, Sacred Heart Church, Shanghai, to General, 19 January 1931. ARSI.

conflict. He recognised the perils of Bolshevism and hoped that the political elements in China would unite around him. To do this, he needed many soldiers.

Jacquinot told the Chiangs that the Jesuit mission was praying for them and for China, 'for peace and good order'. He said that the missionaries were serving China by educating good citizens who believed in God and served Him. While the State only wanted 'the valour of its citizens', the missionaries promoted 'discipline and obedience', educating the people to reject Bolshevism and to follow the Ten Commandments. At a reception, Jacquinot invited Madame Chiang to visit Xujiahui, as she cared for war orphans. They discussed the future of these orphans, and both agreed that they would make good farmers. He also asked the president to help put order into the decisions concerning which districts needed flood assistance the most. He further reflected that it would be good if the apostolic delegate assured the president of the sympathy of the pope and to guarantee his assistance in China, by helping with flood assistance, support for Chiang in the civil wars and in the Bolshevik menace, as well against 'outside dangers'. Chiang should be recognised as the leader of China for the foreseeable future.[42] Jacquinot's influence in Chinese affairs was substantial, much more than most of his Jesuit brethren.

---

42. Confidential report from Jacquinot, Shanghai, 2 December 1931. ARSI.

Chapter 8
New Challenges, 1932—1936

Sino-Japanese War (1931–1932)

The rise of Japanese influence in China, which increased after the Twenty-One Demands of 1915, together with the growth of militarism in Japan in the 1920s, further threatened the security of China. China was seen as a likely area for Japan's expansionist policies, especially in the northeast, which was closest to Japan and Korea, its colony since 1905. The Japanese had lost tens of thousands of troops there during the Russo-Japanese War, 1904–5. Manchuria was also seen as a buffer zone to counteract the expansion of Russia. During the 1920s, the Manchurian warlord, Zhang Zoulin, tried to keep on good terms with Japan, while at the same time maintain his independence. But when the National Government in Nanjing was formed in 1928, Japan became concerned that Manchuria would become part of an integrated China. Zhang Zoulin was assassinated that year, and his son and successor, Zhang Xueliang, a strong nationalist, opposed Japan's presence in Manchuria.

On 18 September 1931, a bomb exploded on the track of the South Manchurian Railway to the north of Shenyang (Mukden). This so-called Mukden Incident was used by the Japanese to attack the Chinese garrison in Shenyang. The Japanese Guangdong Army then took complete control of Manchuria by early 1932, proclaiming an independent state of Manzhouguo (Manchukuo), installing Puyi, the last Manchu emperor as the new emperor. Manchuria became a puppet state of Japan, increasing its colonial empire of Taiwan, Korea and northeast China. The annexation of Manchuria was condemned by the League of Nations on 22 October 1933, but this was completely ignored by Japan. The Guangdong Army meanwhile moved westward, taking control of the eastern part of Inner Mongolia.

This invasion of Manchuria was a direct threat to the Nationalist Government's claim to sovereignty over the whole of China. However, as it was too weak militarily to oppose Japan, it resorted to attempts to gain international support, as well capitalising on a wave of popular anger and rising nationalist sentiment against Japan. The loss of Manchuria was symbolic of the disunity of China, and the weakness of the GMD in its inability to control the north of the country.[1]

Chinese hostility over this incident resulted in a 1932 boycott of Japanese goods in the lower Yangtze region. Japanese business in the region requested military intervention to protect their interests. The Japanese navy had landed marines in Shanghai in 1932, hoping to force Nanjing to end anti-Japanese activities. They later sent in army units to reinforce the navy. However, opposing Chinese military resistance resulted in the withdrawal of the Japanese forces until their shame was erased five years later when they returned.[2]

The apostolic delegation became concerned about Japanese military action in Manchuria soon after it began, and which extended into Shandong, affecting the Shanghai-Beijing railway. Costantini reminded Rome of the decree from the Council of Shanghai, number 696, that if war broke out between China and external nations, missionaries were to abstain in words and action, and remain neutral. There was to be no political stance.[3] In reality, missionaries were a useful source of information concerning Japanese movements. Japanese Christians in Shanghai voiced their plea for peace and toleration between China and Japan,[4] while Chinese Catholics declared that they were nationalists who loved their country, and called for unity, discipline and sacrifice, while praying to God for peace in China.[5]

The Jesuit mission received many wounded and refugees during the surrounding battles, and Haouisée wanted the Catholics to show charity towards these people. He was sad to report on the Japanese occupation of Shanghai, as well as the destruction of Church build-

---

1. Dillon, op. cit., 217–19.
2. David M. Gordon, 'The China-Japan War, 1931–1945', in *The Journal of Military History*, 70/1 (January 2006): 145.
3. Costantini, Beijing, to van Rossum, Rome, 10 October 1931. PF.
4. Costantini, Beijing, to van Rossum, Rome, 3 November 1931. PF.
5. Proclamation by Chinese Catholics, 25 October 1931. PF.

ings in the mission sections.[6] *Fides Service* reported that there were 870 missionaries caught up in the Sino-Japanese war zone, of these there were 430 Chinese religious.[7]

Reporting on the war, comments were made by the missionaries in Shanghai that the city had become a centre for agitation among patriotic students who formed an anti-Japanese association. The agitation was disturbing, as their political patriotism became anti-government, many travelling to Nanjing to agitate. The battle for Shanghai began on 28 January 1932. The international concession had 700 refugees, and religious houses took others. There was calm in the French concession as well as at Xujiahui because of foreign military protection. About 132 wounded soldiers cared for by the Jesuits asked for Baptism before they died (*'in articulo mortis'*). Hostilities ended on 5 May 1932, with many residences relieved, as soldiers from either army had occupied them. The 88th Army (Nanjing) ravaged Tsinpu,[8] while two churches near Song-gang, 40 kilometres from Shanghai, were destroyed. Even Chinese 'notables' wanted protection for their families from the missionaries. Consequently, better relations with the local people resulted.

Demands on the mission at this time were more than they could provide. However, despite war conditions, Christians frequented the sacraments more frequently and the number of catechumens grew. But the downside to the war was that the spirit of 'insubordination' affected some Christians to revolt against the missionary. Some even pillaged their own church, saying it was their property. The vicar apostolic excommunicated them for their action, but they later showed 'repentance'. Members of Catholic Action were also against the missionaries, so much so that they were banded from using church facilities. They were very anti-authority.[9] The missionaries faced challenges, not only from civil unrest that inhibited missionary work, but also from internal challenges from its own Christians who had been so 'docile' in the past. Total control of the mission districts was slipping through their hands in some areas, especially in the main towns and among students.

---

6. Haouisée to Vicariate, Shanghai, 15 February 1932. ASV.
7. *Fides Service,* 11 February 1932. ASV.
8. *Relatio de Chine* (Nanjing, January 1933): 332ff.
9. Chevestrier, Song Kaong, to General, Rome, 3 February 1933. ARSI.

Mission challenges during the war

In addition to enduring the hardships of war, people in the Nan-jing-Xianxian area were subjected to floods from 1931–2. Catholic charities assisted, as well as international lay associations. The pope granted 250,000 lire and the apostolic delegate gave $10,000.

The French Jesuit, Jacquinot, was well known and appreciated in China for his good works and activity in disaster situations. At this time, he was nominated secretary of the Committee to Help Hunger, and was also a member of the committee to help flood victims. He went to the region of Wuchang, then north of Jiangxi to distribute aid. The mandarins held him in esteem for his work, and treated him with friendliness. Through his work he greatly enhanced the prestige of the Church and the missionaries. Soldiers, police and students all knew and praised the 'good father'.

As the floods retreated, famine and disease followed, in the usual cycle of events. Profiteers entered the villages, trading on the misery of the people. It was perceived that conversions during this time usually lacked sufficient motivation. Brigands then followed, especially in the missions of Nanjing and Xianxian. Daming also was bombarded.[10]

In a general appraisal of the mission for 1932, Ives Henry, the rec-tor of the seminary at Xujiahui, noted that there had not been any novices for three years, while some Jesuit scholastics had discouraged candidates. The existing scholastics gave satisfaction and affirmed the seriousness of their vocation. He did not want them to be sent to Europe for philosophy studies, but rather to study locally at Xianxian, which he considered a better place for study than at Xujiahui. Greek should be learned, as this subject was considered necessary for theol-ogy studies. He preferred a Chinese tertianship at Wuhu with Paul Bornet, who commanded much respect, rather than one in Europe. He was pleased that government recognition was given to the two main mission educational institutions, Aurora and St Ignatius' Col-lege, Xujiahui. One concern he had about the arrival of the American Jesuits was that the older ones rarely spoke Chinese and were con-tent to work among foreigners in Shanghai, but some younger ones wanted to go to the 'bush', as they called it. Jesuit authorities in Shang-hai wanted to give them Haikou.[11]

---

10. *Relatio de Chine*, ut supra.
11. Henry, Shanghai, to General, Rome, 21 January 1933. ARSI.

Correspondence continued between the Jesuits and the French legation. The legation suggested that in order to protect the mission from bandits at Tingchow, the missionaries should fly the French flag. This was hardly the most enlightened idea during this time of anti-foreign demonstrations. Verdier, on behalf of the mission, wrote about the need for the church to make a new accord with the Chinese government, in order to give a new legal status to the Catholic Church in China. He wanted China to accept the 'civil personality of the Church', and a 'juridical personality', with the bishop. Then the care for the church would be in the hands of the apostolic delegate to China. This was not acceptable to the French. France could not transfer the goods of the missions guaranteed in the Franco-Chinese Treaties to the Holy See. That was reserved to France alone. Furthermore, the missionaries were reminded that they risked their future by placing their fortunes in the hands of Chinese common law.[12]

Growth of the Catholic Church

The publication of statistics about the Church in China, by the Apostolic Delegation in Beijing between 1923 and 1933, gave some hope to Catholics that the work of missionaries was not in vain, despite the recent war, floods, bandits, famine, epidemics and emigration. The total number of conversions in that period was 550,111, with the lowest number of conversions during the troubled years, 1927–8. Between 1932–3, the net increase over the previous year was 60,715, an increase of 22 per cent. The total Catholic population in China was 2,624,166. In that ten-year period, the number of foreign missionaries increased by 846, and the Chinese clergy by 496. While the increase of foreign missionaries over the decade was 57 per cent, and that of the Chinese clergy was 45 per cent, the number of Chinese currently studying for the priesthood was 6,727.[13] These were encouraging statistics.

---

12. Baudet, Nanjing, to French Minister, Nanjing, 6 October 1932 and 26 June 1933 and 28 June 1933 and 4 July 1933; French Minister, Beijing to Charvet, Tingchow, 3 May 1933; Telegram: Diplomatic Paris to French Minister, Beijing, 17 September 1933. DAC.
13. 'Plus d'un million de conversions en dix ans', *Fides,* in *Relatio de Chine* (Shanghai, January 1934): 219–20.

The new mission of Nanjing was formed on 1 May 1922, and remained the same until 1931, taking in the whole Province of Jiangxi: a province that was the smallest in China, but with the most people; approximately 34,126,000 million that increased rapidly because of continual immigration. In 1926, the vicariate of Hai Men was created from Nanjing, comprising Hai Men and the island of Chongming. It included seven sub-prefectures, with 5,221,500 inhabitants, and was given to the Chinese clergy. Bishop Zhu guided the vicariate of 32,000 Christians. Then in 1931, a new vicariate of Xuzhou, also with seven sub-prefectures and about four million people was given to the Canadian Jesuits, who had been working in the area for some years. George Marin was nominated the administrator apostolic, guiding 54,000 Christians. Nanjing had lost four sections, but retained eight.

In 1922, the vicariate of Nanjing had 199,667 Christians. And after losing 86,500 to the new vicariates, in 1931 it still had about 200,000 Christians. In 1922, it had 26,000 catechumens and 3,265 Baptisms, and after the separation of Xuzhou, in 1932 it had 9,829 catechumens with 1,932 Baptisms. In 1932, there were 106 Jesuit priests, of whom 18 were Chinese. The number of secular clergy increased each year, with 55 current and 43 seminarians. When the territory of the vicariate diminished, the real number of missionaries increased, but the distribution of these clergy was uneven. In the outlying mission districts, there were 52 Chinese to 20 European missionaries, whereas in Shanghai, with its multiple works, there were 20 Chinese priests and 67 Europeans. Since 1921, the mission policy had been to set up Chinese sections with a Chinese priest in charge (a vicar forain). In 1932, the Chinese ran five out of eight sections.

But during the ten-year period, September 1922 to September 1932, the vicariate had lost many clergy: 40 foreign Jesuits, 11 Chinese Jesuits, 17 Chinese secular clergy and four seminarians – a total of 72. The clergy was also ageing: there were six priests over 80 and 15 older than 70. In addition, there were a few premature deaths with four seminarians and missionaries Joseph Hugon and Peter Dühr (from Luxembourg), both less than 40 years old, and had been in the mission only three and four years, respectively. Then there were the deaths of Vanara and Dugout, killed at the ages of 49 and 52, after 24 and 19 years in China. Unexpectedly, over the decade, the European priests lived longer than the Chinese. Maybe this had something to do with diet and care of health in earlier years.

Among the deceased was Bishop Prosper Paris, who had been born at Châtenay, near Nantes on 1 September 1846. He entered the Society of Jesus at Angers on 17 October 1866, and was ordained on 18 September 1880. He arrived in China on 24 October 1883, was superior of the mission, 1893–9, consecrated Vicar Apostolic of Nanjing on 11 November 1900, and died in Shanghai on 13 May 1931, aged 85. He had been vicar apostolic of Jiangnan for 22 years, and of Nanjing for nine. During the time of his episcopacy, the number of Christians doubled, and four new vicariates were created from the original one. Under his government many works of charity, education and scientific were developed. Mission work grew into new areas of evangelisation. He confirmed 135,000 Christians, and ordained 151 missionaries, of whom 103 were Chinese.

Bishop Auguste Haouisée succeeded him. He was born at Evran, France, on 1 October 1877. He had studied for the secular clergy at St Brieue, but during that time decided to enter the Society of Jesus in September 1896, and set off for China in November 1903. He was ordained in China in 1910, and spent several years teaching, before becoming a missionary in Pudong, 1919–25, and then rector of Xujiahui. He was consecrated coadjutor to Paris on 3 October 1928, and succeeded to the vicariate of Nanjing on 13 May 1931.[14]

On the eve of becoming the vicariate of Shanghai in 1933, the city itself was a Catholic centre, with many religious organisations. The most significant for the Jesuit mission were the establishments in their compound at Xujiahui, situated on the border of the French Concession. They operated six parishes, and serviced 10 churches or chapels. There was the Jesuit school, and training colleges for the Jesuits and seminarians, as well as an observatory and orphanage. But there were also two other important works. One was the Museum and the other the Chinese Bureau.

The 'small Museum' started at Xujiahui contained the collected works of Pierre Heude and Frédéric Courtois. It developed into the 'Heude Museum', situated in the grounds of Aurora University and contained material collected over 60 years by the priests: mammals, molluscs, birds, serpents and plants. Henry Belval created a herbarium, which included the entomological collections of Auguste Savio (1882–

---

14. 'The Vicariate Apostolic of Nanjing', in *Relation de Chine* (Shanghai, July 1934): 1–13.

1935) and Octave Piel (Director of Heude Museum, 1935–45). It was the entomology section that grew in significance. Publications appeared: Belval completed the botanic works of Frédéric Courtois (1860–1928)[15] and Savio, together with Piel and the Spanish Jesuit, Longinos Navás made known the insects of the Lower Yangtze in a new revue, '*Notes d'Entomologie Chinoise*'. The library was well consulted by scholars.

The second work was the Chinese Bureau, started on 22 August 1927. Its aim was to help missionaries in their apostolic work in schools, in preparing conferences, articles, and for apologetic publications. Its field was to cover all that related to religious, intellectual and social China. Operating the Bureau was a director and six priests of the mission, two of whom were Chinese. Other missionaries collaborated. Programs included helping teachers through the distribution of journals and reviews, both Chinese and European, and material relating to government legislation and government projects and programmes. They also took charge of producing the annual statistics of the missions in China from the year 1901–2. They helped organise conferences and retreats, defended religious and educational liberty, and studied the Chinese language, as well as its history and literature. Publications included *Renseignements du B.S.* (bi-monthly in French), *Revue Catholic* (monthly in Chinese), and *Missions, Séminaires, Oeuvres catholique en Chine* (annual in French and Chinese). There was also *Mélanges de Xujiahui* (in Chinese), that covered topics of interest such as 'the soul and future life', 'education by the family', 'the history of charity', the encyclical *Rerum Novarum*, and Christian education. Other publications included the 'Summa of St Thomas' in Chinese by Ludovico Buglio, and *Dialectique*, also in Chinese by François Furtado. Other offerings were on the Curé of Ars, the life of Cardinal Robert Bellarmine, a manual of Chinese literature, a history of China in four volumes, and a manual of theology in six volumes. Finally, there was *Variétes Sinologiques,* that began publication in 1892.[16] These were significant initiatives to engage with Chinese culture.

---

15. Courtois went to China in 1901 and collected plants in the eastern part of the country from 1903. He was a keen ornithologist as well as a botanist. In China, he organised expeditions in Jiangsu province, collecting some 40,000 plants from the Anhui and Huangshan mountains. He was director of the Musée Heude for a time. (cf J Stor, Global Plants, plants.jstor.org)

16. 'The Apostolic Vicariate of Nanjing', in *Relatio de Chine* (July 1934): 1–33.

The ordination of 18 priests by Haouisée at Xujiahui on 7 June 1933 brought much needed satisfaction to the mission. They included eight Chinese seculars, one Chinese Jesuit and nine European Jesuits, of whom three were French: Louis Dumas from the diocese of Poitiers, André Bonnichon from Tours, and Fernand Lacretelle from Paris. Nine of these new priests belonged to the Shanghai mission.[17]

New missionaries and missions

The vicar apostolic shared a common view that the Jesuits did not have sufficient men to branch out 'to convert the pagans'. Lefebvre responded by suggesting that there were three Californian Jesuits in Shanghai who wanted to work in Haizhou, but Gonzaga College currently occupied them with work that could easily be undertaken by scholastics. He believed that the Oregon province had many young men who could be sent to Shanghai for regency. This would release priests in the college to work in the 'bush', as the Americans said. The superior general was not keen on Jesuits being sent to the missions for only a short time, despite being told that this arrangement would only be for a few years, lasting until the number of young priests from California increased. These priests presently in the mission were excellent: 'good religious and good apostles'. Haouisée suggested further that other Jesuit provinces might provide men, or if that failed, seek out other congregations who might like to become part of the Jesuit mission in Shanghai.[18] Shortly later, he indicated that there was pressure on the Jesuits from the apostolic delegate, Zanin, to send men to Nanjing. Haouisée wanted the Californian Jesuits to care of a hostel for students, but was aware of the reluctance of the Californian provincial to make such a commitment. Another French-speaking religious group offered to run the hostel, but he wanted to give first choice to the Americans, as the French group did not speak English, nor would they be 'intellectual leaders'. The delegate was informed that the preference for Nanjing was for Jesuits, and the Californian provincial was approached to send two more men, in addition to James Kearney, who was already in Nanjing.[19]

---

17. 'Les ordinations du 7 Juin 1933', *Relatio de Chine*, ut supra, 210.
18. Lefebvre, Shanghai, to General, Rome, 26 September 1934. ARSI.
19. Haouisée, Shanghai, to General, Rome, 14 June 1935. ARSI.

Discussions with the Californian provincial, Zachary Maher, continued, but he strongly opposed sending Charles Simons to Haizhou, despite Simons making strong representation to work in the 'bush'. Haouisée was frustrated about this, as he thought that he should make the final decision about the placement of Jesuits in the mission. It appeared that the American Jesuits did not want to be present in China unless they taught at either Gonzaga College or were in Nanjing. The American scholastics in Nanjing wrote to their provincial saying that the work potential in Nanjing was great, and that they should abandon thoughts of taking on the Haizhou mission. The suggestion was made that they should be given an autonomous region, because the French Jesuit superior in Shanghai always had to ask the rector of Gonzaga before he moved any Californian Jesuit in the mission.[20]

Maher wrote to Lefebvre saying that the superior general had instructed him not to undertake any work in China until the Nanjing project had begun, and at the suggestion that the mission of Haizhou might be assigned to the Californians, he would not consider assigning men there at the present, because to do so would be a formal acceptance of that mission. He pointed out that it was difficult to send men to China, as his own province had great needs. To undertake the running of Haizhou as well as Nanjing, Gonzaga and the Sacred Heart parish would be too much. If the Shanghai mission wanted two priests for Nanjing they should be taken from Gonzaga. Californian Jesuits should be excused from Haizhou at the present, but two scholastics, as well as Francis Rouleau and Thomas Phillips, might be assigned to Nanjing. They would be under the authority of the Californian provincial who would meet the cost of their education, which would prepare them for later ministry in Nanjing. Further scholastics suggested for Nanjing included Paul O'Brien, George Dunne, Albert O'Hara and Wilfred Le Sage. If there were insufficient scholastics at Gonzaga, lay teachers could be employed, as was done in California. Haizhou might be a possibility in the future, but not at present. Many works should not be undertaken at once.[21]

---

20. Extracts from two letters of Lefebvre, Shanghai, to General Assistant, Rome, 23 September 1935. ARSI.
21. Maher, California, to Lefebvre, Shanghai, 2 August 1935. ARSI.

Lefebvre responded to Maher's concerns, suggesting that he visit the mission and see for himself the many existing needs. In the parish of Hangzhou, John Lennon was superior with Francis Xavier Farmer, Francis Borgia Tsang and Henri Frenken, as well as a Californian brother, James Finnegan. In Gonzaga, Leo McGreal, Anthony Sen and scholastics John O'Farrell, Albert O'Hara and Paul O'Brien worked the college, with James Kearney currently in Nanjing. Lefebvre looked forward to at least two more American priests to further the work of education. He apologised for making such requests, but insisted that they were motivated solely 'to save as many souls as possible', and not from 'human respect'.[22]

The Holy See had been keen for the American Jesuits to open a college in Nanjing, rather than a parish, but Lefebvre explained to the superior general that this was impossible, suggesting rather that they build a 'hostel', a student residence, like Hong Kong. The general liked this idea.[23]

Re-establishing itself in Nanjing after 1927 was a challenge for the Jesuits, but Loh Pa-hong[24] was interested in establishing a Jesuit college in the capital, which would reinvigorate the intellectual life of the place. He worked in Nanjing and was aware of the negotiations with the Californian provincial for men to work in the city. He disliked the idea that Maher should have direct jurisdiction over the Californian house, the condition he made for sending money. Loh rightly commented that Maher had no idea of the needs at Nanjing, while Kearney, even given his intellectual gifts, was not practical or prudent. Furthermore, his skills in Mandarin were ordinary, and he lacked understanding of the Chinese people of Nanjing.

---

22. Lefebvre, Xujiahui, to Maher, California, 28 August 1935. ARSI.
23. Lefebvre, Shanghai, to Assistant, Rome, 23 September 1935; General, Rome, to Lefebvre, Shanghai, 2 March 1925. ARSI.
24. **Loh Pa-hong** (Lu Bohong) was engaged in Catholic Action for over 40 years. It began when as a Catholic he joined the Sodality of Our Lady at the age of 22, and worked with the Little Sisters of the Poor and the Sisters of Charity in giving catechetical instructions. In 1911, he founded a Catholic Action society, which had three aims: to propagate Christian ideas, develop educational works and establish charitable institutions. It called for a three-year novitiate, while members were expected to make a daily meditation, examination of conscience and do some spiritual reading. A day of recollection was expected every six months, and every year a retreat of five days. A Chinese terrorist later killed him.

Lefebvre shared Verdier's opinion of Loh Pa-hong by praising him as 'zealous, supernatural, very active' and pious. Theoretically, he respected the authority of the Jesuits, but was himself the 'most authoritative of men, very dominating'. He was a respected leader of any community in which he worked, giving great detail to the rules of schools or hospitals that were in his charge. He had a great reputation for charity, having founded or developed Christian works with the help of non-Christian organisations that acknowledged him as an important authority figure. He had good contacts raising finances. He borrowed from some, even from the Society, but he was not good at paying back.[25]

Observations on the mission by the French provincial, 1935

Another visitation of the mission was considered appropriate in 1935 since the last one in 1927. In his initial observations, the provincial was concerned that many missionaries suffered from discouragement. They were aging, and the apostolate had become more complex since 1927. Once they had official status, which greatly helped the number of conversions, but more recently with anti-foreign agitation, that had passed. Moreover, the Chinese were preoccupied with 'material interests', so they asked why they should change religions. Most wanted their children to follow the traditional religion of '*lao-laei-ku*'. Catholicism and its God were considered foreign, even among the educated Chinese. It was not the religion of China, an idea that the current anti-foreign climate encouraged.

Missionary depression increased with the realisation that the arrival of new missionaries was not coming as quickly as they might have wished. And, when the new men arrived, they were critical of older missionaries, insisting, like many Chinese, of the need for a Chinese-led Church. The older missionaries began to question the correctness of their ideas. If they were mistaken, were all the sacrifices and suffering they had endured in vain?

Criticism was levelled at the missionaries in Shanghai over a Eucharistic Crusade. This gave Chinese nationalists further cause against the foreignness of the French missionaries. Furthermore, the Chinese accused the missionaries of not 'loving them'. This hurt

---

25. Lefebvre, Shanghai, to Assistant, Rome, 23 September 1935. ARSI.

the missionaries, believing that they had sacrificed family, country, health, comfort and food to serve the Chinese. With combined criticism of them from Rome, and from the Chinese asking them to leave, many felt that they should 'shake off the dust from their feet and leave towards other people'.

Some missionaries expressed criticism of the apostolic delegate, showing lack of respect for him because they believed he was anti-French and anti-Jesuit. Some of his decisions were hurtful to the French, but it was wrong to consider him 'the architect of the destruction of the French in China'. The Chinese considered him their great advocate, representing the pope, who was going to put an end to the abuses that they had suffered.

The provincial also found 'a certain narrowness of views' among the French towards other missionaries, even other foreign Jesuits. Some were very critical of them, which did not help unity of purpose among the missionaries. Surprisingly, he had not found any regret about the progressive disappearance of the protectorate or the requirement not to consult the French legation in times of trouble, but rather the missionaries wanted to have better relations with the civil authorities. That being said, when disaster struck, the French Jesuits at Xujiahui were not slow to call out the French sailors for assistance. The young Chinese seminarians accepted this with regret.

The Chinese clergy favourably received Roman directives, which did not help relations with some foreign missionaries who considered these ideas ill conceived. The Chinese liked the way these new ideas changed the ways of proceeding that they had learned from the missionaries, and also because they were at odds with the prevailing influence of the French. The Chinese believed that the French opposed Rome because Rome supported the Chinese against the French. They laid the blame for much of the present anti-Christian attitude in China at the feet of the foreign missionaries. To accept this view would be an injustice. The Chinese also believed that the French Jesuits had no confidence in them; they were considered second rate, and kept in subordinate positions of authority. They were pleased that Rome had forced Jesuit superiors to nominate Chinese vicars forain, and even vicars apostolic. The secular clergy also considered themselves inferior to the Jesuits, which was unfortunate, as these men were an important source of vocations to the Society.

The Chinese priests and Christians suffered much from the injustice from their non-Christian compatriots who called them 'running dogs' of the foreigners. Efforts were made to find suitable Chinese Jesuits as leaders in the mission, but the provincial came to the same conclusion as the mission superiors: there was no one sufficiently 'apt for government'. Was it possible that the Europeans had too high an expectation of the qualities needed for leadership? Their model was European. The Chinese would probably lead differently to the Europeans, even if they did differ in style from the prerequisite qualities demanded by the Jesuit Institute.

The Chinese seculars underestimated the Christians. The Chinese did not believe in the chastity of the Chinese secular priests; they said they had proof of this, but they did accept the chastity of the European priests who they saw as more apostolic than the Chinese seculars. The Christians liked the European priests because they were 'true missionaries'; the Chinese priests were not. The Chinese priests preferred to work with the 'old Catholics' rather than go to the districts and convert the non-Catholics. There was evidence that there was mistrust of the secular priests among some European missionaries.

There was still concern about the teaching of the Chinese language to new missionaries. Many considered the current system of study inefficient. It needed a reasoned and methodical course upon the customs, history, geography, law and culture of the Chinese people. This would be a good supplement to the language study. One specific problem for missionaries to Shanghai was that they were required to learn two languages, *t'ou-wo* and Mandarin. There was diffusion of teaching methods throughout the various missions, with a number of teachers with only a few men. It would seem sensible to rationalise resources and co-ordinate methods of teaching by establishing a two-year course with a strong cultural program in a neutral Mandarin-speaking town with a pleasant climate. Tianjin was suggested. They could live in a rented house with a community during a two-year course. Maybe Beijing could be considered as an alternate location. Another possibility was a two-year course offered to diplomats at the *École des Langues Orientale* in Paris for those destined for China. The Lazarists used this resource, and it was useful, as graduates obtained a State diploma. Studying, writing and speaking the language under competent teachers were considered essential. This subject had been an ongoing concern for many decades, and the issue was never satis-factorily resolved, despite many attempts.[26]

This visitation was focused on the issues facing the mission rather than the religious discipline of Jesuit life. It realistically highlighted challenges for the missionary that required resolution. Tensions between the Chinese priests and the European missionaries would never be resolved as long as the Europeans held on to power and con-sidered the Chinese incapable of assuming responsible positions of authority in the mission.

Mission work in miniature

The Jesuits believed that it was important to inform supporters in France of developments in the mission in China. Occasionally special articles focused on regional sections and highlighted the dedicated work and progress of missionaries in sometimes-hostile territory. One such region was that of Jiang-pei, north of Hai Men, border-ing the sea, and stretching north to the former bed of the Huang-He River. It was a region continually subject to floods, so villagers built walls to protect themselves or moved to land more distant from the Grand Canal and the lakes in the west. It was a fertile area that grew rice and sorted vegetables.

Up to August 1921, no Catholic missionary had been into the interior of the four sub-prefectures: Dongtai, Xinghua, Founing, Yancheng. Henri Doré had explored the region in the south, around Dongtai, but he failed to establish himself in the town. Protestants were already in the interior, around Hai Ho, baptising in the villages, and had established a hospital and school at Yancheng. Missionaries found the area depressing to work in, with 'nothing to do', describ-ing the area as 'a true fiefdom of the devil'. To prove the point, it was registered that at An-feng there were 72 pagodas. It was also an area reputedly controlled by brigands, while the people were experienced as 'energetic but crude'. It was claimed that the big kidnappers of Shanghai came from this area.

---

26. Report of the visit of the French provincial (probably Fr. Lambert), Memorandum 1, 'Moral sufferings of the missionaries'; Memorandum 2, 'Several notes and impressions after my visit to China'; Memorandum 4, 'Study of Chinese', Xujiahui, (no date, but suggest 1934–5). ARSI.

The missionaries lived in poverty, which was the reason that superiors were reluctant to send men to Jiang-pei. In 1921, Charles Bondon, a seasoned missionary since 1891, accompanied by the superior, Verdier, visited the area, and they expressed sadness that so vast a territory had no missionaries. It was under the jurisdiction of Hai Men at that time, while Leopold Gain from Xuzhou had also been a pioneer in the region. Verdier was keen to establish a more permanent mission in the region; so some days later, Bondon was appointed to Rou-gao, a Christian community already established. From there, he was able to penetrate into Dongtai. This decision of Verdier opened a new area of mission activity where former missionaries had planted the Christian faith, and after 15 years it proved to be a 'rich and abundant' mission field.

The stages of conquering the region began at Rou-gao, 1921–2, with excursions into Dongtai. There was a basic problem with the language; it was Mandarin-speaking and the missionaries were forced to learn the language in order to be understood. Added to this was that the language spoken at Dongtai was not exactly the same as that spoken at Fou-ning or Xing Hua. Bondon's first decision was to set up residence at Dongtai, and by 1922–3 he had converted 16 locals. Evangelisation followed at Lin-chi, 1922–4, and then moved into surrounding areas with the help of former students of Aurora, who were originally from Xing Hua. Success followed, but only with difficulty because of the opposition of the people and of some Chinese authorities in particular. This was a middle-class city with little commerce. Powerful families had built strong walls around the town to protect it from both floods and brigands.

Xing Hua followed, 1924–6, with secular priest Li, Francis Xavier Farmer and Gabriel Maujay. Within six years, there were 40 Christians. Between 1926 and 1929, Bondon established schools and developed a catechumen programme at An-feng, and a new Christian community at Zao-ye. By 1934, there were 323 Christians at Dongtai and An-feng. In 1932, Bondon left Dongtai, handing over to priest Zao, already in charge of An-feng, and despite opposition from the people, built at Founing a residence and a school, in readiness for the new missionary André Zhu in 1933. With such growth within 12 years, Haouisée created two new sections, that of Dongtai, given to Chinese secular priests, and that of Founing with Zhu and John Pénot. The evangelisation of the region of Yancheng, 1934–5 completed the growth of the region. Within the 15 years, 1921–36, Bondon had overseen the creation of seven new districts, where there had been 1,671 conversions by 1935. In addition, five new churches had been built, as well as 17 Christian communities established with about 1,000 Christians in each. In 15 schools, 1925–36, there were 611 children who followed religious instruction, and in the four subprefectures there were three secular priests and three Jesuits.

Pioneer missionaries experienced difficulties as they confronted superstition and the right to be accepted. They grew long beards, wore old cloths and spoke fluent Chinese. They were a curiosity, with stares that were not always sympathetic. The Chinese tried to extract as much money as they could over the sale of land to the Church, and local authorities frequently indicated ill will toward them. The all-powerful 'notables' fermented most of the riots over the installation of Catholic centres, with local authorities making registration of land and new buildings difficult. Together with the presence of 'hooligans' and the hostility of the crowds, travel in the region was dangerous. The best means of communication was by the Grand Canal; the wheelbarrow and walking were the only means of transport for Bondon. He would sleep in hostels, and say Mass the next day very early before anyone arose. He frequently encountered 'brigands and soldiers' who were not pleasant, even 'robbing him of his honour'. When they attempted to shoot him, he never lost his calm.

The care of people and the education in the faith were the main aims of all missionaries, and Bondon was no exception. Engaging the people with friendliness and courtesy was probably more important to the people than relying on the 'all-powerful role of Grace'. There was a desire among the people, as well as their children, to be instructed. Schools became an important instrument to meet these needs. At Yancheng, for example, 40,000 students were taught in three middle schools, and a secondary school prepared students for the university. In 1935, at Yancheng, Bondon opened an 'école de livres', where young children, all non-Christians, came to classes, were very attentive, and happy to learn the catechism at the same time. Bondon also educated 500 catechumens, of whom 200 had already received Baptism by 1936.

Bondon, former missionary of Xuzhou, successfully surviving attacks from bandits and even the Boxers, worked this mission by himself for some years, following upon the pioneers, Leopold Gain,

Henri Boucher and Fortunée Marivint. He also faced many calamities, such as floods and famine. At Tangshan, he would visit the prisons where people were held in the most atrocious conditions, to bring comfort especially to those dying of hunger or to those who were soon to be condemned to death, and even administered Baptism to some. He travelled across the region either by the canal or on foot behind his wheelbarrow. Children were his first focus in the villages. His pockets were full of sweets that soon made him friends. Many came to the church where he explained the meaning of the various Christian symbols, and the lines of the catechism displayed on hangings on the walls of the church. Mothers, especially, soon followed the children. This was an important means of evangelisation. His endurance and strength, fortified by his faith and 'supernatural optimism', always sustained him.[27] Similar stories of rural mission life continued to inform Europe of life in China that would stimulate further support. There were also opportunities to rejoice in the progress of mission work, and wonder at the personal sacrifice of the missionary who endured many personal hardships and obstacles.

---

27. De Gassart, D., 'The evangelization of Kiang-pé', in *Lettres de Jersey*, XLVI, Nouvelle Série, T. XIII, 2 (1935–36): 268–83.

Chapter 9
Sino-Japanese War, 1937—1945

Ever since the occupation of Manchuria by Japan as far as the Great Wall of China and the Treaty of Tangkou, 1933, Japan continued to extend its influence southwards, which was resisted by the National Government. By the beginning of 1937, it became clear that the relations between the two countries had reached an impasse: either the Chinese army invade Manchuria, or the Japanese army withdraw from the north. A Chinese invasion was not possible while Chiang Kai-chek was primarily concerned with the growing influence of Communism in China. Meanwhile, the international scene in 1937 seemed to be moving towards a war situation. There was the anti-Communist agreement between Germany, Italy and Japan, the Spanish Civil War, English rearmament, and Stalin shooting his best generals. Chiang Kai-chek was slowly organising his army.[1]

On 7 July 1937, shooting broke out between a 100-man Japanese military unit stationed near Beijing and the local Chinese garrison. Japan had troops in the region under the protection of the 1901 Boxer Protocol. There had been occasional skirmishes between the two sides since 1935, but this was more serious, as it was the intent of the Japanese to launch a full-scale invasion and occupation of China.

This initial skirmish took place at the Lugouqiao or Marco Polo Bridge. The local Chinese commander challenged the Japanese troops who were on night manoeuvres. As they did not respond, the Chinese troops opened fire. No casualties were discovered on either side, but as smaller engagements escalated, the fighting became out of

---

1. 'The Sino-Japanese War', 1937 38, in *Lettres de Jersey*, XLVII, Nouvelle Série. T. XIV, 1, (Pentecost 1939): 84–93.

control for the Chinese by 27 July. On 29 July, Japanese forces occupied Beijing, and by 8 August occupied the city with 3,000 troops. The Chinese army was insufficiently armed or organised to meet this challenge. This not only began the Japanese occupation of China, but also was the beginning of World War II for the Chinese.

While there was no evidence that the Japanese attack was pre-planned, the incident provided an excellent opportunity for the expansionist group in the Japanese army to exploit the situation. The occupation of parts of China followed rapidly. The Japanese army, following the railways southwards, took each city in their path. Tianjin fell on 30 July, while fighting broke out in Shanghai on 13 August, when aircraft of the National Government bombed the Japanese warships anchored off the coast near Shanghai. Wusong, close to Shanghai, was taken on 1 September, and the Japanese navy blockaded the China coast. Nanjing was bombed regularly from 20 September until it fell in December, while Shanghai also finally fell on 12 November. On 20 November, the National Government abandoned its capital, Nanjing, and moved to the relative safety of Chongqing in the south-western Province of Sichuan, where it remained until the end of the war.

The attack on Shanghai resulted in many casualties, even from misdirected Chinese bombing hitting Chinese civilians. Shanghai held out from the bombardment for four months, with thousands of Japanese killed, but the city eventually came under Japanese control. Their brutality after this engagement on its path to Nanjing was probably in retaliation for the loss of Japanese lives in Shanghai.

It was in Nanjing that the massacres reached a climax with the event commonly called the Rape of Nanjing taking place following the entry of the Japanese troops into Nanjing on 13 December 1937. The Japanese troops embarked upon a frenzy of unprecedented looting, burning, murder, mutilations and rape of civilians that was endorsed by the Japanese officers. The scale of this episode was unparalleled in the history of modern warfare, and documented by eyewitness accounts from foreign residents in Nanjing, who published their accounts later in the Western press. While there was no agreement as to the numbers of victims of the massacre, one official account suggested that as many as 200,000 were killed during the Japanese occupation, and at least 20,000 women and girls raped. The International Military Tribunal for the Far East (The Tokyo War Crimes Trial), which took place between May 1946 and November 1948, accepted these figures. The Japanese denied the massacres.[2]

The Jacquinot Zone

At the beginning of September 1937, the Chinese government refused the joint request of the governments of France, Great Britain and the United States to establish a neutral zone in Shanghai to protect the thousands of civilians who were threatened by the war that waged around them in Shanghai. Two months later, by including the Japanese in the discussions, a temporary neutral zone, south and west of the French concession, at Nantao, the old Chinese city near the French concession was established 36 hours before the battle for south Shanghai, but only after a guarantee was given to the Japanese that no Chinese troops would enter the zone.

This neutral zone was essentially the work of the Jesuit, Robert Jacquinot (1878–1946). His credentials as president of an international commission for refugees and vice president of the local Red Cross Committee bolstered his request and, in addition, he was on good terms with the Chinese mayor of Shanghai, and known by some Japanese after his intervention in 1932. He headed a committee that was composed of seven members: three French, two English, one Norwegian and one American. This zone sheltered 250,000 refugees, largely from Nantao and Pudong, after pressuring both the Chinese and Japanese military to respect the neutrality of the zone.

---

2. Dillon, op. cit., 228–30. A review of Iris Chang's, *The Rape of Nanking: The Forgotten Holocaust of World War II*, (New York: Basic Books, 1997), by Oliver August, *Times On Line*, March 17 2005, quoted her figures that Japanese soldiers slaughtered between 100,000 and 300,000 people, and that over a six-week period, up to 80,000 women were raped. The details of the massacres were shockingly detailed. In another review by Sheryl Wudunn in the *New York Times*, 15 December 1998, cf John Rabe, *The Good Man of Nanking, The Diaries of John Rabe*, edited by Erwin Wickert (New York: Knopf, 2000), reflected upon the diaries of the German businessman, John Rabe, who witnessed the massacres and who set up a safety zone for four months, with the approval of the Japanese, that sheltered around 250,000 people. In addition to the killings, 'the Japanese soldiers, looted, smashed and burned people and buildings'. They even entered the safety zone 'to pillage, rape and murder'. As for numbers, Rabe mentioned that out of a total population of 1.2 million, about 800,000 fled before Nanjing fell, so between 50,000 to 60,000 people were probably killed.

Many refugees were also cared for in the international concessions, with the number swelling from 1.5 million to three million. They lived in schools, hospitals and churches. At Xujiahui, there were 20,000 refugees at its height that were fed daily; 4,000 were housed at St Ignatius' College. With the approval of the Japanese authorities, French police and colonial troops took over protection of Xujiahui and its associated works in the neighbourhood. Because of this, the Christian community of Xujiahui received reassurance that they were safe while they continued to work and pray.

Within the Jacquinot zone from 30 November 1937, amid the sufferings and privations for the Chinese, the refugees at least had peace and confidence in Jacquinot and his associates. Among Jacquinot's helpers were Jesuit scholastics who sought out people who were sick and in need of special help. Two Christian doctors, former students of Aurora, worked with the Sisters of St Vincent de Paul, the *Auxiliatrices du Purgatoire,* and the Franciscan Missionaries of Mary in running the hospitals and dispensaries. Chinese merchants were able to obtain rice from Indo-China, while ladies of Shanghai provided clothes, especially for the babies, many of whom had lost parents, and were surrounded by the diseases of influenza, measles and diphtheria. A dozen voluntary Russian police protected the zone. A French inspector of police discretely mingled among the people. Order was well maintained, which was particularly amazing as there was estimated to be about 4,000 bandits in the zone as refugees as well.

In April 1938, Jacquinot went to Hong Kong to collect funds for the refugees, but while there he received a message that the generalissimo, Chiang Kai-chek, wanted to see him in Hankou, and sent a plane to collect him. He explained to the generalissimo his motives for his operation that were totally free of all political questions, and that he worked not for himself, but for the Catholic Church in China. After receiving the gratitude of the president, his wife and other government leaders, he returned to Hong Kong and then to Shanghai.

In May, he visited the United States and was received in the White House by President Roosevelt accompanied by the French ambassador to Washington. This journey rewarded him with $700,000 from the American and Canadian governments for the refugees. He returned to Shanghai via Japan.

Robert Jacquinot de Besange was born in Saintes, France, on 15 March 1878, and was a brilliant student at *Bon-Secours* at Brest. He

entered the Jesuits on 24 September 1894 at Canterbury and, following the noviciate and juniorate, he studied philosophy at Jersey
from 1898–1901. His regency was first in Paris, and then at St Francis Xavier, Liverpool, from 1904–6. Theology followed at Hastings,
1906–10. It was during his fourth year of theology that he worked in
the parish of Rye, Sussex, and during 1910–11 was stationed at *Sainte-
Croix* in Mans. He left France for China on 13 September 1913, and
after a year studying Chinese at Xujiahui, he worked in the Shanghai
parish of the Sacred Heart, living there for 20 years. He also taught
English at Aurora from 1915–22, and he lived there from 1934. In
1927, he saved a group of nuns from a Communist attack and was
commended by the Chinese government for his valour. In 1932, he
secured cease-fires on several occasions, earning a *Croix de Guerre*
from the French government for evacuating more than 2,000 civilians
and setting up camps for some 20,000 refugees. On 15 February 1938,
he was made a *chevalier de la Légion d'Honneur* from the French government to recognise his services and to express gratitude for his
work that was admired throughout the world. France was proud of
him as a missionary and a Frenchman.

He had a strong personality, and was a born organiser and diplomat, with a deep strength of character. His independence worried
his Jesuit superiors who were critical of him for not joining in Jesuit
community life as much as they wanted. His Shanghai zone was a
great success, respected by all parties until the refugees dispersed in
1938. Even the Japanese commander gave Jacquinot money for the
refugees, as did the Chinese mayor of Shanghai. The Canadian Jesuit,
Maurice Belhumeur, helped him in his work. He raised $45,000 from
the French for electricity and clean water in the zone that continued,
with difficulties, until its closure in 1940.

Jacquinot was instrumental in setting up similar neutral zones in
Hankou and Wuchang. The former comprised the area of the former
concessions, the French concession and some neutral territory, about
four square kilometres. The Wuchang zone, separate from Hankou,
was established in the area of the schools and hospitals. As in Shanghai, the Japanese demanded that the Chinese armies respect the zone.
It was estimated that about three to 400,000 refugees entered these
zones. A committee was set up to run them, comprising commercial leaders in Hankou, navigation companies, some Protestants, and
the Catholic Bishop Eugenio Massi OFM (1875–1944), the Italian

vicar apostolic of Hankou. The Japanese army was not permitted to enter the zones, but Japanese police were present. The Red Cross, as in Shanghai, collected funds, and Jacquinot used some of the funds that he had received from America. The Chinese government gave $40,000 initially.

These zones enhanced the face of the Catholic Church in China, and even brought about a number of conversions among the sick and dying, as well as among others who were touched by the charity and zeal of Jacquinot and his workers. Particularly unexpected was a letter of appreciation to Jacquinot from the Japanese Minister of Foreign Affairs, praising his extraordinary courage amid much danger from the opposing armies in establishing the zone. He conveyed to Jacquinot sentiments of 'admiration and respect' from the Japanese nation for his humanitarian work, accomplished in the spirit of complete abandonment.[3]

Unfortunately for Jacquinot, a small group in the Chinese government accused him of collaborating with the Japanese. They expressed

---

3. 'Les Zones Jacquinot', in *Lettres de Jersey*, ut. supra, 93–106; John Meehan, 'The Saviour of Shanghai, Robert Jacquinot SJ, and his safety zone in a city at war, 1937', in *Company* (Spring 2006): 17–21. Cf also, Marcia R. Ristain, *The Jacquinot Safe Zone: Wartime Refugees in Shanghai*, (California: Stanford University Press, 2008).

   Jacquinot returned to France in 1940 with hopes for a Paris Safety Zone. This failed to eventuate, and he suffered depression, especially as his next Jesuit appointment was to parish duties in Paris. The Jesuits failed to utilize his talents and experiences until the Catholic Church requested that he become involved with relief services for the millions of victims of the war. Jacquinot was appointed an envoy of the Central Catholic Committee of Paris to travel abroad and help coordinate relief efforts. He visited England and Ireland, the United States and Canada. These visits were so successful that in December 1945 he was appointed chief of the Vatican Delegation in Berlin for the aid of refugees and displaced persons, and provided spiritual and material services for the displaced persons in the Berlin camps. His health began to decline and he died of advanced leukemia in Berlin, 10 September 1946, aged 68. His funeral was a grand affair, with Cardinal Konrad von Preysing, the archbishop of Berlin presiding. Representatives of the Vatican, the diplomatic corps, the Allied military, and the chief of the Chinese mission, as well as priests, diplomats and academics from the University of Berlin were in attendance. World representatives recognized Jacquinot's extraordinary gifts of organization, his deep concern for justice to those in need, and his 'enormous accomplishments in China and in the world'. His legacy lived on when his concept of safe zones was incorporated into the charter of the Geneva Convention of 1949.

displeasure with this, and with the Society for allowing it to happen. Jesuit superiors suggested that Jacquinot leave China immediately.[4] The apostolic delegate was also involved in this discussion, declaring his disapproval of Jacquinot's conduct towards the Chinese government at Chungking. Zanin told the government that Jacquinot did not represent the Catholic missions, nor that of Shanghai, nor that of the Jesuits and, further, that the Jesuits were sending him out of China. This decision came from the Secretariat of State in Rome. It was believed that he was 'incapable of understanding religious obedience', and that Rome did not want a scandal.[5]

Mission during the war

Soon after hostilities broke out in the north, Haouisée sent a letter to his priests and Christians recommending devotion to China and to help anyone in need during the war. He wanted them, like St Paul the Apostle, to suffer with those who suffer, and to support the Chinese state with all efforts. God had assigned to the missionaries the task of loyally serving China, both its territory and people. This attitude should be shown by completely supporting Chinese soldiers, even to death as an 'auxiliary army'. Above all, prayer for the leaders and soldiers was essential, asking God to care for them and for the wellbeing of the nation. Practically, if required, schools and residences should receive and care for the wounded in association with the Red Cross.[6]

Missionaries in the outlying districts were excellent sources of information about the movements of the Japanese and the effect the battle was having on the villages and among the people. From October, as the Japanese moved closer to Shanghai, it was noted that the Chinese troops withdrew in the face of the rapidly advancing motorised army of the Japanese. Destruction was everywhere. Jiading and Nejiang were in ruin, while the neighbouring population around Shanghai were subject to daily aerial bombing, such as at Cing-pou, north of Sheshan, where roads and bridges in the area were closed. At Psi-pao, the church was damaged, while the Jesuit Gabriel Loiseau, together with the local nuns, opened a dispensary

---

4. Henry to French Provincial, Xujiahui, 9 August 1939. ARSI
5. Henry to General, Xujiahui, 16 September 1939. ARSI.
6. 'Letter of Mgr Haouisée', 31 July 1937, in *Relatio de Chine* (1937): 263–4.

for the wounded. At Song-gang, on 24 October, after bombardment, there were reported to be 200 killed and 400 wounded. Bombs fell around the hospital that had received many wounded. Some of these were taken to the schools of the area, following the directions of the bishop. Pudong was continually attacked: the churches in Zhang Jia Lou, Jin Jia Xiang and Ka-kou-wei were badly damaged.

In Shanghai, the hospice of St Joseph in the Chinese section run by the Sisters of Charity cared for the sick and wounded, many of whom received Baptism. The missionaries made the most of these tragic situations to administer Baptism to those who had nothing to lose except their lives. As the number of refugees increased, the provision of food for them was essential. At Xujiahui, Brother Francis Xavier Lou and his helpers prepared rice meals each day for 7,000 people. Vincent Zi and other priests of the college taught the children of poor families the catechism and basic grammar. In addition, some good families formed a group to study the Catholic faith and later became catechumens. This happened also in Yangchang, a large village west of Wusong that previously had no Christians. These missionaries did not miss an opportunity for evangelisation.

Haizhou was terrorised by the daily bombing by the Japanese, which resulted in a blockade of essential goods such as matches, sugar, petrol and clothing materials. Louis Hermand reported Japanese bombing the ports and railway stations in his area of Hugou. On 28 October 1937, Songjiang was methodically bombed, including the Catholic residence and a small school. At the hospital, it was suggested that they fly the French flag over the buildings. Hopefully the Japanese would respect buildings owned and worked by Europeans.[7] It rarely worked.

Since the formation of the new Chinese vicariate of Nanjing in 1936, distinct from the vicariate of Shanghai, the French mission from Shanghai maintained two houses in Nanjing: Ricci College, directed by Albert Bourgeois, and a hostel for students that was being constructed for the American Jesuits. From the last few days of August 1937, the Jesuit Portuguese architect, José Diniz (1904–89), was forced to stop work on the building because of the incessant Japanese raids in the area, and he was forced to leave the city. Despite

---

7. 'The situation on 28 October 1937', ut supra, 282–5; Farmer to General, Shanghai, 21 January 1938. ARSI.

the dangers, the two houses did not receive direct hits, but the end of the residence at Ricci College was seriously damaged by a large bomb that was aimed at the nearby Ministry of Industry. When the American Jesuits left Nanjing their train was attacked by a Japanese aerial attack, and many people were killed. The only hurt received by the two Americans was their pride when thieves took their baggage.[8]

Since hostilities began in China, it became impossible to accuse the missionaries of being agents of the foreign powers. The response to their accusers was seen in the way the missionaries, in constant danger to themselves, assisted the wounded and gave shelter to the refugees. The whole world knew of the work of Jacquinot, but throughout the Catholic missions affected by the war, the missionaries supported the afflicted. The apostolic delegate supported Haouisée in asking the heads of all the missions to open their schools, residence, seminaries, and even the churches to assist the victims of the war. The missions responded as asked.

These acts of kindness were recognised by the Chinese authorities. At Kaifeng, Henan, the seminary became a military hospital, but when the Japanese threatened the town, it was transferred to a more safe location. But before the Chinese departed, both the wounded and the military doctors gave the missionaries a badge and silver medals with the inscription, 'Glory to those who work', to recognise their assistance. There were other local reports of gratitude from the Chinese military for their support.

The apostolic delegate asked all the Catholic missions to celebrate a service for the Chinese dead on 18 January 1938. This produced a 'profound impression'. At Hankou, the service, led by the delegate, was in the cathedral in the presence of the diplomatic corps, together with civil and military leaders. In his sermon, Zanin prayed for 'peace for the dead', and prosperity for the living, but in order to obtain this result, much work was still needed to support the Chinese people that they might finally have 'tranquillity and eternal salvation'.

Chiang Kai-chek, unable to be present because of military action at the front, sent a message to the service in which he praised the work of the Catholic missions and the Chinese Catholics for works of 'charity, mercy, and education', as well as for their current resis-

---

8. Brière, O., 'The War and the Mission of Changhai: after two months of war: 13 August – 13 October 1937', in *Lettres de Jersey* (1938): 107–15.

tance and defence of China, supporting the many Chinese, military and civilian, who had fallen and died for the country. He prayed with those present for those who had died and for peace for the living.

Later, on 3 March 1938, Madame Chiang Kai-chek spoke directly to the Chinese Christians on radio, asking for prayers that the sacrifices of the people of China not be in vain. On 6 April, she also announced the good news to the missionaries that the generalissimo had decided to revoke the government law that forbade the obligatory teaching of religion in private schools. In the past, this law had hindered the work of the Catholic missions. In her speech, she continued to praise Christianity as a 'source of spiritual and temporal blessings' for China, especially in the field of education and care for the sick, as well as in industry and agriculture. She recognised with gratitude that over the nine months of the war, the foreign missionaries, men and women, and their Christians, had shown a spirit of sacrifice, giving extraordinary care to the wounded, taking in refugees, and assisting all in need. Even non-Christian statesmen declared their admiration and esteem for the Christian religion.[9] These official accolades for the missionaries produced moments of joy and feelings of support that encouraged their painstaking work of attending people suffering from the war.

One moving story was told by the Chinese Jesuit, Brother Lou, who, as mentioned, cared for the many refugees seeking refuge at Xujiahui during the battle for Shanghai. He recounted that, while providing food and clothes, he established a small village to provide for 20,000 people. He also set up a hospital with two doctors from Aurora, and a Chinese doctor who cared for all medical needs. Not having any money, nor receiving any financial assistance from the mission or the Jesuits, he begged assistance from his personal friends, while local charities helped provide rice. With his help, the refugees received two meals each day. He mentioned the good relations that he had with the refugees who were grateful for all that was done for them. But there were problems, some disgruntled refugees and 'vagabonds' caused mischief and tried to swindle the refugees and the people of Xujiahui. Lou defended the refugees against them, and they, together with other Jesuits, then reported him to the Jesuit superior criticising him. They were believed. This caused the brother much pain, both

---

9. 'Across China', ut supra, 385–8.

because the Chinese who accused him were 'uncivilised', and because the Jesuits were jealous of him. Other Jesuits were unaware of all the work he was doing, and did not listen when told. The Federation of the Bureau of Charity recognised his work by giving him $200,000 for provisions, and other friends offered to assist him in setting up an orphanage near Xujiahui, but Lou refused because of foreseen difficulties with the Jesuits.

In sharing his sadness with the superior general, after he heard the news that he was removed from this work, he reasserted that he worked solely for the 'greater glory of God, for the Mission, to save the souls of these poor refugees, redeemed by the blood of the Saviour'. As a result of his work, there were more than 400 new Christians, and 200 catechumens in the camp. He did not sound bitter about the decision of his superiors, left his work and went to Sheshan, where he said he would continue to work 'with all my energy for the greater glory of God'.[10] Such expressions of faith and fidelity to his Jesuit vow of obedience were striking.

Like Jacquinot, Brother Francis Xavier Lou suffered the fate of being too prominent for his superiors. Both were removed from work that brought both them and the mission great fame at home and abroad. It was similarly the Jesuit response to the world famous palaeontologist, Teilhard de Chardin, when he was in China. There are at least two reasons for this: one, that the culture of Jesuit living did not approve of individuals showing initiative outside the common mission; and second, the French Jesuits had continually disapproved of what they called the 'independence' of the Jesuit Chinese brothers. Conformity, obedience, docility and fidelity to Jesuit community duties were among the most admirable virtues expected of Jesuits. Individual initiatives, outside those authorised or controlled by superiors were not acceptable. Unity of purpose and action was paramount. They considered this their strength.

The missionaries were pleased to observe that while attending to the wounded soldiers in the hospitals, a number of them sought conversion to the Christian faith. They had initially appeared to be indifferent to religion, but while suffering much, some turned toward deeper questions about life and the supernatural. Some experienced a return to health and strength following Baptism. There was genuine

---

10. Lou to General, Xujiahui, 9 September 1938. ARSI.

gratitude and admiration for the caring nuns, and appreciation for the visits of the priests: these were their only visitors. Many seemed satisfied with the spiritual answers given to their questions. The Christian God seemed closer to their present needs, feeling comforted by the idea of an all-powerful spiritual being caring for them. Good care was experienced in the Protestant hospitals as well, but it was noticed that discrimination was shown towards those who showed interest in converting. In Catholic hospitals, conversion did not result in temporal advantages.

The main obstacle to conversion was believed to come not from Buddhism, but more frequently from ancestor worship, and traditional Chinese ceremonies surrounding marriages and funerals. They did not want to offend their relatives by abandoning these ancient Chinese customs. When questioned, few seemed to know anything about Communism. Some simply wanted to turn from an evil life to a good one: a life lived by conscience, while others liked the idea of the universality of the Catholic Church. Catechesis was given individually, as the soldiers were almost all bedridden. The catechist used a small book of prayers and the catechism. In this work the missionaries saw themselves as instruments of God's grace bringing salvation to these 'good, vulnerable, but unbelieving people'.[11]

As the mission settled down after the end of hostilities in Shanghai, it was observed that because of the geographical diversity of the mission, especially the difference between the north and south of the Yangtze, it might be wise to use the Europeans in an area that was just opening up for evangelisation and was unified by the Mandarin language. Chinese Jesuits would be best suited to working in the south, working among 'the old Christians'. Shanghai should remain with the French, because of the mission's multiple contacts with Europeans and Americans, and because of delicate issues that arose between the bursars of various religious congregations. The Shanghai vicariate contained a population of three million inhabitants, with 40,000 Catholics.

The mission experienced ruin after the war. Bombing and fires destroyed a dozen churches with residences, while the schools attached were destroyed or badly damaged. The college at Kuang-ki

---

11. Albert O'Hara, 'An Inquiry into the causes and motives of conversion of Chinese wounded soldiers', in *Bellarmino*, 2/20 (October 1938): 23–7.

was ruined, and as the mission was reduced to a third of its revenue, there was insufficient capital to rebuild. In addition, the mission had a considerable debt for the previous 12 years.

As always, there were problems of manpower, with aging and sick missionaries requiring replacement. It was the duty of the superior to work out the placement of the men at his disposal, and he never seemed to have either enough, or men of sufficient quality, to fulfil the job requirements. Chinese studies for Jesuit scholastics, Chinese and European, continued to be a constant concern, while the teaching of French and Latin, as well as Greek, were also to be taught in the seminaries. Teaching at St Ignatius' College, Xujiahui, Gonzaga College and Aurora continued uninterrupted, despite the Japanese occupation.

In the light of stress arising from the political turmoil in which they lived, Superiors continued to stress to their men the importance of the supernatural in their lives. They needed a 'spirit of prayer and a firm attachment to our Rules' as they worked and lived in the districts 'without much control' and amid dangers and rumours that exposed them to 'attacks and denunciations'. For those missionaries sent to the 'bush', they should have 'common sense, courage and solid virtues', without 'nervous dispositions'.[12]

Suspecting that the missionaries might need more universal support, the French provincial, Francis Datin, visited the mission in 1938, and in a warm and encouraging letter to the missionaries, he congratulated and praised them for the great work that they did, bringing 'great glory to God'. The results of the mission over 90 years were magnificent, and despite current suffering, they should remember that the works begun had born great fruit. He assured them of God's protection, united as they were with Him in His suffering. A life of intense prayer was important for the development of the interior life. Jesuits always believed that the fruits of any apostolate were the result of a deeply spiritual life according to the Jesuit rule, whatever natural gifts were exercised.

In commenting on the war, he appreciated the care shown to the refugees in Shanghai, while believing that the Japanese did not deliberately destroy Catholic churches. That only seemed to occur when

---

12. Some problems concerning the mission of Shanghai, Henry to General, Shanghai, 1938. ARSI.

they believed that Chinese soldiers were present in the village. He sympathised with the priests who could not leave residences without a pass from the police.

He reflected further that the best preparation for the China mission was good ecclesiastical studies, and to be as perfect as possible in the Chinese language, while recognising the difficulty experienced by Jesuits who learned Mandarin in Nanjing returning to Shanghai and having to learn and speak another dialect. Schools were a very important part of the mission, as they were the seedbeds of the Christian life. They also put missionaries in contact with non-Christians that missionaries were otherwise unable to reach. The moral and religious development of their teachers was important, as well as guiding their pedagogical skills. In the Christian communities, it was important to seek out leaders who might become good examples to others, especially to the non-Christians, and lead them to conversion. The Society of Jesus had always focused on the development of leaders through the spirit of the Gospel and the *Spiritual Exercises* of St Ignatius'. Retreats might be given to suitable groups. Also, it was among the elite that vocation to the priestly and religious might arise.

Jesuits should also work in 'fraternal unity' with the secular clergy, and with the religious sisters. Social action was an important aspect of the apostolate. When discerning new needs, the choice should always be what was the most fruitful.

The tone of the letter was spiritual, warm, encouraging and practical, even if he frequently reiterated former concerns and common Jesuit practices. At the end, he promised to help the mission as much as possible with financial assistance.[13]

French legation Beijing concerns 1938–1940

As previously, the legation continued to be concerned with protection issues. It announced to Paris that Xujiahui was given protection by French sailors and other foreign troops in December 1937. France remained neutral during the Sino-Japanese War. The French Corps of Occupation in China was ordered to stand down in case of a Japanese attack on their concession. The French authorities attempted to

---

13. Letter from Provincial Datin to Fathers and Brothers in the Mission of Shanghai, Xujiahui, 3 December 1938. ARSI.

prevent the entry of Chinese Nationalists and Communists seeking refuge in the concession in an effort to avoid giving the Japanese an excuse for intervention. Within the French concession in Shanghai in 1937, there were 475,000 people, of whom only 2,342 were French nationals. At the time, 640 soldiers, 2,235 policemen and the ships of the Naval Division of the Far East defended French interests in China. After several skirmishes with the Japanese concerning the French concessions in Tianjin and Shanghai during 1939, in September, Japan demanded the withdrawal of all French land and naval forces from China. In 1943, the Japanese occupied the French concession in Shanghai, and in March 1945 they disarmed the French Corps of Occupation in China and, finally, on 28 February 1946, France relinquished its concessions and special treaty rights with the Nationalist government in exchange for a withdrawal of Chinese Nationalist Army from Tonkin.

Meanwhile, back in 1938, the French ambassador in Beijing objected to the Japanese ambassador about the Japanese attacks on the Catholic missions. The Japanese ambassador replied that the missions should place visible marks on the buildings clearly seen from both air and land, especially in the areas connecting Qingdao, Yenchou and Changte toward the south to the Yangtze River. He later included both Daming and Taiyuan. He also asked for maps of the location of the missions, which the French subsequently sent. The Japanese ambassador also unofficially suggested that all foreign nationals should evacuate the areas of hostility to avoid danger to their lives.[14] Japanese diplomatic responses to requests from the French legation were formal, courteous and practical. The Japanese continued to insist that they did not deliberately wish to attack Catholic missions.

Paris was kept informed about the 'security zones' of Jacquinot in Shanghai, and believed that the Jesuits sent Jacquinot away from China in 1940 because of his political involvement (5 June 1940). But the Jacquinot Zone was 'a precious refuge for the people of Chinese villages and this act of charity had brought new prestige to the French' (29 April 1939). The zone was seen as 'a picture of misery, alive and very active, a sea of vice'. Jacquinot was believed to well serve the

---

14. Japanese legation, Beijing, to French ambassador, Beijing, 1 January 1938. DAC.

interests of France. The legation considered the Zone under French protection (9 August 1938).[15]

The legation continued to report to Paris about the Japanese bombardment of Catholic missions, and that missionaries like Verdier had asked the generalissimo for protection from the Japanese for the missions, especially for the Italians at Anhui (19 April 1938). René Charvet, the French mission bursar, asked for help against the Japanese occupying religious houses in Xianxian, while Bishop Federico Melendro in Anqing reported that flying the French flag was no protection (4 February 1938). Additional safety zones were asked for Xiamen and Wuhu, but were not granted. The Japanese bombing of the Italian mission at Bengbu was reported: 11 bombs fell on the mission with much destruction of mission property. Several Italian Jesuits were wounded, but were taken to the Japanese field hospital and well treated. The Italian ambassador to China objected to the Japanese ambassador (15 February 1938) that the attack took place despite following the Japanese advice to fly the Italian flag on the roofs of houses.

The missionaries gave the French legation excellent information about the Japanese movements around the various missions. József Németh, in Daming, reported that even with the French flag flying, bombs fell hitting the cathedral (12 February 1938). The Japanese later took the town (14 February 1938).[16] The death of Louis Hermand by bandits was reported on 28 April 1939 at Haizhou, having died in a Japanese hospital. Two other priests were held hostage, and one, Aloysius Le Bayon (aged 72), having been set free, died soon after.

The Japanese accused the missionaries in Xianxian of political activity. The missionaries denied the charge, but complicating political matters were the activity of the Communist armies who were also involved in anti-missionary activity when they were in Christian areas. The missionaries said that they kept aloof from political issues, but they certainly reported any abuses by the Japanese or the Chinese Communists to the French legation. Japanese troops arrived

---

15. Security Zones of Fr. Jacquinot, 1938ff, DAC.
16. Letters about the protection of the missions during the Sino-Japanese war, 1938: 17 January, 4 February, 15 February, 6 April, 19 April; Consul, Tianjin to French ambassador, Shanghai, 14 February 1938; Charvet to French Consul General, Tianjin, 12 February 1938, DAC.

in Xianxian on 24 March 1938. They thought that the wounded in the hospital might be Communists, and asked the missionaries if the church ran a Communist school. The suggestion was that perhaps the mission was a sanctuary for the 8th Army. The Japanese decided that the missionary school was both anti-Japanese and Communist.[17]

The legation continued to be concerned about the missions and the treatment of missionaries by both the Japanese and the Chinese Communists, and they made diplomatic complaints when incidents occurred. They reported the capture of a Spanish Jesuit at Wuhu, Anhui, probably by Communists rather than Japanese, when the Communists suspected him of collaborating with the Japanese. Brother Edgar Gauvin's death (aged 31, and two years a missionary) at Xuzhou was noted after a Japanese soldier had wounded him on 28 October 1939. The Japanese had captured three missionaries, thinking that they were Chinese bandits, as they were wearing Chinese clothes. After this incident, the Japanese authorities asked foreign nationals to carry travel documents, inform the Japanese or Chinese authorities that they were passing through, and not to wear Chinese clothes, but if they did, they were to also wear some notice of their nationality, and finally to attach certificates issued by the Japanese to such clothes.[18] The Japanese generally seemed to want to protect the foreign missionaries from harm, but were sometimes confused when they arrived at a particular place. For example in the Xianxian mission, the Japanese arrested Alphonse Gasperment at Zhangjiazhuang on 3 November 1939, on suspicion of collusion with the Communist 8th Army. Decisions concerning a matter of collaboration with the enemy could be very subjective, and such decisions during wartime appeared somewhat arbitrary.

At the same time, the missionaries asked for help from the French legation for compensation from the Japanese for destroyed property. The Japanese ambassador continued to insist that mission property would be respected, provided that it was clearly marked with the French flag.[19] Unfortunately, in wartime, that direction could not always be guaranteed.

---

17. Memo of French legation, 'Japanese accused missionaries in Xianxian of political activities', 20 February 1939. DAC.
18. 'Domei', Hsughow, 11 November 1939. DAC
19. Charvet, Tianjin, to Chargé d'Affaires, Beijing, 13 April 1940. DAC.

Mission concerns 1939–1940

As the Japanese occupied more and more Chinese territory, the apostolic delegate, Zanin, sent a circular letter to all the bishops in China instructing them to observe absolute neutrality in the face of the war. But, in fact, the foreign missionaries were in constant contact with their foreign legations, giving reports of the occupying army's movements and activities, while some even expressed the hope of a final Japanese victory. Some missionaries did not consider that the Christian Chinese ought to love their country in the same way as the European missionaries loved their country of origin. The idea that the representative of the Holy See was radically opposed to supporting the national defence of the country did not impress the Chinese government. The Chinese ordered its ambassador in Paris to protest to the apostolic nuncio for France. There was a movement in China to have Zanin removed, but after an apostolic visitation on the issue, it was only recommended that the Chinese government establish permanent diplomatic relations with the Vatican.[20]

On the occasion of a visit to Xujiahui by Zanin, he claimed optimism about the future of the Catholic Church in China during the present conflict, based on statistics. Before the war, the number of catechumens in China was 400,000, but in 1939 it was 1,500,000. These people did not only come from poor families or those destitute from the war, but there were a growing number of well-off families: commercial, employees, and teachers. Many conversions were from the universities, especially in Beijing, at Aurora and Tianjin. These Baptisms were only permitted with the approval and support of the parents of these students.

Zanin believed that the public face of the Catholic Church in China was good. People saw the good done by acts of charity toward the many people in distress, without distinction, during the war. Moving tributes were also made by the Chinese authorities on the occasion of the death of the pope, expressing respect for him as the head of the Catholic Church. The prestige of the Church was not only appreciated by the Chinese, but also even among the civil and military Japanese, who recognised the unquestionable influence of the Catholic religion that spread throughout China. Even if the attitude of the Catholic missionaries and their flock toward the invasion was

---

20. Louis Wei-Tsing-sing, up supra, 142.

not always without reproach, they, at least, usually gave the Church signs of respect.

While these were signs of hope, there were many sorrowful matters: material ruins of churches and schools, residences destroyed, burnt or robbed, missionaries killed or in prison, suffering of all kinds, as well as fear about the future, especially of the dangers arising from Communism, which was seen as well organised, widespread, and profiting from the sufferings of war in order to spread its propaganda. This was especially seen in the larger Chinese centres.

Sadness was expressed especially at the murder of Louis Hermand at Haizhou, 27 April 1939. He was shot during an attack by about 40 brigands. Before he died, two Japanese doctors attended him, risking an operation that failed.[21]

On 16 July 1939, a decree from *Propaganda Fide* was received in the mission, separating the prefecture of Jingxian from the vicariate of Xianxian, nominating Bishop Leopold Brellinger the first prefect apostolic. At the same time, the superior general decreed that the new mission was to be given to the Jesuit Austrian province. This new prefecture had 30,000 Christians and 332 Christian communities, as well as 25 priests, 10 of whom were Chinese. It comprised 12 subprefectures. In 1935, there was a total population of two-and-a-half million people. Xianxian had 52,000 Christians, while both missions had many vocations. This new vicariate was the region of the deaths of Jesuits Mangin, Denn, Isoré and Andlauer.[22]

One completely unexpected decree from the Vatican concerned the question of the Chinese rites on 28 May 1935, when permission was given to the Manchurian vicar apostolic of Kirin that Chinese Catholics could render homage to Confucius in rites that were considered purely social or civil. The same privilege was given to Japanese Catholics to honour the emperor and national heroes. This overturned the decree of Benedict XIV in 1742, forbidding Catholic participation in traditional Chinese rites because they were considered religious. This decree had resulted in the persecution of Catholics, and set back the evangelisation of China until the present day.

In 1600, there had been 300,000 Christians in China, but only 200,000 in 1800. In 1940, there were three million Catholics. Confu-

21. *Nouvelles de Mission*, Shanghai, 15 May 1939, 2–3.
22. Ibid., 30 July – 15 August 1939.

cius was held in honour during the years of the emperor, with his picture in classrooms, but since the revolution of 1911, honouring him declined because of the world of academics, Western knowledge, the work of Protestant missionaries, and the progress of materialistic and atheistic doctrine. Confucianism as the state religion was suppressed. Prostrations before his image were replaced by a simple inclination of the head and chest. In July 1912, scholarly ceremonies in the temples of Confucius were suppressed: a holiday was substituted. His picture was replaced by that of Sun Yat-sen. According to the apostolic delegate, Costantini, in 1928, bowing to the image of Sun Yat-sen was not an act of idolatry, but rather a greeting to the Father of the Republic, while he saw Confucianism as a 'school of philosophy' that had no theology.

In 1934, on the anniversary of the birth of Confucius, civil and social ceremonies were held to honour the much revered man. Then in Manchuria, 1935, after consulting the Chinese government, the Vatican recognised Confucian rites as exclusively civil, and had no religious character; Confucius was simply honoured, not adored. Finally, on 8 December 1939, in order to show respect for the Chinese civilisation, Rome accepted the Chinese rites as civil and not religious. Christians could participate in ceremonies honouring Confucius, and his image could be placed in Christian schools. Tablets of the dead were also authorised, as they only named the departed. Pius XII insisted on respect for civilisation, and the need to protect and foster local culture.[23]

This approval came too late. The initial decree of condemnation of the Chinese rites had disastrous consequences for the Catholic missions. Persecution of Catholics followed, and missionary methods changed, which adversely affected evangelisation. Subsequent missionaries sent to China had to take an oath to respect the earlier papal decree against the Chinese rites. Now, nearly two centuries later, a time when Nationalist China was battling for its integrity against

---

23. A. Brou, 'Le point final à la Question des rites Chinois', in *Etudes* (January-February-March 1940): 275–83. A recent work by Nicholas Standaert traces Chinese opinions in the debate over the nature of Chinese rites that support the Ricci approach. Cf. Nicholas Standaert, *Chinese Voices in the Rites Controversy. Travelling books, Community Networks, Intercultural Arguments*, Bibliotheca Instituti Historici SJ, 75, edited by Paul Oberholzer SJ (Rome 2012).

Japan and the Communists, the Catholic missionaries hardly gave more than recognition to the decree.

With the Japanese present in Shanghai, and 512 Japanese Catholics who attended Mass at the Sacred Heart Church, the superior general was asked to provide a Japanese Jesuit priest to assist in the parish. Others who needed special assistance were 350 Portuguese and Eurasians, and 400 Germans, as well as a number of Jews from Europe.[24] In this request, the Jesuits were showing their universal pastoral care for any nationals in need.

Letters continued to cross between the Jesuit superior in Shanghai and the Californian provincial concerning more assistance from the Americans. The Californian provincial seemed content with his men working in the Nanjing Institute, but working the mission station in Haikou was something to be considered later, when he had sufficient men and finances to assist. The Shanghai superior replied that he was desperate for men in Haikou, and that if he did not receive assistance from California, he would have to look elsewhere for help.[25]

Since the arrival of the American Jesuits in Shanghai, some of whom were very talented, a resurgence of interest in developing the intellectual apostolate was shown. Pride was always expressed in the work of Aurora University, Shanghai, and *Hautes Etudes*, Tianjin.

Aurora University, situated in the French concession from 1908, was founded in 1903 by Ma Xiangbo, and given by him to the Jesuits. In 1923, there were 301 students: 80 Catholics and 273 non-Catholics, studying in the faculties of medicine, law and civil engineering. In 1924, there were 40 professors that increased to 44 in 1928. For the decade 1929–39, the percentage of Catholic students to non-Catholics rose from 33.22 per cent to 66.73 per cent. During the decade, the number of students educated by the university was 3,762, with an annual increase of 24 students.

The *Hautes Etudes*, established on 9 August 1922 by the French Province of Champagne, opened in September 1925 with ten Jesuits and 16 students. Classes were taught in English, French and Mandarin, with English the official language of the school. Between 1929–39, the percentage of Catholics to non-Catholics was 22.64 per cent

24. Farmer, Shanghai, to General, Rome, 24 January and 9 August 1940. FPA (Province of France Archives, Paris).
25. Seeliger, Provincial California to Henry, Shanghai, 10 October 1940; Henry to Seeliger, 21 December 1940. FPA.

Catholic and 77.35 per cent non-Catholic, while the total student population for the decade was 3,547. On the staff in 1939, there were 22 Jesuit priests, six scholastics and three brothers.[26] These two tertiary institutions gave the Jesuits greater credence among the Chinese for fostering advanced academic studies.

A Chinese outsider comments on the Christian missions

A comment on the missionaries and their work by China's first female professor Chen Hengzhe, Sophia Chen[27], gave a wider perspective to their impact in China. Her attitude to the missionaries changed when she returned to China after being educated in the USA. Writing largely about her experience of Protestant missionaries, she appreciated their motives for going to China, expressing a spirit of sacrifice, and a noble forgetfulness of self. They did great work, especially in education, social work, and in hospitals, helping the suffering poor as well as the rich. They brought a new professionalism for the Chinese women, especially as teachers. She praised the missionaries' use of English, which was an important medium of education for China, while the Protestant University of Peiping fostered the teaching of Chinese culture. But there were challenges. It was difficult for Chinese men and women to worship together, while Chinese converts had

26. T. Carroll, 'The Educational work of the China Mission', in *Bellarmino*, 8/24 (October 1940).
27. **Chen Hengzhe** (1893–1976) was China's first female professor and a well-known writer under the name of Sophia Chen. Born into a prominent family in 1893 in Jiangsu province, Chen embarked on a life of academia. Her grandfather was a prominent scholar during the Qing Dynasty, and her mother came from a wealthy and influential family in the province. In 1911, Chen moved to Shanghai to attend a missionary women's school. In 1914, she was awarded a scholarship to the United States, where she studied western history and literature at women's' Vassar College. She was one of the first female Chinese students to study abroad. In 1918, she was accepted into the University of Chicago for further studies, and returned to China in 1920 with a master's degree, teaching at Peking University. She later taught at the Southeast University in Jiangsu. Believing that Chinese students needed to know more about the West, she wrote *History of the West*. She promoted the movement for a vernacular literature in simplified Chinese rather than the classical Chinese. She was a great promoter of women and their education. With her husband and three children, during the war of 1930s and 1940s, she moved to Hong Kong and then to France. After 1949, she and her husband returned to China, and lived and worked in Shanghai.

not made their mark on the cultural scene. While having done great things, missionaries made many mistakes, essentially because they could not divest themselves from their European background. They were not prepared to engage a new culture or believe that it had the capability of revitalising itself by its own means. They considered the Chinese as 'savage' and 'uncultivated'. They were ignorant of Chinese culture, so the educated and cultivated Chinese were not disposed to their influence. Some missionaries had a little understanding of the old Chinese culture, but probably not about modern China.

There existed a fundamental difference between the missionaries and the intellectual non-Christian Chinese in their attitude towards religion. The intellectual non-Christian Chinese saw religion as a purely personal affair. Chinese intellectuals paid little attention to the religion of their friends. They saw Christianity as just one moral force in the world, but they would never admit that it was the only force. It was difficult for old-style Chinese to accept Christianity as an equal authority to their older culture. Western Christians had only one source of morality, while Chinese culture was comfortable with extremes, such as Christian hymns alongside the chants of Taoists and Buddhists in their funeral processions.

Religion in China was always seen as the servant of philosophy, as in Buddhism, which was part philosophy and part superstition. The Europeans were perceived to bring new superstitions to China, such as the fear of number 13, the desire to go to heaven after death, and the sign of the cross of Christians. For many the Christian religion was considered a collection of superstitions. However, 'the philosophical aspect of Christianity was the only part of Christianity which commanded respect and attention of the Chinese mentality'.

Non-Christian liberal Chinese were tolerant of religion, but the modern generation was 'corrupt and intolerant' and influenced by Russian Communism. The younger generation were not alarmed by the growth of atheism.

Missionaries did well to show the importance of women's education. The missionaries contribution to China should help the Chinese built up a new Chinese culture, influenced by European education, its social system, professionalism and organisation.[28]

---

28. 'The opinion of Mme Sophia Chen on Christianity', in *Bellarmino*, 6/7 (March 1940).

Much in this statement could be applied to the Catholic missions as well, such as her praise of missionaries' self-sacrifice, work in education, health and social services, while her criticism of them as not appreciating the values in Chinese culture, or their inability to adapt European culture and European Christianity to the people, especially to the educated Chinese, was equally true. One difference was the medium of education. She rightly praised those missionaries who taught in English, as that language would open more doors for the Chinese in the future, whereas the French missionaries, by giving emphasis to the teaching of French in their schools and university showed little appreciation of this – they being embedded in the promotion of French culture, and relying on French finance and military support.

Seminary training during the war

Over the decades, the Vatican and *Propaganda Fide* had constantly encouraged the missionaries to foster local vocations, suggesting that they were not pleased with the rate of enthusiasm for the task. The Jesuit mission of Jiangnan showed its enthusiasm from the very beginning of its mission by opening a seminary only one year after they arrived in Shanghai, in 1843. From that time on, fostering vocations to the priesthood and religious life was their major objective and, because of adverse criticism that they did not support an indigenous clergy, they were keen to continually remind superiors in Rome of the progress in this important aim.

In 1842, the mission had eight Chinese priests and 22 seminarians. In 1940, there were 85 'Latinists', considered potential seminarians, at St Ignatius' College, 32 Chinese Jesuit scholastics, 45 seminarians and 102 priests of whom 22 were Jesuits and 80 belonged to the secular clergy.

The mission of Shanghai had 11 sections, of which Chinese priests administered seven. Of the 10 parishes in Shanghai, three were given to the secular clergy. From 1922, six missions were successively detached, of which two were given to the Chinese secular clergy: Hai Men and Nanjing. Thirty-one former Chinese priests from the former Jiangnan mission were in these two new regions. Taking all those Chinese priests belonging to the former mission, there were currently 133 Chinese priests.

Over 100 years, 690 young men entered the seminary: 185 reached priesthood, with the proportion of one in two over the previous 25 years. As the family was significant for vocations, most of these men came from the long-standing Catholics – the 'old Catholics'. Their course in the minor seminary lasted three years, studying Latin, Chinese literature and 'general culture'. In the major seminary, there was two years of philosophy, followed by a year as an apprentice in the districts, followed by four years of theology. Philosophy and theology studies were similar to the courses in the Jesuit house of studies, frequently sharing courses. Counting seven years of primary school, it would take a man until he was 29 years old to become a priest: 22 years of patient and methodical study. Once ordained, they understudied a more experienced priest in one of the sections of the mission, and twice a year they returned to Shanghai for a retreat and a holiday.[29]

Jin Luxian, in his memoirs, gave a detailed account of his life as a seminarian at this time, expressing criticism of the attitude of some French Jesuits towards the Chinese clerics. After graduating from St Ignatius' College, Xujiahui, in 1932, he entered the minor seminary of the Sacred Heart with 22 other students. Out of the 22, ten became priests, six remained laymen and six died prematurely. This was a junior seminary, where, apart from teaching theology, Latin was the main course. Also studied were Chinese classical literature, Church history, and Church liturgy and music. The French Jesuit director of the seminary, Achilles Durand, was experienced as a 'generous, kind and thoughtful person'. He taught religious studies, music and Latin, and stressed the personal need for 'holiness, knowledge and good health'. While being a 'truly sincere' man, he had no real power, that being in the hands of Yves Henry (1880–1963)[30], the rector of St

---

29. Beda Tsang and Joseph Sen, 'Le Clergé chinois de la Mission de Shanghai', in *Bellarmino*, 10/2 (February 1941).
30. **Yves Henry** entered the Society of Jesus at the age of 18, after one year training for the navy. He arrived in China as a scholastic in 1904, where he impressed his colleagues with his energy, amazing memory and articulation. After ordination, he worked for a short time as a missionary and then at Aurora University as an administrator from 1916. In 1927, he was appointed rector of St Ignatius' College, Xujiahui, a time of student revolt. In 1928, he left the college and became rector of the seminaries and the parish in Xujiahui. He later became superior of the mission in 1937, during the war with Japan, and, in 1947 was appointed rector of the regional seminary. The following year he became the vicar of the diocese. He was expelled from Mainland China in 1953 and went first to the Philippines for seven years, and then to Vietnam for three years. He died in Hong Kong. *China Province News* (January 1964), 19–25. CHPA.

Ignatius' College when Jin was a student. He later became rector of the seminary, and then Jesuit superior of the mission for nine years from 15 August 1937, a time when the Japanese occupied Shanghai. He moved Chinese Jesuits from academic positions in the seminary and Aurora University to pastoral work in the mission, a step Jin considered backward. Henry did not trust the Chinese priests, no matter how well qualified, to teach theology.

When the Japanese entered Shanghai in 1932, a seminarian Zhou Junling raised the national flag in the seminary chapel, and together with the other seminaries, prayed for China. Henry forbade this and ordered that the flag be taken down. Zhou refused to obey, sighting that there was a French flag raised in a parish church in Shanghai. Henry wanted to expel Zhou from the seminary, but after discussions with his family and the bishop of Hai Men, Zhu Kaimin, he was sent to Rome for studies, and eventually accepted as a priest for the diocese of Nanjing. The bishop of this diocese sent him to America where he worked among the Chinese overseas students. Jin reflected that the foreign priests not only did not understand, but also even opposed the patriotism of the Chinese seminarians.

In August 1935, Jin entered the major seminary of the Sacred Heart of Mary, which had its own director, Felix Maumus. He was considered more kind than Henry, and taught philosophy, liturgy and pastoral studies. He was later made pastor at St Joseph's for 24 years. Jesuit lecturers at the seminary were French, Spanish and Chinese.

Bishop Haouisée and the Jesuit mission superior, Peter Lefebvre, worked well together for the development of the mission, believing in developing the individual talents of the missionaries at their disposal. They sent men to France, Britain and Rome for studies; one Chinese priest studied sociology and another Church History, with the intention of setting up a Catholic publishing house in Shanghai when they returned. Lefebvre decided to turn the Xuhui Book Repository into a modern-style research library, the aim being to 'bring about a cultural renaissance'. Haouisée and Lefebvre wanted to change the mission custom whereby only Chinese priests worked in the suburbs, and French Jesuits worked the city. In 1933, Haouisée and Lefebvre decided to hand over the cathedral parish, an important Catholic centre, to the control of Chinese priests. They were also given the city church of St Thérèse of Lisieux, thus changing the Church dynamic in Shanghai.

On 20 August 1938, Jin entered the noviciate the Society of Jesus, where Beaucé was novice director, and ran the noviciate just as the one he had experienced in France when he was 20 years old. It was very strict with a European lifestyle, with no attempt to adapt the lifestyle to Chinese social customs. Jin said that Beaucé considered him 'arrogant', and that he was regularly humiliated. He often thought of leaving the Jesuits, but believed that God wanted him to stay. Jin claimed that this experience prepared him well for his later life of 17 years in prison.

Jin was sent to Xianxian, Hebei province, to the Jesuit house designated for philosophy studies for all the Jesuit missions, 1941–2. Soon after arriving at the end of August 1941, they were surrounded by Japanese troops. All Chinese Jesuits were arrested, and not permitted to speak to each other. At the school in Zhangjiazhuang, the soldiers found a KMT flag in one of the classrooms, and took away the headmaster. In the printing house, they found some anti-Japanese material on the press, so they arrested the brother in charge together with his staff. After a day, the Belgian Jesuit, Lichtenberger[31], brought those in prison blankets and provisions from Zhangjiazhuang.

When the news of the siege by the Japanese and the arrest of Bishop Zhao and all the Jesuits reached Tianjin, the president of the university, René Charvet, requested the European and British consulates for assistance. Soon after, the Japanese assembled all the Jesuit prisoners, registered all, and separated those from Hebei from other provinces. After further questioning, Lichtenberger was permitted to take all back to Zhangjiazhuang, but the Hebei people were thrown into prison, where one priest, a lay brother and his print-shop workers were shot. After a year, the remaining prisoners were released.

European Jesuits of many nationalities ran the school of philosophy at this time. When the Japanese army laid siege to Zhangjiazhuang, the Italian bishop of Bengbu, Cassini, came to Xianxian to see if he could help the Jesuits. Meanwhile, the Japanese Jesuits sent a German Jesuit to stay at Zhangjiazhuang during the crisis. The Japanese troops showed him respect, since the Japanese were allies of the

---

31. **Marcellus Lichtenberger** had originally been a nurse, and when all the doctors at the Xianxian hospital took fright with the arrival of the Japanese, they left for Shanghai. So Lichtenberger undertook necessary operations, performing about 1,000 operations without a single casualty. After the war, he was sent back to Belgium to study medicine and to qualify as a doctor.

Germans and Italians in the World War. Thus the international aspect of the Society of Jesus proved its effectiveness. In front of the west door of the church were hung French, German, Hungarian, Spanish, Italian, American and Canadian flags. The Japanese troops were amazed by this display, halting them in their tracks. Life for the Jesuits after that was more comfortable until 8 December 1941, when the Japanese attacked Pearl Harbour, and so war resulted with the United States and Britain. After that, American and Canadian priests and nuns at Zhangjiazhuang were taken away to a concentration camp in Tianjin.

In April 1942, Henry, while visiting the Shanghai Jesuits in Xianxian, told Jin that because of recent victories, it looked as though the Japanese would be in China for a long time, so there was a need for someone fluent in Japanese. Jin was to be sent to Tokyo to study Japanese. In the meantime he was to go to Tianjin to learn some Japanese. This order of Henry's was astonishingly naïve, showing him to be completely unaware of the implications of this decision for Jin. When the Japanese left China, he would be branded as a collaborator, with a possible death sentence. Jin decided on a line of passive resistance. He went to Tianjin, but by his negativity towards the exercise, his teacher told Henry that Jin had no aptitude for the Japanese language. Henry then ordered Jin back to Shanghai to study theology.[32]

Shanghai mission, 1940–1943

For the years 1940–3, the mission of Shanghai was left in relative calm compared to the other Jesuit missions to the north. The Jesuits were left in peace to carry out their apostolate in Shanghai, which became a haven for all Jesuits in the outer regions, especially when there was fighting between the Japanese and the Chinese Communist armies. Jesuits returning to their northern districts frequently met difficulties; one was stripped of all his belongings, another tortured in water, another refused entry into his village, while another was beaten and stripped. There was much movement among the Jesuits, with one, Gaechter, from Innsbruck in the Province of Austria, arriving to teach theology in both Kinghsien and Xujiahui. Henry Milner, from the

---

32. William Hanbury-Tenison (trans), *The memoirs of Jin Luxian, Vol. 1: Learning and Relearning, 1916–1982* (Hong Kong: Hong Kong Press, 2012), 35–67.

English province but belonging to the Byzantine Catholics, had come from Estonia to help the Archimandrite Nicolas with the Russians. Four deaths were recorded for 1940: Anthony Weckbacker (aged 84), Charles Baumert (aged 75), Ignace Zen (aged 35) and George Payen (aged 78). The numbers of Christians in the vicariate from 1939–40 was registered at 139,417, and together with 9,393 catechumens were cared for by 211 priests. Statistics for the same period for the whole of China indicated that in 1850 there had been 18 missions, while in 1940 there were 138, while the number of Chinese priests in the whole of China had increased from 729 in 1912 to 2,261 in 1942. Shanghai, with 107, had the most number of Chinese priests, while in all the Jesuit vicariates there were 241. This was a truly satisfying increase.

It was noted in 1941 that Charles Simons from the Province of California, had been killed at Shuyang in his residence on 31 December 1940, by brigands, while a number of other priests had died of natural causes.

At Xujiahui, there were 98 Jesuit scholastics from 16 different nations studying theology, including four Germans from Hiroshima, and three Dutch Jesuits from Indonesia.[33] Faculty members came from 14 different countries, under the rectorship of Lefebvre, a kind man who showed admirable leadership of such an international group of people that studied together in peace and harmony. This showed that belonging to the Society of Jesus was going beyond individual nationality and, in this case, a unity forged by necessity.

When the Pacific War broke out, the Japanese detained foreign nationals in concentration camps, allowing them no freedom and frequently subjecting them to terrible conditions. The bursar of the Jesuits in Shanghai at that time was Verdier, who arranged with the Japanese High Command for the Jesuits of foreign nationality to be gathered in the Jesuit house in Xujiahui, so enabling those studying theology to continue undisturbed. A Canadian missionary from Xuzhou was also transferred to the Xujiahui seminary. So some foreign nationals managed to secure better treatment. All were permitted to move around freely within the compound, but a Japanese junior officer would visit daily and take a roll call. Anyone wanting to visit the urban area of Shanghai required his permission, which he

---

33. Summary of *Nouvelles de la Mission,* Shanghai Mission, 1940–1943.

always gave. It was coincidental that he was a Catholic and showed respect to the missionaries.

When the Japanese signed the peace treaty on 15 August 1945, the Feast of the Assumption, there was much rejoicing in the streets of Shanghai and, indeed, in most of China.[34]

A reflection on the French protectorate

The French legation continued to work to retain its protectorate over the French missions, and was very protective of this right given to them by treaty with the Chinese. They became aware of an article written by HM Cole, an American instructor of history at the University of Chicago, on the French protectorate. After giving a history of its origins from the Portuguese *Padroado* to Louis XIV and to the modern arrangements after the treaties up to Berthemy in 1865, Cole's thesis was that the French protectorate was one of the means employed by an 'imperialist foreigner' to force open the ports of China in order to increase French influence and prestige. He questioned the effectiveness of this arrangement for France. While the treaty gave France legitimate intervention powers in the internal affairs of China to exact reparation for the murder of missionaries and to demand justice for insults given against the faith, the arrangement 'was not to be seen only as an honourable act to protect religion but a great political act'. French motivation for the protectorate was seen not so much as zeal for the faith as a desire for prestige and power. In fact, French commerce in China was not significant.[35]

Meanwhile, the apostolic delegate informed the French legation of his concern for the missions that were caught up in the Pacific War after the declaration of war on Japan by the Americans on 7 December 1941. He wanted the French to intervene where possible, stressing that he believed the French protectorate to be as strong as always. The French were happy to hear this, as it was somewhat an about face for the apostolic delegate considering his previous comments about the protectorate. The legation said that they would assist when possible,

---

34. William Hanbury-Tenison, op. cit., 71–4.
35. HM Cole, 'The Origins of the French Protectorate on the Catholic Missions in China', in *American Journal of International Law,* 34/3, (July 1940): 473–91; Boissezon, Secretary to the French Ambassador, Beijing, to French Ambassador, Shanghai, 23 October 1941. DAC.

but reminded the delegate that it was Bishop Yu Pin, archbishop of Beijing, who was the 'go between' for the Catholic Church and the Chinese government.[36] Maybe the delegate knew that the Nationalist government was virtually powerless against the Japanese, and thought that the French government might have more success in negotiations with the Japanese. Later in the war, the delegate thanked the French legation for their assistance to French priests and their missions, and again asked for financial assistance to rebuild damaged property. The French responded generously with grants to Nanning, Pakhoi (Tianjin), Kunming and Mukden.[37] In times of great need, the debate over the merits or otherwise of the French protectorate were put aside. The Church appreciated the French protection when there was no one else to help.

During the Japanese occupation of 1943, the Jesuits reflected on how they might be given legal status in China. They produced a pamphlet that dealt with the right of a 'juridical person' (like themselves) in times of war. They argued that the missionaries were supra national, working for the Holy See, a neutral and sovereign state and, therefore, missionaries should be permitted to perform their work uninterrupted, regardless of their original nationality. A 'juridical person', they claimed, did not have political nationality. The Catholic Church had a purely spiritual mission, regardless of politics, a ministry that was recognised by all the powers. The bishops, as representatives of the pope, administered the property of the Church. They even suggested that the local Christians had no nationality, as being part of the Church, and so were supra national.[38] This document was sent to the French consul, who simply acknowledged it, without suggesting any follow up. It would seem that even if there were a case in international law, the complex situation in China at the time would never have allowed any political or legal negotiations of this kind. In fact, the missionaries had agreed that the Japanese had generally treated them with respect, and allowed them to pursue their mission within limits.

---

36. Telegram to French Ambassador Vichy government, Beijing, 18 December 1941. DAC.
37. Apostolic Delegation to French Ambassador, Beijing, 22 January 1945. DAC.
38. Juridical situation of the Catholic Missions, in particular the Chinese missions in regard to international law during the war, T'ou-sé, Xujiahui, Shanghai, 1943. DAC.

Post-war comments

Between 14 million and 20 million Chinese died during this war against Japan. Another 80 million to 100 million became refugees. The conflict destroyed many cities, devastated the countryside and ravaged the economy. The war created a 'sense of national identity'; the people were stirred to defend their country against a hated aggressor, while at the same time had divided loyalties between the Nationalists and the Communists armies. Adherence to either depended upon what the leaders offered.[39]

Once the Japanese had been vanquished, and the two rival Chinese ideologies battled for supremacy among the Chinese people, the role of the Nationalist leader Chiang Kai-Shek was pivotal. Earlier Western critiques of his leadership were not complimentary of him. He was seen as corrupt, personally embezzling financial grants from the United States, and refusing to accept US advice to advance his armies against the Japanese instead of the Communists. The appointment of perceived incompetent generals with insufficient weaponry for his forces were seen as a few reasons for the continual defeat of Nationalist forces. A revisionist view of Chiang portrayed him as a military leader in an impossible position between the Japanese and the Communists forces, having to endure Japanese savagery, and a country in ruin. He survived a militarily superior Japan, and was seen as pivotal in the defeat of the Axis powers by trying down the Japanese forces. Moreover, at the end of the war, China had regained its international status, lost since the Treaty of Nanjing, 1842, by being granted status as one of the Big Four powers that reshaped the post-war world.[40]

---

39. Review by Gordon G Chang of Rana Mitter's *Forgotten Ally, China's World War II, 1937–1945*, (Boston: Houghton Mifflin Harcourt, 2013) in *The New York Times*, 6 September 2013.
40. Ibid. cf also, BarbaraTuchman, *Sand against the Wind: Stillwell and the American Experience in China 1911–45* (Edinburgh: Macmillan, 1970); Jonathan Fenby, *Chiang Kai-shek, China's Generalissimo and the Nation He Lost*, (New York: Carroll & Graf, 2004).

Chapter 10
After the War, 1945—1955

Mission recovery, 1945–1947

After the capitulation of the Japanese on 15 August 1945, relative normality returned to the mission of Shanghai, enabling them to take stock of their situation and plan for the future. Those in the south of the Yangtze and in the environs of Shanghai were not unduly threatened by the Communists, in contrast with those Jesuit missions north of the river. The years of the Japanese occupation resulted in greater collaboration between the Jesuit missions, with Xujiahui growing in importance as the centre for all the Jesuit missions, and a haven for those missionaries seeking protection or peace.

Jin Luxian sent by Henry to Dongtai, Jiangsu, gave an account of the mission to the north of Shanghai. Fighting had broken out in the area between the Nationalists and the Communists. Chiang Kei-shek had broken the ceasefire between the two groups, and Dongtai had fallen into the hands of the Communist New 4th Army. The KMT Army advanced on Dongtai and the battle raged when Jin arrived in the district. He believed that he was sent there to replace the foreign missionaries, as his life was dispensable. Soldiers of the New 4th Army were 'child soldiers', very strict and controlling, and made passage through their area difficult. The KMT Army advanced partly from Taizhou and partly from Yangzhou. They moved south from Xuzhou and encircled the Communist army. The KMT air force passed over Dongtai repeatedly, so Jin felt in the middle of the action. The streets were full of Communist troops rushing about. One war lasting eight years had just ended, and another was beginning again.

A few days after his arrival, Pierre de Prunelé, a missionary since 1908, visited Jin from Yancheng. He knew the county chief of Dongtai, Dong Xibai who was a former student of St Ignatius' College, Xujiahui. While studying in France, he joined the Communist party. De Prunelé took Jin to visit Dong, who greeted the two priests with courtesy and friendship, saying that he always appreciated the special care shown to him at Xujiahui by de Prunelé, and assured the priests that he would help them if needed. The rest of Jin's stay in Dongtai was uneventful. There were very few Catholics in the area, the people being mostly peasants who grew cotton on the wastelands and who lived very simply.

Upon leaving Dongtai for Taizhou, Jin entered the KMT zone, and was questioned by a young officer who suspected him of being a Communist spy. He was later set free to travel on to Shanghai, whereupon his superior, Henry, told him he was returning to the battle region, and the town of Huai'an in Subei. The town, in control of the Communists, was being besieged by the KMT. It was a very dangerous area to be in. When the KMT planes flew over on a bombing raid, one of the nuns tried to save herself by climbing onto the roof to host the Vatican flag, only to be shot by the New 4th Army. Two French priests and three Chinese priests were also shot. *En route* to Huai'an, Jin learned that the Communists had retreated and that the KMT forces had opened up the Grand Canal, the main mode of transport from north to south before the opening of the Tianjin-Pukou railway.

Huai'an was a strong Protestant centre, with a large hospital, a big church and an imposing pastor's residence. The famous author Pearl Buck had been born there. She wrote about 50 novels set in China and won the Nobel Prize for Literature in 1938.

Soon after arriving in Huai'an, Jin was asked by the representative of the United Nations Relief and Rehabilitation Administration (UNRRA) to become his advisor. Together they toured the region. Lianshui was one of the poorest towns; the people had simple homes with little furniture, and wore tattered clothes. They registered each family and after reporting back to their superiors, distributed two bags of flour directly to each of the families. The people were most grateful. But Jin later learned that after they had left, the KMT local authorities visited each family saying that if they wanted more flour from the government officials, they had better share half of what they had been given by UNRAA to them. The corruption of the KMT that later became much more widely known nationally was seen here in miniature.

While the KMT controlled the main highways and the suburban roads, as well as some towns and villages along the Grand Canal, the Communists were in control of the countryside. When the Communist party implemented its land reform by taking fields from landowners and distributing them to the peasants, the landowners fled to the cities and formed their own militias. When the KMT Army moved, the militias followed, intending to settle scores. Armed with weapons, the militias took back land and property from the peasants with much brutality. These actions helped the KMT lose support of the people that led to their inexorable defeat.

In March 1947, Jin was visited by the provincial of the Province of France, Marcel Bith (1883–1963) who was in China to assess the situation in the vicariate of Shanghai. Fernand Lacretelle (1902–89)[1] accompanied Bith, and all three visited the region around Huai'an. It was Bith that changed the direction of Jin's life. He was asked to pursue further studies in Rome for a doctorate in theology, and to eventually return to China to teach theology. Some of the French Jesuits in Shanghai, especially Verdier, objected to this idea, because when Chinese Jesuits went to Europe they did not follow orders, and when they returned they 'no longer respected the French mission-

---

1. **Fernand Lacretelle** was born in Paris, the seventh of eight children. He was educated by the Jesuits at *St Louis de Gonzague*, and entered the Jesuit noviciate on 8 November 1921. After a year juniorate, he spent two years regency in high schools in Eveux and Tours, and, in October 1927 left France for China. After language study and some teaching at St Ignatius, Xujiahui, he studied philosophy and theology from 1929–35 in Xujiahui. Following tertianship in Wuhu, 1936, he was sent to Rome to study canon law for a year, especially those codes relating to matrimony. Back in China, he began many years of administration: four years as director of the minor seminary; rector of the major seminary for four years, 1938–46, and then as superior of the mission and vicar general of the diocese in 1946. In this later role, he was the close collaborator of the new Chinese bishop, helping him support resistance to the Communist regulations. Finally, he was arrested, imprisoned and expelled from Mainland China. After a period of rest in France, he returned to Manila as instructor of tertians, 1956–7, and then went to Vietnam as superior of this mission, where he established a solid basis for the future province. He was then expelled again by the Communists, and ended up in Taiwan where he worked hard until ill health prevented him. As a canon lawyer, he was most exact in demanding conformity to Church laws, whatever the consequences, but he also showed a pastoral sympathy with Catholics in the missions. He was experienced as a most austere man. (Obituary by Stanislas de Geloës SJ, *China Province News*, 1990, 27–31. CHPA.)

aries'. Verdier also said that the Chinese were not qualified to teach theology. During the 100 years that the French missionaries had been in Shanghai, no Chinese Jesuit had been permitted to teach at Aurora University, or at the Observatory or the College of Theology. That was about to change.

The Jesuit missions were divided into two: Shanghai under the Province of France, and Xianxian under the Province of Champagne, which had been formed in 1863. Of the two, Jin believed that the Champagne province paid more attention to the encyclical of Pope Benedict XV, *Maximum Illud,* which required the indigenisation of human resources, and the handing over of dioceses to the local Chinese. This province was more open and visionary than the Shanghai diocese.

When discussion took place about a replacement of Haouisée in Shanghai, Jesuit superiors wanted another Frenchmen appointed. This plan failed, but it showed that even in the late 1940s, the French missionaries were still not prepared to transfer power to the Chinese, not even after the Communists took control of the country. Their eviction from Mainland China was soon to follow.[2]

Jin went to France in 1947 for his tertianship at Paray-le-Monial, near Lyon. He described France as very poor, still suffering from food shortages and lacking finance for reconstruction following the World War. Conditions improved when France eventually accepted aid under the Marshall Plan. Following this year in France, Jin was sent to Rome and the Gregorian University to study for a doctorate in theology on an aspect of the Trinity.

In 1948, there were 880 Jesuits in China, belonging to eleven separate Jesuit provinces. Each province reported back to the headquarters of their individual provinces any significant information. To co-ordinate all these Jesuits in these challenging years, the superior general, Jean-Baptiste Janssens, appointed Franz Burckhardt[3] as visitor of China with powers of the superior general to oversee the whole Jesuit missionary situation. The American, Paul O'Brien, was appointed his deputy. By late 1948, the Vatican realised that the Liberation Army would soon conquer all Mainland China, but miscalculated by think-

---

2. *The Memoirs of Jin Luxian*, ut supra, 75–83. These personal memoires of Jin are an important Chinese account of events during the latter days of the Jesuit mission in Shanghai, and its interaction with the civil government.

3. Franz Burkhardt (1902–2002), cf. Chapter 18, Jingxian mission, footnote 6.

ing that the United States and Chiang Kai-chek would soon regain control of the mainland, and that even if the KMT did not return, the Chinese Communist Party would follow the Yugoslavian model. The Vatican ordered the internuncio Antonio Riberi and all the missionaries to strive to stay on the mainland. If they were driven out, they should not return to their mother countries, but remain in the region and wait for the KMT to return. However, the Jesuit superior general ordered all young Jesuits and seminarians to leave China immediately and continue their studies in Macao or in the Philippines. They could return to China after their studies were completed. Over 1,000 left China and none ever returned.[4]

In Shanghai in 1949, there were 145,962 Catholics, ministered by 118 Chinese and 139 foreign priests; 96 Chinese and 96 foreign brothers; 431 Chinese and 278 foreign sisters. There were also 23 seminarians. In China as a whole, there were three million Catholics, 3,046 foreign and 2,542 Chinese priests; 414 foreign and 663 Chinese brothers; and 2,036 foreign and 4,717 Chinese sisters.[5] Of the 139 Catholics bishops in China, only 26 were Chinese. Rome had not yet accepted that a future Catholic Church in China would be one controlled by the Chinese themselves. That attitude was to change from October that year.

Visitation by the French provincial to the mission

While spending only three months in the vicariate, Marcel Bith wrote a very extensive report on his observation of the mission. He was optimistic about the future of the Catholic Church under the protection of the Nationalist government and, while understating any immediate threat from the Communists, he was aware of its dangerous activities in the north from first-hand experience.

His first observations were about the missionaries themselves, both the French and the Chinese. He was pleased in general with the union between the two groups.

As for the French, no longer did there appear an exaggerated chauvinism among the older missionaries. But there were some excesses. Some priests were still very critical of the faults of the Chinese, and

---

4. *The Memoirs of Jin Luxian*, ut supra, 98–103; 131–3.
5. Louis Wei Tsing-sing, ut supra, 183; 178.

with irritation pointed these out to them. Some preferred to seek out the company of Europeans or Americans, or with the Chinese authorities, while others who had suffered much from the civil strife in China felt exasperation when they read excessive praise given to the Chinese in foreign reviews, usually written by those who lived outside the country. Then there were those who saw 'everything as wonderful', and who had much love for China and its people, grateful to Providence for sending them to evangelise the country.

He noted that the Chinese had a different temperament and psychology from the European. They were seen as sensible, without showing it, susceptible, intelligent, but 'in a fine sense rather than profound', more subtle in 'imitation than in creative genius'. They showed an exquisite politeness, and a happiness that did not desert them, even in difficult times. They were friendly to one's face, but did not manifest externally their interior feelings. They disliked the European 'straight forwardness and freedom'. Their sense of politeness, the Europeans called 'dissimulation', while accepting European actions rather than words.

The Chinese showed accentuated individualism, but had strong affection for the family. They had an excessive love of money and gambling was a passion.

These national traits were combined with limited physical energy, compared to the European. They showed little initiative, or apostolic dynamism. There were areas worked by the Chinese clergy that showed no progress with conversions, whereas schools run by the European priests flourished.

Ignorance of the Chinese mentality, or a readiness to accept it, was the cause of recurring difficulties for some European missionaries, and the reason for their failures. They arrived in China full of enthusiasm but, becoming impatient with the lack of Chinese straightforwardness, showed frustration and so lost face. Patience and politeness were two fundamental qualities for missionaries to China.

During the 20 years of civil war, the greatest impact the missionaries had was the university and the schools. The advent of the Communists was a real threat to these institutions, as they too valued education and set up their own educational units.

The work of the mission was hindered by the presence of armies all over the countryside, and while Catholicism was established with churches and presbyteries in many villages, the areas occupied by the Communists created difficulties for the apostolate. However, the number of Catholics had not decreased, and the priests remained at their posts. But the Protestants, mainly Americans, had been asked by their governments to return home with their families because of the dangers.

The missionaries, working for the establishment of the Kingdom of God, did not hesitate to use their privileged position to help the apostolate. But the title 'foreigner' was an obstacle to success, and subsidies given to the catechumens were a mistake. The Guomindang helped the mission schools, while the non-Christian population generally accepted the presence of the Christians. The support of the Nationalist government should encourage missionaries to continue to open new schools, which was an important means to stimulate interest in the Catholic faith.

The Protestants led the intellectual world of Christian missionaries; Catholicism lagged behind. But progress was being made. Aurora University and its alumni had influence: some alumni were in government, while many were simply favourable towards Catholicism. Bishop Yupin of Nanjing was politically influential. He was not a good pastor, but was an imposing figure and a remarkable orator, who gave a good face to Catholicism and to the Chinese people. The elevation of Bishop Tien Ken-sin (Tienchensing) in Beijing to the cardinalate in 1946 made an impression on the non-Christians.

As for the future, the apostolic internuncio suggested that the Jesuits work more noticeably with the Chinese elite. He wanted the Jesuits to develop their universities, and to educate the Chinese clergy to a level where they have genuine influence on the ruling classes.

At present, there were three Catholic universities in China: Fu Jen in Beijing (the rector was Harold W Rigney, an American Divine Word priest); *Les Hautes Etudes* in Tianjin (the rector was a Chinese priest, Stanislaus Liou, from the Province of Champagne); and Aurora in Shanghai (with Louis Dumas rector).

At Fu Jen, the Chinese directed everything; the American rector did little. It was a progressive university with thousands of students and a few Divine Word priests as lecturers, but its religious influence was weak. At Tianjin, the rector was a Jesuit as it was difficult to find a Chinese priest to lead the institution with authority. Aurora was successful with between 700 and 800 students. Non-Christian students studied philosophy, while Christians did a course in apologetics. *The*

Far Eastern Review (March 1947) claimed that Aurora's faculties of law and medicine had the highest standard among Shanghai universities. It was pleasing to note that since its foundation, the university had 278 Baptisms. However, there were two objections to Aurora, one that it was directed by foreigners, and that part of the instruction was in a foreign language. If a foreign language was needed, then it should be English, the international commercial language. However, if there was a move to replace French with English, the university would not receive its current subsidies from the French government, and the university would have to close. Once again, the missionaries believed that French support was vital to their survival.

There was a move to set up an independent Chinese vice-province, or even two – one north and the other south of the Yangtze. Moving toward this was to establish a combined Jesuit theologate for all the missions at Xujiahui, and a house for philosophers at Xianxian. In addition, the bishop asked the Society to run a regional seminary. Hopes for the future ran high.

In the Xujiahui compound there was a residence, church, noviciate and juniorate, scholasticate for theology, a junior and minor seminary, a junior and senior school (with 1,000 students), 250 catechumens with 500 sympathetic, the observatory and an orphanage. The provincial stressed the importance in the Jesuit apostolate of the education of an indigenous clergy, secular and regular. He noted that in 1946, the diocese had 92 Chinese priests, 24 older seminarians, 20 junior seminarians, and 164 'Latinists'. The Jesuits had 28 priests, 26 scholastics, 25 brothers, 9 novices and 68 Chinese religious. The Jesuits were reputed to educate 'the best clergy in China'.

Shanghai had 12 churches, one Polish and one for the Slavic-Byzantine rite. The Jesuits had charge of five of these churches and the Russian mission. The church of St Peter was on the grounds of Aurora University.

The original mission of Jiangnan had been divided into eight new dioceses. Shanghai had a population of 18 million people with 145,244 Christians and 4,160 catechumens. The mission had three sections, one in the north and two in the south. The northern area, devastated by the Communists, originally gave much hope for conversions. Currently, this area was inaccessible, and was in the most ruined area. It had been difficult for the priests to enter the region. The two sections to the south were more consoling. Yangzhou was situated along the

Imperial Canal, and had 30,000 to 100,000 Christians. There were four main stations, and two flourishing schools. The residences and churches were intact. However, Dongtai was completely occupied by Communists, and one priest had not been able to reach his presbytery for two-and-a-half years. The churches were destroyed, while the residences and schools were damaged. The priests had remained in the region, showing the support of the Church to the faithful Christians. The priests, full of courage, remained in the region supporting the faithful Christians. They continued to work in the school from which they had contact with the armed forces passing through, and ministered to the Catholics among them.

Life in the districts of the north or in the 'bush' was very different from living in Shanghai, where life was similar to a major city in France. In these districts, the missionaries lived more like the Chinese, sharing the same food, lighting, housing and means of transport. It was a hard life, requiring many sacrifices. Discussions were held as to which apostolate was the more important. The provincial thought that the European missionaries ought to be in the 'bush'. They had the better temperament to pioneer the region, and would be more adaptable than the Chinese priests who came mainly from the south, and only understood their local language. Moreover, the Chinese priests usually felt safer if they were associated with a European priest.

The sections of the south had large populations and needed many missionaries. The people were thinner and more intelligent than those in the north. They grew rice in the south, compared to corn and maize in the north. They were not only influential in commerce, but also in the 'movement of ideas'. Two-thirds of students studying in Beijing were originally from the south. Furthermore, Bith suggested that the French should stay in Dongtai, to assist in the region. They had asked to work in schools, but the mission would also like them to work in the 'bush'. They did not seem keen to do so, and it was feared that the Americans would never adapt to the rough missionary life, as they showed 'the tendency to Americanise China'.

Attention was also turned to the successor of Haouisée of Shanghai. Should it be a Chinese? The feeling was that the internuncio would appoint a Chinese secular priest, but the task of finding someone 'sufficiently independent politically', and one that had 'genuine prestige' in the eyes of the local Chinese, was difficult. A French suggestion was to create a new Chinese diocese, and retain a French bishop for

Shanghai. It was noted that Cardinal Tien and the Lazarites had disagreements in Beijing.

The problem of taking on a regional seminary for Jiangsu and Anhui was the different languages between north and south of the region. While the written characters were the same all over the country, the Chinese read differently. Mandarin was generally spoken in the north, but there were many local variations. In the south, each had their own distinct language, especially Shanghainese, Cantonese and their variations. The Jesuits had experienced this problem with their common juniorate in Xianxian. Furthermore, leading such a seminary with students of poor educational background and who had a strong 'critical spirit' would be a challenge. The feeling was generating that because of these language differences the Jesuits should be thinking more of establishing two new provinces, one for the north and one for the south. With 170 priests and brothers from the Province of France, at least as a first step, a new vice-province might be established.

In a country where unity was so difficult to obtain, the local authorities had much authority; it was with them that the missionaries had to negotiate. Armed troops with modern motorised transport occupied towns and controlled many main roads. But these were manageable compared to the 'irregulars' who travelled lightly and sowed terror among the people, above all those in the small villages.

The political situation in China was so complicated that a solution seemed hard to predict. There had been a civil war for 20 years. The war with Japan was only an episode that allowed the Communists to grow and prepare for the next war with the Nationalists.

The strength of Sun Yat-sen's Guomindang was that it appealed to the young, and especially among those who saw China's inferiority when compared to the foreigner. In addition, the missionaries observed in China a 'lack of organisation, absolute and arbitrary power of the mandarins, corrupt officials, insufficient means of communication, lack of industrial output, social injustices, exploitation of the worker, and the tutelage of women'. The Guomindang wanted to change these evils, and revitalise the State with the assistance of an army with modern weapons.

The weaknesses of the party became evident after several years, showing themselves to be just as corrupt as the imperial government. Large fortunes were made by small groups of families associated with the Song family. There were also financial scandals. When moving through the countryside, the Guomindang troops gave a bad impression: 'no discipline, no military spirit, and pillage of occupied villages without shame'. The result was disillusionment among the general public who had placed confidence in the party. Internal fighting with the Communists weakened their influence and showed up weaknesses.

On the other hand, the Communist party benefited from the unpopularity of the KMT. The Russians and Germans had formed them during their union with the KMT. It had the support of extreme right intellectuals, and they were able to gather troops with a strong discipline that became dedicated to the death for an ideal. They expressed a dynamism that gave hope to many Chinese for the future. It was a formidable organisation believed by 80 per cent of the population. They had a military academy, schools, study circles and universities where they taught Marxist doctrine and a 'materialist concept of life, which they portrayed in theatre and in song'. In the country, they organised compulsory assemblies and stirred up hatred against the rich.[6] The provincial gave a seemingly accurate account of the present political situation in China, as well as giving a good assessment of the mission, together with some tentative suggestions to the missionaries for the future. The optimism for the future was tempered with his remarks about the influence of the Communists, and the difficulties they were causing to the mission, especially in the north. Whatever the future, the missionaries were to continue with their work and plan for the future.

In a follow-up letter to the Jesuit superiors in China, Bith gave many recommendations. He encouraged the development of Chabanel Hall in Nanjing, where Jesuit scholastics were being sent to learn mandarin and to continue working in schools, hospitals and dispensaries as places of contact with non-Christians. All were reminded to be politically neutral in the internal struggles of the country.

In the noviciate, he was aware that a number of young Chinese brothers had recently left after taking their first vows. He feared that the mission was too lenient in accepting men who were weak spiritually, and who had only rudimentary religious education. Potential

---

6. Report of Very Reverend Marcel Bith, provincial of Paris, to Fr. General on the mission to Shanghai, 13 April 1947. FPA.

brothers might be admitted initially to perform domestic duties in the noviciate for a few years before commencing postulancy. During this time, they should be given religious instruction, and taught to read and write, if necessary. This education should continue in the noviciate, giving them a good sense of religious life, and the obligations they would undertake specially concerning the vows of poverty and obedience. After vows, they should remain in the house of the noviciate for three years to continue their education.

Bith praised the idea of having one theologate for all the missions of the Society in China, and wanted the Chinese Jesuits to be trained to take leadership roles in administration and lecturing. The language of the theologate should be mandarin.

He praised the work of St Ignatius' College, Xujiahui, for its reputation of serious study among non-Christians, and for the number of catechumens in the school, but as a Christian school, particular attention must be given to the religious and spiritual education of the Christian students, while teaching the non-Christians philosophical and civic ideas about the major human problems that formed the base of their moral life. While there existed a current passion for the 'sciences and industry' in education, there was also the need to recognise China's cultural past by teaching the humanities that would help China's future thinkers, statesmen, lawyers and journalists.

He believed that the work of the observatory gave great service to China, and it was well known in the intellectual world. This gave prestige to the mission. But much of the work of the orphanage at Tushanwan could be done by other than the Jesuits in the mission. They had been in charge of the orphanage for 20 years, helping to form the children to live a happy adult life, through moral and professional education.

Aurora University was considered a great success, not only recognised as important in the Chinese world, but also internationally. The moral course was important, while the faculty of medicine, like that of law, enjoyed a fine reputation. The faculty of science and scientific research was not rated highly by Bith. But considering that the greater part of China was rural, he suggested that there might also be a course in agriculture. The Chinese nature of the university should become more obvious. A Chinese priest as dean would be advisable in the faculty of letters, while a centre of Chinese culture should be created. Bring together specialists to produce a Chinese intellectual periodical, while Chinese scholastics might take a chair in one of the other faculties. Sport, student clubs, an association for alumni, and academic conferences were encouraged.

He recommended parishes to develop a strong sense of Catholic Action among the Christians, encouraging a spirit of 'conquest', while the main challenge in the districts was to 'penetrate the pagan world'. The establishment of a good library might help. The letter ended by encouraging all to have a spirit of hope in a time of threat to the mission.[7]

Bith communicated a new vision of greater partnership between Western and Chinese missionaries. He showed awareness of Chinese sensitivities, and encouraged Chinese leadership. While appreciating the gifts that the Chinese brought to the Chinese Church, he still valued the contribution of Western missionaries in training Chinese clerics and in supporting the Chinese Church.

Living in the districts

Life in the districts for the missionary was much more dangerous and confronting than in urban Shanghai, especially in those areas where the Communists were active.

One report from Peter de Prunelé from Yancheng in 1947 typified the difficulties the missionaries experienced under army occupation, either Nationalist or Communist. When he arrived from Dongtai on 1 September 1947, he found much destruction in the village; the bridges had been burnt down, and north of the river there were many ruins. The Jesuit residence had been damaged and stripped bare; nothing remained. The wall around the village had been partially destroyed, and the bricks taken away. When the Communists arrived, they disarmed the locals and left the village without the intention of staying. However, they put in place a militia comprised of men who knew the village, and who acted as brigands. These made summary executions of those who had profited from the Nationalist government, even taking the sons of Protestant ministers who were not seen again. The Communists had stayed in the Jesuit residence overnight,

---

7. Letter of RP Provincial to the Superior of the Mission to be communicated to superiors of the mission after approval by TRP General, 1947. FPA.

taking anything that they wanted, including a bicycle. Everywhere they went, either by land or by the canal, they ravaged the villages.

By 22 September 1947, Yancheng was a ruined village, taken and retaken five times, always under the threat of a Communist return. All services were disrupted, and 'many shady and curious people' hung around the streets. Some hostages were returned, but about one third became the victims of firing squads, giving the local people a sense of defeat. Many left the town moving southwards when the Communists took the place of the Nationalists after a short battle. About 100 government troops were taken prisoner and a considerable booty was collected. Movement around the region became more difficult as the Communists moved everywhere with extraordinary mobility. Their lives were very frugal, even without money to buy cigarettes, with only the basic necessities for survival. They had a young army, with troops aged from 17 to 23 years, happily moving around, doing what they were told, and 'intoxicated by the Communist virus'. They knew nothing about the human spirit, the 'survival of the soul', or about a 'supernatural religion'. All of this was considered superstition. At one stage, a Communist leader gave de Prunelé a lecture about the Communism doctrine during his brief interrogation. In return, de Prunelé talked about the Christian religion: about seeing the 'Creator Spirit' in everything around us. Despite refusing an invitation to dinner, de Prunelé was given safe conduct out of the town together with six boatmen and some wounded to Dongtai.[8] Missionary comments on the Communists were very useful to a European audience, as they were living in the middle of their rule, and experienced their influence. Their observations were generally accurate, at least from a religious perspective.

Death of Bishop Auguste Haouisée (1877–1947)

Bishop Haouisée had governed the Shanghai mission during most turbulent times, and was generally considered to have governed wisely. The bishop had been born at Évran in the diocese of St Brieuc on 1 October 1877, into a profoundly religious family. His maternal uncle, Daniel, was a provincial of the Jesuits, while a younger brother,

---

8. *Nouvelles de la Mission*, Shanghai, 30 October 1947; 30 August 1947; 30 October 1947; 30 April 1948.

Pierre, was a priest of the diocese of St Brieuc who died in 1946. Two of his sisters were nuns, one of whom worked with him in Shanghai.

Haouisée studied at the College of Cordeliers in Dinan, and philosophy at the major seminary of St Brieuc, before entering the Society of Jesus on 19 September 1896. After his first vows in 1898, he did studies in the classics at Laval for two years, then pursued philosophy studies at Jersey for three years.

On 5 December 1903, Haouisée sailed for Shanghai, where he studied Chinese for a year at Xujiahui. He worked then at Aurora University for some years, teaching English and French, and later philosophy, as well as mathematics to the seminarians in the major seminary nearby. He also taught French for a year at St Ignatius' College, Xujiahui, and at 'Nanyang' College, which was a large non-Christian university.

In 1906, he published *Extraits des Ecrivains français*, of which the seventh edition appeared in 1938. In 1907, he began the study of theology for four years at Xujiahui, and on 11 June 1910 he was ordained priest with Vanara, the Jesuit who was later killed in Nanjing when the southern armies entered there on 24 March 1927.

He was put in charge of the cathedral at Tong-ka-dou in 1911, from where he went daily to Aurora for classes, which was then situated in the French Concession. His years at Tong-ka-dou were rewarded with religious and priestly vocations. He took interest in the younger students, encouraging them to study Latin when they reached secondary school. Some of these later entered the local seminary or the Jesuit noviciate.

Haouisée returned to Europe in 1913 for his tertianship, the final year of studies for Jesuits, at Canterbury. He was mobilised for the French army in 1914, but it was noticed that he had weak health, which was incompatible with military service, and was discharged for chronic dysentery and anaemia. After making his final profession as a Jesuit at Paris-Montmartre on 2 February 1915, he returned to Shanghai on 3 April, and resumed his classes at Aurora.

In 1919, he was put in charge of a large Christian community of two to three thousand at Zhangjialou, a village on the other side of the Huangpu. Here his zeal, devotion to duty, knowledge and leadership qualities as a missionary were recognised.

Following this appointment, he became rector of Xujiahui in 1925, and during his first year he experienced bouts of the illness that had been diagnosed in 1914, which resulted in his being hospitalised for weeks and then put on a very strict regime.

By 1928, Bishop Paris, aged 82, no longer able to visit the regions of the mission, asked for a coadjutor. Haouisée was nominated and consecrated on 3 October 1928.

Upon the death of Paris in 1931, Haouisée became apostolic vicar of Nanjing, and two years later with the division of the vicariate, he was made vicar apostolic of Shanghai. Finally, on 11 April 1946, when the Catholic hierarchy of China was established, he became the first bishop of Shanghai. In 1947, he received from the French government the cross of the Legion of Honour, and from the pope was named 'assistant to the pontifical throne' – a papal honour.

He died on 8 September 1947, aged 70, and was described by a contemporary as 'a man of humility possessing great dignity'.[9]

A Chinese Church

Meanwhile, in the wider ecclesiastical context, on 18 February 1946, Pope Pius XII created the first Chinese cardinal, Thomas Tien SVD, who became archbishop of Beijing on 11 April 1946, at the same time that the pope established the Chinese hierarchy. Twenty archdioceses and 79 dioceses replaced the 99 apostolic vicariates. The *status quo* was maintained for 34 apostolic prefectures and one independent mission. Among the twenty metropolitan sees, only three had Chinese bishops – Beijing, Nanjing and Nanchang – while the 17 other archbishops were still foreigners. Among the 79 dioceses, only 17 had Chinese bishops. Eventually more Chinese bishops were appointed.

Of special significance was the establishment of the Central Catholic Bureau in Shanghai under the administration of the American bishop, James Walsh MM.[10] Its main instrument of activity was called

---

9. Obituary of Bishop Haouisée, *Nouvelles de la mission*, Shanghai, (30 September 1948), 2–3.

10. **James Edward Walsh**, the first Maryknoll bishop, was born in Maryland, USA on 30 April 1891. He entered the newly founded Maryknoll Seminary on 15 September 1912 and left the United States for China on 8 September 1918. He was appointed vicar apostolic of the Maryknoll mission in Kongmoon, Guangdong province, in 1927. He served as superior general of the Maryknoll fathers for ten years from 1936, before returning to China. After the Communists ordered the closure of the Catholic Central Bureau on 8 June 1951, Walsh was under

the Legion of Mary, established for the whole of China to replace the Catholic Action movement.[11] This new movement spread rapidly throughout the Catholic communities and posed a challenge to the Communists, as they created Catholic cells calling for resistance to the atheistic government.

While not having any direct influence on the liturgical life of Catholics at the time in China because of the approaching end of the Catholic missions, a significant decree historically came from Rome on 12 April 1949, authorising Catholic priests to say Mass in Mandarin, except for the Roman canon, which was to remain in Latin. It was not until the mid-1960s that the rest of the Church was permitted to have Mass in the vernacular language. Further Sinification of the Chinese Church followed from Rome with the creation of the Chinese hierarchy. The pope continued to create new bishops, most being Chinese, in order to prepare the local churches for difficult times ahead without the European missionaries. The Communist army took Shanghai on 23 May 1949, and on 9 June, Bishop Gong Pinmei was nominated bishop of Suzhou, but was soon after transferred to Shanghai on 15 July 1950.

The beginning of the end for the foreign missionaries and religious congregations in China began in 1949. China was no longer a mission country in the traditional sense of dependence on foreign powers. The hour had come for the Chinese Christians to become liberated from foreign domination.

It was the Chinese Protestants, on 23 September 1949, that made the first call for the reform of the Christian Church, based on the 'three autonomies': no foreign doctrine, no foreign leadership and no foreign financial support. They recognised that the Christian Church in China for the future would be totally controlled by the Chinese themselves.

The proclamation of the People's Republic of China was made on 1 October, with Beijing as the capital. Archbishop Antonio Riberi[12],

---

surveillance by government officials. Eventually he was arrested in 1958, accused of spying for the Vatican and the United States, and condemned to 20 years in a Shanghai prison, but he served only 12. He was finally released on 11 July 1970 at the time of the visit to China of the American president, Richard Nixon.

11. Louis Wei Tsing-sing, ut supra, 145–7.

12. **Antonio Riberi** was born in Monte Carlo, Monaco on 15 June 1897, and ordained priest of the Roman diocese on 29 June 1922. He was made an archbishop on 28

appointed apostolic nuncio to the Nationalist government replacing Zanin on 6 July 1947, remained in Nanjing, refusing to recognise the authority of the new regime, and in turn was ignored by the Communists. Riberi continually urged Catholics to resist the new government. In 1949, he sent a message to the 5,500 Catholic missionaries spread across the country to remain in their posts and continue their missionary work. Riberi's refusal to cooperate with the new government was totally expected and understandable, considering the wider Catholic Church's total rejection of the 'Godless Marxist ideology', but in his resistance, his stance was suicidal, setting the tone for the cessation of future relations between Mainland China and the Holy See, for the government's control of the Chinese Catholic church, and for the persecution of those Catholics maintaining loyal to Rome.

On 17 December 1949, under the protection of the American 7th Fleet, the Nationalist Government finally left Mainland China for Taiwan.

Rome began to make new Chinese bishops in earnest, aware that the foreigners would no longer be free to exercise any ministry in China. A Chinese Catholic Church was rapidly taking place. Rome also issued a statement on 29 June 1950 saying that anyone collaborating with the new regime would be excommunicated.

The periodical *Chine nouvelle* published an extract from the final declaration of the first Chinese Catholic congress of Kwang Yang on 13 December 1950. It affirmed that they were breaking relations with imperialism, and would work strenuously to reform and establish a new church, independent in administration, resources and apostolate. Relationship with the Vatican in the future was to be purely religious, and they opposed any Vatican interference in Chinese internal politics. The apostolic nuncio condemned this movement.[13]

Pius XII, in 1954, in his encyclical *Ad Sinarum gentem*, declared that those who adhered to the dangerous principles indicated in the 'Three Autonomies', or to other similar principles, could not be con-

---

October 1934 and worked as an official of the Secretariat of State before being sent to China as apostolic nuncio on 6 July 1946. He resigned this post in 1951 after the Communist government expelled him. Subsequent appointments were as apostolic nuncio to Ireland on 19 February 1959, and to Spain on 28 April 1962, where he was made a cardinal on 26 June 1967. He died soon after on 16 December 1967.

13. Louis Wei Tsing-sing, ut supra, 148–53.

sidered Catholic, although he refrained from pronouncing a formal excommunication.

In 1957, the Chinese Patriotic Catholic Association, CPCA, was established by the Bureau of Religious Affairs to exercise state supervision over Mainland China's Catholics. The following year, in his encyclical *Ad Apostolorum Principis,* Pius XII condemned the association, and declared that anyone associated with it, especially in the consecration of new bishops selected by the Patriotic Association, were automatically excommunicated as schismatics. From this time a schism in the China Church occurred. The Church split into an official patriotic church and an underground church loyal to Rome. Rome then turned to Taiwan, supported opponents to the patriotic church as being mere instruments of state control, and encouraged the underground church. Relationships between China and the Vatican became hopelessly blocked.

Since Mao's death in 1976, the Chinese government have exercised a more pragmatic religious policy. Many Chinese Catholics do not wish to have to choose between Beijing and Rome. An alliance between the two is desired, but one that is firmly rooted in their Chinese Church. They believe that Rome has been too fixated on the underground church, which has created problems with the government authorities, as they are not registered with the government. According to official statistics, since 2004 some 100,000 Chinese have joined the official Catholic Church annually and that 300 new churches have been built, taking the existing number to 6,300. Many new bishops have been consecrated, most receiving Roman approval. Since Benedict XVI's letter on China in May 2007, in which he referred to the unity of the Church in China, and the need to engage in respectful and constructive dialogue, it has become easier for underground clergy and laity to join the open Church. The question of the appointment of bishops remains problematic in Chinese/Vatican negotiations. Huns Kung suggests that the Chinese minister for religions informed him that the Swiss model of episcopal election could well be the solutions for China; namely election of bishops in their own country, followed by their approbation by Rome.[14] This suggestion has been part of the ongoing discussion on this issue.

---

14. Hans Küng, *Can We Save the Catholic Church* (U.K.: William Collins, 2013), 184–7.

The Shanghai Diocese after 1949

Jin Luxian was told to return to China after his studies, arriving in Shanghai on 25 January 1951 to find Gong Pinmei as bishop of Shanghai, after the nominated bishop of Nanjing, Gong Shirong, left Mainland China with Yu Bin, bishop of Beijing, for Taiwan. Yu Bin was on the Communist list of the main war criminals, and Gong Shirong, as Yu Bin's secretary, thought that he would also be a marked man. Gong Pinmei was also to oversee the Xuzhou diocese. After his installation in Shanghai, he appointed two Chinese priests as administrators, but he relied heavily on the advice of two French Jesuits, Fernand Lacretelle and Georges Germain.[15] The prevailing belief among the Catholic clergy was that the KMT would return to China in the short term with the help of the Americans. This optimism and sense of hope was all that the missionary Catholic Church could rely upon.

Despite having a Chinese bishop in Shanghai, power still remained in the hands of the French Jesuits. After Gong Pinmei had been ordained priest, he first served as headmaster of the Sacred Heart Middle School in Songjiang, and then eight years as head of the junior middle school department of Aurora University Middle School. He had always worked as a teacher. While at Aurora, the nominal head of the university was the powerless Hu Wenyao, while the real authority rested with the executive director, Germain, a Jesuit much respected by Gong. When Gong set up his diocesan headquar-

---

15. **George Germain** (1895–1978) was born in Rouen, France, and entered the Jesuits in November 1919 at Beaumont-sur-Oise, at the age of 24. After studying philosophy in England from 1921–3, he left for Shanghai, where he studied Chinese and taught at the high school connected to Aurora University. He studied theology in France at Fourvière from 1927–31, during which time he founded a Centre for Chinese Students at Lyon, with André Gaultier, who later became chancellor of Aurora for many years. Returning to China in 1932, he was appointed rector of Aurora for 15 years, where he developed all faculties of the university. His 'high courtesy, his deep understanding of men and affairs, and his humorous outlook on life' made him an attractive personality, gaining many grateful friends over the years. In 1947, he was made bursar of the Jesuit mission and later of the diocese as well, a position in which he thrived for his business acumen. Eventually, in 1952, he was arrested, tried, imprisoned and expelled from Mainland China. He settled in Hong Kong until his death, continuing as bursar of the China province. (Obituary by Frs. L Ladanyi and Jacques de Leffe, *China Province News*, (July-August, 1978): 27–30. CHPA.

ters, Germain was continually at his side. Also before Gong became bishop, the Jesuit superior, Lacretelle, was the vicar general of the diocese. While Gong appointed a Chinese priest as the official vicar general, it was Lacretelle who advised the new bishop in canon law, and regularly visited Gong giving advice. Gong, Germain and Lacretelle ran the diocese, with Gong the public face, and the others the operational agents.

The first mistake they made was to oppose the land reform program of the Communist government, siding with the landowners against the peasants, and requiring Catholics to disobey the law.

Then at the end of 1950, the central government launched the 'Three Self Patriotic Movement'. A few Catholic bishops supported it, and the Protestant churches embraced the policy. Behind the policy was the idea that religion had to separate from colonial control and should be controlled by the Chinese themselves. The papal nuncio, Riberi, followed by Gong Pinmei and Lacretelle, denounced the proclamation. The Shanghai government wanted to apply this policy to education in the city. At a meeting of local headmasters, under the chairmanship of Lacretelle, two of the headmasters spoke against the policy, and were later arrested and imprisoned. The Jesuit Zhang Boda died in prison, November 1951, and Brother Bai, a Marist brother, remained in prison until released under Deng Xiaoping many years later. Most Catholic educational leaders accepted the government proposal; those who did not were later 'condemned as rightists', and sentenced to long prison terms.

When on 30 June 1949 the Chinese Communist Party was close to achieving power, the Vatican issued a decree against Communism, stressing that Communist ideology was opposed to the Catholic faith. Church authorities were forbidden to publish, broadcast or read any Communist publications, newspapers or listen to any radio transmissions. Catholics were forbidden to participate in any activity that promoted Communist theory and, if they did, they were considered abandoning their Christian faith. Most churches did not promulgate this decree, but Gong Pinmei and Lacretelle did disseminate the decree in all its detail. From this act, it became clear that Church and State were on a collision course.

Communist organisation was thorough in its education program, requiring schools, factories and other work places to hold indoctrination lessons. Lacretelle forbade Catholics from attending these meetings. Most Catholics did not attend the classes, and refused to participate in other Communist-organised activities.

During the Korean War, because of anti-United States feeling, the Chinese government sent volunteer troops to assist the North Koreans. Catholics in Shanghai were forbidden to join the volunteer army, or to take part in any anti-American pro-Korean movements. These decrees put great burdens on Catholics, risking them to denouncement and imprisonment.

Faced with opposition from the Shanghai diocese and elsewhere, the government set up the Catholic Patriotic Associations around the country, and pressurised the local churches to join. On 27 April 1951, the Shanghai government authorities arrested 'counter-revolutionaries', among whom were Chinese Catholic priests and student Catholic leaders. Jesuits in Tianjin arrested on 28 March 1951 were Alfred Bonningue, rector of the Catholic University, *Hautes Etudes,* Louis Watine and Henry Pollett, and, shortly after, John Monsterleet, who had urged the Catholic students to resist the revolution and the triple autonomy of the Church. He was expelled from China on 14 Mary 1949.

The activities of the Legion of Mary were banned and its leaders arrested. It was a well-structured group, with a daily regime of prayers, supporting Catholics in their belief and social action. The word 'legion' caught the attention of the CCP that considered the organisation to be political and potentially a military group, and so a direct threat to them. Such a group could not exist, and had to be extinguished. It was declared 'counter-revolutionary', and all members were ordered to leave the organisation. Other motives attributed to the Communists for the assault on the Legion were that if the Legion fell, other Catholic organisations would also collapse. It was also suggested that it was an attack on the Blessed Virgin who was the symbol of crushing the head of the serpent, which stood for the Communists. The handbook of the Legion indicated its opposition to the evil and despotism in the world that had to be counteracted. This indicated to the Communists that the Legion was an earthly army, hiding under the cloak of religion, serving the cause of the imperialists, vowed to oppose them. The CCP decree was draconian in content declaring all members as 'class enemies' and required that members be registered as they left the group. These people in turn were asked to denounce others. Shanghai Catholics, under the orders of Bishop

Gong, refused to co-operate with government officials, which further angered the CCP.[16]

In this social climate, Jin and other Chinese Jesuits organised themselves with the priority to strengthen the spirituality of the Catholics and deepen their faith. They did this mainly through sermons and giving the spiritual exercises of St Ignatius' to various parish groups. Many students who participated became known as Catholic Youth. Despite having no organisation or platform, the Communists eventually declared the group as a 'counter-revolutionary' organisation, and its members came under suspicion, some being imprisoned. Those who did not recant their beliefs were sent to work on state farms.

After the CCP took over Shanghai, initially they protected religion and kept the churches open, but took control of church enterprises. The first was the observatory and weather station, since these were national assets, and could not be run by foreigners. Then they took over the schools. All foreign administered schools were confiscated. The hospitals followed. Gong and Lacretelle moved Chinese priests into the Shanghai parishes, which was all that was left of Catholic activity. The government was closing in on Gong, who resisted any co-operation with CCP officials.

Before Riberi was expelled from China in August 1951, he had instructed Lacretelle to appoint Jin acting-head of the Xuhui Regional Seminary, where there were still the French Jesuits, Henry and Lefebvre. They accepted Jin's appointment and supported him. It was one of the few surviving seminaries after Liberation.

The conflict between Gong and the government came to a climax when Gong and Lacretelle issued an order that refused Holy Communion to all who joined the Catholic Patriotic Association. Gong went further in wanting the pope to excommunicate members of the CPA. At this stage the church was preparing to go underground. Lacretelle ordered the establishment of a secret novitiate for Jesuits, with a Chinese priest as novice master. At Aurora University, the French Jesuit, Emmanuel de Breuvery, recruited several female students to become

---

16. For more details of the attack on the Legion of Mary, see Paul P. Mariani, *Church Militant, Bishop Kung and Catholic resistance in Communist Shanghai* (Cambridge: Harvard University Press, 2011), 76–81ff. This book covers much the same narrative as Jin Luxian, but incorporates documents from the Communist press to indicate inside methods used by the Communists to crush the existing Church.

nuns in an underground convent. Pressure against the influence of the foreign priests continued, so that in November 1952 Germain was arrested and then expelled from China. Then on 15 June 1953, the government forces surrounded the Xujiahui Jesuit house, the Jesuit school of theology and Christ the King Church. Lacretelle, and the head of the Jesuit house Pierre Pelliard, together with American Jesuits James McCarthy and Thomas Philipps, and a few Chinese Jesuits were taken away; the foreigners were later expelled. The residents of the premises were put under house arrest. The persecution of Catholics resulted.

Following this action by the CCP, the Jesuit Visitor, Burckhardt, visited Jin and asked him to be the acting superior of the Jesuits in Shanghai. Jin also had the titles of 'capitular vicar' of Huizhou, and rector of the seminary. In August 1953, Burckhardt was expelled, but he left a note appointing Jin deputy visitor of the Jesuits in China. Any one of these appointments was dangerous for Jin. Then on 8 September 1955, the government launched a campaign against the Gong Pinmei clique, with almost all being thrown into jail. They expelled the foreign Jesuits Maurice Burgaud, Yves Henry and Lefebvre; the latter had a heart attack on arrival in Guangzhou and died.[17]

Gong Pinmei and Lacretelle supporting the underground Church and completely resisting pressure from the Communists was disastrous for the future of the Catholic Church in China. For his public support of the Holy See and following his thirty years in prison, Gong

---

17. *Memoires of Jin Luxian*, ut supra, 161–91. **Jin** was released from prison in 1982, and appointed by the CPA as rector of the Sheshan Major Seminary, outside Shanghai. He was ordained auxiliary bishop of Shanghai without Vatican approval in 1985 and became diocesan bishop in 1988. In 2005 the Vatican recognised him as auxiliary bishop to Joseph Fan Zhongliang, also a Jesuit, the Vatican approval underground Bishop of Shanghai. He died in 2013 at the age of 96. After Jin's release from prison and his acceptance of a position of authority within the CPA, the Vatican and other Catholic Church officials overseas criticised him for collaboration with the Communists. He once told this author that his decision to leave prison and accept the offer of the CPA was not taken lightly. What finally convinced him, after much prayer, was that he would be more use to the Catholics of Shanghai working for them, than remaining in prison. Being ostracised by the Roman Church for many years caused him much pain. He constantly sought official affirmation for his decision to join the CPA. He finally received that consolation when the Vatican recognised his episcopal ordination, and when the current superior general told him in a private audience that he was considered 'a good Jesuit'.

became a hero to the underground Church, while Jin was considered a traitor for ultimately conceding to the Patriotic Church. Ironically, it was Jin's presence later as bishop in Shanghai that protected the underground Church in Shanghai.

The final crackdown on the Church in September 1955 came as a result of the publication of a Confession by Lacretelle, under torture in prison since 1953, who admitted that he and Gong were imperialists, that he had opposed the People's Government and incited others to do the same. He told of clandestine activities, regular meetings, messengers, group leaders and the names of most active Catholics. The Communists had all the information they needed to crush the Church.[18]

Thus ended the French mission to China. Despite the previous reticence of the foreign missionaries to advance the Chinese clergy into administrative positions in the Church, the hour had come when, without restriction from the foreigners, they were required to lead the Chinese church. Subsequent history showed that the Chinese priests, religious and laity showed great resilience in providing leadership to sustain the faith of Catholics in the local communities in a similar way that they once did after the Jesuits left China in the 1770s. The sustainability of local churches without external control should give rise to reflection about the ability of local Christians to educate themselves in the faith. The Chinese Church of the foreign missionaries went underground; it became a church that changed masters from Rome to a Communist government. It suffered from being cut off from the richness of belonging to the universal church, but it was given the ability to develop more fully a distinctive Chinese Church.[19]

---

18. Mariani, op. cit., 156–63; 216–21. In these pages Mariani assessed the impact of Gong and Jin in Shanghai, as well as Jin's later relationship with the Vatican appointed bishop of the underground Church in Shanghai, Joseph Fan Zhongliang from 1985, and how the Vatican finally settled a complex situation.

19. Another significant Jesuit, **Vincent Zhu**, was among 20 Jesuits and 300 lay Catholics who were imprisoned in September 1955. He was born in Shanghai on 17 July 1916, one of thirteen children. One of his uncles was the Bishop of Hai Men, Simon Zhu, who died in prison in 1960. Aged 19, he entered the Jesuits in France, and was ordained in 1944. He was considered a brilliant student. Returning to Shanghai in 1947, he became principal of St Ignatius College, but the school was closed in 1951. Zhu was transferred to the parish of the Sacred Heart in Shanghai where he was arrested first in 1953, but released in 1954. In 1955, he was condemned to 15 years hard labour. But, in 1979, he was released

The clash between the Roman Catholic Church and the new government in Beijing was inevitable. Both governing bodies shared similar characteristics: both exercised strong autocratic control, backed by radically opposing rigid orthodoxies, and were intolerant of dissent. The Communists viewed the Catholic Church as part of the imperialists' invasion of China in earlier years, allies of the United States and the Nationalist government of Chiang Kai-chek. Mao Zedong was determined to break from the past of foreign interference in China, and establish a China governed and controlled by the Chinese. Control of the Catholic Church was part of that determination.

Between 1842 and 1948, 588 Jesuits belonged to the Jiangnan-Nanjing-Shanghai mission. Their nationalities were: 371 French, 142 Chinese, 24 Italian, nine German, eight Belgian, seven Dutch, six Irish, four Luxemburgish, four Portuguese, four Spanish, four Swiss, two Japanese, one British, one Canadian and one Polish.[20] This mission set the tone for other Jesuit missions of the former Jiangnan mission. The growth in the number of Christians and educational works were substantial. The French protectorate, while contributing to the spread of mission works, hindered the growth of an independent Chinese Church. The French Jesuit legacy was essentially a French Church inserted into China.

The Catholic Church in Shanghai survived by going underground, and when religious activity slowly re-emerged after the Cultural Revolution, and especially after the appointment of Jin as bishop in 1985, the revival of the Church, under the supervision of the Patriotic Church, was remarkable and became a model for the whole of China. At the time of Jin's death in 2013, the Chinese government estimated that the Catholic population of Shanghai was 150,000, but local Catholics suggested that the figure was much higher. There were

---

by Deng Xiaoping and returned to Shanghai. He lived with his family but refused to join the Patriotic Church. He was arrested again in 1981, accused of being a spy for the Vatican, and opposed to the independent Church of China. In 1983, he was again sent to prison of 15 years for being a member of a 'clique of counter revolutionary traitors'. However, as his health deteriorated, he was released in 1993, but only lived another few months, dying on 6 July 1993. Zhu became a martyr of the faith for the Catholics of Shanghai. Cited in 'L'Eglise de Shanghai se Souvient, vingt ans après . . .', in *Eglise d'Asie*, Agence d'information des Missions étrangères de Paris (8 July 2013).

20. Mateos, op. cit., 33.

also 70 priests and 80 religious sisters ministering 110 churches. Jin's achievements were truly admirable.

Conclusion

The insertion of well-educated, deeply zealous religious European priests into the totally alien culture of China was an extraordinary challenge for these French Jesuit missionaries. Arriving in China in league with foreign powers eased the entry, but promoting the message of the Christian gospel required the missionaries to engage the Chinese as independently as possible from the influence of the foreign powers. They claimed that their message was entirely spiritual, and had no connection with secular or political ambitions of the Europeans in China. This was not always obvious to the Chinese, as the French Jesuits always relied on the power and support given to them under the French protectorate. The Jesuits from the Province of France during this period of study found it very hard to disengage themselves from their French heritage. Most claimed to be French nationals first, then missionaries. While French nationalism was important to these missionaries, they were not prepared to work with those Chinese who advocated Chinese nationalism. They found it very difficult to understand Chinese culture and customs that they usually strongly criticised because they did not fit into the European cultural categories. What was different required change.

The education in the Catholic faith that the French missionaries gave to China was what they understand as the perennial truths of the Catholic Church as taught and experienced in Europe. The spiritual and theological preparation they had before arriving in China was what they had learned in the French seminaries. To impress people at home in France, they frequently boasted that the training in the Chinese seminaries and the education in the schools were similar and equal to the best offering in France at the time. Some reflecting Chinese students doubted this. They were expected to accept this foreign education that showed little application to the spiritual sensitivities of the Chinese. Some succeeded, many failed. The Ricci method of adaptation to Chinese culture was considered out-dated by some. Even as late as 1946, Verdier did not want Chinese Jesuits teaching theology. Chinese priests were always considered inferior to the Europeans.

When the French Jesuits first arrived in Shanghai, they were unchallenged by Jesuits from other countries. But with new arrivals, critical comments were made about the missionary methods of the Jesuits from the Province of France. These included criticism of their traditional, orthodox missionary style, which was expressed with a confidence that sometimes appeared as arrogant and self-righteous. While continually wanting Jesuit missionaries from other European provinces and the United States, they were not prepared to modify what they believed were tried and proven successful methods of operating. They were not good at co-operating with other missions, and were defensive when challenged by Jesuits from other nations. One Californian Jesuit courageously considered the Jesuits from the Province of France that he knew would have been rated as second-class Jesuits in France.

Despite these limitations in spreading the Catholic faith in China, these Jesuits from the Province of France had remarkable success in planting and expanding the Catholic Church in China. This was clearly seen in the continual growth in numbers of Christians and the number of Christian communities. While sometimes seen by non-Christians as agents of the imperial powers, many Christians were grateful to the missionaries for their spiritual offerings, and for the material support they received in times of troubles. When the foreigners were expelled, they left a strong underground Church that eventually flourished as a genuine Chinese Church. This was always the stated aim of the missionaries, but they would never have imagined that it would emerge as it did without further assistance from them.

Seminarians with Fr Moisan SJ, Shanghai, c 1900's

Courtesy of the archives of the Jesuit Province of France

Jesuit Church of St Ignatius, Shanghai, c early 1930s.

St Ignatius' College, Xujiahui, Shanghai

Courtesy of the archives of the Province of France

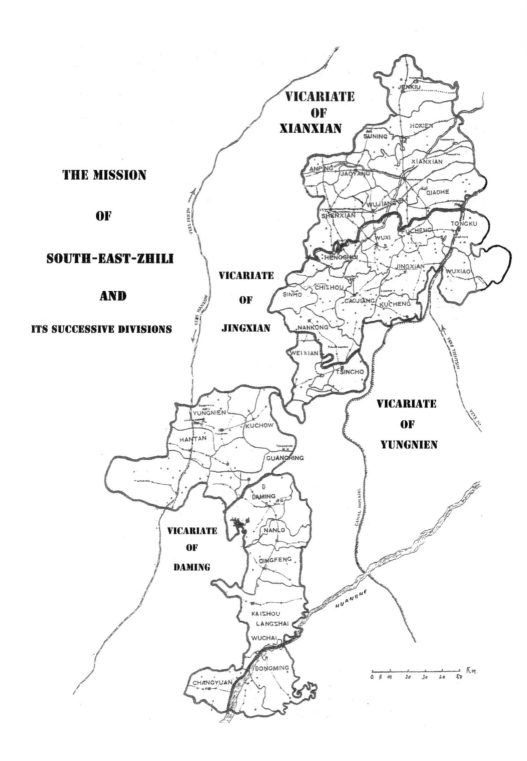

THE MISSION

OF

SOUTH-EAST-ZHILI

AND

ITS SUCCESSIVE DIVISIONS

VICARIATE
OF
XIANXIAN

VICARIATE

OF

JINGXIAN

VICARIATE

OF

YUNGNIEN

VICARIATE

OF

DAMING

JENKIU

SUNING   HOKIEN

ANPING   JIAOYANG   XIANXIAN

QIAOHE

WUJIANG

SHENXIAN

FUCHENG   TONGKU

WUXI

HENGSHUI   JINGXIAN

WUXIAO

SINHO   CHISHOU   CAOJIANG   KUCHENG

NANKONG

WEIXIAN

TSINCHO

YUNGNIEN

KUCHOW

HANTAN

GUANGPING

DAMING

NANLO

QINGFENG

KAISHOU
LANGSHAI
WUCHAI

DONGMING

CHANGYUAN

VERS PEKIN

VERS HANKOW

VERS TIENTSIN

CANAL IMPERIAL

HUANGHE

Km
0 5 10   20   30   40   50

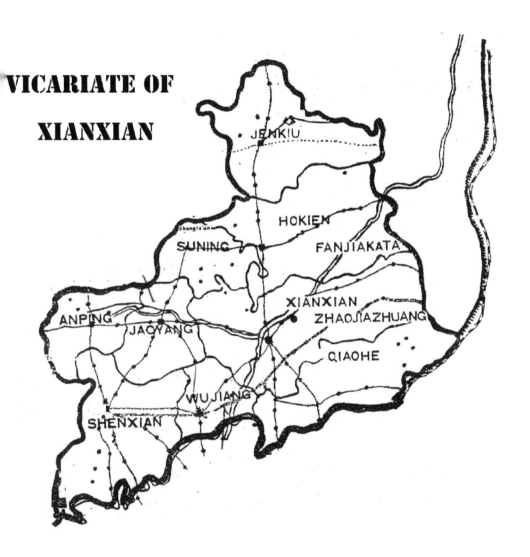

VICARIATE OF
XIANXIAN

JENKIU

Shangts'un
HOKIEN
SUNING
FANJIAKATA

XIANXIAN
ZHAOJIAZHUANG
ANPING
JAOYANG
QIAOHE

WUJIANG

SHENXIAN

Chapter 11
The Mission to South-East Zhili (Xianxian)
Province of Champagne
1856–1926

Beginnings 1856

The founding of the mission of south-east Zhili began with Bishop Joseph-Martial Mouly (1807–68), who set in motion the development of the Catholic Church in northern China. Mouly was a French Lazarist who arrived in Beijing in 1835, where, at the age of 28, he became superior of the mission in Beijing and in Xiwanzi, Inner Mongolia. In 1841, Mouly was appointed vicar apostolic of Mongolia, and was added administrator of the diocese of Beijing in 1846. It was the Catholics here who, a decade earlier, had written to Rome requesting that the Jesuits might be sent to replace the Lazarists, objecting to Mouly's appointment, and refusing to accept him as the new administrator.

In order to settle these disputes, the Holy See, while abrogating the *Padroado* diocese of Beijing, divided it into three vicariates apostolic under the direct control of *Propaganda Fide* in 1856. Mouly became the first vicar apostolic of north Zhili, taking up residence in the Beitang (North Church) in Beijing. Following the Sino-French treaties of 1858 and 1860, which guaranteed French protection for Catholics, Mouly became more confident and reopened the Nantang (South Church) in Beijing in 1860, flying the French tricolour.[1]

Following the advice of Mouly in 1851, the Cardinal Prefect of the Propagation of the Faith told the Jesuit superior general, Beckx, in 1854 that he was happy for the Jesuits to be appointed to the mission

---

1. Arnuld Camps, 'Catholic Missionaries (1800–1860)', in *Handbook of Christianity in China, 1800 to Present*, edited by R. Gary Tiedemann, 2 (Leiden: E.J. Brill, 2000), 128–30.

of Zhili. In February 1856, the Jesuits were informed that south-east Zhili was to go to the *Mission Étrangères*, but they refused, while the south-west was to go to the Jesuits, but the local indigenous clergy objected. At the time, Mouly had two major problems, no money and the fear of schism from the Chinese clergy. The resolution to these discussions by *Propaganda* was a three-fold division. Mouly would govern Beijing and the north; the south-west would go to the Lazarists, and the south-east to the Jesuits.

Propaganda further decreed on 30 May 1856 that the Jesuits of Jiangnan and the Province of France were to administer this new mission, but the new region was later given to the Jesuits from the Province of Champagne, a new province that had been created from the French province from 1863. The Jesuits appointed the rector of Xujiahui, Adrien Languillat, the first vicar apostolic from August 1856 and, with Ignacio Catte, he left Shanghai for the new mission in 1857. Languillat was consecrated by Mouly at Nanjiazhuang, a small Christian community in the suburbs of Paoting on 22 March. Some months later, Luigi Sica, aged 43, joined him as religious superior, together with Louis Caussin.

Languillat first established himself at Zhaojiazhuang, 1857–61. Here with Catte, he set up a small residence with three rooms and an attic. The Christians in this region had affection for the former Portuguese missionaries. Mouly had not spent much time in the area; so the Franciscans from Shandong administered the sacraments during 1847–57. The local Christians wanted the Jesuits. The vicariate contained the prefectures of Hokien, Guangping and Daming with 132 Christian communities, 9,505 Christians and 15 catechumens within a population of 10 million people. In fifteen sub-prefectures there were no Christians. The mission covered a vast plain of alluvial yellow earth that included modern-day Hopeh, a region that experienced dryness in the spring, frequently followed by floods in July and August. The temperature range during the year was between below 15 degrees and more than 40 degrees. In the southern section of Daming, there were about seven million people, mainly illiterate peasant farmers. In a report to Rome covering the years 1857–9, Languillat praised his simple Christians, who suffered occasional abuse from the non-Christians. They attended Mass and prayers, which were often held in private houses. The catechists were also simple people who taught the non-Catholics and educated the Catholics with 'zeal, knowledge, piety and probity'. They were respected in the community, and worked hard. He outlined four main needs of the mission: more missionaries, more schools and churches and more money. The missionaries also needed to spend more time studying the Chinese language.[2] In another letter to the superior general on 15 July 1860, Languillat described the people as 'sober, hard working, accommodating and peaceful' in their poverty. Dwellings were generally very simple and badly built.[3]

Initially, the missionaries explored the region, moving around by bicycle or in a Chinese chair giving missions, but as both Prosper Leboucq and Mathurin Joubaud knew no word of Chinese, their effectiveness was limited. They travelled up to 25 kilometres, visiting between 40–50 places. The first Baptisms registered were in 1857. The Chinese priests were indispensable and they worked mainly among the non-Christians. Between 1858–9, six schools were established, as well as the decision to build a seminary, of which Leboucq was the architect.

There were initial setbacks with the deaths of Jesuit missionaries recently sent to work in the new mission. Ignatio Catte, aged 37, died on 23 June 1859, and Louis Caussin, aged 34, died in 1860. The Neapolitan, Francisco Giaguinto, aged 40, arrived on 31 March 1858, after having spent nine years in Jiangnan. He could not endure the hot winds, and returned to Shanghai, while Louis Sica also left when he became sick. On 25 March 1859, Brueyre and Joubaud arrived, but the latter died soon after on 21 July. Leboucq arrived on 23 June 1859, and went to the north of the mission. The Jesuits lived in very poor conditions and extreme privations, with insufficient food, no vegetables or fresh meat. Leboucq became seriously ill, but recovered, while Caussin died of typhus on 21 May 1860.

Unhappy with this initial foundation, and the area having suffered from the effects of war, Languillat decided to move his residence to the small Christian village of Zhangjiazhuang in 1862, built from indemnities after the destruction of mission buildings during the war. This village was only two kilometres from Xianxian, with 142

---

2. Languillat, A report on the Zhili mission, 1856–9. ARSI.
3. Languillat, to French provincial, 15 July 1860, in Maquet, *Vicariate of Tcheu-li-S-E, 1857–1907*.

Christians. In the surrounding districts, there were 15 to 20 Christian communities, with about 3,000 Christians.

Following the Franco-Chinese Treaty of October 1860, the freedom to establish Christians missions was accepted, and with the help from the indemnities paid for destruction of the mission during the war, Languillat built a new 25-room episcopal residence, followed by a small seminary, which opened on 4 February 1861 at Xianxian with 13 students and Brueyre as director. He also built a school for catechists, orphanages for boys and girls, two pharmacies, as well as the foundation for a new cathedral at Xianxian. His co-missionaries in three sections consisted of seven Jesuits, two secular priests, one Jesuit brother and 12 catechists. In the seminary, the students studied Chinese, Latin, chant and spiritual subjects.

Leboucq reported in 1861 that being in the interior of China, the missionaries did not have the same back-up from the French protectorate as they would in the cities, especially in the disputes between Christians and the mandarins. He experienced the Chinese people as humiliated after the war, and as a conquered people, with head bent under the power that had subdued them. This turned them against the Christian religion. At Kuchow, the 'satellites' of the mandarins decapitated four seminarians, and this occurred when there was official peace. The liberty that the Chinese government gave the missionaries in favour of religion had added to their misery, especially from those who worshipped idols. Leboucq wrote that the Jiangnan mission was in ruins, with Christian villages burnt, churches destroyed, and many men and women held in captivity by the rebels. Recently they had enlisted more than 10,000 young men to their cause. In the advance of the rebels, many Chinese fled their villages.[4] Despite these setbacks, Leboucq reported two years later that he had 200 conversions in one month, and worked with 4,000 new catechumens.[5]

In 1863, the White Lotus brigands, a branch of the Taipings, invaded the extreme south of Zhili. They had first pillaged the region in the north of Shandong for many weeks, and then moved south into Zhili with an army of 20,000. They killed the military mandarin in Daming, destroyed much of the mission, burnt villages, with Chris-

---

4. Leboucq to a priest in France, Zhili, 7 December 1861. Letter 405, *Lettres des Nouvelles de La Chine,* Tome II, 1846–1863.
5. Leboucq, Zhili, to Basmain, 23 December 1963, ibid., letter 510.

tians killed or taken prisoners. Many people fled the region, but some 500 Christians held their ground and defended the seminary, with the Jesuit brother, Joseph Guillon in charge. The Chinese government forces were impotent in the crisis, but assistance came from a British detachment of 800 men.

The following year, Leboucq reported much missionary success in his area. He was proud of the number of catechumens, with 8,000 studying the catechism and preparing for Baptism. There were already 5,600 Christians in the mission living in 160 Christian communities, but 58 of these were without churches or chapels. Visiting 150 non-Catholic villages, he found that the people were well disposed toward the foreigners, but the mandarins were not. He believed that penetration of the interior of China would be 'tiresome, the struggle long and unrelenting'.

The Bishop Edouard Dunbar years (1865–1878)

In 1865, Languillat was transferred from Xianxian to Shanghai, and his successor was Edouard Dunbar, consecrated in the cathedral on 19 February. He had only been in China for four years. At this time, the mission comprised ten priests and two Jesuit brothers, 11,230 Christians and 2,265 catechumens in 174 Christian communities. There was also a minor seminary with 22 students, 18 boys' schools with 180 students, and four girls' schools with 108 students. Two orphanages cared for 270 children.

Soon after the departure of Languillat from Zhili, the superior general sent the provincial of France, Michael Fessard, as visitor to the two Jesuit missions in China. He spent two months in Xianxian. One of his decisions was to appoint Joseph Gonnet (1815–95)[6] as superior in Zhili. He was one of the original missionaries to Shanghai, arriving

6. **Joseph Gonnet** was described as 'a simple man of unpolished nature', but a strategist for conversions. As superior of the mission from 23 November 1869, he lived through difficult times with rebellions and the deaths of many Jesuits. After 1878, he installed many catechists, founded schools for both sexes and ran the vicariate as vicar after the death of Dubar in 1878 until the appointment of Bulté in 1880. That year he was declared 'the apostle of Jingzhou and Kou Techeng'. He worked in the centre of the vicariate and was the founder of providing resources for the mission, from both overseas and from the European concessions in Tianjin. He died in 1895, aged 80. (cf Bornet, below, 113–19).

in October 1844, and typified traditional missionary methods, suggesting to new missionaries that they follow the methods of former Jesuits, which included attempts to be friendly with the mandarins and to seek out non-Catholics who had been unjustly treated, and take up their cases with the mandarins. If the case was won, a whole family might be converted. He believed that the obstacles to conversion among the non-Catholics were 'corruption of the human heart and enslavement to passions'. He advocated teaching the catechism, and learning the Chinese language, as well as teaching European sciences: mathematics and physics.[7]

Gonnet was considered a good administrator by his collaborators for establishing a solid base for missionary activity in Zhili. Together with Pierre Octave, a missionary since August 1861, Clément Couvreur, who arrived in 1863, and Xavier Xi, a secular priest, they developed the south of the vicariate at Daming, but they encountered opposition from the educated Chinese at Guangping. After recourse to the French legation, progress was made, and relations with the Chinese authorities improved, with the Christian community at Guangping growing in strength.

Conversions continued to grow, from 13,000 baptised in 1865 to 28,000 in 1878. Leboucq was considered 'the great converter', especially in Hokien. The Chinese government decorated him with the 'blue pearl' for his work with the English military against the bandits. He also improved relations between mandarins and foreigners.

The 'Long Hair' bandits returned in mid-January 1868. They pillaged Xianxian, killed the mandarin, and burnt buildings, leaving the city devastated. Some people fled the city, while others took refuge with the missionaries who were not harmed. Imperial soldiers arrived and massacred the rebels on 26 March. In a letter to the bishop of Beijing on 17 June 1868, Gonnet wrote about the disasters, spiritualising the events by claiming that 'God permitted these things for a greater good', and that profit might be gained by people exercising the virtues of 'patience, abnegation and mortification'. Gonnet tried to stir up hope among those who had been affected by the disasters, but he also went to Tianjin to report the disaster to the French consul. One result of this mission by Gonnet was the establishment of a Jesuit

---

7.   Emile Becker, *Le demi-siècle d'apostolat en Chine, Le Réverend Père Joseph Gonnet SJ* (Hokien, 1900).

house in Tianjin in 1869 for a mission bursar, who worked importantly as a conduit between the mission, the Chinese government and the French legation, especially relating to indemnities.

Business between the missionaries and the French legation became frequent from this time. Languillat had asked the consul for help to buy property, and to seek reparations for the destruction of property in 1861.[8] By 1868, assistance was sought to help buy houses, and many letters sought military assistance against the attacks by bandits and soldiers, as the mandarins were usually unhelpful. Months of correspondence occurred concerning retribution for an attack upon Leboucq and his catechist, with the consul requesting much detail before he would send his memorandum to the French minister in Beijing.[9] The missionaries were ruthless in pursuing their own interests against the Chinese authorities, without any reflection about addressing the underlying causes of the attacks upon them. There was also polite diplomatic weariness in the correspondence from the French consul to his superiors about the constant demands of the missionaries, who were, at the same time, very flattering toward the French consul, inviting him to lunch and telling him what a great job he did on their behalf, expressing much gratitude for his assistance.

After these devastating years, the mission flourished. New Christian communities were established, and older ones reorganised, all with a small local school for between 10 to 15 children. There was a college at Xianxian, a school for catechists, and a minor seminary. The missionary activity of Leboucq at Hokien in the north, together with the zealous Gaetano Stévani at Nankung in the south, and Octave in the extreme south, resulted in the establishment of 12 new Christian communities.

With the Franco-Prussian War raging in Europe in 1870, and Dubar at the Vatican Council, the missionaries were unable to get much help from France at a time when they were victims of anti-Christian and xenophobic attacks, which resulted in the massacre at Tianjin on 21 June 1870. The French consul, M Fontanier, two missionaries and Sisters of Charity were the more notable victims. The mission lost its house. The missionaries suggested that the mandarins were behind the incident in order to embarrass the foreigners.

8. Languillat to French consul, 20 September 1861 and 3 April 1861. DAC.
9. French consul, Tianjin, to French Minister, Beijing, 1 June 1969. DAC

This was followed by drought at the end of summer 1870, and famine and typhus in the autumn, which led to high prices for grain. Then floods occurred in 1873, submerging Hokien. Famine again prevailed from 1876–7, and pestilence from 1878, from which seven out of ten people either emigrated or died. It was observed that every year of natural or human disaster, Christian converts increased. Leboucq reported with joy that in 1871 he had 1,333 adult Baptisms, and 1,928 catechumens. Christians recognised that it was the French who protected the missionaries whenever possible, and assisted them in the reconstruction of the village after bandit attacks.

Typhus was the great killer in those years. Many priests died of this disease during the years 1871–8. The Jesuits lost Alexis Meyer who was a scientist, scripture scholar and fluent in the Chinese language on 16 September 1871. Jules Denizot followed on 15 May 1872, and Jean Petitfils on 3 April 1874. Pierre Octave soon followed. It was a similar story at the orphanage and the minor seminary. The brother, Auguste Pelte, after caring for more than 300 sick people, succumbed to the disease, as well as Xavier Edel, who was in charge of the observatory, after only five years on the mission. Six Jesuits died in 1878.

By 1872, the vicariate had one Chinese priest, 12 Jesuits, two scholastic novices and six Jesuit brothers, serving 21,280 Christians in 314 communities. Floods had ravaged the north and east of the vicariate resulting in much misery. Entire villages had disappeared under water, hardly leaving any time for the unfortunate inhabitants to flee. Several Christian communities had disappeared, chapels were destroyed, and people travelled great distances to find food. In the districts to the north, the Christians were more than usually poor, and were reduced to extreme need.

In the southern parts of the vicariate, there were no floods, but drought. The lack of water caused crop failure and destruction. Facing these disasters, the poor peasants had recourse to their traditional superstitions. Many refugees took shelter with the vicar apostolic at Zhangjiazhuang, but resources needed to care for them were insufficient. The misery increased with habitual sickness, fever and deaths. The missionaries were tired and brave in the face of the dangers from epidemics. Jules Denizot, who had only arrived in the mission in November 1870, died after three days while ministering to people with typhoid and burying eleven people in his community. The missionaries were reduced to ten men who were supposed to minister to ten million non-Catholics.

Support came with the arrival of six priests in October 1872, while hope was expressed for the future with mention of 33 students studying at the seminary. Non-Christians admired the success of the established schools. The number of catechists increased to 15, while 10 chapels and 45 oratories had been built. The four orphanages prospered and conversions continued.

The missionaries in the north suffered from adverse propaganda against them following the massacres at Tianjin, reminding them that French protection was tenuous. In this section, conversions slowed down, and catechists decreased.

In the centre of the vicariate, the number of Christians was stable; the efforts of Brueyre and Cyril Bonnomet resulted in 300 adult Baptisms, but there were insufficient catechists.

The southern part of the mission was the most uncultivated and most fruitless section of the mission. When Octave arrived there some years before, there were scarcely 50 Christians, but overcoming obstacles, he was rewarded with 1,200 Christians in 1872. Dubar believed that God had rewarded Octave's 'patience and persevering efforts'.[10]

A report on the mission by Gonnet in 1878 indicated an increase in the number of missionaries to 24 Jesuit priests, of whom four were Chinese. There were also two European scholastics studying theology, five Chinese scholastics, six Jesuit brothers and two Chinese secular priests. The number of Christians had increased to 26,152 in 470 Christian villages. There had been 2,490 Baptisms and there were 5,000 catechumens. But sadness was recorded at the death of the vicar apostolic, Dubar, the Jesuit superior, three missionary priests and a brother. There were more floods, famine and disease, which resulted in many deaths. Scarcity of resources was a chronic situation. In 1876, the harvest had been insignificant; in 1877, there was nothing. During the summer, heat burned the crops; while in autumn, emigration began in the search for food. Many went to Tianjin where the Chinese government had arranged some distribution of food.

In the villages, the situation was worse with many houses destroyed. Even dead bodies could not be given suitable rites of burial. Those

---

10. Dubar, Report of the mission of Zhili S-E, 1872. ARSI.

who took to the road risked dying on the way from cold and famine. Typhoid occurred, especially at the Chinese school where 150 children contracted the disease, but only two died. Following a cold and dry winter, with the temperatures falling to below 20 degrees, despair set in among many. These situations greatly affected the missionaries. Generosity from France helped, but it was insufficient.

As frequently happened on the mission, adversity brought its own rewards in the form of an increase of conversions. With insufficient priests, the missionaries had enlisted talented Chinese Christians to help in their work, even if this had been limited by sickness and famine.

The faith of the Christians was a source of consolation. Despite their poverty, they would travel great distances to inform the priest that someone needed the Last Sacraments. Much gratitude was expressed for this service. Seeing this visit by the priest, who also gave alms to the Christians, impressed many pagans, who, hoping for similar support from the missionaries, agreed to join the catechumenate. Caution was expressed before these people could receive Baptism. They had to understand the catechism and prayers, and 'finally renounce completely their idols and superstitions'. The catechists were the teachers, but other Christians also showed great zeal in assisting the education of the non-Christians.

The seminary had received 21 new students, and the Chinese school received more students than in the previous year. The mission provided them with food as well as an education. The care of orphans and abandoned children continued, despite some fear among families of giving children to the missionaries. The mission was already at straining point with the number of children. Sometimes five or six children would be handed over in one night. Many were abandoned.[11]

When Dubar went to Shanghai to ordain priests because Languillat was ill, the misery and despair in the north of China was evident. The bishop asked for help from the missionaries in the south. When he arrived in Wukiao, Jingxian, to care for the sick Henri Maquet, he contracted typhus and died in 1878.[12] Other Jesuits, Ignace Azere and Louis Duvelle, soon followed him. Since May, fourteen Jesuits had

---

11. Gonnet to General, Zhili, a report, 1 July 1877 – 1 July 1878. ARSI.
12. Joseph Jaeggy, SJ, 'La Mission de Sienhsien', in *Bellarmino*, 9 (Shanghai: Xujiahui, 3 December 1940): 137–47.

contracted typhoid, and six had died. This added to the burden of the remaining missionaries.

Much of the reporting about the mission was full of misery and gloom from floods, disease and bandits, but the growth in the number of conversions, the strong faith of many new Christians, the increase in the number of seminarians, as well as the satisfaction gained from caring for the sick and abandoned, strengthened the resolve of the missionaries in their work.

Bishop Henri Bulté years (1880–1900)

Bulté was appointed vicar apostolic of Zhili on 15 July 1880, having been the vice-rector of Xujiahui, Shanghai. Gonnet remained as the Jesuit religious superior until 18 April 1884, when Emil Becker succeeded him. Xianxian became the centre of the mission. The year 1880 recorded 28,000 Christians in the mission. The early years of Bulté's reign were described as peaceful and fruitful, the number of catechumens grew, while the primary schools of the mission developed and inculcated a spirit of faith among the children.

Bulté and Becker worked together to develop the education of the Chinese collaborators, which had been encouraged at the Synod of Beijing in 1886. Becker desired to form the virgins into a religious congregation, but this did not eventuate. It was finally agreed that the catechists should have at least two years education. Of the 108 accepted for the school of catechists between 1886 and 1896, 78 graduated and worked in the mission.

There was a decline in the number of conversions in 1886. One suggestion given for this was that the Chinese were fearful of the growing influence of the Boxers. Others believed that they did not want to be under the political control of the Europeans. There was a general feeling at the time that difficult days were ahead for the missionaries, even the possibility of the 'shedding of blood'.

From 1889, letters from missionaries indicated concern about the influence of the White Lotus rebels and the Boxer movement. Omer Neveux, in July 1889, expressed concern about 690 catechumens who had been recruited by a Chinese priest. Many of these became affiliated to the White Lotus group, and 'only came to Church because they were escaping the police'. Others, however, became good Christians.

In his annual report, 1888–9, Bulté was less satisfied than he would have desired. But he was pleased that the Holy Infants had 11,818 Baptisms, which indicated the zealous work of the priests and virgins who worked in the pharmacies. He thought that Catholics were known 'as a religion of charity'. Challenges for him included the need for better instruction of the catechumens, but this required better catechists. He would like to establish a 'house for catechumens', and provide better instruction for the catechists. Lapsed Catholics (apostates) were more trouble than the non-Catholics. The work in the schools and boarding houses were very important providing vocations to the Society and to the seminary, as well as possible future catechists. Christians became more zealous as a result of retreats and the promotion of the 'Devotion to the Sacred Heart'. He praised the zeal of the priests who spared no pain or fatigue, especially caring for the children in the communities, giving them monthly Holy Communion. This was particularly evident in Weixian.[13]

One missionary, Clotaire Bandoux, reported in 1891 that he believed the Western powers were arming the rioters to bring about the end of the Imperial Dynasty. He also mentioned the report in which the Holy See had indicated its desire to establish a nunciature in Beijing, as well as a hierarchy. In the mission, he found it difficult making conversions. However, he saw the Christians as the 'crème in a mass of iniquity', of good character, sober, temperate, affable, polite, flexible, without exaggerated vices, patient and materialistic. But he found them hard to understand. He also made one of the rare comments from Jesuit missionaries about the Chinese Rites. One educated Chinese had told him that in these rites, the Chinese simply made memory of Confucius, and nothing else.[14] This subject was taboo among the missionaries, one that they had taken an oath not to discuss.

What pleased Bulté most in his annual report on the mission for 1892 was the growth in the number of Christians. There were currently 551 communities with 39,744 Christians and 3,807 catechumens, in contrast with numbers in 1856 when there were only 132 communities with 9,475 Christians and 62 catechumens. He thought

---

13. Bulté, the mission of Zhili S-E, annual report, 1888–9, to Provincial, in *Lettres de Jersey*, VIII/11 (December 1889).

14. Letter from Clotaire Bandoux, Zhaojiazhuang, 3 October 1891, 61–3.

that these statistics should hearten the missionaries and be a 'reward
for leaving their own country'. He thought that they had 'accommodated to the climate, language and customs of China'. He praised the
good work of the co-missionaries, especially the virgins who worked
in the pharmacies, as well as the leaders of the seminary, the college,
the school for catechists and the school for training the virgins. The
priests communicated a good spirit in their communities. There were
some vocations to the priesthood, and to the Society, and to the catechists who came from 'the solid piety of the Christians'. He desired
to have a priest in each sub-prefecture, but the number of Chinese
priests available was currently insufficient to realise this desire. The
priests were generally absorbed in meeting the needs of the present Christians and were less concerned with conversion of the non-
Christians; he needed more priests for this work. However, there had
been growth in the number of Christians in Daming, an area where
previously there had been few Christians.[15]

Emil Japiot, a missionary in the section of Guangping and Daming, expressed hopes for more Christian communities at Qingfeng.
The catechumens of Kaizhou who took their work seriously and were
'less occupied with earthly occupations' pleased him. He had baptised five adults that he had been preparing for two years, and was
happy with the school at Kaizhou that had 18 children and two catechists. However, in those areas that did not know the missionaries,
'there were great obstacles'.[16]

One celebrated missionary in the region of Xuzhou was Léopold
Gain (1852–1930). He arrived in China in November 1876, and was
sent to Anhui in 1881 with the advice from Garnier 'to be prudent,
simple and trust in God'. It was not a successful beginning, as he was
soon attacked and driven from his house and the village, accompanied by his catechists. He went to Wuhu for safety. After a few years
in Hai Men, Gain went to Xuzhou in 1887, where he was praised for
his energy. He frequently battled with the local mandarins, and was
subjected to attacks by bandits. In 1894, at Ma-sin, the residence was
attacked, and damage done to the church. Mission residences in the
region were usually well protected with high walls; the one at Xuzhou

15. Bulté, a report on the mission of Zhili, S-E, Xianxian, 25 July 1892, *Lettres de Jersey*, 12, 1893.
16. Letter of Japiot to Bishop Bulté, 24 August 1892, in *Lettres de Jersey*, 12 (1893): 34.

was a substantial building with two stories and verandas. At Fengxian on 22 January 1888, the Boxers attacked, destroying many houses, but they were beaten off. During the massacre of Christians in 1900, the residence at Xuzhou was completely destroyed, with many other building pillaged. The rebels had been told to pillage but respect the people, while the mandarins were no help, showing sympathy towards the rebels.

Gain's best years were 1900–11, when he acted as mediator between warring factions in Anhui, gaining the respect of the mandarins. He continually moved into new mission areas where there were few Christians, and converted many. He built the large church at Xuzhou. In a letter in 1910, he wrote about great floods at Xuzhou around October, but was pleased with the number of conversions. The first Baptisms occurred in 1888, and by 1910 he had baptised 39,999, of whom 23,118 were adults. There were currently 34,918 catechumens. By 1929, the number had increased to 52,298.[17]

Missionary reflections

The Jesuit missionary was sent to China for the remainder of his life, adapting his lifestyle in what ways he could among the Chinese, 'had few resources, was aware of local superstitions, prayed for the emperor and preached one doctrine'. Of the missionaries, the martyr was considered the most heroic person, much envied by the missionaries, as the spilling of blood made them resemble their leader, Jesus of Nazareth. The faith of the missionaries was compelling. They believed in the providence of God who would sustain them in attacks by their enemies, and in a God who would advance their work despite setbacks because they were doing what he wanted them to do. This was affirmed and strengthened their resolve when they reflected that in 1854 there had been only 9,000 Christians in the mission, while in 1888 there were 47,000. Progress was being made, despite the difficulties.

---

17. P.L. Gain SJ (1852–1930), *Apostle of Xuzhou, Vicariate of Nanjing* (Xujiahui, 1931); Cindy Yik-yi Chu, *Catholicism in China, 1900-Present: The Development of the Chinese Church* (London: Palgrave Macmillan, 2014). Gain spent the years 1911–12 in Nanjing, and then 1919–25 in Shanghai. His final years were at Tongjia-tou.

The mission headquarters at Zhangjiazhuang was situated in a very large compound, surrounded by a wall, that included a large church, the priests' residence, a residence for the virgins, a seminary, college, and orphanage, as well as a farm and stables. The flag over the compound read: 'The Grand Kingdom of France, temple of the Master of Heaven'. The missionaries believed that France shared in the glory of the success of the missionaries in the conversion of China, but this was not a widely held belief.

Observations about the character of the Chinese varied among the missionaries. Joseph Hoeffel, in the Daming section of the mission, believed them to be dishonest, but he thought that the Chinese peasant was similar to the French peasant of Alsace or Bretagne in that they valued money too much. They were not civilised in the European sense, but why should they be? They were generally outwardly courteous, but could be insulting, and the mandarins were frequently unjust. But were they any worse that the enemies of Christianity in France? This was a more balanced reflection that tried not to excessively condemn the Chinese character and way of life.

Some missionaries noted more positive attributes among the Chinese. These admired 'their patience, sobriety, religious instinct, respect for tradition, deference to absolute power, politeness, and rules of civility', qualities that differed from the West. Negative qualities included infanticide and the abandoning of children, as well as opium smoking. The latter was not accepted among Christians. Suicide occurred, but not frequently. This was more common among women who were avoiding violent or angry husbands, after taking a strong dose of opium. Sometimes men took their lives because of a ruined life or to take vengeance upon an enemy.

Among the Chinese Christians there were both martyrs and apostates. The faith was not sufficiently deep to sustain some Christians in times of persecution. There were other Christians who converted for the material help given to them by the mission, or in the hope of gaining support against the mandarins. Hoeffel recognised that this was not a 'high motive' for being a Christian, but 'God understands'. Among the catechumens, some persevered and became good or even excellent Christians, but others returned to 'their errors and superstitions'. Being a non-believing country, China could not be compared with a Christian country. Conversions were frequent among the 'poor and simple', but rare among 'the men of letters', the educated class.

Hoeffel further reflected that 'it is not our great sermons that convert the non-Christians; nor our preaching in the public places, but rather by friendship'. He did not believe that in his district he had converted any person directly. For the most part, the people were illiterate. The role of the priest was to direct the catechist, bring together the neophytes and to supervise their education in the faith. By doing this, he believed that God would bring about conversions. Xavier Edel, a veteran missionary since 1873, and who worked in the observatory at Zhangjiazhuang, wrote about the simple faith of the peasant Christians who had affection for their priest, seeing him as 'pastor, judge, arbiter, doctor, defender and counsellor'. He found it 'impossible not to love these brave people'. Other missionaries believed that the Chinese converts saw the priest as 'good, religious, in service, honest in morals and manner' and not engaging in commerce. The missionary did not seek his own welfare or a comfortable life, but was motivated only to promote 'true religion'.

A mandarin asked a missionary why it was that the French government persecuted Christians in France, but protected Christianity in China? He was not satisfied with the answer that the Church only had a spiritual mission.[18]

The Boxer Rebellion

Some missionary letters reflected upon the causes for the Boxer rising. The more remote causes included the Russian building of a railway through Manchuria in 1875, while the 1894 Japanese war in Korea was believed to increase the hatred of foreigners in the northern provinces up to 1900. More immediate causes as seen by Ignatius Mangin included the 'hatred of the mandarins against foreigners' with the slogan 'protect the dynasty, destroy the foreigner'.[19]

By July 1898, the number of missionaries in the vicariate had increased to 53 priests (48 Jesuits and five Chinese seculars), 11 Jesuit brothers, 382 catechists and 245 religious sisters, serving four districts. The centre of the mission was still at Zhangjiazhuang.

---

18. H-J.Leroy, *En chine au Tché-le S-E* (Paris: Desclée,1899).
19. Paul Bornet, SJ. *Mission de Chine, Le Tcheu-li Sud-est,* 1857–1900; Mgr. Henri Maquet, SJ, vicar apostolic, *Vicariate de Tcheu-li Sud-est, 1857–1907,* manuscripts, FPA, Vannes.

Following the German occupation of Jiaozhou, bandits attacked and destroyed a Christian village and killed some people. The arrival of the Germans was seen as a 'great cross for the missionaries in certain districts of the interior'. Attacks on Christian communities increased in number from May 1898.[20]

In his journal, Rémi Isoré, based in Zhaojiazhuang, and minister of the section Quang-ping, was responsible for 600 Christians, a primary school and a school for catechists. At Weixian, Albert Wetterwald had a girls' school and an orphanage. They prepared for an attack from bandits promoting the catch-cry: 'obey the Ch'ing . . . death to Europeans'. On 3 November 1898, Hongtao, Jiangsu, was attacked, pillaged and burnt with three people killed. Ti-san-gou was set on fire. Fortunately, government troops came to the rescue and routed the rebels on 6 November.

Sadness was expressed with the death of Constant Hennequin on 1 October 1898, aged 53, at Hokien. This district, that also included Chen-zhou, had 2.8 million people and nine missionaries working among 379 Christian communities and 241 schools. Hennequin was a popular priest among the Christians, and had expressed his desire for martyrdom.[21]

The Boxers had been condemned in 1890 by the Emperor Kia-King. Their aim at that time was to save the Ch'ing and destroy the foreigners. They became active in Shandong by 1898, destroying missions of the vicariate apostolic of southern Shandong led by Bishop Johann Baptist von Anzer SVD. This was followed by attacks on the Christian communities of Bishop Machi. They then moved south to Zhili, Kaizhou and Weixian. They attacked a Protestant village for six weeks in 1899, followed by attacks on European property in September. The government sent troops that killed some Boxers, but the rest dispersed. It appeared that the governor of Shandong favoured the Boxers. The Catholics seemed to suffer more than the Protestants. In the Italian Franciscan vicariate, more than 5,000 Christians were without protection and resources to defend themselves against the Boxers who attacked the prefecture of Hokien in the spring in 1899. Mangin asked local authorities for assistance. Christians combined with government troops to prevent more destruction of local villages.

---

20. Letter of Paul de Cray, Tianjin, 16 May 1898, *Chine et Ceylon*, 1, November 1898.
21. Journal of Isoré, *Chine et Ceylon*, 2, April 1899.

Within the vicariate, 15 Christian centres were ravaged. The mandarins were too weak to stop the rebels, and gave orders not to shoot, arrest or to apply force. The Christians were compelled to defend themselves. The French consul and Chinese viceroy tried to intervene when the Jesuit residence at Xianxian was threatened. Finally, at the battle of Kuancheng on 15 December 1899, the Christians won.

Mangin reflected that, 'we have not yet been established in China, and neither the foreign missionaries nor the religion that they preach are acceptable to the mass of the population'. He believed that Christians were seen as the enemy of the people, and so must be removed. Yet, like most missionaries, he saw the struggle as being more anti-European than anti-Christian. Mangin praised the patience of the Chinese Christians, mentioning that there were very few apostates. Some were for a short time, but repented and returned later to the community.[22]

Other letters told of the activities of the Boxers in their region. The superior of the mission, Henri Maquet, believed that the 'Secret Societies' wanted an end to the Europeans and Christianity. He reported that a chapel was burned down in Feoutcheng, where Peter Zhou worked. There was disorder in the areas of Kaizhou (Japiot), in Kou-zheng (Denn) and in Jingzhou (Mangin). The mandarins were unable to prevent the disorders. Denn further reported in his area that the bandits had attacked with a 'so-called imperial letter to protect the throne and destroy the foreigner'. They fired the chapel and were armed with guns, swords, pistols and lances. The villagers knew their leaders. Denn had been threatened, and they demanded of him '500 ounces of money'.[23]

Louis Ghestin, who had only spent a month in China, wrote about the increase in the number of Boxers in his area as they went from village to village recruiting and invoking magic spells, as well as the devil, which was supposed to give them special protection, making them invulnerable to attacks. The mandarins did little to stop them.[24]

---

22. Letter of Mangin concerning the origin and aim of the Boxers, and a reflection 23 April 1900, *Chine et Ceylon*, 5 (1900–1901); letter of Wetterwald, Zhaojiazhuang, 20 September 1899, in *Lettres de Jersey*, XIX/2 (October 1900); Memo, History of the Boxers in Zhili, S-E, 20 March 1902. DAC.
23. Letter, Maquet to French Provincial, 29 November 1899, *Lettres de Jersey*, ut supra.
24. Letter of Louis Ghestin to a Father in Enghien, Xianxian, 17 December 1899; Joseph Wanz, 1 January 1900, *Lettres de Jersey*, ut supra.

Boxers attached the Christian community of Pang-jia-xiao, seven kilometres south-east of Wuxiao, on 1 January 1900. The Christians defended themselves as best they could, but several were killed and wounded. The chapel was destroyed before the brigands went north into Shandong. By 15 January, Maquet reported the devastation of 45 Christian communities. When the rebels arrived they first asked the Christians to apostasise or watch their homes burnt and destroyed. Most Christians stood firm and refused to co-operate. By March, it was reported that the mission found it impossible to defend the Christians against the Boxers, as they received government support because they were anti-foreign and anti-Christian. However, the government did fear the intervention of the foreign powers. The great danger for the missionaries was when the struggle evolved into a battle between the Chinese government and the foreign powers. The Chinese people, for the most part, supported the Boxers, while the Chinese soldiers who had been guarding the missionaries abandoned them, resulting in a critical situation for the mission.

The journal of Albert Wetterwald narrated many of the events of 1900 in the mission. In May, the village of Wo-fou-tang was attacked but well defended. The Boxers first attacked the non-Christian section of the village, but the imperial soldiers arrived too late and did not stop the Boxers. The Christians then abandoned the village, taking some of the wounded. The Boxers headed north, devastating villages they passed through on the way to Beijing. Between Po-ting and Beijing, at Gao-jia-kou, 60 Christians were killed and burnt in their chapel.

The Boxers attached Wo-fou-tang. The routes to Tianjin were very dangerous. Zai-jian was destroyed on 15 June, with women, children, the aged, or sick killed in 'a horrible fashion'. Refugees were in great numbers, while the mandarins exercised no authority. Wetterwald was critical of the weakness of some catechists who fled south rather than face death or apostasise. He considered this action cowardly. These events coincided with dry weather, with few crops available for food. Wetterwald was isolated in Fan-jia-ka-ta, a village that was strongly fortified. It was too dangerous to venture outside the walls. The Boxers were sighted on a dike to the southwest, 800 metres from the village on 3 July 1900. On 8 July, the Boxers burnt and pillaged four neighbouring Christian villages. Wetterwald wondered if missionaries should leave their stations. In large villages like his that were well defended, he thought that all should stay, but if defence became impossible, the choice would be to die or to flee. He believed that the Christians should be encouraged to die for the faith, but such a decision must depend on circumstances. The siege for Kata began on 10 July.

In a letter received from the sub-prefect of Weixian, he mentioned that the Boxers were faithful to the Empire, that Chinese Christians needed to convert and renounce 'their past aberrations', and that European missionaries should leave China under a sound escort. This was completely rejected.

The missionaries stayed with their people and continued to assist them in defending the villages. Wetterwald commanded forces in three villages, with Zhaojiazhuang providing 200 men and 50 Puncun. They were better armed than the Boxers.

On 17 July, the Boxers appeared on the flats of Daming and attacked Weixian. Wetterwald led the Christian militia in battle formation and engaged the Boxers, forcing them to retreat. About 68 Boxers were killed or wounded. Another battle on 20 July appeared to be against the odds. The Christians had fewer numbers than the Boxers who had hundreds of men. The wind 'blew powder in our eyes, the enemy was well armed and attacked on two fronts'. But again, the Christians were victorious. There was a further attach on the 22nd, but the Boxers retreated. Meanwhile, a massacre of Christians occurred at the undefended villages of Zhongguanying and Mazhuong.

Non-Christians also suffered at the hands of the Boxers, being forced to feed them. Some landowners were also held for ransom. The fortified compounds of the Jesuit missions and the defence of many Christian communities at this time displayed great courage, and were better protected than most non-Christian groups. On the 28th, there was a massacre at Zhujiahe. Over the month of July in the mission, there had been over 3,000 victims.[25]

Henry Wibaux, missionary in the north Hokien section at Chenzhou, kept a diary of events, June–July 1900. He noted the deaths of

---

25. Journal of Albert Wetterwald, Weixian, May – 28 July 1900, in *Lettres de Jersey*, 5 (1900–1901); Robert Bickers & R. Gary Tiedemann, *The Boxers, China and the World* (USA: Langham, Rowan & Littlefield, 2007) at <https://books.google.com.au/books?printsec=frontcover&vid=LCCN2007002569&redir_esc=y#v=onepage&q&f=false>. Accessed 15 June.

Rémi Isoré and Modest Andlauer[26] at Wuxi on 23 June, together with six catechists. They had been caught in the wrong place at the wrong time, killed in the Jesuit residence. One hundred Boxers then went on to Lao-pai-zun, but the villagers were well armed and killed seven Boxers. The others returned to Wuxi. While deaths were reported, some villages were saved. On 26 June, the mandarin of Chen-zhou went to Wang-la-si appealing the Christians to lay down their arms and renounce their faith. They refused, saying they would rather die than renounce their faith.[27]

Fears were spreading among the missionaries at the reports of deaths and destruction. On 20 July, Ignatius Mangin [28] and Paul

---

26. **Rémi Isoré** was born in the small French town of Bambeque on 22 January 1852. Encourage by his parish priest to become a priest, he entered the seminary in Cambrai, studying philosophy and theology. After teaching primary students at Roubaix, he entered the Society of Jesus in 1875 at St Acheul. Theology studies in 1881 were on the British island of Jersey. He asked his provincial to go to the mission in Zambia, where he thought he had a good chance of martyrdom. The provincial thought he had better chances of martyrdom in China, so he was sent there in 1882. After language study and ordination, he was sent to the school in Zhangjiazhuang and spent most of his missionary life there. He died on 16 June 1900, aged 48.

  Modeste Andlauer was born on 22 May 1847, in Rosheim, near Strasbourg. He entered the Society of Jesus on 8 October 1872, having already completed seven years' study in a minor seminary, and some years in the major seminary. After further studies he was ordained in Laval on 22 September 1877, and subsequently taught in schools at Amiens, Lille and Brest, from 1877–1880. As a talented linguist, he was sent to China, arriving in 1882, were he undertook the study of the Zhili dialect of Mandarin at Zhangjiazhuang. Pastoral duties in Wuxiao and Wuxi followed. He died 19 June 1900, aged 53. He was buried in Xianxian. Cf. Anthony E. Clark, *China's Saints, Catholic Martyrdom during the Qing (1644–1911)*, (Bethlehem: Lehigh University Press, 2011), 92–9.

27. Journal of Henry Wibaux, Persecution at Chenn-zhou, 20 June – 10 July 1900, in *Lettres de Jersey*, XIX/2 (October 1900).

28. **Léon Ignace Mangin** was born at Verny, France on 30 July 1857. His early schooling was in Thionville and Metz, where fellow students found him 'tall and imposing, with a purposeful but affable personality'. He entered the Society of Jesus on 5 November 1875, at Amiens, and in 1881 was assigned to a school in Liège. Meanwhile his frequent request to be sent to the foreign missions was accepted in 1882, and he arrived in China and Tianjin on 22 November 1882. Theology studies and ordination followed. His first pastoral assignment was to Gucheng, and then transferred in 1897 to Jingzhou where he found the Boxers strong in this section. He feared how he might protect three to 4,000 people when he knew that he would not have adequate protection either from the French or

Denn,[29] together with 2,000 Christians were killed at Zhujiahe. This happened when the Imperial Army was on its way to Beijing together with the Boxers. They 'all hated the Christians'. About 2,500 men bombarded Zhujiahe on 18 July. The Jesuit residence at Xianxian was destroyed, as was much of the mission. Great misery followed the deaths or apostasy of several thousands of Christian refugees. In July, the mission lost 50,000 Christians. Of this number, about 30,000 had their houses destroyed and their goods pillaged.

On 8 August, six Jesuits in the Daming section were reported dead, but were later found alive, but 'stripped of everything'. The residence and church at Daming was destroyed, with 20 killed and 100 wounded. Many Christians believed that the presence of European soldiers was their only hope.[30]

In October, the arrival of French troops in Xianxian was welcomed, and in December, thirty government soldiers appeared to defend the mission. The mandarins were supportive out of fear of the European soldiers. The question of indemnities was discussed, as the residence was a mass of rubble. About a dozen Christians were killed on the eve of Christmas and on Christmas day. After the distribution of food, the bandits arrived, killed the peasants and took the food.

---

from the mandarins. With his Christians, he suffered during times of flood and famine, as well as sickness. He worked hard in negotiations with the Chinese authorities, which required generosity and humility. Frequently speaking about his desire to be a martyr, his wish was accepted on 20 July 1900. He was only aged 43 years. The wider district of Hokien from 1890 had 20,000 Christians, 240 parishes and nine assistant priests. Cf. *Chine et Ceylon*, 8 (1901); Clark, op. cit., 99–102.

29. **Paul Denn** was born in Lille on 1 April 1847, one of five children. He was recognised as a strong-willed youth, but also pious, being an altar boy in his parish and helping with the Association of the Holy Children. He joined the Society of Jesus on 6 July 1872, aged 25 years, and only a few weeks later was sent to China. On 1 November, he was at Zhangjiazhuang to prepare for the priesthood, and was ordained on 17 December 1880. His first assignment was to the small rural community of Fanjiageda for three years, before his appointment as rector of the school at Zhangjiazhuang. In 1897, he was reassigned to the parish at Gucheng village where Mangin joined him. Early 1900 he helped Mangin fortify the village of Zhujiahe, and it was here that he died with Mangin on 20 July 1900. For a longer description of the battle against the Boxers at Zhujiahe, see Clark, ut supra, 102–10.

30. Letter Eugene Bosch, Tianjin, 31 August 1900; Letter Maquet, Zhaojiazhuang, 8 September 1900, *Chine et Ceylon*, 5 (1900–1).

About 5–6,000 died, many confessing their faith. Some Christians verbally apostatised to save their lives, but returned later, admitting their fault and seeking forgiveness.[31]

In October, a European force started clearing out the Boxers from Tianjin, while 3,000 German troops, together with the Japanese, cleared the Imperial Canal. The Boxers fled before them. It was estimated by Japiot that 8,000 Christians had been killed in the Zhili vicariate.[32]

Other reports in October mentioned that drought added to the burden of the people. Many moved inland with very few possessions. Almost all the Christian villages in the south of the mission had been destroyed. The missionaries were powerless to help the people as they had nothing themselves. Many continued to die from depravations. Bandits still roamed the countryside, so European missionaries feared to move around, but the Chinese priests were better able to do this. During this time, nineteen missionaries, 13 French and six Chinese, served the mission.[33] By 1901, with pressure from the French troops, French missionaries were slowly returning to some districts, but the Boxers were still killing Christians and missionaries. Famine had increased attacks from armed groups.[34] One missionary was angry that some Christians had stolen some food because they were hungry. He claimed that they were not excused, as 'hunger did not justify the means'![35] Such strict interpretation of Catholic moral theology was not common.

The Boxer rebellion resulted in serious losses in the mission. The number of Christians declined from 50,575 to 45,422; the churches reduced from 674 to 58; priests from 55 to 48; schools from 221 to 49; students from 4,078 to 950; pharmacies from 88 to zero; and orphanages eight to three. However, 5,164 catechumens and 447 catechists, as well as 285 'holy women' remained.[36]

31. Paul Reimsbach to Amblard, Xianxian, 11 October 1900; Maquet, Zhangjiazhuang, 27 December 1900, in *Lettres de Jersey,* XIX/2 (1900).
32. Bonnet, ut supra, 1900.
33. Letter of Victor Lomüller to his mother, Zhangjiazhuang, 25 October, 1900; Augustine Finck, Zhaojiazhuang, 29 October 1900, *Chine et Ceylon,* ut supra.
34. Letter from Henri Maquet, April 1901, *Chine et Ceylon,* March 1901.
35. Letter, 20–26 August 1900, *Chine et Ceylon,* ibid., 307.
36. State of the mission in 1900, *Chine et Ceylon,* ibid.

Effect of the rebellion on the Zhili mission

In reflecting upon the effects of the war, Albert Wetterwald believed that the Chinese learned very little from the experience. The taking of Beijing was not a mortal blow to the regime, and subsequent peace talks were only in order to gain time. Prince Duan, discovered in Mongolia, tried to raise a resistant force among the Mongols, and in March they attacked Christian communities in Mongolia. Jesuit superiors went to Tianjin and Beijing to see the occupying authorities, especially General Émile Jean François Régis Voyron (1838–1921) and Marshal Alfred de Waldersée (1832–1904), the latter taking up residence in the palace of the empress, as allied commander. The imperial palace had not been touched, and was guarded by the Japanese and Americans: special permission was required to visit. The eunuchs continued to care for the place, while several concubines had returned, but their residence was closed. The French troops returned to Europe, while 'the colonials' alone remained and began the work of reconstruction. Wetterwald reflected about the aftermath of the war on China, and how the missionaries would continue their evangelisation. He suggested that if China was to revive, she needed more emphasis on European sciences. If not, the end of the imperial dynasty was inevitable. Missionaries would continue their work as before once peace was assured. Priests, especially the Chinese, had already begun to return to their districts.[37]

From Xianxian, Celestin Cézard reported that the village suffered less than Daming, because of its 'old strong Christians', who were able to defend themselves with arms. The new Christians to the south, not as numerous or undistinguishable from the non-Christians, were not able to resist. Boxers did not annihilate them, but were content to fleece them and demolish their churches or chapels. In the north of the mission, the persecution was more violent, with massacres of Christians. In the centre of the mission, persecution was milder and less violent, consisting mainly of the pillage of churches and rich Christians. Missionaries were returning to their regions, even to Wuxi, where Rémi Isoré and Modest Andlauer had been murdered. Their bodies had been buried by order of the mandarin in the same village behind a pagoda during the night, but were later transferred

---

37. Wetterwald to his mother, Fan-jia-ka-ta, 14 April 1901, in *Lettres de Jersey*, ut supra, 90–1.

to the cemetery in Xianxian. Non-Christian sources said that the two priests had been killed while kneeling before the altar in the church by blows from lances. Mention was also made of the deaths of Jesuits Ignatius Mangin and Paul Denn who were killed in the midst of their Christians, and their bodies left for three months, because no Christian dared visit the place of massacre. It was difficult to find their bones among the three to four thousand bodies. A monument was erected in memory of these victims once peace was restored. Foreign troops left the region.

In Beijing, the emperor was once again proved impotent. The government was still in the hands of the empress and her favourite, Rong-lu; the two of them were the principal authors of the revolution that began three years previously with the condemnation of the reformists. Surprisingly, despite the devastating efforts of the war, Cézard believed that the great flood had more terrible effects on the local people than the religious persecution, because it desolated the region from Daming to Guangping, and resulted in famine and three years of drought. He prayed for an end to the calamities and for the restoration of peace. The mandarins, with some knowledge of the local situation, remained loyal to the imperial court. They were superficially polite to the missionaries, but showed inertia in assisting the Christians. If the defeat of the Europeans did not occur, the mandarins hoped at least that the popular movements might strengthen in their favour. Prayers were asked for the missionaries and for 'our poor Christians'.[38]

Wetterwald continued this narrative of misery among the Christians in south-east Zhili, caused by the war and the drought of the previous two years. Christians had been stripped of their belongings and were dying of hunger. The mandarins compensated those Christians, who were likely to recover, but at Weixian, Qing-he, and at Qinzhou, after many months of discussions and promises, nothing has been granted, so the distress was really upsetting. Chinese diplomats were good at conning the Europeans.

In describing the aftermath of the war, many details emerged of its effects in the Christian communities. Wetterwald wrote later with pride about a young man recently baptised who had been pressurised to apostatise, but he energetically refused, so they tortured him to

---

38. Cézard to Godefroy, Xianxian, 30 April 1901, in *Lettres de Jersey,* up supra, 91–3.

death. This was one example of a new Christian who converted by conviction, and not simply for the benefits of connection with the missionaries and Europeans. Wetterwald told similar stories of other deaths and destruction, while at Wuxi, the scene revered because of the deaths of Isoré and Andlauer, nothing remained. These stories of death and fidelity to the Christian faith were powerful testimonies to the importance of religion to the local non-Christians, and even to Protestant Chinese. The future was hard to predict; the foreign troops had retired from the interior, while the Chinese forces remained before Tong-fou-xiang. The empress was annoyed that the allies had not evacuated Beijing. Wetterwald hoped that in the future the Europeans would be greater respected, but the missions would probably suffer bad days ahead. He, too, asked for prayers, to be saved 'from the mouth of the dragon'.[39]

The violent death of fellow Jesuits was recorded with much detail, expressing sadness, but proclaiming them martyrs of the faith, which should be the cause of joy because they suffered the same fate as their leader, Jesus of Nazareth. The massacre of Mangin and Denn, as well as two to 3,000 Christians at Zhujiahe, was another tragedy. The bandits and regular troops marched on the Jesuit residence in the compound, and the massacre began. The residence was destroyed, the mission ruined: a scene of misery, death or apostasy of several thousand Christian refugees. Praise was given for those Christians who remained faithful to their new beliefs.[40]

Mission reconstruction

Around Daming, by 1901, after two years of drought, the Chinese were beginning to produce some grain and cloth, which generated money. Many had been forced to sell their houses at low prices, so poverty was everywhere. To avoid death through hunger, many families sold their daughters or young wives. As many as 15,000 Christians were in this situation.

---

39. Wetterwald to Leurent, Weits'ounn, 18 May 1901; and Wetterwald to a priest of Champagne, Zhang-jia-zhuang, 18 July 1901, in *Lettres de Jersey*, ut supra, 93–5.
40. Reimsbach to Amblard, Xianxian, 11 October 1900, *Lettres de Jersey*, ut supra. Further letters from Jesuits Désiré Mignan, Pierre Colvez, Pierre Lémour and Léopold Gain describing destruction and turmoil in their regions are to be found in Boucher, op cit. (1899–1901): 8–17.

At this time, the Christians were guarded by European troops. In the south, around Daming and Guangping, local bandits were still killing Christians, who continued to suffer from famine and misery. Brigands came at night, pillaged, murdered, and took children. The missionaries had no money to support the needy. Moreover, roadways were infested with robbers who took whatever they wanted, especially money. Even children were sold by weight for favours. At Jiu-zhou, 30 Christian girls were sold to non-Christians.

It had been a very cold winter as well, and deaths were common. At Shanxi, it was reported that the Chinese were eating human flesh. Meanwhile, the mandarins were demanding higher taxes, which the people could not pay. This meant that the Chinese government found it difficult to pay the indemnities required after the 1900 rebellion.

By April 1901, with the presence of foreign troops, some degree of calm returned to the north of the mission, after violence and extreme persecution against the Christians. There was less persecution and violence in the central districts, while in the south, as the number of new Christians was indistinguishable from the non-Christians, they were not killed, but rather ransomed. Churches and chapels were destroyed.

As the year progressed, some churches and residences were restored, as at Jiu-zhou and Guangping, while the Jesuits opened a noviciate with five scholastics and three brothers, and Vanchon as director.

To end the year, on 8 December, Henri Maquet (1843–1919) was consecrated bishop in the cathedral at Tong-ka-fou by Bishop Paris.[41]

Peace was gradually re-emerging in parts of the mission by the end of 1901. After only a month in the mission, Paul Jubaru reflected that the English were more influential than the French in China, but the latter were the 'only ones who take evangelisation seriously'. While the countryside and much of the mission stations were in ruin, the European quarters were being re-built.[42]

41. Paul Bornet, SJ, *Histoire de 100 ans de la mission et du diocèse de Sienhsien (Hopei), 1901–1949,* letters from Neveux, Daming, 6 January; Maquet, 13 January, 20 January; Albert Wetterwald, 29 January; Seneschal, 27 April; Lomuller, 30 April; Maquet, 18 August, Japiot, 26 August 1901.
42. Paul Jubaru, Tianjin, 6 December 1901, *Chine et Ceylon,* 19 (1902).

The episcopal years of Bishop Henri Maquet (1902–1917)

Mission challenges continued into 1902 with an outbreak of cholera in July. Four Jesuits died that year: one from cholera, and one from exhaustion, but six new Jesuit missionaries had arrived in the mission in April, which raised spirits during a time of depression resulting from death and destruction. Some reconstruction of buildings took place: nine churches and 45 chapels, as well as 12 oratories that included schools and presbyteries.

The issue of which language to teach in the schools of the mission was again discussed. The French became anxious when they heard that Yuan Shi kai wanted English taught in his prefecture. But they were realistic in admitting that teaching the English language was important for the future economic growth of China. However, in the sole surviving schools at Daming, Paul Reimsbach continued to teach French to the non-Christians. He believed that by doing so he was 'enhancing the influence of France'.[43] The missionaries were slow learners. The attachment to France still dominated missionary practice.

Returning to Kaizhou, in the Daming region, in May 1902, Emile Japiot saw material ruin everywhere, but found the Christians strong and resilient. They flocked to see him, assuring him that they had kept the faith. However, they were upset about the indemnities the government had imposed upon them to restore the Christian missions. There was general resistance to these taxes and the Chinese militia had to intervene. On 3 March, regular Chinese soldiers fought against a group of 2,000 rebels. They were dispersed, but lost 800 men in the fighting. Two villages were completely burnt. There was another revolt at Daming because of the taxes, and the missionaries were seen to be the reason for them. Japiot hoped that the mandarins could contain the riots and work to localise them.[44] The missionaries did not appear to think that the new taxes on the peasants were too much for them, considering all that they had already suffered.

Wetterwald noted that the remnants of the Boxers were still attacking Christian communities at Kiom-chai and elsewhere. A group known as the *toan* threatened the priests in Weixian, especially

---

43. Bornet, ut supra, 19–31.
44. Letter of Japiot, K'ai-tcheou, 24 May 1902, in *Lettres de Jersey,* XXI/2 (August-September 1902).

at Zhangjiazhuang, the community of Victor Lomüller.[45] The Christians turned to him for help. On the way, he was attached at Sizhuang and killed with his catechist and his driver on 26 April 1902, and their heads were attached to the south gate of Jianzhou. The missionaries had been warned not to move around without an armed escort of Chinese soldiers, but Lomüller ignored the escort. This event put fear into the Jesuits at Weixian, seeing him as a victim of the large indemnity required of the Chinese. The French minister was besieged with letters for support; so he sent his envoy to investigate the case. Yuan-Shi-kai was also supportive, but recriminations and negotiations over indemnities were lengthy.

The Boxers and allies were finally defeated, with 500 killed by the Chinese soldiers on May 1902, at Sizhuang. The rebel leader Jing-ting-pin and his 16-year-old son were finally beheaded.[46]

As peace was gradually restored to the mission by 1903, the number of catechumens and conversions increased. Throughout the mission there were 1,700 new catechumens in 35 communities and four new Christian villages. The new catechumens were not rich, but were free from financial concerns. Zhangjiazhuang boasted that they had 47 martyrs during 1900, which included the two Jesuits, Isoré and Denn. It was a strong belief among the missionaries that persecution and martyrs led to the increase of Christians. Many of the 72 seminarians in 1904 were the sons of martyrs. While 5,000 Christians died during the persecution, 6,682 new Christians replaced them. This increase was seen as 'the grace of God'. As the Chinese schools also flourished, and the rebuilding of churches continued, the missionaries expressed 'joy and confidence' in their work.

Henri Viot, recently arrived in China in 1902, was very quick to judge the non-Christians. He thought that underlying an external 'bonhomie', there was 'nothing solid, nothing generous, no noble or serious idea', whereas the virtues of 'honour, distinction, politeness, order, and taste, even *proprieté*' came from the faith of the European missionaries.[47] Viot had much to learn from the Chinese.

---

45. **Lomüller** had worked in China for 13 years. He had a cold temperament, but was very energetic and was only 50 years old when he died.
46. Albert Wetterwald's journal, *Chine et Ceylon*, no. 10, September 1902; Becker to Leurent, 1 May 1902, in *Lettres de Jersey*, XXI/2 (August-September 1902).
47. Viot, Daming, 22 November 1903, *Chine et Ceylon*, 1904.

Reflections upon the work of the Protestants continued. Elias Hopsomer, who had also only arrived in 1902, observed that the Protestants had a high standard of living, and recruited five to six times the number of catechists than the Catholics.[48]

In a lengthy letter on the same subject by Philippe Leurent, also only recently arrived in China, he wrote about the Protestant pastors. English and American Protestants were in different prefectures in Zhili. In Daming, they had recently developed a large area. They also had large establishments in other major cities. The Boxers had destroyed many of these buildings, but with the help of indemnities, many had been rebuilt, some better than they were previously. Besides a church at Siao-tchang, they had a large school, a catechumenate, as well as a hospital with an English doctor who spoke excellent Chinese and gave his services free. This hospital was held in high regard.

In the eyes of some mandarins, Catholicism was seen as the religion of France, while Protestantism was the religion of the English. As it was convenient to be on good terms with both countries, the local people had good relations with both the Catholic missionaries and the Protestant pastors. The pastors had little contact with the Chinese, simply conducting services, and then left. They did not have meals with the Chinese, as they had family obligations and recreated with them. The Chinese did not approve of this, as their custom forbade spouses to go outdoors together. The Chinese Protestant catechists worked like the Salvation Army. They set themselves up in the market places and preached the doctrine in the open air, where they freely distributed religious books.

What were the fruits of this missionary method? There was no particular answer, but it was observed that it was easier for the Chinese to become a Protestant than to become a Catholic. Some did so just to escape justice or creditors. Laurent reflected that he was sad when non-Christians attacked Catholics because they were Europeans, as all they wanted to do was to 'teach the Chinese to be good patriots while professing Christianity'. Many Chinese did not distinguish between Catholics and Protestants. This was seen as an obstacle to the spread 'of the true faith'.

Leurent further reflected on the non-Christians in Xianxian, where they had few pagodas. Where he was stationed a Kaizhou,

---

48. Bornet, ut supra, 44–73.

they had 'magnificent pagodas'. They were not places of prayer, as in Christian churches, but rather meeting places where men gathered 'to smoke the pipe, take in the cool air, sit under the trees and discuss their affairs'. They provided shelter for beggars at night, sharing space with thieves and their loot. Non-Christians only went to the pagodas on determined days, such as to perform funeral rites. Some pagodas were the focus of pilgrimages for merchants of the region. On these days, the guardian of the pagoda would make a fortune. On one very hot day in summer, a devout lady spent the day fanning the statue of Buddha! Ordinary devotions consisted of burning sticks of incense in order to obtain good fortune, offering money and making prostrations before the statues of demons.

In his district, Leurent was sad that among the million non-Christians he was unknown, and even seen as an enemy. However, since the Boxer rebellion, the Catholic religion had seen resurgence. When Christians encouraged non-Christians to embrace Christianity, many replied that while they admired Christianity, they were 'too poor to embrace it'. They could not rest on Sundays or find time for prayers as they must work. There was also 'the practice of certain commandments' that they could not accept. In summary, Laurent believed that the main obstacles to conversion were 'indifference and a superstitious cult'.

Around Xiaochang, he had 250 catechumens and, in six months, 100 adults were baptised, which were the work of catechists. Those preparing for Baptism learned prayers by heart, and were then given an explanation of the texts. He praised his catechists for being 'good, generous and poor'. They read his sermon during Mass. He also had 15 schools for boys and 18 schools for girls, as well as two boarding schools.[49] It was impressive that these European missionaries were so zealous and successful, even when their language skills were poor or non-existent. The catechists were essential for conversions and mission expansion.

The question of who had control over the mission schools became an issue in 1906. The government wanted official recognition of all schools. The missionaries were uncomfortable with this decree. Jubaru believed that it would not be good for the mission schools, as

---

49. Leurent, 'Pagans and Protestants, Ki-tcheou', in *Lettres de Jersey*, XXIV, no. unique (1905): 174 ff.

students would have to submit to official government exams. Bishop Maquet was less concerned, as he believed that the government was trying to Europeanise the schools with a scientific and literary curriculum, and so the mission must follow this lead or be left behind. Even the seminary curriculum needed updating. On 7 February 1907, Becker announced that the government refused to accredit schools held by foreigners within China, but despite that, the mission schools would continue to teach medicine, the arts and trades.

Drought and famine continued into 1908, followed by flood that led to cholera in 1910. With the end of the monarchy and establishment of the republic at the end of January 1912, many Protestant missionaries left China, but the Catholics stayed at their posts. Foreign troops moved into Beijing and Tianjin. The famine in 1913 was considered worse than the disasters resulting from the Boxers. With the declaration of World War on 4 August 1914, three Jesuits left China with French forces returning to Europe to fight for France. On 30 July 1917, Henri Lécroart was appointed coadjutor bishop to Maquet, whose health was declining. Maquet finally died on 23 December 1919, aged 76 years.

Bishop Henri Lécroart years (1918–1926)

Floods came again from the end of July 1917 into 1918. The worst effects were felt in Daming, which led to many beggars. The missionaries responded to this calamity by supplying soup daily to about 200 people.

On 2 February 1918, Lécroart was consecrated bishop of the vicariate of S.E Zhili, in a grand ceremony, which impressed the Chinese. The name of this vicariate was changed by decree from *Propaganda* on 3 December 1924 to the vicariate of Xianxian. Charles Héraulle was the earlier Jesuit regional superior, replaced by John-Baptist Debeauvais on 6 July 1921.

During the years 1914–18, the number of missionaries and catechists decreased. On 28 April 1918, Emil Becker died aged 82. He had been a missionary in China since 1878, and Jesuit superior of the Zhili mission from 1884–94, and again between 1901–9. Between those years, he was in charge of the Hokien section of the mission. He was described as 'a liberal, practical, profoundly religious, full of courage and zeal, and a man of the Institute'. During his missionary life, the number of Chinese secular priests increased from 13 to 25, with increases in the number of Christians from 89,046 to 99,462, and the number of churches and chapels from 421 to 484.

In 1919, Bishop Guébriant from Guangzhou made an apostolic visitation of the mission, and it was reported that he seemed happy with what he saw. He offered the mission the island of Sancian, where St Francis Xavier had died, which had 5,000 Christians, and suggested that the mission might set up a university at Tianjin and annex the city to the mission. As a result, three Jesuits went to Tianjin and set up a residence. They were Edward Desreumaux, Aloysius Duquesne, the mission bursar, and Emil Licent, the scientist and explorer.

As a result of further drought and famine in August 1920, animals were being killed for food, and people emigrated from the country-side to Tianjin. Brigandage followed this usual cycle of events. But with welcome rain in September, seeding occurred, and the famine ended by June 1921. During the time of famine, the mission schools gave each child money for one meal a day, and baptised many dying non-Christian babies. They cared for Christian girls who were aban-doned or sold or married to non-Christians. Care was also given to the aged and deserted women with children, with the help of the Red Cross. Some missionaries believed that worse than the famine was the presence of brigands and soldiers, but others thought the oppo-site. Both were disastrous for the mission. The soldiers that ravaged the countryside had not been paid, and they sought compensation from the people. This was seen especially in Hokien.

During 1920, mention was made in a letter about the civil war in China between the northerners, who were pro-Japanese and opposed to the government, and the southern nationals, that included the gov-ernor of Zhili, who was anti-Japanese. The missionaries thought that another war was approaching.

On 9 December 1920, Bishop de Vienne gave Lécroart permis-sion without conditions to establish a college in Tianjin. It was inau-gurated on 4 December 1921, as the 'Hautes Etudes Industrielle & Commerciales', or the 'Institute of the Sacred Heart', with Paul Jubaru as the superior.[50] Jubaru believed that this new venture was important to counteract the educational work of the Protestants in Tianjin. He was concerned that Protestant influence was spreading throughout

---

50. Bornet, ut supra, 1918–21.

China. The new school was to be built on seven hectares of land that the mission had bought, and the design would resemble the Jesuit colleges in France. Students would live together in rooms with five beds and study desks.[51] By early 1923, there were 200 students enrolled. There was need for teachers of mathematics, physics and chemistry.[52]

Mission issues at this time included the request for more European missionaries. Apart from five new men, there had not been any sent from Europe from the end of 1913 until 1920, when six were sent. The effect of the Great War on the French provinces was considerable, as many French Jesuits had been called up to fight for France.[53] Eight new European Jesuits arrived from 1920–1, which helped, but was still considered insufficient to meet the needs of the mission. Many priests were elderly and some were sick, while there were only five students in the seminary.[54] The possibility was raised about inviting Jesuits from other provinces to come to China, such as the Canadians, the Austrians and the Hungarians. Moreover, it was felt that insufficient work was done to attract Chinese to the priesthood.[55]

The schools in the mission were thought to perform well, especially the one in Daming under Paul Jung. Chinese Jesuit scholastics were reported to be good at teaching catechumens.[56]

Missionary concerns about the presence of Cotta and Lebbe in Tianjin were ongoing. The French legation in China had been concerned about their presence since 1917, when, considering them 'great menaces', they had asked that they be expelled from China as they were undermining the French protectorate. Lebbe's superiors agreed and Lebbe left for Shanghai on 26 March 1917.[57]

Then Cotta, considered an Egyptian, was charged with sympathising with the enemy, placed in police custody and would probably be expelled. However, this was an unjust accusation. In fact, he had been helping flood victims and was much appreciated by the Chinese. Furthermore, Cotta was identified as an Austrian, and therefore consid-

---

51. Jubaru, Tianjin, to General, 21 January 1922. ARSI.
52. Debeauvais, Xianxian, to General, 3 March 1923. ARSI.
53. Cézard to General, Xianxian, 3 January 1921. ARSI.
54. Mission consultor to General, Xianxian, 2 January 1922. ARSI.
55. Debeauvais, regional superior, Zhili, to General, 1 January 1922. ARSI.
56. Leurent, Daming to General, 13 January 1921; Héraulle, Daming, to General, 1 February 1921. ARSI.
57. Memo, the affair Lebbe and Cotta, 1917. DAC.

ered an enemy of the French. Cotta himself claimed to be an Egyptian by race, but an Austrian by nationality.[58] It was highly possible that the French legation was primarily responsible for the expatriation of Cotta.

A few years later, in 1922, it was reported that *Propaganda* advised de Vienne that Lebbe would return to Tianjin, because both *Propaganda* and Lebbe wanted more Chinese clergy in the missions. Paul Jung believed that would be bad for Tianjin, for the vicariates of the north and for the whole of China. He knew that Lebbe was popular with the Chinese clergy and against the European missionaries. There had been calm in Tianjin since Lebbe departed.[59]

The Jesuit superior, Debeauvais, was upset about what he perceived as the calumnies of Lebbe against the Jesuit mission in Shanghai. Lebbe wanted to publish in his Chinese periodical a private letter of the Jesuit superior general to the mission of Shanghai. Debeauvais was pleased when his own congregation censured Lebbe for his indiscretion.[60]

Over the next few years, missionaries were concerned about the continuing lack of missionaries required for the work, especially teaching priests. Many priests were elderly or tired. This meant that the more energetic work among the non-Christians was curtailed. Some believed that more emphasis should be placed on recruiting more Chinese secular priests rather than fostering Chinese Jesuits, as even Bishop Paris had been doubtful if the Chinese were really 'apt' candidates for the Society of Jesus. However, there were other Jesuits who disagreed with this attitude, and believed that many Chinese were suitable potential Jesuits.[61] It appeared that the Jesuits from the French Province of Champagne were more open to accepting Chinese priests into administrative positions of leadership than those from the Province of France.

Bandits were still active in the area around Daming. Despite this, missionaries were rewarded with an increase in the number of converts and catechists, but there were insufficient funds to pay the latter.[62]

58. Letter, Director General of Flood Relief and Conservation, Beijing, to French Minister, Beijing, 20 February 1919; telegram, Consul, Tianjin, to French Minister, Beijing, 24 February 1919. DAC.
59. Jung, Daming, to General, 15 January 1922. ARSI.
60. Debeauvais, Xianxian, to General, 3 March 1923. ARSI.
61. D'Herbigny, Hokien, to General, January 1923; Mertens, Xianxian, to General, 28 January 1923. ARSI.
62. Gaudissart, Daming, to General, 16 January 1923. ARSI.

Disagreements and conflict between the missionaries and the Chinese were numerous. One such incident occurred in 1923 when four Chinese from Xianxian wrote to the apostolic delegate complaining that they had been unjustly accused by a domestic of the Jesuit Raphael Gaudissart in Daming of stealing 18 chalices. They reported that they had been arrested without investigation, with the mandarin accepting the word of the priest, and were imprisoned and tortured. Their reputation and that of their families was ruined. They asked if this was 'the will of the Holy Father who sent priests to China'. Was this 'the way to propagate the doctrine of Providence among non-Christian Chinese'? They asked for help from the delegate to redress this injustice.[63] This complaint went to *Propaganda* for settlement. Lécroart later reported to the delegate that the congregation rejected the accusation against Gaudissart.[64]

Mertens, a lecturer in philosophy at the seminary in Xianxian, expressed anxiety to the superior general that 'atheistic, evolutionist and materialistic books from the West' were flooding China. To counterbalance this, he suggested that Jesuits translate French books on apologetics into Chinese. At present, there was no one opposing these philosophies that were being published from the Commercial Press of Shanghai and the National University of Beijing.

He also mentioned that both the bishop and Chinese Christians enjoyed the celebration of solemn High Masses. The Chinese were impressed by the 'external manifestations of grandeur'. But, unfortunately, a Chinese priest rarely celebrated these Masses, much to the disappointment of the Chinese Christians. These ceremonies reinforced the idea among many Chinese that Catholicism was 'the religion of the stranger'. Chinese priests needed to be seen as having equal status to the European.[65]

The mission bursar, Stephen Jacquart, shared with Rome the frightening statistics about the current ages of the missionaries with an eye to the future. Of the 60 priests in the mission, six were over 70; 18 were between 60–70; 18 between 50–60; 13 between 40–50, and only five under 40.[66] Insufficient missionaries to realise mission dreams was a constant complaint.

---

63. Letter of four Chinese, Xianxian, to Apostolic Delegate, 12 March 1923. ASV.
64. Lécroart to Apostolic Delegate, Xianxian, 13 August 1923. ASV.
65. Mertens, Xianxian, to General, 22 December 1923. ARSI.
66. Jacquart, Tianjin, to Boynes, French Assistant, 11 February 1924.

Plenary Council of China, 1924

Previous mention has been made about the significance of this Council for the mission in the account of the Jiangnan mission, but the Jesuit superior of the Zhili mission, Debeauvais, gave his reflections on the Synod. He thought that there were too many people present, but appreciated the display of unity and charity among the delegates. The main thrust of the council related to common works rather than to individual vicariates, which may have been expected. The final document was 'a little utopian', detailing a Chinese 'canon law' for everyone, which was 'illusory and contradictory'. Debeauvais rightly commented that the Catholic missions were in a constant state of flux and could not be directed by rigid formulas. The council wanted all missions to conform to a universal canon law, whereas in reality, all were in different stages of development. Moreover, it was too simplistic to view China as a country like France, as China was very large and diverse geographically and culturally. China was not politically unified. Even when the Chinese wanted unity, they discovered many differences and opposing ideologies. They were only united in 'hating the foreigner' and 'boycotting his goods'. Priests from the south disagreed with priests from the north of the country, yet the council wanted unity and control. Each vicariate believed that it was in step with the greater China, but they were not even in contact with one another to truly assess this belief.

In discussions about the regional seminaries, the apostolic delegate wanted the larger seminaries to share with smaller vicariates. All wanted to have their noviciate in China, except for the Scheut Fathers, who sent their novices to Belgium. It had been well established that many lay Chinese students who went to Europe lost more than they gained. It was similar with ecclesiastical students; Rome was not a good place for them, as they could not cope with the intellectual rigour of the seminaries. If some vicariates were small, and yet wanted to establish seminaries, some help might be given to them in terms of lecturers and students from other missions. It was accepted that the more flourishing seminaries were those in the vicariates with greater numbers, such as Shanghai with 172 priests and 202,000 Christians or in Xianxian with 80 priests and 118,000 Christians.

There was a call for a united protest against the papal encyclical, *Maximum Illud*, of 1919. There were expressions of 'depression, discouragement and decreasing confidence in superiors among foreign missionaries'. The belief was expressed that the Church was trying to govern the vicariates too theoretically (*a priori*), and from a distance, without understanding the local situation. Moreover, the encyclical had aroused the xenophobia of the Chinese priests, and among those who would want to see the end of the foreign missionaries. This was an open disagreement with the pope on his evaluation of the state of the Church in China and its vision.

Surprisingly, some delegates wanted another interpretation of the Chinese rites. They believed that times had changed significantly since the establishment of the Chinese republic. The apostolic delegate said that he was open to such a discussion, but seemed to be unaware of the full implications of any change. The Chinese priests were generally in favour of a revision, while Chinese lay Christians formed a group to discuss the question with the delegate in Beijing. Debeauvais was in favour of a revision, but believed that the discussions would be complex.

The apostolic delegate wanted a Chinese secretary in Beijing. If this occurred, some expressed the idea that as the Chinese were generally known to be indiscrete, many vicars apostolic would not send confidential material to the delegate, but would send such documents directly to *Propaganda*. This comment highlighted another example of cross-cultural mistrust among missionaries.

Education in the schools received a strong endorsement from the synod delegates, but all lacked money for teachers. Schools were the main means of Christian propaganda, 'the sole efficacious means of genuine Christian formation for those from paganism'. The Marist brothers were currently expanding their schools, but they were not seen as good enough teachers for the 'children of the upper classes'.

Finally, *Propaganda* was keen to initiate an institute of higher learning in Beijing, just as it had approved the Jesuit institute in Tianjin. The Benedictines were invited to open a school of 'arts and trade' in Beijing. The council understood that it would be a Catholic university with chairs in philosophy, theology and canon law. Debeauvais urged the Jesuits in Tianjin to collaborate with this new university and to provide help as required.[67]

---

67. Debeauvais, Some Notes on the Plenary Council of China, Shanghai, May-June 1924, 6 September 1924. ARSI.

The reactions to this Synod showed that the missionaries tried to relate the ideals of the Synod to the reality in the various regions. Debeauvais was realistic in his interpretation of the decrees as he saw appropriate for his mission. All the foreign missionaries at the Synod expressed the tension they experienced in balancing Roman decrees with their assessment of local needs. They frequently claimed that Rome did not realistically understand the local situation and only listened to a vocal, marginal group of missionaries who were out of touch with reality. This expressed the perennial problem of how to accept the outsider telling the insider how to act. The other problem for the missionaries was how to apply the decrees of the Synod in the local region. While strongly endorsing the desire for unity and collaboration, as well as recognising common challenges, they also accepted the need for regional diversity. Some suggestion about accommodation to the local milieu was encouraging.

Internal issues

There were always challenges within the Jesuit communities, whether it concerned the governing ability of the local superior, such as Paul Wonner as rector of the college in Xianxian in 1926, who was considered by his superior as 'excessively prudent, no risk taking nor initiatives', or problems relating to the Jesuit brothers. Superiors regularly considered the brothers too independent, but in 1926, Debeauvais thought that the European brothers were also 'given to pride, and even in open rebellion'. Some had given scandal and should be sent back to Europe. Control by superiors in community was always paramount in Jesuit government. Individual independence or initiative was not always appreciated among those who were only expected to obey. Initiatives were the prerogative of superiors.

The health of the missionaries was a frequent concern of superiors. One more serious case related to Seraphin Rivat, a science teacher in the Xianxian College, who suffered from depression and had an alcohol problem, but despite efforts to reform his life, he had not sufficiently improved. However, trying to be positive, Debeauvais reported that amid these difficulties, the younger scholastics were progressing well, as were the Christians in the mission.[68]

---

68. Debeauvais, Xianxian, to General, May 1926. ARSI.

Writing to the superior general after only one month in China in 1926, Joseph Subtil expected to experience more discipline in the college in Daming, and noticed clashes between the Chinese and European missionaries. Furthermore, while the Europeans were not 'sufficiently charitable in conversation in recreation', the Chinese told fellow teachers and students about disagreements with the Europeans. Moreover, he thought that the Chinese teachers were 'too close to the students', which resulted in the deterioration in studies and discipline.[69] Distance from students in Jesuits school was always encouraged.

Bishop Lécroart wrote to the vicariate in 1926 about the importance of recruiting priestly vocations. There were many difficulties with the seminarians. Some had to contend with parents who did not wish them to be priests, some were unsuitable or had financial troubles. Many had personal issues with struggles against their vocation. There were also a number who died. Lécroart asked all in the vicariate to value the priesthood, to pray for vocations and to encourage anyone who would be suitable. All should 'water the seed'.[70]

While coming to terms with internal challenges relating to the mission, the missionaries also experienced external disturbances from the movement of regular troops from the south of China to the north, as well as brigands appearing in the east and in Xianxian. French protection was constantly sought against these disruptions.[71] It was ironic that while the Jesuits regularly wrote about believing that God was their only protector, they were not slow to seek help from the powerful French legation, and not only in major crises.

The intellectual apostolate

The development of the intellectual apostolate in whatever region of the world they lived was always important for the Jesuits. The early Jesuits in China were accepted largely for their knowledge of Western science and understanding of the Chinese classics. The Jesuits of this modern period likewise strived to revive that tradition. One

---

69. Subtil, Daming, to General, 25 December 1926. ARSI.
70. Lécroart, Xianxian, Pastoral letter to the faithful of the vicariate on priestly recruitment, 11 October 1926. ASV.
71. French minister, Tianjin, to French consul, Beijing, 18 October 1924; de Vienne, Tianjin, to French consul, Tianjin, 6 January 1926. DAC.

such Jesuit of the Zhili mission was Èmile Licent (1876–1952)[72], who, reflecting on the future of the Catholic Church in China and Mongolia sent long documents to Cardinal van Rossum[73] of *Propaganda Fide*. He advocated 'The School of the Far East', specialising in Sinology, a Catholic university in the north of China as part of the Catholic apostolate among the Mongols, and finally expressed some thoughts on Chinese psychology. He mentioned that he had travelled some 33,000 kilometres around northern China in order to give foundation to his reflections. He was not impressed with Aurora University, saying that it was 'too old to make a difference'. He thought Shanghai was geographically too distant from Beijing and Tianjin to foster the intellectual apostolate. He wanted to develop Catholic intellectual life in the north.

The first document was mainly about China and his hope for a Catholic university in the north. He wrote with respect for those missionaries who had 'sinified' themselves: making themselves 'all things to all men'. These missionaries not only learned the Chinese language, but also about the institutions, philosophy, religions, economy, law, and geography of these ancient peoples. But in order to reach the more highly educated Chinese, they needed to show the Chinese that they knew the country and the character of those they served. Too many missionaries found the study of Chinese, and especially writing and reading in Chinese, difficult. The expansion of Chinese studies was necessary. Even the Chinese priests would benefit from a Chinese institute. The missionaries had mainly given the Chinese 'European science', seen in the considerable influence of the observatory at Xujiahui and the museum in Tianjin. Protestants had already given the lead by establishing a university in Beijing in 1925.

---

72. Émile Licent was a historian of nature. He spent more than 25 years researching in Tianjin, with expeditions across northern and central China with his colleague Pierre Teilhard de Chardin in the late 1920s. When he arrived in Tianjin in 1914, he established a museum, which was one of the earliest of its kind in China. He left China in 1939 and was awarded an honour by the French government for his pioneering scientific work.
73. **Cardinal Willem van Rossum, CSsR**, born 3 September 1854, was the first Dutch cardinal since the Reformation, serving as Prefect of the Congregation of the Faith, 1918–32, having been a member of the Congregation since 1896. He was a former professor of dogmatic theology and a consultor to the Commission for the Codification of Canon Law, 1904. In 1914, he was appointed president of the Pontifical Biblical Commission. He died 30 August 1932, aged 77.

The second report traced the development of his museum in Tianjin, which he had founded in 1914. It did not teach students, but was a centre of scientific research for European and Chinese scientists. Many publications had appeared. The Jesuits had established an industrial and commercial institution, *Hautes Etudes,* in 1923, which had developed well. Currently, there were 95 students, with 35 of these Catholic. Conversions had resulted. There was a good spirit at the institution and it was expected to grow. The French government modestly supported both the museum and the *Hautes Etudes.* In suggesting further for the establishment of a Catholic university, it was hoped that it would receive the support of both the Chinese and French governments. Currently, the Catholic University of Beijing was under the direction of the Benedictines, and also trained Chinese priests. Licent also suggested the creation of an agricultural institute, as the Chinese were essentially farmers. This would encourage evangelisation. Greater collaboration between the university in Beijing and the Jesuit institute in Tianjin would be beneficial.

A further report related to Licent's 12 years of experience and reflection on the 'psychological traits of the Chinese'. He commented on their pride in their ancient civilisation, and their 'docility, unused to self-determination'. The 'old Christians' became Europeanised, and were 'more open, pleasant, charitable, compassionate and gentle', as well as being a 'docile people'. The idea of a 'Chinese nation' was new: the idea of statehood, embryonic. There was a new patriotic spirit among the young Chinese, which was essentially negative: they attacked anything that prevented self-determination. Most Chinese lived in small villages, usually centred on a clan that did not have connection with other clans. The idea of sub-prefectures was mainly for tax purposes, which were very high. Beijing, the political centre of China, had little impact on village life. The people were mainly peasants who were 'tranquil, frugal, patient, hard working, economic, and hospitable', but they had become xenophobic against anyone from outside their clan or region. Licent believed that their attitude toward the foreigner was 'jealous, disenchantment, and coldness'. They were fearful of the Westerner, and aware of their inferiority. Education would help them to overcome this feeling. He experienced the Chinese as 'deceitful; difficult to know him or trust him'. This was especially true of the peasants who had been oppressed and even frequently attacked by bandits: they were naturally mistrustful. However, he thought that Chinese business people were fundamentally honest, but they had no idea of the European concept of a 'just price'. Rates of interest were high. He did not believe that the Chinese were generally interested in the teaching of science: they were 'copyists', like the Japanese, wanting immediate results. Geology was taught in Beijing, but botany and zoology was less valued. Only recently had interest been shown in agriculture and forestry. But this was not the opinion of the young educated Chinese who were very strong on the importance of teaching Western science. When Chinese students who had studied abroad returned to China, many were disenchanted with what they experienced, and this lead to 'fierce nationalism'. They saw their inferiority in relation to the West. Many leaders believed that the Chinese were an 'oppressed people'. Hence, there was the need for the Chinese to engage more in higher learning.

Finally, Licent believed that Bolshevism would not succeed in China, 'as the Chinese were very protective of their property'. They lacked the ability 'to critique anything'. This was a naïve assessment in the light of future events in China. He thought further that generally the Chinese were like all non-Christians – morally weak: they were 'sexually alive and precocious', tending toward 'softness and sensuality'. However, they showed wonderful artistic talent with ceramics, and vases, while their literature and 'former philosophy' was admirable. Education was the best means of enhancing their culture.[74]

While praising those missionaries who had accommodated themselves to the Chinese, he believed that both missionaries and the Chinese still needed to deepen knowledge of China's heritage. Higher learning in Chinese studies and Western scientific knowledge was an important ambition for the missions. Those Jesuits from the Province of Champagne seemed more determined than those from the Province of France to expand institutions of higher learning.

Pierre Teilhard de Chardin (1881–1955)

One significant Jesuit was Pierre Teilhard de Chardin, who, following in the Jesuit scientific tradition, contributed significantly to the promotion of the intellectual apostolate by his scientific research in China from the 1920s. His work, in collaboration with others, opened

---

74. Licent to Cardinal van Rossum, Rome, 8 April 1926. ARSI.

up the importance of China to the West for further geological and paleontological research. Teilhard was a scholar in four fields: science, spirituality, philosophy and theology. He was born on 1 May 1881 in Auvergne, the fourth of eleven children. He was educated by the Jesuits in the college at Mongré, Villefranche-sur-Saône, gaining his baccalaureate in philosophy and mathematics. He entered the Jesuits and the Province of Champagne on 20 March 1899, at Aix-en-province, and began his 13 years training as a Jesuit. These studies were in Jersey and Hastings, while his regency was at the Collège de Saint Famille, in Cairo, from 1905–8, teaching physics and chemistry. He was ordained on 24 August 1911, aged 30. From 1912–14, he worked at the *Museum d'Histoire Naturelle* with Marcellin Boule, a specialist on the Neanderthal Man, who trained Teilhard in research into human palaeontology.

During the Great War, 1914–19, he became a stretcher-bearer in the 8th regiment of the Moroccan infantry and received several awards for bravery, including the *Médaille Militaire* and the *Légion d'Honneur*. During these years, he developed ideas that were later published in a book, *The Making of a Mind*. In 1919, at Jersey, he wrote *The Spiritual Energy of Matter*.

Teilhard's relationship with the Jesuits was such that he almost never worked for a Jesuit institution. He spent most of his Jesuit life outside Jesuit houses. In Beijing, he lived with the Lazarists. Some Jesuits made him welcome, but most ignored or criticised him for not being a traditional, conformist Jesuit. The superior general Ledóchowski was not sympathetic toward him, but Janseens was basically on his side. Some provincials distrusted him; some local superiors were hostile toward him. They allowed him to follow his scientific career, but would not allow him to accept lecturing positions offered to him, nor publish his scientific works and essays. Rome believed that his works were not in conformity with traditional Catholic theology. His friends asked him why he did not leave the Jesuits, but he said that the spiritual, intellectual and cultural life of the Jesuits still drew him.

In Paris, he graduated from the Sorbonne in the natural sciences, geology, botany and zoology, his thesis being on *French Lower Eocene Mammals and their Deposits*. He also lectured at the *Institut Catholique*, teaching palaeontology in 1920. Of particular interest was the dating of rocks by means of fossils in them. He believed in evolution at a time when the Church was opposed to it.

It was then that he discovered China in 1923 with Emile Licent, working with him in his museum in Tianjin. Visiting Paris, he resumed lecturing at the *Institut*, and gave a series of lectures. One paper concerning his meditations on Original Sin, addressed to theologians was misunderstood, and consequently he lost his lectureship and was sent back to China, with the instructions to restrict his thinking to science and not to promote unscientific speculations. He was in China from 1926–46.

During this time, he travelled both within China and overseas. He was based in Tianjin with Licent until 1932, and then in Beijing, living with the Lazarists who had a house near his laboratory. He lived there for nine years. Teilhard made five geological expeditions in China, which enabled him to draw up the first general geological map of China. But he also wrote on spirituality during this time with his famous *The Divine Milieu* and his reflective *Mass on the World*. He did not have faculties for priestly work in China, and his contacts were with the scientific and European community. He had almost no contact with ordinary Chinese people. He researched China's geology, not its culture. He also seemed to accept the opinion of some missionaries that the Chinese were backward because they were an inferior race.

During 1929, he was adviser to the Chinese National Geological Department, and in that capacity supervised the geological aspects of the work and non-human palaeontology in the Zhoukoudian excavations near Beijing. He stayed with Licent in Mongolia for a time, but soon disagreed with him, and they went separate ways. During the year he drafted the beginnings of *The Phenomenon of Man*.

In 1931, Teilhard discovered that the *Sinanthropus*, or *Pekin Man* of Zhoukoudian, closely related to the *Pithecanthropus* of Java, was a *Homo Faber*, one who used fire and stone tools. He also took part in the *Croisière Jaune* expedition through Central Asia with a group of scientists. The group were taken prisoners for several months in Ürümqi, the capital of Xinjiang. The following year, 1932, the Sino-Japanese War broke out.

He was back in Paris again, from 1932–3, depressed that *Le Milieu Divin* was refused the imprimatur and so would not be published. On 1933, the superior general forbade him to accept any teaching position in Paris. In the years that followed, he returned to China, living in the Jesuit residence Chabanel Hall when in Beijing. This increased his depression as his superior forbade him to go out at night, and thought that he was a bad influence on the Jesuit scholastics that also lived in the Hall because of his theories on evolution. He wanted him out of the country. Teilhard continued to join expeditions in southern China, India, Java and Burma in following years.

During the war years, 1939–46, Teilhard was prevented from travelling overseas. In May 1940, Licent's museum was transferred to Beijing into a Geobiological Institute run by Teilhard and Pierre Leroy. Teilhard moved out of Chabanel Hall and away from its superior, and lived with Leroy and another priest in the Institute. In May 1946, he left China for France, never to return. He remained in Paris from 1946–51, where he was elected a member of the French *Académie des sciences* in 1950, to the *Institut de France* in May 1951 and the Linnean Society in London. He had previously, in 1947, been promoted officer of the *Légion d'Honneur*, section Foreign Affairs, for his work in the fields of geology and palaeontology. He suffered a heart attack on 1 June 1947. His final residence was in the USA, living in the Jesuit house in New York from 1952. During this time, he went on expeditions to South Africa and Zimbabwe. His final relationship with the Jesuits was sad, as they largely ignored him. They still tried to place restrictions on his movements. He finally died of a cerebral haemorrhage on Easter Sunday in 1955, at the home of friends. Almost no one attended his funeral.[75]

China was the context of much of Teilhard's seminal writing, including ideas for his two major works, *The Divine Milieu* and *The Phenomenon of Man*. He was not concerned with Chinese culture or mores, nor was he at ease with traditional missionary methods. Yet it was in China that he made his most famous discoveries.

He is remembered as 'one of the three founding fathers of Chinese palaeontology'. When leaving China, he expressed gratitude to the country that had helped him 'to reflect in new ways on humankind's and cosmic destiny'. From the 1990s, Chinese scholars had renewed interest in Teilhard's work, acknowledging his contribution to Chi-

---

75. Cowburn, John, SJ, Pierre Teilhard de Chardin: a Selective Summary of his Life, August 1994; The life of Pierre Teilhard de Chardin, at <http:/www.mnhn.fr/Teilhard/VieE.htm>. Accessed 16 September.

nese geology, and for his 'Mass on the World', which evoked 'the physical relationship that still links humankind to matter and the earth'. Thierry Meynard, a current Jesuit scholar teaching in China, saw Teilhard's influence as 'envisioning the future of humankind beyond national and ethnic barriers and the way such vision was congruent with the United Nations ideals developed at the same time'.[76]

While in China, Teilhard received mixed reception from his Jesuit superiors. But when attached to the *Hautes Etudes* residence in Tianjin in 1934, some Jesuits appreciated his occasional presence, especially for the assistance he gave to Licent in his museum. His absences from the community were regretted, and it was commented upon that he was a good religious who 'always says the Breviary', and regretted not being able to say Mass on his long expeditions.[77]

It is ironic that this brilliant Jesuit scholar, whose ideas were unacceptable to the Church and Society to which he had given his life, should have found China as a fertile land for the development of his scientific and theological investigations. It is one modern example of where China enlightened Western thought.

---

76. Benoit Vermander, 'As China changes, Teilhard de Chardin reappears', in *Global Pulse* (29 October 2014).
77. Charvet, rector Tianjin, to General, 18 January 1935. ARSI.

Chapter 12
The Vicariate of South-East Zhili (Xianxian)
1927–1952

Division of the vicariate

Planning for the future was continually in the minds of Jesuit superiors, and one most important discussion centred on the division of a vicariate into other vicariates when the numbers in the mother vicariate reached the point that the missionaries were no longer able to minister adequately to the large numbers. The initiative in the case of the Jesuit missions usually comes from the vicariate itself, but usually supported by the apostolic delegate and Roman officials, Jesuit or the Vatican.

The vicariate of South-East Zhilli had reached that point when discussions about a division became a priority. Much talk took place on whether to give an independent vicariate to the Chinese clergy. The Jesuits were generally cautious in recommending such a move, but seemed to realise that it would be inevitable that the Chinese would shortly be given an independent vicariate with a Chinese bishop. As might be expected, Jesuits expressed various opinions on the future division of the vicariate. Peter Xavier Mertens, a theology lecturer in the seminary at Xianxian, wrote about the attitude of the Chinese priests in the vicariate. Most of them were from the northern part of the vicariate, with no one from the south. If the Chinese priests were given a vicariate in the south, they would return north to visit families. He advocated that the French keep the south and leave the north to the Chinese, because in the north there were many Christians, who were well instructed and literate. The south was a barren field for Christian conversions, whereas the north was fertile for future growth. The north had no need for European missionaries, and had aspirations of autonomy, whereas the south would be an easier apostolate, where the people were more docile.

An important Jesuit missionary principle in choosing an apostolate was to consider the greater good. Following that principle,
the mission should give the more settled region in the north to the
Chinese, where the increase in Christians was mainly through birth.
Greater opportunities for conversions were in the south. However,
there were objections to this plan. Many Jesuits were attached to their
well-established residence in Xianxian, the centre of many mission
works. The bishop liked the idea of moving to Daming, because of the
grand church there and the pilgrimage to Our Lady of Lourdes at Kaizhou, as well as the opportunity for more conversions. It was a region
that would foster growth in the seminary and the Jesuit noviciate.[1]

The superior of the mission, Debeauvais, wanted the old prefecture in the centre of the region to form the new Chinese vicariate.
The Province of Champagne should keep the remaining regions
north and south with the help of Austrian and Hungarian Jesuits. The
disadvantage would be travelling through another vicariate to reach
the extremities of this vicariate. He was open to various suggestions,
but appeared to want to keep the region to the north centred around
Xianxian for the French, where there were 80,000 Christians.[2]

A detailed description of the vicariate outlined various possibilities
for the division. The length of the vicariate was 400 kilometres, divided
into two sections by a sub-prefecture belonging to the Province of
Shandong. It had a population of nearly eight million, with no large
town throughout the mission. The largest village was Daming in the
south. The Catholic population in the vicariate in 1926 was 130,000,
a pleasing increase from 10,000 in 1857 when the Jesuits took charge.

The vicariate comprised five prefectures, with 36 sub-prefectures.
From north to south, Hokien contained 11 sub-prefectures with
52,000 Catholics; Shenzhou, four sub-prefectures with 5,863 Catholics; Jingxian, six sub-prefectures with 9,416 Catholics; Guangping,
10 sub-prefectures with 36,400 Catholics and Daming, five sub-prefectures with 25,676 Catholics. The division suggested a three-way
division centred on Hokien, Guangping and Daming. There were
currently 28 Chinese secular priests in the vicariate of Xianxian.

Which region was the best for the Chinese clergy? The apostolic
delegate favoured the Guangping region. It was more recently evange-

---

1. Mertens, Xianxian, to General, 7 January 1927. ARSI.
2. Debeauvais, Xianxian, to General, Memo concerning the division of the vicariate
    of Xianxian, 9 August 1927. ARSI.

lised than that of Hokien and was growing rapidly. The Catholics were fervent and the number of catechists numerous. Vocations flourished, especially in the region of Weixian in the north. There were currently 15 Chinese priests working in the area. The advantages of this vicariate were that the Catholic population was growing, and it was situated far distant from the centres of political and nationalist trouble, Beijing and Tianjin, the best centre for the recruitment of secular clergy. Moreover, the secular clergy 'loved this territory' which they wanted to administer entirely themselves without any foreign priests.

The second area was Hokien, with 2,600 catechumens. It was geographically very central being on the train line: Tianjin-Pukow-Nanjing. It contained the nucleus of the 'most ancient Christians', who were very fervent. It also had some very lukewarm Christians and even some apostates: the result of troubles and persecution from 1900. But it also produced the most vocations. The advantage of this vicariate was that it had the greater number of secular priests in their region of origin. But the Chinese priests were considered layback in their ministry, while the European priests were the animators of the works of the vicariate. Being close to Beijing and Tianjin made the Catholic population more restless and more difficult to govern than in other regions. This might be a good region for the Chinese priests to operate.

The third region, all the southern parts of the vicariate of Xianxian, south of Guangping to the Yellow River, would be too far away from their origins for the Chinese clergy. This region had good potential for evangelisation, but the territory would be perhaps too large for the secular clergy.[3]

After a visitation of the vicariate by a visitor, it was suggested that the Daming region should be given to the Hungarian Jesuits because of the presence of Hungarian nuns in Daming. The central region might be given to the secular clergy and the northern region divided between the Austrians and the French. The former should start a school at Nunkong.[4] The Chinese secular clergy were finally given the vicariate of Yungnien, the central region of the vicariate of Xianxian, in 1929, a region of 39,000 Christians with 18 secular priests.

The idea of giving the Daming region to the Hungarian Jesuits grew. It would include seven sub-prefectures that included the major

---

3. Memo concerning the new vicariate-apostolic for the Chinese secular clergy, 1927. ARSI.
4. Extracts from a visitation of the region (Xianxian), May 1927. ARSI.

towns of Daming and Kaizhou. The section had a population of about 1,657,000 people, of whom 27,834 were baptised. There was a 'beautiful cathedral', a hospital, orphanage, dispensary, as well as a school for Catholic children and a French school. Daming should be the centre of the new vicariate, as it already had a large Jesuit residence with chapel attached. Vocations were on the rise in this part of the mission, and the Chinese priests were open to the change. The suggestion was made that in preparation for a hand-over in about seven years, the Hungarian Jesuits already in the mission be given administration of some sections, while the Hungarian province might send some Jesuit brothers each year, as well as a few priests and scholastics. When the number of Hungarians present in the region was considered sufficient, there could be further talk about a Hungarian superior.[5]

In this proposed vicariate, there were 51,633 Catholics in 1926, cared for by eight European missionaries and 13 Chinese priests. In the Jesuit College at Daming, there were seven European priests, three Chinese and eight brothers, seven of whom were Chinese. In preparation was a new school at Hantan, and a boarding school for girls run by Hungarian nuns. A house for the new bishop and land for a future seminary was also bought. Finances for the new vicariate would come from the Jesuit procurator in Tianjin. It was hoped that the new vicar apostolic would be a Jesuit.[6]

Similar plans were developing for the distribution of territory to the Province of Austria that would be given the northern part of the mission; ten sub-prefectures, centred on the two towns of Chenzhou and Jingxian. The latter included six sub-prefectures with a population of 1,353,000 and 9,601 Christians, while Chenzhou consisted of four sub-prefectures with a population of 806,800 and 6,125 Christians. The two areas together would have a Christian population of 15,724. The French Jesuits wanted the Austrians to take this mission because they had more men available than the Hungarians, and also because there was the rumour that the new apostolic prefecture of Lihsien was approaching Rome to attach to itself Chenzhou. If the Austrians accepted the offer, that would cut short this plan. Details for a hand over to the Austrians were meticulously outlined, which included listing the major missionary works of the new mission. This included a

5. Memo. 'Project distributing territory to the Province of Hungary, 1928. ARSI.
6. Lécroart, Xianxian, Memo re detaching Daming from Xianxian at the end of 1928. ARSI.

school, ten orphanages, and dispensaries in the Chenzhou section, with schools for non-Christian boys and girls at Nunkong in the Jingxian section. The Jesuits of the Province of Champagne would retain the north-east section of the current vicariate, which had 54,325 Christians.[7] These plans were further developed in 1932, when Lécroart urged the provincial of Champagne to agree to the division. He highlighted that there would be sufficient missionaries to work the region. At the end of May 1932, there were nine Austrians Jesuit priests, seven Chinese seculars and one Chinese Jesuit in the region, as well as ten seminarians and three Jesuit brothers. Vocations were good. The bishop wanted this division, as well as the Austrians, who thought that they would fit into the current works of the area. No one was against it.[8]

Plans for the erection of the new vicariate for the Hungarian Jesuits were well advanced by 1934. The French Jesuits saw this further division of the original vicariate as necessary as they did not have sufficient men to meet the demands of this region. There was obvious concern that currently only a few Hungarians were in the region. Twenty-three priests worked the area, eleven of whom were Chinese, seven French, and five Hungarians, as well as three scholastics studying Chinese. The first Hungarian to arrive in China was Miklós Szarvas in November 1921. By the end of 1934, twenty Hungarian Jesuits had joined the Xianxian mission. With these small numbers, it was believed that if more Hungarians did not arrive shortly, the vicariate of Yungnien would have to expand south.

Discussions continued about the divisions in the northern region that included the towns of Nunkong and Chenzhou next to Xianxian. Andrew Joliet, a missionary in Kaizhou, was not clear why this was being considered, as it was so close to Xianxian, which was the centre of the mother vicariate. He also thought it to be too close to the secular vicariate in the south. The Austrian Jesuits continued to be targeted to administer this new vicariate. Eighteen Austrian Jesuits had joined the Xianxian mission up to 1934, but only eight were in the areas assigned to them. But there were also eleven Chinese priests originally from this region, seven seculars and four Jesuits. There were also five major seminarians and five Jesuit scholastics who were born in this territory.[9]

7. Memo re distribution of territory to the Province of Austria, 1928. ARSI.
8. Lécroart and Bornet to Provincial Champagne, Thoyer, 16 June 1932. ARSI.
9. Joliet, Andrew, Memo concerning the division of the Vicariate of Xianxian, 22 February 1934. ARSI.

The Sacred Congregation of the Propagation of the Faith finally decreed the erection of the new apostolic vicariate of Daming on 26 March 1935, with Miklós Szarvas appointed the new vicar apostolic on 5 February 1936. He had been vice-superior of the mission in Daming and Kaizhou from 3 March 1931. The superior general detached the mission of Daming from that of Xianxian on 11 February 1936. On 23 November, the general appointed George Marin his visitor in China to prepare future divisions of the mission.

Civil War

Meanwhile, the civil war continued to harass the mission. The presence of 'armed revolutionaries' concerned Lécroart in 1927, especially after the assassination of priests. The people were scared. Soviet agents in the villages announced the destruction of the Catholic Church. There had been violence in the south of the vicariate and catechumens had been arrested, which led to fewer conversions. The Nationalist armies experienced difficulty in conquering the provinces in the north. The bishop also expressed concerned about the 'draconian rules for mission schools' set by the Nationalist government.[10]

Paul Wonner, rector of the seminary at Xianxian, recounted difficulties resulting from the civil war in the villages from the beginning of 1926. Many towns and villages had bonded together to withstand the military and the bandits, but all were unharmed. The military had instructed the soldiers not to enter the Christian villages. The missionaries, especially the Jesuit Maurice Verdun, a doctor, had tended wounded soldiers from both sides and to those suffering from typhoid. The sick appreciated the care received, even the Communists.[11]

In January 1928, the southern armies reached Daming, where it was reported that the bandits had invaded the village and destroyed buildings. They had previously pillaged the churches at Qingfeng and Kaizhou. As war was all around the villages, most priests left Daming, and Kaizhou as well. Soldiers occupied the school.[12] The southern armies occupied Tianjin on 12 January.

Lécroart reported that by May the southern army (Sudists) was in Xianxian, but he was grateful that the soldiers had left the mission

---

10. Lécroart, Xianxian, to Apostolic Delegate, 1927. ASV.
11. Wonner, Xianxian, to General, Xianxian, 10 January 1927. ARSI.
12. Gabor, Daming, to General, 11 January 1928. ARSI.

alone, did not live with them and also showed respect to the missionaries. But other actions by the army did not disillusion him that they were capable of disturbances. At that time, Xianxian was at the southern-most part of the civil war, while the northern front was 20 to 30 kilometres away.

The French legation asked Lécroart to take measures for departure from the region in case of invasion, and no responsibility would be taken if the advice were ignored. Lécroart told them that all missionary personnel and religious wanted to remain at their posts, but he thanked the French minister for his advice and absolved him of any responsibility for mission personnel. [13]

Visitation of the mission in 1927

The provincial of the French Province of Champagne, Joseph Subtil, visited the mission and submitted a number of reports to the superior general that were very comprehensive.

He described the mission as situated in an agricultural region, with no large city nearby. Conversions were difficult, except in Daming in the region's south. In many towns there could be up to 40 Christians, but in the established Christian communities there could be up to 600 Catholics, with most of these from the lower social classes. They were poor and relied on the missionaries for assistance. Since taking over the mission from the Lazarists, the number of Christians had increased from 9,500 to 130,000. In the three parts of the mission, 'Old Christians' were in the north, whereas in the south there were mainly new Christians. Many of the missionaries were elderly, sick, incompetent, eccentric or restricted because of scandal, and needed to be replaced. Some of these should be returned to Europe. After the recent war, many Jesuits on the mission had died and were not replaced by younger Jesuits. These were sent to the school in Tianjin or Xianxian or to the seminary. The main problem for the foreign missionaries was to adapt to different Chinese ways. All Jesuits in formation were required to be proficient in the Chinese language and culture. The teaching of the scholastics and seminarians was considered mediocre because teachers had too many jobs, or were old or sick. Superiors from 1900 to 1915 did not think that the mission

---

13. Lécroart to his sister, Xianxian, 27 May 1928. ARSI.

had any future capacity for evangelisation among the non-Christians. While there had been few conversions in the north of the mission, there were many in the south.

Subtil was concerned, as were many Jesuits, about the 'ultranationalism' of the Chinese students in the college at Xianxian, many of whom were uneducated. All Church authorities condemned this attitude. The leaders in this college appeared to be the lay teachers, and indirectly, the prefect of the Chinese college. The Jesuits had centred all their major works in Xianxian, situated in a desert, 70 kilometres from the main town. They included the house of formation for Jesuits, a primary and secondary school, a major and minor seminary, as well as the bishop's residence. The Jesuits worked too hard, despite their age, and it was impossible to find replacements for them. The bishop suggested that if no younger priests were made available, then the college should close.

Subtil found difficulties in the administration of the college in Daming run by the Hungarian Jesuits. He thought that the rector was too controlling, while the studies needed stronger direction. With this in mind, he did not think that the college was productive, whereas in contrast the Protestant college flourished.

In Tianjin, *Hautes Etudes* was still going through growing pains. Some European priests were not good at speaking Chinese, and so could not relate to the students. There were no Chinese priests with sufficient education or discipline to direct students. Raymond Liou was being sent there, but his main work was to write Chinese books. Most of the European priests said that they were too busy to learn Chinese. He wanted superiors to ask the Americans to send two scholastics to teach English. Other difficulties Subtil discovered included insufficient finance, especially to pay the salaries of the teachers. One of the missionaries, Max Laplazie, was praised for being gifted at speaking Chinese, but was criticised for poor judgment in showing favour toward the Chinese! But it was also suggested that Jesuits spend more time speaking Chinese with the local people.

Subtil had praise for the work of Licent in his museum that was annexed to the college for promoting science, with a section of the museum open to the public. Licent worked there alone, with some help from Teilhard de Chardin who came twice in two years to help in the geology and palaeontology section. Licent had difficulty relating to people, but Teilhard was 'excellent' in his relationships. Licent was very unhappy with the lack of resources to fund his work, and wanted an assistant. The museum was highly valued in China and in Europe, and he wished that it could have the same scientific impact on China that Ricci had in earlier days. He did not want a 'second rate man', and asked for 'even a brother'! Brother Theo Moegling would be helpful as he was a 'naturalist and had knowledge of pharmacy', while speaking German and understanding English. He was himself too busy to reply to letters received, or to attend conferences at home or abroad, such as in Tokyo. His domestic work was 'overwhelming and urgent'. At 51 years of age, he could no longer meet his obligations to the European Concessions. He had written five times asking for assistance and would ask no more. He was a sad man.

Overall, Subtil concluded his report by believing that the mission had a good future, but he could see future problems resulting from the civil war, and older missionaries mixing with younger one. He hoped that the Hungarian and Austrian provinces would send more 'ardent missionaries'.[14]

French or English teaching?

War and destruction, as well as internal deficiencies, never diverted the missionaries from their evangelical mission and in looking for better ways to promote the reign of God among the non-Christians. They continued to make the most of what resources were available. The discussion about which language was the best medium of instruction for teaching the Chinese was continuous. Augustine Bernard, the rector of the college in Tianjin, observed that English was the main language spreading throughout China, and it was the common language between the Europeans and the Chinese officials. This was because English was the language of commerce throughout the world, and because of American influence in their universities and in the YMCA. It was the obligatory language of all secondary schools in preparation for tertiary education. Moreover, the Chinese used English in their schools. Many educational books were in English, because the Chinese language was not able to express scientific data,

---

14. Visitation of Xianxian, 1927; Subtil, Tianjin, to General, 5 March 1927; Copy of letter of Licent to Subtil, communicated to General requested by Licent, Tianjin, 10 November 1927

and because English was the common language among those of the many local dialects in China. The villages of China, from the point of view of language, were an English colony.

From the Catholic perspective, 'atheists or Protestants' wrote the English texts. The Catholic religion was not represented in English: not in the press, nor in the manuals or books translated from English. The Catholic schools generally used the French language in the large towns such as Beijing, Tianjin, Hankou, Shanghai and Guangzhou. In all other schools, government and Protestant, in the same towns, tuition was in English. The French language had no future in China; English was spreading everywhere.

The college, *Hautes Etudes*, in Tianjin, was established by *Propaganda* to teach the children of the upper classes. In teaching French, student recruitment was inferior in both number and in quality. Many families were put off by the extra years required for the study of French, while those who wanted good positions in government and commerce needed English to deal with the Europeans and with the Chinese in other provinces. Why were the French Jesuits different from others? The Catholic bishops of Beijing and Tianjin had English as the medium of teaching in their 'middle schools'.

The result of this discussion was that Catholics in the mission villages needed English under pain of being continually disadvantaged. In *Hautes Etudes,* there was the need to replace French with English and Chinese. French could be maintained as a second language, as it was in many of the Chinese universities.

The advantages of doing this would be to give the college better recruitment possibilities and give the Jesuits greater rapport with educated Chinese. In doing this, the Jesuits would be seen as not opposing nationalism, and the 'Catholic religion' would no longer be seen as 'the French religion'. It would give the Jesuits better relations with the non-French missionaries, and would facilitate better relations with the Protestants, who, up to the present, completely ignored Catholics.

The main obstacle to this plan was the French government. In 1926, the French minister told Licent to keep teaching the French language as it communicated French culture to the Chinese. Moreover, the French language was clearer and more adaptable to Catholic teaching: French textbooks were more numerous. The Catholics could translate the French books into English and Chinese, if necessary. It would be hard to get agreement among the different French missions on this question. Maybe French Jesuits ought to be encouraged to learn English, while negotiating for assistance from American Jesuits.

Conclusions to this discussion relating to the *Hautes Etudes* were that English should replace French for new students in the first years of the preparatory course. English should be introduced as soon as possible in such courses as physics, chemistry, geography, economics, mathematics and finance. French Jesuits destined for Tianjin should be expected to know English before they arrived, as they would be engrossed in learning Chinese immediately. This had already begun.[15] The French minister in Beijing wrote that he was not happy that the Jesuits had given up teaching in the French language.

In the college at Daming, the students progressed well in their studies but were not keen on learning French. The authorities had added English to the third- and-fourth level studies. Gaspar Lischerong was the English teacher.[16]

Raymond Liou, in Xianxian, also wanted the translation of religious books from the European language into Chinese, 'either to refute superstitions or to foster piety and devotions' as a necessity. He thought that there were currently an insufficient number of such books available. The ones that they did have were old and the style of expression was difficult to understand by a modern Chinese. Priests with expertise in Chinese were needed for this task.[17] Leo Wieger was editing Chinese books, especially those on health issues. Seraphin Couvreur had produced his *Dictionnaire français-chinois* in 1885, and *Chinoise-françois* in 1890. He also edited and translated many Chinese classics.

Jesuit life

There were ongoing relational problems in communication between the European and Chinese clergy. The Europeans were perceived to work harder than the Chinese. Frustration resulted. During rec-

---

15. Bernard, 'A discussion concerning English as the language of communication', Tianjin, July 1927. ARSI.
16. Gabor to General, Daming, 11 January 1928. ARSI.
17. Liou, Xianxian, to General, 5 January 1927. ARSI.

reation in the Jesuit houses, many topics of conversation had to be avoided in order to keep the peace.

Jesuit superiors also perceived depression among the missionaries concerning the differences of opinion about missionary ideas that clashed with those of the apostolic delegate and so also of the Roman authorities. This malaise verged on discouragement. The missionaries felt that the Holy See did not appreciate their hard work, did not trust them and treated them as suspects. Any compliments given were received as a mere formality. The French visitor responded to this concern that the missionaries were too sensitive. It was true that there were contradictory affirmations, one from the Europeans and another from some Chinese source, with the Europeans usually deemed to be wrong. In some Catholic newspapers, they were judged, criticised and condemned without being able to defend themselves. The reproaches of the Holy See were made public in China, where nothing was a secret. The consequences to this were that the Chinese must save face, while the prestige and authority of the European missionaries was being undermined. The Vatican, *Propaganda* and the apostolic delegate opposed their administration and decisions. Contending with this attitude of Church superiors, combined with their concerns about Chinese 'hypernationalism', the apostolic effectiveness of the missionaries was diminished.[18] The tension between central administration and the local mission continued.

The rector of *Hautes Etudes*, Bernard, was happy with the institution and its progress, and believed that all the missionaries, European and Chinese, lived in harmony with one another. He delighted in the number of Jesuit scholastics and the effectiveness in the ministry of the young priests, but regretted that Stephen Jacquart, the mission procurator, worn out and weak, was forced to return to France. There was no one to replace him. There was further sadness when Louis Giebens, who had only been in China for three weeks, died of typhus. He had been unwell before he left Belgium for China, and so was weak in health when he arrived.

There were 110 students in the institution, of whom 35 were Catholic. This was considered a sufficient number of students considering the troubled times in Tianjin. As English was the language of teaching, this caused some difficulty for students coming from primary

---

18. 'Extracts from a visitation of the region', May 1927. ARSI.

schools that did not teach English. It was difficult to give instruction in 'morals and religion' at the university. Some Jesuits were considered good teachers, but others were 'not apt to teach', except in teaching general subjects. Licent's museum was praised for fostering good relations with the Chinese, but he needed an assistant. Overall, the mission had great need for good Jesuit teachers from other provinces.[19]

Another idea was raised that the mission might begin a Chinese secondary school in Tianjin that would give instruction in English and feed students to the *Hautes Etudes*. Bishop de Vienne liked this idea, as it would seem to be the best way for the university to receive more students. The main difficulty with this would be to obtain competent teachers. The American Jesuits had been approached, but they were not interested. This disappointed the French who thought that the Americans did not have a missionary spirit! Bornet thought that the presence of the Americans would be advantageous for the mission as they had a different attitude to the French. He recognised that the Province of Champagne was unable to send more men.[20] In fact, the province did send some missionaries, but only 20 between 1928 and 1939. During that same period, 59 Chinese Jesuits joined the mission.

On the overall status of Christianity in China, Paul Jung, the regional superior of Jingxian, believed there were two threatening dangers, one external and one internal. The internal threat was from the Chinese government's schools' policy, which aimed to laicise the mission schools. They were not happy that the missionaries used their schools for evangelisation, and so the schools required to be registered with the government or be closed. The external threat was the ultra nationalism of the Chinese clergy. They 'denigrate' the European missionaries.[21] The continuing differences between the Europeans and the Chinese, especially during the time of rising Chinese nationalism, dampened the spirits of all the missionaries.

French legation support

The apostolic delegate, Costantini, under instructions from the Holy See, made a formal protest to the Chinese minister objecting to a land

19. Augustin Bernard to General, Hautes Etudes, Tianjin, 20 January 1928. ARSI.
20. Bornet, to General, Tianjin, 9 April 1928. ARSI.
21. Jung, Xianxian, to General, 8 January 1929. ARSI.

act that changed the right of the Catholic missions to acquire land, and asked for a revision of the Act. He gave an example of Matthew Loh attempting to buy property in perpetuity at Wuchuang, Kiangsu, with permission refused. He took this case to the French legation. Similarly, the Church at You-li-zang was refused registration by the local authorities. The legation saw these examples as an infraction of the Berthemy Convention. The Nationalist foreign minister responded to the delegate that the purpose of the Act was to ease 'the operations of control and protection'. Furthermore, it was a purely administrative order that regularised laws regarding property, and in no way intended to interfere with the legitimate rights of the missions. He asked the delegate to assist the government in applying the laws, reassuring him that the missions would be treated with respect. The letter showed great courtesy towards the delegate and the pope, but the delegate still sent a copy of the letter to the French legation.[22] Later, the French legation expressed reservations about the missionaries having perpetual rights to Chinese land. Maybe a lease could be negotiated for perhaps 10 or 20 years.[23] French Jesuits continually barraged the legation over difficulties with local authorities concerning rights to Church lands. Verdier, the Jesuit procurator in Shanghai, in one letter listed six such examples and saw these infractions as a 'breach of the treaties with France'.[24]

There was agitation by some citizens of Guangzhou for the government to resume control of land ceded under the Treaty of Tianjin. The dispute arose when missions were seen to build houses on acquired land and then rent it to people for personal gain. To support this claim, the *Canton Gazette* reported the text of the Land Decree: all property of a mission was to conform to the laws and taxes of China; in buying property, the missions needed to seek approval of the local authority; requests would be refused if requests went beyond what the mission actually needed; no property could be used for commerce; even if the property was shown to belong to the mission, this could not be considered as a perpetual rent.[25]

22. Costantini, Beijing, to Nationalist Minister, Nanjing, 16 August, 1928; Nationalist Foreign Minister, Nanjing, to Apostolic Delegate, Beijing, 27 October 1928. DAC.
23. French consul, Shanghai, to legation, Beijing, 1 March 1934. DAC.
24. Verdier to French Consul General, Shanghai, 23 April 1934. DAC.
25. *Canton Gazette*, 8 December 1928. DAC.

More generally, the French legation continued to be concerned about the future of the protectorate in the face of opposition, especially from the apostolic delegate and his sympathisers. They thought that Costantini would appoint like-minded bishops to vicariates in China and upset the balance. An apostolic visitor had been appointed, Bishop Fouquet, who was hostile to French politics and the protectorate. Fouquet wanted to make Lebbe vicar apostolic of Tianjin, with Bishop de Vienne appointed elsewhere. This was a concern for the legation, as Lebbe was well known to be hostile to the French cause. Fouquet recommended to Costantini that Lebbe go to Tianjin and de Vienne appointed coadjutor bishop of Beijing. The Lazarists opposed the move and de Vienne refused to move. The French legation did not trust Costantini or Fouquet for their anti-French attitudes. However, they did seek help from the legation for common action against the Chinese Land decree, which was given.[26] Both the apostolic delegate and the French legation were pleased to use each other when opportunity demanded.

Concern was raised in 1930 when the legation learned that the Holy See and the Italian government wanted to care for Italian missionaries. This was a development of the policy several years before of the Vatican and the Chinese government to make each Catholic mission responsible to its own country of origin. The apostolic delegate forbade the raising of the French flag in Catholic missions.[27] This resulted in further tension between the legation and the apostolic delegate.

The State of the Mission 1930–1931

When writing about the state of the mission in 1930, the mission superior Bornet continued to lament the lack of missionaries from the Province of Champagne, especially for the *Hautes Etudes* in Tianjin. Finding and then educating lay collaborators was given high priority.

26. M Mantel, French Minister, Beijing, to M Briand, Paris, 22 December 1928; Telegram, Beijing to Guangzhou, 4 January 1929; Telegram, Minister, Nanjing to Diplomatic Paris, 28 January 1929; Telegram, French Consul, Shanghai, to French Minister, Paris, 4 February 1929; Letter of *Agence Fides*, Paris, 18 October 1929; Noury to French Minister, Shanghai, 20 September 1929. DAC.
27. Dr G Bechamp, French consulate Tchentou to French Ambassador, Beijing, 16 June 1930. DAC.

He put much hope in the presence of Jesuits from the Austrian province, who currently had sufficient men to operate their own vicariate. They showed good will, but were obviously inexperienced. He was pessimistic about the presence of Hungarian Jesuits. Their province had not yet been generous with new missionaries.

The future of the vicariate looked promising with the presence of 12 Chinese scholastic novices and four brothers. In the minor seminary of the secular clergy there were 32 'Latinists' or beginners, 11 philosophers and 11 theologians. Unfortunately, at least four of these were considered unsuitable for the priesthood and required sending away, but Lécroart feared that he would be accused of prejudice against the native clergy to do so. Moreover, the secular clergy had little taste for developing the intellectual life. Once they left the seminary, there was little enthusiasm for further study. They found administering the new Chinese vicariate hard to maintain.

The increasing number of students in the schools was pleasing, because the schools gave vocations to the secular clergy and to the Jesuits, as well as providing future school teachers and leaders in the Christian communities.

Religious sisters ran dispensaries in Xianxian and Daming, small hospices for female non-Christians, and an orphanage for girls. The presence of the nuns was invaluable, and all female congregations were receiving local Chinese vocations as a result of their work. A Chinese congregation of sisters was founded to work in the main towns of the vicariate. The Chinese catechists and virgins were well-educated and considered good workers, and were essential in the formation of new Christian communities, but they needed to be supervised by the missionaries. European control was never distant.

Jesuit ministry included giving 'closed retreats' – that is, silent ones – to 3,000 people the previous year. Catholic Action was not a great success, as it seemed to have created jealousies and divisions among the Christians, despite 5,000 being theoretically involved.

Difficulties continued to be experienced from Chinese nationalism, even among the Chinese clergy, as well as attacks from brigands, famine and war. Not to be permitted to provide religious teaching in the schools was an added burden.

While generally satisfied with the running and ministry of Jesuit houses in Xianxian and Daming, Bornet was concerned that Tianjin was a difficult place for the Chinese priests, because of the constant demands for nationalism, as well as for the European scholastics, who needed more discipline than they were receiving from local superiors.

Finally, the mission of Xianxian wanted to make the customs of the French assistancy their own.[28] This indicated that while there was much action in developing the local Chinese Church, control was still strongly in the hands of the foreign missionaries, and that the Jesuits themselves still wanted to follow the customs of the mother country. There was very little reflection on adapting their lifestyle to that of the Chinese. The Jesuits were still basically outsiders in a foreign, and even hostile environment.

Reporting from Kaizhou, Henri Bernard expressed concern over the death of Stephen Gabor who had been in China from Hungary since 1924. Kaizhou had gathered 'malcontents' against the missionaries, and against Maurice Cannepin, the vicar of the region, in particular. Henri d'Herbigny was imprisoned for a short time. The main issue seemed to stem from the alleged stealing of $6,000 from the mission. The Christians supported the missionaries, but while the mandarins were initially hesitant to take sides, they finally agreed to attempt to retrieve the money. The Christians calmed down, but Cannepin would not remain with them as he feared the rebels and was unsure of protection from the mandarins.[29]

The Jesuits generally could not cope with the rise of Chinese nationalism. They worked against it vigorously. This resulted in further tension between the European and Chinese clergy, and between the missionaries and many young Chinese.[30]

Praise was given to Leo Wieger, a medical missionary in China since 1888, who worked for 42 years before his golden jubilee in the Society on 21 January 1932. His medical expertise as a doctor, as well as his writing, greatly assisted his ministry. He was well versed in Chinese language and ancient Chinese history. He completed works on Taoism, and wrote works on modern China and on religious topics. He was currently teaching Chinese philosophy at the seminary

28. Bornet, State of the mission in Xianxian, Nancy, 22 May 1930, ARSI.
29. Henri Bernard to the bishop, (with a copy to the French Assistant in Rome), Kaizhou, 21 July 1930. ARSI. Help in this matter was referred to the French legation, cf. letters, 4 August 1930 and 14 August 1930. DAC.
30. Aizier to General, Xianxian 13 March 1931. ARSI.

in Xianxian.[31] Wieger was symbolic of those foreign Jesuits who took immersion into Chinese culture seriously.

A further visitation from the provincial of the Province of Champagne, 1933

Xavier Thover visited the mission in 1933 and praised the missionaries for their hard work and for the good relations they had with the vicar apostolic. He thought that the one important work missing from the mission was an 'ambition for the intellectual life'. The formation of young Jesuits was 'too limited to instruction and preservation', and needed more practical application. He thought highly of the excellent leadership of the superior Bornet, but did not consider him an innovator, nor was he open to necessary progress in the mission. He had confidence in the bishop, but was concerned about the need for Chinese superiors. Chinese Jesuits were reluctant to take on positions of responsibility. However, Francis-Xavier Zhao gave the Chinese Jesuits a good example of leadership.

Thover was pleased with the progress and influence of the colleges, which should produce a 'militant elite' who would help with conversions.

He showed insight by raising the question of how European missionaries might better adapt to Chinese culture. He thought that some missionaries were 'a little haughty, distant and pessimistic', while some tried to adapt themselves, but not happily. He advised that all common Jesuit activities were to be conducted in Chinese. Furthermore, there was need to renew relations with the secular clergy. Henry Jomin, a future superior from 1938, was considered influential with young Chinese priests helping them to develop spiritually. Finally, in this context, he believed that the mission needed full independence and freedom from all French influence.

Continuing this theme, Thover dreamed about the possibility of creating a Jesuit Province of China. But he recognised current

---

31. Memo re jubilee of Léon Wieger, 1931. ARSI. Wieger edited *Rudiments de parler et de style chinois*, in a dozen volumes, published in 1905.

     Léon Wieger was born in Strasbourg, Bas Rhine, France, on 9 July 1865. He entered the Jesuits in the Champagne province on 21 January 1881, and arrived in China and Zhili-Xianxian mission on 15 October 1887. He died in Xianxian on 25 March 1933, aged 67. CHPA.

problems that included questions of distance with poor transport, diversity of local needs, and different European missions requiring financial assistance from home provinces. In preparation for this, the mission might send Joseph Chang to Rome to study missiology.

Finally, he believed that social involvement in the midst of the misery of the majority of Chinese was very important. He hoped that Tianjin could become an important centre for this ministry, especially in regards to publications, as the Jesuits in Shanghai claimed that they could not be involved in any more activities.[32] Thover showed genuine empathy for the Chinese and made genuine attempts to encourage the mission to become more deeply immersed in Chinese culture. The Province of Champagne Jesuits were more alert to the importance of this issue than their brethren from the Province of France.

Mission reports 1934–1936

In his report to Rome in 1934, Lécroart traced the history of the mission from 1856, when there were 9,505 Christians grouped into 132 Christian communities with five missionaries: three Jesuits and two Chinese secular priests. In 1929, there were 138,910 Christians, with 57 European and 47 Chinese priests. By a papal decree of 24 May 1929, the pope detached from Xianxian the civil prefecture of Yungnien to form a new vicariate with 38,889 Christians in 10 sub-prefectures with 19 Chinese secular priests. On 6 March 1933, the new vicariate received Bishop Joseph Tsoei, a secular priest, as the first vicar apostolic. Pius XI consecrated him in Rome on 11 June 1933.

When this vicariate separated from the vicariate of Xianxian, that left Xianxian on 1 July 1934 with a Jesuit bishop, 68 European Jesuit priests, and 45 Chinese priests, of whom 15 were Jesuits. There were also 48 Jesuit scholastics, 32 being Chinese, and 33 Jesuit brothers, 19 of whom were Chinese. The number of Christians was 110,902.

Lécroart also wrote about the Daming region, which was to be given to the Hungarian Jesuits. In this region, there were 36,012 Christians, a major Jesuit college with a large residence and a cathedral at Daming. There were also three Hungarian religious houses and some good churches with comfortable residences attached. In this region in 1857 there were no Christians, but in 1934, Christians

---

32. Report of the visitation of the mission by Xavier Thover, 1933. FPA.

lived in 920 communities. The local people were mainly farmers and labourers who were open to evangelisation. This region had given the best number of adult Baptisms of the vicariate.

The work of the Protestants flourished in this region with schools and many charitable works, with a hospital and live-in doctor. Catholic missionaries had good relations with them, and they worked together in distributing food during famine times.

Good relations with the local Chinese officials also existed, and students from the schools only occasionally became involved with political issues.

Because of the poverty of the Catholics, they were not able to become involved with the apostolate. Recent flooding of the Huanghe River during 1933 destroyed many Christian communities.[33]

With the endless demands of pastoral work, and external pressures from local authorities, government decrees and civil war, missionaries needed time for reflection on the mission and plan for the future. The occasional visitations from French provincials were opportunities for someone outside the mission to give an objective comment on the situation in the mission. But the missionaries themselves also expressed opinions on perceived needs.

One such reflection occurred in 1936 when Francis Xavier Tchao (Zhao Zhen-sheng), the superior in Hokien and a mission consultor, suggested that superiors needed to make a serious study of the needs of China: a study of movements, tendencies of the younger generations, and recent codes, laws and decrees of the government. He had the impression that superiors were mainly interested in the immediate needs of the mission, without sufficient consideration of the needs of the Church in China. He thought the current mission superior, Nicholas Vagner, was more open to this course of action than the former superior Bornet, but much more was required. The bishop needed a coadjutor to lessen his burden of work. But overall, to make such changes many more men were needed in the mission to ease the workload of the present missionaries who might then have time for reflection.[34] Zhao was so highly thought of by superiors that he was

---

33. Copy of a letter to *Propaganda* by Lécroart, Xianxian, sent to General, 30 August 1934. ARSI.
34. Zhao, Hokien, to General, 17 January 1936. ARSI.

appointed vicar apostolic of Xianxian on 2 December 1937. Henry Jomin became the Jesuit regional superior from 1 May 1938.

In preparation for a conference of Jesuit superiors in June 1937, the agenda included a number of questions for reflection: why had the rate of conversions slowed down? Why had conversions been the least in the older, more established Christian communities? To what degree did the lay helpers, catechists and teachers serve the mission? Were the non-Christians taught the main points of Catholicism? Was too much time given in attempting to make Catholicism better known 'to the better class of Chinese society'? How could the press be better used for evangelisation? Why were relations with the civil authorities not 'what they should be'? Were there sufficient 'virgins' to contact non-Christian women?[35]

The French Jesuits in Xianxian continued to make genuine attempts to adapt to the local culture, but were always limited by their own education and earlier experiences. During 1935, they translated four books into Chinese: *The Secret of the Confession; Martyrs of the Roman Catacombs; Life of St. Aloysius;* and *the Demon – his temptations, his obsessions, his possessions.*

Preparation for the Jingxian mission

Soon after his appointment as vicar apostolic in 1938, Francis-Xavier Zhao Zhen-sheng wrote about the proposed erection of the new vicariate of Jingxian. The territory was centred on the town of Jingxian. In 1938, this region contained 293 Christian communities, with 30,000 Catholics and 2,764 catechumens. The people were generally farmers, but there were also some commercial centres at Nunkong and Jingxian with good transport connections to Tianjin and Beijing. The Imperial Canal was also a good transport route. Jingxian was the centre for education, with government schools. There had been many surrounding village schools, but they were destroyed during the civil war. Zhao believed that evangelisation in the region progressed, but not rapidly. At Nunkong in the south-east, a new Jesuit residence had been constructed able to house twelve priests, as well as a new college, while at Jingxian, the Jesuits had a residence and a college with 78 students, as well as a minor seminary.

---

35. *Relatio de Chine*, Shanghai, January 1936.

Alfonse Duscheck and Leopold Brellinger were the first Austrian Jesuits to arrive in the mission in June 1926. Currently, there were seven Chinese secular priests, all under the age of 40 who worked hard among the people. Assisting the priests were 100 catechists and 120 virgins.[36]

Acceleration of the civil war from 1938

Meanwhile, from 1938, battles between various Chinese forces increased. In January 1938, it was reported that 'the Red Army', the southern forces, were between Hokien and Xianxian, causing much 'pillage and destruction', and were moving towards Xianxian. Much fear was expressed about the possible outcome of this invasion. 'God help us'. The missionaries suffered many privations from the cold, lack of fuel, houses destroyed, and walls broken. Many wounded were evacuated. In an attempt to hold out the invaders, the missionaries in Xianxian flew a flag, '*Mission Catholique*', over the compound. However, the 'Reds' occupied Xianxian after a bloody battle on 23 March 1938. Many refugees went to the Church compound for safety. Hokien was also occupied. They came in floods.

Troubles also came from the Japanese forces. Four Jesuits were killed at this time, as well as nine seminarians and eleven catechists. The French legation was kept busy negotiating with the Japanese legation over these murders. The Communists had also killed some. The Japanese had maltreated some Jesuits in Xianxian, and 24 Chinese Christians had been killed. Particular mention was made of the Japanese bombing the mission of Zhangjiazhuang, near Xianxian, with much material loss on 21 September 1937, and more violence occurred against mission staff on 28 April 1938. Jesuits from Anqing mission were arrested on 18 February 1939 by the Chinese, suspected of collaborating with the Japanese. Meanwhile, following troubles with the Japanese, the Japanese legation replied that members of the Catholic missions spread anti-Japanese propaganda among the

---

36. Zhao, Xianxian, Report of the erection of the Vicariate of Kinghsien within the Vicariate of Xianxian, 27 October 1938. ARSI. Francis-Xavier Zhao (1894–1970) was born in Kinghsien, took vows in the Society of Jesus in 1913, ordained priest on 26 August 1923, and appointed vicar apostolic of Xianxian, 2 December 1937. He was ordained bishop on 27 March 1938, and appointed bishop of Xianxian, 11 April 1946.

people and were helping the enemy (the Chinese). They required the neutrality of the missions. Chinese students had been arrested for 'anti-Japanese feeling', but after been admonished they were released. At Hokien, the Jesuits was accused of helping the Chinese 8th Army and of distributing anti-Japanese textbooks to students. This claim was rejected, but it was admitted that students were learning the Japanese language. The Japanese legation wanted the Catholic mission to continue activities as usual during the occupation, especially in the schools of Xianxian. They would not interfere, and asked that all 'previous misunderstandings' be forgotten.[37]

By 1939, the Japanese had taken over the mission, already experiencing the effects of floods and famine. Licent's museum was transferred to Beijing, and the seminary in Xianxian was transferred to Hokien in January. Also this year, the Austrian Jesuits were officially given the apostolic vicariate of Jingxian, with 30,000 Christians, separate from Xianxian. Leopold Brellinger, who had arrived in China in June 1926, was appointed the new vicar apostolic on 4 May 1939.[38]

From 1940–5, the Japanese incarcerated or killed many Christians. In 1940, the Japanese occupied the villa house at Xianxian and many Jesuits went to prison, including the bishop, as a result of some Japanese helpers having been killed. By 1941, no school in the mission remained open. On 22 November, the bishop and 60 priests were released from prison, but 20 remained incarcerated. The war with USA from 8 December worsened the situation. American and Canadian nuns were apprehended and the mission came under military control. During this time, the minor seminary was occupied and a Jesuit brother was killed. Spanish and French missionaries were left alone, as their home country was either neutral or allied to the Axis Powers.

Conditions worsened in 1942 when 18 Christians were executed on 24 January 1942, as well as the Jesuits Joseph Ho and scholastic André Fong, at Huaizhen on 25 January 1942. Canadian and American Jesuits were sent to Chabanel Hall in Beijing during 1942. The Jesuit tertians also went there the same year. Chabanel became a Jesuit

---

37. Capture and murder of missionaries since 1933; French legation to Japanese legation, 26 January 1939; Japanese embassy, Beijing to French ambassador, Shanghai, 4 April 1939; Hokien affair, July 1939; reply of the Japanese legation; answers to accusations against the Catholic Church at Hokien, 1939. DAC.
38. Bornet, up supra, 1938–9; History of the Mission, 1938–9. FPA.

prison camp. Henri Réal, rector of the scholasticate, and two brothers were apprehended on 30 May 1944, after the Japanese found the body of a Japanese buried in the Jesuit garden, killed by the Communists. The brothers were tortured, but all released on 14 June. In order to show tolerance and respect, the Japanese embassy invited all religious superiors in Beijing to dinner, which turned out to be a grand banquet. The ambassador asked the superiors for 'moral collaboration for the work of Japan in China'. There was no recorded response.

Stanislas Liou became the first Chinese Jesuit appointed rector of *Hautes Etudes* in Tianjin in 1943, while on 22 April, Paul Jung was murdered in the Xianxian section. George Marin reported that missionaries of both sexes from enemy countries were interned in four religious houses, two for each sex. Men went to the Procure (head house) of the Franciscans and Lazarists, as well as Xujiahui. They were forbidden to go outside the compound, to telephone or receive visitors or write except one per month under censorship. Fifty Jesuits were in Xujiahui and twelve non-Jesuits. Overall, in Shanghai, there were 230 interns, including two bishops. Six Jesuits acted as chaplains to the civil internment camps, as well as eight others from diverse congregations. Gonzaga College had closed, as well as other Jesuit works in Wuhu and other missions. Jesuits in Xuzhou had restricted movement.[39]

Post-war mission life amidst the battle with Communists

The Communists replaced the Japanese at the end of the war in 1945 and soon occupied the whole mission, causing maximum disturbance. The major seminary was the first house occupied, followed by part of the episcopal residence, the church and other mission buildings. Much destruction of property followed, while some priests were killed and others imprisoned. Communists took over the Jesuit printing press for their own daily journal. All valuable furniture and goods were taken, while they occupied the Jesuit residence to set up their own bank and centre of instruction. Following the seizure of grain, the poor people suffered further. Jesuits were brought before the crowd and insulted; property was seized, statues destroyed, cemeteries profaned from 13 December onwards. Everyone was heavily

39. Marin to O'Brien, Xujiahui, 22 June 1943. FPA.

taxed. From the beginning of 1946, many fled the mission for Beijing or Tianjin, but those who stayed, despite the danger and suffering, were continually harassed by the Communists, especially through the written word. Letters and papers of the missionaries were taken in an attempt to discredit them.

Japanese concentration camps ended soon after the armistice that had housed 340 missionary priests, ten brothers and 16 religious sisters. Most subsequently went to Beijing, but the Jesuits went to Chabanel Hall, where the work of learning the Chinese language continued.

Reflecting on the Xianxian mission soon after the end of Japanese occupation, Alfred Bonningue, who had been in China for only two years, remarked that Catholicism was not making its mark in Chinese life, as were the Protestants. Catholic missions gained conversions and prepared the Church for martyrs, but had not changed the country. Chinese Catholics had not reached out to non-Christians. With admitting that the Jesuits provided good teachers in the university of Tianjin, Chinese converts had not provided leadership for important Chinese enterprises, such as politics or literature. Jesuits had not provided leadership in philosophy, science or spirituality. Nothing had been produced since the death of Wieger. The kind of superiors needed in China was not the same as in Europe. China needed men who could 'see clearly, imagine intelligently, give solutions to original problems, and who did not fear of entering into bold ways, capable of dominating events rather than being submissive to them, and capable of strong leadership'. Jesuits needed to foster the intellectual life, as did the Protestants.[40] Bonningue was reflecting what a number of the younger Jesuit priests were thinking about future work in China. They wanted to revive the Jesuit traditionally honoured intellectual apostolate. They wanted to influence the changes that were taking place in China after the war with Japan. However, such attitudes were not universally shared among superiors. The superior of Tianjin, probably Stanislas Liou, said that 'he feared Bonningue. He was a utopian and inflexible'. He feared that he thought too much.[41]

---

40. Bonningue to French Provincial, Xianxian, 15 November 1945. FPA.
41. Superior to French Provincial, Tianjin, 3 December 1945. FPA.
    Alfred Bonningue (1908–97) was born on 20 January 1909 in Hallines, France. He entered the Society of Jesus on 1 October 1926 and was ordained priest on 24 June 1937. He was missioned to China in 1940, and until 1954,

Xianxian was in ruin by the end of 1945, causing great sadness among the missionaries after 50 years hard work. Communications with Shanghai by rail were cut. Missionaries were divided in attitude toward the Communists. Some saw them as 'rebels', others as a 'party'. Government soldiers were not organised or disciplined, and did not seem to have the will to combat the Communists.[42]

In Xianxian, from 1946, the Jesuits lived on alms. Nothing could reach them from Tianjin. On 11 April 1946, Pope Pius XII created the Catholic Hierarchy of China, replacing most the vicariates apostolic. Cardinal Tien (Tienchensing) was installed as archbishop of Beijing. Rene Charvet, in Tianjin, reported that the Jesuits were not free to move around the mission. What buildings the Communists did not destroy they occupied, taking over 15 mission churches and residences. No new schools were possible, so the Christians were restricted to public prayers on Sundays. French citizens were preparing to leave China, but religious houses in the mission carried on as best they could, encouraging the Christians and giving them spiritual assistance through retreats and counselling.

In this time of uncertainty, Jesuits appeared to struggle with the lack of leadership of some superiors. Besides the mission superior, Rene Charvet and Henry Réal, the rector of the college in Beijing, it was thought that others lacked 'virility, decision and savoir-faire'. Chinese Jesuits were still considered to lack 'stature' in leadership roles.[43]

---

studied Mandarin and taught science in Beijing and Tianjin, where in 1949 he became rector of the Catholic University of Tianjin. With the Communist takeover of China, he was imprisoned during his last three years from 1951 to 1954 when he was expelled from China. After a brief rest in France, he went to Bangkok on 2 April 1955, joining the first Jesuits in their new mission, where he studied Thai and taught French at Chulalongkorn University, wrote, and laid the foundations for involvement in the social apostolate. In 1961, he opened a social centre, and formed the first Credit Union in Thailand. From this work grew the Catholic Church's Committee for Justice and Peace. In 1968, he was sent to Hong Kong and Manila to found the Bureau of Asian Affairs. Afterwards, he returned to Bangkok, living in the slums, but with declining health he returned to French on 2 June 1985 with heart disease. Alzheimer's disease also attacked him over the following twelve years. Finally, he died on 28 June 1997, a much-respected scholar in Thailand. Obituary by Sigmund J Laschenski, SJ, 4 July 1997, *China Province News* (August-September 1997): 24–5. CHPA.

42. Monsterleet to his father, Tianjin, 21 December 1945. FPA.
43. Klok, Mission procurator, Tianjin, to Jeannet, 29 June 1946. FPA.

Support for Bonningue's plea for strengthening the intellectual apostolate came from Jean Monsterleet, currently doing postgraduate studies in France. He, too, wanted to influence the educated classes, which he saw as necessary for saving the apostolate to the 'bush' or mission stations. He wanted the Jesuits to prepare Chinese specialists to work in schools and universities, as well as become technicians for *Hautes Etudes*. Europeans still considered the Chinese Jesuits as a second-class group. Specialists in English were essential.[44]

A top-level Jesuit visitation of the mission in 1947 by the Jesuit provincials of the Champagne, France, and California provinces attempted to make recommendation about Jesuit personnel in a time of great fluidity. At Chabanel Hall, they suggested that George Marin be replaced as he was 'unadaptable and his methods purely administrative without any human contact'. They recommended John Desautels from the Canadian mission as the new superior. They did not want this international house to be controlled from Xianxian. They agreed on the great need for money in rebuilding the missions, and suggested the establishment of a fund. Finally, they wanted to provide better spiritual assistance to the scholastics by providing a suitable 'spiritual father'. Emile Muller, from the Canadian mission, was the preferred candidate.[45]

Chabanel Hall became a significant Jesuit residence in the mission fostering the intellectual life, and preparing Jesuit scholastics for the future. Réal believed that the Chinese studies were well done, but thought that an extension to the two-year period might be more profitable. He did not believe that the rector, George Marin, was suitable. While a good religious, he was 'very correct, and rigid', but not well supported by the community. The scholastics were 'calm, simple, without difficulties, and did not suffer much'. Some of the recent arrivals were ardent but not adaptable. The rector could not handle the diversity of these scholastics.[46]

---

44. Monsterleet, Memo on the mission, 24 September 1946. FPA.
45. Jeannet, Champagne Provincial to Dragon, Canadian provincial, Beijing, 24 May 1947. FPA.
46. Réal, Chabanel, General State, 22 August 1948, in History of the House of Probation, 1 July 1948–30 June 1949. FPA.

Increased Communist pressure on the mission from 1947

Pressure upon the Catholic missions tightened during 1947–8. When the Communists arrived in a Christian community, they spoke words of peace and liberty of conscience. But soon after, they prevented evangelisation and closed schools, while requisitioning churches and presbyteries for their own use. Men fled the villages because they did not want to be incorporated into the Communist army. In Hebei, Shandong and Shanxi, churches were burnt down, which affected the morale of the Christians. While worrying about children without schools, without catechists, and without education, infanticide increased. Twenty flourishing missions were ruined and completely disorganised. The Communists pretended that they did not torture anyone, but that was not true; Bishop Szarvas at Daming was one such victim.[47]

Andrew Joliet, at Qiaohe, together with some Christians, was arrested, but some were later released. Those living in the episcopal residence were all arrested on 21 October 1947, but the bishop had already left for Beijing. Mass was forbidden, and the residence trashed. Religious sisters went to prison in 1948, while others, including the Jesuits, were given 'house arrest'. In Beijing, American Jesuits, followed by the Canadians left China, but those Jesuits from Spain, France, Hungry, Austria and Italy remained. The Sisters of the Precious Blood returned to America. Despite these calamities, the Jesuits received thirteen vocations between 1939 and 1950.[48] The superior general, Jean-Baptiste Janssens, told all European Jesuit missionaries not to leave China for Europe or America, but to stand firm with the Chinese Christians.[49] The active ones obeyed until expelled, but the scholastics, novices, the elderly and the sick were soon repatriated.

Réal was appointed regional superior of the mission of Xianxian from 12 September 1948, when there were 15 priests, 31 scholastics and six brothers left in the mission.[50] He reported that in Janu-

---

47. *Chine, Ceylon, Madagascar*, new series, 10, May 1948. FPA.

48. Bornet, ibid, 1940–9.

49. Janssens to Lacretelle, Rome, 29 November 1948. FPA.

50. **Henri Réal** (1904–96) was born in September 1904 at St-Omer, Pas-de-Calais, North France, one of four boys. The four brothers studied at a diocesan high school during the beginning of WW1. Although an 'impetuous, choleric boy' in his youth, after his decision to become a priest, he resolved to 'become kind and obsequious'. In 1917, when the battlefront approached St-Omer, the Réal

ary 1949 he was preparing to send the 11 Jesuit novices to Shanghai, then to Macao and finally to Manila. Tianjin had been bombed, and it was impossible to have communications with that city. He wanted a new rector at Tianjin and suggested Bonningue to replace Liou. Life at Chabanel Hall in Beijing was normal for the 80 Jesuits living there, but the house lacked resources. The mission could not afford to pay the Chinese lecturers. Working in the parish continued, but was becoming 'more menacing'. When the Communists took over, normal life would gradually become more complicated.[51]

---

brothers were sent to Southern France to study at the Jesuit high school in Tours. After the armistice was signed, the brothers went back to the North to study at the Jesuit school in Lille. It was here that he decided to become a Jesuit. He entered the Jesuit noviciate at Florenne on 2 November 1922, after which, during his juniorate, he studied classics, botany and chemistry. During the years 1925–7, he completed military service in Bayreuth by teaching sciences and Latin at the Jesuit St Joseph University. Philosophy studies followed at Vals, 1927–30, during which time he studied for a Master of Natural Sciences degree for the Sorbonne University in Paris that he received in 1931. That year he was assigned to the China mission, arriving in Tianjin, via Siberia, on 29 August 1931.

Two years of regency was spent teaching science at the *Hautes Etudes* in Tianjin, while privately studying Mandarin. Theology studies in Shanghai followed, 1933–7. After ordination, just when the Japanese army invaded North China, from 1937–45, Réal was appointed to Xianxian, and successively worked as prefect of the minor seminary, assistant to the director of novices and rector of the scholasticate. These were dangerous times with the mission occupied at different times by the Japanese or the Communists. In May 1944, Réal was jailed for a month by the Japanese, because the body of a Japanese soldier, killed by the Communists, was founded in a pond near the scholasticate. In January 1946, he moved with the scholastics to Beijing. After René Charvet, the superior of Xianxian, was arrested, condemned and expelled from China by the Communists, Réal was appointed superior of the mission until the police jailed him in Paoting on 3 February 1950, accused of the usual crimes against the State. Here, he was interrogated for twenty months, and on 3 October 1951 was sentenced to seven years' hard labour, where he suffered much physically. On Easter Sunday, 18 April 1954, he was expelled from China, his 'crimes' expiated.

After his release, he began a long apostolic life in East Asia, initially in the Philippines and then Taiwan. In 1966, he was assigned to Dalat, South Vietnam, as a theology lecturer in the Pontifical Seminary. Here, he once again encountered the Communists. He was eventually expelled by them from Vietnam on 9 July 1976, and returned to Taiwan for the rest of his life. Obituary by Fernando Mateos, *China Province News* (August-September 1996), 30–4. CHPA.

51. Réal to provincial, 9 January 1949. FPA.

Bonningue was appointed rector of *Hautes Etudes*, Tianjin, on 4 January 1949, and left Beijing on foot for Tianjin. He was challenged on the way by Communists, but eventually allowed to pass. He was well received in Tianjin by the civil administration.[52] Reporting to the Champagne provincial in February 1950, Bonningue mentioned that Réal was in prison. In August 1949, the government imposed a course of dialectic materialism at *Hautes Etudes*. This being done, the Jesuits introduced a course on Catholicism, which was attended by 100 students. Communist students challenged this move. In September, the Jesuits agreed to three hours of dialectic materialism. By December, the Communist students were demanding the removal of the Catholic 'heads' of the institution. This was followed by lengthy negotiations. By May, Catholic activities were coming to an end. The Communists were tightening the grip on the missionaries.[53] They claimed that the missionaries were 'the patrols of evil imperialists . . . you are the assassins of our revolution . . . quickly depart to your den. If not as quickly as we command, then your blood shall be upon your head . . .'[54] Soon after this proclamation, some Chinese faculty members of the Fu Jen University, Beijing, started a movement for control of the institution to pass into Chinese hands. Any religious element in courses was gradually removed, and administration passed into Chinese control.[55]

Charvet, who was replaced as the mission superior by Réal on 12 September 1948, wrote about the misery in the mission during 1948–9. The 35 missionaries, 12 of whom were Jesuits, who lived among the ruins of the mission, represented 'the charity and humility of Christ'. The Catholic Church in China, as the European missionaries knew it, was lost 'for the moment'. But hope remained that it would be restored sooner rather than later. The legacy left to the Chinese was 'the poverty, patience and charity of Christ'. The Chinese Church had 'lost its foreign appearance, its life, regime and habits of the missionaries'. But, because of the work of European missionaries,

52. Bonningue to Charvet, Tianjin, 14 March 1949. FPA.
53. Bonningue to Provincial Champagne, Tianjin, 7 February 1949; Bonningue to Pillaine, Tianjin, 7 May 1950. FPA.
54. Letter from the Patriotic Socialist Party, 6 February 1949. FPA.
55. North Daily News, 17 February 1949, Beijing. FPA.

the Catholic Church was planted in China. Now, all was Chinese.[56] The Catholic mission in Xianxian was reported to supply intelligence to the Americans and Guomindang spies. As a result of this allegation, Charvet was deported.[57]

In 1949, there were estimated to be three million Catholic in China, served by 5,000 priests and 8,000 religious. The proportion of Chinese priests to the European priests had risen considerably. Figures for 1947 showed that 560 Chinese priests and 660 foreign priests worked in Communist-controlled zones. Since the end of the war with Japan up to 1947, the Communists had killed forty-seven Catholic missionaries, and 27 had died in prison. Ten foreign missionaries had been killed, two had disappeared and ten died in prison. Despite these statistics and surrounded by devastation of the missions, it was truly remarkable to read of the optimism and hope of the missionaries. Some believed that the witness of the Catholic Church that embraced all classes of people, gave signs to a life lived in poverty that would out witness the Communists. 'Communism will pass . . . what will not pass will be the example we give the Communists in this time. Look to the future with hope and confidence that the Church would triumph.' Meanwhile, the Vatican excommunicated Communists and all collaborators in 1949, which did not impress the Communists.[58]

The gradual take over of all mission activities by the Communists continued from 1950. Bonningue, Louis Watine and the secular priest Sun were removed from the administration of *Hautes Etudes* from December 1950. Bonningue, Watine and Henry Pollet were later accused of espionage and imprisoned on 28 March 1951. Missionary priests continued to be imprisoned or expelled during 1951 and 1952. Réal was condemned to seven years in prison. By 2 June 1952, all foreign scholastics had left China. Shanghai was the last post for Jesuit missionary activity by 1952.[59]

---

56. Charvet, in *Chine* . . ., ut supra, 18, September 1949.
57. French consul, Shanghai, to French Ambassador, Nanjing, 23 August 1948. DAC.
58. *Chine* . . . 17 July 1949; *China Missionary Bulletin,* Hong Kong, September 1949. FPA.
59. Letters of missionaries, 1951–3. FPA.

A testimonial to the mission

On the centenary of the Xianxian mission in 1956, a touching memorial was given on the achievements and losses over those 100 years. It was a testimony to the extraordinary dedicated service of the Jesuit missionaries from the Province of Champagne. It spoke about the number of deaths to the mission itself, the central residence, the seminary, the college, the work of the religious sisters, the primary schools, the parish school in Beijing, the three residences in Beijing, the printing apostolate, the pharmacies and the hospital. All these works that took 100 years to build were all destroyed in a short number of years. Who would remember the sacrifices made to develop the mission? The history of the mission was told, with all the challenges required to secure possession of land on which to build the mission, as well as the opposition from local Chinese, authorities and non-Christians, bandits and rebel armies. Many missionaries had died of disease or hard work or were even killed. Within this framework, by 1946, the last reliable statistic, there were 61,000 Christians in the original mission. The Provinces of France and Champagne gave the mission 224 Jesuits, to which were added 49 Austrian or Hungarian Jesuits who worked in the mission before the creating of their own vicariates. Of the secular clergy, from 1876 to 1954, 102 Chinese priests were formed. In December 1947, there were 32 secular priests. Over the 100 years, the mission formed 76 Jesuit priests, 31 scholastics and 31 brothers.[60] This was a story of the great faith of the missionaries that sustained them in their mission. Their spirituality strengthened their courage and determination to overcome all obstacles. They continued to serve until they were expelled or imprisoned. Bishop Jin believed that the Jesuits from the Province of Champagne were 'more open and visionary' than those from the Province of France. They paid greater attention to the request of the pope to indigenise human resources, and establish a Chinese run diocese.[61] Many missionary letters supported this belief.

---

60. *Le centenaire de la Mission de Xianxian*, 30 May 1856 – 30 May 1956. *In memoriam – in spem*. FPA. Cf also, Joseph Jaeggy, SJ, 'La mission de Sienhsien' *Bellarmino*, 9 (Shanghai: Xujiahui, 3 December 1940): 137–58.
61. Chapter 10, page 2.

In 1981, a meeting of Catholic representatives in Hebei decided to rename the dioceses in the province in line with the government's administrative divisions. Xianxian diocese was renamed Cangzhou diocese. Currently, this diocese has more than 200 churches with 70,000 Catholics, served by 260 nuns and 110 priests. The present bishop is Joseph Li Liangui, a former rector of the local seminary who is approved by the Vatican.[62] The Church once established by the Jesuits and secular clergy of Xianxian currently flourishes in another form after decades of challenges.

62. UCAN directory, Database of Catholic Dioceses in Asia, Diocese of Cangzhou.

Bibliography

1. Primary Sources

A Manuscripts

Archivum Romanum Societatis Iesu – Jesuit archives, Rome (ARSI)

Letters, reports, maps, statistics and catalogues from the Province of France on the Jiangnan/Nanking/Shanghai mission in China, 1840–1939.

Letters, reports, statistics, maps and catalogues from the Province of Champagne on the Tchely S-E/ Xianxian mission in China, 1828–1939.

Letters, reports, statistics, maps and catalogues (1923–1949) from the Province of León on the Anqing mission in China, 1922–1939.

Letters, reports, obituaries, maps and statistics from the Province of French Canada on the Xuzhou mission in China, 1934–1938.

Letters, reports, statistics, maps and catalogues (1918–1950) from the Province of Castile on the Wuhu mission in China, 1917–1939.

Letters, reports, statistics, maps and catalogues (1949–1950) from the Province of Austria on the Jingxian mission in China, 1936–1939.

Letters, reports, statistics, maps and catalogues (1921–1950) from the Turin Province on the Bengbu mission in China, 1923–1939.

Catalogues for the Province of California, 1935–1950.

Catalogues for the Province of Hungary, 1929–1950.

Acta Congressus Missionum SJ, Romae, Curia Generalis, 1925.

Collectanea Commissionis Synadolis (1924–1941). Dossiers de la commission Synodale (Digest of the Synodal Commission).

Missions entrusted to the Society of Jesus among the heathen. Statistics & information (Roma: Grafia, 1925).

Diplomatic Archives Centre, Nantes, France. (DAC)

Pékin/Shanghai: Legation A/B/C/D.
    a) Shanghai (Consulat General)
        Serie A: 1914–1962
        Serie B: 1844–1921
        Serie C: 1847–1952

    b) Pékin: Serie A: 1721–1969.
        Serie D: 1843–1964.
Kiang-nan, 1846–1911. Carton 31 Serie A
The French Protectorate, Carton 59, Box 60, 62, 62 bis, 63, 63 bis, 64, 64 bis, 67: 1844–1943
Tche-li sud-est, Box 21, 1860–1941.
Shanghai Box, A 30, 1948–1951.
Shanghai Box 32, 1922–1932.
Shanghai Box 123, Aurora, 1922–1934.
Shanghai, Box 81, Security Zones, 1938–40.
Shanghai, Box 349, Protection of Missionaries during Sino-Japanese war, 1938ff. Includes protection of Hungarian mission of Taming, Xianxian mission, Wuhu mission, Xuzhou mission,

Letters, reports and statistics to French consular officials in China and from French Ministers in China to French Foreign Ministry, Paris, and replies.

Propagation of the Faith Archives, Rome (PF)

Rubrica, no. 21, NS vol. 1000, 1929 and 1931.
Rubrica no. 21, vol. 804, no.79, and vol. 806, 1923; vol. 807, 1924,
vol. 899, 1926–27; vol. 900b, 1928.

Canadian Jesuit Province Archives, Montreal (CPA)

Biographies of Chinese missionaries in *Le Brigand, Rumeurs, Litterae
Annuae, Provinciae Canadae Inferioris Societatis Iesu, a die 1 August
1941 ad diem 1 August 1944,* and *Lettres du Bas-Canada, 1963–1970.*

Catalogus Missionis Nankinensis (1842–1937).

Diary of Jacques Bouchard, 8 December to 31 December 1937,
Anqing, 1 January 1938.

Journal of Mission of Suchow, October 1931

Le Brigand, 1930–1950
Le Messager Canadien, 1924

Letters, reports, obituaries, statistics, maps and catalogues of the
Xuzhou mission, 1924–1950.

Nouvelles de Chine, 1931,1933, 1948

Semaine d'étude des methods d'apostolat en usage dans le Vicariat
Apostolique de Süchow, 26 June to 2 July 1944.

Status Missionis Süchowensis Societatis Jesu, 1932–1949 (Shanghai,
Xujiahui: Tushanwan, 1950).

Semaine d'étude des methods d'apostolat en usage dans le Vicariat
Apostolique du Süchow, Xujiahui, 26 June -2 July 1944. (Held during
internment by Japanese in Xujiahui).

Status Missionis Sienhsien Societatis Jesu, anno 1929–1947.

Status Missionis Taming Societatis Jesu, anno 1935–1941.

Status Missionis Pengpu Societatis Jesu, anno 1931–1932; 1939–1940.

Status Missionis Wuhuensis Societatis Jesu, anno 1931–1932.

Status Missionis Ankinensis Societatis Jesu, anno 1936–1937.

Jesuit Austrian Province Archives, Vienna, (AASI)

Actus conventus Superiorum missionum SJ in Sinis, Xujiahui, a die 20 Maii ad diem 28 Maii 1948.

Father General Janseens, Ad Omnes Superiores Regulares Missionum SJ in Sinis, Consultationes Missionis, Rome, 24 October 1948.

Catalogues of the Champagne and Austrian Province, 1926–1954.

Das neue Missionsgebiet der österreichischen Jesuiten: Die Apostolische Prefektur Kinghsien, 1939.

Decretum Wlodimirus Ledóchowski, Praepositus Generalis SocietatisIesu, Romae, 28 May 1939.

Ein Jahr Aufbauarbeit in der Mission Kinghsien, July 1940.

Ein kurzer Überblick über die Arbeit unserer Missionare (A brief review of the work of our missionaries), n.d., unsigned.

Einigen über das Regional seminar kin Kinghsien (jetzt in Peiping), (Some things about the regional seminary in Kinghsien, now in Peiping), Beijing, 8 September 1948.

Joseph Dehergne to Provincial Heinzel, Curriculum Vitae, Father Albert Tschepe SJ, 13 November 1956.

Father Emil Büchler SJ, King-Hsien – Mission (1), Kleine Geschichte derselben bis 1939 (King Hsien – Mission short history to 1939), Salzburg, den, 22 April 1958.

Father Francis Xavier Tchao SJ (Zhao Zhen-sheng), Rapport sur l'erection d'un vicariate apostolique de Kinghsien dans le vicariate de Sienhsien, Xianxian, 27 October 1938.

Freinberger Stimmen (Journal of the Collegium Aloisianum at Freiberg near Linz, School for vocations to religious orders and missionaries), 1935–1940.

Historia Seminarii Regionalis, Kinghsien, Hopeh, Sinis, 1939–1946.

Letters, reports, statistics relating to the Jingxian Mission, 1928–1950.

Lumen Service, Beijing, reports on the Jesuit missions, 31 May 1940.

Matthias Leitenbauer, Eine Stadt tut die Tore auf, 16 July 1941.

Nachrichten der österreichischen Prorinz SJ (Newsletter of the Austrian Province for members of the Society of Jesus), 1927–1949.

Was von unserer Seite zur Vorbereitung der Katastrophe beigetragen haben mag (What, on our side, might have contributed to the preparation of the catastrophe?) n.d. no author.

Augustin Zehetner, On the class struggle and the Communist takeover of the mission, Beijing, Maison Chabanel, 18 February 1947.

Jesuit Hungarian Archives, Budapest (HPA)

Letters from the Daming mission to the Jesuit General, Rome, 1932–1954.

Jesuit Californian Province Archives, Los Gatos, California, USA. (CaPA)

Letters, reports, statistics, catalogues, maps of the Yangzhou Mission, 1924–1947.

China Letter, The Jesuits of California, no. 33, Haichow Number, Fall, 1939.

China Jesuit Province Archives, Taipei (CHPA)

Biographies of many Jesuit Missionaries who worked in China during the period of this study.

Noticias generales Provincia Legionesis, (January-March 1960)

Jesuit Province of France, Archives, Vanves, Paris (FPA)

Letters, reports, articles (manuscripts), catalogues, periodicals, photos relating to the China missions of the Province of France (Jiangnan/Nanking/Shanghai) and Province of Champagne (Tchli-S-E/ Xianxian), 1840–1950.

Brou, A. *Les missions des Jésuites de France, 1928–1929*, pamphlet.

Institutions et opera, Missionis Nankinensis SJ, Shanghai, 1888.

Correspondence of provincials, 1941–1955.

Diary of the Jesuit Minister, Xianxian, 1945–1947.

Documents relating to the Daming mission from 1930s, including statistical data, letters between Hungarian provincial and provincial of the Champagne province (1932), description of the prefecture apostolic of Daming.

History of the Mission in Xianxian, 1938–1949.

La mission du Kiangnan, son histoire, ses ouvres, pamphlet, Paris, 1900.

Le centenaire de la Mission de Sienhsien, 30 Mai 1856- 30 Mai 1956, *in memoriam – in spem*, manuscript.

Maquet, H., SJ, *Vicariat du Tcheu-le sud-est . . . 1857–1907*, manuscript, Hokien, 1907.

Memoire sur l'état actuel de la Mission du Kiang-nan, 1984–55 (Paris, 1855).

Quelque notes sur l'état et les progress de la mission du Kiang-nan en 1897 (Vanves 1897).

Réal, Henri, SJ. Memoriale domis (Chabanel Hall), 1948–1949

Rapport sur la visite du Kiang-sou (October 1926–1927).

Reports of French Provincials after visiting the missions, 1911–33.

Semaine d'étude des methods d'apostolat en usage dans le Vicariat Apostolique de Süchow, 26 June to 2 July 1944.

Becker, Emile, SJ, 'Un demi-siècle d'apostolate en Chine, Le Réverent Père Joseph Gonnet, SJ' (Hokien 1900), manuscript.

Maquet, Mgr, SJ, Vicar Apostolic, 'Vicariate of Tcheu-li S-E, 1857–1907'. Manuscript.

Taming Mission, 1933. Statistics, letters to 1933.

Jesuit Spanish Province Archives, Madrid (SPA)

Wuhu Mission (Province of Castile)

Letters, statistics, annual reports, photos from the Wuhu mission, 1918–1948.
Costumbres de la Mision Anking, manuscript, n.d.

Statistics 1925–1926.

Mission to Wuhu, 1922–1947, manuscript.

'Misión de la PP Jesuitas de Anhwei', *Sursum Corda*, Burgos, 1924.

Wuhu y suo Missioneros,

Cartas de Ujú (Wuhu), 1927, 1930

Mission de Wuhu, 1946, manuscript.

Noticias de la Provincia de Cast. Occ, Abril-May 1956.

Anqing Mission (Province of Leon)

Letters reports, statistics, relating to the Anqing Mission. 1918–1948.

Armancio Arnáiz, SJ, Un martir desaparecido, El Pardr Avito, SJ, Misionero de China, manuscript, 1995.

Fr J. Manrique (pp. 12–18) & Cautiverío de los PP Avito Gutierrez y Zacarias Hidalgo, (pp. 30–53) *Primicias de Martres*, Vicariate de Anking, 1935.

Cartas Edificantes de la Provincia de Castilla, Tome XIII, 1925, Oña, Spain.

El Correo de China, 1936

Historic Points for a history of the mission of Anking, 1940–1949, manuscript.

Misio de Wuhu – Estudio de Chino – informe, 1928. Manuscript.

Jesuit Turin Province Archives, Gallarate, Italy (TPA)

Letters, reports, statistics, articles, catalogues, photos, maps from the archives of the Turin Province, 1909–1944

Notizie della Missione di Pengpu, 1924, 1937, 1938, 1940

Notizie Generali e Stato del Vicariato, 1 July 1938.

La Missione dell-Hwai-sè (Cina), for benefactors, pamphlet, 1925.

La Missioni della Compagnia de Gesù, 1921–1944.

Marchesa, Stefano, SJ, *La Nuova Missione Cinese dei Patri Gesuiti della Provincia di Torino,* pamphlet, (Torino: Artigianelli, 1923).

Litterae Annuae Missionis Pengpu, 1938–1941, manuscripts.

Rerum Gestarum relatio, a die 1a Julii 1932 ad diem 30 Junii 1935, Missio Pengpu, Anhwei, Cina, manuscript.

Primo Decennale del Vicariato Apostolico di Pengpu, 1929–1939, pamphlet for benefactors, 1940.

Vatican Secret Archives, Vatican City (ASV)

Letters, reports, and statistics to and from Apostolic Delegates and Vicars Apostolic of the Jesuit missions in China, 1927–1933.

Cina – Archive della Reppresentanze Pontifice, Indice 1251, 1922–1933.
1. Box 9, Delegazione apostolica in Cina, Mons Celso Costantini (1922–1933), ff. 718.
Fasc. 20, III Regione ecclesiastica Hopei – Xianxian, 1922–1933 (1857–1928; 1922–1933), Olim A1; b 13 fasc. 19, nos. 1, 3, 6.
2. Box 25, ff. 976, fasc. 55, VIIIa Regione ecclesiastica Kiangsu-Vicariato apostolico Nanking, (1923–1933), ff. 719 (Olim A2, b 36, fasc. 55), nos, 1–10.
3. Box 26, ff. 312, fasc. 56, VIIIa Regione ecclesiastica Kiangsu—Vicariato apostolico Nanking, ff. 228; fasc. 57, VIIIa, Regione ecclesiastica Kiangsu—Prefecttura apostolica Suchoufu, 1931–33, ff. 84. Nos. 1–3.
4. Box 27, ff. 809, fasc. 58, IXa, Regione ecclesiastica Anhwei, Vicariato apostolico di Anking, 1929–33, ff. 207, nos. 1–4; fasc. 59, Pengpu, 1929–1933; fasc. 60, IXa, Regione ecclesiastics Anhwei – Vicariato apostolico di Wuhu, 1922–1933, ff. 424, nos. 1–6.

B PRINTED

Official Material

Arrupe, A, SJ, Letter to the Society of Jesus on Inculturation (Rome: May 1978).

Catalogue of Christian archival material, 1836–1963, in the Shanghai Muncipal Archives, Shanghai, (2002).

Chan, Albert, SJ, *Chinese Books and Documents in the Jesuit Archives in Rome*, A Descriptive Catalogue, Japonica-Sinica I-IV (New York: M.E. Sharpe, 2002).

Instruction de la sacrée Congrégation de la Propagande adressee aux archevêques, vicars apostoliques et autres supérieurs des missions. (Rome, 1845), in Joseph Gabet, CM, *Les Missions Catholiques en Chine en 1846* (Paris: Valmonde, 1848).

Benedict XV, *Maximum Illud* (1919) on line.

Jesuit General to Chinese missionaries, on the subject of Chinese studies for missionaries, Rome, 3 September 1926, *Lettres de Jersey*, vol. XL, Nouvelle Série, T.VII (1926–27).

Noll, Ray, R (ed.), trans Donald F St. Sure, SJ, *100 Roman Documents concerning The Chinese Rites Controversy (1645–1941)*, Studies in Chinese-Western Cultural History, no. 1 (University of San Francisco: The Ricci Institute for Chinese-Western Cultural History, 1992).

Primum Concilium Sinense, 14 May to 12 June 1924 (Shanghai: Xujiahui, 1930).

Pius X, *Vehementer nos*, 'On the French Law of Separation', 11 February 1906. Papal Encyclicals online.

Pius XI to Chinese bishops, Rome, 15 June 1926, *Lettres de Jersey*, vol. XL, nouvelle série, T. VII, (1926–27).

Sacred Congregation of the Propagation of the Faith, re division of the Apostolic Vicariate of Xianxian, 26 March 1935.

Decree of the Sacred Congregation of Propaganda (concerning the Chinese rites), 8 December 1939.

Terrien, Constant, SJ, (ed.), *Monita ad Missionarios Provinciae Nankinensis et Adjumenta Varia, pro recta et uniformi agenda ratione in ministerio,* (Shanghai, Xujiahui: Tushanwan, 1899).

2. Secondary Sources
A Bibliographical and Historiographical

Cartier, Michel (ed.) *La chine entre amour et haine,* Actes de VIIIe colloque de sinology de Chantilly (Paris: Desclée de Brouwer, 1998).

Dehergne, J., SJ, *Répertoire des Jésuites de Chine de 1552 à 1800* (Paris: Legouzey, 1973).

Heyndrickx, Jeroom, CICM, *Historiography of the Chinese Catholic Church, Nineteenth and Twentieth Centuries,* Louvain Chinese Studies I, (Louvain: Ferdinand Verbiest Foundation, 1994).

McCoog, Thomas M., *A Guide to Jesuit Archives* (St Louis: The Institute of Jesuit Sources, 2001).

'Scriptis Tradere et fideliter conservare', Archives as 'Places of Memory' within the Society of Jesus (Rome: General Curia, 2003).

Tiedemann, R.G., 'Ludovico de Bési', Ricci Roundtable on the History of Christianity in China, biographies, on line.

Vamos, Peter, obituaries of Hungarian Jesuits in Ricci Roundtable, Ricci Institute, San Francisco, University of San Francisco, Biographies.

Wurth, Elmer, MM, researched and compiled, Maheu, Betty Ann, MM, (ed.) *Papal Documents Related to China, 1937–2005* (Hong Kong: Holy Spirit Study Centre, 2006).

B Manuscript Histories and Studies

Bornet, Paul SJ, *Mission de Chine, Le Tcheu-li Sud-est, 1857–1900*; Mgr Henri Maquet,SJ, vicar apostolic, *Vicariate de Tcheu-li Sud-est, 1857–1907*, manuscripts, FPA.

Butcher, Beverley Joan, *Remembrance, emulation, imagination: the Chinese and Chinese American Catholic ancestor memorial service*, PhD, University of Pennsylvania, (UMI: Ann Arbor, 1994).

Breslin, Thomas A., 'American Catholic China Missionaries, 1918–1941', University of Virginia, PhD, 1972. CaPA.

Conférences données à l'Institute Catholique de Paris, 1927–1928, *Les Missions Catholiques et l'oeuvres de civilization* (Paris: Librairie Bloud et Gay, 1929). Articles included, 'La condition de la femme du people en Chine' by P. Robert, pp. 104–125; 'L'Apostolat Intellectual dans les Missions de la Compagnie de Jésus' by A. Brou, SJ.

Fleming, Peter J, 'Chosen for China: the Californian province Jesuits in China, 1928–1957: a case study in Mission and Culture'. PhD, Graduate Theological Union, Berkeley, California, April 1987. CaPA.

Fleury, Samuel C, *Le financement canadien-francais de la mission des Jésuites au Xuzhou de 1931–1949*, MA thesis, Québec, Canada. CPA.

Strong, David, SJ, 'Catholicism and Traditional Chinese belief: A study of Catholic missionary methods in the late Ming and early Ch'ing', dissertation for Master of Arts (prelim), Department of History, University of Western Australia, 1982.

International Conference on the Boxer Movement and Christianity, Taipei and Hong Kong, 10–14 June 2004, manuscript.

Mateos, Fernando, Lists of Jesuits in the China Mission, 1842–1949, manuscript. CPA.

C Printed Material

Newspapers and Periodicals

Annales de l'Observatoire astronomique de Zô-sè (Chine): vol. 1, 1901–1905. Centre Sèvres library, Paris.

Archivum Historicum Societatis Iesu, 1962. ARSI.

Bellarmino, (Shanghai: Xujiahui), 1938–1940. CPA.

Carroll, T, SJ, 'The Educational work of the China Mission', no. 8, 24 October, 1940.

'L'opinion of Mme Sophia Chen sure le Christianisme', no. 6, 7 Mars, 1940.

O'Hara, Albert, SJ, 'An inquire into the causes and motives of conversion of Chinese wounded soldiers', no. 2, 20 October 1938.

Tsang Bede, SJ, 'Le Clerge Chinois de la mission de Shanghai', no. 10, 2 February 1941.

'Un siècle d'apostolat en Chine par la Compagnie de Jesus' no. 9, 3 December 1940.
  1. L'apostolat des Jésuites dans la Chine central.
     a. Cesbron-Lavau, Etienne, SJ, 'La Mission de Shanghai', 33–78.
     b. Mendiburu, Benjamin, SJ, 'La Mission de Wuhu', pp. 79–106.
     c. Vasquez, Modeste, SJ, 'La Mission de Anking'.
     d. Cerutti, Sergio, SJ, 'La Mission de Pengpu', pp. 107–117
     e. Jaeggy, Joseph, SJ, 'La Mission de Sienhsien', pp. 137–158.
  2. L'apostolat des Jésuites dans la Chine septentrionale.
     a. Lévesque, Léonard, SJ., 'La Mission de Suchow', pp. 119–134.
Bulletin Catholique de Pèkin, 1946–1947
Cartas de Ujú (Wuhu), 1927, 1930. SPA.
China Province News (formerly Province News, Provincia Extremi-Orientis 1963, 1965)) (1969 – 2001). CHPA.
China Missionary Bulletin, Hong Kong, September 1949-juillet 1951 CPA.

Chine et Ceylon 1898- *(Later Chine, Ceylon, Madagascar* to 1949).
Letters of Jesuit missionaries from the Province of Champagne,
November 1898- May-June 1903. FPA.
East Asian Pastoral Review, Manila 1982
Ephemerides, Shanghai, 1910–1914. FPA.
Etudes 1901 (Library, Jesuit residence Rue de Grenelle, Paris)
Freinberger Stimmen. AASI
Gerbes Chinoises, Lille, 1934. FPA.
Ignatiusbote, (Newsletter of the Austrian Province for friends of the
Society) 1939–1948.) AASI.
La Missioni 1926,1937, 1939. TPA.
Le Brigand, 1930–1970. CPA.
Le Messager Canadien, 1924. CPA.
Lettres des Nouvelles Missions de la Chine, 1841–68, (7 vols.), Centre
Sèvres, Paris.
Lettres de Jersey 1887–1939. Letters of the Province of France. FPA.
Lettres du Bas-Canada, 1957. CPA.
Memorabilia Societatis Iesu, vol. VIII, (January 1950). ARSI.
Nachrichten der österreichischen *Provinz SJ.* AASI.
North China Herald, 1900–1903, 1927. Australian National Library,
Canberra, Australia.
North China Daily, Shanghai, 1927, 1931. FPA.
Nouvelles de la Mission, Shanghai, 1939–1949. FPA.
Oeuvres de la mission de Kiang-nan, 1891–1936. Centre Sèvres
Library, Paris.
Primicias de Mártires, Anqing, 1935. SPA.
Relatio de Chine 1903–1948, FPA & Centre Sèvres Library, Paris.
Rumeurs Xujiahui, 1942–1945. CPA.
UCAN Directory, Database of Catholic Dioceses in Asia, on line.

Books

Abbott, Walter, SJ, *The Documents of Vatican II* (Dublin: Geoffrey
Chapman, 1966).
Austin, Alvyn J, *Saving China, Canadian Missionaries in the Middle
Kingdom, 1888–1959* (Toronto: University of Toronto press, 1986).
Bangert, William V, SJ, *A History of the Society of Jesus* (St Louis: The
Institute of Jesuit Sources, 1986).

Bays, Daniel H. (ed.) *Christianity in China. From the Eighteenth Century to the Present*, (Stanford, California: Stanford University Press, 1996).

Becker, Emile, *Le demi-siècle d'apostolat en Chine, Le Réverend Père Joseph Gonnet SJ* (Hokien, 1900).

Bernard, Prosper & Bernard, Prosper M Jr. *De L'autre côté de la terre: la Chine* (Montreal: Science et Culture, 1999)

Bevans, Stephen B. SVD & Schroeder, Roger, P. SVD, *Constants in Context. A theology of Mission for Today* (Maryknoll, New York: Orbis, 2004).

Bickers, Robert A, and Tiedemann, R. G., *The Boxers, China and the World*, Langham (Md: Rowan and Littlefield, 2007), on line.

Bornet, Paul, SJ, *Mission de Chine. Le Tcheu-li Sud-est, 1857–1900*. FPA.

Bornet, Paul, SJ, *Histoire de 100 ans de la mission et du Diocèse de Sienhsien (Hopei), 1901–1949.*

Bosch, David J, *Transforming Mission, Paradigm Shifts in Theology of Mission*, American Society of Missiology Series, No. 16 (Maryknoll, New York: Orbis Books, 1992).

Boucher, Henri, SJ, *La Mission du Kiang-nan, Son histoire, ses oeuvres* (Paris: J. Mersch, 1900).

Brou, Alexandre, SJ, *Les Jésuites missionaires au XIXe siècle* (Bruxelles: Dewitt, 1908).

Brou, Alexandre, SJ & Gilbert, Gustave, SJ, *Jésuites Missionaires un siècle, 1823–1923* (Paris: Editions Spes, 1924).

Brou, Alexandre, SJ, *Cents ans de Mission 1815–1934. Les Jésuites Missionaires au XIXe et XXe siècles* (Paris: Editions Spes, 1935).

Brouillon, N, SJ, *Mémoire sur l'état actuel de la Mission du Kiang-nan, 1842–1855* (Paris: Julien, 1855).

Brown, Thompson, G, *Christianity in the People's Republic of China* (USA, Atlanta: John Knox Press, 1986).

Buckley, C.M, SJ, *When Jesuits were Giants, Louis-Marie Ruellan, SJ, 1846–1885 and his contemporaries* (San Francisco: Ignatius Press, 1999).

Bush, Richard, C, Jr. *Religion in Communist China*, (New York: Abingdon Press, 1970).

Carlson, E.C, *The Foochow Missionaries, 1847–1880*, East Asian Research Centre, (Cambridge Mass: Harvard University Press, 1974).

Cary-Elwes, Columba, OSB, *China and the Cross*, A survey of Missionary History (New York: Kennedy and Sons, 1956).

Cent ans sur le fleuve bleu, une mission des Jésuites, n.a. (Shanghai: Xujiahui, 1942).

Cerezo, Elías, SJ, & Villasante, Roberto, SJ, *Spanish Jesuits in China, 1552–2014* (Taiwan, Taipei: Inforchina, 2015).

Chan, Wing-Tsit, *Religious trends in Modern China* (New York: Octagon Books, 1978).

Chang, Mark, K, SJ, *A historical sketch of Christianity in China* (Taiwan: Window Press, 1985).

Charbonnier, J, *Histoire des Chrétiens de Chine* (Paris: Desclée, 1992).

Christensen, Torben, *Missionary ideologies in the Imperialist era, 1880–1920,* (Århus, Denmark: Aros, c1982)

Yik-yi Chu, Cindy, *Catholicism in China, 1900 – Present: the Development of the Chinese Church* (London: Palgrave Macmillan, 2014).

Ch'en, Jerome, *Yuan Shih-k'ai* (Stanford, California: Stanford University Press, 2nd edition, 1972).

Ching, J, *Confucianism and Christianity* (Tokyo: Sophia University, 1977).

Clark, Anthony E, *China's Saints, Catholic Martyrdom during the Qing (1644–1911)* (Bethlehem: Lehigh University Press, 2011).

Clements, Paul H, *The Boxer Rebellion* (Columbia: Longmans, 1915).

Cohen, Paul A, *Discovering History in China,* American Historical Writing on the Recent Chinese Past (New York: Columbia University Press: 1984).

Colombel, Augustin-M, SJ, *L'histoire de la Mission de Kiang-nan,* 3 vols. (Shanghai: Imprimerie de la Mission Catholique à L'Orphelinet de Tushanwan, 1899).

Chang, Iris, *The Rape of Nanking: The Forgotten Holocaust of World War II* (New York: Basic Books, 1997).

Chesneaux, Jean, et al (eds.) *China from the 1911 Revolution to Liberation,* trans from the French by Paul Auster and Lydia Davis (U.K: The Harvester Press, 1977).

Chesneaux, Jean, et al (eds.) *Movements populaires et sociétés secrètes en Chine aux XIXe et XXe siècles* (Paris: Maspero, 1970).

Clarke, Jeremy, *Catholic Shanghai,* A Historical, Practical and Reflective Guide (St Louis: The Institute of Jesuit Sources, 2012).

Cronin, Vincent, *The Wise Man from the West* (London: Rupert Hart-Davis, 1955).

Datin, R, SJ, *Un centenaire de la Mission de Chang-hai, 1842–1942* (Paris, 1942).

Dawson, Raymond, *The Chinese Chameleon, an analysis of European conceptions of Chinese civilization* (London: Oxford University Press, 1967).

Delacroix, S. (ed.) *Histoire Universelle des Mission Catholiques*, 4. vols, (Paris: Librairie Grund, 1954–1959),

D'Elia, Pasquale, M, SJ, *Catholic Native Episcopacy in China* (Shanghai: Tushanwan Printing Press, 1927).

D'Elia, Pasquale, M, SJ, *Les missions Catholique en Chine* (Shanghai: Tushanwan, 1934).

Dillon, Michael, *China, a Modern History* (London/New York: Tauris, 2010).

Dragon, Antonio, SJ, *En Mission parmi les Rouges* (Montréal: Le Messager Canadien, 1946).

Dragon, Antonio, SJ, *Le Père Bernard* (Montréal: Le Messager Canadien, 1948).

Duara, Prasenjit, *Culture, Power, and the State*. Rural North China, 1900–1942 (Stanford, California: Stanford University Press, 1988).

Esherick, Joseph W, *The Origins of the Boxer Uprising* (California: University of California Press, 1987).

Etiemble, R, *Les Jésuites en Chine, la querelle des rites, 1552–1773* (Paris: Julliard, 1966).

Fairbank, J.K, *The United States and China* (Cambridge, Massachusetts: Harvard University Press, 1949).

Fairbank, J.K, *The Great Chinese Revolution, 1800–1985* (New York: Harper & Row, 1986).

Fenby, Jonathan, *Chiang Kai-shek, China's Generalissimo and the Nation He Lost* (New York: Carroll & Graf, 2004).

Fenby, Jonathan, *History of Modern China* (England: Penguin, 2008).

Franke, O.W, *China and the West* (Oxford, Blackwell, 1967).

Franke, Wolfgang, *A Century of Chinese revolution, 1851–1949*, trans Stanley Rudman (Oxford: Blackwell, 1970).

Fu, Patrick, *Passivity, Resistance and Collaboration*. Intellectual choices in occupied Shanghai, 1937–1945 (Stanford, California: Stanford University Press, 1993).

Gabot, P, *Les Missions Catholiques en Chine en 1846* (Paris: Valmonde, 1848).

Gamble, Sidney D, *North China Villages*. Social Political and Economic activities before 1933 (Berkeley: University of California Press, 1963).

Gernet, Jacques, *China and the Christian Impact* (UK: Cambridge University Press, 1985).

Giunipero, Elisa, 'The Boxer movement through the eyes of European missionaries',
The International Conference on the Boxer Movement and Christianity in China (Hong Kong, June 2004).

Granet, Marcel, *The Religion of the Chinese People* (Oxford: Basil Blackwell, 1975).

Guibert, Joseph de, SJ, *The Jesuits their spiritual doctrine and practice,* a historical study, William J Young SJ translator, George E. Ganss SJ editor (Chicago: The Institute of Jesuit Sources, 1964).

Becker, Emile, SJ, *Un demi-siècle d'apostolat en Chine:* le reverend Père Joseph Gonnet de la Compagnie de Jésus (China: Hokien, 1900).

Hanbury-Tenison (trans*), The Memoirs of Jin Luxian, vol. 1*: Learning and Relearning, 1916–1982 (Hong Kong: Hong Kong University Press, 2012).

Harrison, Henrietta, *The Missionary's Curse and Other Tales from a Chinese Catholic Village.* Series: Asia, Local Studies/Global Themes (USA: University of California Press, 2013).

Hayhoe, Ruth & Yongling Lu (eds.) *Ma Xiangbo and the mind of Modern China, 1840–1939* (New York: Sharpe, 1996).

Hermand, Louis, SJ, *Les* étapes *de la Mission du Kiang-nan, 1842–1922 (1923) et de la mission de Nanking, 1922–1932* (Shanghai, Xujiahui: Imprimerie de la mission, 1933).

Howe, Christopher (ed.) *Shanghai, Revolution and Development in an Asian metropolis* (Cambridge: Cambridge University Press, 1981).

Huang, Philip C.C, *The Peasant Economy and Social Change in North China* (Stanford, California: Stanford University Press, 1985).

Hughes, E.R. & Hughes K, *Religion in China* (London: Hutchinson's University Press, 1950).

Hugon, Joseph, SJ, *La Mission de Nankin et mes paysans* (Paris: Vanves, 1925).

Hugon, Joseph, SJ, *Mes Paysans Chinois* (Paris, Vanves: 1930).

Jen Yu-wen, *The Taiping Revolutionary Movement* (Haven & London: Yale University Press, 1973).

Johnson, Chalmers, A, *Peasant Nationalism and Communist Power,* (Stanford, California: Stanford University Press, 1962).

Johnston, Reginald, F, *Twilight in the Forbidden City* (New York: Appleton-Century, 1934).

Li, Dun, J. (ed.) *China in Transition, 1517–1911* (New York: Reinhold, 1969).

Joly, Léon, *Le christianisme et l'Extrême-Orient* (Paris: Leithielleux, 1907).

Kuang-sheng, Liao, *Antiforeignism and modernization in China, 1860–1980* (Hong Kong: The Chinese University Press, 1984).

Kung-Chuan Hsiao, *Rural China*, Imperial Control in the Nineteenth Century (USA, Seattle: University of Washington Press, 1960).

Küng, Hans, *Can we save the Catholic Church?* (UK: Collins, 2013).

Lafortune, Edouard, SJ, *Canadiens en Chine*, (Montreal: L'Action Paroissiale, 1930).

Langlais, Jacques, *Les Jésuites du Québec en Chine, 1918–1955* (Québec: Presse de Université Laval, 1979).

Latourelle, K.S., *A History of Christian Mission in China* (New York: The Macmillan Company, 1929).

Laurentin, René, *Chine et christianisme, après les occasions manquées* (Paris: Desclée, 1986).

Leclercq, Chanoine J, *La Vie du Père Lebbe* (Paris: Tournai, 1964).

Lee, Robert, *France and the Exploitation of China, 1884–1901*. A study in Economic Imperialism (Oxford: Oxford University Press, 1989).

Leroy, H-J., *En chine au Tché-le S-E* (Paris: Desclée, 1899).

Levaus, Leopold, *Le Père Lebbe, Apôtre de la Chine Moderne* (Paris/Brussels, 1948).

Leys, Simon, *The Hall of Uselessness*, the work of László Ladány, 1914–1990 (Melbourne: Black Inc., 2011).

Liao, Kuang-sheng, *Antiforeignism and Modernization in China, 1860–1980*, (Hong Kong: Chinese University Press, 1984).

Lou Tseng-Tsiang, *Ways of Confucius and of Christ* (London: Burns Oates, 1948).

Louis Wei Tsing-sing, *Le Saint-siege et la Chine de Pie Xi à nos jours* (Paris: Allais, 1968).

Lutz, Jessie, G, (ed.), *Christian Missions in China, evangelists or what?* (Boston: Problems in Asian Civilizations, 1965).

Lutz, Jessie, G, *Opening China*, Karl F.A. Gützlaff and Sino-Western Relations, 1827–1852, Studies in the History of Christian Missions (U.K., Cambridge, William B. Eerdmans, 2008).

Madsen, Richard, *China's Catholics*, Tragedy and Hope in an Emerging Society (Berkeley: University of California Press, 1998).

Malatesta, Edward J, SJ, *The Society of Jesus and China, a historical-theological essay* (St Louis: The Institute of Jesuit Sources, 1997).

Malovic, Dorian, *Le Pape jaune*, Mgr. Jin Luxian, soldat de Dieu en Chine communiste, (Asie: Perrin, 2006).

Mariani, Paul P, *Church Militant, Bishop Kung and Catholic resistance in Communist Shanghai* (Cambridge: Harvard University Press, 2011).

Marin, George, SJ, *Une Mission Canadienne* (Montréal: Procure de la Mission, 1925).

Maryks, Robert A, & Wright, Jonathan (eds.) *Jesuit Survival and Restoration, A global history, 1773–1900*. Articles by Paul Mariani, Paul Rule, and Jeremy Clarke.

Mateos, Fernando, SJ, *China Jesuits in East Asia, Starting from Zero, 1949–1957*, (Taipei, 1995).

Mertens, Pierre-Xavier, SJ, *La Légende dorée en Chine*. Scènes de la vie de Mission au Tche-li sud-est (Paris: Desclée, 1920).

Mertens, Pierre-Xavier, SJ, *L'Eglise de Chine, situation actuelle* (Montreal: L'Oeuvres des Tracts, no. 354, December 1948).

Meynard, Thierry, SJ, *Following the Footsteps of the Jesuits in Beijing* (St Louis: The Institute of Jesuit Sources, 2006).

McAleavy, Henry, *Black Flags over Vietnam* (London: George Allen and Unwin, 1968).

Minamiki, George, SJ, *The Chinese Rites Controversy from its beginnings to Modern Times* (Chicago: Loyola University Press, 1985).

Mitter, Rana, *Forgotten Ally, China's World War II, 1937–1945* (Boston: Houghton Mifflin Harcourt, (2013).

Moidrey, J, SJ. *Notes sur les vingt-quatredemiers années des cinq regions synodales de Chine*, pamphlet (Shanghai: Xujiahui, 1930).

Morse, Hosea Ballou, *The International Relations of the Chinese Empire*, The Period of Conflict, 1834–1860, & vol. III, The Period of Subjection, 1894–1911 (New York: Paragon Book Gallery, 1917).

Niebuhr, H.R, *Christ and Culture* (London: Faber and Faber, 1952).

Padberg, John, W, SJ, *Colleges in Controversy*, the Jesuit schools in France from Revival to Suppression, 1815–1880 (USA: Harvard University Press, 1969).

Payne, Robert, *Chiang Kai-shek*, (New York: Weybright & Talley, 1969).

Perry, Elizabeth J, *Rebels and Revolutionaries in North China, 1845–1945* (Stanford, California: Stanford University Press, 1980).

Planchet,J.M, *Documents sur les Martyrs de Pékin pendant la persecution des Boxers* (Pékin: Imprimie des Lazaristes, 1920).

Po-Chia Hsia, R, *A Jesuit in the Forbidden City*, Matteo Ricci, 1552–1610 (Oxford: Oxford University Press, 2010).

Preston, Diana, *The Boxer Rebellion* (New York: Berkley Books, 2000).

Proulx, Armand, SJ, *Mon T'ang-li* (compound) (Montréal: Bellarmin, 1957).

Rabe, John, *The Good Man of Nanking, The Diaries of John Rabe*, Erwin Wickert, editor (New York: Knopf, 2000).

Renaud, Rosario, *Süchow, Diocèse de Chine, 1882–1931*, Tome I (Montreal: Bellarmin, 1956).

Renaud, Rosario, *Süchow '48* (Montreal: Procure des Mission 1949).

Renaud, Rosario, *Le Diocèse de Süchow (Chine)*, vol. 2, 1918–1954 (Montreal: Bellarmin, 1982).

Ristain, Marcia R, *The Jacquinot Safe Zone: Wartime Refugees in Shanghai* (Stanford, California: Stanford University Press, 2008).

Roberts, S.H, *History of French Colonial Policy*, 2 vols. (London: King and Son, 1929).

Rule, Paul, *K'ung-tzu or Confucius?* The Jesuit Interpretation of Confucianism (Sydney: Allen & Unwin, 1986).

Rule, Paul (ed.) *The Church in China* (Adelaide: Interface, Australasian Theological Forum Inc., 2010)

Ryan, Thomas, F, SJ, *Jesuits in China* (Taiwan: Kuangchi Cultural Group, 2007).

Schutte, J.F., *Valignano's Mission Principles for Japan*, vol. 1 (1573–1582), trans by J.J. Coyne (Arand-India: Gujarat Sahitya Prakash, 1980)

Servière, Joseph de la, SJ, *Histoire de la Mission du Kiang-nan*, Tome 1, 1840–1856, & Part II, 1856–1878 (Shanghai: Xujiahui, 1914).

Servière, Joseph de la, SJ, *La Nouvelle Mission du Kiang-nan*, 1840–1922, pamphlet, (Shanghai, Xujiahui, 1925).

Soetens, Claude, *L'Église Catholique en Chine au XXe Siècle* (Paris: Beauchesne, 1997).

Sohier, Albert, 'Père Vincent Lebbe: Prophet and Missionary', *Prophets in the Church, Roger Aubert (ed.)* (New York, 1968).

Spence, Jonathan, D, *To Change China: Western Advisers in China, 1620–1960* (U.K.: Penguin, 1980).

Spence, Jonathan, D, *The search for Modern China* (New York: WW Norton, 1999).

Standaert, Nicholas, *Chinese Voices in the Rites Controversy. Travelling books, Community Networks, Intercultural Arguments,* Bibliotheca Instituti Historici SJ, vol. 75 Paul Oberholzer SJ, editor (Rome 2012).

Tsing, S. & Fairbank, J.K. (eds.) *China's Response to the West* (Cambridge: Harvard University Press, 1965).

Tsing-Sing, Louis Wei, *Le Saint Siège et la Chine de Pie XI à nos jours* (Paris: Allais, 1968).

Tuchman, Barbara, *Sand against the Wind: Stillwell and the American Experience in China 1911–45* (Edinburgh: Macmillan, 1970).

Vamos, Peter, *Körösi Csoma Kiskönyvtár*, Magyar jezsuits misszió Kínában (Budapest: Akadémiai Kiadó, 2003).

Weber, Max, *The Religion of China, Confucianism and Taoism,* (New York: The Free Press, 1951).

Whyte, Bob, *Unfinished Encounter, China and Christianity,* (Collins London: Sands and Company, 1988).

Wiest, Jean-Paul, *Maryknoll in China, A History, 1918–1955* (New York: ME Sharpe Inc. 1988).

Wolfenstan, Bertram, SJ, *The Catholic Church in China, 1860–1907* (London: Sands and Company, 1909).

Wright, Jonathan, *God's Soldiers*, Adventure, Politics, Intrigue, and Power – A History of the Jesuits (New York: Doubleday, 2004)

Wei, Tsing-sing, Louis, *La politique missionaire de la France en Chine, 1842–1856* (Paris: Nouvelles Editions Latines, 1960).

Wei, Tsing-sing, Louis, *Le Saint-Siege et la chine, de Pie XI à nos jours* (Paris: Allais, 1968).

Young, Ernest P, *Ecclesiastical Colony: China's Catholic Church and the French Religious Protectorate* (Oxford: Oxford University Press, 2013).

Articles

Adigard, S, 'Protestant establishments at Nanjing and Chang-King (Sichuan)', Varia, *Lettres de Jersey,* vol. xvi, no. 1 (May 1894).

Ancel, 'Catholics and Protestants in China', *Relatio de Chine* (September-December 1923).

Barry, Peter, MM, 'Sun-Yat-sen and Christianity', *Tripod*, vol. 31, no. 162 (Autumn 2011).

Beckmann, Johannes SMB, 'Dialogue with Chinese Religion', *The Church Crossing Frontiers* (Uppsala: Gleerup, 1969), pp. 124–138.

Benigno, Michael, 'Fr. Terrence Curry, SJ: Voluntary Vulnerability in China', *Midwest Jesuits* (25 September 2014).

Bernard-Maître, Henri, 'L'attitude du P. Matteo Ricci en face des coutumes et rites chinois', *Recherches de Science Religieuse*, vol. 28 (1938), pp. 31–47.

Bernard-Maître, Henri, 'The Chinese and Malabar Rites', *Concilium*, vol. 7, no. 3 (1967), pp.38–45.

Bonnichon, André, 'The peasants of Xuzhou', *Lettres de Jersey*, no. 45, (1933).

Bornet, Paul, SJ, 'Les origins de Tcheu-li mission', *Bulletin Catholique de Pékin*, no. 30 (1943).

Boxer, C.R, 'The Jesuits at the Court of Peking', *History Today*, vol. VII (1957), pp. 582–589.

Brou, Alexandre, SJ, 'La mission du Kiang-nan. Coute histoire de soixante-cinq ans', *Relatio de Chine*, no. 2 (1907), p.2.

Brou, Alexandre, SJ, 'L'encyclique sur les mission. Le clergé indigene. Sa formation', *Etudes*, no. 2 (1920), pp. 592–612.

Brou, Alexandre, SJ, 'Concerning an article on Aurora', *Lettres de Jersey*, no. 41 (1927–28).

Brou, Alexandre, SJ, 'Le premier jubilee de l'université l'Aurore', *Etudes*, 197 (November 1928), pp. 284–85.

Brou, Alexandre, SJ, 'Le point final à la Question des rites Chinois', *Etudes*, vol. 242, (January-February-March 1940), pp. 275–282.

Brucker, Joseph, 'Les missionaries catholiques aujourd'hui et autrefois', *Etudes*, no. 5 (July 1901).

Camps, Arnulf, OFM, 'Celso Costantini, Apostolic Delegate to China, 1922–1933. The changing role of the foreign missionary', *Tripod*, no. 44 (1988).

Carroll, T, 'The Educational work of the China Mission, *Bellarmino*, no.8, *24* (October 1940).

Charbonnier, Jean, MeP, 'How Chinese Catholics Renewed the Church in China', *Tripod*, vol. 29, no. 155 (Winter 2009).

Chong, Francis, CDD, 'Cardinal Celso Costantini and the Chinese Catholic Church', *Tripod*, vol. 28, no. 148 (Spring 2008).

Clooney, Francis, X, SJ, 'A Charism for Dialog. Advice from the Early Jesuit Missionaries in Our World of Religious Pluralism', *Studies in the Spirituality of Jesuits*, no. 32/2 (March 2002).

Cohen, P.A, 'The anti-Christian tradition in China', *Journal of Asian Studies*, vol. 20, no. 2 (February 1961), pp. 169–180.

Cole, H.M, 'The Origins of the French Protectorate on the Catholic Missions in China', *American Journal of International Law*, vol. 34, no. 3 (July 1940).

Corniot, Christine, 'La guerre des Boxeurs d'après la presse française', *Etudes Chinoises*, vol. VI, no. 2, (Automine 1987).

Cothonay, Bernard, OP, 'A Missionary's view of the Chinese question', *The Catholic World*, vol. LXXIII, no. 436, (July 1901), pp. 415- 426.

Cummins, J.S, 'Two missionary methods in China: Mendicants and Jesuits', *Archivo ibero-americano*, vol. 38 (1978), pp. 33–108.

Cerutti, Sergio, SJ, 'La mission de Pengpu', *Bellarmino*, no. 9 (Shanghai: Xujiahui, 3 December 1940).

Datin, Françoise, SJ, 'Un centenaire: la mission de Shanghai, 1942–1942', *Missionaires de la compagnie de Jésus*, no. 7 (1942), pp. 232–247.

Davy, Jacques, "La condemnation en Sorbonne des 'Nouveaux Memoires sur la Chine' du P Le Comte' *Recherches de Science Religieuse*, no. 37 (1950), pp. 366–397.

De Gassart, D, 'The Evangelization of Kiang-pé', *Lettres de Jersey*, vol. XLVI, Nouvelle Série, T. XIII, no. 2 (1935–36).

Dehergne, J, 'Noes sur la bréve histoire de l'Aurore (1901–1951), *Etudes*, 350 (May 1979, pp. 613–14.

Dehergne, J, 'La mission du Kiang-nan (Chine) pendant les deux premières siècles de 'époque modern (1599–1800)' *NZM*, no. 27, 1971, pp.253–272.

Dragon, Antonio, 'En Mission parmi les Rouges' *Le Messager Canadien*, (Montreal: 1946).

Dragon, Antonio, 'Le Père Bernard', *Le Messager Canadien*, (Montreal:1948).

Dreffer, Jean, 'The future of the French Missions in China', *Le Journal de Pekin* (30 December 1928).

Dumeige, Gervaise, SJ, 'L'idée de mission et la compagnie de Jésus', in Retif, A, SJ, (ed.) *Les Heritages de Saint François* (Paris: Artheme Fayard, 1956).

Entenmann, Robert, 'Christian Virgins in Eighteenth Century Sichuan' in Daniel H Bays (ed.) *Christianity in China: From the Eighteenth Century to the Present* (California: Stanford University Press, 1996).

Fay, Peter W, 'The French Catholic Mission in China during the Opium War', *Modern Asian Studies*, 4, 2, (1970), pp. 115–128.

Gordon, David M, 'The China-Japan War, 1931–1945', *The Journal of Military History*, vol. 70, no. 1 (January 2006).

Harris, G.L, 'The Mission of Matteo Ricci, SJ: a case study of an effort at guided culture change in the sixteenth century', *Monumenta Serica*, vol. 25 (1966), pp. 1–168.

Hoffman, Ronan, OFM Conv, 'The Development of Mission Theology in the Twentieth Century', *Theological Studies*, vol. 23, no. 3, (September 1962), pp. 419–441.

Jaeggy, Joseph, SJ, 'La Mission de Sienhsien', *Bellarmino*, no. 9 (Shanghai: Xujiahui, 3 December 1940).

Kang Zhijie, 'The Yeast of Evangelization: a Study on the Contribution of the Virgin Catechists', *Tripod*, vol. 33, no. 170 (Autumn 2013).

Krahl, Joseph, SJ, 'China Missions in Crisis', Bishop Laimbeckhoven and his times, 1738–1787, *Analecta Gregoriana*, vol. 137 (Rome: Gregoriana University Press, 1963), p. 99ff.

Lam, Anthony, 'Archbishop Costantini and the First Council of Shanghai (1924', *Tripod*, vol. 28, no. 148 (Spring 2008).

Leurent, 'Pagans and Protestants, Ki-tcheoui', *Lettres de Jersey*, vo.XXIV, no. unique, (1905).

L'Eglise de Shanghai se Souvient, vingt ans après…', *Eglise d'Asie*, Agence d'information des Missions Étrangères de Paris, (8 July 2013).

'L'université de Aurora', *Bulletin de la Jeunesse Catholique Chinoise*, l'Associatio Catholic Juventutis Sinensis, ACJS, Louvain, no. 37 (January 1928).

Marin, George, SJ, 'Les croyances religieuse des Chinois', *Le messager Canadien*, XXXIII, no. 11 (Montréal: November 1924), pp. 504–509.

Marin, George, SJ, *'La Chine à Dieu. Une mission canadienne, le Siu-Tcheou –Fu,* (Montréal: Procure de la mission de Chine, 1925).

Maron, Joseph, SJ, 'La Mission de Taming', *Bellarmino*, no. 9 (Shanghai: Xujiahui, 3 December 1940).

Meehan, John, SJ, 'The Saviour of Shanghai, Robert Jacquinot SJ, and his safety zone in a city at war, 1937', *Company* (Spring 2006), pp. 17–21.

Mendiburu, Benjamin, 'The Mission du Wuhu', *Bellarmino*, no.9 (3 December 1940).

Mungello, David, 'The return of the Jesuits to China in 1841 and the Chinese Christian Backlash', *Sino-Western Cultural Relations Journal*, vol. 27, (2005), p. 9–46.

O'Hara, Albert, 'An Inquiry into the causes and motives of conversion of Chinese wounded soldiers, *Bellarmino*, no. 2, 20 (October 1938).

Renaud, R, SJ, 'Le bienheureux Ignace Mangin SJ et ses compagnons, martyrs', *Lettres du Bas-Canada*, no. 9 (1955), pp.133–157.

Rule, Paul, A, 'The Confucian Interpretation of the Jesuits', *Papers in Far Eastern History*, no. 6 (September 1972), pp. 1–61.

Saimpeyre, Antoine, 'La Mission dans la Tourmente', *Lettres de Jersey*, vol. XLI, Nouvelle serie, T. VIII, (1927–28).

Servière, Joseph de la, SJ, 'The work of the Catholic Church in China', *The Oxford and Cambridge Review*, June 1912.

Shan, Paul Cardinal, SJ, 'Acknowledging Mistakes, Clarifying Misunderstandings: Keynote Address', trans by Arthur Chung & Peter Barry, International Conference on the Boxer Movement and Christianity in China, Taiwan and Hong Kong (2004). Cf. *Tripod*, vol. 24, no. 134 (Autumn 2004) for details of the Conference.

Standaert, Nicholas, SJ, 'The Chinese Mission without Jesuits', *Yearbook of the Society of Jesus* (2014), pp. 58ff.

Servière, Joseph de la, SJ, 'The work of the Catholic Church in China', *The Oxford and Cambridge Review*, (June 1912).

Servière J, de la, SJ, 'Une Université française en Chine', *Relatio de Chine*, 2 (April, 1925), pp. 3–4.

'Shanghai Université l'Aurore', *Bulletin*, vol. 10, no 40, n.a.(Shanghai: Imprimerie de Tushanwan, 1949)

Starkloff, Carl, C, SJ, 'Pilgrimage Re-envisioned. Mission and Culture in the last five General Congregations', *Studies in the Spirituality of Jesuits*, no. 32/5 (November 2000)

Taveirne, Patrick, CICM, 'The Missionary enterprise and the endeavours to establish an ecclesiastical hierarchy and diplomatic relations with China, 1307–1946', *Tripod*, vol. 54 (December 1989), pp. 53–66.

Taveirne, Patrick, CICM, 'Catholic Higher Education in China', *Tripod*, vol. 26, no. 142 (Autumn 2006).

Ticozzi, Sergio, PIME, 'Celso Costantine's Contribution to the Localization and Inculturation of the Church in China', *Tripod*, vol. 28, no. 148 (Spring 2008).

Tiedemann, R.G, 'Christianity in a violent environment. The North China Plain on the Eve of the Boxer Uprising', Jerome Heyndricks (ed.) *Historiography of the Chinese Catholic Church, 19th and 20th Century* (Leuven 1984).

Tiedemann, R.G, 'Catholic Religious Communities of Women (Foreign)', in R.G. Tiedemann (ed.) *Handbook of Christianity in China*, vol. 2: 1800 to the Present, Part Two: Republican China (USA: Brill, 2010), pp. 526–531.

Tsang, Beda & Sen, Joseph, SJ, 'Le Clergé chinois de la Mission de Shanghai', *Bellarmino*, no. 10, 2 (February 1941).

Vamos, Peter, 'Hungarian Missionaries in China', Whalley, Stephen Jr. & Wu, Xianoxin (eds.) *China and Christianity. Burdened Past, Hopeful Future.* (Armonk, New York: M.E. Sharpe, 2001), pp. 217–232.

Vamos, Peter, *Magyar jezsuita misszió Kínában*, Körösi Csoma · Kiskönyvtár 26 (Budapest: Akadémiai Kiadó, 2003).

Vamos, Peter, *Két Kultúra* ölelésében *Magyar misszionáriusok a Távol-Keleten* (Embracing Two Cultures: Hungarian Missionaries in the Far East) (Budapest: Jésus Társasága Mayaroszági Rendtartománya, 1997).

Vamos, Peter, (ed.) *Bevégeztetet. Koch István naplója a magyar jezsuiták kínai missziójának pustulásáról* (The Diary of István Koch on the Destruction of the Hungarian Jesuit Mission in China). (Budapest: Terebess, 1999).

Vásquez, Modeste, SJ, 'La Mission de Anking' (Jésuites Espagnols de la Province de León), *Bellarmino*, no.9 (Shanghai: Xujiahui, 3 December 1940).

Vermander, Benoit, SJ, 'As China changes, Teilhard de Chardin reappears', *E-Renlai Magazine*, (28 October 2014).

Vermander, Benoit, SJ, 'Missionaires jésuites en monde chinois: le tournant du concile Vatican II', *Missionnaires chrétiens, XIXe – XXe siècle*, Asie et Pacific (2008), pp. 50–64.

Vermander, Benoit, SJ, 'Jesuits and China', *Oxford Online Publicatio*, (April 2015).

Wieger, Léon, 'La Chine Actuelle', *Etudes*, vol. 64, no, 191 (Avril-Mai-June, 1927).

'Xu Guangqi', *Asian News* (2 January 2015).

Wiest, Jean-Paul, 'Bringing Christ to the Nations: Shifting Models of Mission among Jesuits in China', *The Catholic Historical Review*, vol. 83, no. 4 (October 1997), pp. 654–681.

Wiest, Jean-Paul, 'From Past Contributions to present opportunities' in Whalley, Stephen Jr. & Xiaoxin Wu (eds.) *China and Christianity* (Armonk, New York: M.E. Sharpe, 2001).

Yang Chien, 'The Communist Menace in China', *La Politique de Pekin*, no. 30 (1931).

Young, John D., 'Comparing the approaches of Jesuit and Protestant missionaries in China, *Ching Feng*, no. 22 (1979), pp. 107–115.

Zhao Jianmin, "Matteo Ricci: he Pioneer of 'Renaissance' in China", *Tripod*, vol. 30, no. 158 (Autumn 2010).

Zhang Ruguo, 'Les 25 and de l'Aurore, 1903–1928', box 3, 'Université l'Aurore', PFA.

Zhang Shijiang, John B., 'Towards a Wider Reconciliation', A cultural-theological reflection on the division within the Church in China, *East Asian Pastoral Review* vol. 34, no.1/2 (Manila, 1997).

Name Index

De Vienne, Jean, 213, 411, 413,
    418, 439, 441.
De Vienne, Jean, 213, 411, 413,
    418, 439, 441.
Debeauvais, Jean, 205, 220, 244,
    410, 412, 413, 415, 416, 417,
    428.
Delorme, Paul, 94, 95.
Denizot, Jules, 386.
Denn, Paul, 116, 331, 396, 400f,
    403, 404, 407.
Desjacques, Marin,
Dillon, Michael, 11, 47, 48, 49,
    82, 84, 107, 108, 130, 135, 141,
    171, 214, 247, 289, 296, 315.
Diniz, José, 320.
Donovan, Cornelius, xiii.
Doré, Henri, 93, 114, 309.
Doré, Henri, 93, 114, 309.
Dowager, Emperess, 80, 90, 107,
    114, 115, 132, 135.
Dreffer, Jean, 264, 265, 484.
Dubar, Bishop, 69, 383, 385, 387,
    388.
Ducis, Jean-François, 35, 71.
Ducoux, Joseph, 174, 176, 186,
    224.
Dumas, Louis, 303, 351.
Dumas, Louis, 303, 351.
Dunne, George, xiii, 304.
Dupanloup, Félix Antoine Philib-
    ert, 2.
Durand, Achilles, 337.

E

Edel, Xavier, 386, 394.
Elgin, Lord, 49.
Emperes Eugénie, 1.
Estève, François, 1.

F

Fairbank, John King, 10, 11, 477,
    482.
Faivre, M, 4.
Farmer, Francis Xavier, 305, 310.
Favier, Pierre-Marie Alphonse, 85,
    120, 122, 129, 274.
Fay, Peter W, 2, 485.
Ferrand, Léon, 100, 138, 139.
Fessard, Michael, 61, 383.
Fessard, Michel, 61, 383.
Finegan, James, 305.
Finnegan, James, 305.
Fitch, GH, 144.
Fornier, Léon, 54.
Foucault, Auguste, 73, 74.
Frederick II, xx.
Frenken, Henry, 145, 305.
Frenken, Henry, 145, 305.
Froget, Louis, 35.
Furtado, François, 302.

G

Gabet, Joseph, 17, 470.
Gaillard, Louis, 103.
Gain, Léopold, 99, 139, 310, 311,
    391, 392, 404.
Garcia, Anselmo, xii.
Garnier, Valentin, 75, 76, 77, 78,
    99, 114, 200.
Gasparri, Pietro, 271.
Gasperment, Alphonse, 329.
Gauvin, Edgar, 329.
Geertz, Clifford, xxiv, xxvi.
Gernet, Jacques, xxiii, 112, 478.
Ghestin, Louis, 396.
Giaquinto, Francesco, 36, 60.
Gilot, Henri, 163, 224, 254.
Gonnet, Joseph, 3, 7, 383, 384,
    387, 388, 467, 475, 478.

Place Index

A

Anhui, 3, 4, 6, 8, 54, 62, 66, 72, 73, 76, 90, 93, 94, 98, 118, 126, 135, 137, 141, 150, 163, 165, 176, 183, 184, 185, 205, 209, 215, 218, 220, 222, 227, 243, 246, 257, 258, 277, 284, 287, 288, 290, 302, 328, 329, 354, 391, 392.

Anqing, 62, 63, 65, 66, 67, 133, 135, 183, 184, 185, 191, 277, 328, 448, 461, 463, 468, 474.

Aurora University, 169, 177, 181, 187, 189, 206, 222, 224, 232, 243, 248, 250, 251f, 260, 280, 284, 286, 290, 301, 310, 316, 333, 337, 338, 348, 351, 352, 356, 359, 364, 367, 419.

Aurora, 220, 321, 330, 483.

Austrian Jesuit Province, 228, 331, 412, 428, 430, 431, 442, 458, 464, 474.

B

Beijing, xviii, 3, 4, 5, 6, 7, 8, 39, 40, 49, 52, 53, 58, 64, 66, 68, 71, 74, 80, 82, 84, 85, 87, 114, 115, 116, 117, 118, 119, 121f, 129, 130, 133, 137, 140, 154, 156, 157, 171, 198, 204, 205, 206, 210, 215, 223, 230, 231, 232, 233, 238, 239, 240, 244, 247, 251, 252, 253, 261, 262, 264, 265, 274, 277, 278, 287, 288, 292, 296, 299, 308, 313, 314, 326f, 330, 342, 343, 351, 353, 354, 361, 363, 364, 370, 379, 380, 384, 385, 389, 390, 397, 400, 402, 403, 404, 410, 413, 414, 416, 418, 419, 420, 421, 422, 423, 424, 429, 436, 437, 440, 441, 447, 449, 450, 451, 452, 453, 454, 455, 456, 458, 480.

Benedictine University, Beijing, 253, 416, 420, 464, 465.

Bengbu, 183, 184, 185, 197, 277, 287, 328, 339, 461.

Boxers/ Boxer Revolution, 90, 91, 92, 108, 111ff, 112, 116, 117, 118, 120, 121, 123, 122, 124, 127, 129, 130, 133, 135, 137, 152, 156, 198, 216, 240, 241, 311, 313, 389, 392, 394f, 397, 398, 399, 400, 401, 402, 406, 407, 408, 409, 410, 475, 476, 477, 478, 481, 486, 487.

Bozhou, 128.

176, 177, 187, 198, 204, 205,
206, 208, 213, 214, 216, 217,
222, 223, 224, 226, 227, 228,
230, 231, 232, 233, 234, 235,
237, 238, 240, 242, 243, 244,
245, 246, 248, 249, 250, 251,
254, 256, 258, 260, 261, 262,
269, 270, 271, 272, 273, 274,
278, 279, 283, 286, 287, 289,
290, 292, 293, 296, 297, 298,
300, 301, 303, 304, 306, 308,
309, 314, 315, 316, 317, 318,
319, 320, 322, 324, 325, 326,
327, 333, 334, 336, 337, 338,
340, 341, 342, 345, 346, 347,
348, 349, 351, 352, 353, 354,
355, 357, 358, 359, 360, 361,
364, 365, 366, 367, 368, 369,
370, 372, 373, 374, 380, 381,
383, 388, 389, 412, 413, 414,
415, 416, 419, 436, 440, 445,
447, 450, 452, 455, 462, 466,
470, 474, 476, 481, 484, 485.
Shuyang, 341.
Songjiang, 20, 54, 67, 75, 164, 227,
320, 364.
St Ignatius College of, Xujiahui,
27, 127, 147, 148, 153, 155,
187, 189, 193, 200, 254, 260,
273, 298, 316, 325, 336, 337,
338, 346, 356, 359, 375.
St Ignatius Church, 26, 374.
Suining, 138.
Suzhou, 20, 50, 54, 115, 122, 230,
361.

T

Taiwan, 295, 347, 362, 363, 364.
Tangshan, 312.
Tianjin, 49, 81, 118, 124, 157, 340,
385, 387, 411, 413, 418, 419,

429, 435, 436, 437, 439, 441,
451, 452, 455, 456.
Turin Jesuit Province, vii, 183,
461, 468.
Twenty-One Demands, 141, 171,
295.

W

Wuhu, 94, 98, 183, 184, 185, 233,
242, 243, 244, 245, 246, 247,
255, 276, 298, 328, 329, 347,
391, 450, 461, 462, 464, 467,
468, 469, 473, 486.

X

Xujiahui, 1, 18, 21, 26, 27f, 37, 38,
42, 43, 44, 50, 53, 54, 55, 56, 58,
59, 61, 67, 70, 72, 75, 76, 79,
114, 119, 125, 126, 127, 147,
148, 149, 150, 153f, 154, 155,
169, 176, 179, 180, 185, 187,
189, 193, 194, 200, 217, 220f,
222, 235, 243, 246, 249, 254,
258, 260, 261, 271, 272, 273,
278, 279, 286, 294, 297, 298,
301, 303, 307, 309, 316, 319,
320, 322, 323, 325, 326, 330,
337, 341, 345, 346, 347, 352,
359, 375, 389, 392, 450, 463,
464, 471.

Y

Yangtze, 72, 118, 327, 345.
Yangzhou, 62, 73, 75, 77, 169, 176,
177, 218, 258, 345, 352, 466.
Yaowan, 172.
Yingzhou, 205.
Yungnien, 429, 431.